NEWSPAPER DESIGNING

NEWSPAPER DESIGNING

By John E. Allen, Editor of *The Linotype News*

Author of *Newspaper Makeup* and *The Modern Newspaper*

HARPER & BROTHERS PUBLISHERS

New York and London

NEWSPAPER DESIGNING

Printed in the United States of America

F-X

Contents

PART I

Preface vii

1. Modern Scene 3
2. Attractive, Legible Makeup 5
3. Page Sizes and Column Widths 10
4. Makeup Limitations 37
5. News Head Faces 40
6. News Body Faces 78
7. Leading and Spacing 95
8. Nameplates and Ears 101
9. Date Lines and Running Heads 115
10. Dashes, Cutoffs and Column Rules 121
11. Boxes and Box Effects 131
12. Feature Heads 137
13. Jump Heads 142
14. Illustrations 154
15. Front-Page Makeup 172
16. Makeup of Other Pages 190
    - Editorial Pages 193
    - Feature Pages 202
    - Woman's and Society Pages 206
    - Sports Pages 210
    - Financial Pages 214
    - Radio Pages 218
    - Magazine and Book Sections 220

17. Display Advertising 221
18. Placing Display Advertisements 239
19. Theatrical Advertising 252
20. Classified Advertising 255
21. Gravure, Offset and Color 265
22. School Papers 275
23. Influences of World War II 277

PART II

1. Modern Comment 293
2. Parade of Progress—Typographic 315
3. Parade of Progress—In Other Ways 362
4. Modern Suggestions 399
5. Modern Pages 411
6. The Modern Tabloid 424
7. Prize Winners 447
8. The Newspaper of Tomorrow 465
Glossary of Technical Terms 468
Index 473

Preface

In the spring of 1936 a book by this writer entitled *Newspaper Makeup* was published by Harper & Brothers, and four years later a companion volume, also by this writer, was brought out by the same publishers under the title *The Modern Newspaper.*

Both books were well received and ran through several printings, but *Newspaper Makeup* has been out of print several years now, and many important developments in the way of newspaper makeup have taken place since it and *The Modern Newspaper* were published.

This present volume combines features from both of those books with much new material. And for the convenience of readers, it is presented in two parts.

Part I is concerned chiefly with the historic background and past development of newspapers, and with the fundamental principles of sound newspaper design.

Part II has to do chiefly with the present-day application (and misapplication) of those principles, describes and illustrates more recent significant developments in the way of news transmission and presentation, and includes pertinent comments on the newspaper of the future.

Many influences have been at work since *Newspaper Makeup* first appeared and some of those influences have brought about improvements more important and farther reaching than any merely typographic betterments.

While the adoption of a modern type dress has helped many a paper, and could help many another, the *story* continues to be the thing.

Of course, the *content* of a paper is of first importance. Physical appearance is secondary. The reader does not buy a paper, and keep on buying it, merely because it pleases the eye. The best typography cannot make a superior newspaper of one that is basically inferior.

In several chapters, but particularly in Chapter 1 of Part II, many different points of view are presented. While it would have been possible to include there many more quotations—and decidedly worthwhile quotations—because many people have made many excellent suggestions for newspaper improvements, the statements presented are representative of most of the better arguments in favor of the modern newspaper.

In other chapters, too, extensive use is made of direct quotations. It would have been easy enough to present indirectly the gist of most of those quoted statements, but it seems to this writer that in a volume such as this it is better to state who said it, when he said it, and exactly what he said. This treatment has been applied to the extent that quotation marks are employed with many of this writer's own statements.

While no one newspaper is employing all of the modern techniques of news presentation illustrated and discussed in these pages—possibly for what may seem to be good reasons, in various individual instances —it is encouraging to note that more and more newspaper executives have become aware that techniques that were effective years ago are not necessarily just as effective today. A growing number of newspaper executives realize that better methods of news presentation than many now being applied are possible of attainment, and are trying to attain them.

Many of the illustrations employed here are of pages from the *Linotype News*, which long has served as a typographic laboratory for newspapers, and of which this writer has been the editor from its beginning, in 1922.

Most of the type faces specifically referred to are, frankly, Linotype faces, with, of course, Linotype names. Faces in various typographic categories manufactured by various companies have many different names. But the same principles of selection and arrangement apply, of course, whether the faces are composed on the Linotype, by hand, or on other machines.

In the examples made from rough paste-ups and from other experimental pages, the wording of nearly all of the type lines is merely incidental and so are any illustrations on the pages. Most of the units on such pages are employed solely for physical effect—not for content.

In the examples where the *type faces themselves* are the chief points of discussion, descriptions of the faces are given; in the examples where the *arrangements* of the type faces and other units of composition are the main points, rather than the faces themselves, such descriptions are omitted as superfluous.

As to phraseology, the writer has attempted a middle course—to be technical enough to be followed accurately and economically by the experienced practitioner of newspaper makeup, and yet to be informal enough to be understood by the less experienced—no easy dual task.

No descriptions of the various mechanical processes employed in newspaper making are presented, except for occasional brief parenthetical remarks, as descriptions of most of those processes may be found in encyclopedias or dictionaries; but a glossary of technical terms is included toward the end of this volume.

In preparing this book, the writer, who is familiar with the formats of hundreds of newspapers of today, has examined originals, facsimiles or other reproductions of many old newspapers, and has consulted, among many other works on journalism in this and other countries, Isaiah Thomas's *The History of Printing in America,* published by Isaiah Thomas Jr., Worcester, Mass., 1810; Frederic Hudson's *Journalism in the United States from 1690 to 1872,* Harper & Brothers, 1873; James Melvin Lee's *History of American Journalism,* Houghton Mifflin Company, 1917; Stanley Morison's *The English Newspaper,* Cambridge University Press, 1932, and *The Continuing Study of Newspaper Reading* conducted by the Advertising Research Foundation.

The writer is grateful to Harry L. Gage, C. H. Griffith and Walter B. Patterson, all executives of the Linotype Company and all with rich backgrounds of printing experience, for checking parts of the manuscript and offering helpful suggestions.

The writer is grateful, too, to Julien J. Soubiran, president of the Horan Engraving Company of New York City, who supplied most of the engravings shown in Chapter 14 of Part I. The photograph reproduced in various ways in that chapter was made by Harry Day of Forest Hills, N. Y.

Gerry Powell of New York City designed the series of folders presenting comparative showings of pages from "The Ordinary Newspaper" and "The Distinguished Newspaper," some pages from which are shown in Chapters 15 and 17 of Part I.

To A. H. Burns, mechanical superintendent of the *New York Herald Tribune,* and to O. Alfred Dickman, advertising production manager of that paper, thanks are expressed for having made it possible for the writer to examine consecutive copies of the *Tribune* from its inception to its merging with the *New York Herald*, and for reading certain chapters of the manuscript; and to John E. Martin of the *New York Sun* for providing plates of heads from back issues of the *Sun*.

And the writer expresses his indebtedness and thanks to all individuals and publications quoted for permission to quote.

John E. Allen

PART I

1

Modern Scene

A SOFT-VOICED but insistent alarm clock sputters. James Q. Citizen stirs reluctantly beneath his bed covers. In his gradually awakening mind the regular matutinal rebellion flares. But habit wins again, as usual, and he reaches out and silences the call to wakefulness and the day's routines.

A moment later he leans over the facsimile receiver in his den and scans the roll of news stories and pictures that has come to him over night.

In a few minutes he has finished with the facsimile, and soon appears in the dining room, with his favorite morning newspaper, for a few minutes' look at it before breakfast.

"I did hope," sighs Mrs. Citizen, "that the new gadget would help you get to breakfast sooner."

"Not yet," chuckles James Q., coming up from a detailed story about pig iron in Pittsburgh. "Facsimile is fine. And it'll keep getting better. It whets the appetite for news. But I'll keep on reading the *Daily News*, unless it goes back on me."

"But haven't you just seen, on the facsimile roll," questions Mrs. Citizen, "a lot of the same stuff you're looking at now?"

"Sure," replies James Q. "And that's what I just said. It whets the appetite.

"Take that new television set, now. That was a good program last night. But is that set going to keep us home, glued in front of it all the time? Won't we still want to hear an occasional concert, see an occasional play; want to see tennis matches, boat races, football games and other things—all in the flesh and in person?

"Television is fine, and it'll keep getting better. But we and a lot of others will keep wanting newspapers for a long time to come."

Before leaving for the station and the eight-thirty-seven train, James Q. listens a few moments to a news broadcast coming from the radio in his living room, and continues with the same broadcast, from the radio in his car, right down to the station.

With seventy-two seconds to spare, he watches the big screen at one end of the waiting room and takes in the news bulletins being received by radiotype—giant-sized words being thrown on the screen at the rate of a hundred a minute.

"All the same," muses James Q., as he unfolds his *Daily News* in a smoking-car, "things surely are speeding up. Gibbs of the *News* was saying at the club that maybe in a few years newspapers wouldn't need any presses at all; that maybe they'd simply stack up sheets of sensitized paper, thousands in a pile, and wave a sort of fairy wand over them. And that wand, a beam of light, a sort of printing electric eye, would print a whole stack at once, in a few seconds. Think of thousands of *Daily Newses,* without presses, in a few seconds!"

James Q. chuckles to himself as he thinks of his forming thoughts: "When they get facsimile and television to a point where you can carry a set in your pocket, like a watch, then they'll be getting places in a hurry. Think of pulling out your portable 'fac' or 'tel' any place, any time, and seeing and hearing what's going on somewhere else!"

And there we are—or soon may be, discounting any seeming exaggeration.

The facsimile newspaper is here. Television is here. The radiotype is here.

For several years, of course, we have had the radio. We have had news reels at the movies. We have had weekly news digests, news-picture magazines—many things that have competed with newspapers.

And what have the newspapers themselves done about it?

Many have done little or nothing. Many others, however, have been getting abreast of the parade of progress.

What those many others have been doing about it is set forth in Part II of this book.

But readers interested in the historic background of newspaper makeup—in the evolution of newspaper format from earlier days—and in a discussion of certain fundamentals of makeup, may find the other chapters in Part I interesting, and possibly helpful.

2

Attractive, Legible Makeup

Books, we were told in childhood, should not be judged by their covers. Perhaps they should not be, but they often are. People and things *are* judged by appearances. They are judged instantly—favorably or otherwise. Such judgments may be erroneous and only temporary; but first impressions are tenacious.

To make a favorable first impression, a newspaper must be attractive physically. For the dress of a paper—its physical makeup—is seen, and liked or disliked, before its contents can be appreciated.

While attractive appearance cannot make the contents of a poorly written and edited newspaper better, it can make a well-written and well-edited paper doubly effective.

But what, in a newspaper, constitutes physical attractiveness? One type of reader likes vigorous headlines; another prefers more restrained display faces.

But virtually all newspaper readers are agreed as to one requisite of physical attractiveness in a paper—the chief requisite—*legibility*. They want their newspapers to be easy to read—at least as easy as is reasonably possible.

Millions of newspaper readers today, particularly in large cities, do most of their reading in a hurry, on the way to and from business—in vibrating commuters' trains, jolting buses, crowded and dimly lighted subways, swaying and jerking surface cars. If they are to get much from their papers, they must get it quickly.

Even in small towns and rural communities, where people are supposed to have more time for newspaper reading, whether they actually do or not, legibility is an important asset to a newspaper. For not always are reading conditions in such places of the best, and many of the newspaper readers there are elderly people who have retired from more bustling centers, and whose eyesight is not good.

Important, however, as legibility is, many newspapers are not as easy to read as they could be—in a practical, profitable way—or as attractive otherwise.

Many newspaper publishers who have spent millions of dollars to modernize their plants keep on turning out newspapers that look about the same as they did a generation or two ago and that are just as hard to read and otherwise unattractive now as then, despite the fact that more appropriate type faces are available.

Magazine publishers, as a class, have been more progressive in this respect. Imagine an influential magazine of today—a magazine that hoped to be influential—greeting its readers through a typographic plan of thirty years ago! Who would buy it? A few enthusiasts, perhaps, but not the average magazine reader. Magazine publishers, even the most conservative, know this. That is why they employ attractive front covers, attractive type faces, attractive typographic and art plans—attractive in a modern way. They know that such things catch and hold the attention of magazine buyers.

Big advertisers of today, with comparatively few exceptions, would not think of trying to sell today's merchandise as they did a generation or two ago. Some alert advertisers, it is true, have revived and are using to good effect certain typographic and pictorial treatments employed in advertising many years ago; but even "modernistic" advertising, based, as much of it is, on lines that waxed and waned in a bygone era, has unmistakable touches of today about it.

Candy manufacturers offer their products in new and more attractive containers; so do perfume makers, soap makers, food manufacturers—hundreds of other manufacturers. But many newspapers—even many that stress editorially the importance of keeping up with the times—look much the same today in their news and editorial columns as they did many years ago.

Compare today's advertising columns of metropolitan newspapers with their advertising columns of no more than twenty years ago. In most cases a decided change for the better typographically will be observed in today's.

Then compare today's news and editorial columns of the same papers with their news and editorial columns of ten, twenty or even thirty years ago. In many instances comparatively little improvement will be noticed.

Even many a new paper, with a chance to begin where so many older journals might well have left off, patterns its appearance after some paper that has been using the same head faces for a generation, or entrusts the important task of dress selection to too many people, and not always well qualified, who often throw together a type dress the various elements of which clash with each other and which causes the paper to be heavily handicapped in appearance from the start.

How would an office building look, a house, a church, a school, if designed by several people with only a superficial knowledge of architecture, and particularly if the plan agreed on and carried out incorporated several different and unrelated sets of ideas?

Yet the appearance of many a newspaper suggests such a structure —many a paper published from an expertly planned and handsome building—many a reputable and well-edited paper copies of which are seen by thousands of people who never see the fine structure from which the copies come, nor meet the ones who produce them, but who, consciously or otherwise, judge the paper and the people behind it by the printed copies they see and read.

An effective head schedule does not "just happen." It is the result of the efforts of one person or closely working group of persons thoroughly familiar with and agreed on certain fundamentals of newspaper makeup and striving for a definite preconceived objective.

Any section of such a schedule will be consistent throughout. (The word *section* is used here with the thought of big newspapers in mind —papers which, because of their large size, might well employ one kind of head dress for their general-news columns, another kind for their society columns, another for their editorial pages, and still another for their classified-advertising departments, and so on.)

Each element in any section of such a schedule—even any decidedly contrasting elements—will harmonize with all other elements in its section. There will be no indiscriminate mixing of unrelated faces or other units of composition. All rules and dashes and any ornaments in any section will harmonize with the type faces employed in that section and with themselves.

"I can hear some of the old-time editors say: 'Bunk! The story is the thing!'" stated Malcolm W. Bingay, editorial director of the *Detroit Free Press*, in an article in *Editor & Publisher* urging newspaper publishers to give more thought to the appearance of their publications. "And the story *is* the thing. But a Booth, a Barrett, a Sothern playing Hamlet has the same story—word for word—as has the barnstorming tragedian. It is the manner in which the story is presented that counts; not consciously always, but subconsciously.

"Some front pages give the reader the impression that he is being spoken to by a scatterbrained woman who is trying to talk about everything at once. Others give him the feeling that he is talking to a cultured, pleasant personality with a finely disciplined mind which takes up each topic in its proper sequence; places the emphasis on the important and, with just the right touch, lightly dwells on those matters which are interesting and entertaining but not wholly essential."

Back in 1908, William R. Nelson, founder and first editor of the *Kansas City Star*, wrote a letter to a newspaper friend of his who had purchased a daily in the Middle West and had sent Mr. Nelson a copy of the paper to criticize.

"I am not enthusiastic over your paper," wrote Mr. Nelson, as quoted in the *Iowa Publisher*. "It makes the same sort of impression on me that a man would who came into my presence dressed in ill-fitting, gaudy clothing, and talking in loud and vulgar tones. Such a man, I would know at first glance and hearing, was without stability or character.

"In my judgment, good taste and good form speak as well for a newspaper as for a man. Nothing pays a man better than fine character and an outward appearance that befits that character. Nothing pays better in the newspaper business than worth and character. Make your appeal to the best people and deserve their confidence and support and you will be a sure winner. Be a gentleman among newspapers. But, to be recognized as a gentleman, one must really be a gentleman and dress like a gentleman, which your paper does not."

Another reason why many newspapers might well be more particular about their appearance than they are is that national advertisers or their agents, in the absence of authentic data as to circulations, reader interest and buying power represented by newspapers in the territories the advertisers wish to cover, often select the better looking paper in a town and pass up the less attractive.

As the editor of the *Imperial Type Metal Magazine* observed in that publication, in writing of the growing volume of national advertising that has been appearing in American newspapers in recent years:

"The agency men and other advertising executives who were used to scrutinizing magazines and other mediums with high-class production standards were sensitive to newspaper appearance.

"It soon became apparent that while the local store chose its media on what it knew of circulation and reader interest, the national space buyer, working at a distance, was swayed in many cases by which was the better looking paper in a town. Besides this the actual material submitted by the national advertiser called for exacting production methods. He expected it and payment came much more promptly and gracefully when he got what he wanted."

Careless makeup can be costly—by wasting space, and by discouraging readers and advertisers. An attractive makeup not only attracts readers and advertisers but often helps to minimize production costs.

These statements are proved by many specific demonstrations in the chapters that follow.

3

Page Sizes and Column Widths

Early day newspapers were considerably smaller than most newspapers of today. They contained fewer pages, which were seldom larger than those of our present-day tabloids (which, of course, are not at all new as to page size), and they presented fewer columns and fewer words to the page. With the exception of the title lines (now usually called nameplates) at the tops of front pages, and occasional heads seldom larger than our 14-point faces of today, they employed no display types, although many early day news-pamphlets presented display lines on their title pages. And even the most pretentious early day papers rarely used pictures with stories.

Although the Chinese are supposed to have printed from blocks many centuries ago, and Europeans to have used similar methods in the twelfth century for the ornamenting of fabrics, and in the fourteenth century for the printing of playing cards, printing as we think of it today began with the invention of movable types about the middle of the fifteenth century. "This invention," according to the Funk & Wagnall's *New Standard Dictionary of the English Language*, "is probably due to Laurens Janszoon Coster of Haarlem, but Johann Gutenberg, with the aid of Johann Fust and Peter Schoeffer of Germany, is generally credited with being the first to put it to practical use."

The *New Standard* states that the earliest known wood-cut, one picturing Saint Christopher carrying the infant Christ, from the Chartreuse of Buxheim, Bavaria, dates from 1423. But *Compton's Pictured Encyclopedia* states: "The earliest wood-cut probably dates from before 1400, but the first dated one known, a Virgin Mary probably of German origin, carries the date 1418."

For that matter, though, what is stated by the *New Standard* to have been the first newspaper as we use that term today—although daily bulletins are said to have been issued in Rome as early as 691 B.C., concerning the movements of the Roman armies—did not appear until

1566, when the Venetian government issued its *Notizie Scritte*, which "might be read on payment of a gazetta, a small coin, whence our word gazette."

"But," states Frederic Hudson, in his *Journalism in the United States from 1690 to 1872*, "if we may believe *Galignani's Messenger*, always a reliable chronicler, neither Venice nor London have any claims to this great honor of issuing the first newspaper. According to a statement in the *Messenger*, a paper called the *Gazette* was printed as early as 1457 . . . in Nuremberg, Bavaria." Regarding the name *Gazette*, Hudson continues: "Some hold that the name comes from the Italian word *gazza* or *gazzara*, which means a magpie, a chatterer, a gossip, and not from the small piece of money called *gazetta*."

What is sometimes referred to as the first newspaper in our colonies was issued September 25, 1690, when *Publick Occurrences* of Boston appeared. (See Example 1.) That paper, however, was suppressed before a second issue could be circulated.

That first (and only) number of the "first newspaper" published in what is now the United States consisted of four pages about 7¼ inches wide by 11⅜ inches deep, with the fourth page blank. The body type was about the size of our 12 point of today, in columns about 17 picas wide, with two columns to the page. And the columns were separated by strips of white space, rather than column rules.

(*Note well those strips of white space, instead of column rules—a treatment followed by many newspapers more than two and a half centuries ago. Yet certain newspaper men and certain typographers sometimes say today, "Let's go modern by leaving out column rules."*)

The main lines of the title were in two sizes of roman capitals, the first line about 24 point, the second about 36 point. Two three-line initial letters were employed on the first page. At the bottom of page three was a credit line reading: "Boston, Printed by R. Pierce, for Benjamin Harris, at the London-Coffee-House. 1690."

What is more generally referred to as the first newspaper published in our colonies, and one that existed seventy-two years, was the *Boston News-Letter*, which first appeared April 24, 1704. (Example 2.)

The first number of that paper consisted of two pages about 8 inches wide by 11¾ inches deep. The body type was about the size of our 11 point of today, in columns about 19 picas wide, two to the page, and separated by column rules. (Isaiah Thomas said of that

Numb. 1

PUBLICK OCCURRENCES

Both *FORREIGN* and *DOMESTICK.*

Boston, Thursday *Sept.* 25*th.* 1690.

IT is designed, that the Countrey shall be furnished once a moneth (or if any Glut of Occurrences *happen,* oftener,) *with an Account of such considerable things as have arrived unto our* Notice.

In order hereunto, the Publisher will take what pains he can to obtain a Faithful Relation *of all such things ; and will particularly make himself beholden to such Persons in* Boston *whom he knows to have been for their own use the diligent Observers of such matters.*

That which is herein proposed, is, First, *That* Memorable Occurrents *of* Divine Providence *may not be neglected or forgotten, as they too often are.* Secondly, *That people every where may better understand the Circumstances of Publique Affairs, both abroad and at home ; which may not only direct their* Thoughts *at all times, but at some times also to assist their* Businesses *and* Negotiations.

Thirdly, *That some thing may be done towards the* Curing, *or at least the* Charming *of that* Spirit of Lying, *which prevails amongst us, wherefore nothing shall be entered, but what we have reason to believe is true, repairing to the best fountains for our Information. And when there appears* any material mistake *in any thing that is collected, it shall be* corrected *in the* next.

Moreover, the Publisher of these Occurrences *is willing to engage, that whereas, there are many* False Reports, *maliciously made, and spread among us, if any well-minded person will be at the pains to trace any such* false Report *so far as to find out and Convict the* First Raiser *of it, he will in this Paper (unless just Advice be given to the contrary) expose the Name of such person, as* A malicious Raiser of a false Report. *It is suppos'd that none will dislike this Proposal, but such as intend to be guilty of so villanous a Crime.*

THE Christianized *Indians* in some parts of *Plimouth,* have newly appointed a day of Thanksgiving to God for his Mercy in supplying their extream and pinching Necessities under their late want of Corn, & for His giving them now a prospect of a very *Comfortable Harvest.* Their Example may be worth Mentioning.

'Tis observed by the Husbandmen, that altho' the With-draw of so great a strength from them, as what is in the Forces lately gone for *Canada*; made them think it almost impossible for them to get well through the Affairs of their Husbandry at this time of the year, yet the Season has been so unusually favourable that they scarce find any want of the many hundreds of hands, that are gone from them ; which is looked upon as a Merciful Providence

While the barbarous *Indians* were lurking about *Chelmsford,* there were missing about the beginning of this month a couple of Children belonging to a man of that Town, one of them aged about eleven, the other aged about nine years, both of them supposed to be fallen into the hands of the *Indians*

A very *Tragical Accident* happened at *Water-Town,* the beginning of this Month, an *Old man,* that was of somewhat a Silent and Morose Temper, but one that had long Enjoyed the reputation of a *Sober* and a *Pious Man,* having newly buried his Wife, The Devil took advantage of the Melancholly which he thereupon fell into, his Wives discretion and industry had long been the support of his Family, and he seemed hurried with an impertinent fear that he should now come to want before he dyed, though he had very careful friends to look after him who kept a strict eye upon him, least he should do himself any harm. But one evening escaping from them into the Cow-house, they there quickly followed him found him *hanging by a Rope,* which they had used to tye their *Calves* withal, he was dead with his feet near touching the Ground.

Epidemical *Fevers* and *Agues* grow very common, in some parts of the Country, whereof, tho' many dye not, yet they are sorely unfitted for their imployments ; but in some parts a more *malignant Fever* seems to prevail in such sort that it usually goes thro' a Family where it comes, and proves *Mortal* unto many.

The *Small-pox* which has been raging in *Boston,* after a manner very Extraordinary, is now very much abated. It is thought that far more have been sick of it then were visited with it, when it raged so much twelve years ago, nevertheless it has not been so Mortal, The number of them that have

EXAMPLE 1

N. E. Numb. 1

The Boſton News-Letter.

Publiſhed by Authority.

From Monday April 17. to Monday April 24. 1704.

London Flying-Poſt from *Decemb.* 2*d.* to 4*th.* 1703.

LEtters from *Scotland* bring us the Copy of a Sheet lately Printed there, Intituled, *A ſeaſonable Alarm for* Scotland. *In a Letter from a Gentleman in the City, to his Friend in the Country, concerning the preſent Danger of the Kingdom and of the Proteſtant Religion.*

This Letter takes Notice, That Papiſts ſwarm in that Nation, that they traffick more avowedly than formerly, and that of late many Scores of Prieſts & Jeſuites are come thither from France, and gone to the North, to the Highlands & other places of the Country. That the Miniſters of the Highlands and North gave in large Liſts of them to the Committee of the General Aſſembly, to be laid before the Privy-Council.

It likewiſe obſerves, that a great Number of other ill-affected perſons are come over from *France*, under pretence of accepting her Majeſty's Gracious Indemnity; but, in reality, to increaſe Diviſions in the Nation, and to entertain a Correſpondence with *France*: That their ill Intentions are evident from their talking big, their owning the Intereſt of the pretended King *James* VIII. their ſecret Cabals, and their buying up of Arms and Ammunition, wherever they can find them.

To this he adds the late Writinge and Actings of ſome diſaffected perſons, many of whom are for that Pretender: that ſeveral of them have declar'd they had rather embrace Popery than conform to the preſent Government; that they refuſe to pray for the Queen, but uſe the ambiguous word Soveraign, and ſome of them pray in expreſs Words for the King and Royal Family; and the charitable and generous Prince who has ſhew'd them ſo much Kindneſs. He likewiſe takes notice of Letters, not long ago found in Cypher, & directed to a Perſon lately come thither from St. *Germains*.

He ſays that the greateſt Jacobites, who will not qualifie themſelves by taking the Oaths to Her Majeſty, do now with the Papiſts and their Companions from St. *Germains* ſet up for the Liberty of the Subject, contrary to their own Principles, but meerly to keep up a Diviſion in the Nation. He adds, that they aggravate thoſe things which the People complain of, as to *England's* refuſing to allow them a freedom of Trade, *&c.* and do all they can to foment Diviſions betwixt the Nations, & to obſtruct a Redreſs of thoſe things complain'd of.

The Jacobites, he ſays, do all they can to perſuade the Nation that their pretended King is a Proteſtant in his Heart, tho' he dares not declare it while under the Power of *France*; that he is acquainted with the Miſtakes of his Father's Government, will govern us more according to Law, and endear himſelf to his Subjects.

They magnifie the Strength of their own Party, and the Weakneſs and Diviſions of the other, in order to facilitate and haſten their Undertaking; they argue themſelves out of their Fears, and into the higheſt aſſurance of accompliſhing their purpoſe.

From all this he infers, That they have hopes of Aſſiſtance from *France*, otherwiſe they would never be ſo impudent; and he gives Reaſons for his Apprehenſions that the *French* King may ſend Troops thither this Winter, 1. Becauſe the *Engliſh* & *Dutch* will not then be at Sea to oppoſe them. 2. He can then beſt ſpare them, the Seaſon of Action beyond Sea being over. 3. The Expectation given him of a conſiderable number to joyn them, may incourage him to the undertaking with fewer Men, if he can but ſend over a ſufficient number of Officers with Arms and Ammunition.

He endeavours in the reſt of his Letters to anſwer the fooliſh Pretences of the Pretender's being a Proteſtant and that he will govern us according to Law. He ſays, that being bred up in the Religion and Politicks of *France*, he is by Education a ſtated Enemy to our Liberty and Religion. That the Obligations which he and his Family owe to the *French* King muſt neceſſarily make him to be wholly at his Devotion, and to follow his Example; that if he ſit upon the Throne, the three Nations muſt be oblig'd to pay the Debt which he owes the *French* King for the Education of himſelf, and for Entertaining his ſuppoſed Father and his Family. And ſince the King muſt reſtore him by his Troops, if ever he be reſtored, he will ſee to ſecure his own Debt, before thoſe Troops leave *Britain*. The Pretender being a good Proficient in the *French* and *Romiſh* Schools, he will never think himſelf ſufficiently aveng'd, but by the utter Ruine of his Proteſtant Subjects, both as Hereticks and Traitors. The late Queen, his pretended Mother, who in cold Blood when ſhe was Queen of *Britain*, advis'd to turn the Weſt of *Scotland* into a hunting Field, will be then for doing ſo by the greateſt part of the Nation, and, no doubt, is at Pains to have her pretended Son educated to her own Mind: Therefore, he ſays, it were a great Madneſs in the Nation to take a Prince bred up in the horrid School of Ingratitude, Perſecution and Cruelty, and filled with Rage and Envy. The *Jacobites*, he ſays, both in *Scotland* and at St. *Germains*, are impatient under their preſent Straits, and knowing their Circumſtances cannot be much worſe than they are, at preſent, are the more inclinable to the Undertaking. He adds, That the *French* King knows there cannot be a more effectual way for himſelf to arrive at the Univerſal Monarchy, and to ruine the Proteſtant Intereſt, than by ſetting up the Pretender upon the Throne of Great *Britain*, he will in all probability attempt it; and tho' he ſhould be perſuaded that the Deſign would miſcarry in the cloſe, yet he cannot but reap ſome Advantage by imbroiling the three Nations.

From all this the Author concludes it to be the Intereſt of the Nation, to provide for Self-defence; and ſays, that as many have already taken the Alarm, and are furniſhing themſelves with Arms and Ammunition, he hopes the Government will not only allow it, but encourage it, ſince the Nation ought all to appear as one Man in the Defence

EXAMPLE 2

issue: "It is printed on half a sheet of pot paper, with a small pica type, folio.") The title line was in roman capitals and lower-case about 36 point in size. Below the title line and above the date line appeared the significant statement, in old-English between a pair of light rules, "Published by Authority." The old-English was about 18 point in size. The days of the week, too, in the date line, were in old-English, with the rest of the line in roman. One five-line initial was used at the beginning of the first story on the first page, and three two-line initials were employed on the second page. At the bottom of the second page was a credit line reading: "Boston: Printed by B. Green. Sold by Nicholas Boone at his Shop near the Old Meeting-House."

John Campbell, then postmaster of Boston, was the first proprietor and publisher of the *Boston News-Letter*, and Nicholas Boone was associated with him only a short time.

There were not so many newspaper readers in any country in 1704, or even a hundred or a hundred and fifty years later, as now, of course; the transmission of news from one country to another, even from one section of a country to another section, was much slower then than at present, and the business of producing the papers themselves involved slow and laborious work by hand.

Many an early day paper was produced by one man (often a scholarly craftsman who was proud to be known as a printer) or one man and a single apprentice, or "devil." They were the ones who gathered, wrote, set and printed the contents of the paper—set it by hand, printed it on hand-made paper, from ink prepared by hand on the premises, and on presses operated by hand. And the printer's name, with the title of printer, as we have seen, usually appeared on the paper—quite commonly on the first or last page.

Naturally enough, then, as early day news-pamphlets and newspapers were shaped throughout by printers—craftsmen who, though men of many interests, expressed themselves chiefly as printers—as printers of books—early day news-pamphlets and newspapers had a "bookish" appearance. In fact, the early day news-pamphlet *was* a book. The same type faces that were used for books in the more conventional sense were used for news-pamphlets—the same line widths, the same presses, the same kinds of ink, and the same kinds of paper. The news-pamphlet usually was a quarto—a fairly large sheet folded twice into eight comparatively small pages, the first page a title page. And the newspapers that succeeded the news-pamphlets usually were half sheets, of two pages, or were folios—fairly large sheets folded once into four comparatively large pages—with two columns of type to the page.

This writer has a series of old London newspapers—nearly one hundred and fifty consecutive copies dating from April 24, 1786—which have come down through the years with little deterioration, and which, with the exception of words containing unfamiliar long s's and certain obsolete phrases, still are easy to read. And he is familiar with copies of other newspapers considerably older, but which, like the papers just referred to, still are in good condition, whereas even file copies of many newspapers printed no more than fifty or even twenty-five years ago have become brittle and discolored with the years, and the inks used for their printing appreciably faded.

Up to about the middle of the nineteenth century most newspapers were printed on paper made from rags. Such paper was quite expensive, and, moreover, the many newspapers which by that time had come into being were consuming it at a rate of speed that threatened soon to exhaust the available supply, as the paper-makers were finding it difficult to secure enough rags to meet the demands for rag paper. ("About the beginning of the nineteenth century," states *Compton's Pictured Encyclopedia*, "the modern process of paper-making by machinery was invented, and by the middle of the century it had supplanted the hand processes for all but the very finest grades.")

For more than one reason, then, newspaper producers were willing enough to change from the higher priced paper they had been using to the cheaper substitutes that began to appear—first in the form of newsprint made from straw, and later in the form of our newsprint of today, made chiefly from wood pulp.

(Quaintly enough, many long-dead Egyptians unwittingly helped many newspapers in America through a print-paper shortage during our Civil War, and to some extent before, according to Louis Calder, president of the Perkins-Goodwin Company. In a brochure issued in 1946 to commemorate the hundredth anniversary of his company, Mr. Calder stated: "A decade earlier, when the rag shortage had become desperate, paper-makers of New York state had imported Egyptian mummies and used their wrappings for paper-making; now, during the

Civil War, when his groundwood paper was not commercially successful, August Stanwood of Gardiner, Maine, brought several shiploads of Egyptian mummies to Maine and used the woven wrappings as well as the papyrus filling to make his pulp. He stated that the only objections he encountered in getting the mummies out of Egypt came from the Egyptian railroads, which were using them as firewood!")

However, it is not the purpose here to discuss at length the physical qualities of early day newspapers, nor to suggest that papers of today should be published to be read in the dim future. (Some newspapers of the present, of course, do turn out a limited number of copies of each issue on high-grade paper and make use of a good quality of ink, for their own files, public libraries and private collections. And some newspapers now photograph their pages on microfilm for their files and for some subscribers.)

The chief points to be noted are that early day newspapers in general were set in larger types than those generally used for the body matter of most news stories today; in wider columns—usually no more than two, three or four to the page, and in many instances with strips of white space between the columns, rather than column rules—and on pages considerably smaller than the size employed by many newspapers of today.

With the speeding up of transportation, printing machinery and human life in general, the producers of newspapers naturally found it possible to compose, print and distribute papers much more quickly than before. Moreover, they had much more news to present than previously, and desired to present it before an increasing number of competitors could do so.

These things, coupled with a growing interest in news on the part of more and more readers and a greater willingness on the part of more and more merchants and others to advertise in papers, brought about the shifting of newspaper making from a *printing* to a *publishing* basis.

(In many instances postmasters—often men with only a superficial knowledge of printing, but in direct contact with various news sources through the couriers who passed their stations—established small presses and published small papers more or less regularly while their postmasterships lasted. In many more instances politicians and booksellers became the financial backers of newspapers, and merely employed the owners of printing plants to do their printing for them.)

With non-printers becoming the guiding spirits of journalism, and with printers, as printers (although many of them left the workroom for the sanctum and the counting house), beginning to play subordinate roles, newspapers began to lose their "bookish" appearance.

The desire of those in control to meet or surpass competition—to run as much advertising and news, along with editorial comment, or propaganda, as they could cram into each issue—gradually brought about marked changes of makeup.

The elaborate margins that characterized earlier newspapers were abandoned as being too costly. Smaller type sizes took the place of the larger faces formerly used, with a corresponding narrowing of column widths, with more and deeper columns, and with less leading (pronounced ledding) between the lines. Column rules on narrower bodies took the place of the wider strips of white space or wider shouldered rules formerly used between columns, as reduced strips of white failed to separate the columns as satisfactorily as did the narrow and space-saving rules.

In Great Britain in 1712 some pronounced changes of makeup took place. August 1, 1712, a stamp tax was placed on newspaper paper —a tax of ½d. on a half sheet or smaller, and 1d. on a sheet larger than a half sheet. To hold down production costs, many newspaper owners at first crowded their pages. They reduced the depths of their title lines, narrowed their margins, and employed smaller body types. But soon the proprietors of several British papers found a flaw in the tax ruling and went to six pages (using one and one-half sheets), as the law made no provision for the taxing of papers consisting of more than one sheet. Many of the six-page papers had a page size a little smaller than that of our own *Publick Occurrences*, with two columns to the page; employed comparatively deep title lines, wide margins, and, in some cases, body types as large as our 14 point, and leaded—to pad out beyond four pages to escape the tax.

However, in 1725, the tax ruling was amended to cover papers consisting of more than one sheet, and the six-page papers were taxed for one and one-half sheets. Consequently, there was a shifting back to four crowded pages—pages usually about 2 inches wider than the pages of the six-page papers, but less than 11 inches deep, and with two wider columns, in smaller types, to the page.

Although the tax on British newspapers was originally planned to run only thirty-two years, it was in effect as recently as the beginning of our own Civil War days.

By 1816 the tax had been so increased (and it continued unusually high until 1836, because of the Napoleonic Wars) that many British papers began to use the equivalent of our 6-point faces. By that time there were actually three taxes—a stamp tax, a paper tax, and a tax on each individual advertisement run. By that time, too, several British papers had adopted modern type faces proportionately heavier than the old-style faces formerly used, with the result that the pages were considerably blacker than before.

In 1853 the tax on advertisements was removed, in 1855 the stamp tax was discontinued, and in 1861 the tax on paper was abolished, with the result that several British papers began to undo some of their crowding, and many other cheaper papers were established.

The British stamp act proposed for newspapers published in the American colonies, along with a proposed tax of two shillings on each advertisement run, had little direct effect on newspaper makeup in this country, although it caused some American papers to cease publication temporarily. That stamp act, planned to take effect November 1, 1765, was repealed March 18, 1766, and it is doubtful that any of our colonial newspapers used any stamped paper or paid any advertising tax.

Some papers appeared for a while without their customary title lines or addresses, and others stated prominently in print: "No Stamped Paper To Be Had."

Thursday, October 31, 1765 (the day before the stamp act was supposed to go into effect), William Bradford of Philadelphia presented his *Pennsylvania Journal* as suggested by Example 3.

The three other pages of that issue were also given "mourning-rule" treatment. And at the bottom of column three on the last page, under a cut of a coffin, appeared the statement: "The last remains of the *Pennsylvania Journal*, which departed this life the 31st of October, 1765, of a stamp in her vitals, aged 23 years." (Note, also, the line along the right edge of Example 3: "Adieu, Adieu to the LIBERTY of the *PRESS*.")

However, the *Pennsylvania Journal* continued to appear in its customary way.

But certain taxes imposed on newspapers by our colonies themselves, and, later, by the federal government, did have a bearing on makeup here—in many instances made for a tightening of pages.

Thurſday, *October* 31, 1765. THE NUMB. 1195.

PENNSYLVANIA JOURNAL; AND WEEKLY ADVERTISER.

EXPIRING: In Hopes of a Reſurrection to LIFE again.

I AM ſorry to be obliged to acquaint my Readers, that as The STAMP-ACT, is fear'd to be obligatory upon us after the *Firſt of November* enſuing, (the *fatal To-morrow*) the Publiſher of this Paper unable to bear the Burthen, has thought it expedient to STOP awhile, in order to deliberate, whether any Methods can be found to elude the Chains forged for us, and eſcape the inſupportable Slavery; which it is hoped, from the juſt Repreſentations now made againſt that Act, may be effected. Mean while, I muſt earneſtly Requeſt every Individual of my Subſcribers, many of whom have been long behind Hand, that they would immediately Diſcharge their reſpective Arrears, that I may be able, not only to ſupport myſelf during the Interval, but be better prepared to proceed again with this Paper, whenever an opening for that Purpoſe appears, which I hope will be ſoon. WILLIAM BRADFORD.

Remember, O my friends! the Laws, the Rights,
The generous plan of power deliver'd down,
From age to age, by your renown'd forefathers;
O let it never periſh in your hands!
But piouſly tranſmit it to your children.
Do thou, great Liberty, inſpire our ſouls,
And make our lives in thy poſſeſſion happy,
Or our deaths glorious in thy defence. ADDISON's Cato.

LIBERTY is one of the greateſt Bleſſings, which human beings can poſſibly enjoy: When we are deprived of this earthly happineſs, we are fettered with the Chains of inimical ſervitude. Nations, who are born for the mutual ſupport of each other, ſhould preſerve a ſteady attachment to the welfare and happineſs of that nation with whom they are united, that their mutual alliance of friendſhip might be ſincere and permanent. When this union is ſeparated by the illegal encroachments on that Liberty, which is the Soul of Commerce, and the ſupport of Life, it degenerates into implacable Enmity, which in time grows inveterate, and finally recoils upon thoſe who have been the means of its unhappy diſſolution. The *Liberty of the Preſs* has very juſtly been eſteemed one of the main Pillars of the Liberty of the People. While this is maintained, the firſt Steps to Oppreſſion are detected, and the Attention of the People ſeaſonably awakened. When this is ſuppreſſed, the Suſpicion of the People, and their Ruin may admit of ſo ſudden a tranſition, as renders the Succeſs of the firſt impracticable, and the Miſeries attending the latter unavoidable. So dangerous is this to lawleſs Power, that the fartheſt approaches to it are reſolutely oppoſed, or rigorouſly puniſhed. So eſſential is this to Freedom, Property, and Happineſs, that the moſt plauſible Attempts to curtail it even in the ſmalleſt Degree, have always been moſt ſtrenuouſly oppoſed by the virtuous, free, and unbiaſſed Patriot. It is the Priviledge of Britons to ſpeak Truth with impunity, and even to fear no Danger from ſpeculative Error whether in Religion or Politicks. The want of attending to this has produced needleſs Enquiries, and unjuſtifiable Cenſures of what is true in Fact or no more than falſe in Speculation.---But how unhappily is it to be debarr'd from this laſt Relief in a dangerous and ſickly State! How melancholly to pine and die while no kind Phyſician is allowed to explore the Cauſe, or preſcribe the Cure of our manifold Diſorders? The love of Eaſe, and abſence of Pain in ſome Diſtempers, is a fatal Symptom of the deſperate Circumſtances of the Patient. And in all political Diſorders the more contented we are under them, ſo much the worſe are they, and ſo much the worſe are we for them. It is a very happy Circumſtance attending public Virtue and public Spirit, that the more it is vilified, the more illuſtrious it always appears. No Falſhood formed againſt it can proſper, for it at once detects and confutes the darkeſt and moſt inveterate Calumny. But although public Virtue cannot be affected by the Indulgence of the moſt unlimited Freedom of ſpeaking or writing, yet Oppreſſion and Tyranny as it derives all its Influence from its Secrecy, may be extremely benefited by the Reverſe. For this reaſon, in Countries ſubjected to the inſatiable Demands of Power and Avarice, the firſt Attempts to inſpire People with a juſt Senſe of their Condition, are commonly nipt in the Bud. It is of the laſt Importance to the Views of deſigning Men to ſhut up the moſt ſucceſsful and univerſal Channel of Information from the People, when they are forming ſuch Schemes as need only to be known in order to be Oppoſed. Beſides the Deprivation of our whole Liberty may be juſtified on the ſame Principles as the Deprivation of any individual Part, ſuch as the Liberty of the Preſs undoubtedly is.

How amiable is the Enjoyment of Liberty! But how deteſtable are the Bonds of Servitude! 'Tis therefore ſincerly to be hoped, that the old *New-England* Spirit ſo exemplarily free in former Times, will never condeſcend in Submiſſion to new and unwarrantable Reſtrictions.

A Day, an Hour of virtuous Liberty,
Is worth a whole Eternity in Bondage.

May we all as loyal Subjects, and free born Britons exert our utmoſt to preſerve the Rights and Liberties of our Country, in a Manner that ſhall add Honour to our Endeavours; that future Poſterity may reap the Benefit, and bleſs the Hands which were the Inſtruments of procuring it.---

That Glory then, the brighteſt Crown of Praiſe,
Which every Lover of his Country's Wealth,
And every Patron of Mankind deſerves,
Will gracefully adorn ſuch Patriot's Deeds,
And leave behind an Honour that will laſt
With Praiſe immortal to the End of Time.

Thurſday laſt arrived here the ſhip Philadelphia Packet, Capt. Budden, from London, by whom we have the following advices

ROME, *July* 24.

THE harveſt in this country hath not proved ſo good as we hoped. This event hath engaged the congregation eſtabliſhed for inſpecting into the ſupplies of proviſions for this capital, to ſeek all poſſible means to prevent a freſh ſcarcity.

St James's, Auguſt 17. The king has been pleaſed to appoint the moſt honourable the Marquis of Rockingham to be lord lieutenant of the weſt-ridings of the county of York, and of the city of York, and county of the ſame city: and alſo Cuſtos Rotulorum of the north and weſt ridings in the ſaid county of York and of the city of York, and county of the ſame city; and Ainſty, otherwiſe Aynſtry, of York.

The king has been pleaſed to appoint the right hon. William Earl of Dartmouth, Soam Jenyns, Edward Elliot, John York, George Rice, John Roberts, Jeremiah Dyſon, and William Fitzherbert, Eſqrs; to be commiſſioners of trade, and for inſpecting and improving his majeſty's plantations in America, and elſewhere.

The king has been pleaſed to grant unto the right hon. Richard Viſcount How, the office of treaſurer of his Majeſty's navy

St. James's, Auguſt 27. By the laſt letters from Col. Deſmaretz, his majeſty's commiſſary at Dunkirk, we are aſſured, that orders were given by the French miniſtry, for immediately ſetting about the demolition of the Jettees, which are the ſupport of the harbour of Dunkirk.

Warſaw, Auguſt 1. The tribunal of Great Poland, held at Poſnania, has granted permiſſion to the Lutherans at Lobſcutz to open their church, which has been ſhut near twenty years, to provide a miniſter, and to perform divine ſervice in public.

Corunna, July 17. The detachment of one hundred men deſtined for Louiſiana, are on the march for Ferrol, where they are to embark on board the Unicorn frigate with a governor, two capuchin friars, a commiſſionary at war, and ſome civil officers.

Cadiz, July 23. Letters brought by the laſt poſt from Gibralter ſay, the report before ſpread, that the Algerines have killed their Dey, and declared war againſt all the European powers except England and France, proves not true.

LONDON.

Auguſt 17. On Thurſday at the king's arms tavern in Cornhill, an elegant entertainment was given by the committee of North-American merchants to Richard Glover, and Charles Garth, Eſqrs; when thoſe gentlemen received the thanks of that body, for their endeavours to prevent the ſoldiery from being billeted upon the private houſes of their fellow-ſubjects in America.

Part of a letter from an officer in the Eaſt-India ſervice, dated from the Arielur camp, January 8, 1765.

"In my laſt I acquainted you that we did at laſt reduce Madure. The army has ſince conquered the Arielur country for the Nabob, of 100,000l. revenue a year. We are now under orders to attack another chief, or polyagor contiguous to this country, both chiefs have mutually maintained an independency of the Nabob till now; merely on account of the impenetrable woods they are poſſeſſed of. You certainly have heard before of the memorable battle Major Munro gained at Bengal over Suja Dowla, one of the moſt formidable powers of India: The conſequence of this battle gives the company the command of trade in the greateſt part of the Mugul's dominions; and, without exaggeration, the Eaſt-India company at preſent may be brought in comparriſon with Alexander the Great, whoſe command, from the river Indus to the river Ganges, was not ſo much reſpected as their's."

It is ſaid the new m----y, taking into conſideration the preſent deplorable ſituation of the Canadians, have determined to take up all the Canada bills at par, with intereſt to the preſent time; and afterwards to demand, in the moſt ſpirited terms, *immediate* and *full* payment of France, under pain of all the conſequences that can reſult from a refuſal.

The new lords of trade and plantations will hold a board on Monday next, for the firſt time, at the Cockpit Whitehall.

We hear the rent rolls of the ſeveral proprietary eſtates in America, obtained by former grants under the crown are ordered to be made out, as alſo an eſtimate of the annual produce of their land tax, in order to introduce a more equitable form of levying his majeſty's revenues in that part of the world.

They write from Gibralter, that Engliſh officers and ſeamen are engaging both there and at Minorca by foreign agents, to ſerve on board his Sardinian majeſty's ſhips of war in the Mediterranean.

Auguſt 20. The right honourable the Earl Cornwallis, lieutenant colonel to the 12 regiment of foot, is appointed one of his majeſty's aids de camp, with the rank of colonel of foot in the army.

We are informed, that a gentleman lately very popular in this country, is ſoon to reſide at Louſanne, in Switzerland, where he intends publiſhing his friend Mr. Churchil's poems, with explanatory notes; and we are likewiſe informed, that he has an intention of publiſhing, at the ſame place, a hiſtory of England wrote by himſelf.

By a veſſel arrived at Guernſey from Belleiſle there is advice, that the French are erecting ſeveral batteries at Sandy Bay, on the ſouth eaſt of the iſland, and in the great road where the deſcent was made in the late war by the ſeamen and troops under Admiral Keppel and General Hodgſon.

Aug. 21 We hear lord Viſcount Spencer is ſhortly to be created an earl.

All thoughts of any farther changes are ſaid to be entirely laid aſide.

It is reported, that a perſon of high rank, on being lately offered a great employment, refuſed it, ſaying, "that he could not poſſibly accept of it, conſiſtently with the love he bore to the Britiſh nation, which would ever be the object of his care and attention."

Monday ſome diſpatches ſaid to be of importance, were received here from Holland, but the ſubject has not yet tranſpired.

Private letters from Paris mention; that the true reaſon

Adieu, Adieu to the LIBERTY of the PRESS.

EXAMPLE 3

The Provincial Legislature of Massachusetts imposed a tax of ½d. the copy on each newspaper printed in Massachusetts from April 30, 1755, to May 1, 1757. The colony of New York imposed a like tax on New York papers from January 1, 1757, to December 31, 1759. Other taxes were imposed on Massachusetts papers from March 18, 1785, to July 2, 1785, and a tax was placed on each advertisement run in Massachusetts newspapers from July 2, 1785, until early in the year 1788. From September 30, 1842, to September 30, 1848, Virginia taxed its newspapers, but limited the tax to ten dollars or less a year on any one paper, depending on the subscription price. The lower the subscription price, the lower the tax. While our Civil War was going on, the federal government taxed newspapers on the gross receipts from advertising, but all such taxes were removed March 2, 1867.

As more and more advertising began to appear in newspapers in this country, with a corresponding increase in the amount of news presented, page sizes kept getting larger and larger.

As even the fastest presses in use several generations ago were ever so much slower than presses of today, it was considered, in many instances, more expedient to increase the page size than the number of pages, as the actual printing of a larger sheet—the pressroom part of the work—took no longer, or little longer, than the printing of a smaller sheet. Besides, many publishers considered the larger sheets more impressive than the smaller.

The old hand press had a capacity of only about 200 impressions an hour, or 100 sheets printed on both sides. Thus only 100 four-page papers printed two pages at a time could be turned out in an hour from such a press. Even when the first cylinder presses and steam power began to be used for the printing of newspapers, early in the nineteenth century, no more than 2000 impressions an hour could be run off by one pressman, who still was obliged to feed separate sheets of paper by hand. Later, cylinder presses were developed to accommodate as many as ten hand-feeders and had a capacity of ten times 2000 impressions, or 10,000 sheets printed on both sides. But it was not until the latter half of the nineteenth century, when stereotyping—experimented with by several individuals early in the eighteenth century, but practically applied by several American newspapers only after the Civil War—had been developed to a high point of efficiency, and the web perfecting rotary press, which was electrically driven and automatically fed from rolls of newsprint, also had been highly developed, that it was possible to print newspapers of many pages at a high rate of speed. Modern stereotyping methods, of course, make it possible to produce duplicate plates from original page forms quickly, and the duplicates can be printed from simultaneously and speedily on one or several modern press units.

And thus the size of the newspaper page grew, until it reached the stage of the "blanket sheets" of our more recent forefathers—papers with as many as nine or more columns 13 or 14 picas wide to the page and several inches deeper than the columns of most newspapers of today.

One of these "blanket sheets," the *Morning Courier and New-York Enquirer*, attained a page size of 27 by 32½ inches, with eleven columns to the page, each column a little more than 14 picas wide. The issue for January 1, 1851—typical of many issues of that paper—appeared with eleven columns on each of its four pages, with the first five columns of the front page filled with small advertisements, most of them beginning with two-line initial letters. And many similar advertisements appeared on the other pages. Double oxford rules were used above and below the front-page date line.

Eight and one-half years later, however, July 4, 1859, an ambitious journalist from Boston, George Roberts, published one issue of a paper in New York City designed to set a high mark for "blanket-sheet" papers. His *Illuminated Quadruple Constellation* embraced eight pages, with a page size of 35 by 50 inches, with thirteen columns to the page, each column about 13½ picas wide. As suggested by Example 4, columns one and thirteen of the front page were high columns. The nameplate, an elaborate affair eleven columns wide, was 8 inches deep. Ten other engravings were employed on the page, including large cuts of President Buchanan, Edward Everett and the Reverend Henry Ward Beecher. Many other engravings were run on the inside pages, along with considerable verse and quite a number of advertisements.

In a preface that began at the top of the first high column on the front page, the editor and publisher stated:

"We do not wish to conceal the honorable pride which we take in this magnificent sheet. It is the offspring of Invention, Taste, Enterprise and herculean Industry; it is without a compeer or rival; it

ILLUMINATED QUADRUPLE SHEET

The Constellation.

New York, 1859. George Roberts, Editor & Publisher. Price Fifty Cents.

EXAMPLE 4

cannot be excelled in its mammoth dimensions—because a sheet of any greater length and breadth would be absolutely unmanageable. The elephant might be caught, but what would you do with him? It cannot be excelled in its typographical beauty—in its artistic splendor—in its general imperialism of thought and design. It will be the pride of every true-hearted American and the wonder of Europe. Does language like this cause you to call us 'vain'? So be it. But it is not vanity that irradiates our brow; it is honest pride—pride such as Michael Angelo felt when he gazed on his St. Peter's—pride such as thrilled Napoleon when he beheld the Simplon conquering with its enormous and fearless length the terrible Alps.

"We were the pioneers in this extraordinary enterprise, of which the old *Boston Notion* is the monument. That sheet, superb as it is, pales its fires before the *Illuminated Quadruple Constellation.*

"Then, with our great Artists, Poets, Prose Writers and Printers who have been engaged with us, we offer this glorious Typographical Tribute on the shrine of Patriotism, and in the atmosphere now hallowed by the Glorious Fourth, exclaim, in the words of Ross Wallace, 'The Love of Country Is the Love of God.' "

In ten columns on the front page of the *Constellation* appeared a story continued from the fourth page—a "break-back" arrangement that would seem inexcusable now—but the *Constellation* introduced the front-page continuation by stating that inasmuch as pages one and eight were printed last, "we placed the first part of these 'wonderful discoveries' on Page Four, to which the reader's attention is directed before commencing here." The story was a reprint of the "Moon Hoax" tale published by the *New York Sun* in 1835.

A half dozen and more "story-advertisements," a book notice, an essay, three sets of verses and several pieces of miscellany appeared on the front page, but nothing that now would be regarded as straight news. Several of the engravings on the front and other pages were from the volume referred to in the book notice, *The History of the United States, for Families and Libraries,* by Benson J. Lossing. Extra shoulders of white space were used with all column rules.

A few somewhat modified "blanket-sheet" newspapers still are being published in this country. And a great many papers in other countries still appear with most of their columns 14 picas or more in width.

But the "blanket sheets" were too unwieldy to be popular with many newspaper readers, and, with the coming of faster presses and improved stereotyping, newspapers began to revert to smaller page sizes—but to print more pages to the copy, and to employ narrower columns than before.

However, while newspapers in general many years ago tended steadily to become larger as to page size, as well as to present more and narrower columns to the page, many an individual newspaper changed from smaller to larger and from larger to smaller several times in the course of its existence. Sometimes these changes of format were made necessary by a temporary shortage of paper of a certain size; sometimes by a pronounced falling off or decided increase of advertising patronage; sometimes by a change of press equipment; sometimes by a change of ownership and the application of new ideas.

It should be interesting here to trace, sketchily, with occasional interruptions and "flash-backs," the physical evolution of one of our leading metropolitan dailies of today—a newspaper that has undergone many changes of format—the *New York Herald Tribune.*

Although the *Herald* was launched by James Gordon Bennett May 6, 1835, six years before Horace Greeley first issued the *Tribune,* and the papers were not merged until March 19, 1924, this study is confined to the *Tribune* and the *Herald Tribune.*

One reason for this, obviously, is that the physical evolution of one of these papers can be sketched more briefly than that of both could be; and another reason is that, with the merging of the papers, the *Herald Tribune* continued to follow the format of the *Tribune.*

When the *New-York* (observe the hyphen) *Tribune* first appeared, April 10, 1841, it consisted of four pages. The page size (Greeley referred to it in his announcement as "a fair royal sheet") was about 15 by 20⅝ inches, with five columns to the page. The columns (our present point system was not adopted as standard until 1886) were a little wider than 16 picas—about 16¼ picas. (See Example 5.) Most of the body matter was in types about the size of our present 6-point or 5½-point types, although some of the early issues were partly set in types even smaller.

(In those days some newspapers computed the widths of columns, as well as the depths, in agates, rather than in picas or inches.)

The title line of early issues of the *Tribune* was in large outlined old-English letters with shading between the outer lines. A masthead, or flag (condensed statement of ownership, principles, purposes,

New-York Tribune.

BY HORACE GREELEY. "I desire you to understand the true principles of the Government. I wish them carried out—I ask nothing more."—Harrison. OFFICE NO. 30 ANN-ST.

PRICE ONE CENT. NEW-YORK, SATURDAY, APRIL 10, 1841. VOL. I. NO. 1.

CASE OF RECORDER MORRIS.

Opinion of Willis Hall, Attorney General, on the legality of the conduct of Robert H. Morris, Recorder of the City of New-York.

EXAMPLE 5

address, and so on), was at the top of column one on the front page of early issues, although no masthead appeared on page one of the first issue. The only head below the date line of the *Tribune's* first front page consisted of one centered line of 8-point capitals, above three hanging-indented lines of a 6-point bold face. And nearly 1000 lines of 6-point body matter were presented on the page, unrelieved by any leading.

One of the chief features of early issues was a front-page serialization of Dickens' *Barnaby Rudge*, with a line under the title reading "A New Work by Boz." Number eight of volume one presented "Fifteen Songs by Thomas Moore."

Although early issues of the *Tribune* continued to present fiction stories and verse, a decided change appeared on the front page of the paper about a fortnight after its launching. Number fourteen of volume one had appeared with the first two and one-half columns devoted to *Barnaby Rudge*. But number fifteen came out with column one of the front page given over to small advertisements.

Later issues of early numbers presented as many as four columns of small advertisements on front pages—a practice still followed (sometimes to the extent of entire front pages) by some newspapers in other lands. (But World War II, with its newsprint and other material shortages, as pointed out in Chapter 23 of Part I of this book, caused many papers in other lands to give up running classified advertisements on front pages, in favor of news stories.)

About five months after the first issue of the *Tribune* appeared, the paper changed its format. September 13, 1841, it came out with the same page size, but with six columns to the page—columns about 13¾ picas wide. A new title line, in a sort of Condensed Bodoni Bold, with a pictorial device between *New-York* and *Tribune*, appeared at the top of the front page. Columns one and six of that page were "high columns"; that is, they started higher than the top of the title line and flanked it on both sides, with the four inside columns starting under the title line. See Example 6.

(In recent years certain newspapers have appeared with front pages given this "new" treatment, which, of course, is not at all new.)

April 6, 1844, the *Tribune* appeared with a title line reading *New-York Daily Tribune* (to differentiate it from the *Semi-Weekly Tribune* and the *Weekly Tribune*) on a page 17 by 21¼ inches, with seven

NEW-YORK TRIBUNE.

BY GREELEY & McELRATH.

OFFICE NO. 30 ANN-STREET.

EXAMPLE 6

columns about 13½ picas wide to the page. A copy still consisted of four pages.

In the 1840's several metropolitan newspapers presented unusually important news stories under displayed heads, a practice which was further developed through the Civil War days. Such heads, the most prominent lines of which seldom were larger than 24 point, consisted of a succession of single-line decks in various kinds and sizes of types (sometimes a dozen or more) separated by dashes. When a deck could not be presented with the desired degree of display, in a single line, it was presented in one full line and one or more following centered lines or hanging-indented lines. And from such decks our heads of today have been developed. (Our Civil War encouraged the use of comparatively large display types for newspaper heads, but the Spanish-American War encouraged greater display and the use of banner lines, and World War I still larger display, with larger banners and more of them. For a while, during World War II, many of our papers went in for still more vigorous display. But with the clamping down of government restrictions on newsprint and other publishing materials, space-saving became necessary for many newspapers, and a toning down of display and a general tightening up of pages resulted. More and more newspapers started using space-and-time-saving flush-left heads of the sort pioneered by the *Linotype News* in 1929 and ever since ardently championed by that publication. (See Chapter 2 of Part II.)

In 1850 the *Tribune* went back to a smaller page size—15 by 19⅞ inches—and to six columns, but of the same width as before—about 13½ picas. And one of the chief reasons for this change was that the *Tribune* had quit being a four-page and had become an eight-page paper.

However, three years later, April 11, 1853, the *Tribune* increased its page size to 17½ by 22½ inches, and again appeared with seven columns to the page—columns about 15¾ picas wide. The title line now appeared in old-English, and incorporated a cut of a printing press of that day.

Less than seventeen months later, though, September 1, 1854, the *Tribune* went back to a smaller page size, back to six columns, and with the column width reduced to about 14½ picas. The new page size was about 16¼ by 21⅜ inches.

By May 1, 1855, the page had been shortened to 20¾ inches, but by January 1, 1856, it had been lengthened to 21¼ inches.

In August, 1861, the *Tribune* began to print from curved stereotype plates of entire pages, following many experiments carried on in the *Tribune* plant by Charles Craske.

Early in July of 1886 the first commercially successful Linotypes were operated by the *Tribune*, the first newspaper to be composed on such machines. Incidentally, Whitelaw Reid, who at that time was the leading spirit of the *Tribune*, is said to have been the one who gave the new machine, which composed and cast type in a solid line, or slug, rather than in individual types, its name—Linotype. This machine revolutionized printing and publishing, as it enabled one man to compose as many lines as five or six compositors setting type by hand. It speeded up, lessened the cost and increased the amount of printing of all kinds. Such machines have been developed to produce composition from small 4-point faces up to 144-point faces—faces 2 inches high. Composing machines of different makes and models are now in use in most printing and publishing plants throughout the world, and today comparatively little type is set by hand.

In the meantime, several other inventions and mechanical developments had speeded up the transmission of news and had been at least partly responsible for the establishment of more and more newspapers, as well as for an increase in the number of pages in many papers.

January 24, 1838, according to *Dots and Dashes*, a house publication of the Western Union Telegraph Company, "Samuel F. B. Morse transmitted the historic message, 'Attention, the Universe! By kingdoms, right wheel!' at the first formal demonstration of the electromagnetic telegraph before an audience of distinguished guests at New York University on Washington Square, New York City. . . . Morse next demonstrated his invention before the Franklin Institute of Philadelphia, and then before officials in Washington, D. C. After years of struggle, he obtained governmental backing for an experimental line between Baltimore and Washington, D. C., and on May 24, 1844, sent the message, 'What hath God wrought?' over that line to Vail in Baltimore, who sent it back." (The Vail referred to was Alfred Vail, son of Judge Stephen Vail and nephew of George Vail, owners of the Speedwell Iron Works at Morristown, N. J., all of whom assisted Morse with his experiments.)

In 1858 the first message by cable between Europe and the United States was sent.

Three years later—in 1861—the first transcontinental telegraph line in this country was completed.

In 1865 William Bullock of Philadelphia invented a press fed from a continuous roll, or "web," of paper.

March 10, 1876, the first spoken message successfully transmitted by wire was sent by Alexander Graham Bell to an assistant in a Boston hotel.

One of the first practical applications of wireless came in 1898, according to *Compton's Pictured Encyclopedia*, "when Guglielmo Marconi followed the Kingstown Regatta races in a tug and flashed the results to a Dublin paper. . . . On October 27, 1920, Station KDKA at Pittsburgh obtained a license, and on November 2 it broadcast the 1920 election returns. . . . Other scientists added their improvements to Marconi's and by 1921 'wireless' had become 'radio,' with broadcasting successfully established." (See, also, Chapter 3 of Part II.)

As recently as 1909 the *New York Tribune* continued to present six columns to the page, although the page size and column width had been changed several more times. For some time before October, 1909, however, seven columns appeared on pages containing classified advertising—three columns of news 16 picas wide, and four columns of classified advertising 12 picas wide. (This same column plan has been retained to this day for the *Herald Tribune* editorial page.)

October 21, 1909, the *Tribune* changed all of its news pages from six to seven columns—columns 13½ picas wide—with a page size of 17½ by 24⅛ inches. And a seven-column paper the *Tribune* continued to be until 1914, although, by that time, it had narrowed its column width to 13 picas.

June 23, 1914, it became an eight-column paper, with columns narrowed to 12½ picas, and thus it continued, with a page size of 18 by 23 inches, until April 6, 1932, when it decreased its column width to 12 picas and its page size to 17⅛ by 22¾ inches.

"Up to the latter years of World War I," ran a typographic announcement in the *New York Herald Tribune* for February 28, 1937, "the notion that news printing could be a thing of practical beauty, far removed from the brashness of a screaming headline, had not dawned in America. But in 1916 the *Tribune's* editors and compositors, working with the famed typographer Ben Sherbow, conducted a year-long series of typographic experiments. These experiments took the form of stop-watch reading tests using various combinations of display type looking to a more pleasing, more striking and more quickly readable headline style.

"The net of those tests was the *Herald Tribune* headline typography substantially as it is today, but the changes leading to the present style were gradual. The first major change appeared in the *Tribune* of February 12, 1917, when headlines, for the first time in modern newspaper history, were set in upper- and lower-case (capitals and small letters). Up to that time, news headlines—as they are in many newspapers to this day—had been set all upper-case (all capitals), despite the fact that the eye, by reading habit, is accustomed to a combination of capitals and small letters almost from the time it begins to read."

December 3, 1918, the *Tribune* changed over to a Sherbow-designed news head schedule in capitals and lower-case of Bodoni

Bold and Bodoni Bold Italic—a news head schedule that the *Herald Tribune* continues to use.

(It was this writer's privilege several times in 1919 and 1920 to watch Benjamin Sherbow at work on some of his newspaper experiments, in his offices off Union Square in New York City. Another youngster, William G. Lownds, and this writer, both of the Linotype Company, used to drop in on Sherbow on Saturday afternoons to watch him at work and to do odd jobs of type checking and galley sorting for him. That experimenting typographer, a wide-hipped little man with a high-pitched voice, usually had a curved-stem pipe going full blast and a cloud of tobacco smoke about his head as he worked away on his unconventional newspaper pages. A brother of his who worked with him often stood by playing a violin as Benjamin did his experimenting. And some of that music, it seemed, managed to get into his newspaper heads—always in capitals and lower-case; never in "all-caps." At any rate, Benjamin Sherbow's heads were "sweet singers" on the printed page.)

Up to World War I the 13-pica (or 13-em) column was regarded as the standard width for newspapers in this country, and quite a number of weeklies still adhere to that standard. But since World War I, most of our dailies have reduced their column widths—first to 12½ picas and then to 12, the present standard. And many of our weeklies also are now employing 12-pica columns.

An editorial in the *Publishers' Auxiliary* for September 22, 1945—an editorial headed "The Case for 12 Ems"—included these statements:

"The crusade for a change-over from 13 to 12 ems started in World War I, when metropolitan dailies switched over to this measurement to save newsprint, due to its scarcity and increasing prices. Weeklies likewise began to adopt 12 ems. But, in addition to being a paper-saving expedient, the idea demonstrated practical, profit-making advantages. It caught on and in the years that followed, the *Auxiliary* and other trade papers helped promote it.

"World War II brought another newsprint crisis. Early in 1943 the War Production Board urged country weeklies and small-town dailies, although exempt from paper-curtailment orders, to standardize on a 12-em column. By this means it was proposed to save 50,000 tons of newsprint a year.

"In the last two years more than 1000 weeklies have changed over from 13 to 12 ems. None of them, so far as we know, is contemplating going back to 13 ems, now that the war is over. That is a testimonial worth thinking about.

"Thus what was a patriotic wartime gesture has now become a peacetime asset.

"From all available evidence, the advantage lies with the editor who changes to 12 ems. Decreasing the column width gives him an extra column to the page, thus making a seven-column page out of a six; an eight out of a seven. That will be important in postwar years ahead from both an advertising and editorial standpoint.

"Changing from 13 to 12 ems automatically raises the advertising rate, since the publisher is getting the same amount of money for a smaller space. National advertisers as a whole have adopted the 12-em measure. Advertising plates and mats received in weekly offices are in 12-em measure almost exclusively. The publisher who runs 12-em ads in 13-em space, or their equivalent in multi-column ads, is supplying space for which he receives no pay.

"Then there is the matter of appearance and readability. Publishers report the change-over greatly improves the makeup of their papers. Their statements are corroborated by the fact that most of the winners in newspaper contests, especially where typographical appearance is taken into account, are 12-em papers.

"The final test lies with readers and advertisers. And here again 12-em shows its advantage. Publishers report that readers and advertisers are usually pleased with the change. The increased number of columns looks to them like a forward step, an indication of growth. Moreover, they say the change makes the paper easier to read."

Dailies of many pages and large circulations have effected large savings by reducing their column widths to 12 picas, and many of them have done so without any loss of word count.

A large metropolitan daily that reduced its column width from 12½ to 12 picas prepared for the change by replacing the regular spacebands on its composing machines with extra-thin spacebands to bring about a closer spacing of words.

The change was made without confusion in any department. Stories continued to run virtually line for line as before. Head-writers on the copy desk followed the same unit count. Operators continued to keep their machines going at high speed on body matter, and those on the head machines sent the larger lines through as speedily as ever.

Advertising plates, nearly all of them made for 12-pica columns anyhow, were quickly fitted to the forms, and the makeup men kept the forms rumbling to the stereotypers on scheduled time.

"We figure that the saving on newsprint alone amounts to four per cent," the business manager of the paper informed this writer, shortly after the change of column width was brought about. "And there are other savings, of course, along the line. Less metal, for one thing, is now needed in the composing room and in the stereotyping and engraving departments. These savings and others connected with the change of column width are considerable in the aggregate, and we get an even more attractive and legible paper, due largely to the closer spacing between words made possible by the use of extra-thin spacebands."

The editorial department was enthusiastic, too.

"Stories continue to go through virtually line for line," said the managing editor. "The copy desk experiences no trouble at all with heads for the narrower columns. The head-writers knew, of course, the night of the change, that they had 6 points less to work with, but the narrower measure proved no handicap, as they continued to follow the same character count used before. Closer spacing between words made up the difference. So, in one sense, there hasn't been any change in the editorial department, as the heads are written to the same plan as before, and as story length virtually has been unaffected by the narrower columns."

The present type-page depth of a printed copy of that paper is the same as before the change (21½ inches), and the paper depth is the same as before (22¾ inches). The type-page width of a printed copy, however, with each of the eight columns 6 points narrower than before, is 4 picas, or ⅔ of an inch, narrower than it was.

The paper width formerly was 18 inches. At present, with 4 picas, or ⅔ of an inch, deducted from the over-all type width, and allowing for dry-mat shrinkage in stereotyping, and for slightly narrower margins, the paper width is 17⅛ inches—⅞ of an inch narrower than before.

Thus a strip of newsprint 22¾ inches long and ⅞ of an inch wide (or nearly 20 square inches) is saved to the page under the new arrangement. For a 48-page issue, say, the saving in newsprint alone amounts to more than 900 square inches to the copy, a saving of more than two full pages of newsprint to the copy.

Thus that newspaper, with a daily circulation of more than 325,000 copies, effects a saving of more than 650,000 pages of newsprint every day it produces a 48-page paper.

Apply those figures to the Sunday editions, with a circulation of more than 450,000 and with the average number of pages more than twice forty-eight, and it will be seen that the saving amounts to more than 1,800,000 pages of newsprint to the issue.

Apply the figures to a year's issues, translate the pages of paper saved into tons of newsprint saved, and those tons into money saved; include the savings on metal, and other savings along the line, and it will be seen that the annual saving runs into many thousands of dollars.

And yet that large saving has been brought about by the adoption of a single simple and easily applied phase of makeup—the reducing of the column width by a mere 6 points.

Moreover, as stated before, the resultant closer spacing of words has made for an even more attractive and legible newspaper.

Of course, advertising rates were unaffected by the change to the narrower measure, as the depth of columns was kept the same as before, and the previous agate-line rate to the column was maintained.

During World War II, some of our daily newspapers (and some dailies even before World War II) started setting their news stories in column widths a few points or even 6 points less than 12 picas, to conserve newsprint, while retaining the conventional 6-point column rules. Other dailies started indenting news stories 3 points or so at the beginning and end of each slug line, to compensate for decreased shoulders on space-saving 4-, 3-, 2- and even 1-point column rules. (See Chapter 10 of Part I.)

The many thousands of newspapers published in this country use many different page sizes and for many different reasons—some of them having to do with press sizes and other mechanical considerations. Consequently, it would be naive to suggest that one particular size seems more desirable than any other. But it is quite practical to suggest that, roughly, a page might well be about one-third longer than it is wide, as such proportions make for an attractive oblong. A page as wide as it is long would not be so attractive; nor would one, say, twice as long as it is wide. A page of the latter sort would suggest lankiness, and would be awkward to handle; a square page, or one nearly square, would suggest squattiness, and be awkward to handle; but a page about a third longer than it is wide suggests gracefulness, and is comparatively easy to handle.

While a newspaper that is a large buyer of newsprint can have its paper made to its own specifications without having to pay a premium for such service, smaller buyers must order more or less standard sizes.

A large organization which, among other things, supplies many newspapers throughout the country with partly printed newspapers (with ready-prints, or patent-insides) uses certain definite page sizes.

For columns 13 picas wide, its page sizes are:

	5 columns—13	x	20	inches
	6 columns—15	x	22	inches
Short	7 columns—17½	x	22	inches
	7 columns—17½	x	24	inches
Short	8 columns—20	x	24	inches
	8 columns—20	x	26	inches

For columns 12 picas wide, its page sizes are:

	5 columns—11¾	x	16½	inches (tabloid)
	6 columns—14	x	22	inches
Short	7 columns—16	x	22	inches
	7 columns—16	x	24	inches
Short	8 columns—18	x	24	inches

To this writer, elaborate margins on a newspaper page seem as inappropriate as narrow margins usually would seem on a book page. The eye takes in the general outlines of most book pages—of two facing pages—all at once, and has a chance to appreciate the relation of margins to type lines—the relation of the frame to the picture. But most newspaper pages are too large and too complex to be taken in at a glance. One of the practical reasons why book margins are comparatively wide is to afford room for the thumbs to help hold the book while it is being read—room beyond the type lines. But most newspaper pages are not held by the outer edges while being read, but are folded for convenience, with the thumbs resting on adjoining columns of reading matter. Elaborate margins on newspaper pages would necessarily increase the page size over what it would be with narrower margins and consequently would make the pages, particularly already large pages, more difficult to handle.

To this writer, newspaper pages with side margins much more than 4 picas wide, top margins much more than 4 picas deep, and bottom margins much more than 5 picas deep, suggest carelessness, rather than artistry. To him such margins are so much superfluous "pie crust" that the publishers have neglected to remove for the convenience of the reader.

Many metropolitan dailies employ scantier margins than those suggested in the immediately preceding paragraph, chiefly for economic reasons, but many small-town newspapers appear with side margins an inch or more in width, with even greater top and bottom margins—with too much superfluous "pie crust."

4

Makeup Limitations

Newspaper designing is hedged about by many "must nots." It is markedly different, for instance, from fine-book designing. A designer of books not restricted to the limitations of the trade-book field is used to a comparatively free and wide choice of materials. He is accustomed to specifying, in addition to the kinds and sizes of type faces and the degrees of leading to be employed, the kinds of paper and ink, the page dimensions, the line widths, the margin sizes, the kinds of decorative and illustrative mediums, the binding treatments, and so on, including, even, the kinds of press processes to be used. But the designer of a metropolitan daily has no such freedom of choice.

Would he suggest a better grade of paper? Paper costs are high enough as they are, declares the publisher.

A better quality and higher priced ink? Too expensive, says the publisher.

Would he increase the column width? Thousands of national and local advertisers who prepare millions of advertisements to be duplicated in many newspapers work to the 12-pica column width as standard.

How about a larger body face—an artistic book face—and more leading between body lines? But no, the designer reconsiders, those things would not do, either. A larger face—one very much larger—would not space so well in a 12-pica column, and artistic book faces were not designed for use on newsprint nor to be printed on high-speed presses with rubber rollers. No; a much larger face would not do, agrees the editorial department, with more news and feature material on hand than it can get into print as things are. Besides, continues the designer, think what stereotyping, with its tremendous pressure, might do to the fine lines of certain book faces.

Yet he well knows that it would never do to suggest that stereotyping be abandoned for electrotyping. The latter would be far too slow, to say nothing of the new and expensive equipment that would be required. Nor would it do to suggest running direct from type, for the presses of big newspapers are not built to run that way. Besides, many duplicate plates of pages are required to take care of large circulations quickly. Besides, again, several hundred thousand impressions would be quite hard on many units of composition in the original forms, many of which units—particularly halftones and line-cuts—are salvaged to be used again and again. Besides, still again, several original forms are broken up and remade several times daily for the various editions published, and often while their predecessor pages—in the form of stereotype plates—still are being used on the presses.

Would he suggest halftones of a much finer screen than that at present used, with the hope of securing more detail in the printed pictures? Not when he thinks of what would happen to fine-screen halftones—how they would fill up and the resultant pictures appear "muddy"—when printed on coarse-fibered newsprint.

How about eliminating the comic strips? While that might be quite agreeable to the publisher or editor personally, it probably would affect the circulation adversely.

Up to this point the designer of a metropolitan daily would have contributed nothing toward an improved appearance for the newspaper. He would have had no chance to do so. The limitations he would have encountered have become too widely and firmly standardized to be suddenly and radically disregarded without possibly disastrous economic consequences to the owner of the paper.

A skilled designer could do considerably more, comparatively, for a small weekly newspaper than for a large daily, and, working under ideal conditions in such a field, might well turn out a distinguished-looking product.

But conditions in the weekly field, at best, rarely are ideal. The weekly paper, too, must approximate the column width followed as standard by many large advertisers, unless its publisher has equipment enough and men enough—and, moreover, would be *permitted* by advertisers—to reset all plated or "matted" advertising matter received from them, to fit his wider columns.

Few weekly publishers could afford to follow such a procedure, even if minded to do so.

But many weekly publishers with small circulations can and do run the greater part of their pages direct from type, and some few use paper better than the average newsprint, finer screen halftones, and ink of better quality than that used by most newspapers.

With the advantages afforded by running direct from type, finer screen halftones, better paper and ink, the designer would be in a position to turn out an attractive-looking paper—provided he were given a fairly free choice in the selection and treatment of type faces, and were assured of *expert make-ready and running in the pressroom.*

But such happy possibilities are predicated on conditions that do not prevail in the average newspaper plant—the newspaper mass-production factory, if you will—and so it may be well to leave off thinking for the moment of newspaper-printing ideals, however reluctantly, and to return to the consideration of more prosaic but more closely approachable possibilities.

5

News Head Faces

MANY NEWSPAPERS continue to use headline faces dating from before the Civil War—faces the selection and use of which were dictated by economic conditions that do not apply to the same degree today—and that are just as unattractive now and as hard to read as they were then. (Not, however, that age should be held against the quality of type design. Far from it. Certain faces designed years ago—even centuries ago—are just as good today as they were then, and will continue to be good for years to come. But there were unattractive and illegible types in the past—as there also are today—and some of them still appear in newspapers.)

Many newspapers have discarded certain headline faces in favor of better ones, but have nullified their effectiveness by using them in conjunction with faces they do not harmonize with.

Type faces fall naturally into specific categories, the chief of which, for newspaper headline purposes, are old style, modern, sans serif and square serif. Some typographers use the terms square serif and flat serif interchangeably.

The term old style applied to a type face does not necessarily mean an obsolete, or even obsolescent, type face; nor does the term modern necessarily mean a recently designed face.

To attempt a brief and non-technical definition, old-style faces are more freely flowing than modern faces, appear "less premeditated," have slanting or dipped serifs, and but slight contrast between their lighter and heavier elements. On the other hand, modern faces are more precise, more severe, have evened-off serifs, and incorporate contrasting thick and thin strokes.

Serifs, in a type sense, are the ending strokes of most letters in the English and many other alphabets, and are the offshoot of the ending chisel strokes of the ancient carvers of letters into stone, and of the ending stylus or pen strokes of the writers of ancient manuscripts.

An excellent illustration of old style is provided by the original

Caslon types, and a good example of modern is afforded by Bodoni. Yet both faces were designed considerably more than a century ago. William Caslon was a noted English type founder who lived from 1692 to 1766, and Giambattista Bodoni was a noted Italian scholar and printer who lived from 1740 to 1813.

A sans-serif face, as the name implies, is a face without serifs; and it usually has little if any variation in the thickness of its strokes. It is commonly referred to in this country as gothic. In England and Scotland it is often called sans serif; in France and Spain, antique; in Germany, grotesque. (In various sections of Europe and to designers the sort of type we usually think of as old-English is more generally known as gothic or black-letter.)

Examples 7 to 10 show faces that come within the old-style, modern, sans-serif and square-serif classifications, in the order named.

And Example 11 shows the sort of face generally referred to in Europe as gothic or black-letter, but in this country as old-English.

18-point Caslon Old Face

EXAMPLE 7

18-point Bodoni

EXAMPLE 8

18-point Spartan Heavy

EXAMPLE 9

18-point Memphis Bold

EXAMPLE 10

18-point Lino Text

EXAMPLE 11

While it would be too arbitrary to insist, in these commercial days, that old-style, modern, sans-serif and square-serif faces never should be used one with another in multiple-deck newspaper heads, it is no more than fair to state that such mixtures often result in unattractive and not-easy-to-follow heads. And it would be too arbitrary to insist that condensed faces should not be used with medium-width or expanded faces, in a multiple-deck head.

In newspaper designing, the weight of faces is something to be considered along with letter shape. And in some instances the result is less discordant when an old-style face has been used with a modern in the same multiple-deck head (supposing that the type limitations of a plant offer no better combination "to hold color") than it is when a heavy modern has been used with a light modern, or a heavy old style with a light old style, or a heavy sans serif with a light sans serif.

The use of news heads comparatively heavy throughout, alongside department or feature heads comparatively light throughout, is something quite different, and sometimes can be highly acceptable as affording desirable contrast between adjacent heads, if the faces in both kinds of heads are held to the same type family or closely related families. (But no more than a few decidedly contrasting heavy-and-lights should be used on the same pages, for reasons set forth in Chapter 12 of Part I.)

As stated in a preceding chapter, one type of reader likes a vigorous head dress, while another prefers a more restrained one. But both types appreciate legibility. They want their newspapers to be easy to read—at least as easy as is reasonably possible.

It is possible for a head dress to be vigorous and legible at the same time, or to be restrained and at the same time easy to read. Neither vigor nor restraint need be opposed to readability. But the trouble with many newspapers that go in for vigorous head dresses is that they overplay display. They use too many large display lines too close to each other and in too many different kinds of faces—often in faces that do more "shouting," as well as more clashing with each other, than informing. In attempting to attract attention to several different stories at once, such papers succeed in distracting attention from one story to another and another—unless a particular story in itself is of outstanding interest to the reader. Even then, the other adjacent and clashing headlines keep interrupting his reading, consciously or otherwise.

Such head dresses can attract attention to a paper as a purchasable commodity on the newsstand—an important consideration in communities with competing papers that depend on newsstand sales, and particularly on sales to transients, for any considerable part of their circulations—but, having attracted attention to the point of purchase, they proceed to distract it.

Some readers become aware of those distractions at once, and resent them; other readers take longer, but eventually become consciously disturbed by such papers, and still others—many others—and without realizing why, grow tired of such papers and change to others.

The head dresses of such papers suggest display windows packed with so many attention-arresting objects that no one object has a chance to stand out on its own. Windows of that sort do stop the passerby, but they give him little opportunity to appreciate individually the objects offered for sale. Or, again, such head dresses suggest a closely packed and competing group of husky-throated auctioneers clamoring so loudly that no one of them can be comprehended.

There is an old and true saying that "all display is no display." Many a headline good in itself has been "killed" by an inexpertly handled adjacent headline. Effective display is secured by contrast—harmonious contrast.

As a general rule, lines set entirely in capital letters are more difficult to read than lines set in capitals and lower-case or in lower-case without capitals.

There are at least three good reasons why this is so.

One is that, as most capitals in a font of type are of the same general shape—usually oblong—they are not sufficiently varied in appearance to form a distinctive word pattern. That is why a skilled typographer, when, to secure an evened-off or more formal effect in a piece of fine printing or an advertisement, he occasionally composes lines entirely in capitals, usually letter spaces such lines—so that each letter will be given a better chance to stand out on its own and thus the lines be easier to read than they would be without the extra spacing between letters. (Different degrees of spacing are employed between some capitals than between others, as, for example, in the word "LANE" more extra space is required between the N and the E than between the L and the A and between the A and the N, as the natural body space above the lower stroke of the L, and on either side of the upper portion of the A, makes little if any extra spacing necessary. See Examples 12 and 13.)

LANE	LANE
(No letter spacing)	**(Letter spaced)**
EXAMPLE 12	EXAMPLE 13

Another reason is that, from childhood on, most readers of English, as well as many other languages, have been accustomed to reading ever so many more lines in capitals and lower-case, or in lower-case alone, than in capitals—in books, magazines, newspapers, personal and business correspondence—and have formed the habit of reading, not letter by letter, but by word forms—by the forms of words in lower-case letters.

And still another reason is that the blank space above the lower-case letters without ascenders, and alongside some of the lower-case ascenders, lets more light into a line and consequently makes for a greater contrast between the printed characters and the paper background than is afforded by most capitals—a contrast that enhances legibility.

Through the years, the makers of the Linotype have made an intensive study of the elements that make for legibility in type faces —a study the findings of which have been supported and applauded by many hundreds of oculists, psychologists and educators in various parts of the world.

That part of the resultant report bearing directly on the subject here discussed ran as follows:

"Our second principle dealt with the question of the way in which words of a familiar language are read. Here, investigation amply bore out the conclusion that all such reading is a matter of recognizing word forms, rather than a spelling out of the letters which compose them.

"In order to realize the soundness of this finding, you have only to remember that the reason matter set in capitals makes comparatively hard reading lies in the unfamiliar aspect of the resulting word forms. Except for the size of the parallelograms by which they are bounded, the appearance of corresponding words is almost identical. So, best to convey these familiar word forms is to gain again in legibility.

"The accompanying diagram illustrates what is meant by word forms:

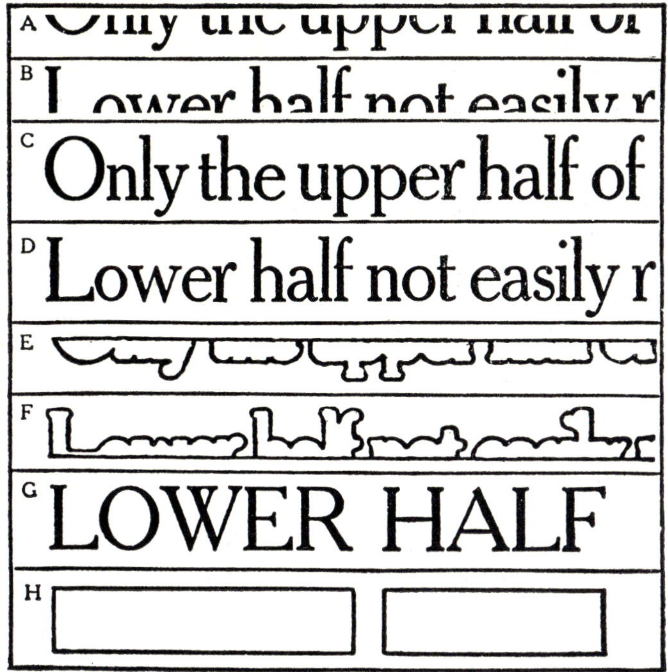

"Figure A cannot be read. Figure B can. Yet, in each instance, the line is cut at precisely the same point. Figure C is the completion of Figure A; Figure D that of Figure B. Figure E is the word shape of Figure A; Figure F that of Figure B. Both Figure A and Figure B, as shown by Figures G and H, would be parallelograms only if set in capitals."

THESE LINES YOU ARE NOW READING, SET, AS THEY ARE, ENTIRELY IN CAPITALS, ARE MORE DIFFICULT TO READ THAN THE LINES IN THE PRECEDING AND FOLLOWING PARAGRAPHS.

Of course this does not mean that lines never should be presented entirely in capitals. In some forms of printing, when evened-off effects or formal treatments are desirable, lines presented in such a way can be quite effective. And, of course, lines entirely in capitals seem quite appropriate for such dignified and formal things as inscriptions on monuments or on the entablatures of certain buildings of classic design —on dignified and formal things to be appreciated leisurely—not in a hurry.

Sparingly used, lines entirely in capitals can be quite effective in newspaper advertising—even for newspaper headlines. But they should be used sparingly, as newspaper advertising and headlines usually must be read hurriedly if they are to be read at all.

As a general rule, sans-serif, or gothic, faces (particularly in the smaller, body-matter sizes) are more difficult to read than faces with serifs, as we are more accustomed to reading faces with serifs than without them. The serifs help to shape the word forms we have learned by years of practice to recognize at a glance.

As a general rule, again, faces of medium, or normal, width are easier to read than expanded, widened faces, or condensed or extra-condensed faces, as such faces are departures from the type forms to which we have become most accustomed through years of reading.

As a general rule, still again, italic faces are more difficult to read than roman faces, as we are more accustomed to reading roman faces than italic. Sparingly used, however, italics can be quite effective on a newspaper page. As the slant of such faces gives them more "movement" than roman faces generally possess, they can be made to contribute liveliness and sparkle to the dress of a paper. But very many consecutive lines in italics would be too lively, too disturbing, for easy reading. After the first few lines (as this paragraph begins to suggest, if, indeed, it has not done so before this) the very fanciness of such faces causes the mechanics of the lines to intrude on the consciousness of the reader—to get between him and the message they are supposed, but erroneously so, to convey particularly effectively.

As newspaper columns are comparatively narrow, the characters of comparatively large display faces used in single-column widths must be somewhat condensed to give a satisfactory unit count—an important consideration to the head-writer.

Headlines that must be confined to ten or fewer units each are more difficult to write than lines that may contain from twelve to fifteen units each. Given more units to work with, of course, the head-writer has a freer choice of words at his command and can work at higher speed and otherwise more effectively. (In certain condensed faces the figures and most capitals are counted as one unit each, with the letter I, most punctuation marks and spaces counted as a half unit each, and with the M, W and the dash counted as one and one-half units each. But the M and W of certain other faces are several times as wide as the thinnest lower-case letters in the same fonts—sometimes five or six or more times as wide—and, consequently, other definite systems of unit counting must be worked out to be followed when such faces are used.)

Many newspapers that now use condensed capitals for single-column heads could enhance the legibility of the lines, and without a lessening of unit count, by substituting capitals and lower-case of less-condensed faces of the same point size. Or they could use even larger sizes of the same condensed faces and maintain the same unit count, and with enhanced legibility, by using capitals and lower-case of the larger size instead of capitals alone of the smaller. Or, again, they could secure a larger letter count, with increased readability, by using capitals and lower-case of a condensed face of a certain size, rather than capitals alone of the same face and size.

To illustrate: A line set, say, in 30-point capitals of a certain condensed face affords a unit count of twelve.

The same unit count can be maintained by using capitals and lower-case of a less-condensed 30-point face—and such lines will be easier to read than the others, and for two reasons: Medium-width faces are easier to read than condensed faces; capitals and lower-case are easier to read than capitals. (It is assumed, of course, that the sort of medium-width faces referred to are inherently good ones. Medium width in itself does not make a face good.) Or the same unit count can be maintained, and readability enhanced, by using 36-point condensed capitals and lower-case, rather than 30-point condensed capitals. Or the unit count can be increased, and legibility enhanced, by setting the lines in 30-point condensed capitals and lower-case, rather than in 30-point condensed capitals.

A single-column line in 30-point condensed capitals, as has been stated, is comparatively hard to read. But when the same size and kind of capitals are presented in lines two, three or four columns wide, the lines become increasingly hard to read. Even the lower-case letters of the same 30-point condensed face, when presented in lines two or more columns wide, become increasingly difficult to read with each additional column of width.

A fairly safe general rule to follow is: The wider the line the larger the type face—larger as to point size or width or both point size and width.

To illustrate: A paper that uses a 36-point condensed face for the main lines of single-column heads might consistently use a 42-point condensed face for heads two columns wide, or a 48-point condensed for heads three or four columns wide. Or it might well use a 36-point medium-width face for heads two columns wide, or a 42- or 48-point medium-width for heads three or four columns wide.

This applies, of course, to heads for important news stories—not necessarily to heads for minor feature stories or secondary news stories —which often might well be presented under two-column heads (either italic or roman) no larger than 18 or 24 point, even when 36-point condensed faces are used for the main lines of important news heads presented in single columns.

Up to our Civil War times nearly all newspaper headlines were confined to single-column widths, and for various reasons. One of the chief of these was established by the limitations of even the fastest presses used by even the largest and most enterprising metropolitan newspapers. For twenty years or so following 1846 many of our enterprising metropolitan dailies were printed direct from type on what were known as type-revolving presses. The type lines were assembled in a curved container called a turtle (a term, by the way, that has been handed down to the page-form trucks used in many newspaper plants today, as the turtle was moved about on a truck, as well as by means of a crane) and the curved container was fastened to and revolved with a cylinder on the press. As the column rules played important parts in helping to hold the thousands of individual types in the form as it rotated with the cylinder, the rules usually were regarded as "unbreakable" by editors and advertisers unless higher rates were paid for the special treatment made necessary by such "breakings." (See Example 155.)

And it was not until stereotyping processes had been developed to a fairly practical state that large newspapers in general began to "break" their column rules more or less regularly for advertising and for heads over stories.

Old-time single-column heads often ran many decks deep—much deeper than most of our heads of today.

When enterprising newspapers of today wish to give an unusually important story prominent head treatment, they do much of the displaying horizontally, rather than vertically, and wisely so, as, properly treated, such display can be much more quickly comprehended by the reader than could many comparatively large display faces presented in many consecutive short lines.

Lines of the latter sort would call for too frequent shifting of attention on the part of the reader—too frequent shifting back and forth, over and over again, from the ends of preceding lines to the beginnings of succeeding ones—to be read with comfort.

The tendency of most large dailies in recent years has been toward fewer decks in news heads, with two decks as the maximum number for any but exceptionally important stories—even though Americans have come to be quite generally referred to as forming a nation of headline readers.

Many Americans undoubtedly do read more newspaper headlines than stories, but, even so, or possibly because of that fact, they want to be able to do their headline reading as easily and quickly as is reasonably possible.

Display heads from old-time papers can be quaintly interesting when looked at occasionally and individually; but if we were obliged to look at many of them side by side and day after day, we should soon grow weary of their multiplicities of unattractive, unrelated and hard-to-read faces and be glad enough to switch to heads of fewer decks and in fewer and more harmoniously associated type faces.

Yet, as previously stated, many newspapers of today employ heads just as inexpertly planned (even if they do not use quite so many different kinds of faces in the same heads), and many of our papers of today continue to use some of the same unattractive and hard-to-read faces that were used in papers many years ago.

Economic reasons were largely responsible for the comparatively wide use of gothic capitals for newspaper heads many years ago. Gothics were selected and used by many newspapers then largely because, in those days of hand setting, gothics would wear longer than most other type faces. Gothics had no light lines or serifs to wear down or break off from oft-repeated use—an important consideration when the putting in of a new font of display type was something of an occasion in many a newspaper plant.

And many more newspaper heads were set in gothic capitals then than in capitals and lower-case, because a font of capitals could be purchased at about half the price of a font of capitals and lower-case. In fact, the demand for gothic lower-case in the old days was so slight that many type founders offered only capital fonts of many of their gothics.

And gothic capitals were popular in newspaper plants years ago for another reason. Nearly all newspaper plants then did job work as well as newspaper publishing. Much of that commercial printing consisted of sales bills for farmers, and gothic capitals seemed quite the thing for farmers' sales bills—so much so, in fact, that certain of those gothics became known, in composing-room parlance, as "stud-horse gothics."

Consequently, many a newspaper publisher and job printer of other days, when planning a head dress for his paper, had at least one eye on the requirements of his job department and its sales bills, and he usually chose gothic capitals.

Habit is a strong thing in the newspaper business, and many a newspaper continues to use the same kind of unsightly and hard-to-read gothic capitals that it used a generation or two ago, even though the economic reasons that originally dictated the use of such faces no longer apply in the same degree. In these days, when most of the lines in a newspaper are composed by machine, a font of matrices of one kind of face should last as long as a font of any other kind.

Some newspaper publishers hesitate to change the head dresses of their papers for fear that any decided change will militate against the recognition value of the heads as they are, which, such publishers contend, have become valuable trademarks. But this, of course, is fallacious reasoning. Such a publisher might as well contend that he himself should keep on wearing the same sort of clothes that he wore thirty or forty years ago, for fear that he would not be recognized in the garb of today, or the kind that his grandfather wore when he established the paper, perhaps eighty or ninety years ago.

Every successful long-established newspaper that this writer can think of has changed its head dress, and body dress, too, at least several times (in many cases many times) in the course of its existence.

Let us look at some heads from old-time issues of a big metropolitan daily that was established more than a hundred years ago, and that has changed its head dress many times in its five score and more years of publication—the *New York Sun*.

Example 14 suggests the upper part of the front page of the first issue of the *Sun*, published September 3, 1833.

THE  SUN.

NUMBER 1.] NEW YORK, TUESDAY, SEPTEMBER 3, 1833. [PRICE ONE PENNY.

PUBLISHED DAILY,

AT 222 WILLIAM ST............BENJ. H. DAY, PRINTER.

The object of this paper is to lay before the public, at a price within the means of every one, ALL THE NEWS OF THE DAY, and at the same time afford an advantageous medium for advertising. The sheet will be enlarged as soon as the increase of advertisements requires it—the price remaining the same.

Yearly advertisers, (without the paper.) Thirty Dollars per annum—Casual advertising, at the usual prices charged by the city papers.

☞ Subscriptions will be received, if paid in advance, at the rate of three dollars per annum.

FOR ALBANY--PASSAGE ONLY $1.

The large and commodious steamboat COMMERCE, Capt. R. H. Fitch, will leave the foot of Courtlandt street on Friday, at five o'clock, P. M. for Albany stopping at the usual landing places to land and receive passengers. Passage $1. For particulars apply to the Captain on board.

REGULAR DAYS.

From New York, Mondays, Wednesdays, Fridays.
From Albany, Tuesdays, Thursdays, Saturdays. a29

FOR NEWPORT AND PROVIDENCE.

The splendid steamboat BENJAMIN FRANKLIN, Capt. E. S. Bunker, and

AN IRISH CAPTAIN.

"These are as sweet a pair of pistols as any in the three kingdoms;" said an officer, showing a pair to a young student of his acquaintance, "and have done execution before now; at the slightest touch, off they go, as sweet as honey, without either recoiling or dipping. I never travel without them."

"I never heard of highwaymen in this part of the country."

"Nor I." replied the officer, "and if I had I should not trouble myself to carry the pistols on their account—Highwaymen are a species of sharks who are not fond of attacking us lobsters; they know we are a little too hard to crack. No, my dear sir, highwaymen know that soldiers have not much money, and what they have they fight for."

"Since that is the case, how come you to travel always with pistols?"

"Because," answered the officer, "I find them very useful in accommodating any little difference I may accidentally have with a friend, or which one friend may chance to have with another."

"Do you often settle differences in that way?"

"Why, I was twice *out* before I arrived at your age.—The first time was with a relation of my own, who said he

"Provided you had a good cause," replied the young student.

"I should not be squeamish respecting the cause, provided I had a good battle: that, my dear, is what is the most essential to a conscientious officer, who wishes to improve himself in his profession. I have much reason, therefore, to wish for a war; and at the present juncture, it would be much to the advantage of the nation in general, as it is dwindling into a country of ploughmen, manufacturers, and merchants. And you must know, too, that I am pretty fortunate, having already stood thirteen shots, and I never was hit but once."

"Thirteen! what, have you fought thirteen duels?"

"No, no!" replied the captain, "the last shot fired at me completed only my sixth duel."

Wonders of Littleness.—Pliny and Elian relate that Myrmecides wrought out of ivory a chariot, with four wheels and four horses, and a ship with all her tackling, both in so small a compass, that a bee could hide either with its wings. Nor should we doubt this, when we find it recorded in English history, on less questionable authority, that in the twentieth year of Queen Elizabeth's reign a blacksmith of London, of the name of Mark Scaliot, made a lock of iron, steel, and brass, of eleven pieces, and

EXAMPLE 14

That issue consisted of four pages 8¼ inches wide by 11¼ inches deep, with three columns about 14½ picas wide to the page. Most of the last column on the last page, however, was set in two 7-pica columns—a listing of the names of banks in the United States and Canada, under the head "New York Bank Note Table." No head on any page was larger than 10 point (and only three heads in type that large were used in the whole paper), with the exception of the title line, in a face suggesting Bodoni Bold and about as large as our 48 point of today; running heads in the same face about as large as our 14 point, and one head in old-English, "Sales by Auction," on an inside page and about as large as our 14 point. Column one on the front page presented ten brief transportation advertisements, each with a small illustration of a steamboat or sailing vessel. The main story on the page, which filled all of column two and the upper quarter of column three, was an anonymous fiction story entitled "An Irish Captain." The rest of column three was devoted to sketches on the "Wonders of Littleness," and about a whistling boy in Vermont.

Example 15 is a reproduction of a head from the *Sun* of April 13, 1844, where it appeared over the balloon-hoax story by Edgar Allan Poe.

Observe the many decks of this single-column head, the many

different kinds and sizes of faces, with most of the lines (twenty out of twenty-six) entirely in capitals.

SUN OFFICE
April 13, 10 o'clock A. M.

ASTOUNDING
NEWS!
BY EXPRESS VIA NORFOLK:
THE
ATLANTIC CROSSED
IN
THREE DAYS!
SIGNAL TRIUMPH
OF
MR. MONCK MASON'S
FLYING
MACHINE!!!

Arrival at Sullivan's Island, near Charleston, S. C., of Mr. Mason, Mr. Robert Holland, Mr. Henson, Mr. Harrison Ainsworth, and four others, in the

STEERING BALLOON
"VICTORIA,"
AFTER A PASSAGE OF
SEVENTY-FIVE HOURS
FROM LAND TO LAND.
FULL PARTICULARS
OF THE
VOYAGE!!!

EXAMPLE 15

THE LATEST NEWS.

BY TELEGRAPH TO THE N. Y. SUN.

Civil War Begun!

THE MADNESS OF TREASON.

FORT SUMTER
ATTACKED!

FURIOUS BOMBARDMENT.

GALLANT DEFENCE OF THE
FORT.

"Our Flag is Still There"

Arrival of the Relief
Fleet!

PRELIMINARY OFFICIAL CORRESPONDENCE.

EXAMPLE 16

Seventeen years later, to the day, April 13, 1861, the head a reproduction of which is shown in Example 16 appeared in the *Sun*.

Again observe the many lines (but not so many as appeared over the less important story referred to by Example 15), the different kinds and sizes of faces (but not so many as before), and that ten of

BLIZZARD WAS KING

The Metropolis Helpless Under Snow.

HARDLY A WHEEL TURNS

Business Knocked Flat as if by a Panic.

PLAYS, TRIALS, FUNERALS. ALL POSTPONED.

Fifty Train Loads of Passengers Stuck on the Main Lines.

WHERE THEY ARE, HEAVEN KNOWS.

A Wonderful Change in Our Ways of Living and Moving Sprung on Us in a Night.

ELECTRIC LIGHTS OUT.

MIGHTY LITTLE NEWS GOT INTO TOWN OR GOT OUT OF IT.

GOING TO LET UP NOW

The Elevated Roads After a Day's Paralysis Get a Half Hold Again on Travel.

EXAMPLE 17

EXTRA

DYNAMITE

Russell Sage's Office Blown Up.

A CRANK DID IT

Came in and Demanded $1,200,000.

THE LUNATIC KILLED

After the Explosion Ruin and Chaos.

SEVERAL PERSONS BADLY INJURED

Others Killed by the Explosion.

EXAMPLE 18

the fourteen lines appear entirely in capitals. On the whole the head is simpler and easier to read than the one shown in Example 15.

But the *Sun* came out March 13, 1888, with the head part of which is reproduced in Example 17 over the story of the famous blizzard of 1888.

Observe the dozen decks, with all lines in condensed or extra-condensed faces, but with only nine of the twenty-one lines entirely in capitals. At that, though, this head as a whole is more difficult to read than those shown in Examples 15 and 16.

December 4, 1891, the head a reproduction of which is shown in Example 18 appeared in the *Sun*.

Back to fewer decks, with much more leading between decks, and with only five of the thirteen lines entirely in capitals. However, nine of those thirteen lines are in condensed or extra-condensed faces. But the head as a whole is easier to follow throughout than any of the other heads previously reproduced from the *Sun*, partly because it consists of fewer lines, but mostly because the type faces used throughout it do less clashing among themselves, and because more generous leading has permitted much more light to come through between the lines.

Although, as has been stated, this head appeared back in 1891, some newspapers of today continue to use the same sort of comparatively hard-to-read faces used for nine of the lines in the head. But not so the *Sun*.

Twenty-one years later, April 16, 1912, we find it using the head part of which is reproduced in Example 19 over the story of the sinking of the *Titanic*.

Eight single-column decks were used, with only one of the decks in a condensed face, and with the seven other decks set entirely in Bodoni. Only three of the fifteen lines in Bodoni—the three crosslines —were set entirely in capitals.

Today the main single-column heads of the *Sun* usually are limited to four decks, and all four decks are in the same type family—the Cheltenham family—with six of the ten lines in capitals and lowercase, as shown in Example 20.

The extent to which other metropolitan newspapers sometimes went, fifty or seventy-five years ago, in the way of decks over unusually

GIANT LINER GONE ERE HELP CAME

Only Her Boats Found, Carrying 866 Passengers and Boat Crews.

WOMEN LIVE, MEN DIE

Many Noted American Families Are Plunged Into Mourning.

ICEBERG HIT IN NIGHT

Within Less Than Four Hours the Magnificent Liner Foundered.

RAN ONLY 30 MILES MORE

Sea Strewn With Wreckage and Corpses When the Carpathia Came.

EXAMPLE 19

BOONEVER SON FACES REBUKE IN CAR CRASH

Tom, With Brother Roger as Passenger, Barely Escapes Death.

MOTOR HIT SIDE OF TRUCK

Frederic, Jr., Who Also Has Had Some Automobile Troubles, Wires Story to Father.

EXAMPLE 20

important news stories, is demonstrated by Example 21, which suggests the front page of the *Chicago Tribune* for October 11, 1871, when the famous Chicago fire was raging.

Observe the head—fifteen decks, forty-two display lines, mostly in condensed or extra-condensed faces—that occupied three-fourths of column one.

That page, with two high columns, was given over almost entirely to stories about the fire, some of them under heads about the size of

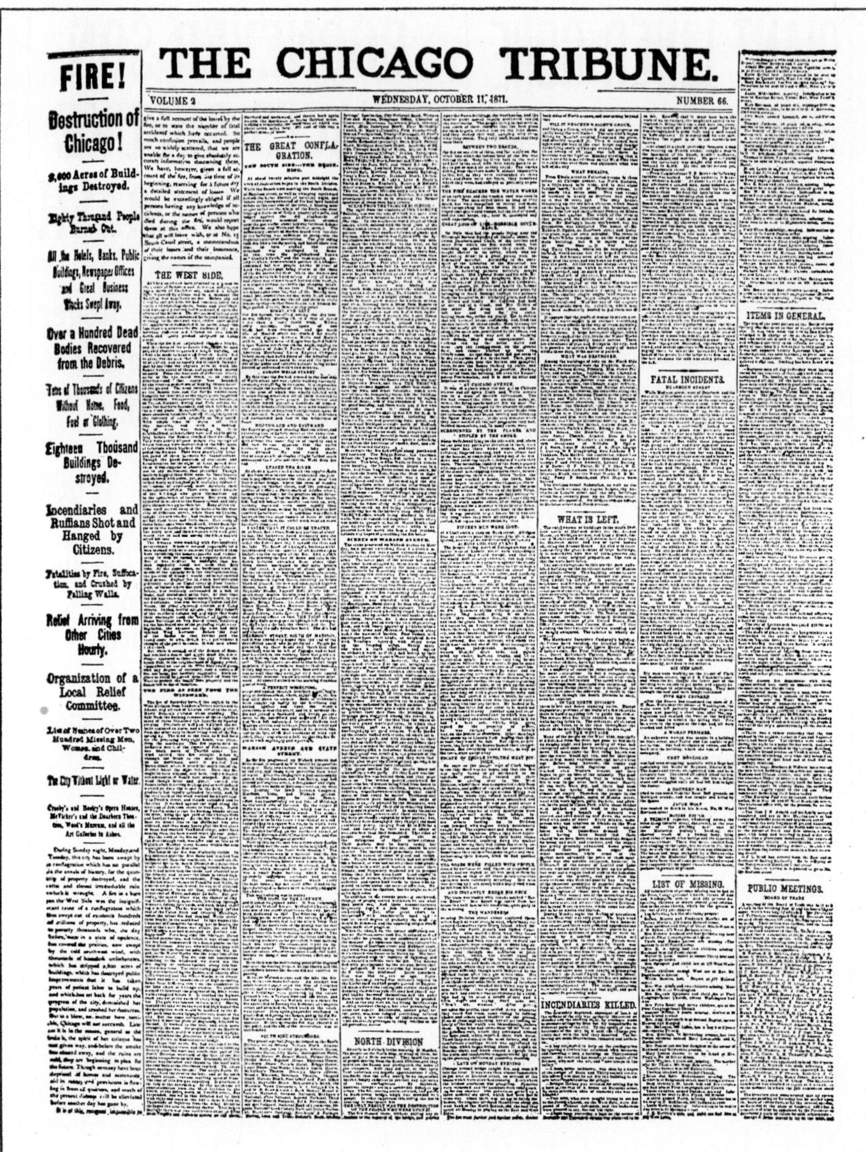

THE CHICAGO TRIBUNE.

VOLUME 2 — WEDNESDAY, OCTOBER 11, 1871. — NUMBER 66.

FIRE!

Destruction of Chicago!

2,000 Acres of Buildings Destroyed.

Eighty Thousand People Burned Out.

All the Hotels, Banks, Public Buildings, Newspaper Offices and Great Business Blocks Swept Away.

Over a Hundred Dead Bodies Recovered from the Debris.

Tens of Thousands of Citizens Without Home, Food, Fuel or Clothing.

Eighteen Thousand Buildings Destroyed.

Incendiaries and Ruffians Shot and Hanged by Citizens.

Fatalities by Fire, Suffocation, and Crushed by Falling Walls.

Relief Arriving from Other Cities Hourly.

Organization of a Local Relief Committee.

List of Names of Over Two Hundred Missing Men, Women and Children.

The City Without Light or Water.

Crosby's and Hooley's Opera Houses, McVicker's and the Dearborn Theatres, Wood's Museum, and all the Art Galleries in Ashes.

During Sunday night, Monday and Tuesday, this city has been swept by a conflagration which has no parallel in the annals of history, for the quantity of property destroyed, and the utter and almost irremediable ruin which it wrought. A fire in a barn on the West Side was the insignificant cause of a conflagration which has swept out of existence hundreds of millions of property, has reduced to poverty thousands who, the day before, were in a state of opulence, has covered the prairies, now swept by the cold southwest wind, with thousands of homeless unfortunates, which has stripped 2,600 acres of buildings, which has destroyed public improvements that it has taken years of patient labor to build up, and which has set back for years the progress of the city, diminished her population, and crushed her resources. But to a blow, no matter how terrible, Chicago will not succumb. ...

... give a full account of the losses by the fire, or to state the number of fatal accidents which have occurred. So much confusion prevails, and people are so widely scattered, that we are unable for a day to give absolutely accurate information concerning them. We have, however, given a full account of the fire, from the time of its beginning, reserving for a future day a detailed statement of losses. We would be exceedingly obliged if all persons having any knowledge of accidents, or the names of persons who died during the fire, would report them at this office. We also hope that all will leave with, or at No. 15 South Canal street, a memorandum of their losses and their insurance, giving the names of the companies.

THE WEST SIDE.

THE GREAT CONFLAGRATION.

NORTH DIVISION

WHAT IS LEFT.

INCENDIARIES KILLED.

FATAL INCIDENTS.

LIST OF MISSING.

ITEMS IN GENERAL.

PUBLIC MEETINGS.

EXAMPLE 21

our 14 point, but with body matter almost entirely in unleaded lines in a type face about the size of our 5 or 5½ point.

In those days, too, when many newspapers ran long stories on their front pages, with no jumps to inside pages, main stories often were started at the top of column one and continued at the tops of adjoining columns. There was no aversion in those days to running "dead ends" of stories at the tops of columns on front pages. And it was not until considerably later (when newspaper publishers came to regard the front page as the show window for the displaying of many important stories) that the upper right of the front page came to be rather generally regarded as the most eye-arresting position on the page—the logical place for the presentation of the most important story. See Chapter 15 of Part I.

There are several type families that may be used to better advantage for news heads than certain families still being used by many papers.

While it is not the purpose of this volume to attempt to serve as a type catalog—to attempt to list all of the many faces that can be used advantageously for heads in newspapers—it is the purpose to name and show several appropriate faces, and, in this chapter, several faces particularly appropriate for general-news heads.

Most of the faces to be named and shown, or faces with other names but in the same general classifications, are available both on composing machines and in hand types and in various point sizes ranging from the comparatively small to the unusually large. Many of the machine-set fonts, in point sizes from the smallest up to and including 24 point, may be had with two different characters (in different casting positions) on the same matrix in various combinations of both roman and italic (some including small capitals) or both light and bold face, or with faces from two quite-different type families, and of different point sizes, on the same matrix. But it should suffice here to show only a few sizes of each face, even in cases where many other sizes are available, as the showing of additional sizes, smaller and larger, would consume too much space.

Some of the type faces more appropriate for general-news heads than certain other faces now used by many newspapers are Bodoni, Bodoni Italic and Bodoni Condensed; Bodoni Bold, Bodoni Bold Italic and Bodoni Bold Condensed; Poster Bodoni and Poster Bodoni

Italic; Caledonia Bold; Caslon No. 3, Caslon No. 3 Italic and Caslon Bold Condensed; Century Bold, Century Bold Italic and Century Bold Condensed; Cheltenham, Cheltenham Italic and Cheltenham Condensed; Cheltenham Medium Condensed; Cheltenham Bold, Cheltenham Bold Italic, Cheltenham Bold Condensed, Cheltenham Bold Condensed Italic, Cheltenham Bold Extra Condensed and Cheltenham Bold Extra Condensed Italic; Cloister and Cloister Italic; Cloister Bold and Cloister Bold Italic; Erbar Light Condensed, Erbar Medium Condensed and Erbar Bold Condensed; Ionic Condensed; Memphis Medium, Memphis Medium Italic and Memphis Medium Condensed; Memphis Bold, Memphis Bold Italic and Memphis Bold Condensed; Metrolite No. 2, Metrolite No. 2 Italic and Metrolite No. 4 Italic; Metromedium No. 2 and Metromedium No. 2 Italic; Metroblack No. 2 and Metroblack No. 2 Italic; Ryerson Condensed; Spartan Medium and Spartan Medium Italic; Spartan Heavy and Spartan Heavy Italic; Spartan Black, Spartan Black Italic, Spartan Black Condensed and Spartan Black Condensed Italic.

Of the twelve type families represented by these faces, four of the families—the Caslon, Cheltenham, Cloister and Ionic Condensed—come within the old-style classification; three of the families—the Bodoni, Caledonia and Century—within the modern, and four others—the Erbar, Metro, Ryerson and Spartan—within the sans-serif classification. The Memphis family is in the square-serif category.

Of course various other faces can be used to advantage for general-news heads. And still other faces, including lighter weights (not shown in this chapter) in some of the families specifically named here, can be employed advantageously for occasional department and feature heads on the same pages with general-news heads in heavier members of the same families, and for heads in certain departments of a newspaper—for the society columns, woman's pages, magazine and book sections, and so on, as well as in the advertising columns—and some of those faces to better advantage than some of the faces named in the preceding paragraphs. Several such faces are shown in succeeding chapters.

Most of the faces specifically named here are colorful enough, particularly in the larger sizes available, to be attention arresting, and yet most of them afford a workable unit count.

Here is how the faces specifically referred to appear in various sizes, confined to lines 24½ picas wide, so that the single- or double-column unit count of those shown can be readily determined:

12-point Bodoni

Some Newspapers Are Easier to Read Than Others and Are

18-point Bodoni

Some Newspapers Are Easier to Read Th

30-point Bodoni

Some Newspapers Are Easi

12-point Bodoni Italic

Some Newspapers Are Easier to Read Than Others and Are

18-point Bodoni Italic

Some Newspapers Are Easier to Read Th

30-point Bodoni Italic

Some Newspapers Are Eas

24-point Bodoni Condensed

Some Newspapers Are Easier to Rea

30-point Bodoni Condensed

Some Newspapers Are Easier

12-point Bodoni Bold

Some Newspapers Are Easier to Read Than Others and

18-point Bodoni Bold

Some Newspapers Are Easier to Read

30-point Bodoni Bold

Some Newspapers Are Easi

12-point Bodoni Bold Italic

Some Newspapers Are Easier to Read Than Others and

18-point Bodoni Bold Italic

Some Newspapers Are Easier to Read

30-point Bodoni Bold Italic

Some Newspapers Are E

18-point Bodoni Bold Condensed

Some Newspapers Are Easier to Read Than Othe

24-point Bodoni Bold Condensed

Some Newspapers Are Easier to Read

30-point Bodoni Bold Condensed

Some Newspapers Are Easier t

12-point Poster Bodoni

Some Newspapers Are Easier to Read Than

18-point Poster Bodoni

Some Newspapers Are Easier

30-point Poster Bodoni

Some Newspapers

12-point Poster Bodoni Italic

Some Newspapers Are Easier to Read Than

18-point Poster Bodoni Italic

Some Newspapers Are Easier

30-point Poster Bodoni Italic

Some Newspaper

16-point Caledonia Bold

Some Newspapers Are Easier to Read Than

21-point Caledonia Bold

Some Newspapers Are Easier to R

30-point Caledonia Bold

Some Newspapers Are E

12-point Caslon No. 3

Some Newspapers Are Easier to Read Than Others

18-point Caslon No. 3

Some Newspapers Are Easier to

30-point Caslon No. 3

Some Newspapers A

12-point Caslon No. 3 Italic

Some Newspapers Are Easier to Read Than Others

18-point Caslon No. 3 Italic

Some Newspapers Are Easier to

30-point Caslon No. 3 Italic

Some Newspapers A

14-point Caslon Bold Condensed

Some Newspapers Are Easier to Read Than Others

18-point Caslon Bold Condensed

Some Newspapers Are Easier to Read Tha

30-point Caslon Bold Condensed

Some Newspapers Are Easi

12-point Century Bold

Some Newspapers Are Easier to Read Than Others

18-point Century Bold

Some Newspapers Are Easier to Read

30-point Century Bold

Some Newspapers Are E

12-point Century Bold Italic

Some Newspapers Are Easier to Read Than Others

18-point Century Bold Italic

Some Newspapers Are Easier to Read

30-point Century Bold Italic

Some Newspapers Are

18-point Century Bold Condensed

Some Newspapers Are Easier to Read Than Othe

24-point Century Bold Condensed

Some Newspapers Are Easier to Read

14-point Cheltenham

Some Newspapers Are Easier to Read Than Others a

20-point Cheltenham

Some Newspapers Are Easier to Read Tha

30-point Cheltenham

Some Newspapers Are Easier

14-point Cheltenham Italic

Some Newspapers Are Easier to Read Than Others a

20-point Cheltenham Italic

Some Newspapers Are Easier to Read Tha

30-point Cheltenham Italic

Some Newspapers Are Easie

14-point Cheltenham Condensed

Some Newspapers Are Easier to Read Than Others and

18-point Cheltenham Condensed

Some Newspapers Are Easier to Read Than Oth

30-point Cheltenham Condensed

Some Newspapers Are Easier to

18-point Cheltenham Medium Condensed

Some Newspapers Are Easier to Read Than Oth

24-point Cheltenham Medium Condensed

Some Newspapers Are Easier to Rea

30-point Cheltenham Medium Condensed

Some Newspapers Are Easier to

12-point Cheltenham Bold

Some Newspapers Are Easier to Read Than Others a

18-point Cheltenham Bold

Some Newspapers Are Easier to Rea

30-point Cheltenham Bold

Some Newspapers Are E

12-point Cheltenham Bold Italic

Some Newspapers Are Easier to Read Than Others a

18-point Cheltenham Bold Italic

Some Newspapers Are Easier to Re

30-point Cheltenham Bold Italic

Some Newspapers Are

12-point Cheltenham Bold Condensed

Some Newspapers Are Easier to Read Than Others and Are More

18-point Cheltenham Bold Condensed

Some Newspapers Are Easier to Read Than

30-point Cheltenham Bold Condensed

Some Newspapers Are Easier t

12-point Cheltenham Bold Condensed Italic

Some Newspapers Are Easier to Read Than Others and Are More

18-point Cheltenham Bold Condensed Italic

Some Newspapers Are Easier to Read Than

30-point Cheltenham Bold Condensed Italic

Some Newspapers Are Easier

18-point Cheltenham Bold Extra Condensed

Some Newspapers Are Easier to Read Than Others an

24-point Cheltenham Bold Extra Condensed

Some Newspapers Are Easier to Read Than

30-point Cheltenham Bold Extra Condensed

Some Newspapers Are Easier to Rea

24-point Cheltenham Bold Extra Condensed Italic

Some Newspapers Are Easier to Rea

18-point Cloister

Some Newspapers Are Easier to Read Than Ot

30-point Cloister

Some Newspapers Are Easier t

18-point Cloister Italic

Some Newspapers Are Easier to Read Than Ot

30-point Cloister Italic

Some Newspapers Are Easier to

12-point Cloister Bold

Some Newspapers Are Easier to Read Than Others and Are

18-point Cloister Bold

Some Newspapers Are Easier to Read Than

30-point Cloister Bold

Some Newspapers Are Easi

12-point Cloister Bold Italic

Some Newspapers Are Easier to Read Than Others and Are

18-point Cloister Bold Italic

Some Newspapers Are Easier to Read Than

30-point Cloister Bold Italic

Some Newspapers Are Easie

18-point Erbar Light Condensed

Some Newspapers Are Easier to Read Than Others an

24-point Erbar Light Condensed

Some Newspapers Are Easier to Read Tha

34-point Erbar Light Condensed

Some Newspapers Are Easier to R

18-point Erbar Medium Condensed

Some Newspapers Are Easier to Read Than Others an

24-point Erbar Medium Condensed

Some Newspapers Are Easier to Read Than

34-point Erbar Medium Condensed

Some Newspapers Are Easier to R

18-point Erbar Bold Condensed

Some Newspapers Are Easier to Read Than Others an

24-point Erbar Bold Condensed

Some Newspapers Are Easier to Read Tha

34-point Erbar Bold Condensed

Some Newspapers Are Easier t

18-point Ionic Condensed

Some Newspapers Are Easier to Read Than Others and A

24-point Ionic Condensed

Some Newspapers Are Easier to Read Than

30-point Ionic Condensed

Some Newspapers Are Easier to Rea

12-point Memphis Medium

Some Newspapers Are Easier to Read Than Others a

18-point Memphis Medium

Some Newspapers Are Easier to Rea

30-point Memphis Medium

Some Newspapers Are

12-point Memphis Medium Italic

Some Newspapers Are Easier to Read Than Others a

18-point Memphis Medium Italic

Some Newspapers Are Easier to Rea

30-point Memphis Medium Italic

Some Newspapers Are

12-point Memphis Medium Condensed

Some Newspapers Are Easier to Read Than Others and Are More

18-point Memphis Medium Condensed

Some Newspapers Are Easier to Read Than Ot

30-point Memphis Medium Condensed

Some Newspapers Are Easier t

12-point Memphis Bold

Some Newspapers Are Easier to Read Than Others a

18-point Memphis Bold

Some Newspapers Are Easier to Rea

30-point Memphis Bold

Some Newspapers Are

12-point Memphis Bold Italic

Some Newspapers Are Easier to Read Than Others a

18-point Memphis Bold Italic

Some Newspapers Are Easier to Rea

30-point Memphis Bold Italic

Some Newspapers Are

12-point Memphis Bold Condensed

Some Newspapers Are Easier to Read Than Others and Are More

18-point Memphis Bold Condensed

Some Newspapers Are Easier to Read Than Ot

30-point Memphis Bold Condensed

Some Newspapers Are Easier t

12-point Metrolite No. 2

Some Newspapers Are Easier to Read Than Others an

18-point Metrolite No. 2

Some Newspapers Are Easier to Read

30-point Metrolite No. 2

Some Newspapers Are

12-point Metrolite No. 2 Italic

Some Newspapers Are Easier to Read Than Others an

18-point Metrolite No. 2 Italic

Some Newspapers Are Easier to Read

30-point Metrolite No. 4 Italic

Some Newspapers Are Easie

12-point Metromedium No. 2

Some Newspapers Are Easier to Read Than Others and Ar

18-point Metromedium No. 2

Some Newspapers Are Easier to Read Th

30-point Metromedium No. 2

Some Newspapers Are Eas

12-point Metromedium No. 2 Italic

Some Newspapers Are Easier to Read Than Others and Ar

18-point Metromedium No. 2 Italic

Some Newspapers Are Easier to Read Th

30-point Metromedium No. 2 Italic

Some Newspapers Are Easi

12-point Metroblack No. 2

Some Newspapers Are Easier to Read Than Others an

18-point Metroblack No. 2

Some Newspapers Are Easier to Rea

30-point Metroblack No. 2

Some Newspapers Are

12-point Metroblack No. 2 Italic

Some Newspapers Are Easier to Read Than Others an

18-point Metroblack No. 2 Italic

Some Newspapers Are Easier to Rea

24-point Metroblack No. 2 Italic

Some Newspapers Are Easier

18-point Ryerson Condensed

Some Newspapers Are Easier to Read Than Oth

24-point Ryerson Condensed

Some Newspapers Are Easier to Read T

30-point Ryerson Condensed

Some Newspapers Are Easier to Re

12-point Spartan Medium

Some Newspapers Are Easier to Read Than Others and Are

18-point Spartan Medium

Some Newspapers Are Easier to Read T

30-point Spartan Medium

Some Newspapers Are Easie

12-point Spartan Medium Italic

Some Newspapers Are Easier to Read Than Others and Are

18-point Spartan Medium Italic

Some Newspapers Are Easier to Read T

30-point Spartan Medium Italic

Some Newspapers Are Easie

12-point Spartan Heavy

Some Newspapers Are Easier to Read Than Others and A

18-point Spartan Heavy

Some Newspapers Are Easier to Read T

24-point Spartan Heavy

Some Newspapers Are Easier to

12-point Spartan Heavy Italic

Some Newspapers Are Easier to Read Than Others and A

18-point Spartan Heavy Italic

Some Newspapers Are Easier to Read T

24-point Spartan Heavy Italic

Some Newspapers Are Easier to

12-point Spartan Black

Some Newspapers Are Easier to Read Than Others

18-point Spartan Black

Some Newspapers Are Easier to Rea

24-point Spartan Black

Some Newspapers Are Easie

12-point Spartan Black Italic

Some Newspapers Are Easier to Read Than Others

18-point Spartan Black Italic

Some Newspapers Are Easier to Rea

24-point Spartan Black Italic

Some Newspapers Are Easie

12-point Spartan Black Condensed

Some Newspapers Are Easier to Read Than Others and Are More

18-point Spartan Black Condensed

Some Newspapers Are Easier to Read Than Oth

30-point Spartan Black Condensed

Some Newspapers Are Easier to

12-point Spartan Black Condensed Italic

Some Newspapers Are Easier to Read Than Others and Are More

18-point Spartan Black Condensed Italic

Some Newspapers Are Easier to Read Than Oth

24-point Spartan Black Condensed Italic

Some Newspapers Are Easier to Read T

Any experienced designer of modern newspapers knows that there is nothing mysterious about modern makeup principles. He knows that the chief fundamental is simplicity, and he builds on that.

Before working out a general-news head dress for a paper, he usually selects a good body face or faces, and decides on the point sizes of such faces and the degrees of leading to be employed.

For a general-news head dress, he will select a single good type family or no more than a few closely related families, and will try to get along with as few faces and sizes as possible.

He will keep the head schedule simple, or comparatively simple, for at least three good reasons—to hold down the original cost, to minimize the work of head writing, and to save time and money in the composing room.

Suppose, for example, we want a sans-serif general-news head dress.

With only six fonts of matrices it is possible to take care of all of the single- and double-column head requirements, and they, of course, constitute by far the greater part of any head schedule. A few larger sizes for three- and four-column heads, for spread heads, and banners, and the schedule would be complete—with no more than a dozen fonts required.

But let us see what we can do with the six fonts referred to before —with, say, 34- and 24-point Erbar Medium Condensed, 30-point Metromedium No. 2, and 24-, 18- and 14-point Metromedium No. 2 with Italic.

34-point Erbar Medium Condensed

Some Type Faces Are Easier to Re

24-point Erbar Medium Condensed

Some Type Faces Are Easier to Read Than Oth

30-point Metromedium No. 2

Some Type Faces Are Easie

24-point Metromedium No. 2 with Italic

Some Type Faces Are Easier to R

Some Type Faces Are Easier to R

18-point Metromedium No. 2 with Italic

Some Type Faces Are Easier to Read Than

Some Type Faces Are Easier to Read Than

14-point Metromedium No. 2 with Italic

Some Type Faces Are Easier to Read Than Others a

Some Type Faces Are Easier to Read Than Others a

With these six fonts we can get, in addition to several other possibilities, the twenty-five different single- and double-column heads shown here:

1—1

34-point Erbar Medium Condensed
14-point Metromedium No. 2

Seventeen Men
Leap 196 Yards
In Eleven Jumps

Then They Turn Round
And Turn Cartwheels
Quickly Out of Town

1—2

34-point Erbar Medium Condensed
14-point Metromedium No. 2

Seventeen Men
Leap 196 Yards

Then They Turn Round
And Turn Cartwheels
Quickly Out of Town

1—3

24-point Erbar Medium Condensed
14-point Metromedium No. 2

Twenty-three Youths
Prance 22,237 Yards

Then They Turn Round
And Turn Cartwheels

1—4

24-point Erbar Medium Condensed

Twenty-three Youths
Prance 22,237 Yards

1—5

18-point Metromedium No. 2

Seven Local Women
Enter Golf Contests

1—6

18-point Metromedium No. 2 Italic

Seven Local Women
Enter Golf Contests

1—7

18-point Metromedium No. 2

Seven Local Women

1—8

18-point Metromedium No. 2 Italic

Enter Golf Contests

1—9

14-point Metromedium No. 2

Seventeen Local Women
Enter Two Golf Matches

1—10

14-point Metromedium No. 2 Italic

Seventeen Local Women
Enter Two Golf Matches

1—11

14-point Metromedium No. 2

Seventeen Local Women

1—12

14-point Metromedium No. 2 Italic

Enter Two Golf Matches

2—1

30-point Metromedium No. 2
14-point Metromedium No. 2

Ninety-seven Young Men
Run From Here to There
And Quickly Back Again

Then They Turn Round and Turn Cartwheels
And Street Corners Rapidly Out of This Town
And Toward Many Other Fine Large Cities

2—2

30-point Metromedium No. 2
14-point Metromedium No. 2

Ninety-seven Young Men
Run From Here to There
And Quickly Back Again

Then They Turn Round
And Turn Cartwheels
And Street Corners
Rapidly Out of Town

2—3

30-point Metromedium No. 2
14-point Metromedium No. 2

Ninety-seven Young Men
Run From Here to There

Then They Turn Round and Turn Cartwheels
And Street Corners Quickly Out of This Town

2—4

30-point Metromedium No. 2
14-point Metromedium No. 2

Ninety-seven Young Men
Run From Here to There

Then They Turn Round
And Turn Cartwheels
Quickly Out of Town

2—5

30-point Metromedium No. 2

Ninety-seven Young Men
Run From Here to There

2—6

24-point Metromedium No. 2
14-point Metromedium No. 2

Seventy-seven Lively Kangaroos Leap From Home to Breakfast

Then They Turn Round and Turn Cartwheels And Street Corners Quickly Out of This Town

2—7

24-point Metromedium No. 2
14-point Metromedium No. 2

Seventy-seven Lively Kangaroos Leap From Home to Breakfast

Then They Turn Round And Turn Cartwheels Quickly Out of Town

2—8

24-point Metromedium No. 2

Seventy-seven Lively Kangaroos Leap From Home to Breakfast

2—9

24-point Metromedium No. 2 Italic
14-point Metromedium No. 2 Italic

Seventy-seven Lively Kangaroos Leap From Home to Breakfast

Then They Turn Round and Turn Cartwheels And Street Corners Quickly Out of This Town

2—10

24-point Metromedium No. 2 Italic
14-point Metromedium No. 2 Italic

Seventy-seven Lively Kangaroos Leap From Home to Breakfast

Then They Turn Round And Turn Cartwheels Quickly Out of Town

2—11

24-point Metromedium No. 2 Italic

Seventy-seven Lively Kangaroos Leap From Home to Breakfast

2—12

18-point Metromedium No. 2

All Factories Humming, Workers Also, As Humming Birds Besiege This Town

2—13

18-point Metromedium No. 2 Italic

All Factories Humming, Workers Also, As Humming Birds Besiege This Town

The 24-point Erbar Medium Condensed used for two of those general-news heads may be had in combination (on the same matrices) with 24-point Erbar Light Condensed, a weight that can be used to advantage on society, woman's and certain other pages calling for comparatively light physical treatment. (Of course, Erbar Light Condensed can be employed effectively for general-news heads, also, as witness several illustrations of pages in this book.)

And so, by availing ourselves of that 24-point combination, and by adding only one other font—34-point Erbar Light Condensed—we can get, among other possibilities, these four additional and lighter heads:

X—1

34-point Erbar Light Condensed
14-point Metromedium No. 2

Seventeen Men
Leap 196 Yards
In Eleven Jumps

Then They Turn Round
And Turn Cartwheels
Quickly Out of Town

X—2

34-point Erbar Light Condensed
14-point Metromedium No. 2

Seventeen Men
Leap 196 Yards

Then They Turn Round
And Turn Cartwheels

X—3

24-point Erbar Light Condensed
14-point Metromedium No. 2

Twenty-three Youths
Prance 22,237 Yards

Then They Turn Round
And Turn Cartwheels

X—4

24-point Erbar Light Condensed

Twenty-three Youths
Prance 22,237 Yards

Of course the possibility of getting many different heads from only a few fonts of matrices is not at all limited to members of the Erbar and Metro type families. Effective head schedules in other type families can be worked out just as readily with comparatively few fonts of matrices in each instance.

In fact, several years ago this writer worked out fifteen different and effective head schedules, each based on only six fonts of matrices, which the Linotype Company presented in a booklet entitled *So You Want to Change Your Head Dress!*

Many newspaper executives secured copies of that booklet and put them to work for their papers.

6

News Body Faces

In a commercial sense, the front page is the show window of the newspaper, and the headlines used throughout the paper are the salesmen of the various items of news, opinion and entertainment offered for sale.

If the appearance of the front page is inviting, it will help to invite attention to the individual headlines, and if the headlines are good salesmen they will help to sell the lines below them—the body lines.

But if the body lines themselves—physically—are not easy to read—as easy as is reasonably possible—the buyer will not be so well served as the show window and the salesmen have led him to expect.

Type was made to read, and type that is not easy to read—as easy as is reasonably possible—is not good type.

The statement that one particular type face is the best face for all kinds of printing would be absurd. Many different type faces have been designed for many different kinds of printing, and even the inherently good ones—the ones of sound design—perform their chief function with varying degrees of effectiveness when used for various purposes and in different ways.

Many a type face good in itself would not be a good face for newspaper body matter.

As previously stated, newsprint has much coarser fibers than many other printing papers. To appreciate this, observe Example 22, a reproduction of a microphotograph of a piece of newsprint.

Observe the decidedly rough surface—the pronounced hills and valleys. (See, too, Figure 1 in this chapter.)

Moreover, news ink is inferior to many other printing inks; stereotyping is too hard on many kinds of faces for them to be used advantageously, and high-speed presses with rubber rollers—equipment made necessary by a rate of speed that would be too hard on composition rollers—are not so well qualified to turn out good printing as certain much slower presses with composition rollers.

And yet, with all these handicaps, most newspaper body types must be considerably smaller (at least in the present scheme of things—because of narrow columns and the economic necessity of presenting many words to the page) than the types used, say, for a modern novel—an item of printing that usually is read less hurriedly and under better lighting conditions than the pages of newspapers usually are.

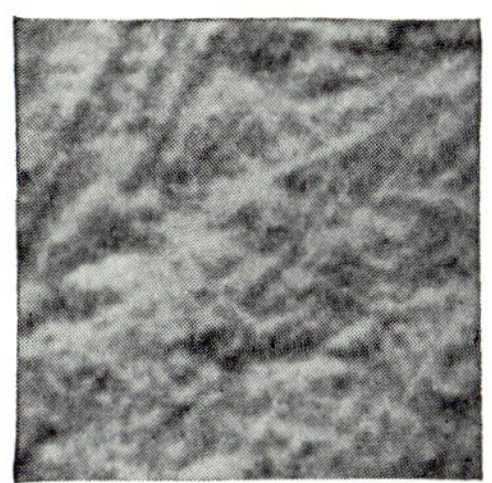

EXAMPLE 22

Prior to the year 1900 and for many years thereafter the most popular news body type in the United States was a face known as Roman No. 2. Most of our newspapers, both large and small, used it, in various sizes, but the most generally used sizes were the 6 and 8 point—the 6 point by the dailies, and the 8 point by the weeklies. But the trend now is toward larger body faces. Many of our dailies now use 7-, 7½- and 8-point body faces cast on a 7½-, 8-, 8½- or 9-point body. Some dailies, and even more weeklies, now use 9-point faces on a 10-point body.

(During World War II some of our dailies went back temporarily to smaller body faces, because of newsprint and other shortages, and many dailies temporarily reduced the leading between body lines. But most of the papers that did such retrenching planned to return to larger body faces and more generous leading as soon as publishing restrictions were lifted.)

In 1904 came a face known as Century Expanded, and many of the larger papers, but not so many of the smaller, changed over to it.

And for many years those two faces—Roman No. 2 and Century Expanded—were the most popular news body faces in this country. And as newspaper presses several years ago were considerably slower than they are now, those faces served fairly well.

But newspaper presses did not remain as they were several years ago. The speed of them kept getting faster and faster.

Nor did stereotyping processes remain the same. They, too, took on increased speed. The wet, or steamed, stereotype matrix, which for many years had been well nigh universally used by large newspapers, but each one of which had taken several minutes to produce, gave way to the dry matrix, which can be turned out in a small fraction of the time required for the wet. (Even the "dry" matrix, of course, contains some moisture.)

The wet matrix had subjected type faces and other units of composition to great pressure, but to nothing like the tremendous pressure they became subjected to by the dry and harder surfaced matrix.

That increased pressure and the faster presses rendered the Roman No. 2 and Century Expanded faces inadequate. That pressure, far beyond what those faces had been designed to withstand, broke down the fine lines of the faces. The faster presses revealed ink traps in their design that the slower presses had not revealed. A comparatively thin flow of ink over such faces, with their fine lines broken down, resulted in printed pages with insufficient color—with a grayed-out appearance that made for difficult reading. But a heavier flow of ink contributed to even more unsatisfactory results. The printed pages were too smudgy for easy reading.

Obviously, what was needed to meet the new conditions—to print well despite tremendous stereotyping pressure and at high speed—was a type face or faces with sturdier fine lines and as devoid as possible of features that would catch and fill up with ink and ink-soaked fibers from the speeding newsprint.

Composing-machine manufacturers went after the problem with several new type faces, most of which are available in several point sizes and in combination with italic and small capitals or with bold face or gothic.

"Prior to 1922," C. H. Griffith, Linotype vice-president in charge of typographic development, informed this writer, "there is no recorded instance of a definitive analytical study of the printing and reading qualities of small body types in relation to the specialized technique of newspaper printing processes. Type was type, whether for printing a book or a newspaper. All the newspaper body types in use up to that time were merely small sizes of faces originally designed for printing on flatbed presses with composition ink rollers. Some of them had their origin even in the days when damp paper was used and the forms inked with an ink ball.

"With the advent of machine composition, which provided new type for each issue, and the stereotype printing plate, the legibility of newspaper body types began to decline, and probably reached its lowest ebb about 1920, when superspeed presses, rubber rollers and the dry flong imposed further and intolerable burdens on traditional type faces that for a half century had been struggling to keep pace with the constant development of the newspaper printing press and its related processes.

"The Linotype Company recognized the fact that the type faces of that period, which were characterized chiefly by contrasting thick-and-thin lines and small counters, would not perform a satisfactory job of printing under the new technical standards that were rapidly being established in stereotype and pressrooms throughout the country. The approach to a solution involved problems of an economic nature, as well as those of a combination of engineering and art.

"Increasing the size of the type would effect a partial solution, but it would not be practical from a purely economic standpoint. At that time, nearly all the daily papers were set in solid 6-point type, and a few in 7 point, a practice largely influenced by the economics of the piece-scale. On the mechanical side, deference had to be made to the inherent characteristics of the molding properties of the dry flong and the inking performance of rubber rollers. The delicate lines of the letter would frequently be crushed by the tremendous pressure on the flong, and the rubber rollers lacked sufficient resiliency to suck excess ink from the small counters, which resulted in broken and blurred letters. Thin lines could be made thicker and small counters larger, but here we face two interrelated problems, one physical and the other esthetic: the problem of fatigue, and the problem of monotony. A purely monotone letter, all lines of equal weight, with large counters, would be fatiguing and monotonous for extensive reading.

"Ionic No. 5, which was Linotype's first answer to these difficult problems, was developed in 1925 and introduced to the newspapers in the fall of that year. It is a fairly dark face, with just enough contrast in thick-and-thin lines to avoid the monotony of a monotone and still print with a vigorous color and maximum legibility under adverse conditions. Careful designing and letter-fitting effected material space economy in comparison with other types of the same size that were in use at that time.

"Ionic No. 5 was a success from the moment of its introduction, and 3000 newspapers adopted it within eighteen months.

"Excelsior came into the field in 1931 under circumstances that were both natural and unusual. The popularity of Ionic was so strong that competition frequently developed among local newspapers for its adoption, and in some cases the loser was not inclined to imitate his competitor. This situation called for the creation of a new design —in the form of Excelsior. While embodying all the scientific factors of legibility and printing performance of Ionic, the design of Excelsior cleaves more closely to the traditional design of the roman letter. The thin-and-thick lines have slightly more contrast than in Ionic, but the finest lines are sturdy enough to withstand the punishment of the modern stereotype matrix molding machine. The counters are large enough to prevent blurring, and other design details were applied to eliminate ink traps and produce a clear and sharp impression. The shape of the lower-case a easily distinguishes Excelsior from other modern types.

"Opticon was introduced in 1935 in response to a demand for a body type of the Excelsior design that would print with full color on an imported newsprint having a semi-hard glazed finish that lacked the absorptive characteristics of domestic newsprint. Opticon is exactly the same design as Excelsior, but with slightly heavier strokes.

"In all three legibility types—Ionic, Excelsior and Opticon—the visibility factor is rather high, which is a desirable element in effecting maximum legibility. This is accomplished by carefully developed proportions in thick-and-thin strokes and the elimination of very fine lines.

"In many of the tabloid publications which are crowded with pictures, as well as a few standard newspapers that feature very black type in advertising display, an abnormal flow of ink is needed for adequate coverage. Under these conditions the reading type in news columns usually prints so black that it smuts the hands of readers hours after delivery.

"To meet this peculiar condition, another addition was made to the legibility group in 1935, in the form of Paragon. This is a fairly light face, with large, well-proportioned counters, free of ink traps, which will print clean and sharp and without smudging under a literal flood of ink. Under normal printing conditions, Paragon produces a gray page texture, but nevertheless sharp and clear and with a high degree of legibility. It possesses all the scientific elements of design that make for reading ease and printing qualities.

"Corona, introduced in 1940, is frankly a composite of the entire legibility group, with especial emphasis on the factor of space economy. A given size of Corona has the reading visibility of any other face at least 1 point larger, and the space economy of the average face 1 point smaller in size. In addition to these desirable features, Corona embodies a new principle of letter design and fitting which, in brief, anticipates and corrects the natural distortion and loss of printing quality that results from the shrinkage of the dry flong in the stereotyping process."

Shortly after the introduction of Excelsior, Harry L. Gage, Linotype vice-president, referred to that face as follows:

"Imagine a surface of matted crisscross soda-fountain straws and picture the result of printing on such a surface with metal types however large. This is what happens, as the microscope sees it, on every bit of modern newsprint when it goes through the press.

"Ground wood is just such a mass of slivery fibers. Put a bit of printed news under a moderate microscope and the result looks very much like Figure 1. Sometimes it's almost impossible to discern the whiskery shapes as letter forms at all.

"So type designing for news requirements has become a highly specialized art. The elements of beauty which can be studiously embodied in book and commercial-printing types have been forced to submit to the ever-increasing necessities of newspaper stereotyping and printing on high-speed presses with rubber rollers.

"From the days of the early news sheets in Caslon (not so many generations ago) through the first years of Linotype composition, the conventional types amply served the purpose of slow and simpler printing methods. With the development of higher and higher speeds began a contest between type designer and machinery builder which is paralleled only by the familiar rivalry of gun-builder and armor-plate maker.

"Properly to understand this problem of letter design for these exacting requirements we must look at each letter form in its final appearance on a news page. Microscopic study is not very helpful. The problem becomes so fuzzy, as in Figure 1, that we only realize the extreme difficulties to be met.

"Obviously, however, the blurred and fibrous images of our letter forms indicate the first approaches to redesigning. Figure 2 shows four letters of a familiar news face, Roman No. 2, which is closely related to the old favorite, Century Expanded (Figure 6). The latter, in its days of first adoption, was regarded as the most legible type for news work. Nobody of discerning taste ever called it beautiful. But it served through many years to produce thousands of papers, year after year.

"If we superimpose the same letters in the Excelsior design over the characters of Roman No. 2 (Figure 3), we have a clear illustration of the cleaning-up process that produces clearer type impressions today. The designer has had to study the *background* of paper in each letter, rather than the printed image, which may be noticed by the illustration Figure 4.

"Counting on a fringe of whiskers on every stroke, curve and serif to add weight or color, the designers ruthlessly chopped away weight. Excelsior's anatomy is much thinner but nowhere wiry.

"Attenuated finishing strokes, as in a and e, were found to be ink traps.

"Thinly drawn, almost-touching serifs, as in w, sometimes break in stereotyping. Often their newsprint crop of whiskers joins them together. More ink traps and blackened characters. Excelsior serifs are sturdier and shorter.

"Lower-case g, the most complex of the alphabet, could not be reduced to a more elemental form (as has been attempted in certain 'modernistic' types) without losing the familiarity of form which is essentially a reading habit in the public eye. So in the Excelsior it is given maximum openness. The ball serif gave way to an equally traditional shape which left a full opening instead of a three-quarters surrounded area of background. The intersections of the curving strokes are less acute. The counters, or backgrounds of the loops, are themselves more open.

"Meantime word count remains as a designer's strict limitation. It would have been easy to open up a thinner, sturdier face to meet the soft rubber rollers, soupy ink, and fuzzy newsprint of present-day printing. Excelsior doesn't exact that penalty with its legibility. Its alphabet length is almost identical with Ionic. And Ionic has compressed many thousands of dollars into higher content of news and classified matter. This is the ultimate test of Excelsior design, final proof of the skill in shaving off superfluous thousandths of an inch in all the intricacies of caps and lower-case to do away with blurs and smudges."

FIGURE 1. *Enlargement of a typical newspaper face of yesterday as it appears under the microscope, printed on newsprint*

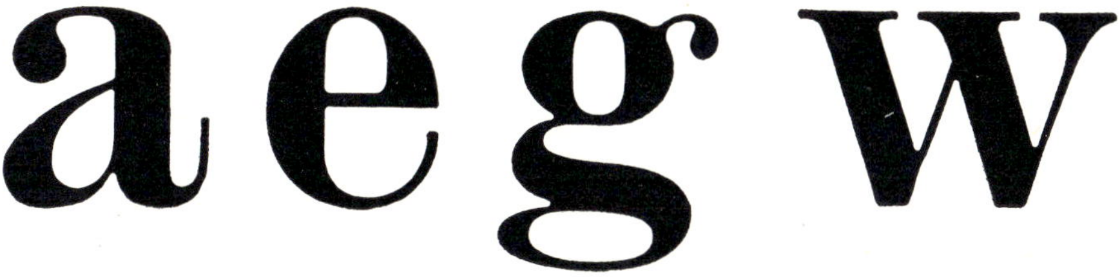

aegw

FIGURE 2. *A "clean" enlargement of the original type characters of* FIGURE 1, *photo-engraved from the type patterns*

aegw

FIGURE 3. *Excelsior superimposed over* FIGURE 2 *to show how the ink traps have been eliminated*

aegw

FIGURE 4. *The characters of Excelsior, shown in* FIGURE 3, *photo-engraved from the type patterns, revealing the clear, free design of the background of each letter* a e g w

FIGURE 5. *The same characters of Caslon Old Face, similarly reproduced. This was one of the early types used for the forbears of modern newspapers*

a e g w

FIGURE 6. *Century Expanded, for decades a popular news face, contains, nevertheless, the treacherous background pockets, to trap inky fibers*

In referring to Corona, not long after it was introduced, C. H. Griffith stated:

"Several years of careful research devoted to the problem of stereotyping in its relation to the quality of printing resulting from the use of rubber rollers and high-speed newspaper presses clearly disclosed that the horizontal shrinkage of the page, averaging about four per cent, due to the use of dry flongs, reduced the white area inside the letters and the normal space between letters to such an extent that the plate lost a very considerable amount of its sharpness of impression as compared to the printing surface of the slugs as delivered from the composing machine.

"A flong with a shrinkage of $\frac{2}{3}$ of an inch across the page played havoc with the size, shape and printing characteristics of the lowercase letters, to a greater or lesser degree according to individual design details.

"Experiments clearly disclosed that merely increasing the thickness of the sidewalls (space between the letters) uniformly on all letters in the alphabet would not correct the condition, because the distortion characteristics under shrinkage varied according to the shape of the letter. For example, a closed form like the lower-case o would not shrink as much as the lower-case e; the shrinkage of the lower-case m amounted to almost ten per cent of its original width, while the lower-case n shrinkage was only about four per cent. The counters of such letters as the lower-case g, a, e, and so forth, were shrunken to an extent that they would fill up with ink.

"This disclosure eventually resulted in the development of a scientific formula of shrinkage factors and distortion characteristics of each letter in the alphabet, which we were able to apply to the design of individual letters and provide for the necessary compensations to produce letters of normal shape and printing qualities when finally cast on the stereotype plate.

"In other words, all the defects in printing quality and shape of letters caused by dry-mat shrinkage were anticipated and corrected in the original design of the letters.

"The compensations apply not only to the shape of the letters and the space or sidewalls between the letters but to the weight of the lines and other elements of the design.

"Corona has been designed and cut according to this new formula, and it has been my observation that newspapers printed in Corona show the texture and clear-cut impression that characterized newspapers of the days before the advent of the dry mat, rubber rollers and high-speed presses.

"Another important point is that any size of Corona has a readability equivalent to that of a normal face fully 1 point-size larger, while its space economy is equal to that of a normal face approximately 1 point smaller."

• Ionic No. 5, Excelsior, Opticon, Paragon and Corona are available in various sizes, most of them from 5 or 5½ point up to and including 12 or 14 point, and in various combinations of roman and italic, or roman and bold. Some sizes of some of the faces are available, also, with regular, short or long descending letters—g, j, p, q and y.

Two widths of Excelsior—Excelsior No. 1 and Excelsior No. 2—are available in the 7- and 8-point sizes. Excelsior No. 1 is slightly wider than Excelsior No. 2.

Examples 23, 24 and 25 show, respectively, 7-, 8- and 10-point Ionic No. 5 set solid.

There are two hurdles news must surmount in its quick trip from the copy desk to the reader's mind. One is in the newspaper plant; the other is in the reader's eye. Modern newspaper printing conditions offer many hazards. To survive the ordeal of dry-mat stereotyping, a type face must be sturdy, free from thin lines and delicate serifs. It must be designed with due regard for the slurring effect of rubber rollers, and the tendency of

7-point Ionic No. 5 on a 7-point body

EXAMPLE 23

There are two hurdles news must surmount in its quick trip from the copy desk to the reader's mind. One is in the newspaper plant; the other is in the reader's eye. Modern newspaper printing conditions offer many hazards. To survive the ordeal of dry-mat stereotyping, a type face must be sturdy, free from thin lines and delicate serifs. It must be designed with due regard for the

8-point Ionic No. 5 on an 8-point body

EXAMPLE 24

There are two hurdles news must surmount in its quick trip from the copy desk to the reader's mind. One is in the newspaper plant; the other is in the reader's eye. Modern newspaper printing conditions offer many hazards. To survive the ordeal of dry-mat stereotyping, a type face must be sturdy, free from thin lines and delicate serifs. It must be designed with due regard for the slurring effect of rubber rollers, and the tendency of thin inks to collect in sharp

10-point Ionic No. 5 on a 10-point body

EXAMPLE 25

Examples 26, 27 and 28 show, respectively, 7-point Excelsior No. 1, 7-point Excelsior No. 2 and 10-point Excelsior set solid.

There are two hurdles news must surmount in its quick trip from the copy desk to the reader's mind. One is in the newspaper plant; the other is in the reader's eye. Modern newspaper printing conditions offer many hazards. To survive the ordeal of dry-mat stereotyping, a type face must be sturdy, free from thin lines and delicate serifs. It must be designed with due regard for the slurring effect of rubber rollers, and the

7-point Excelsior No. 1 on a 7-point body

EXAMPLE 26

There are two hurdles news must surmount in its quick trip from the copy desk to the reader's mind. One is in the newspaper plant; the other is in the reader's eye. Modern newspaper printing conditions offer many hazards. To survive the ordeal of dry-mat stereotyping, a type face must be sturdy, free from thin lines and delicate serifs. It must be designed with due regard for the slurring effect of rubber rollers, and the tendency of

7-point Excelsior No. 2 on a 7-point body

EXAMPLE 27

There are two hurdles news must surmount in its quick trip from the copy desk to the reader's mind. One is in the newspaper plant; the other is in the reader's eye. Modern newspaper printing conditions offer many hazards. To survive the ordeal of dry-mat stereotyping, a type face must be sturdy, free from thin lines and delicate serifs. It must be designed with due regard for the slurring effect of rubber rollers, and the tendency of thin inks to collect in sharp angles and narrow openings. The

10-point Excelsior on a 10-point body

EXAMPLE 28

Examples 29, 30 and 31 show, respectively 7-, 8- and 10-point Opticon set solid.

There are two hurdles news must surmount in its quick trip from the copy desk to the reader's mind. One is in the newspaper plant; the other is in the reader's eye. Modern newspaper printing conditions offer many hazards. To survive the ordeal of dry-mat stereotyping, a type face must be sturdy, free from thin lines and delicate serifs. It must be designed with due regard for the slurring effect of rubber rollers, and the

7-point Opticon on a 7-point body

EXAMPLE 29

There are two hurdles news must surmount in its quick trip from the copy desk to the reader's mind. One is in the newspaper plant; the other is in the reader's eye. Modern newspaper printing conditions offer many hazards. To survive the ordeal of dry-mat stereotyping, a type face must be sturdy, free from thin lines and delicate serifs. It must be designed with due regard for the

8-point Opticon on an 8-point body

EXAMPLE 30

There are two hurdles news must surmount in its quick trip from the copy desk to the reader's mind. One is in the newspaper plant; the other is in the reader's eye. Modern newspaper printing conditions offer many hazards. To survive the ordeal of dry-mat stereotyping, a type face must be sturdy, free from thin lines and delicate serifs. It must be designed with due regard for the slurring effect of rubber rollers, and the tendency of thin inks to collect in sharp angles and

10-point Opticon on a 10-point body

EXAMPLE 31

Examples 32, 33 and 34 show, respectively, 7-, 8- and 10-point Paragon set solid.

There are two hurdles news must surmount in its quick trip from the copy desk to the reader's mind. One is in the newspaper plant; the other is in the reader's eye. Modern newspaper printing conditions offer many hazards. To survive the ordeal of dry-mat stereotyping, a type face must be sturdy, free from thin lines and delicate serifs. It must be designed with due regard for the slurring effect of rubber rollers, and the

7-point Paragon on a 7-point body

EXAMPLE 32

There are two hurdles news must surmount in its quick trip from the copy desk to the reader's mind. One is in the newspaper plant; the other is in the reader's eye. Modern newspaper printing conditions offer many hazards. To survive the ordeal of dry-mat stereotyping, a type face must be sturdy, free from thin lines and delicate serifs. It must be designed with due regard for the

8-point Paragon on an 8-point body

EXAMPLE 33

There are two hurdles news must surmount in its quick trip from the copy desk to the reader's mind. One is in the newspaper plant; the other is in the reader's eye. Modern newspaper printing conditions offer many hazards. To survive the ordeal of dry-mat stereotyping, a type face must be sturdy, free from thin lines and delicate serifs. It must be designed with due regard for the slurring effect of rubber rollers, and the tendency of thin inks to collect in sharp angles

10-point Paragon on a 10-point body

EXAMPLE 34

And examples 35, 36 and 37 show, respectively, 7½-, 8½- and 10-point Corona set solid.

There are two hurdles news must surmount in its quick trip from the copy desk to the reader's mind. One is in the newspaper plant; the other is in the reader's eye. Modern newspaper printing conditions offer many hazards. To survive the ordeal of dry-mat stereotyping, a type face must be sturdy, free from thin lines and delicate serifs. It must be designed with due regard for the slurring effect of rubber rollers, and the

7½-point Corona on a 7½-point body

EXAMPLE 35

There are two hurdles news must surmount in its quick trip from the copy desk to the reader's mind. One is in the newspaper plant; the other is in the reader's eye. Modern newspaper printing conditions offer many hazards. To survive the ordeal of dry-mat stereotyping, a type face must be sturdy, free from thin lines and delicate serifs. It must be designed with due regard for the slurring effect of rubber rollers,

8½-point Corona on an 8½-point body

EXAMPLE 36

Some newspaper executives believe that the setting of important paragraphs in bold-face type emphasizes the importance of those paragraphs, and that the alternating of light and dark paragraphs can lend interest to a column.

In so thinking, they are partly right and partly wrong. Lines set

There are two hurdles news must surmount in its quick trip from the copy desk to the reader's mind. One is in the newspaper plant; the other is in the reader's eye. Modern newspaper printing conditions offer many hazards. To survive the ordeal of dry-mat stereotyping, a type face must be sturdy, free from thin lines and delicate serifs. It must be designed with due regard for the slurring effect of rubber rollers, and the tendency of thin inks to collect in sharp angles and narrow openings. The

10-point Corona on a 10-point body

EXAMPLE 37

in bold face can be more conspicuous, but they can also be harder to read than lines set in roman. And the alternating of light and dark paragraphs can give a column or a page an unattractive spotty appearance.

This is not an argument against the judicious use of bold face for body lines. Sometimes body lines seem to call for bold-face treatments.

But when more than a few consecutive body lines are presented in bold face, those lines should be generously leaded—more generously than their complementary roman body lines—or those important lines will be harder to read than the less important lines.

In the midst of newsprint shortages in World War II, the publisher of a leading metropolitan daily asked the writer of this book for suggestions on space saving. And this writer replied, in part:

"Of course we know that unless any particular issue can be cut two full pages, or a smaller page size employed, no paper saving can be made, as all normal issues, of course, consist of an even number of pages—never an odd. And I am assuming that you have set up some definite standard by which to determine the number of pages to be run in any particular issue—based on the amount of advertising available or acceptable and the amount and importance of news and feature material available.

"So the thing to do now is to see how much more news and feature material can be run on a definitely limited number of pages—how much more tightening up can be done—without sacrificing too much in the way of attractiveness, legibility and general effectiveness."

After having pointed out several ways in which pages might be tightened up, this writer continued, with reference to that publisher's general-news body matter:

"You now set most of your news body matter in 7½-point Corona on an 8½-point body. This gives you approximately 1093 words to a

21½-inch column. I think this is an excellent combination, and wouldn't suggest that you change it. But it seems only fair to add that 7½-point Corona on an 8-point body affords approximately 1164 words to a 21½-inch column—seventy-one words more than when 7½ is presented on 8½.

"However, as we know, most news columns are not given over entirely to body matter, but usually contain display heads and illustrations as well. So any actual saving usually would be less than seventy-one words to the column."

The following tables suggest the approximate number of words to the column that may be attained when certain news body faces are set solid, or with various degrees of leading. (In all instances, the column width is assumed to be 12 picas and the column depth 21½ inches.)

IONIC NO. 5

Size and Body	Approx. Words
7 on 7	1345
7 on 7½	1258
7 on 8	1180
7½ on 7½	1202
7½ on 8	1126
7½ on 8½	1067
8 on 8	1077
8 on 8½	1015
8 on 9	966

EXCELSIOR

Size and Body	Approx. Words
7 on 7	1348
7 on 7½	1258
7 on 8	1180
7½ on 7½	1221
7½ on 8	1142
7½ on 8½	1077
8 on 8	1133
8 on 8½	1066
8 on 9	1004

OPTICON

Size and Body	Approx. Words
7 on 7	1320
7 on 7½	1245
7 on 8	1168
7½ on 7½	1202
7½ on 8	1127
7½ on 8½	1067
8 on 8	1078
8 on 8½	1016
8 on 9	970

PARAGON

Size and Body	Approx. Words
7 on 7½	1233
7 on 8	1168
7½ on 7½	1223
7½ on 8	1140
7½ on 8½	1078
8 on 8	1100
8 on 8½	1040
8 on 9	990

CORONA

Size and Body	Approx. Words
7½ on 7½	1242
7½ on 8	1164
7½ on 8½	1093
8 on 8	1164
8 on 8½	1093
8 on 9	1033

When selecting type faces for news body matter, and the degrees of leading to be employed, newspaper executives should give due consideration to the important subject of eyesight—the eyesight of their average readers.

In the spring of 1937, a man who signed himself "Just a Reader" wrote this writer as follows:

"I am a free-born American, aged forty-five, never wore glasses and, by jinx! I don't intend to for some time to come. Anything tending to weaken the orbs goes into the discard. I let others strain their eyes in my stead.

"About a year ago the local paper came out with new body type. Readers didn't know what it was, but eyestrain was lessened—that they knew. Whether Ionic or what not, they little cared. This new type was wider and better spaced, and everybody knew the difference.

"I have a sister who spent some time in a hospital and consequently read considerable. She received several newspapers daily. 'What's the matter with the paper from L————?' she asked me one day. 'It's hard to read, and makes my eyes dizzy.' I looked at the sheet in question. Sure enough. 'Rotten type,' I said.

"The thought came to me that we take elaborate precautions on health matters, but when it comes to ruining the most precious of the senses—eyesight—the malefactors at the bottom are allowed their liberty.

"Should the ordinary citizen be forced to put on 'cheaters' when he picks up a newspaper? How did he get that way? While doctors have their line, dentists theirs, and so on, you fellows should be specialists in protecting that thing which must be employed to make your business go—eyesight. If we were all blind, the great aggregation which makes its bread and butter from the graphic arts and its allied industries would have to look elsewhere for a livelihood."

In May, 1938, this writer stated editorially:

"According to Lewis H. Carris, managing director of the National Society for the Prevention of Blindness, approximately 3,000,000 school children in the United States—one-eighth of the school population—are handicapped by defective eyesight.

"Newspaper publishers and editors would do well to consider these figures in relation to the type dresses of their publications.

"And bear in mind that these 3,000,000 are the *young* readers of newspapers.

"How about the eyesight of most *middle-aged* readers?

"Of course we know that *elderly* readers—and there are millions of them in this country—do not see as well as they once did.

"Are you sure that your newspaper can be read with ease by most of your readers?"

In May of 1943, in the midst of World War II, in a booklet entitled *Eyes—No. 1 Production Tool*, the Better Vision Institute, Inc., of New York City stated: "Eighty per cent of all human motions are controlled by the eyes, which also convey eighty-three per cent of the knowledge that reaches the brain. Victory literally hinges on eyesight. Yet nearly three-quarters of all adults have defects of vision, and only a minority of them have had these defects corrected through professional eye care."

So newspaper executives, when selecting type faces and degrees of leading for their papers, and particularly for news body matter, which occupies by far the greater part of their papers, should make sure that the faces are easy to read—as easy as is reasonably possible.

7

Leading and Spacing

Leading (pronounced ledding), the amount of white space *between lines,* and spacing, the amount of white *between character groups or single characters within lines,* deserve careful consideration, as both play important parts in the *appearance* and in the *cost* of newspapers. Yet leading and spacing work in opposite ways.

Type lines usually are easier to read when leaded 1 or 2 points than when set solid. But the same lines are harder to read when widely spaced than when closely spaced.

The more clearly defined separation of lines brought about by leading helps the reader to follow through from line to line by lessening the possibility of his gaze's returning by mistake to the beginning of the line he has just finished reading, instead of dropping to the beginning of the next line. But of more importance is the fact that leading, by putting a strip of white space above the tops of ascending letters (b, d, f, h, k, l, t) and below the bottoms of descending letters (g, j, p, q, y) causes the word forms to stand out more clearly on the page and thus be more readily recognizable. In lines set solid, the word forms in one line often blend or nearly blend with word forms in the following line, as the descending letters in one and the ascending letters in the other often nearly touch each other.

Leading, too, can change the color of a paragraph, a head, or an entire page. Lines set solid make for heavier masses than would be the case were the same lines leaded. The greater the leading, the lighter the masses. Unusually black heads can be toned down somewhat by generous leading.

While leading can make a newspaper page more legible, practical considerations suggest definite leading limits for news body lines. The greater the leading, of course, the fewer the lines to the column, page and issue, unless pages are added, which necessarily increases the cost of production.

As stated in Chapter 6 of Part I, the tendency of dailies in this country at present is to set their news body matter in 7-, 7½- and 8-point faces cast on a 7½-, 8-, 8½- or 9-point body. But many of our dailies now set the body matter of their classified-advertising columns in 5-point faces, solid, or in 5½-point faces with short descenders on a 5-point body, which gives them fourteen lines to the inch and, consequently, more income than they would receive at the same line rate from lines in larger point sizes and leaded, or from the 5½ point leaded, or even set on its own body size, 5½ point. Although such small and closely set lines are harder to read than the larger and leaded body lines in the news columns, the important item of income dictates their use—that and the considerations that such lines form but a comparatively small part of the paper as a whole; that the reader probably is interested in no more than a few classifications at any one time, and that, therefore, he is put to comparatively little inconvenience in reading such lines.

Example 38 shows 7½-point Corona on an 8-point body, and Example 39 shows 7½-point Corona on a 9-point body.

There are two hurdles news must surmount in its quick trip from the copy desk to the reader's mind. One is in the newspaper plant; the other is in the reader's eye. Modern newspaper printing conditions offer many hazards. To survive the ordeal of dry-mat stereotyping, a type face must be sturdy, free from thin lines and delicate serifs. It must be designed with due regard for the slurring effect of rubber rollers, and the

7½-point Corona on an 8-point body

EXAMPLE 38

There are two hurdles news must surmount in its quick trip from the copy desk to the reader's mind. One is in the newspaper plant; the other is in the reader's eye. Modern newspaper printing conditions offer many hazards. To survive the ordeal of dry-mat stereotyping, a type face must be sturdy, free from thin lines and delicate serifs. It must be designed with due regard for the slurring effect of rubber rollers, and the

7½-point Corona on a 9-point body

EXAMPLE 39

Notice how much darker the lines seem in Example 38 than in Example 39.

If a news story deserves a multiple-deck head, the head itself surely deserves enough leading to cause the lines to stand out and to be read as easily and quickly as possible.

Many newspapers are prodigal with multiple-deck heads, but are strangely thrifty with leading in them.

Example 40 shows a badly leaded two-deck head, and Example 41 shows the same lines properly leaded.

Local Boy's Club
To Meet Today
At Court House

Business Problems
To Be Discussed—
Program Outlined

EXAMPLE 40

Local Boy's Club
To Meet Today
At Court House

Business Problems
To Be Discussed—
Program Outlined

EXAMPLE 41

Example 41 is less than 2 picas deeper than Example 40, but notice how much more attractive it is and how much easier to read. The marked difference between the two heads was easily brought about by the insertion of 4 points of leading between the lines of the first deck, 8 points between the decks, and 2 points between the lines of the second deck, for a total of 20 points (4, 4, 8, 2, 2), or less than 2 picas.

It is well to bear in mind that, if a story deserves a multiple-deck head, the head itself deserves proper leading. A few additional points of leading should not be withheld when those points—as often is the case—constitute the difference between an unsatisfactory head and a satisfactory one.

When, before a page form is locked up for the press or the stereotyping department, the columns are being justified to fill, care should be taken with any extra leading necessary.

The extra leads—and they should be 1-point leads, not 2-point or thicker leads—should be placed between the first few consecutive lines of body matter of each story in a column; or, if only a few points are required, between the first few consecutive body lines of the first story in the column.

Often the temptation is strong, when a page form has to be justified in a hurry, to drop several of the extra leads together before or after "30" dashes, or subheads, or between or immediately below the lines of main heads. But such haphazard leading disfigures any pages so treated.

When definite standards of leading have been adopted for heads and dashes—and definite standards must be followed by papers that hope to turn out attractive pages—no deviations from those standards should be tolerated.

If there are five stories, say, in a column, and the column is 20 points short of filling (and no filler lines are readily available or desirable), 1-point leads should be placed between the first five consecutive body lines of each story, making four extra 1-point leads to each story. But if, say, a column is only 6 points short of filling, it usually is advisable to put six 1-point leads between the first seven consecutive body lines of the first story in the column—supposedly the most important story in the column.

Extra 1-point leading at the beginning of a story usually helps the reader to "get into it better" without seriously marring the appearance of the story or the page. But the use of 2-point or thicker leads for the extra leading of the first few body lines does have a marring effect. The difference in appearance between the extra-leaded lines and the following regularly leaded or solid lines is too pronounced to be acceptable to careful makeup editors.

Closely spaced body lines are easier to read than widely spaced.

One reason for this is that wide spacing makes it necessary for the reader, however unconsciously, to "jump" from word form to word form, instead of gliding along smoothly from one group of characters to another. That "jumping," if long continued, becomes a conscious effort and, consequently, an intruding, attention-distracting thing. The gliding, of course, is done with little if any conscious thought on the part of the reader that his gaze *is* gliding. He does not pause to consider the mechanics of spacing until something occurs—something like wide spacing—to make him conscious of it—that things are not going as smoothly as they might.

And another reason (or an extension of the reason already discussed) why wide spacing makes for difficult reading is that it causes "rivers of white" to flow down through the lines. Such "rivers" often become so pronounced as to form patterns of their own—patterns that compete with the reading matter for attention—and that mar the appearance of the type lines, the columns, the paper as a whole.

Correct spacing is easily attainable on composing machines. Various thicknesses of spacebands are available—spacebands for comparatively large faces, for medium-size faces, for comparatively small faces. And many thicknesses of non-variable spaces are available.

Type lines should be composed with no more space between sentences than between the character groups within sentences.

A common practice in composition is the placing of more space between sentences than between the word or figure groups within sentences.

This writer distinctly remembers that his first printing instructor told him, when teaching him to set type by hand, to put a full "mutton," or em, quad between sentences—three times as much as between word or figure groups within sentences.

And this writer continued to follow that practice longer than he usually cares to admit. He followed it from hand cases to composing machines. On the machines, he continued to drop the equivalent of a full em quad between sentences—an equivalent usually made up of a "nut," or en, quad and a spaceband.

And many operators today follow that same practice.

To those who suggest, as some have who hesitate to revise a plan of typesetting they have followed for years, that there should be a longer pause at the end of a sentence than at the points of punctuation within the sentence, and that that longer pause is partly brought about by additional space, it can be said with logic that the punctuation point at the end of a sentence ends the sentence in its own right. The space immediately following the ending point has nothing to do with the duration of pause indicated by the point.

If the spacing did have anything to do with the duration of pause, it would naturally follow that two em quads immediately following an ending point would call for a longer pause than one em quad, and three em quads a still longer pause than two. To pursue this line of reasoning further, it would seem just as logical to assume that the pauses after commas in widely spaced lines should be greater than the pauses after commas in closely spaced lines.

But we know that this is not true. The comma calls for a definite degree of pause, in its own right, regardless of spacing; the semicolon calls for a longer pause, and the period for a still longer. Wide spacing, medium spacing or close spacing do not affect those degrees of pause.

But let us do some graphic comparing of widely spaced lines with closely (and correctly) spaced lines.

The lines in Example 42, purposely made up of short sentences, to emphasize the point being made, are widely spaced, with at least the equivalent of a full em quad between sentences.

Obviously, Example 42 is unsightly and difficult to read. The fault does not lie with short sentences, but with the wide spacing between and within the sentences.

Not so good. Unsightly. Notice the holes. There's a reason. Em quads. They do not belong here. Too wide for use between sentences. One spaceband is enough. One extra-thin spaceband. Be careful with spacing. Do not set lines like these. Avoid em quads between sentences. Be careful. Be correct. Be exact. Use spacebands. Use extra-thin spacebands. Your lines will be better looking. You will like them better. They will be easier to read. Type was made to read.

EXAMPLE 42

Much better. Attractive. No holes. There's a reason. No em quads. They do not belong here. Close spacing between sentences. One spaceband is enough. One extra-thin spaceband. Be careful with spacing. Set lines like these. Avoid em quads between sentences. Be careful. Be correct. Be exact. Use spacebands. Use extra-thin spacebands. Your lines will be better looking. You will like them better. They will be easier to read. Type was made to read.

EXAMPLE 43

Example 43 is made up of the same number of short sentences, but they have been set with extra-thin spacebands throughout—not only between the words in the sentences but between the sentences.

Particular typesetters, when setting type for a fine book or other item of fine printing, and with plenty of time for the setting, use (for typographic effect) different degrees of spacing between some of the words, depending on the shapes of the punctuation marks involved and on the shapes of the letters at the ends and beginnings of words; but such careful spacing usually requires too much time to be followed advantageously on the busy news machines, which usually must turn out body lines at high speed.

As stated in Chapter 3 of Part I, a metropolitan daily, in reducing its column width from 12½ picas to 12, found it possible to present just about the same number of words to the column in the narrower measure as it had in the wider, by equipping its composing machines with extra-thin spacebands.

Many other papers have followed the same procedure to advantage.

8

Nameplates and Ears

BACK IN THE "BOOK STAGE" of journalism, nameplates, or title lines, were simple, restrained, dignified, and they harmonized with the other typographic units with which they were used. And for at least two reasons: First, newspapers then, as previously stated, were controlled and produced by printers—not publishers as we use that term today—by skilled craftsmen more interested in turning out well-organized pages from a printing standpoint than in "selling" their wares to the public. Second, as there was comparatively little competition between newspapers at the equivalent of our newsstand, as many readers bought their copies direct from the printer at his own shop, or received them by post, or read them at coffee-houses the proprietors of which often handled one paper exclusively, there were few important "outside" reasons for newspapers to go in for more eye catching nameplates.

The nameplates of many English-language newspapers, back in the early days, were set in roman capitals or capitals and lower-case, or in both roman capitals and capitals and lower-case—often in larger sizes of the same sort of faces used for body matter.

Example 1 suggests how *Publick Occurrences* of Boston, back in 1690, employed roman capitals for the main lines of its nameplate; Example 2 suggests how the *Boston News-Letter* employed roman capitals and lower-case back in 1704, and Example 44 suggests how the *London Packet* used both roman capitals and capitals and lower-case back in 1786.

Although early day newspapers used no ears of the sort employed by many newspapers of today, some early day papers presented their issue numbers above their nameplates, to the left (see Example 1) or right (see Example 2), or occasionally presented a few other incidental lines in an ear position.

Some early day newspapers employed pictorial devices in their nameplates, usually in the form of wood-cuts—pictures of postmen or postboys, afoot or mounted on horses, with trumpet in hand or at the lips. Other early day papers presented pictures of packets (ships), or other pictorial devices, in their nameplates.

In England before 1712, when a stamp tax was placed on newspaper paper, several British papers employed comparatively deep title lines, but the tax caused some of those papers to lessen the depths of those lines. Some of those papers not only lessened the depths of those lines but presented the first and last columns on their front pages as high columns to get more lines on the page and thus to hold down production costs.

When competition between papers became keener, the title lines of many papers became bolder and more ornate, with a rather general shifting from roman types to black-letter, or old-English—the blackest type then available in many newspaper shops.

When several influential papers had shifted from roman to old-English for their nameplates, in the 1670's, many less important papers followed suit, and for twenty-five or thirty years old-English was employed quite extensively for newspaper nameplates.

Imitativeness was a characteristic of the newspaper business in those days (as of course it still is), and many lesser papers then did not dare be much different in appearance from important papers—not if those lesser papers hoped, as of course most of them did, to appear important themselves.

For twenty-five or thirty years, as has been stated, many papers used old-English for their nameplates. Along toward the end of the seventeenth century, however, several important papers shifted from old-English back to roman—with a natural trailing along on the part of many less important papers.

For many years then many newspapers on both sides of the Atlantic used roman types for their nameplates.

Then several important papers shifted to old-English again, as also did innumerable imitators, and old-English continues to be used by hundreds of newspapers to this day.

Many newspapers started in this country no more than twenty-five years ago—in some instances no more than ten years ago, or less—adopted old-English for their nameplates chiefly because many other papers, many of them quite important, were using old-English. And many considerably older papers have hesitated to change from old-English to other faces, because they want "to appear their age"—to have "a long-established look"—and are unwilling to let go of what they regard as the trademark value of their old-time nameplates.

When the *Linotype News* was launched, in 1922, it followed tradition by appearing with a nameplate in old-English. But it since has employed several other faces for nameplates, and sometimes has shifted nameplates from one issue to another, depending on the head dress used, as suggested by several examples in this volume.

Newspaper ears as we know them today—displayed ears often used with nameplates to call attention to important features in papers, to advertise the papers, to promote community affairs, to present weather or tide information, to identify particular editions, and for many other purposes—are comparatively recent inventions. They are a manifestation of the competition that has developed between newspapers, particularly newsstand competition.

Certain it is that newspaper ears, because of the positions they occupy at the top of a page, can be attention arresting, and many newspaper editors and publishers are convinced that appropriately worded and displayed ears have strong "pulling power" or "sales appeal."

The nameplates suggested by the examples that follow (and of course many other and different nameplates could be shown if space permitted) cover a wide range typographically, and employ various means to present various statements in their ears—those that have ears.

Example 44 suggests the nameplate on a copy of the *London Packet* issued in 1786.

As may be observed, the word "THE" was in widely letter-spaced roman capitals centered in a line by itself above a pictorial device that interrupted the second and third lines; the words "LONDON PACKET" were in letter-spaced roman capitals of a size fully twice as large; the word "OR" in the third line was in roman capitals of the same size used for the first line, and the words "New Lloyds Evening Post" were in roman capitals and lower-case of the same size used for the second line.

It should be interesting to note, in passing, that a line immediately below the nameplate and above the date line stated: "Printed by F. Blyth, No. 2, Queen's-Head-Alley, Pater-Noster-Row. A Letter-Box on the Gate." Note that that credit line stated *printed*, not *edited*, or

THE

LONDON PACKET;

OR, New Lloyds Evening Poſt.

Printed by F. BLYTH, No. 2, QUEEN'S-HEAD-ALLEY, PATER-NOSTER-ROW. [*A Letter-Box on the Gate.*

Price Three-pence. From WEDNESDAY, MAY 31, to FRIDAY, JUNE 2, 1786. [No. 2435.

EXAMPLE 44

THE Numb. 7

VIRGINIA GAZETTE.

Containing the freſheſt Advices, Foreign and Domeſtick.

Founded 1736 From Friday, February 8 to Friday, February 15, 1946

NEW SERIES — VOLUME XVII. WILLIAMSBURG, VIRGINIA 5c PER COPY

EXAMPLE 45

published. Yet Mr. Blyth was only one of several printers who printed that paper before it was merged with another London journal.

Example 45, which suggests a nameplate used by the *Virginia Gazette* of Williamsburg, Va., a paper founded August 6, 1736, has a colonial flavor.

Note the letter-spaced "THE" in a line by itself; the word "*VIRGINIA*" in italic capitals; the third line, in italic capitals and lower-case; the periods at the ends of the second and third lines.

Example 46 suggests a nameplate (in a rather condensed old-English) that has been used by the *Alexandria* (Va.) *Gazette.*

The ear at the left played up a "Brotherhood Week"; the one at the right referred to the weather, tides and sun. Two tapered dashes were used with each ear. A comparatively small line in italic capitals under the nameplate stated: "America's Oldest Daily Newspaper—Established 1784."

The *Rhinebeck* (N. Y.) *Gazette* has used a nameplate of distinction, one drawn by a master designer, Frederic W. Goudy, not only to harmonize with the type faces used for heads by the *Gazette*—Bodoni Bold, Bodoni Bold Italic and Bodoni Bold Condensed—but to suggest the spirit and flavor of our colonial days, when Rhinebeck was founded. (See Example 47.)

Note that the words "The" and "Gazette" were given italic treatment, with a swash T for "The" and a swash z for "Gazette," with "Rhinebeck" in roman, and all words in capitals and lower-case.

"Since Rhinebeck reaches back into colonial times," Jacob H. Strong Jr., editor of the *Gazette*, informed this writer, "Mr. Goudy decided that the introduction of italics into the heading would, in a way, carry out the colonial tradition and, as well, add to the variety and interest of the line."

While this particular nameplate from the *Rhinebeck Gazette* appeared without ears, the *Gazette* has used ears of various kinds.

Example 48 suggests how a pair of line-cuts, placed to face into the page, were used with a nameplate in 72-point Narciss, with ears in Bodoni Bold Italic and Bodoni Bold centered between the cuts and the nameplate.

The *Ottawa* (Ont.) *Journal* has used a nameplate of the sort shown in Example 49. Note that the leading display is in outlined characters filled in with conspicuous dots; that prominently displayed near the

BROTHERHOOD
WEEK
FEB. 17—24

The Alexandria Gazette

AMERICA'S OLDEST DAILY NEWSPAPER—ESTABLISHED 1784

Weather, Tides And Sun

Clear and continued damp.

Maximum temperature, 39 at 1:30 a. m.; minimum, 30 at 6:40 a. m.

High tide, 11:02 a. m., 11:23 p. m.; low tide, 5:32 a. m., 5:59 p. m.

Sunrise, 6:53 a. m.; sunset, 5:51 p. m.

VOL. CLXIII—No. 15 | ASSOCIATED PRESS and UNITED PRESS LEASED WIRES | ALEXANDRIA, VIRGINIA, THURSDAY, FEBRUARY 21, 1946 | ALL THE LOCAL NEWS OF TODAY | FIVE CENTS

EXAMPLE 46

The* Rhinebeck *Gazette

VOL. C, NO. 44 | RHINEBECK, NEW YORK, FEBRUARY 28, 1946 | SINGLE COPIES SEVEN CENTS

EXAMPLE 47

55-90-34
See Page Three

The Linotype News

72-90-34
See Page Eight

VOLUME XI | BROOKLYN, DECEMBER, 1932 | NUMBER THREE

EXAMPLE 48

center are three lines reading: "Late News and Sport on Page 4"; that a single rule is used immediately below the nameplate matter.

The *Milford* (Conn.) *News* has used a deep nameplate with a line-cut toward its center and with scrolls to the left and right listing the names of a dozen neighboring communities in which the paper circulates, as suggested by Example 50.

Three lines in small type between light rules to the left of the central line-cut stated: "A Home-Town Newspaper, Dedicated to Perpetuation of Milford's Own Ideals and Traditions"; and three lines to the right, between the same kind of rules: "Town of Milford, Founded in 1639, the Sixth Oldest Town in Connecticut, But Still Young."

The *Marin Journal* of San Rafael, Calif., has used a nameplate of the sort suggested by Example 51, with the two main words presented in outlined old-English.

The *New York Herald Tribune*, which has used many different kinds of nameplates since the establishment of the *Herald* and the *Tribune*, has been using in recent years the rather strong old-English treatment suggested by Example 52.

Note that the left ear presents information about the weather, and that the right ear identifies the edition.

The *New York World-Telegram* has used its right ear to identify the edition, and to specify the price of the paper. As a left ear it has used the Scripps-Howard emblem, a lighthouse. A small line below the nameplate presented information about the weather, and a smaller line above that presented copyright data. See Example 53.

The *Journal-Times* of Ritzville, Wash., a prize-winning seven-column weekly with heads in Memphis and other square-serif faces, employs nameplates of different widths—four, five and six columns—depending on the kind of makeup desired for a particular edition.

Example 54 shows the six-column nameplate used with a high first column. Note that nearly all of the type characters in the nameplate are in square serifs, to tone in well with the paper's head dress, but that *Journal-Times* has been given a strong script treatment for effective contrast. Only one rule was used with that nameplate—a rule interrupted to accommodate the lower end of the descending *J* in *Journal*.

One newspaper, the *San Diego* (Calif.) *Daily Journal*, far from believing that a change of nameplates works against a paper, has used

EXAMPLE 49

The Milford News

Devon
Myrtle Beach
Walnut Beach
Laurel Beach
Silver Beach
Fort Trumbull Beach

A Home-Town Newspaper, Dedicated to Perpetuation of Milford's Own Ideals and Traditions

Town of Milford, Founded in 1639 the Sixth Oldest Town in Connecticut But Still Young

Woodmont
Morningside
Pondpoint
Bayview
Bayview Heights
Point Beach

Vol. XIX—No. 3 Published Weekly by The Milford News Publishing Co., Inc Yearly Subscription $2.50 Single Copy 5 cents. MILFORD, CONN., MARCH 8, 1946 Entered as Second Class Mail Matter, April 17, 1928, at the Post Office at Milford, Under Act of March 3, 1879 Eight Pages

EXAMPLE 50

THE Marin Journal
ESTABLISHED 1861

VOL. 84—No. 29. SAN RAFAEL, CALIFORNIA, THURSDAY, OCTOBER 4, 1945. PRICE FIVE CENTS

EXAMPLE 51

THE WEATHER

Today: Considerable cloudiness and mild; highest temperature near 70; gentle to moderate southerly winds shifting to north.
Tomorrow: Partly cloudy and cooler.
Temperatures Yesterday: Max., 73, Min., 55
Detailed Report on Page 16

VOL. CV No. 36,294

NEW YORK
Herald Tribune

Copyright, 1946, New York Tribune Inc.

SATURDAY, MARCH 30, 1946

LATE CITY EDITION

THREE CENTS In New York City

EXAMPLE 52

SCRIPPS-HOWARD

New York World-Telegram

7TH SPORTS
Final Stock Tables
Five Cents

Copyright, 1946 by New York World-Telegram Corporation. All rights reserved.

Local Forecast· Cooler today. Clear and much cooler tonight. Moderate temperatures tomorrow.

VOL. 78—NO. 229—IN TWO SECTIONS—SECTION ONE

NEW YORK, SATURDAY, MARCH 30, 1946

Entered as second class matter Post Office, New York, N. Y.

EXAMPLE 53

Men in Service
★ ★ ★ ★ ★ ★ ★

Report From The Philippines
Pfc. Clarence Fleming, son of Mrs. Fred Selcho of Ritzville, tells interestingly of life in the Philippines in a recent letter:
"Work goes on just as monotonously as ever day after day

The RITZVILLE Journal-Times

Vol. XLVI, No. 22

Ritzville, Washington

Thursday, May 31, 1945

Subscription $2.50 per year

EXAMPLE 54

EXAMPLE 55

EXAMPLE 56

SAN DIEGO'S HOME-OWNED NEWSPAPER

SAN DIEGO DAILY JOURNAL

THE JOURNAL SET THE PACE WATCH

Vol. 3 No. 37 1127 2nd Ave. SAN DIEGO (1), CALIF., FRIDAY, APRIL 5, 1946 * Tel. F-7651 5c per Copy

EXAMPLE 57

The *Journal* of San Diego, Calif., has used as many as three different nameplates in a single day, as suggested by the three examples on this page.

as many as three different kinds of nameplates in a single day's issues, as suggested by Examples 55, 56 and 57.

In a single day the *Daily Journal* has used a vigorous square-serif and script nameplate for its bulldog edition, a reverse plate of a night scene of downtown San Diego for its night final, and a decidedly different and quite conservative nameplate for each of its two home editions.

Two of the nameplates suggested here—those for the bulldog and the night final—were four columns wide and were "floated" below the tops of front pages. The other nameplate—used for each of the home editions—was spread across eight columns at the top of each front page, with a pair of ears.

The *Brewery Gulch Gazette* of Bisbee, Ariz., has used in its nameplate a full-width drawing of a street scene—fanciful or otherwise—in Brewery Gulch. Under the drawing appeared the line: "The sun shines on Brewery Gulch 330 days in the year, but there is moonshine every day."

The *Blair* (Wis.) *Press* has used a nameplate in old-English, without ears, but with a line in rather heavy gothic capitals just below it stating: "The Only Paper in the World That Cares Two Whoops for Blair, Wisconsin."

Some weekly papers have used two monthly calendars for ears with their nameplates—a calendar of the current month, and one of the month to come.

Sometimes when one newspaper absorbs another, the dominant journal runs for a while a smaller nameplate of the other above its own and larger nameplate, to attract the attention of former readers of the other, and later presents both names in a new nameplate. The *New York Telegram* followed that procedure for a while after February 27, 1931, when it absorbed the *New York World* papers, as suggested by Example 58, which shows three different nameplates near the top of the page.

A curiosity in the way of nameplates is suggested by Example 59, which shows how ten New York City morning newspapers, back in September of 1923, put out a combined edition under ten different nameplates when a strike of pressmen kept the papers from appearing in the usual way.

The New York evening papers, also, followed a similar procedure during the strike.

The Evening World

The World

Complete Wire Reports of UNITED PRESS and ASSOCIATED PRESS

The New York Telegram

Metropolitan

VOL. 63.—NO. 203.— IN TWO SECTIONS—SECTION ONE | NEW YORK, FRIDAY, FEBRUARY 27, 1931 | PRICE THREE CENTS.

WORLD PURCHASED BY THE TELEGRAM

HUNT TAXI MAN SEEN BY THREE IN VICE SLAYING

Police Try to Block Questioning of Three Witnesses to Miss Gordon's Murder.

ATTACKED BY TWO MEN NEAR PARK, THEY SAY

Patrolman, on Leave, Who Once Arrested Her, Sought by the Investigators.

HAS HUSBAND HELD

SENATE READY TO UPSET VETO OF LOANS BILL

Upper Chamber Unlikely to Give Hoover Much Over a Dozen Votes.

HOUSE VICTORY 328 TO 79, DEFEAT FOR MELLON, TOO

Administration Faces Another Bitter Denunciation in Debate Today.

Merger Means Re-Birth of World, Says Howard, Pledging Faith to Ideals

PULITZERS PRESENT THREE MONTHS PAY TO THEIR EMPLOYES

Foley Authorizes the Consolidation, Ruling Trustees Are Sole Judges of the Contract—Deal Delayed Sixty Hours.

COURT RULES THAT TERMS OF CONTRACT ARE PROVINCE SOLELY OF TRUSTEES

Permits Greatest Consolidation of Newspapers in Years, Concluding Gallant Fight for Their Purchase.

EXAMPLE 58

The Combined New York Morning Newspapers

New York American

THE NEW YORK HERALD

The Journal of Commerce

DAILY NEWS

The Morning Telegraph

The New York Times.

New York Tribune

The World.

New-Yorker Staats-Zeitung

IL PROGRESSO ITALO-AMERICANO

VOL. LXXXIII No. 28,067 | THURSDAY, SEPTEMBER 20, 1923

Ward Witness Admits State Coached Him

Trooper Forced by Counsel for Defense to Tell of Instructions Regarding Caliber of Revolver

Woman, 60, Walks Past Bars to Die on Track

Battleship Hits Destroyer Off Cape Cod Canal

McFarland Limps to Boston Yard With One Dead and Several Hurt After Being Rammed by the Arkansas

O'Connor and Thor Reveal Bribe Silence

Inspector Takes Stand, Lahey Already Knew; Ex-Inspector General Quit When Suspected

ZR-3 to Fly From Germany to U. S. in 140 Hours in November

Teuton-Built Sister to Navy's Latest Airship Will Cover 4,500 Nautical Miles on Trip "Without Intermediate Stop"

Two-Year Coal Pact Signed at Pinchot's Home

Publishers Demand New Press Union

Refuse to Deal With Outlaw Strikers and Call on President Berry to Revoke Their Charter

Martial Law for Year, if Needed, Walton's Threat

Baden General Strike Halts Rails and Press

Hunt in Vain After Distress Call in Sound

Vote Ending Ruhr Fight Due Sept. 26

Stresemann Will Urge Decision by Reichstag; Baldwin and Poincare Confer; Parley Expected

EXAMPLE 59

During World War II, newsprint and other scarcities prompted some newspapers to shift to shallower nameplates to save paper; to do away with one or even both ears on front pages, to pack in more stories;

to do away with the use of nameplates on front pages of second and following sections.

To this writer it seems that a nameplate should be presented in a type face (or hand lettering) in the same family used for the main news heads on a front page, or in a decidedly different type face (or lettering)—not one just a little different. A nameplate to be effective should be closely related to the main-head type, or offer decided contrast to it. It should not be somewhere in between. And when an illustration is used in a nameplate, the design and color of the illustration should tone in well with the design and color of the type face or lettering of the nameplate—should not be so "off color" as to attract too much attention to itself and away from the name of the paper. And the type faces and any rules or ornaments used for ears should harmonize in design and color with the nameplate or with the head dress of the paper.

Some of our modern scripts can be used effectively for nameplates of newspapers, particularly for newspapers with head dresses in modern sans serifs and square serifs.

Some publishers of newspapers with nameplates that do not get along well with the head dresses used hesitate, as has been stated, to change to more appropriate nameplates for fear that any change would impair the recognition or trademark value that long usage of the old nameplates has given the upper part of their papers—that any such change would disturb readers accustomed to the old nameplates, and would work against the papers on the newsstands.

But it is difficult for this writer to believe that any change that enhances the attractiveness of a paper would militate against it—at least for long. Indeed, the best answer to the line of reasoning opposed to such a change is offered by many a long-established and successful newspaper that has changed its nameplate, and its head and body types as well, many times in the course of its existence.

When a nameplate is made (from type lines or slugs or a drawing), it usually is advisable to have a master plate made—a plate not to be used in the forms itself—but to be used for electrotype reproductions for employment in the forms. The master plate preferably should be deep-etched in copper, and the electros be steel-faced and mounted on metal, to assure their standing up well under stereotype pressure or on the printing press and their reproducing clearly despite oft-repeated use.

Some newspapers use nameplates engraved in steel or in bronze.

Nameplates and ears in many papers are so battered or broken or smudgy that they mar the appearance of the papers.

When a nameplate begins to show appreciable wear, the master plate should be brought out from the files and a new electro made. And the ears, too, should be kept in good condition—like those of a small boy.

9

Date Lines and Running Heads

THE KIND OF RULES used with the date line of a newspaper, and the leading between the rules and the type line, have considerable to do with the appearance of the page as a whole.

Several papers use with their date lines rules that are good in themselves, but that are inappropriate for date-line use. Other papers use the right sort of rules with date lines, but fail to employ the right amount of leading between the rules and the type lines.

Back in the "book stage" of journalism, some newspapers employed no rules toward the tops of their pages. (See Example 1.)

Other papers (see Example 2) employed plain light rules above and below their date lines, or above and below a statement such as "Published by Authority," with liberal leading between the type line and its accompanying rules.

That sort of leading seemed appropriate then, when papers employed comparatively large body types, wide columns and generous page margins; but in these days of larger and tighter pages, deep leading seems out of place for date lines.

Also, back in the days when papers employed little if any display, and that little in comparatively light faces, light parallel rules seemed appropriate for use with date lines on front pages (see Example 6) and under running heads on other pages.

But habit is a strong thing in the newspaper business, and many papers, even when they increased the size and weight of their head dresses, continued to use light parallel rules with date lines and running heads—as many strongly headed papers do to this day.

Another rule treatment of date lines that became popular many years ago (possibly because some relatively important paper—a paper of course imitated by many less important ones—had only a limited supply of rules and attempted to make the most of what it had to work with) involved the use of a fairly light parallel rule above the date line and a fairly heavy oxford rule (sometimes called a Scotch rule or a double rule) below the date line. And hundreds of newspapers continue to employ that sort of rule combination with their date lines.

(Parallel or single rules and oxfords often can be used together advantageously for composite borders for advertisements and in certain other forms of printing, but they form a less effective combination when used in pairs with type lines between them, as in date lines.)

It is possible here to show only fragments of date lines, but these fragments should serve to illustrate the points to be brought out. In each illustration the type line is in the same face and size—12-point Bodoni Bold—to show how a face of that sort—one with a decided difference in weight between its thick and thin strokes—gets along well with some kinds of rules, and not so well with others.

Of course, the type face used for the main line of a date line might well be in the same type family, or one of the same families, used for the head dress of the paper, as the date line is a part of the head dress and should harmonize with the other parts.

As a general principle, date-line rules used with head faces the thick and thin strokes of which are *not* in marked contrast with each other should be either single rules or parallel rules, while date-line rules used with head faces with decided differences in weight between their thick and thin strokes should be either single or oxford rules.

But fairly light parallel rules (and, as has been stated, many newspapers continue out of habit to use such rules with their date lines, regardless of the kinds of head faces employed) seem out of place, even when used with monotone faces, unless those faces are comparatively light in weight.

Too Much Space Above and Below Type Line

EXAMPLE 60

Example 60 is typical of date lines carried by many weekly papers. The rules are all right in themselves, but they do not get along well with a face like Bodoni Bold, and there is too much leading between the rules and the type line. Nine points of leading appear above the line and 9 more (including any shoulder on the type-line slug) below it. Some weeklies use as much as 12 points of leading both above and below. Space is wasted, and the result is unattractive.

Other papers, some of them metropolitan dailies, use date lines like the one in Example 61. The rules are appropriate, but there is not enough leading between the rules and the type line. The whole thing is too crowded, and the result is unattractive.

Rules Are Too Close to Type Line In This

EXAMPLE 61

Still other papers use date lines like the one in Example 62, for, as previously stated, many papers began using such rules together many years ago and have kept on doing so out of habit. Each of these rules is all right in itself, but the general effect is not good when they are used together in this way.

This Is an Unattractive Combination

EXAMPLE 62

Some papers use oxford rules that are entirely too heavy for such use, like the ones in Example 63.

These Oxford Rules Are Too Heavy

EXAMPLE 63

The parallel rules used in Example 64 (and several papers use date lines such as this) do not go well with a face like Bodoni Bold, and the rules are too "deep" for date-line use with any face. There is too much space between the lines of each rule. The general result is unattractive.

These Parallel Rules Are Too "Deep"

EXAMPLE 64

Many papers, some of them metropolitan dailies, use oxford rules as they appear in Example 65. The rules are appropriate, and the leading between the rules and the type line is about right. But the fact that the lower oxford has been placed with its light stroke down keeps the whole from appearing as finished as it would be were the light stroke up.

The Lower Rule Should Be Inverted

EXAMPLE 65

In Example 66 the amount of leading between the rules and the type line is about right—4 points of space, including any shoulder on the type-line slug. (Of course, the parallel rules are not so appropriate for use with Bodoni Bold as they would be with light monotone faces.)

Four Points Above and Below About Right

EXAMPLE 66

Example 67 shows a date line as it might well be treated when 12-point Bodoni Bold is used. Four points of leading have been used above, and 4 more below the type line, including any shoulder. As the lower rule appears with the thin stroke up, or inside, the type line is attractively framed by the rules.

Four Points Above and Below About Right

EXAMPLE 67

The single rules used in Example 68 are too heavy. They attract attention to themselves and away from the type lines they are supposed merely to complement.

These Single Rules Are Too Heavy

EXAMPLE 68

But the plain rules used in Example 69 form an attractive frame for the line.

Four Points Above and Below About Right

EXAMPLE 69

The same type face used for the main line of the date line might well be used for running heads also, as well as the same kind of rule, for running heads have the same relation to inside pages as date lines do to front pages.

When an oxford rule is used with a running head, the rule should be placed with its light stroke down.

During World War II, when newsprint saving became a necessity in many newspaper plants, many a newspaper gave up using a pair of rules immediately below its nameplate in favor of only one rule, as suggested as far back as 1930 by the *Linotype News*. (See, among other illustrations, Examples 185 and 48.)

Some papers that "tightened up" their rule treatments inserted their date-line and related matter between one rule and the nameplate. Other papers presented the date-line and related matter in the form of a front-page ear—usually the right ear.

Along with the "tightening up" of date-line rules on front pages came a "tightening up" by many newspapers of running heads, on other pages.

Some papers reduced the width of running heads to four columns and started the other columns high on the page. Other papers reduced running-head widths to three, two or even single columns. Still other papers started using various widths of running heads in the same issue, depending on the amount and width of advertising carried. Some newspapers started using full-width running heads on some pages in some sections, and various widths on other pages in other sections.

Many newspapers, in "tightening up" their pages, gave up the use of nameplates on the front pages of second and following sections, and some papers reduced their subordinate nameplates to running heads of the sort suggested by Example 70.

Many years before World War II, some newspapers started presenting their running heads vertically in the outer margins of pages. Some of those papers employed specially punched matrices on their composing machines so that the resultant lines could be read straight down from the top to the bottom. Other papers set and cast the lines in the usual way and presented them to be read sidewise from the bottom to the top of the line.

In the spring of 1939, as a newsprint-conservation measure, the *New York Daily News* started presenting its running heads in the outer margins of pages. The shifting of those lines from the tops to the sides of pages, with, of course, the necessary press and stereotype-machinery readjustments, made it possible for the *News* to run from 61-inch, rather than 62-inch, rolls of newsprint, just as many lines to the page as formerly at a saving of several thousand tons of newsprint, and many thousands of dollars, annually. (However, the *News* continues to present running heads in the usual way on some of its pages —across the tops of those pages.)

Washington Post Sports

**** *Sunday, January 6, 1946* **2R**

Bee Bee, Mandell to Open D. C. Sock Market Tomorrow

By Tony Neri
Post Staff Writer

Methodical Bee Bee Washington, the pride of Foggy Bottom and top drawing card in Turner's Arena last year, returns to the W st. emporium tomorrow night to face Jimmy Mandell, an Italian scrapper

EXAMPLE 70

Some newspapers present the running heads on some of their pages as "running feet," at the bottoms of pages, and in various widths.

10

Dashes, Cutoffs and Column Rules

MANY NEWSPAPER MAKEUP MEN make the mistake of putting the same amount of leading above "30" dashes (the dashes at the ends of stories) as below them. Some makeup men actually put more leading above than below.

As "30" dashes are supposed to *end* stories, not merely to separate them, and surely *not to form parts of following heads*, it is advisable to put more leading below than above them.

And if body lines of stories are set on slugs of larger point sizes (if the lines themselves are cast leaded), that leading on the slugs themselves should be allowed for when extra leading is placed above "30" dashes. More leading should be used above "30" dashes when body lines are cast solid than when cast leaded. But in either case more leading should be used below the dashes than above.

Where the final line of a story is short—where the printed characters fill less than one-half of the line—it is advisable to omit any extra leading above the "30" dash, as the comparatively long blank portion of the final line gives the effect of leading. But extra leading should be placed below the dash, unless the dash, instead of being centered vertically on its slug, has been cast above center to secure extra following leading automatically.

Theoretically, when type characters in the final line of a story fill less than one-fourth of the line, the slug presenting that line should be cut so that the "30" dash may be placed closer to the next-to-last line of the story than would be possible without cutting, for, in such cases, it is the next-to-last line, rather than the unusually short final line (commonly referred to as a "widow"), that should dictate the amount of leading needed.

Practically, however, that plan would not always work out well in the busy newspaper plant. Many newspaper pages have to be made up at high speed to meet exacting schedules, and not always do the makeup men have the time, even when they think about it and ordinarily would prefer to do it, to attend to such details as cutting slugs above "30" dashes.

But they usually do have time, when making up feature columns and departments, which often may be put together more leisurely than can straight-news matter, to treat "30" dashes, as well as any ornaments used between items, in such a way when the dashes or ornaments follow "widows."

Various kinds of "30" dashes, both ornamental and plain, are available for various forms of printing. In newspaper news and editorial columns, plain "30" dashes usually are more appropriate, and more effective, than ornamental dashes. And white space often can be more effective than dashes of any kind.

Of course, when "30" dashes are used, they should not be so heavy or so fancy that they attract undue attention to themselves, or so light that they fail to hold their own with the other units of composition. They should harmonize in design and weight with the other typographic elements.

"Thirty" dashes used in 12-, 12½- or 13-pica columns should not be much more than 8 picas wide nor much less than 7 picas. If they are much wider than 8 picas, they suggest cutoff rules (rules that reach clear across the column and one purpose of which often is to divert attention to the column to the right).

"Thirty" dashes used in columns wider than 13 picas but less than two regular columns in width should be about the same width, proportionately, as those used in regular columns—about two-thirds of the column width. But "30" dashes used in columns wider than two regular columns should be somewhat less than two-thirds of the wider column, to keep the dashes from being too conspicuous.

Some papers continue to use, or recently have gone in for, ornamental "30" dashes. Many such papers squeeze those dashes between the ends of stories and following heads, with little or no relieving white space between the units. In some instances the dashes are closer to the following heads than to the stories they are supposed to end.

Note, in Example 71, the crowded appearance of the various units, and that the "30" dash competes with the following head and keeps it from standing out clearly on its own.

A plain "30" dash with white space immediately below it would be better, as suggested by Example 72.

evening, and that all other plans would be held in abeyance until the main plan was working properly.

Doe, Jones and Smith Get Eight-Year Plaques

At a meeting at the local high school last night, John Doe, Richard Jones and James Smith, all resi-

EXAMPLE 71

evening, and that all other plans would be held in abeyance until the main plan was working properly.

Doe, Jones and Smith Get Eight-Year Plaques

At a meeting at the local high school last night, John Doe, Richard Jones and James Smith, all resi-

EXAMPLE 72

But a pica of white space, with no dash, would be better still, as suggested by Example 73.

evening, and that all other plans would be held in abeyance until the main plan was working properly.

Doe, Jones and Smith Get Eight-Year Plaques

At a meeting at the local high school last night, John Doe, Richard Jones and James Smith, all resi-

EXAMPLE 73

Newspapers that employ heads no smaller than 12 point, say, might well do away with the use of "30" dashes and employ white space instead. But when heads smaller than 12 point are employed, "30" dashes or cutoff rules seem necessary. Small heads without dashes or cutoffs immediately above them might confuse the reader. He might think that the heads were subheads of preceding stories, rather than heads over other stories.

For many years many newspapers have employed jim dashes (dashes narrower than "30" dashes) between and immediately below the decks of multiple-deck heads, and immediately below single-deck heads.

Jim dashes so used seldom performed any useful service, but many newspapers have kept on using them as a matter of habit. Jim dashes used with heads not only are superfluous; they actually compete with the type faces they are supposed merely to complement.

It is much better to use white space than jim dashes in the news and editorial columns of today's newspapers. In fact, any "modernly designed" newspaper that continues to clutter up its heads with jim dashes has not been modernly designed.

However, jim dashes—comparatively narrow dashes—are not inappropriate in modern newspapers when used as "separators" of unheaded paragraphs in departments, or immediately above such things as editorial notes or footnotes at the ends of departments.

Cutoff Rules

Cutoff rules (the rules used clear across columns to separate advertisements, or advertisements from story matter above them; or to even off the bottoms of stories presented in two or more adjoining columns and followed by other stories; or used between heads of stories and accompanying cuts; or used over, and sometimes under, jump heads; or used to divert attention from one column to an adjoining column to the right) should harmonize with the head dress employed.

Cutoffs may be oxford rules if oxford rules harmonize with the head dress and oxfords are used with the date line on the front page and with running heads on inside pages. Or they may well be parallel rules if such rules get along well with the head dress and parallels are used with date lines and running heads.

But cutoffs in the form of single light rules can fit in well with any kind of head dress, date-line or running-head rules, and the single light rules are more appropriate for the news and editorial columns of modern newspapers than any other kinds of cutoffs.

Several years ago wavy rules were used as cutoffs by many newspapers, but today comparatively few papers use wavy rules for such a purpose. Wavy rules, which are livelier than oxford, parallel or single rules of corresponding weight, usually have too much movement to be used appropriately for cutoffs, which are not supposed to speed things up, but to slow them down—to divert or interrupt attention.

However, some newspapers of today do use wavy rules on classified-advertising pages, with the thought that the liveliness of such rules helps to liven up what often are the dullest looking columns in a paper.

Many papers still follow the custom of placing cutoffs between display advertisements and between stories and advertisements even when the advertisements have enclosing rules or full-width top and bottom rules of their own, and even when advertisers are not charged for the space from cutoff to cutoff. But many other papers have abandoned the practice, and properly so, it seems to this writer, as unnecessarily space consuming and making for unattractive congestions of rules.

The oxford cutoff rule employed in Example 74 does not harmonize with the head face it accompanies, and the rule is too conspicuous.

Seventy-seven Lively Kangaroos Leap From Home to Breakfast

EXAMPLE 74

Nor does the parallel cutoff rule used in Example 75 get along well with that sans-serif face, and the rule attracts too much attention to itself.

Seventy-seven Lively Kangaroos Leap From Home to Breakfast

EXAMPLE 75

The plain cutoff rule employed in Example 76 is too heavy. It serves to distract attention from the head to the rule itself. Rules of that weight often can be used to advantage with department heads, but they are too conspicuous for use as cutoffs over news and feature heads, particularly down in the body of a page.

The single hairline rule used in Example 77 does its work quietly

Seventy-seven Lively Kangaroos Leap From Home to Breakfast

EXAMPLE 76

but effectively. It cuts off the head from the matter above, yet does not intrude on the consciousness of the reader.

Seventy-seven Lively Kangaroos Leap From Home to Breakfast

EXAMPLE 77

Note that plenty of white space—6 additional points—has been used between the cutoff-rule slug and the first head slug. That inconspicuous rule and the additional white space give the head a chance to stand out attractively on its own.

When column rules drop from the ends of cutoff rules, the cutoffs and the column rules should be joined with some sort of ornament, rather than be left unjoined, as a joining ornament contributes to a more finished appearance. One of the most acceptable ornaments for such use is a simple diamond-shaped ornament—an outlined diamond for medium- or light-weight head dresses, and a black diamond for heavier head dresses.

As column rules ordinarily cannot be joined properly to parallel or oxford cutoff rules by means of ornaments, single cutoffs should be used when any such joining needs to be done. And this is a good argument in favor of the use of single rules for cutoffs, instead of parallels or oxfords, as it is inconsistent to use parallel or oxford cutoffs at various points on a page or pages and plain cutoffs at other points on the same page or pages.

Usually single-rule cutoffs should be light-weight rules—1-point or even hairline rules. But when single-rule cutoffs are used immediately below unusually heavy banner lines, those cutoffs should be heavier than 1-point rules. In such cases 2-point and sometimes even 3-point rules are more appropriate.

Many of our daily newspapers use hairline rules on 1-point bodies —steel rules—as space savers on their classified-advertising pages.

Column Rules

The sort of column rules still most commonly used by newspapers in North America are hairline rules centered on 6-point bodies.

During World War II, as stated in Chapter 3 of Part I, some of our daily newspapers (and some dailies even before World War II) started setting their news stories in column widths a few points or even 6 points less than 12 picas, to conserve newsprint, while retaining the conventional 6-point column rules. Other dailies started indenting news stories 3 points or so at the beginning and end of each slug line, to compensate for decreased shoulders on space-saving 4-, 3-, 2- and even 1-point column rules. (Most of the 2- and 1-point column rules were steel rules, as softer rules on such long-and-thin bodies would not stand up well and would tend to "wave" in the forms.)

December 23, 1941, little more than a fortnight after the attack on Pearl Harbor, the American Newspaper Publishers' Association discussed 4- and 3-point column rules in its *Mechanical Bulletin No. 266.*

assess and evaluate a	pleasant to their
of its esthetic	is always practical
the pace-makers	what they see in
printing rave over a	is, partly, its excel
type? What do they	ness to perform
is it so superlatively	"heft" and balance

assess and evaluate a	pleasant to their eyes?
terms of its esthetic	is always practical
the pace-makers	what they see in a
printing rave over a	is, partly, its excellent
type? What do they	ness to perform its
is it so superlatively	"heft" and balance

assess and evaluate a	pleasant to their eyes?
terms of its esthetic	is always practical
the pace-makers	what they see in a
printing rave over a	is, partly, its excellent
type? What do they	ness to perform its
is it so superlatively	"heft" and balance

EXAMPLE 78

Of 500 A.N.P.A. member-newspapers then reporting, 212 newspapers, or 42.4%, were using 4-point column rules, and twenty newspapers, or 4.0%, were using 3-point column rules.

After 1941 many other newspapers adopted 4-, 3-, 2- or 1-point column rules, but many of the papers that gave up 6-point rules in favor of rules on narrower bodies did so merely as a temporary thing. They hoped to return to the 6-point standard as soon as newsprint restrictions were lifted, and some of the papers already have done so.

In fact, some of our newspapers continued to use, right through the war days, hairline rules on 8- and even 9-point bodies, for their general-news columns.

And there is no doubt that wider shouldered column rules (or generous strips of white space between columns) help to make the columns more attractive and easier to read.

The top fragment in Example 78 shows the use of a hairline rule on a 6-point body between columns; the second fragment, a hairline rule on a 4-point body, and the third fragment, a hairline on a 3-point body.

Of course, column rules should be presented without breaks, or gaps of white space, when pieced together. Breaks mar the appearance of the rules (and of the page as a whole) and suggest carelessness.

Several newspapers employ comparatively wide shoulders of white space beside column rules on some of their pages, notably editorial pages, as such treatments can help considerably to set off such pages from other pages in the same papers—to give them an individualized and opened-up appearance.

In recent years several papers have replaced column rules with white space, with the thought that that treatment is new and modern.

Of course there is nothing new about it, as many of our papers published more than two and a half centuries ago appeared without column rules on any of their pages.

Such treatments—"bookish" treatments—often work out well on feature and editorial pages, but not always so well on news pages that include display advertising, unless column rules are employed to separate the advertisements from each other and advertisements from the news columns.

Confusion often is caused by the lack of column rules between advertisements placed side by side, particularly between advertisements without enclosing rules or borders of their own, as display lines in some such advertisements often "run into" and, at first glance, seem to form parts of display lines in neighboring advertisements.

Confusion also frequently results, even on feature and editorial pages, when the intervals of white space between columns are too narrow, as heads in adjoining columns often "run into" each other, and, sometimes, even the body lines.

When column rules are lifted in favor of white space, it seems to this writer that the intervals of white between columns should be no narrower than 10 points.

After all, the reader should be considered. If a certain treatment is not an advantage to the reader, then it is unwise to adopt it merely to secure an "arty" effect.

Some early day papers used parallel rules for column rules, and some even used ornamental rules to separate columns.

Formerly it was customary for papers, when their owners or chief editors died, to "turn" the column rules on their editorial or even front pages for one issue or even several issues—to print from the heavier bottom edges of the rules, rather than from the hairlined upper surfaces—as marks of respect for the departed. And sometimes, in such cases, it was customary to surround the pages with the same sort of "turned" rules. (See Example 3.)

Often, in the past, "mourning rules" have been used on front and other pages chronicling the death of some public figure.

And some newspapers of today occasionally "turn" column rules.

Before leaving the subject of column rules *versus* white space, let us consider this statement recently made to this writer by the publisher of a small weekly paper:

"I've started using white space instead of column rules, because my plant's not properly equipped to have nice fresh rules for each issue. And I believe that no column rules are better than smashed and badly aligned rules."

This writer felt obliged to admit that that publisher "had something there." Surely, worn or battered or improperly joined column rules can disfigure a newspaper.

Another argument in favor of strips of white space instead of column rules was presented by executives of the *Spartanburg* (S. C.) *Herald*, the *Spartanburg Journal* and the *Sunday Herald-Journal*, in a story in *Editor & Publisher* for September 8, 1945, about two months after those Spartanburg papers had given up most of their column rules in favor of white space.

In that story William A. Townes, publisher of the papers, stated that the plan was adopted because he believed that "it would make the papers more attractive and more readable."

And Publisher Townes continued, in part, as follows:

"The style has not been uncommon for some time on editorial

pages and we saw no reason not to extend it throughout the papers, except around advertisements.

"It makes the paper open-appearing much the same as a display ad with white space; it makes heads, art and body type stand out."

In the same story, Clarence E. Webber, mechanical superintendent of the Spartanburg papers, stated that the elimination of column rules would make for a saving of at least four hundred dollars a year on press rollers and a big saving on press blankets.

"We are no longer bothered with column rules not showing up or punching through the mat when rolled," Mr. Webber asserted. "This makes it easy for the stereotypers to get better casts and prints.

"Indentions are made by a special device attached to the Linotype machines, holding in the line 3 points on each side, thus giving us 10 points of white space between the columns.

"The device, an inch-long sleeve, is attached to the jaw of the Linotype machine for indentions and is removable for setting type full measure.

"Veteran operators readily adapted themselves to the new style and the same speed is maintained in mechanical operations as before the new style was adopted."

11

Boxes and Box Effects

THE CHIEF EXECUTIVE of a large chain of metropolitan dailies is said to have expressed the belief that a brief story in a box, or set off with extra shoulders of white space, at the top of the front page has ten times as much chance of getting read by the average reader as does the leading news story on the page, even though that story be played up with a multiple-deck head in large type faces.

Perhaps the very brevity of the boxed or extra-shouldered short story is what attracts attention and gets it read. Perhaps its "different" treatment, its "exclusiveness," the fact that it is set apart from other stories by enclosing rules or extra shoulders of space, has something to do with its popularity. Perhaps years of newspaper scanning has convinced the average reader that papers are accustomed to serving up in boxes or box effects their choicest bits of "human interest" and unusual bits of news.

Boxes the type lines of which are too wide, too near the enclosing rules, and not sufficiently leaded, are not as attractive as they could be, nor as easy to read.

The shape is important. Square or nearly square boxes are unattractive. They look squatty. Oblongs are better. The ancient Greek artists gave us an excellent model in their "golden oblong." The enclosing rules should harmonize in weight with the head and body matter they enclose.

Leading is important. The head should be sufficiently set off from the body, and both the head and body from the enclosing rules, to avoid the appearance of being crowded. The lines in the body usually should be leaded at least 2 points. A box should be opened up enough to give it a "chance to breathe."

Example 79 shows a box with many faults.

The bold-face type used for body matter is not bad in itself. It is an acceptable face for certain uses. But it was not designed to be used in general-news columns unrelieved by leading. Properly leaded and

THIS BOX IS NOT GOOD

It is not attractive. It doesn't invite attention. It is hard to read. It is not the right shape. It should be deeper. Square or nearly square boxes look squatty. The type lines are too wide, too close to the rules. And the lines are too close to each other. The face is too small and too black to be used in masses such as this. The rules are too heavy. They have been butted, instead of mitered, and the corners are carelessly "joined." The head is too small, and is too close to the body matter. As the type face in the head is the same as that in the body, there is not enough contrast between the two elements.

EXAMPLE 79

* * * * * * * * * * * * * * *

* **INTERNATIONAL** *
* **NEWS SERVICE** *
* **FOR BLANKVILLE** *

* Beginning today The Blank * carries a telegraph service sup- * plied by the International News * Service. "INS" is a well-known * "credit line" on news matter ap- * pearing in daily papers. It is with * the desire to supply our readers * with news that is up to the minute * that we have added this feature to * The Blank. A bulletin giving daily * reports from our wire service is * to be established in a few days. *

* * * * * * * * * * * * * * *

EXAMPLE 80

used with a head of appropriate size and design, and within enclosing rules of a weight to harmonize with the head and body, it could form an effective box. As it is here, the head is too small and too close to the body. The type lines are too wide, and the rules are too black. Body lines are not leaded, and the rules have been carelessly "joined" at the corners.

Rules should not be put together in hit-or-miss fashion. Carelessness in this detail will spoil the whole. They should be joined exactly. This can be done at the corners by mitering—by cutting the rules at an angle of forty-five degrees where they are to meet at the corners—and care in makeup and lockup.

Unattractive boxes also result from the use of inappropriate border units as enclosing elements. Example 80 shows how the misuse of asterisks, for one thing, makes for an unattractive box.

The asterisks in this case are considerably lighter than the boldface capitals used for the head, with all three of the staggered lines too short to present an attractive stagger. The body lines are too full, too close to the asterisks on either side; and not enough leading has been used below the asterisks at the top or above the ones at the bottom.

The box shown in Example 81 is much better than those in Examples 79 and 80. The head, in 14-point Bodoni Bold Italic, is attractive. Crowding has been avoided. Sufficient shoulders of white space have been employed, and the body lines are leaded 2 points. All three elements—head, body and enclosing rules—get along well together. The rules have been mitered, and care has been exercised in makeup and lockup. The box is attractive and easy to read.

This Box Is Better

It is attractive. It does invite attention. It is easy to read. It is pleasing in shape, after the golden oblong of the Greeks. The type lines, of a pleasing point size and color, have been set ten and one-half picas wide, allowing eighteen points of space for the rules and a sufficient shoulder of white space between the rules and the body. The lines have been leaded two points. The rules harmonize with the type lines in weight. They have been mitered, and the corners carefully joined. The head, in 14-point Bodoni Bold Italic, is sufficiently set off from the body to stand out prominently. The head, the body matter and the rules go well together—harmonize.

EXAMPLE 81

BITING!

Just to prove that the present fishing season is a good one in these parts, John Doe of this city exhibits a couple of largemouth black bass he caught last week in a local lake. The larger weighed an even six pounds and the smaller four and a quarter.

EXAMPLE 82

Oxford rules can be used to advantage for boxes when the head faces employed have decidedly contrasting thick and thin strokes.

Example 82 shows a single-column box making use of oxford rules, which get along well with the Poster Bodoni head employed, and a picture that tones in well with the head, the rules and the body matter, in Bold Face No. 2.

Notice that the body matter has been well leaded, and that the generous shoulders of white between the contents of the box and the enclosing rules cause the contents to stand out attractively.

Light parallel rules can be employed advantageously for boxes when fairly light monotone or nearly monotone faces are used for heads, and the body-matter faces are not heavy, as suggested by Example 83, with the head in Cheltenham.

Crosstown Routes Get New Coaches

Twenty-one new transit type coaches, seating thirty-one passengers each, will be placed in service in the next few days on the crosstown routes of the Fifth Avenue Coach Company, it was announced Tuesday. The coaches are streamlined and the engines are mounted in the rear.

The routes the coaches will serve extend on Fifty-seventh Street from Sutton Place to Eighth Avenue and on Seventy-second Street from York Avenue to Central Park West, via Fifth Avenue, Fifty-seventh Street and Broadway.

EXAMPLE 83

Our Crosstown Routes Get 21 New Coaches

Twenty-one new transit type coaches, seating thirty-one passengers each, will be placed in service in the next few days on the crosstown routes of the Fifth Avenue Coach Company, it was announced Tuesday. The coaches are streamlined and the engines are mounted in the rear.

The routes the coaches will serve extend on Fifty-seventh Street from Sutton Place to Eighth Avenue and on Seventy-second Street from York Avenue to Central Park West, via Fifth Avenue, Fifty-seventh Street and Broadway.

EXAMPLE 84

And single rules with round corners can help to form attractive boxes, as suggested by Example 84, with the head in Cloister Italic.

Various ornamental rules also can be used to advantage at times for boxed stories in newspapers, but, as it usually is better for newspapers to employ simpler rules for such boxes, it seems inadvisable here to consider the many possibilities (and hazards) of ornamental rules for news or feature boxes.

In fact, more and more newspapers, particularly modernly designed papers that have discovered or rediscovered the high merit of simplicity in makeup, are doing away with the complete boxing of brief news stories in favor of the simpler box effect.

The box effect is easily brought about by setting the head and body lines of the brief story about 18 points narrower than the regular column width, with no rules on the sides (other than regular column rules), but with head and tail rules or borders that tone in well with the type faces used for heads. Many modern papers go a step farther

Crosstown Routes Get New Coaches

Twenty-one new transit type coaches, seating thirty-one passengers each, will be placed in service in the next few days on the crosstown routes of the Fifth Avenue Coach Company, it was announced Tuesday. The coaches are streamlined and the engines are mounted in the rear.

The routes the coaches will serve extend on Fifty-seventh Street from Sutton Place to Eighth Avenue and on Seventy-second Street from York Avenue to Central Park West, via Fifth Avenue, Fifty-seventh Street and Broadway.

EXAMPLE 85

Crosstown Routes Get New Coaches

Twenty-one new transit type coaches, seating thirty-one passengers each, will be placed in service in the next few days on the crosstown routes of the Fifth Avenue Coach Company, it was announced Tuesday. The coaches are streamlined and the engines are mounted in the rear.

The routes the coaches will serve extend on Fifty-seventh Street from Sutton Place to Eighth Avenue and on Seventy-second Street from York Avenue to Central Park West, via Fifth Avenue, Fifty-seventh Street and Broadway.

EXAMPLE 86

Crosstown Routes Get New Coaches

Twenty-one new transit type coaches, seating thirty-one passengers each, will be placed in service in the next few days on the crosstown routes of the Fifth Avenue Coach Company, it was announced Tuesday. The coaches are streamlined and the engines are mounted in the rear.

The routes the coaches will serve extend on Fifty-seventh Street from Sutton Place to Eighth Avenue and on Seventy-second Street from York Avenue to Central Park West, via Fifth Avenue, Fifty-seventh Street and Broadway.

EXAMPLE 87

Crosstown Routes Get New Coaches

Twenty-one new transit type coaches, seating thirty-one passengers each, will be placed in service in the next few days on the crosstown routes of the Fifth Avenue Coach Company, it was announced Tuesday. The coaches are streamlined and the engines are mounted in the rear.

The routes the coaches will serve extend on Fifty-seventh Street from Sutton Place to Eighth Avenue and on Seventy-second Street from York Avenue to Central Park West, via Fifth Avenue, Fifty-seventh Street and Broadway.

EXAMPLE 88

and, in place of any special head and tail rules, simply employ regular hairline cutoff rules.

An important point is that all of the lines of box effects—the heads as well as the body lines—should be generously indented and leaded. Many an otherwise-attractive box effect has been marred by the use of heads set wider than the body lines they accompany.

Another important point, from the standpoint of production in the composing room, is that box effects can be made up much more easily and quickly than completely boxed items. The box effect, having no corners to be mitered, fitted and carefully locked up, can be put through with the speed of regular news stories.

Example 85 shows a box effect with wavy rules heavy enough to harmonize with the Metroblack No. 2 used for the head, set flush at the left.

Example 86 shows an unusual box effect secured by the use of head and tail pieces consisting of braces the thick and thin strokes of which get along well with the Caslon No. 3 Italic head.

An attractive box effect can be secured by the use of tapered dashes at the top and bottom, with body and headlines held in, and no side rules (other than regular column rules), as in Example 87, with the head in Century Bold.

Another box effect, and one of the simplest to secure, is one like that shown in Example 88.

No side rules (other than regular column rules) were used, and no top and bottom rules (other than regular cutoff rules). The box effect was secured by merely setting the type lines of both head and body matter 18 points narrower than the regular column width. The head, it will be noted, is in two flush lines of Memphis Medium.

Boxed stories or box effects seem much more "at home" when placed toward the top of a newspaper page, or when hanging from a row or group of heads in the body of the page, or when placed at the bottom of the page, than when "floating" in the body of a page. They seem to need something substantial to hang from or rest on.

But sometimes when a brief boxed story is closely tied up as to subject matter with a more important top-of-page story and there is no space available for the box at the top of an adjoining column, it seems advisable to insert the box between the first few lines of body matter of the main story—the same sort of plan followed for the reference lines in Example 109.

12

Feature Heads

THE USE of both heavy and light type faces in the same multiple-deck news heads usually should be avoided.

News heads of that sort ordinarily should be avoided because a news page has a way of calling for several or many news heads, and more than a few heavy-and-light heads on a page would give it an unattractive spotty appearance.

But this does not mean that heavy and light faces cannot be used to advantage in department and feature heads. Sometimes they can. For usually no more than a few such heads appear on a page or even, in many instances, in a whole edition. Thus heavy-and-light department or feature heads are hardly likely to give a page or an edition a cluttered-up appearance—cluttered up with many disturbing heavy-and-lights.

Several years ago this writer received from the editor of a southern daily a letter that started with the question, "How about getting out your catalogs and making suggestions for a headletter type that we have fairly clearly in mind but can't find?"

That editor went on to explain that he was looking for a feature head that would get along well with his general-news heads but that readers would readily recognize as a head over an interesting feature and not as the preamble to a straight-news story.

"What we want, in addition to variety," that editor explained, "is a type that will say to the reader, 'Now here, old fellow, is a story that isn't necessarily important, but stands a chance of being interesting or funny or at least something to read out loud to your wife.' "

As that paper's general-news head dress was in Bodoni Bold and Bodoni Bold Italic, and as Poster Bodoni was employed on its editorial page, it occurred to this writer that his friend could work out some appropriate feature heads simply by mixing a small amount of Poster Bodoni with a larger amount of Bodoni Bold Italic. So this writer had some heads set for him—heads like the one shown in Example 89—and sent along some proofs.

Air Hero

Tells Newspaper Scribes How He Bagged 6 Planes

EXAMPLE 89

The idea, this writer suggested, was to start each head with a "kicker" line that emphasized a single key word or phrase that would stand out on its own but also would flow into the more informative lines to follow.

(In some newspaper offices the "kicker" lines are referred to as "teasers" or "come-ons.")

"After a few days of using such heads over feature stories," this writer wrote that southern editor—"when readers have become used to the idea—it should be easy for readers quickly to associate such heads with features, rather than straight-news stories. In other words, these 'different' heads will stand out for what they are."

That editor liked the idea, promptly applied it to his paper, and later wrote that he found the new heads a "useful distinction."

Of course, various other combinations of faces can be used to advantage for the same kind of feature heads for use with other general-news head dresses. Among these combinations are Spartan Black with Spartan Medium Italic, as demonstrated by Example 90, and Memphis Extra Bold with Memphis Medium Italic, as demonstrated by Example 91.

Dove of Peace

Flies Into Tents of Soldiers And Sets Many Fists Flying

EXAMPLE 90

Black Bass

Now Biting Heads Off At Head of Head Lake

EXAMPLE 91

Naturally, an over-generous use of feature heads of this sort would give a page an unattractive spotty appearance. Used sparingly, however, they can be quite effective.

Two-tone feature heads of another sort are shown in Examples 92 and 93.

Opportunity *Knocks Thrice, At Front, Side and Back Doors*

EXAMPLE 92

Sweet Spring **Frolics North, But Scampers South Again**

EXAMPLE 93

Note that, in Example 92, the first word is in a heavy sans serif and the other words in a light sans-serif italic (24-point Metroblack No. 2 and 24-point Metrolite No. 2 Italic), and that, in Example 93, the first two words are in a light sans-serif italic and the others in a heavy sans serif (24-point Metrolite No. 2 Italic and 24-point Metroblack No. 2).

Although there is marked contrast between the light and dark elements in both heads, it is harmonious contrast, as both of the faces employed are members of the same type family.

Other combinations of the same two faces that could be applied effectively in two-tone heads are Metroblack No. 2 in the same head with Metrolite No. 2, and *vice versa*, and Metroblack No. 2 Italic in the same head with Metrolite No. 2 Italic, and *vice versa*.

Example 94 suggests how one newspaper handles certain two-tone feature heads: One line of 24-point Metroblack No. 2 followed by two lines of 18-point Bodoni Book Italic.

Degrees for Fourteen Pupils

—three local girls and eleven boys
to be graduated from Design School

EXAMPLE 94

The head is not so effective as it could have been, because the Metro and Bodoni families are in different typographic categories and do not mix well with each other.

The head shown in Example 95, again with the first line in 24-point Metroblack No. 2, but the second and third lines in 18-point Metrolite No. 2 Italic, is more effective, because both decks of that head have been set in members of the same family.

Degrees for Fourteen Pupils

—three local girls and eleven boys
to be graduated from Design School

EXAMPLE 95

A variation of the theme, with even more contrast between the two decks, is carried out in the head in Example 96—in 24-point Metroblack No. 2 and 18-point Memphis Light.

Degrees for Fourteen Pupils

—three local girls and eleven boys
to be graduated from Design School

EXAMPLE 96

While the Metro family (a sans-serif) and the Memphis (a square-serif) are in different typographic categories, the two families are more closely related to each other and get along better when used together than either would with a family like Bodoni (a modern) or one such as Caslon (an old-style).

In Example 96, the sans and square serifs do not clash with each other. In fact, they get along fairly well together.

But, to repeat, heavy and light type faces should not be used together for general-news heads, as the employment of more than a few heavy-and-lights on a page would give the page a cluttered-up and unattractive appearance.

13

Jump Heads

MANY PAPERS have cut down on jumped stories—stories continued from one page to another, but particularly from the front page. The editors of such papers feel that readers do not like jumps, and they undoubtedly are right.

Some editors have done away entirely with jumps, while others, as previously stated, have cut down on the number of them. These latter editors try to limit the jumps to continuations on page two of long main stories opened in the right-hand column on the front page, or else jump front-page stories to final pages (final pages of the same sections, of course, when an issue consists of more than one section), so that readers can continue reading without opening up the paper.

There are several ways of treating jump heads in newspapers—heads appearing over parts of stories continued from other pages in the same issues.

Some papers follow the plan of repeating the entire head, even in the case of the multiple-deck head, when stories are jumped. Some do the repeating in the same faces and sizes used in the original head; some repeat all of the lines, but in smaller type faces.

Such treatments, of course, call for two settings of a head, or a recasting of the original head.

In many newspaper plants where such treatments of jump heads are followed, two heads are cast for every long or fairly long news story, to facilitate the makeup if it becomes necessary or advisable to jump the story. The makeup men have the second heads right there before them on the imposing stones and do not have to wait for jump heads to be set to order.

Other newspapers follow the practice of using jump heads with the same number of decks as appear in the original settings, and in the same type faces and sizes (or only slightly smaller), but with the lines reworded to "sell" the stories over again to the readers when they get to the continuations, or with features played up in the jump heads that were not referred to in the original heads and were not mentioned in the body lines that preceded the jumps.

Some papers follow the practice of repeating by-lines under jump heads when by-lines are used under original heads.

Other papers, when continuing stories by unusually prominent writers, use jump heads consisting only of the writers' names, in large display, followed by small "continued from" lines.

Because a front-page story has a two-column head is no good reason why its jump head should be two columns wide. The jump might well be a full eight-column head if the story seems important enough, long enough, or illustrated enough, to call for such treatment. On the other hand, the jump of a two-column or wider head might well be a single-column head if the runover is not long enough to warrant the use of a wider jump, or if the makeup of the page on which the jump is to appear will be facilitated by the employment of the narrower head.

Some papers, in jumping stories, and with space and time saving in mind, repeat only one line from the first deck of the original head.

Other papers, also to save space, confine to a single display line the supposedly most important and most readily identifying words from the original head. For instance, a multiple-deck head, say, over a front-page story discussing the murder of a Mr. High might call for a jump head like that shown in Example 97.

High Murder Story

(Continued from front page)

EXAMPLE 97

—SUICIDE

(Continued From Page One)

EXAMPLE 98

And a multiple-deck front-page head in another paper might call for a jump head like that shown in Example 98.

Some newspapers use jump heads presented between pairs of parallel rules, with each jump consisting of a single key-word set flush at the left and followed by a dash, above a "continued from" line in italic—the key-word being a repetition of a "summing-up word" centered in bold face at the end of the first section of the story and above a "continued on" line in italic.

To illustrate, a front-page story under a two-column two-line head reading "Vaudeville Actress Turns to Selling Oil From Truck" would present the single word "Actress" centered, say, in a 7-point bold face at the end of the first section of the story and above a line in a 7-point italic reading "*Continued on Page Ten.*"

And the jump head on page ten would appear as in Example 99.

Actress—

Continued from the First Page

EXAMPLE 99

Still other papers, both to save space and to do away with the resetting or recasting of original heads, employ differently numbered heads for jumps. These jump heads, either in slugs or as electrotypes, and numbered, respectively, from 1 to 10 or higher, depending on the maximum number of jump heads used by a paper, are kept standing from issue to issue and within easy reach of the makeup men.

Another argument advanced by some for the use of jump heads of this kind is that the marked difference (but it can be a *harmonious* difference) in appearance between such jump heads and the regular news heads on the same page makes it easier for the reader to recognize continuations.

As an example of this form of jump head, let us suppose that a front-page news story is continued on page two. At the bottom of the front-page section of that story appears a line in italic reading "(*See page two, No.* 3)." And on page two, at the beginning of the continuation of the story, appears a jump head like that shown in Example 100.

Number 3

(Continued from front page)

EXAMPLE 100

1 CONTINUED FROM FIRST PAGE

EXAMPLE 101

Some newspapers use jump heads similar to the one suggested by Example 101, with, at the end of the front-page section of the jumped story, a line in bold face reading, say, "(Turn to Page 2, Number 1)."

Other papers use jump heads like those shown in Examples 102, 103, 104 and 105.

HERE'S MORE ABOUT
THREE LINE LOCAL
Continued from Page 1

EXAMPLE 102

HERE'S MORE ABOUT
BRAZOS HOTEL
STARTS ON PAGE ONE

EXAMPLE 103

Concluded From Page One

Use Of Injunction Scored In State Labor Disputes

EXAMPLE 104

PRESIDENT ACTS ON COAL STRIKE

CONTINUED FROM PAGE ONE

EXAMPLE 105

Jumps like those shown in Examples 102 and 103 often are used in the form of electrotypes mortised to receive new center lines for each new head. In other words, the borders or rules and top and bottom lines are kept standing as electrotypes, and the only changes in such heads from issue to issue and head to head are changes of the center lines, in the form of slugs inserted in the mortises in the electrotypes. The top panels of jump heads like that shown in Example 104, and the lower panels of jump heads like that shown in Example 105, also usually are kept standing as electrotypes, but the lines used with such panels are changed to fit specific jump-head requirements.

Some papers employ an out-of-the-ordinary line at the end of the first section of a continued story—a line making use of an index character, or "fist," followed by gothic capitals, as suggested by Example 106.

Other papers employ jump heads with emphasis on the position and typographic treatment given the word "Continued." To illustrate, a story started under a multiple-deck head has been continued under a jump head of the sort suggested by Example 107.

☛ PAGE FOUR, COL. 1

EXAMPLE 106

CONTINUED
From page one

Midwestern Policemen Set Traps for Kidnaper

EXAMPLE 107

Notice the prominence given the word "Continued" by placing it above the head, and by giving it comparatively large display.

Still another way of treating jump heads is one involving the use of several different kinds of ornamental border units, and slugs that have been given various color treatments for the guidance of makeup men. But, as that system has been copyrighted and a fee has been charged for the use of it, it seems inadvisable to discuss it in detail or illustrate it here.

Some papers follow the practice of jumping stories to left-hand pages, with the thought that such pages are less attention arresting than right-hand pages and, consequently, are the logical pages for continuations of stories that already have been "sold" by headlines on preceding pages, and that the right-hand pages should be employed for the original presentations of other important stories.

Other papers try to concentrate most of their jump heads on one page for the convenience of readers, in some instances the final page, so that continuations can be easily turned to by the reader, even when he is riding in a crowded street car or other means of conveyance.

Still other papers try to place their jump heads in the last page, or last pages, to be made up, to avoid "remakes" if jumped stories are revised or lifted.

In the fall of 1934 the *Toronto* (Ont.) *Evening Telegram* did away with the direct jumping of stories. It did away with it, even in the case of what ordinarily would have been a long story, by breaking the story into various divisions and presenting each division under a head of its own. But a brief paragraph at the end of the front-page division directed attention to other divisions on other pages.

Many newspapers place the jumps of certain kinds of stories on certain departmentalized pages. For instance, the jump of a front-page story about Wall Street affairs would be placed on a financial page; the jump of a baseball story, on a sports page; the jump of a story about a socially prominent wedding, on a society page, and so on.

Some papers sometimes call attention to stories on inside pages by referring to such stories in front-page ears. Other papers, particularly tabloids that present only headlines, pictures and legends on their front pages, often refer to stories on inside pages by presenting small "*Story on Page Blank*" lines under front-page headlines, or by including similar references in cut legends on front pages.

When a news story about an important speech or ruling is run on a front page and the text of the speech or ruling is presented on an inside page or pages, an effective way to call attention to the speech or ruling is to run a reference box immediately below the front-page head, as suggested by Example 108, or after the first few lines of body matter, or to present the reference information between a pair of wavy or plain rules after the first few lines of body matter, as suggested by Example 109.

Byrnes Says U.S. Will Play A World Role

Tells American Club in Paris There Should Be No Doubt of U.S. Policy

Text of the Byrnes speech— Page 10

PARIS, Oct. 3.—Secretary of State James F. Byrnes told the American Club of Paris today

EXAMPLE 108

By the United Press.

WASHINGTON, June 26.—President Roosevelt created by executive order today the National Youth Ad-

The text of the President's order appears on Page 48.

ministration. He allocated $50,000,000 from the $4,000,000,000 work relief fund to assist 500,000 needy youths obtain a good start in life.

"I have determined that we shall do something for the nation's unemployed youth because we can ill afford

EXAMPLE 109

The *Inland Bulletin* of the Inland Daily Press Association for March 11, 1936, reported a convention talk on jump heads made by D. D. Mich, then managing editor of the *Wisconsin State Journal* of Madison, Wis., but at this writing executive editor of *Look*. Mr. Mich joined the staff of *Look* in 1937, became managing editor in 1940, and executive editor in 1942.

In speaking of jump heads, Mr. Mich stated, in part:

"Lest anyone feel that I am unduly bold in assuming that I know what the pet peeve of the newspaper reader is, I hasten to assure you that I am not assuming anything, but simply relaying to you what the newspaper reader himself has told me—the norm, or average, of all the people who read our newspapers.

"This fellow has told me—and a good many other editors—in no uncertain terms, that his pet peeve is the newspapers' habit of continuing ('jumping') stories from one page to another. Sometimes he grows a little nasty in his criticism of this habit, especially when he is told that a story is continued on page eight, column three, and after what seems like a very long search he finds it on page four, column six. But his annoyance is not, by any means, confined to the mistakes that are made on jump lines.

"Even when every jump line tells the truth, our reader is greatly put out when he has to turn to some other page to complete a story started on page one. His peeve grows upon him terribly if he is a family man and finds that the jump page containing thirds, quarters and halves of stories which he has started to read is in a part of the paper which has been appropriated by his wife or his children. If he finds that front-page stories have been jumped to several widely separated inside pages, he feels completely betrayed.

"For several years, I wondered if anything could be done about jump stories. They were always my pet peeve as a newspaper reader, and I knew they must annoy others as much as they annoyed me. From time to time, at the *State Journal* in Madison, Wis., we would make an effort to hold down the number of jumps, but a reaction always set in and we frequently found ourselves using as many as ten or twelve a day. We came to regard them as a necessary evil about which nothing could be done.

"One night last November, in looking through the *Saturday Evening Post,* I came across a short article called 'Front Page.' It was written by Gurney Williams, managing editor of *Life*. . . .

"Well, in this article, he told the story of a man who had been arrested on a charge of murder. The man readily confessed to the police that he had killed the editor of a newspaper who had refused to pay any attention to his complaints against jump stories. The police, also newspaper readers, were completely sympathetic. They released the prisoner and sent him out gunning for another editor.

"Now, I wasn't afraid that a reader of the *Wisconsin State Journal* would get murderous ideas from reading the article, but I did take Mr. Williams' clever criticism to heart. (Incidentally, the *Post* made the article doubly effective by jumping the last four or five lines of it from page twenty to page eighty-six, or something like that.)

"I gained the courage to try to eliminate jumps from the *State Journal.* We tried it as an experiment. We asked the readers what they thought of it, but we used only a little one-column box.

"The response was terrific.

"In the fourteen years that I have worked for newspapers, I have never experienced such a deluge of commendatory messages as we received—in the mail, in person, over the telephone. There were more than one hundred the first day. Even now, after our no-jump policy has been in effect for three months, we still frequently receive word of approval from grateful readers. Some readers have told us that the *State Journal* is worth twice as much as it was before. Not a single unfavorable comment have we received.

"We had some trouble at the start, but our makeup now goes along more smoothly than it ever did when we were jumping from five to fifteen stories off page one every day. At first, we eliminated jumps only from page one, but within a week we had also knocked them out of the sports section and the Sunday society section, which formerly had used a considerable number.

"Our only real distress in making up a jumpless paper has come in the handling of extremely long stories. . . . For a while, we let them run all over page one, but I am willing to confess that some of those pages did not look so good. Now, on an occasion when we have a very long story, we run it from column eight of page one to column one of page two, without a jump head. Most papers with no-jump policies do likewise, and there is really no inconvenience to the reader, since the story can be followed with a mere flip of the page. . . .

"I have a hunch that the portion of a story which is continued on an inside page is read by a surprisingly small percentage of readers—except in the case of a story of tremendous interest.

"Our no-jump policy has had several effects—all beneficial, in my opinion. It has made inside pages more attractive and more readable. It has put a higher premium on concise writing and sharp editing. It has eliminated the necessity of holding two and sometimes three pages open to the last minute in order to place the jumps.

"Best of all, it has pleased the readers, whose only complaint is that we didn't take this step a long time ago."

After several years of following a no-jump policy, the *Wisconsin State Journal* modified that policy, for competitive reasons, to be able to start more stories on its front pages. However, in the summer of 1946, Don Anderson, publisher of the paper, informed this writer: "If I were running a paper in a non-competitive field, I would certainly have a no-jump policy. All of the continuing studies prove that a story loses about half its readership when it is continued to an inside page. In a competitive field, I feel we are doing the smart thing."

A weekly publisher once told this writer that if a story—even an important story—is too long to be presented in its entirety on one of his front pages, he presents the whole story on an inside page. He does that not only to keep jumps out of his paper, but to help to convince readers that all pages in his paper are important—that his inside pages are just as important as his front pages.

In the case of another weekly, however—a ten-page paper studied by the Research Company of America under the sponsorship of the American Press Association—the last page, which contained several jumps, was as thoroughly read as the front page.

"One interesting finding," ran a paragraph in the study referred to, "was that the back page of the ten-page newspaper was read with just as much interest as the front page. In fact, the readership of several stories which were continued from the front page to the back was greater for the continuation than for the beginning of the story. One explanation for this is that when people devote a couple of hours to reading their newspaper they actually spend more time with the last page, before putting the paper aside, than they do with the front page when they are eager to see what the rest of the paper contains."

In June of 1946, the *Christian Science Monitor*, Boston, adopted a no-jump policy that was introduced in all editions of the *Monitor* for June 24, 1946, with a front-page story that ran as follows:

"With today's editions, the *Christian Science Monitor* begins a new front-page makeup. We have, first of all, eliminated that ancient aggravation to readers—'jumps' from page one to inside pages. The

THE CHRISTIAN SCIENCE MONITOR

AN INTERNATIONAL DAILY NEWSPAPER

VOLUME 38 NO. 177 — BOSTON, MONDAY, JUNE 24, 1946 — CENTRAL EDITION — TWO SECTIONS — FIVE CENTS A COPY

Uneasy China Waits As Wily Generals Talk Out the Truce

By Ronald Stead

Drys Flay Wet Links In Indiana

When Victory Was in Making

Montgomery . . . Eisenhower . . . Bradley

Eisenhower Puts Epic Tale of War In Victory Report

Allied Commander Credits Aides And German Mistakes for Success

By William H. Stringer

Big Four Scan Formulas for Istria And Central European Free Trade

By Saville R. Davis

The Monitor's New Make-Up

State of the Nation

By ROSCOE DRUMMOND

United Nations Emblem

Latin Communists Assail Anglo-U. S. 'Imperialism'

Inside Reading:

New Appeal to U. N.
India asking the nations' help in Africa . Page 2

Behind Operation Crossroads
H. B. Nichols bares Bikini details Page 3

Japan and Democracy
Robert Peel studies the mind of Nippon Page 5

Iowa's Centennial
U. S. pantry feeds world's hungry Page 7

EXAMPLE 110

THE CHRISTIAN SCIENCE MONITOR

AN INTERNATIONAL DAILY NEWSPAPER

VOLUME 38 NO. 177 BOSTON, MONDAY, JUNE 24, 1946 ATLANTIC EDITION

Soviet Plans to Cling To Veto Power In Any Atom Control

The World's Day

Europe: Soviet Never to Give Up Atom Veto?

Boston: Parking Violators Visit Hub Court

Washington: Truman Accepts Purcell Resignation

National: German Occupation Revision?

Philippines: Roxas Hits Ickes Statement

India: Interim Plan Reported Rejected

Weather Prediction: Warm

New Boston School Post Thrown Out

By Laura Haddock

State Takes Over Castle Island

Left to right: Maj. Gen. Clarence R. Kells, Port Authority Director; Maj. Gen. Douglas L. Weart, United States Corps of Engineers; Governor Tobin, and Judge James E. Nolan of Port Authority. [Story: Page 2]

Victory Report: War Epic Told By Eisenhower

Allied Commander Credits Aides And German Mistakes for Success

By William H. Stringer

Fighting Spirit Won War

German Miscalculation

Points at Issue in Eisenhower Report: Page 13

Big Four Scan Formulas for Istria And Central European Free Trade

By Saville R. Davis

Plan Outlined

Advantage to Russia

Effect of Past

Tangible Solutions

The Monitor's New Make-Up

State of the Nation

By ROSCOE DRUMMOND

Chief of the Washington Bureau of The Christian Science Monitor

United Nations Emblem

Americans Go Meatless—Yet Warehouses Bulge

By Josephine Ripley

Meat Should Move

Many Workers Laid Off

Test Vote Possible

Inside Reading:

Behind Operation Crossroads — H. B. Nichols bares Bikini details .... Page 3

Japan and Democracy — Robert Peel studies the mind of Nippon ..... Page 6

New Appeal to U. N. — India asking the nations' help in Africa .. Page 7

Iowa's Centennial — U. S. pantry feeds world's hungry .... Page 11

EXAMPLE 111

design you see on this page—which will vary inevitably from day to day as the news changes—converts page one from a heavily laden assortment of beginnings to a selective and strongly accented group of outstanding dispatches.

"The new makeup puts desired typographical emphasis on our own special stories; it presents them in self-contained units; it emphasizes the long-range values which will mean most to readers. It seeks to express the basic elements of reader interest: clarity, significance, vigor."

Example 110 presents a reduced showing of the front page of the Central edition of the *Monitor* for June 24, 1946, and Example 111 presents a reduced showing of the front page of the Atlantic edition issued the same day.

Note, in each example, the two-column box effect at the bottom of columns five and six—a box effect calling attention to important stories on inside pages. Note, also, that, while column rules are employed to separate most of the stories from each other, no column rules are used within a story when the story is presented in two or more side-by-side columns.

Reference to this "rule and no-rule" treatment was made by the *Monitor* in a front-page story June 26, 1946:

"Selected outstanding dispatches, beginning and ending on page one, again today feature the *Christian Science Monitor's* new front-page makeup.

"The inside pages gain, too. For, instead of being heavily laden with 'jumps' from page one, these pages have their own major stories presented as integral units.

"On page one, it will be noted, we leave out the column rules within a dispatch, emphasizing unity and helping to produce a strong, well-blocked page. How do you like it?"

Undoubtedly, many readers were pleased with both the no-jump and the "rule and no-rule" treatments.

Note that, in Example 111, summations of important stories from various parts of the world were presented across two columns at the upper left of the page, under a three-line display head and a subhead reading "The World's Day."

14

Illustrations

A SINGLE PICTURE often tells more than hundreds of words. And appropriate and appropriately presented pictures can brighten up news and feature stories and enliven the makeup.

As stated in Chapter 3 of Part I, even the most pretentious early day newspapers rarely used pictures with stories; but today most newspapers employ pictures, some papers many pictures.

The earliest illustrations in newspapers were printed from wood-cuts, but such cuts seldom are used in newspapers at present.

In 1846 several metropolitan papers that previously had used wood-cuts occasionally or oftener, abandoned the use of cuts—for mechanical reasons. For twenty years or so following 1846 many metropolitan papers were printed on type-revolving presses direct from type in curved containers that rotated with the cylinders of presses, and flat-surfaced cuts could not be used on such presses. The comparatively small number of cuts used on such presses had to be given special treatment to make them agree with the curved printing surface. (The old *New York Daily Graphic,* one of the papers that used type-revolving presses, employed a trade stereotyper who had a casting box for the casting of stereotyped plates of certain widths and with curved surfaces corresponding to the curve of the type-carrying cylinders of such presses, and such plates sometimes were used in presenting illustrations. Stephen Henry Horgan engraved for the old *Graphic,* on curved stereotypes two columns wide, the first daily weather maps. Those maps showed up as white lines on United States maps in line tints. Prior to March, 1884, newspapers employing stereotyping found that wood-cuts sometimes would split when stereotype matrices were being made in the steam molding presses, so engravers occasionally did their engraving on metal instead of wood. Mr. Horgan engraved billiard shots for the old *Graphic* on type-high metal blocks, and the shots appeared in the paper as white lines against black backgrounds.) But with the further development and fairly general adoption of over-all stereotyping by our larger city papers, more pictures began to appear in such papers, and more and more of them have been used ever since.

Among the more popular illustrative mediums for newspapers since the wood-cut have been the chalk-plate (invented by Maurice Joyce, a stereotyper of Washington, D. C.), the line-cut (or line-etching) and the halftone.

Back in our Civil War days James Gordon Bennett the elder ran many war maps in his *New York Herald.* The maps were engraved in wax and electrotyped, and the electrotypes were made up in the forms with the other printing units.

The old *New York Daily Graphic* is said to have been the first daily newspaper to print a halftone. That halftone—a straight-line halftone of a subject entitled "Shantytown"—was the work of Stephen Henry Horgan, and was published in the *Daily Graphic* of March 4, 1880.

What is said to have been the first cross-line halftone used in a newspaper printed on a web perfecting press employing stereotype plates—a reproduction of a portrait of Senator Thomas C. Platt of New York—was published in the *New York Tribune* January 21, 1897. That halftone, too, was the work of Mr. Horgan.

Mr. Horgan died August 30, 1941, at the age of eighty-seven, and a story about his life and work, in the *New York Herald Tribune* the next day, was accompanied by reproductions of his halftones of "Shantytown" and of Senator Thomas C. Platt.

After having agreed with the statements about Mr. Horgan already made in this chapter, the *Herald Tribune* story continued:

"Although the *Tribune* is generally credited with having printed the first halftone from a high-speed perfecting press, two other newspapers disputed the claim. In March, 1940, a member of the *Youngstown* (Ohio) *Vindicator* said that that newspaper had turned the trick on December 26, 1893, printing a picture of a banker, Chauncey Andrews. In March, 1922, a representative of the *Minneapolis Times* said that his newspaper had turned out halftones from fast stereotyping presses as early as 1895. . . .

"In 1924 the American Telephone and Telegraph Company perfected a process of sending pictures by wire, and Mr. Horgan suggested that they could send color pictures as well as the plain black-and-whites they were using. On July 15, 1924, the first color picture was sent by wire from Chicago to New York.

"The picture, of the late Rudolph Valentino, motion-picture actor, was first photographed through a filter that permitted only red to pass through, then through a yellow filter, and finally a blue. The three plates were wired exactly as if they were black-and-whites. At their destination they were developed and inked for their separate colors and printed one atop the other. The result was a perfect reproduction of the original color picture.

"On March 4, 1930, Mr. Horgan was guest of honor at a dinner in London commemorating the fiftieth anniversary of the first halftone. There he received a medal with his portrait in high relief stamped on it. A group of engravers from Japan gave him a painting, acknowledging the benefits they had received from his invention; an organization of Chinese photo-engravers donated a rare Chinese vase, and the American Institute of Graphic Arts gave him the institute's medal."

The story ended with the statement that Mr. Horgan "was the first honorary member of the International Photo-engravers' Union."

In 1881, Frederic E. Ives of Philadelphia, according to John Clyde Oswald in his *Printing in the Americas*, published in 1937 by the Gregg Publishing Company, "invented a process of photography through cross-lined screens and then employing chemicals to etch metal plates, which process has almost supplanted the former method of cutting away parts of the surface of a block with a burin."

"After the World War," states *Compton's Pictured Encyclopedia*, referring to World War I, "newspapers began printing pictures of happenings in distant localities the day after the event. An explanatory line said, 'transmitted by wire.' "

Soundphotos, first made available to newspapers in 1936, and now widely used, make possible rapid transmission of pictures by radio.

The most commonly used halftones in newspapers at present are of 50-, 55-, 60- and 65-line screen—comparatively coarse screens. Finer screened halftones usually would not print so well on coarse-fibered newsprint on high-speed presses and with little make-ready.

A 50-line-screen halftone has fifty dots to the inch crosswise and fifty dots lengthwise, or 2500 dots to the square inch; whereas a 65-line-screen halftone has 4225 dots to the square inch—1725 more than the 50-liner. But both such cuts are considered coarse screened when compared with, say, a 150-line-screen halftone, with 22,500 dots to the square inch. The 150-line screen is the one most commonly used for gravure and colorgravure printing.

In newspaper halftones, depth—the depth of the depressions between the dots—is more important than tone and color, as the cuts always darken in printing. And one reason why more zinc than copper halftones are used for newspaper illustrations is that zinc is a softer metal than copper and offers less resistance to the acid used for etching, thereby making it possible to secure greater depth. Also, zinc halftones can be made quicker than copper, and are less expensive.

The safest means of pictorial presentation in a newspaper is the line-cut, if the lines in the original drawing are not too close together. They should be far enough apart in the original to make certain that, *in the reduction,* at least 2 points of white space will appear between the black lines. If the intervals of white are less than 2 points thick, *in the reduction,* they are likely to fill in during the press run.

The retouching of photographs—the strengthening of important areas and the toning down or eliminating of unimportant—often is necessary for the securing of good contrast in halftones. In cuts of scenery, for instance, where the sky is of no great importance to the object or objects to be featured, the sky might well be eliminated by silhouetting the features, to avoid the "muddiness" that often results from the printing of skies on newsprint.

It is not the purpose here to explain the various illustrative mediums at present employed by newspapers, including cuts of crayon drawings made on Ross boards, mezzographs, cellographs, high-light halftones, combination cuts, and quarter-tones, except to state that many advertising men regard the quarter-tone as the most "foolproof" screened cut known for newspaper use, and to comment briefly on that kind of cut.

After checking up on the making of quarter-tones in several large plants, Julien J. Soubiran, president of the Horan Engraving Company, New York City, told this writer:

"Some plants handle this type of plate one way, and others another. But when you get right down to it, any plate made from a 'blow up,' or an 'enlarged halftone,' or made as an 'indirect,' as we term it, can be referred to with assurance as a 'quarter-tone.'

"Let us assume that a quarter-tone plate 6 inches wide and of 50-line screen is desired.

"One popular method of producing such a plate is to make a halftone one-half the width desired and of 100-line screen, and finish it properly as though it were a regular job. A good proof of the halftone is taken, or the plate is chalked up, and either the proof or the chalked plate is used as copy for a photographic enlargement. Then a negative twice as wide as the copy is made, is printed on metal in the usual way, and goes through for reproduction as a 50-line-screen plate. By this method the detail from the 100-line-screen plate is retained.

"Another method of making quarter-tones is by what is known as velox reproduction.

"Assuming, again, that a quarter-tone plate 6 inches wide and of 50-line screen is desired, a negative is made, say, 5 inches wide and of 60-line screen. From this an enlargement is made, say, 10 inches wide. A velox print is made from the large negative, mounted on art board, and retouched with black and white. When the retouching is finished, the velox print is rephotographed down to 6 inches in width by the engraver and put through the usual course of production. The finished plate will be 50-line screen, and a good type of plate for newspaper use."

Vignetted halftones (cuts with gradually fading away backgrounds) usually do not print well on newsprint, as the outer edges that are supposed to fade away usually show up as hard lines. (But sometimes make-ready in the stereotype department or the pressroom can alleviate that objectionable feature.)

Cuts given "square" halftone treatments for newspapers—particularly fairly small cuts—might well incorporate an outer line, to keep the outer edges from appearing ragged.

Although, of course, the paper used for this book is not newsprint, Example 112 shows a vignetted halftone of 50-line screen, and Example 113 shows the same subject silhouetted in 55-line screen.

Example 114 shows the same subject given an oval treatment in 65-line screen, and Example 115 the same subject as a "square" halftone in 85-line screen.

The upper and right-hand section of Example 116 shows the same subject in a 42½-line-screen quarter-tone "blown up" from the 85-screen halftone in the lower and left-hand section.

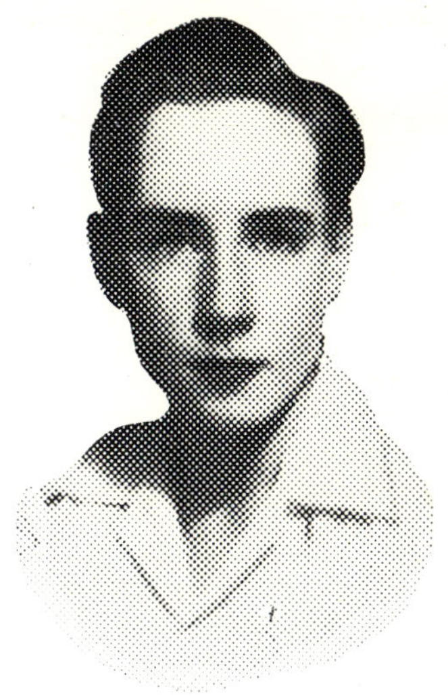

EXAMPLE 112

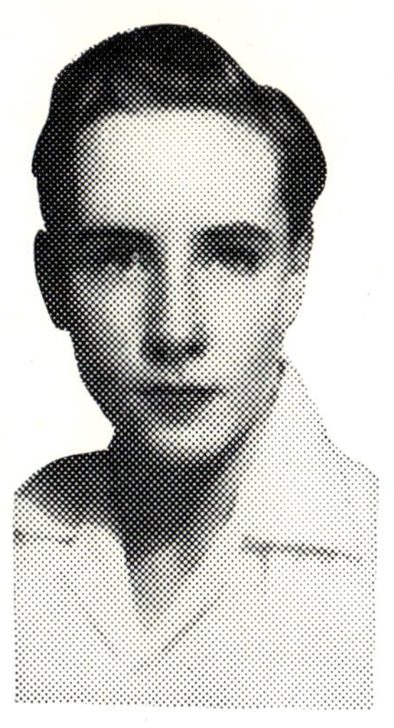

EXAMPLE 113

Example 117 shows a mezzograph, or mezzotint, made through a grained screen, and Example 118 is a high-light, or drop-out, combination plate—partly in line and partly screened, with the high-lighted area in the halftoned hat tooled out.

EXAMPLE 114

EXAMPLE 115

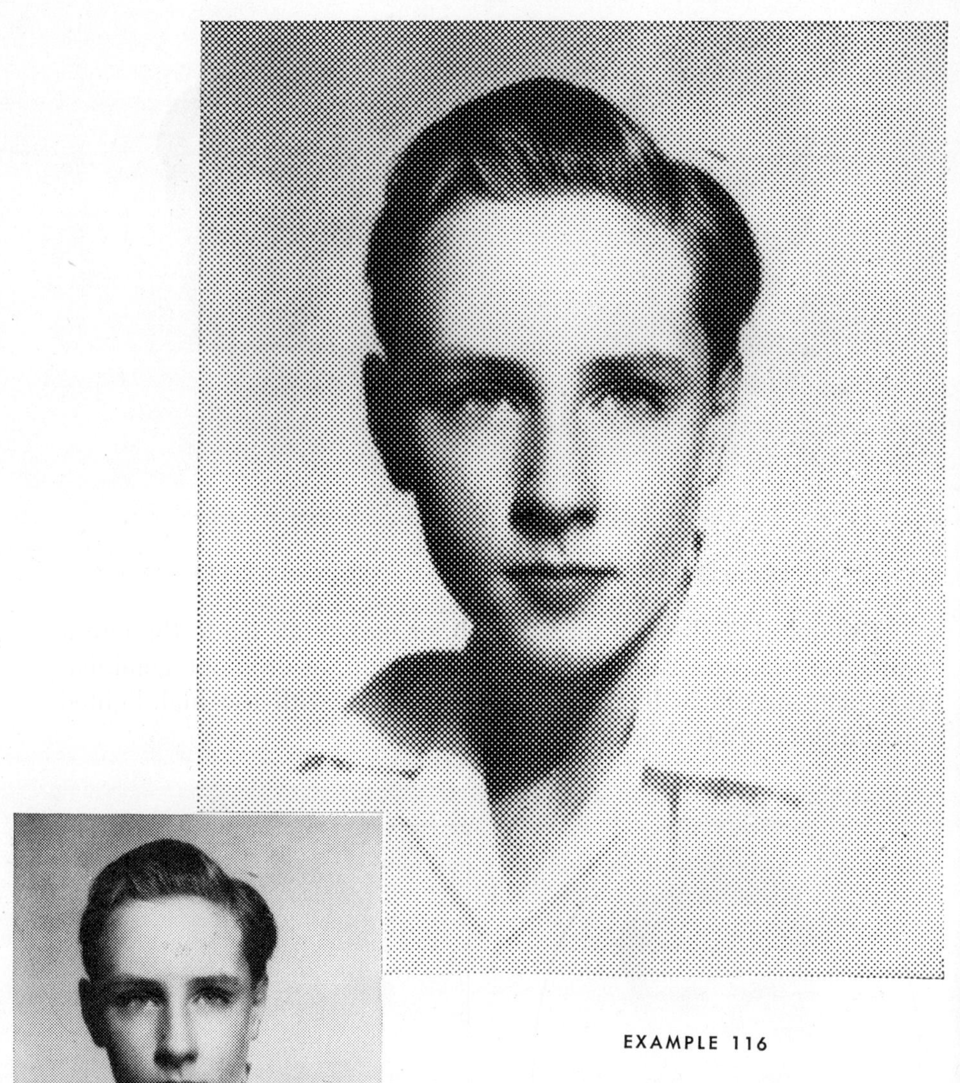

EXAMPLE 116

Example 119 is a straight combination silhouetted line-and-half-tone, with no whites tooled out; and Example 120 is a straight high-light, or drop-out, halftone, with no line work—made from a wash drawing.

The Ben Day process is the name of a process involving many different kinds of screens of lines or dots for use over parts or all of certain

EXAMPLE 117

EXAMPLE 118

cuts, and sometimes over unusually large and heavy type characters or rules or other units of composition.

Example 121 shows a dozen popular Ben Day patterns used by newspapers.

Example 122 shows a line-cut with a solid-black background—too black to be acceptable to some newspapers.

But Example 123 shows how the use of a 65-line screen approximating Ben Day pattern No. 505, over most of the cut, lightens up the heavy areas and makes the cut acceptable. In fact, that treatment gives the cut a three-tone effect, with whites, grays and blacks.

Not so many years ago many newspapers, particularly metropolitan dailies, when presenting two or more cuts in a group, "tied the cuts together" with drawn-in ornate lines and ornaments often slightingly referred to by artists as "candle grease" or "spinach." But that ornate way of tying up cuts is dying out, for most newspapers today present

EXAMPLE 119

EXAMPLE 120

their picture groups more simply, and often with no connecting lines or ornaments.

Even when most of the heads in a paper are presented flush at the left, it seems to this writer that cut overlines usually should be centered—not set flush at the left.

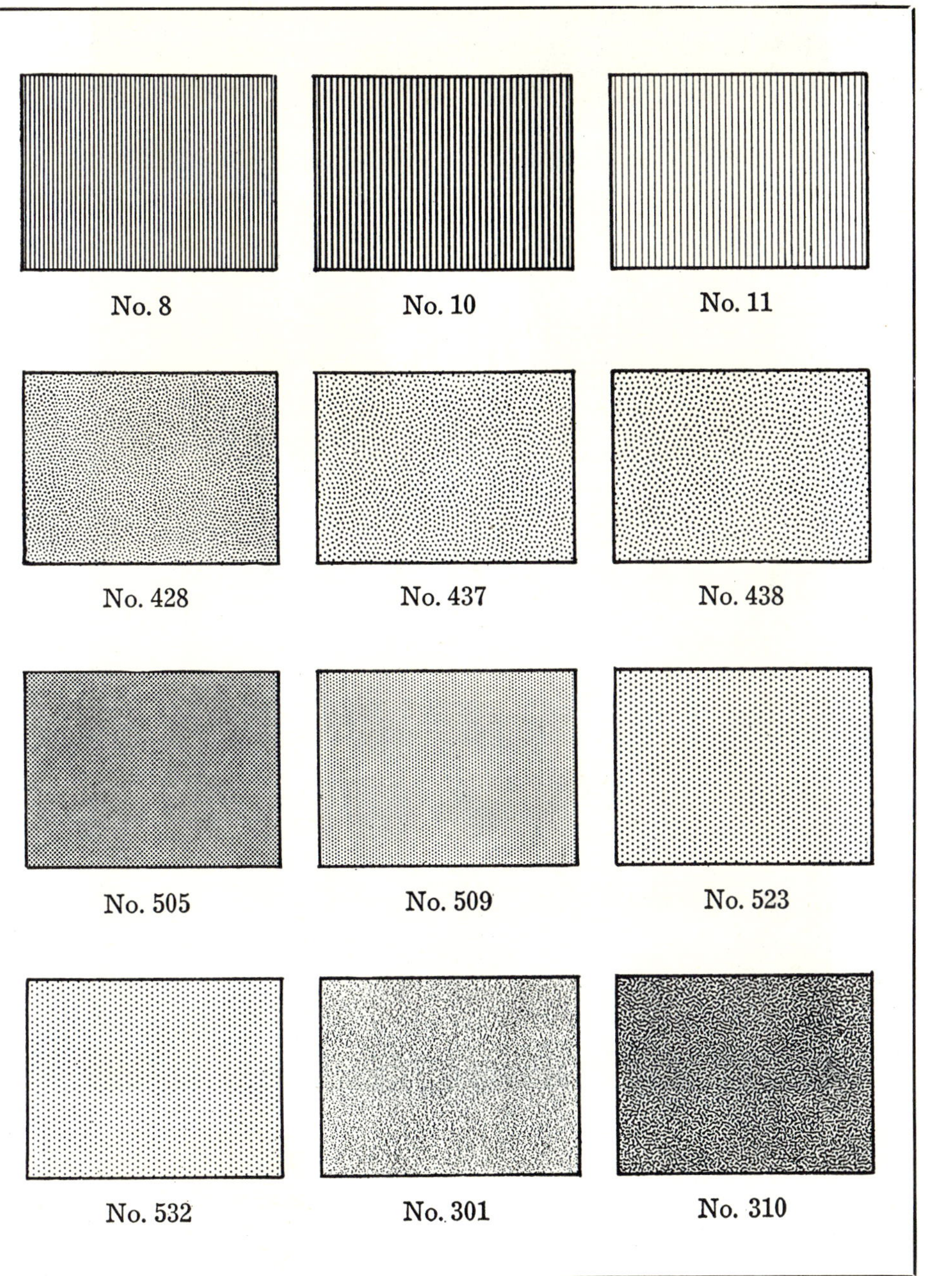
No. 8
No. 10
No. 11
No. 428
No. 437
No. 438
No. 505
No. 509
No. 523
No. 532
No. 301
No. 310

EXAMPLE 121

EXAMPLE 122

EXAMPLE 123

A flush-left cut overline usually looks accidental—appears to have slipped out of place—particularly if it is a short line.

Note the unfinished appearance of the picture treatment suggested by Example 124.

Not only is the overline in Example 124 faulty, but the legend lines, too, are not as they should be. They have been set full double-column measure, whereas the actual *printing surface* of the cut is only 23 picas

New President

John Doe of this city, who was elected president of the Civic Club at the meeting of that organization held last night at the Hotel Modern in this city

EXAMPLE 124

wide and the legend lines should have been held within the width of that *printing surface*.

In Example 125 the legend lines are too wide, and so is the box of the overline. That box, too, extends beyond the *printing width* of the cut, and the result is unattractive.

Besides, that box is superfluous—and costly. It contributes nothing of value to the picture treatment, and it wastes valuable time in the composing room. Those rules must be trimmed to fit and mitered at the corners. And if they are not expertly joined and carefully locked up, the result will be an eyesore.

Note the simpler, less expensive and more effective treatment suggested by Example 126, in which the legend lines have been held within the width of the *printing surface* of the cut, and the overline has

New President of Civic Club

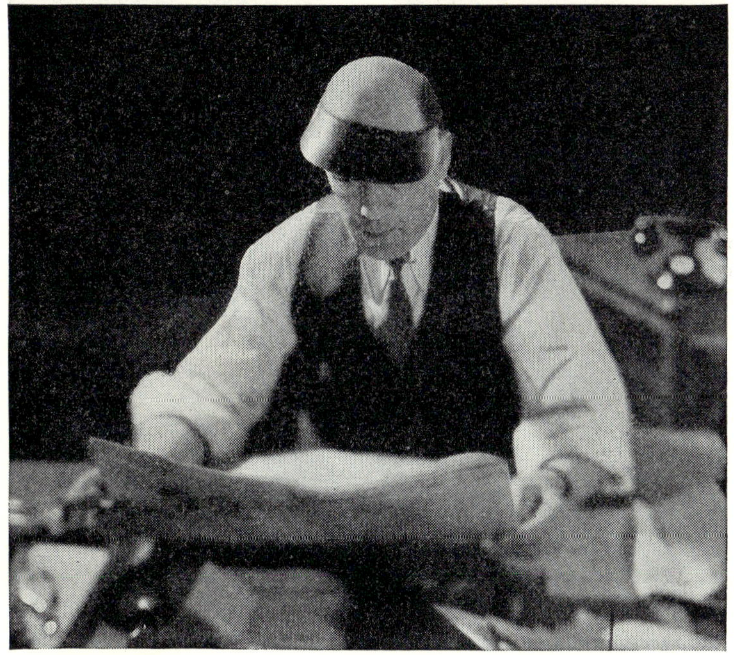

John Doe of this city, who was elected president of the Civic Club at the meeting of that organization held last night at the Hotel Modern in this city

EXAMPLE 125

been centered and presented without complicated and complicating rules.

Some modern newspapers use no overlines with cuts, and such simplified treatments often can be quite effective.

Although comparatively few newspapers use half-column cuts of individuals with news stories, such cuts could be used by many papers to advantage—with full justice to the subjects of the pictures, and at a considerable saving of space.

Certain metropolitan papers make liberal use of such cuts, as space saving is an important item to such papers; but surely many papers in smaller cities and towns also are interested in saving space.

New President of Civic Club

John Doe of this city, who was elected president of the Civic Club at the meeting of that organization held last night at the Hotel Modern

EXAMPLE 126

A half-column cut, obviously, takes up only one-fourth of the space required for the same picture when it is a full column wide. Regardless of any difference in price between the smaller and larger cuts, the saving in space is well worth considering. Engravers have minimum charges, of course, but the smaller cut at most will cost no more than the larger.

Another important point is that the smaller and space-saving cut often can be quite effective pictorially, and often is more appropriate than a larger cut would be.

Often stories with half-column cuts can be more easily handled in making up than stories with larger cuts, and there is less likelihood of the cuts in one story clashing with those of an adjacent story.

Still another important point is that the half-column cut does not interrupt the reader as does the larger when presented in the body of a story. In the case of the half-column cut, the reader is not obliged "to jump over the picture" to continue reading. The type "run-around" presented beside the smaller cut enables him to read along without interruption. But care should be taken with the spacing of those narrow lines beside the smaller cuts. Wide spacing is objectionable in any part of the paper, but sometimes it is not easy to avoid in narrow lines. And sometimes it is advisable to avoid the starting of new paragraphs in the narrow lines, to get away from too much white space beside the narrow cuts.

The half-column cut presented in Example 127 has been given "square" halftone treatment; the one in Example 128 has been silhouetted. Either form of presentation is appropriate for newspaper use. However, as the silhouetted cut calls for more attention from the engraver, it usually costs more than the "square" treatment.

EXAMPLE 127

EXAMPLE 128

It is advisable to have the picture "face into the story," rather than away from it. This helps to focus the reader's attention on the story.

A satisfactory size for these small cuts, for the average newspaper column width, is 6 picas in width by 9 picas in depth, or 5 picas by 7½ picas, with the sides trimmed flush, to get away from any indention on the outside. When shoulders are used for tacking, they should be at the top and bottom of the cuts. Six points of space between the inside edge of the cut and the narrow type lines is about right. Halftones much smaller than 5 by 7½ picas would not show up well in a newspaper. Cuts 7 or 8 picas wide for use in single-column widths would not leave enough room for the setting of attractive "run-around" lines to accompany them.

Some papers, when presenting a story between columns topped with pictures, or alongside pictures, make use of arrowheads inserted beside indented body lines, to direct attention to a picture or group of pictures connected with the story.

Quite a number of newspapers use arrowheads or full arrows with picture legends, particularly in their gravure or colorgravure sections.

Papers printed on flatbed presses and using paper better than ordinary newsprint can and often do use finer screen halftones than metropolitan newspapers, and advisedly so.

When stereotype matrices of cuts include overlines and legends in type faces that do not harmonize with the other faces used on a page, the overlines and legends should be trimmed off the "flat casts" and the lines reset in appropriate type faces.

Sometimes the makeup editor of a newspaper and his associates are confronted with the problem of how best to present in print a long story without benefit of illustrations.

Perhaps the first thing that will occur to them in such a case, assuming that they are experienced in the business of makeup, will be to have all body lines of the long stories set about 6 points less in width than the regular news columns. This will make possible the use of wider shoulders of white space between the column rules and the type lines. White space has a way of helping the looks of a long story. (Extra leading of body lines undoubtedly would help, too, but the very length of the story usually precludes the use of extra leading.) They probably will make certain that plenty of single-column subheads are sprinkled through the story—several subheads to each column. Subheads help to break up the long story, and help the reader to locate the points of chief interest to himself. If the story is long enough to fill an entire page, the ones responsible for putting it into type probably will give the story a banner line, with subordinate decks at least two columns wide dropping at the left. Also, several sectional heads two columns wide would help the looks of the page, and so would, say, a two-column box or box effect near the top of the page—a box presenting the outstanding points of the story.

Of course, when illustrations are available, the long newspaper story can be presented more attractively.

"Will pictures supplant the printed word?" Robert U. Brown of *Editor & Publisher* asked in the issue of that publication for September 29, 1945, and he answered the question, in part, as follows:

"We feel that words will never be a 'last resort' nor will pictures 'fail.' Someone once said that a good picture can take the place of a thousand words. That's true and Joe Rosenthal's picture of Marines planting the flag on Mt. Suribachi is evidence of it. But what kind of a picture can tell the story of General MacArthur's address at the Jap surrender ceremony, or of President Truman's remarks after that?

"A decade ago some men with vision thought pictures could tell the whole story about everything and the slick-paper picture magazines were launched. They went all right at first, but it was soon realized a few words were needed. The word percentage has increased gradually until only a little more than fifty per cent of those so-called picture magazines are pictures.

"Pictures and words supplement each other. They don't fight. We could get along without pictures if we had to, but we couldn't get along without words."

15

Front-Page Makeup

YEARS AGO, when a young friend of this writer's had made up a studiously symmetrical front page after much planning and considerable revising, he carried a proof of the page to a shrewd and seasoned newspaper editor and printer in whose judgment he had much confidence.

"What do you think of it?" the young man asked.

The editor-printer surveyed the proof critically, and looked embarrassed. "Well, if you must," he grinned, "it doesn't look natural. It's too studied—artificial. It looks like a page turned out by someone who had just listened to a theoretical lecture on what a theoretical front page should look like. It looks like a piece of job printing—like an advertising circular. It looks as if you had decided just where each story was to go—each head, cut, box and everything else in the way of composition—before you had seen the copy."

"That's true," the young man blushed. "You've got me there. I'd been thinking about such a page several days. And I had to do some chopping here and some padding there to get just the effects, and the general effect, I wanted to get."

"Of course you did," grinned the editor-printer, "and any careful observer of the page, if it came off the press that way, would suspect it. And he wouldn't have to be a newspaper man or a printer, either.

"The average run-of-the-newsstand or run-of-the-mail-list reader probably wouldn't notice it so much the first time or two, but he certainly would eventually—and he'd begin to sense that he was being served with typography instead of news.

"What your page needs is to have a nice important story come in just before press time—a front-page *must* story that will knock a lot of its too-studied symmetry into something much more natural looking.

"A page should be planned, of course—carefully planned—but it should be planned to fit the news—not the other way round. The news shouldn't be jammed or padded to make pretty designs on a page.

The various units of composition should be used to play up the important stories, and to hold down the less important. And the page should be made up in a way that will give each story what it seems to have coming to it in the way of display and position."

In passing, it may not be amiss to state that a front-page *must* story did come in shortly before press time and that considerable symmetry went out of that front page.

And this writer has tried to keep too-studied symmetry out of many a newspaper page since then, although he often has heard studied symmetry referred to as a desirable quality by judges in newspaper contests and by students of journalism.

Once a young woman student asked this writer, following a discussion of newspaper makeup, what he thought of "geometric makeup." The one questioned felt obliged to suggest that she forget about it.

"Geometric makeup" often can be followed to advantage in advertising layouts or on magazine or special feature pages when the copy for heads, body matter and pictures is available for consideration by the layout men before the layouts are made, but seldom for the fluent and fluctuating news pages, with new copy and new pictures continually coming in.

Any experienced newspaper makeup editor realizes that any arcs, angles, gridirons, brackets, or other "geometric" effects he gets on a news page are the result of his having given each story and its head the typographic treatment and position it seemed to deserve—not the other way round. The main head or heads on a page set the stage, and less important stories should be headed and placed to attract the attention that they themselves, individually, in competition with each other and with the main heads, seem to deserve. Surely, minor heads are not placed on a page to focus attention on main heads. Well-treated and placed main heads get attention on their own, and suggest how less important heads should be, or advisedly could be, handled.

But to get back, for a moment, to studied symmetry.

Why should studied symmetry—unnatural balance—be a desirable quality for a news page? What high merit attaches to it? Experienced painters of pictures purposely avoid it. Artistic photographers instinctively shy away from it. So why should such a cramping, inhibiting and unnatural thing as studied symmetry be striven for on a news page when a page can be such a dynamic, fluently alive thing when it seems natural and spontaneous?

Of course when, as sometimes happens, but comparatively infrequently, the display elements on a news page just naturally result in a symmetrical page, it is better to leave those elements as they are than to cut or pad certain stories "to get away from unnaturalness." For the story is the thing.

Inasmuch as news stories have a way of varying in importance and length from day to day and from column to column in the same day, any plan of newspaper makeup should be flexible enough to be easily adaptable from day to day to the news of the day—not so rigid that important stories have to be radically cut, or less important stories overplayed, to form exactly predetermined patterns on a page.

An air of naturalness—of spontaneity—of attractive spontaneity—is the thing to aim at in newspaper makeup, as the experienced newspaper makeup editor is well aware. But the less experienced, if he has reached the planning stage at all, often holds so rigidly to an exact balancing of paired units that the result is an obviously artificial page—one in which carefully counted lines of incidental body matter have been employed to hold certain heads, boxes and cuts together, rather than a page in which those elements have been used to bring out the stories—to give them the physical treatment they seem to deserve.

Many a newspaper attractive at the top of its front page is unattractive below the center fold of the page.

This condition usually is caused by the starting of comparatively long stories at the top of the page and letting them run to the bottom, or within a few lines of the bottom, with the ends of the columns filled out with short items under single-column heads.

The heads at the top give color, variety, contrast, character to the upper half of the page; but the absence of sufficiently colorful heads below the center fold makes for monotony, bleakness, lack of character in the lower half. The lower half peters out. It is anticlimactic in appearance. It makes the page appear topheavy.

One good way to enliven the appearance of the lower half of a front page is to use one or two or even three double-column heads below the center fold, depending, of course, on the number of columns to the page.

Example 129 suggests the lower half of an effectively handled eight-column front page.

Three double-column heads were used in that lower half, supplemented by ten single-column heads over ten comparatively short items—thirteen stories and heads below the center fold. (That page also presented ten stories and heads above the center fold—a total of twenty-three stories and heads on the page.)

But the point to be brought out here is that the use of the double-column heads below the center fold made for a lively looking, interest-holding lower half—a lower half with character in keeping with that of the upper half.

James M. Lynch Dies From Blood Poisoning

James Pym 57 Years With Boston Paper

N. Y. Spanish Daily Promoter of Good Will

Says Ionic Attracted Thousands of Readers

Printing Craftsmen to Have Lively Time in Los Angeles

Oshkosh Firm Installs Five Model 8 Linos

Sends Ancient Press To Ford Museum

Lancaster Newspapers, Inc., Gives Ad Men Sound Advice

New Text Book on Operating Boon to Keyboard Workers

70 Years in Trade—Swinburne Retires

Sultan of Swat Sells Truckload of Papers

Chicago Post Adds Lino and Metro Faces

Cleveland Press Adds Four More Linotypes

EXAMPLE 129

Although the makeup of nearly all newspaper pages should start at both the top and bottom of the page, front pages particularly should be made up this way. No unnecessary chances should be taken with the lower half of the page.

When the page illustrated in part in Example 129 was made up, those three double-column stories below the center fold were placed in the page before any stories were placed at the top of the page. Those three were treated, but not too arbitrarily, as stories that had to go there, or about there, regardless of the length of stories to be placed above them. It so happened that all three were short enough to go on the page without jumping. But there was no meticulous line-counting in connection with their placing—no artificiality. Any one of the three stories could have been a half dozen lines longer, or shorter, than it was without marring the makeup plan.

It happened that the story at the top of column one was too long to go on the page in its entirety, so it was permitted to run down to the top of the first double-column head below the center fold and then jumped to another page. This same treatment was given the comparatively long story at the top of column eight. Other top-of-page stories were then placed in the form, and the makeup of the page progressed from the top toward the bottom.

Some alert editors and publishers who appreciate the importance of dressing up the lower halves of their front pages present feature stories under double-column or wider heads below the center fold. These newspaper men believe that, while such stories ordinarily do not deserve top-of-page position along with the biggest news stories of the day, they do deserve fairly prominent treatment in the show window of the well-rounded newspaper.

For many years it has been the custom of many makeup editors of English-language newspapers to present the leading news story of any issue at the top of the right-hand column of the front page. The top of that column is supposed to be the most eye-arresting point on the page. This assumption is based on the thought that, inasmuch as readers of English are accustomed to reading from left to right, the average reader, as he contemplates a front page, glances at the various heads from left to right, and pauses at the top of that right-hand column.

This probably is sound reasoning. At any rate, many makeup editors usually follow this plan, and, even when a banner line is run across the top of the page, its drop heads and story usually are presented in that right-hand column. (On inside pages presenting advertisements pyramided to the right, however, it often is more expedient to present the drops from banners in left-hand columns, where, usually, more space is available for the drops and their stories than in the right-hand columns.)

Another reason for presenting the leading story in the right-hand column of the front page is that a long story presented there can be continued to the top of column one on page two without a jump head. However, as previously explained, too many jump heads irritate readers and should be avoided.

The top of column one is regarded by many makeup editors as the second most eye-arresting point on the front page. The average reader is supposed to see the top of that column when he glances across the top of the page. Even when his glance moves to the right-hand column and he reads the story there, if interested, his attention is supposed to return to the top of column one on the front page (although sometimes he follows that right-hand-column story to an inside page and fails to return to page one). And when two banner lines are used across the top of the front page, the drop heads and body lines of the secondary important story usually are presented in column one.

When banner lines are not used, but spread heads—multiple-deck heads with first decks three or more columns wide, but less than the full width of the page—are, the head over the most important story usually is presented at the upper right of the front page, and that over the next most important usually at the upper left.

But the fact that reading habits strongly built up through the years seem to have given the tops of first and last columns on a front page natural eye-appeals, sometimes induces makeup editors to present their strongest displays in other columns, with the thought of building up a third strong point of interest at the top of a page in addition to the two natural points. Note many examples on following pages.

Example 130, which suggests a fragment of a front page from what might be termed the "ordinary newspaper," contains many faults—several of them previously discussed.

The nameplate was in an old-fashioned and homely type face, and entirely in capitals. And too many different kinds of type faces, and unrelated faces, were used on the page.

The first deck of the head at the upper left was in heavy gothic capitals, and the second deck (with far too many words in it) was in an unrelated condensed face. The four-deck head in column one should not have been placed in the position it was given. If used at all, such a head should have been placed at the top of the page, not permitted to "float" in the body of the page. If it did not deserve top-of-page position, then it did not deserve four decks, and at least two of them should have been eliminated. But the head itself had several faults. The first deck was in rather heavy condensed capitals, the second and fourth decks were in a light expanded face, and the third deck (intended to be a crossline, but in reality merely a centered short line) was in wide and rather heavy capitals. The shifting from deck to deck from

THE ORDINARY NEWSPAPER

VOLUME I — AMERICAN CITY, NOVEMBER 13, 1926 — NUMBER 1

MIXING TYPE FACES IN MAIN HEADS IS A COMMON FAULT

Right Underneath the Gothic Head Comes Another Deck Set in Cheltenham Bold Extra Condensed—No Harmony Between the Two Faces—The Caps in the Top Deck Are Hard to Read; There Are No Hooks For the Eye to Catch Hold Of.

The only excuse for mixing type faces in main heads is the lack of sufficient quantity of type to set all the main heads uniformly.

The style head reproduced above and the others that surround it were not conceived in an effort to be facetious, but were copied from a recent issue of a daily paper printed in an eastern city. The makeup, too, as it appears on this page is similar.

CAPS DIFFICULT TO DECIPHER IN THESE 3 LINES

Word Count Reduced By Extended Face Used Thus

TYPE TOO WIDE

This Deck Should Be Smaller and Relate To the One Above

Apparently no head schedule was used by the paper that allowed its front page to be thrown together in this manner.

The purpose of the head is to outline the story as completely as possible in a very limited number of words.

Space is at a premium for head writing. Large, extended type faces are impractical for this purpose. All caps require more space than caps and lower case of the same size and make the job of writing heads much more difficult.

Some makeup men in an effort to play up every possible story set the head out of proportion to the news value of the article.

The old axiom "all display is no display" seems to have been forgotten in some newspaper offices.

SQUARE BOXES "SQUATTY"

Because the shape of a newspaper page is proportionately deeper than it is wide, objects placed within that page should conform in general to this shape. A square box is out of harmony with its surroundings.

Indenting both sides would have extended the depth several lines and would have improved the appearance of this feature.

Heavy rules and black face type are not pleasing to the eye.

PARALLEL HEADS OF THE SAME SIZE PUZZLE THE EYE

When two single column heads of the same size occur in a parallel position they appear at first glance like a double column head, especially so when the top line of the left hand head is too long as happens in this case.

Three Steps Taken When Two Would Have Been Enough

The use of heads like this might be compared to taking one step backward in every three forward. A short article like this does not warrant three lines of 18 point type for a head.

The depth of the head is equal to half the entire text. Nevertheless, we frequently find examples like this in the makeup of the ordinary newspaper.

THIS APPEARS TO BE A DOUBLE COLUMN HEADING

Confusion Caused By Haphazard Style Of Makeup

The first impulse of the reader on encountering two single column heads like this is to read right across the top line into the adjoining column.

The weight of the type face is so much greater than that of the column rule, the division between the columns is hardly noticeable at first glance.

Newspapers have been accused by eye specialists of contributing to a considerable extent toward the increasing number of sufferers from eye trouble and as the newspaper constitutes the main reading matter of the majority this may not be without some foundation in fact.

Whether true or not, anything that contributes toward greater legibility is an object well worth obtaining.

THE ORDINARY NEWSPAPER

CONTAINS MANY EXAMPLES OF VARIOUS STYLES AND SIZES OF

TYPE FACES

INCLUDING BOLD, ITALIC AND CAPS

They Make the "Ad"

CONFUSING TO THE READER
DISAPPOINTING TO ADVERTISER
INJURIOUS TO THE PAPER

EXAMPLE 130

dark to light, to dark to light, and in unrelated type faces, gave the head an unattractive spotty appearance. The box in column two was square and squatty looking. The enclosing rule was too heavy. The body lines were not opened up enough, and the shoulders of white space between those lines and the enclosing rules were insufficient. The head was not conspicuous enough, even though it was set entirely in capitals. The whole thing seemed crowded, and was uninviting. The bumped, or tombstone, heads at the tops of columns three and four competed with one another for attention, to the disadvantage of each. At first glance they seemed to form one double-column head. The second deck of one of them was in a type face that did not harmonize in design or color with the face used for the first deck. The three-line stagger head in column three wasted space. Two lines would have been more appropriate. The semblance of an advertisement presented too many different kinds of faces and unrelated faces. The enclosing rule was much too heavy.

Although it was not intended that that fragment of a page should suggest that advertising be run on a front page, that semblance of an advertisement was intended to suggest the kind of advertising often run on inside pages (and sometimes on front pages) of the "ordinary newspaper."

The first column rule on the page should have been topped with a black diamond and joined to a plain cutoff rule. The parallel rule used for the cutoff was inappropriate.

All heads on the page would have been easier to write, to set and to read had they been set flush at the left in capitals and lower-case of related type faces, with second decks uniformly indented at the left, and with white space employed in place of jim dashes.

The pages of many weekly papers and small dailies are made up without the use of layout sheets, or dummies. When the time for making up arrives, the editor or makeup man approaches the imposing stones with a fairly definite mental picture of the important items to be run, and he builds up the pages, or supervises their building up, "as he goes along." That is, he transfers stories and cuts and advertisements from galleys directly into the chases, or causes them to be transferred, without actually having previously seen just how the various units will look when placed together in the pages.

A good makeup man with plenty of time and working on a comparatively small paper can turn out attractively constructed pages in such a way; but the makeup men of large-city dailies often have to work fast and on many pages—have to deal with so many problems of makeup, and so hurriedly, that it usually is not feasible for them to work without the assistance of dummies.

Such dummies usually are blanked-out sheets comparatively small in size, ruled off into columns, with the page depths indicated by inches or agate lines in figures to the right and left, and with the various makeup instructions or suggestions penciled into the various columns.

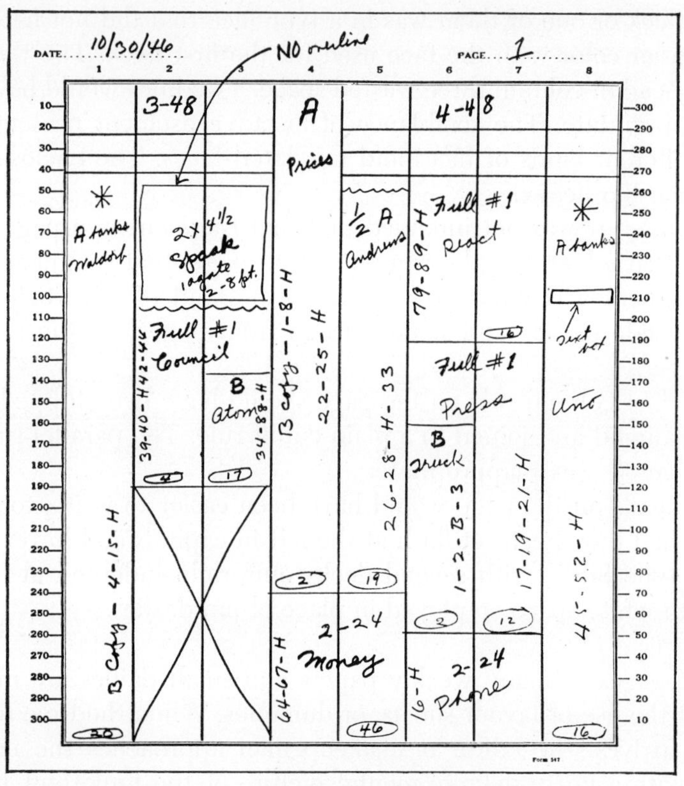

EXAMPLE 131

In a metropolitan newspaper office, an editorial conference is held at a certain hour each day to plan the paper about to be put through.

The *New York Herald Tribune*, a morning paper, holds an editorial conference at seven o'clock each evening six days a week, and at five o'clock on Saturdays.

NEW YORK

Herald Tribune

LATE CITY EDITION

VOL. CVI No. 36,508 — WEDNESDAY, OCTOBER 30, 1946 — THREE CENTS

Baruch at Forum Bars Release of Atom Secrets Unless Veto Is Given Up

Asserts U. S. Will Sign No Pact Until Accord on Veto Is Arrived At

Spaak Hails Truman On Address to U. N.

Boyd Orr Urges Action on Food; La Guardia Hits British Stand on D. P.s

THE PRESIDENT OF THE GENERAL ASSEMBLY—Paul-Henri Spaak, addressing the second session of the Forum yesterday

Citizens' Group Suing to Block Retroactive Subway Pay Rise

Challenges City's Right to Give 20c an Hour Back to July 1 and Manner of Raising $18,500,000; Council Asks Increase for 110,000 Workers

By David McConnell

Atomic Board Asks Army to Carry On Now

Will Take Over Manhattan Project Gradually; Urges Scientists to Stay on Job

Price Ceilings GoOffRadios. Fats and Oils

Kitchenware Also Freed Among Hundreds of Items in O. P. A. Order

Other Articles Still On the Waiting List

Small Hails Increase in Employment; Attacks 'Pessimistic Forecasts'

Molotov Asks World Arms Cut, Calls for Ban on Atomic Bomb, Warns End of Veto Is End of U.N.

Stalin's Views Seen Echoing Byrnes Aims

Appraisal of Statements Shows Both Seek Unified Economy for Germany

By Bert Andrews

'Smart and Tough,' Says Austin, Liking Parts of Molotov Speech

Won't Answer Charges Now; Connally and Dulles Have No Comment; British Disappointed; India and Canada Are Impressed by Proposals

By Peter Kihss

Russian Tells Assembly U. S. Atom Plan Would Upset Charter of U. N.

Delivers a Personal Attack Upon Baruch

Says Other Side in a War May Use Bomb, Too, 'and Something Else'

By John C. Rogers

Investigation of Britain's Press Ordered by Commons, 271-157

Royal Commission Created to Inquire Into Charges of Monopolistic Control, Which Government Holds Is Distorting Freedom of Press

Trucks Rushing Supplies to City, Embargo Eased

Rail Shipments Will Be Freed; Warehouses and Terminals Now Humming

$3,500 Left on L. I. Train Seat Ordered Split 5 Ways by Court

U.S.-to-Moscow Radiotelephone Open to Public for First Time

News on Inside Pages

CITY AND VICINITY — FOREIGN — NATIONAL — WASHINGTON — SPORTS — EDITORIALS AND MISCELLANY

EXAMPLE 132

Each conference is attended by the managing editor, an assistant managing editor, the night editor and usually by the foreign editor and the city editor.

While the conference is going on, reports and recommendations on the leading news stories of the day are received from the cable editor, the telegraph editor, the night city editor and the picture editor.

When the stories have been appraised by the managing editor and his chief conferees, a front-page dummy is marked up and copies of it sent to the copy desk, the composing room "and others."

The actual marking up usually is done by the night editor, on a sheet of newsprint 10½ by 12 inches in size, ruled into eight numbered columns, and numbered from 10 to 300 on each side. The side figures, which run down on the left side and up on the right, refer to agate lines. (The full type depth of a *Herald Tribune* eight-column page is 300 agate lines, or about 21½ inches.)

Example 131 presents a front-page dummy marked up at the conclusion of a *Herald Tribune* editorial conference, and Example 132 suggests the resultant front page.

In many newspaper plants, two dummies of each page containing advertising are marked up in the advertising makeup department—one (for the composing room) indicating just which and what size advertisements are to go on a page, and the other (for the editorial department) showing just how much space, and in which columns, is available for news and feature matter.

In the *Herald Tribune* plant the dummy sent to the editorial department indicates the width and depth of each advertisement, but does not identify the advertisers. The dummy sent to the composing room *does* identify each advertisement, along with its width, and its depth in agate lines, for the guidance of the makeup men.

The pages containing advertising usually are made up without written instructions from the editorial department—are "filled out" by the makeup editor and makeup men working together in the composing room—except in the case of unusually important stories and pictures, when specific instructions are sent through by the editorial department.

Example 133 shows a dummy sent to the editorial department by the advertising makeup department for a certain page in the *Herald Tribune*, Example 134 shows the companion dummy marked up for the composing room, and Example 135 suggests the resultant page.

While the discussion of dummies for pages containing advertising might properly be presented in a later chapter in this book—in the chapter on "Placing Display Advertisements"—it seemed appropriate to this writer to present that discussion here along with the discussion of front-page dummies.

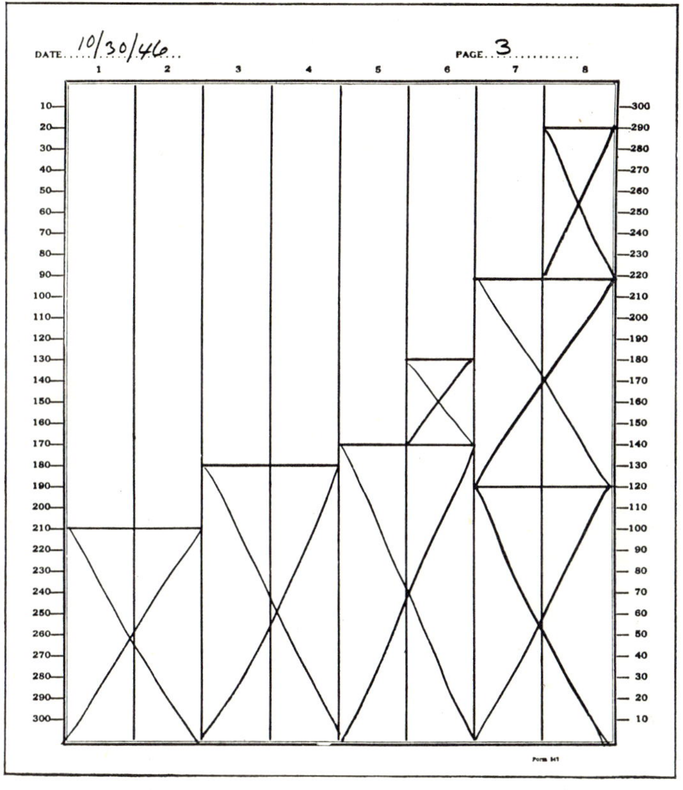

EXAMPLE 133

Dummies for editorial pages, book-section pages, and other special pages without advertising, usually are marked up in the departments of origin.

Metropolitan dailies usually are issued in two or more sections, a practice also followed by some smaller city dailies, as well as by some of the larger weekly papers. Some editors treat the front pages of second or following sections as they would any of their inside news and advertising pages and present them under the usual running heads. Others employ nameplates at the tops of such pages, and run editorial pages or feature pages in such positions. Still other editors treat such pages as "additional front pages," but usually with the multiple-deck display heads confined to smaller type sizes than those employed for main front pages.

Most of the metropolitan papers that issue large Sunday editions, or occasional special editions, present such editions in several sections, usually with a nameplate at the top of the front page of each section, and, in many cases, with different head dresses from section to section.

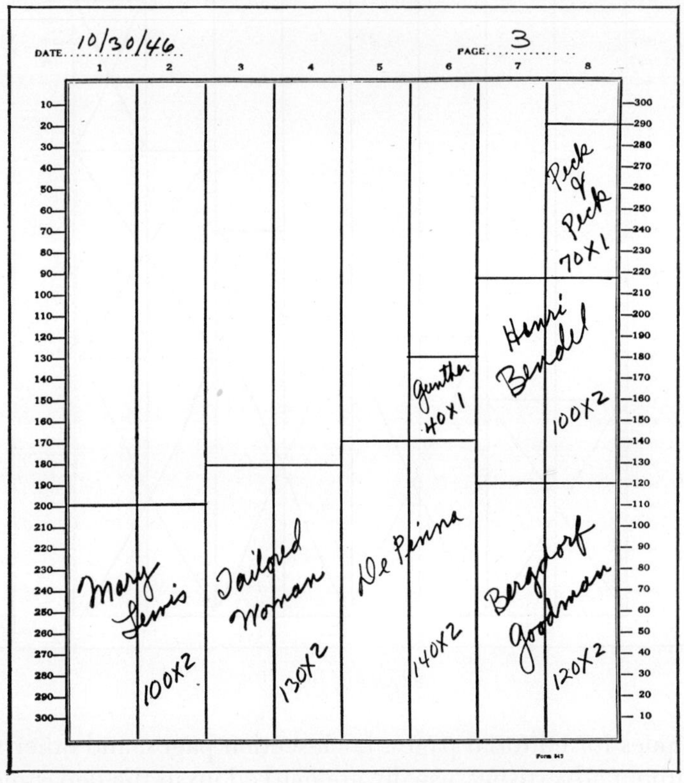

EXAMPLE 134

Some metropolitan papers with many readers in certain suburbs follow the plan of localizing a section or the front page or several pages of a section of copies distributed in each of those suburbs.

Some newspapers can improve the effectiveness of their front and other pages without purchasing any additional type faces at all, by dis-

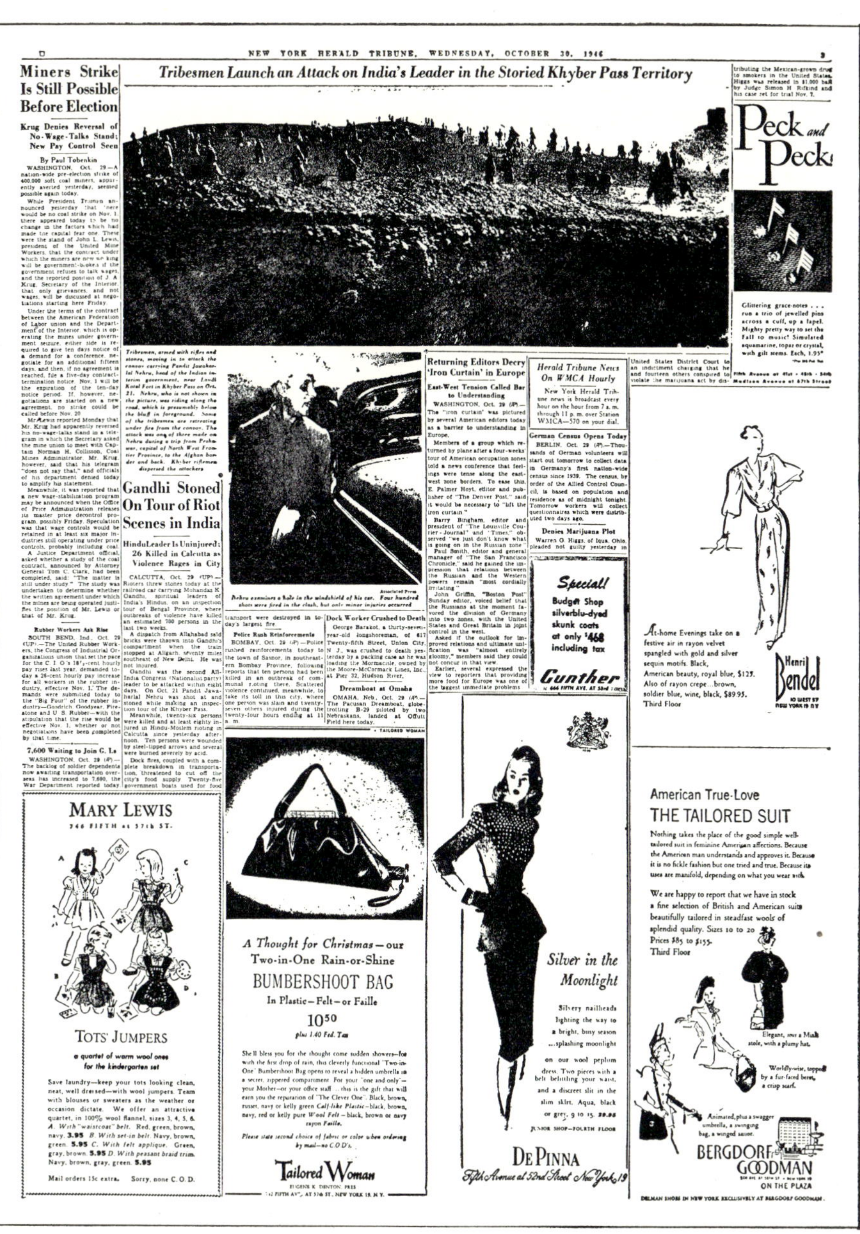

NEW YORK HERALD TRIBUNE, WEDNESDAY, OCTOBER 30, 1946 3

Tribesmen Launch an Attack on India's Leader in the Storied Khyber Pass Territory

Tribesmen, armed with rifles and stones, moving in to attack the convoy carrying Pandit Jawaharlal Nehru, head of the Indian interim government, near Landi Kotal Fort in Khyber Pass on Oct. 21. Nehru, who is not shown in the picture, was riding along the road, which is presumably below the bluff in foreground. Some of the tribesmen are retreating under fire from the convoy. The attack was one of three made on Nehru during a trip from Peshawar, capital of North West Frontier Province, to the Afghan border and back. Khyber riflemen dispersed the attackers

Associated Press

Nehru examines a hole in the windshield of his car. Four hundred shots were fired in the clash, but only minor injuries occurred

Miners Strike Is Still Possible Before Election

Krug Denies Reversal of No-Wage-Talks Stand; New Pay Control Seen

By Paul Tobenkin

WASHINGTON, Oct. 29.—A nation-wide pre-election strike of 400,000 soft coal miners, apparently averted yesterday, seemed possible again today.

While President Truman announced yesterday that there would be no coal strike on Nov. 1, there appeared today to be no change in the factors which had made the capital fear one. These were the stand of John L. Lewis, president of the United Mine Workers, that the contract under which the miners are now working will be government-broken if the government refuses to talk wages, and the reported position of J. A. Krug, Secretary of the Interior, that only grievances, and not wages, will be discussed at negotiations starting here Friday.

Under the terms of the contract between the American Federation of Labor union and the Department of the Interior, which is operating the mines under government seizure, either side is required to give ten days notice of a demand for a conference, negotiate for an additional fifteen days, and then, if no agreement is reached, file a five-day contract-termination notice. Nov. 1 will be the expiration of the ten-day notice period. If, however, negotiations are started on a new agreement, no strike could be called before Nov. 20.

Mr. Lewis reported Monday that Mr. Krug had apparently reversed his no-wage-talks stand in a telegram in which the Secretary asked the mine union to meet with Captain Norman H. Collisson, Coal Mines Administrator. Mr. Krug, however, said that his telegram "does not say that," and officials of his department denied today to amplify his statement.

Meanwhile, it was reported that a new wage-stabilization program may be announced when the Office of Price Administration releases its master price decontrol program, possibly Friday. Speculation was that wage controls would be retained in at least six major industries still operating under price controls, probably including coal.

A Justice Department official, asked whether a study of the coal contract, announced by Attorney General Tom C. Clark, had been completed, said: "The matter is still under study." The study was undertaken to determine whether the written agreement under which the mines are being operated justifies the position of Mr. Lewis or that of Mr. Krug.

Rubber Workers Ask Rise

SOUTH BEND, Ind., Oct. 29 (UP).—The United Rubber Workers, the Congress of Industrial Organizations union that set the pace for the C. I. O.'s 18½-cent hourly pay rises last year, demanded today a 26-cent hourly pay increase for all workers in the rubber industry, effective Nov. 1. The demands were submitted today to the "Big Four" of the rubber industry—Goodrich, Goodyear, Firestone and U. S. Rubber—with the stipulation that the rise would be effective Nov. 1, whether or not negotiations have been completed by that time.

7,600 Waiting to Join G. I.s

WASHINGTON, Oct. 29 (AP).—The backlog of soldier dependents now awaiting transportation overseas has increased to 7,600, the War Department reported today.

Gandhi Stoned On Tour of Riot Scenes in India

Hindu Leader Is Uninjured; 26 Killed in Calcutta as Violence Rages in City

CALCUTTA, Oct. 29 (UP).—Rioters threw stones today at the railroad car carrying Mohandas K. Gandhi, spiritual leaders of India's Hindus, on an inspection tour of Bengal Province, where outbreaks of violence have killed an estimated 700 persons in the last two weeks.

A dispatch from Allahabad said bricks were thrown into Gandhi's compartment when the train stopped at Aligarh, seventy miles southeast of New Delhi. He was not injured.

Gandhi was the second All-India Congress (Nationalist party) leader to be attacked within eight days. On Oct. 21 Pandit Jawaharlal Nehru was shot at and stoned while making an inspection tour of the Khyber Pass.

Meanwhile, twenty-six persons were killed and at least eighty injured in Hindu-Moslem rioting in Calcutta since yesterday afternoon. Ten persons were wounded by steel-tipped arrows and several were burned severely by acid.

Dock fires, coupled with a complete breakdown in transportation, threatened to cut off the city's food supply. Twenty-five government boats used for food transport were destroyed in today's largest fire.

Police Rush Reinforcements

BOMBAY, Oct. 29 (AP).—Police rushed reinforcements today to the town of Sasnor, in southeastern Bombay Province, following reports that ten persons had been killed in an outbreak of communal rioting there. Scattered violence continued, meanwhile, to take its toll in this city, where one person was slain and twenty-seven others injured during the twenty-four hours ending at 11 a. m.

Dock Worker Crushed to Death

George Barakot, a thirty-seven-year-old longshoreman, of 617 Twenty-fifth Street, Union City, N. J., was crushed to death yesterday by a packing case as he was loading the Mormacisle, owned by the Moore-McCormack Lines, Inc., at Pier 32, Hudson River.

Dreamboat at Omaha

OMAHA, Neb., Oct. 29 (AP).—The Pacusan Dreamboat, globe-trotting B-29 piloted by two Nebraskans, landed at Offutt Field here today.

Returning Editors Decry 'Iron Curtain' in Europe

East-West Tension Called Bar to Understanding

WASHINGTON, Oct. 29 (AP).—The "iron curtain" was pictured by several American editors today as a barrier to understanding in Europe.

Members of a group which returned by plane after a four-weeks' tour of American occupation zones told a news conference that feelings were tense along the east-west zone borders. To ease this, E. Palmer Hoyt, editor and publisher of "The Denver Post," said it would be necessary to "lift the iron curtain."

Barry Bingham, editor and president of "The Louisville Courier-Journal" and "Times," observed "we just don't know what is going on in the Russian zone."

Paul Smith, editor and general manager of "The San Francisco Chronicle," said he gained the impression that relations between the Russian and the Western powers remain "most cordially irritating."

John Griffin, "Boston Post" Sunday editor, voiced belief that the Russians at the moment favored the division of Germany into two zones, with the United States and Great Britain in joint control in the west.

Asked if the outlook for improved relations and ultimate unification was "almost entirely gloomy," members said they could not concur in that view.

Earlier, several expressed the view to reporters that providing more food for Europe was one of the biggest immediate problems.

Herald Tribune News On WMCA Hourly

New York Herald Tribune news is broadcast every hour on the hour from 7 a. m. through 11 p. m. over Station WMCA—570 on your dial.

German Census Opens Today

BERLIN, Oct. 29 (AP).—Thousands of German volunteers will start out tomorrow to collect data in Germany's first nation-wide census since 1939. The census, by order of the Allied Control Council, is based on population and residence as of midnight tonight. Tomorrow workers will collect questionnaires which were distributed two days ago.

Denies Marijuana Plot

Warren O. Higgs, of Iqua, Ohio, pleaded not guilty yesterday in United States District Court to an indictment charging that he and fourteen others conspired to violate the marijuana act by distributing the Mexican-grown drug to smokers in the United States. Higgs was released in $1,000 bail by Judge Simon H. Rifkind and his case set for trial Nov. 7.

Special! Budget Shop silverblu-dyed skunk coats at only $468 including tax

Gunther 666 FIFTH AVE. AT 53rd

Peck and Peck

Glittering grace-notes . . . run a trio of jewelled pins across a cuff, up a lapel. Mighty pretty way to set the Fall to music! Simulated aquamarine, topaz or crystal, with gilt stems. Each, 1.95*

Fifth Avenue at 41st · 48th · 54th Madison Avenue at 67th Street

At-home Evenings take on a festive air in rayon velvet spangled with gold and silver sequin motifs. Black, American beauty, royal blue, $125. Also of rayon crepe...brown, soldier blue, wine, black, $89.95. Third Floor

Henri Bendel 10 WEST 57 NEW YORK 19 N.Y.

MARY LEWIS 746 FIFTH at 57th ST.

TOTS' JUMPERS

a quartet of warm wool ones for the kindergarten set

Save laundry—keep your tots looking clean, neat, well dressed—with wool jumpers. Team with blouses or sweaters as the weather or occasion dictate. We offer an attractive quartet, in 100% wool flannel, sizes 3, 4, 5, 6. *A. With "waistcoat" belt.* Red, green, brown, navy. **3.95** *B. With set-in belt.* Navy, brown, green. **5.95** *C. With felt applique.* Green, gray, brown. **5.95** *D. With peasant braid trim.* Navy, brown, gray, green. **5.95**

Mail orders 15c extra. Sorry, none C. O. D.

TAILORED WOMAN

A Thought for Christmas—our Two-in-One Rain-or-Shine BUMBERSHOOT BAG In Plastic—Felt—or Faille

10.50 *plus 1.40 Fed. Tax*

She'll bless you for the thought come sudden showers—for with the first drop of rain, this cleverly functional "Two-in-One" Bumbershoot Bag opens to reveal a hidden umbrella in a secret, zippered compartment. For your "one and only"—your Mother—or your office staff . . . this is the gift that will earn you the reputation of "The Clever One". Black, brown, russet, navy or kelly green *Calf-like Plastic*—black, brown, navy, red or kelly pure *Wool Felt*—black, brown or navy rayon *Faille*.

Please state second choice of fabric or color when ordering by mail—no C.O.D's.

Tailored Woman EUGENE K. DENTON, PRES. 742 FIFTH AVE., AT 57th ST., NEW YORK 19, N. Y.

Silver in the Moonlight

Silvery nailheads lighting the way to a bright, busy season ...splashing moonlight on our wool peplum dress. Two pieces with a belt belittling your waist, and a discreet slit in the slim skirt. Aqua, black or grey, 9 to 15. 29.95

JUNIOR SHOP—FOURTH FLOOR

DE PINNA *Fifth Avenue at 52nd Street New York 19*

American True-Love THE TAILORED SUIT

Nothing takes the place of the good simple well-tailored suit in feminine American affections. Because the American man understands and approves it. Because it is no fickle fashion but one tried and true. Because its uses are manifold, depending on what you wear with.

We are happy to report that we have in stock a fine selection of British and American suits beautifully tailored in steadfast wools of splendid quality. Sizes 10 to 20 Prices $85 to $155. Third Floor

Elegant, says a Mink stole, with a plumy hat.

Worldly-wise, topped by a fur-faced beret, a crisp scarf.

Animated, plus a swagger umbrella, a swinging bag, a winged sailor.

BERGDORF GOODMAN ON THE PLAZA

DELMAN SHOES IN NEW YORK EXCLUSIVELY AT BERGDORF GOODMAN.

EXAMPLE 135

GIVE to the Red Cross

New Guide for Business Planners (p. 11)

THE FINANCIAL POST

The Canadian Newspaper for Businessmen and Investors

Vol. XXXIX | 10c. a Copy, $5.00 a Year | Publication Office: Toronto, March 3, 1945 | Member of Audit Bureau of Circulations | No. 9

The Nation's Business

What Are Tax Officers Doing to Farmers?

Socialists going "where the cream is."

Garson should stay where he is--for now.

Price Gains In U.S. May Aid Canada

Current Pressure for Adjustments Important to Raw Material Producers

By DWIGHT L. MOODY

TRADE PILOT

New president of the Toronto Board of Trade is Edward William Bickle, of the investment firm of Wills, Bickle & Co. Born (1890) and schooled in Toronto, he has actively supported the community's education (as treasurer of Victoria College), its charity (as president of Toronto's Hospital for Incurables) and its sports as well as its business. His business experience has been broad: he is at present chairman of the board, Sterling Rubber Co., president, Maple Leaf Gardens, vice-president Industrial Food Services, director, Canadian Food Products. To wartime problems he brings first-hand war knowledge: he left his newly-established business to enlist in 1914, went overseas with the first division, was gassed and wounded. In his new job he will face, on behalf of Toronto business generally, the already emerging postwar problems of business.

Provinces Help Build Machine To Distribute the Baby Bonus

Co-operate With Ottawa On Essential Parts of National Program Despite Verbal Opposition

By KENNETH R. WILSON

Ottawa's Slant on Provincial Co-operation

Here's Ont. Government Argument For Its New Securities Legislation

Co-ops Are Social Organ Claim of Quebec Groups

Novel Argument for Tax Exemption Advanced Before McDougall Probe by Quebec Superior Council of Co-operation

By GORDON L. SMITH

Won't Let Election Collide With Victory Loan, Belief

By STAFF WRITER

Less U. S. Steel for Canada But Cut Is Said Temporary

By STAFF WRITER

International Air Board To Get Revised Charter

Change in U. S.-U. K. Attitudes Opens Prospect of Change in Agreement Before the Permanent Organization is Launched

Sask. To Invade 'Where Cream Is'

McColl Given Tax Rebates

Pace of Business

Retail Sales Rise

EXAMPLE 136

Engineer in Insurance

St. Clair McEvenue, newly elected president of the Canada Life Assurance Co., is a mining engineer who found his destiny in the life insurance business. Graduating from McGill University in 1913, he soon changed. After extensive experience in life insurance underwriting and management, he joined Canada's oldest life insurance company as western supervisor in 1927. In 1929 he became assistant superintendent. In 1938 he was made general manager and a few months ago vice-president. A football star at McGill, he later coached the Toronto Argonauts to win the Dominion championship, after World War I. During it, he served overseas as a captain with a Montreal battalion and later with the Royal Flying Corps.

The Financial Post

The Canadian Newspaper for Businessmen and Investors

Vol. XL | Ten Cents an Issue, Five Dollars a Year | Publication Office: Toronto, March 23, 1946 | Member of Audit Bureau of Circulations | No. 12

'Orderly Retreat' Forecast From Fixed Price Ceilings

Steel, Farm Implements, Milk Expected to Go Up in Major Ceiling and Subsidy Overhaul — Rents and Installment Buying to Stay Frozen

By KENNETH R. WILSON

OTTAWA—(Staff)—The Government will shortly be advised that it must now face "an orderly retreat" from the present level of ceiling prices.

Here's what is looked for:

1. A boost in steel prices, followed by creeping advances in consumer durable goods.
2. Higher ceilings for farm implements.
3. Possible elimination of the consumer milk subsidy, followed by a one-point rise in the cost-of-living index.
4. No retreat on rent control or installment buying curbs.

Full extent of the "retreat" has not yet been determined. It will depend on timing and the government policy on subsidies. Every attempt will be made to maintain "order in the traffic" as Canadian prices are adjusted.

Demand Jumps For New Tires

With milder weather a marked increase in the demand for new passenger car tires has been noticed within the past week or so, dealers and distributors tell The Financial Post.

Nearly all tire sizes are available except some odd sizes although this varies between dealers so that it might be necessary to "shop around" to get a particular size. Inventories, while showing some improvement since the first of the year, are still reported not up to normal and likely to show a declining trend now. Dealers handling brands of manufacturers who make tires for new cars have been in an easier position due to the strikes in the automobile industry.

Additions To Loblaw Chain Seen

Renovation of Existing Premises Is Also Planned in $2.5 Millions Program Outlined

Ontario Moves to Ease Death Duty Regulations

Inside News

THE NATION'S BUSINESS

Tax Dictatorship Must Be Ended

It appears that Ottawa plans to throw away, on a tax case appeal to the Privy Council, a sizeable amount of money painfully supplied by much-taxed Canadians.

Cut Discretionary Powers

A Real Step Forward

Canadian-Built Power Plants to Help in China

Mass Building Plan Revived

Canada, U.K. Plan Income, Estates Tax Reciprocity

Clearer Will Is Advised When 'Strings' Attached

Citroen Seeks Sorel Plant? Has Not Approached Owners

Say Mining Union Demands Would Result In Sharply Curtailed Operations for Industry

By GORDON M. GRANT

Imperial Tobacco Plans Expansion

Pace of Business

EXAMPLE 137

carding certain clashing faces and using in place of them certain other faces already available in their plants.

A case in point is afforded by the *Financial Post* of Toronto.

In the spring of 1945 Douglas M. Gowdy, manager of the *Post*, and Ronald A. McEachern, editor, decided to make a critical study of their paper's format. And, as so often happens, they found it possible to make several decided improvements at virtually no cost at all. Better than that, the simplified production that accompanied the improved makeup helped to save time and money all along the production line.

At that time, as suggested by Example 136, the *Post* employed a nameplate that was inappropriate for an alert, forward-looking publication. The nameplate was old fashioned, clumsy looking, too heavy. Its black capitals dominated the page and thus tended to overshadow—to subdue—the headlines over even the most important front-page story. The paper's head dress mixed heavy sans serifs with lighter Bodonis—unrelated type faces that clashed with each other and marred the makeup. Its index of inside features was presented in the right ear on the front page, but uninvitingly. Despite its favored position, the earmatter was not so conspicuous as it deserved to be, and the individual type lines were too small for easy reading. And the *Post* regularly featured a two-column halftone in the upper center of the front page—a fixed position that worked against variety in makeup.

Mr. Gowdy visited the *Linotype News* with several copies of the *Post* and a list of the machine faces available in his plant.

It was soon determined that his composing room had enough members of the Bodoni family for an excellent head dress and need not install any additional display faces. It had enough sizes of Poster Bodoni for the contrast desired in certain parts of the makeup, and could get along without using in its head dress any of the clashing sans serifs.

So changes of the sort suggested by Example 137 were recommended by this writer.

Moving the regular two-column halftone from the upper center of the front page to the upper left gave the page a livelier beginning and greatly increased possibilities for variety in makeup from issue to issue. The main story on such a page may now be presented in anything from a six-column spread head on down to a single, and several other stories featured on the upper half of a page if desired.

A cap-and-lower line of Narciss cast on a Linotype was enlarged by

Post engravers to give the paper a modern nameplate—a nameplate truly representative of an up-to-the-minute publication fully aware of current trends and of future possibilities—and yet a nameplate with dignity and restraint. The new nameplate stands out clearly and readily identifies the paper for readers. Yet it does not keep the headlines from standing out as they should.

The ineffective index was dropped from the right ear and developed into an "Inside News" feature that gives the *Post* staff a front-page chance to sum up and "sell" important stories on inside pages.

Shortly after the new makeup was adopted, Mr. Gowdy wrote this writer: "The changes on page one have been very well received, both within the organization and without. The new nameplate, in upper-and-lower Narciss, has smartened the appearance of the paper substantially. 'Inside News' has already achieved a wide degree of popularity. In fact, it is a feature which we have been contemplating for some time, and the new page-one format provided a splendid opportunity to inaugurate this new feature. The picture-of-the-week seems much better placed in its new location, and offers much more variety in the way of makeup."

In the next chapter "before" and "after" editorial pages from the *Post* are illustrated and discussed.

16

Makeup of Other Pages

Extensive studies made in recent years of the reading habits of newspaper readers continue to suggest that men usually read more editorials than women, more comics, more financial news and more sports news, and that women read more radio programs and news, more society news, more amusement advertising and, in fact, more advertising of all sorts—national, local, department-store, classified—than men.

Since July of 1939 the Advertising Research Foundation of the Association of National Advertisers and the American Association of Advertising Agencies, in co-operation with the Bureau of Advertising of the American Newspaper Publishers' Association, has been conducting a series of field studies of many daily newspapers in the United States and Canada. The studies are based on personal interviews with readers of those papers—interviews carried on for the Advertising Research Foundation by the Publication Research Service of Chicago.

An individual report on each newspaper thus studied has been presented in a booklet entitled *The Continuing Study of Newspaper Reading.*

At this writing, more than one hundred daily newspapers, large and small, have been studied and as many individual reports issued.

When five years of *The Continuing Study* had been completed, the Advertising Research Foundation issued a summary of the studies of seventy-two dailies that had been made—seventy-two dailies that ranged in size from eighteen to fifty-six pages, and in circulation from 8570 to more than 250,000, with a combined circulation of 5,777,639. The conclusions in that summary, the Advertising Research Foundation stated, "are based upon 31,704 interviews with adult men and women eighteen years and older."

It is not the purpose here to quote extensively from that summary, which discussed in detail, with many tables and charts, "Reading by Type of Content," "Wartime Reading *Vs.* Prewar Reading," "Reading by Occupational Groups," "Readership Results by Position," "National

Advertising," "Local Advertising," "Continuing Features," and so on.

But a few quotations from that summary should be of interest to many readers of this book:

"Since the inception of these studies, it has been shown repeatedly that to the vast majority of readers the advertising columns are an extremely important part of the newspaper. The median readership percentage for those who read some advertising is eighty per cent for men—third only to the comics and the editorial page. For women, the median readership percentage of ninety-five for advertising exceeds any of the editorial departments. . . .

"Practically every reader reads something in all sections of his daily newspaper.

"The median readership percentage for 2282 pages (regardless of the type of page) is sixty per cent for men and seventy per cent for women. The median readership percentage for 1065 general-news pages which also carried advertising is sixty-three per cent for men and seventy-two per cent for women. . . .

"Additional studies have not changed the conclusion made in the previous summaries that left- and right-hand pages are equally well read. Position on a left-hand page *versus* position on a right-hand page still does not appear to be a factor in influencing readership. . . .

"The picture pages and good society and sports pictures continue to command large audiences. Comics, cartoons and well-done news stories are also high on the list of well-read features. The median for seventy-two best read news stories for men is sixty-eight per cent; for women sixty-three per cent. War stories are far more interesting to men than to women. . . . It is evident that women prefer local news to the war and battle stories."

In December of 1946, after seven years of *The Continuing Study* had been completed, the Advertising Research Foundation issued a summary of the studies of one hundred newspapers that had been made—a summary that made it possible to compare prewar, wartime and postwar reading habits of newspaper readers.

A story about that summary released for publication December 6, 1946, included the following statements:

"During the war, both men and women paid more attention to editorials, editorial-page items and classified advertising than they did in the prewar era. There also was a wartime increase in women's readership of national advertising. But their averages for readership of other editorial and advertising departments either remained static or dropped below the averages compiled during the prewar years.

"Since the end of the war, the sharpest increases in readership percentages have been recorded for department-store advertising and society items. Men's readership of department-store ads has increased eighteen percentage points over the wartime figure, while women's has risen eight percentage points. Similarly, male readership of society items has advanced twelve percentage points over the wartime average, while that of women is up six percentage points in the postwar studies.

"Men prefer front-page national and international news, while women strongly favor local stories and will shop through the inside of the paper for news items which are of interest to them.

"And readers like pictures. Picture pages and outstanding news photos have consistently drawn high attention, even topping the readership of best read news stories. Human-interest, crime and national-defense pictures have won highest attention.

"As might be expected, society news and pictures command high attention among women, as do sports news and photos among men. But local sports columnists get higher male readership than sports stories, and personal items on the society pages outpull best read society stories among women.

"More men than women read editorials and editorial pages. What may be surprising is the fact that editorial pages and comics hold a slight edge over sports pages among male readers. With women, top attention is given to society items—with editorial pages and comics strong runners-up.

"Editorial cartoons are the most popular continuing feature among men. Women give most attention to gag-line humor panels, although editorial cartoons rank a close second in popularity.

"Next to editorial cartoons, men are attracted by oddities and humor panels, comics, the weather, and local sports columnists. But among women the next best read features are deaths, comics, humor panels with balloons, oddities panels, and the weather. About half the women read advice to the lovelorn.

"Among columnists, competition is keen for top readership honors —particularly among local, New York and political writers.

"Humor panels of both the balloon and gag-line types show they can give comic strips a run for their money. Averages for best read humor panels compare most favorably with those for best read comics."

It would be possible here to illustrate many effective editorial, feature, woman's and society pages, as well as many effective sports, financial and radio pages; but it seems more advisable to devote the available space to a discussion of the fundamental principles of makeup for such pages, and to show only a few pages or parts of pages.

Editorial Pages

In these days, when the average newspaper reader has less time for reading than formerly—when he does more glimpsing than reading, and confines most of that glimpsing to the headlines and leading news stories or entertaining features—he has less time for the reading of newspaper editorials. If his attention is to be captured and held by the editorial page, that page must be unusually attractive physically. It must be even more inviting looking than the general-news pages, and even easier to read.

True it is that the number of editorial readers is greater now than it was before World War II, for the war, with its many important news stories written from different and often-conflicting points of view, caused more people to look to editorials for explanations and interpretations not to be found in the news stories themselves.

Habit, of course, is a strong thing, and that habit formed in war days has been carried over to the present by many people who paid little or no attention to editorials before 1939.

But many more editorial readers could be attracted by more attractive editorial pages or easier-to-find and easier-to-read editorials.

There are several ways of making the editorial page of a newspaper attractively different in appearance from the other pages, no matter how physically attractive those others may be.

One popular way of doing this is by using fewer columns on the page, with some of the columns wider than others and in larger faces.

Many newspapers—particularly small-town papers—make the mistake of setting editorials (and other feature matter on their editorial pages) in lines that are too wide for the sizes of type used. Comparatively small type faces are designed for use in comparatively narrow measures. Comparatively wide measures call for the use of larger faces.

While an 8-point face, say, is appropriate for a single-column width, the same face is too small for a measure two columns wide or wider. Comparatively wide lines set in comparatively small faces are difficult to read.

Generous leading would help some, but usually not enough.

Newspapers that now present editorials (and certain feature matter) in 8-point faces or smaller in lines two columns wide would do better to employ larger faces or to decrease the column width.

Newspapers that do not wish to increase the type size, but want their editorial columns to be at least a little wider than the regular news and feature columns, can secure attractive effects by converting three regular columns into two columns from 17 to 19 picas in width, or four regular columns into three columns 16 picas or so wide, or by employing other column breakups.

Some eight-column papers employ seven columns of equal width on their editorial pages; others employ six, and others five.

Some papers employ one double column, in larger type, along with six regular-width columns; others employ two doubles, in larger type, along with four regulars, and still others employ other combinations.

Some tabloid papers that present five columns on most of their pages present four columns of equal width on their editorial pages; others present three.

Still other tabloids present one double, in larger type, along with three regular-width columns, or two doubles, in larger type, separated by a single column.

Many papers that accept advertising for editorial pages employ regular-width columns on the right half of the pages to accommodate such advertising without resetting, even when wider columns are employed on the left half.

More and more newspapers are separating the columns on their editorial pages with generous strips of white space, or with wider shouldered rules, instead of regular-width rules. And wisely so, because such treatments give the pages a more open and more inviting appearance.

However, many papers that accept advertising for editorial pages, separate advertisements from editorials and from each other with regular-width column rules even when they employ strips of white instead of rules to separate other columns at the left on the pages.

Some positive opinions concerning editorials were expressed by the improvement committee of the Weekly Newspaper Bureau of the National Editorial Association in a report made to the Association in the summer of 1946. Composing the committee were A. Edwin Larsson, editor of the *Wellesley* (Mass.) *Townsman;* Walter D. Allen, publisher of the *Brookline* (Mass.) *Chronicle*, and William W. Loomis, publisher of the *La Grange* (Ill.) *Citizen.*

"Every newspaper," they stated, "should have an editorial column —if not an editorial page. It is a sad reflection on many weekly publishers (and some small dailies) that they do not carry *any* editorials. Hardly more than thirty per cent of the weekly newspapers throughout the country have an editorial page. Even among those that do, there is an increasing tendency toward the use of 'canned' editorials furnished free and written by some hack writer who knows nothing of local conditions or problems.

"It is said that if we don't stand for something, we'll fall for anything. Newspaper editors, and the columns of their papers, serve as the 'mouthpiece' of their communities. Some editors are not qualified to write good editorials; some insist that they haven't the time; others are afraid of giving offense and endeavor to play safe by expressing no opinions on local, state or national issues. This is a great mistake.

"Editorials give character to a newspaper and develop greater reader interest. Even the readers who do not agree with the views expressed respect an editor who has opinions and presents them clearly and fairly. The day has gone when editors can tell their readers what to do or how to vote; but they can stimulate interest in local issues. One column of home-made editorials, even those not so well written, is better than two or three columns of 'filler' editorials sent in to beat the drums for an outside cause."

Some papers continue to use on editorial and feature pages, or recently have gone in for, many display initial letters.

On certain forms of printing, display initials serve a useful purpose, the chief of which often is the breaking up of long and otherwise unrelieved "stretches of gray."

But an average editorial or feature page usually contains many heads and comparatively few long "stretches of gray." And on such a page display initials often not only are superfluous; they actually compete with the headlines.

Example 138 suggests a treatment of the sort employed on many an editorial page.

announced shortly before evening, and that all other plans would be held in abeyance until the main plan was working properly.

HERE THEY COME!

FOR several days now the ducks and geese have been arriving from the North, and already many local hunters have reported good bags of mallards and pintails.

EXAMPLE 138

Note that the headline there not only has to compete with the superfluous oxford-rule dash but with a display initial.

As the head is the thing to be emphasized, why not emphasize it and rid it of competition?

In Example 139 the head has been set in capitals and lower-case of a larger type face, the dash has been replaced by white space, and the display initial is absent. And note how much more effectively the editorial has been introduced.

announced shortly before evening, and that all other plans would be held in abeyance until the main plan was working properly.

Here They Come!

For several days now the wild ducks and geese have been arriving from the North, and already many local hunters have reported bags of mallards, pintails and teal.

EXAMPLE 139

In the spring of 1945, when Douglas M. Gowdy, manager of the *Financial Post* of Toronto, and Ronald A. McEachern, editor of that paper, decided to improve the format of the *Post*, and Mr. Gowdy visited the *Linotype News* with copies of the paper, the *Post* had an editorial page like the one suggested by Example 140.

It was a page above the average, but its four largest head treatments wasted space and employed rather heavy black dots ("cannon balls") that actually competed with—worked against—the heads they were supposed to enhance.

(As the *Post* had in its plant many members of the Bodoni type family, this writer suggested that an attractive revision of the page could be brought about by the use of certain of those Bodonis in place of certain others, and that no new display faces would be necessary.)

The head at the upper left, "The Editorial Page," by far the largest on the page, seemed superfluous at best, as other elements on the page clearly identified it as an editorial page. So the suggestion was offered that that head be eliminated in favor of a double-column head over the leading editorial, thus switching the emphasis from a mere label line to the leading article on the page.

The suggestion was offered, also, that the makeup be simplified by continuing the three wider columns to the bottom of the page, instead of interrupting them with the four narrower columns, and that one of the wider columns be shifted to the extreme right, for variety and to give the cartoon an inside position and thus the top of the page a more interesting and effective breakup.

The additional suggestion was offered that the resetting of the comparatively large department heads in smaller sizes of Poster Bodoni and Poster Bodoni Italic would give those heads plenty of emphasis and at the same time save considerable space.

And it seemed advisable to do away with all "30" dashes in favor of white space.

The suggestions were applied by Manager Gowdy and Editor McEachern, with the result that the *Financial Post* started turning out more attractive editorial pages than before—pages of the sort suggested by Example 141.

Note how the simplified makeup has improved the page.

The portrait cuts might well be somewhat smaller than they are, from issue to issue. And the consequently wider lines alongside the smaller cuts would make possible better spacing of those lines, from issue to issue.

Soon after the new makeup was adopted, Mr. Gowdy wrote this writer, in the same letter referred to in Chapter 15 of Part I of this book: "The editorial page looks much better, in our judgment, following the recent changes. The deletion of the large heading 'The Editorial Page' running across three wide columns has permitted us to put

Page 6 THE FINANCIAL POST Feb. 3, 1945

The Editorial Page . .

Let's Hear Public Opinion On This

Gadgets Won't Do the Trick

Labors' Responsibility

Choosing the Right Business

"ONE VERY UNPOPULAR GUY"

Cartoon by Gassick

The Postwar World . . .

In this department The Financial Post notes current comment, opinion and research on the world that will face us after the war has been won.

A Free Press in a Free World

Post-Scripts . . . .

He Hunts Industry

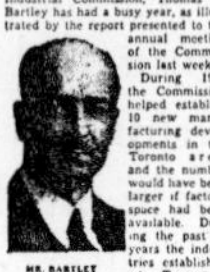

MR. BARTLEY

Leather, Bagpipe and Pigs

MR. STEWART

Heads Biggest Trade Board

MR. COTTERELL

The Financial Post

Other Peoples' Views . . . .

The Canadian Editorial of the Week

The CCF and Profits

Winnipeg Free Press

As Others See Us . .

Action at Long Last

Hamilton Review

Watch Tourist Opportunities

Huntsville Forester

Municipalities' Postwar Needs

Elora (Ont.) Express

What The Papers Say

Industrial Education at UBC

Vancouver Sun

Light Drinkers

Windsor Star

Why Milk is 10c.

Ottawa Citizen

Sayings of the Week

Stop Me If . . . . .

EXAMPLE 140

The Editorial Page

Can We Afford This Sacrifice?

When the auto salesman starts calling on his prospect list this summer he is likely to discover that there has been a vast change in buying habits since 1939. Old customers in the medium salaried class who used to buy a new car regularly every other season may have to be convinced that they can afford a new vehicle after waiting five years. And purveyors of radios, furniture, rugs, refrigerators and a score of other goods in the semiluxury class are going to meet the same resistance, because the "surplus" money that used to be available for such purchasing now largely goes to Mr. Ilsley and to meet the higher cost of necessities.

The story of what has happened to the $5,000 a year man since 1939 is told on page 13 of this issue of The Financial Post. Before the war he was able to meet his essential needs, food, clothing shelter, etc., for well under $3,000 in most parts of Canada.

To provide those same necessities over $4,000 must be spent today, and with his taxes up from five to ten times from pre-war it does not take a magician to discover where the balance of his present salary goes. To put it another way, where the $5,000 a year citizen had well over $2,000 left for such things as automobiles, travel, rugs and even necessities like insurance and pension fund in 1939 he now has less than $1,000. Many of the semiluxuries, too, like the food and shelter he must provide, would cost him much more than pre-war if he could get them.

The fact that there are now almost twice as many Canadians earning $5,000 a year as there were in 1919, and the same proportion would hold for the $3,000 and $4,000 citizens too, makes no difference. Sharply higher taxes and an increase of more than 20% in the bare necessities of life has drained away the bulk of the surplus purchasing power of the medium salaried classes.

Not only is there a direct threat of the loss of one of our most important markets for durable and semiluxury goods, but we also risk losing a vital testing field for the introduction of new goods.

It was the $5,000 a year man who bought the first commercial automobiles, the first radios, the better houses and the better furniture. The market he provided permitted the manufacturer to get into larger and lower cost production, to open a broader mass market, and thus new work creating industries were established and expanded. If the wartime sacrifice of the salaried man's standard of living is to become permanent, then the whole country loses with him.

The Farmer and the Income Tax

The Alberta Wheat Pool Budget, a pamphlet issued by the Alberta Wheat Pool, says that The Financial Post is the "guilty one" responsible for the income collection drive among farm communities of western Canada.

Full tribute to the powers of The Post is paid as follows:

Need Leadership in Food Drive

For More Builders

These WAC Bonfires

Give the Tourist a Break

Stop Me If —

Post Scripts

Heads Big Drug Firm

MR. LESLIE

Rhodes Scholar Labor Minister

MR. ARNOLD

MR. SMITH

Up Through Grain Trade

HOW THAT PUP HAS GROWN SINCE 1940

—Cartoon by Grassick

Batteries Damaged to Sell as Scrap?

WAC Charged With Destroying Saleable and Needed Equipment

The Official Version

What Others Are Saying

Editorial of the Week

Rewrite Whole Income Tax

Winnipeg Free Press

Other People's Views

The Financial Post

EXAMPLE 141

punch into the leading editorial. Other changes have resulted in the deletion of unattractive 'cannon balls' at several points on the page, and more effective use of the available space."

One of many modern editorial pages worked out in the typographic laboratory of the *Linotype News*—a page employing sans-serif faces—is suggested by Example 142.

Note that the main editorial was presented prominently at the upper left on the page, and that space for the masthead was provided at the lower left—an arrangement that might well be followed by many a paper that presents its masthead at the upper left, to the disadvantage of leading editorials.

Body matter of the first three columns (each 15½ picas wide, with a full pica of white space between each of them and the first column rule) was in 10-point Corona leaded 2 points. Body matter of the four narrower (12-pica) columns was in 7½-point Corona on a 9-point body. Heads were in 36-, 18- and 14-point Metromedium No. 2 Italic and 24- and 14-point Metromedium No. 2.

Typographically, the page was kept simple throughout. Nothing fancy or complicated about it. And observe how inviting it is, and how easy to read.

At a meeting of the American Society of Newspaper Editors, in Washington, D. C., in April of 1940, the late Douglas C. McMurtrie of the Ludlow Typograph Company had the following to say about editorials:

"I was out in an Ohio city a while ago, and a publisher said to me, almost with tears in his eyes, or his voice, 'We spend so much time and effort writing editorials and people never read them.'

"I looked at him in amazement and said, 'Do you want people to read your editorials?'

"He said, 'Yes, indeed we do.'

" 'Well,' I said, 'why don't you take advantage of some of the typographic resources of your paper to get those editorials read?'

"That was something that he had never given any thought to. That is something I think all of us can learn from Mr. Hearst. You know when he writes a statement or has written a statement he wants read rather widely, it is not set in 7 point on page eight. It is set in 14 point two columns wide and leaded on page one.

The Paths Ahead Are Marked

News arrives from the edge of town that the cold, wet weather, which has annoyed bees and butterflies and made early flaunters of straw hats feel foolish, has been greeted by our outlying bird populations with what disgruntled suburbanites have thought was unnecessary enthusiasm. For a suburbanite, attached painfully to a lawn mower and straining to keep up with rain-boosted grass seed, is not, one hears, entirely in tune with the serene carols of an evening robin or the careless trills of a song sparrow.

It is at the end of a shower that birds are particularly vocal, our rural correspondent has noticed. This, he rather surprisingly declares, seems to be mostly a matter of joy over an increase in the local food supply. For any nestwife with a hungry family is free to exercise her own ability in rustling red meat. Rain, of course, our observer asserts, brings the early worm earlier to the surface, resulting, with nature's nice balance, in supply equaling demand and hymns of joy following the happy process.

Unfortunately, cold rains and time and a half at the lawn mower have no such melodic effects upon the suburbanite. But they do increase his appetite. And showers that have encouraged cabbage plants in Victory gardens have not increased the supply of T-bone steaks in our markets. The result, then, has been that robins have been growing fatter and more cheerful during the last wet weeks, while our correspondent has glumly been eating tripe, kidney stew and something dubbed veal tongue with sauce piquante—none of which, he feelingly states, is conducive to gustatory paeans.

News arrives from the edge of town that the cold, wet weather, which has annoyed bees and butterflies and made early flaunters of straw hats feel foolish, has been greeted by our outlying bird populations with what disgruntled suburbanites have thought was unnecessary enthusiasm. For a suburbanite, attached painfully to a lawn mower and straining to keep up with rain-boosted grass seed, is not, one hears, entirely in tune with the serene carols of an evening robin or the careless trills of a song sparrow.

It is at the end of a shower that birds are particularly vocal, our rural correspondent has noticed. This, he rather surprisingly declares, seems to be mostly a matter of joy over an increase in the local food supply. For any nestwife with a hungry family is free to exercise her own ability in rustling red meat. Rain, of course, our observer asserts, brings the early worm earlier to the surface, resulting, with nature's nice balance, in supply equaling demand and hymns of joy following the happy process.

Unfortunately, cold rains and time and a half at the lawn mower have no such melodic effects upon the suburbanite. But they do increase his appetite. And showers that have encouraged cabbage plants in Victory gardens have not increased the supply of T-bone steaks in our markets. The result, then,

meat. Rain, of course, our observer asserts, brings the early worm earlier to the surface, resulting, with nature's nice balance, in supply equaling demand and hymns of joy following the happy process.

Unfortunately, cold rains and time and a half at the lawn mower have no such melodic effects upon the suburbanite. But they do increase his appetite. And showers that have encouraged cabbage plants in Victory gardens have not increased the supply of T-bone steaks in our markets. The result, then, has been that robins have been growing fatter and more cheerful during the last wet weeks, while our correspondent has glumly been eating tripe, kidney stew and something dubbed veal tongue with sauce piquante—none of which, he feelingly states, is conducive to gustatory paeans.

It is at the end of a shower that birds are particularly vocal, our rural correspondent has noticed. This, he rather surprisingly declares, seems to be mostly a matter of joy over an increase in the local food supply. For any nestwife with a hungry family is free to exercise her own ability in rustling red meat. Rain, of course, our observer asserts, brings the early worm earlier to the surface, resulting, with nature's

For Open Mindedness

News arrives from the edge of town that the cold, wet weather, which has annoyed bees and butterflies and made early flaunters of straw hats feel foolish, has been greeted by our outlying bird populations with what disgruntled suburbanites have thought was unnecessary enthusiasm. For a suburbanite, attached painfully to a lawn mower and straining to keep up with rain-boosted grass seed, is not, one hears, entirely in tune with the serene carols of an evening robin or the careless trills of a song sparrow.

It is at the end of a shower that birds are particularly vocal, our rural correspondent has noticed. This, he rather surprisingly declares, seems to be mostly a matter of joy over an increase in the local food supply. For any nestwife with a hungry family is free to exercise her own ability in rustling red meat. Rain, of course, our observer asserts, brings the early worm earlier to the surface, resulting, with nature's nice balance, in supply equaling demand and hymns of joy following the happy process.

Unfortunately, cold rains and time and a half at the lawn mower have no such melodic effects upon the suburbanite. But they do increase his appetite. And showers that have encouraged cabbage plants in Victory gardens have not increased the supply of T-bone steaks in our markets. The result, then, has been that robins have been growing fatter and more cheerful during the last wet weeks, while our correspondent has glumly been eating tripe, kidney stew and something dubbed veal tongue with sauce piquante—none of which, he feelingly states, is conducive to gustatory paeans.

Unfortunately, cold rains and time and a half at the lawn mower have no such melodic effects upon the suburbanite. But they do increase his appetite. And showers that have encouraged cabbage plants in Victory gardens have not increased the supply of T-bone steaks in our markets. The result, then, has been that robins have been grow-

Local Administrator

News arrives from the edge of town that the cold, wet weather, which has annoyed bees and butterflies and made early flaunters of straw hats feel foolish, has been greeted by our outlying bird populations with what disgruntled suburbanites have thought was unnecessary enthusiasm. For a suburbanite, attached painfully to a lawn mower and straining to keep up with rain-boosted grass seed, is not, one hears, entirely in tune with the serene carols of an evening robin or the careless trills of a song sparrow.

It is at the end of a shower that birds are particularly vocal, our rural correspondent has noticed. This, he rather surprisingly declares, seems to be mostly a matter of joy over an increase in the local food supply. For any nestwife with a hungry family is free to exercise her own ability in rustling red meat. Rain, of course, our observer asserts, brings the early worm earlier to the surface, resulting, with nature's nice balance, in supply equaling demand and hymns of joy following the happy process.

Unfortunately, cold rains and time and a half at the lawn mower have no such melodic effects upon the suburbanite. But they do increase his appetite. And showers that have encouraged cabbage plants in Victory gardens have

We Stand Together

News arrives from the edge of town that the cold, wet weather, which has annoyed bees and butterflies and made early flaunters of straw hats feel foolish, has been greeted by our outlying bird populations with what disgruntled suburbanites have thought was unnecessary enthusiasm. For a suburbanite attached painfully to a lawn mower and straining to keep up with rain-boosted grass seed, is not, one hears, entirely in tune with the serene carols of an evening robin or the careless trills of a song sparrow.

It is at the end of a shower that birds are particularly vocal, our rural correspondent has noticed. This, he rather surprisingly declares, seems to be mostly a matter of joy over an increase in the local food supply. For any nestwife with a hungry family is free to exercise her own ability in rustling red meat. Rain, of course, our observer asserts, brings the early worm earlier to the surface, resulting with nature's nice balance, in supply equaling demand and hymns of joy following the happy process.

Unfortunately, cold rains and time and a half at the lawn mower have no such melodic effects upon the suburbanite. But they do increase his appetite. And showers that have encouraged cabbage plants in Victory gardens have not increased the supply of T-bone steaks in our markets. The result, then, has been that robins have been growing fatter and more cheerful during the last wet weeks, while our correspondent has glumly been eating tripe, kidney stew and something dubbed veal tongue with sauce piquante—none of which, he feelingly states, is conducive to gustatory paeans.

News arrives from the edge of town that the cold, wet weather, which has annoyed bees and butterflies and made early flaunters of straw hats feel foolish, has been greeted by our outlying bird populations with what disgruntled suburbanites have thought was unnecessary enthusiasm. For a suburbanite, attached painfully to a lawn mower and

MASTHEAD

IN THIS

POSITION

has been that robins have been growing fatter and more cheerful during the last wet weeks, while our correspondent has glumly been eating tripe, kidney stew and something dubbed veal tongue with sauce piquante—none of which, he feelingly states, is conducive straining to keep up with rain-boosted grass seed, is not, one hears, entirely in tune with the serene carols of an evening robin or the careless trills of a song sparrow.

We Strongly Protest

News arrives from the edge of town that the cold, wet weather, which has annoyed bees and butterflies and made early flaunters of straw hats feel foolish, has been greeted by our outlying bird populations with what disgruntled suburbanites have thought was unnecessary enthusiasm. For a suburbanite, attached painfully to a lawn mower and straining to keep up with rain-boosted grass seed, is not, one hears, entirely in tune with the serene carols of an evening robin or the careless trills of a song sparrow.

It is at the end of a shower that birds are particularly vocal, our rural correspondent has noticed. This, he rather surprisingly declares, seems to be mostly a matter of joy over an increase in the local food supply. For any nestwife with a hungry family is free to exercise her own ability in rustling red meat. Rain, of course, our observer asserts, brings the early worm earlier to the surface, resulting, with nature's nice balance, in supply equaling demand and hymns of joy following the happy process.

Unfortunately, cold rains and time and a half at the lawn mower have no such melodic effects upon the suburbanite. But they do increase his appetite. And showers that have encouraged cabbage plants in Victory gardens have not increased the supply of T-bone steaks in our markets. The result, then, has been that robins have been growing fatter and more cheerful during the last wet weeks, while our correspondent has glumly been eating tripe, kidney stew and something dubbed veal tongue with sauce piquante—none of which, he feelingly states, is conducive to gustatory paeans.

News arrives from the edge of town that the cold, wet weather, which has annoyed bees and butterflies and made early flaunters of straw hats feel foolish, has been greeted by our outlying bird populations with what disgruntled suburbanites have thought was unnecessary enthusiasm. For a suburbanite, attached painfully to a lawn mower and straining to keep up with rain-boosted grass seed, is not, one hears, entirely in tune with the serene carols of an

Basic Conflict of Policy

It is at the end of a shower that birds are particularly vocal, our rural correspondent has noticed. This, he rather surprisingly declares, seems to be mostly a matter of joy over an increase in the local food supply. For any nestwife with a hungry family is free to exercise her own ability in rustling red

The Eyes Have It—Today and Every Day in the Week

What Some of Our Readers Think

Hazing the Press

The statement came as a welcome surprise to most of the non-medical delegates, representing labor, farmers' groups and other lay organizations interested in medical care from the public's point of view. It had been generally believed here that the national health program outlined yesterday at the conference by the government's Technical Committee on Medical Care, calling for additional expenditures of $850 000 000 a year for a ten-year period, half to be contributed by the American Medical Association.

Dr Abell's statement followed a plea for "a spirit of cooperation and constructive service" offered by Dr F L Bishop, executive secretary of the interdepartmental committee, who presided at this morning's session.

Dr Bishop assured the conference that the program and the recommendations presented yesterday were not final but were open to suggestions and amendments.

Before calling on the first scheduled speaker Dr Bishop recognized Dr Abell who spoke as follows:

The statement came as a welcome surprise to most of the non-medical delegates representing labor farmers' groups and other lay organizations interested in medical nate Health and Welfare Activities heard this morning a dramatic statement by Dr Irvin Abell president care from the public's point of view. It had been generally believed here that the national health

Downstream Classic

"The officials of the American Medical Association come to this meeting at the express instructions of its House of Delegates. We come not imbued with a controversial spirit but with a determination to give this conference our very best thought, our experience and the information which has been accumulated in our bureaus through the years that have passed since the organization of the American Medical Association.

"The heads of our technical departments are here, carrying with them the information which we have in our files and which we will gladly place at the disposal of this conference.

"You may rest assured that in any of the efforts which you make for betterment in the health care of the people of this country you have our whole-hearted cooperation. We shall be most glad and most happy to give our services to heard this morning a dramatic tional Health Conference being dent of the American Medical Association, assuring the conference of the organized medicine's "wholeheld by the President's Interdepartmental Committee to Coordi-

In Rebuttal

The statement came as a welcome surprise to most of the non-medical delegates representing labor farmers' groups and other lay organizations interested in medical care from the public's point of conference by the government's

"On behalf of the interdepartmental committee we accept."

The statement came as a welcome surprise to most of the non-medical delegates, representing labor farmers' groups and other lay organizations interested in medical care from the public's point of view. It had been generally believed here that the national health program outlined yesterday at the conference by the government's Technical Committee on Medical ditures of $850.000.000 a year for a

give this conference our very best not imbued with a controversial spirit but with a determination to thought our experience and the information which has been accu- program outlined yesterday at the conference by the government's hearted cooperation in any of the efforts which you make for betterment in health care of the people of this country."

The statement came as a welcome surprise to most of the non-medical delegates, representing labor, farmers' groups and other lay organizations interested in medical care from the public's point of view. It had been generally believed here that the national health program outlined yesterday at the conference by the government's Technical Committee on Medical Care, calling for additional expen- most happy to give our services to ditures of $850 000 000 a year for a ten-year period, half to be contributed by the American Medical Association.

Captions of Captions

Dr Abell's statement followed a plea for "a spirit of cooperation and constructive service" offered by Dr F L Bishop executive secretary of the interdepartmental committee, who presided at this suggestions and amendments.

Dr Bishop assured the conference that the program and the recommendations presented yesterday were not final but were open to morning's session.

Before calling on the first scheduled speaker, Dr Bishop recognized Dr Abell, who spoke as follows:

"The officials of the American Medical Association come to this meeting at the express instructions of its House of Delegates. We come not imbued with a controversial spirit but with a determination to give this conference our very best

Before calling on the first scheduled speaker Dr Bishop recognized of this country."

"The officials of the American Medical Association come to this meeting at the express instructions of its House of Delegates. We come thought, our experience and the information which has been accumulated in our bureaus through the years that have passed since the organization of the American Medical Association.

"The heads of our technical departments are here, carrying with them the information which we have in our files and which we will

'I Love Thee, But—!'

The statement came as a welcome surprise to most of the non-medical delegates, representing labor, farmers' groups and other lay organizations interested in medical care from the public's point of view. It had been generally believed here that the national health program outlined yesterday at the conference by the government's Technical Committee on Medical Care, calling for additional expenditures of $850.000.000 a year for a ten-year period, half to be contributed by the American Medical As-

"You may rest assured that in any of the efforts which you make for betterment in the health care of the people of this country you have our whole-hearted cooperation. We shall be most glad and be of help to you in that respect.

"On behalf of the interdepartmental committee, we accept."

Dr Abell's statement followed a plea for "a spirit of cooperation and constructive service" offered by Dr F L Bishop, executive secretary of the interdepartmental program outlined yesterday at the

Black Is Not White

Dr Abell's statement followed a plea for "a spirit of cooperation and constructive service" offered by Dr F L Bishop, executive secretary of the interdepartmental committee, who presided at this morning's session.

Dr Bishop assured the conference that the program and the recommendations presented yesterday were not final but were open to suggestions and amendments.

Before calling on the first scheduled speaker Dr Bishop recognized of this country."

"The officials of the American Medical Association come to this meeting at the express instructions of its House of Delegates. We come not imbued with a controversial spirit but with a determination to give this conference our very best thought, our experience and the information which has been accumulated in our bureaus through the years that have passed since ten-year period, half to be contributed by the American Medical Association.

"The heads of our technical departments are here, carrying with hearted cooperation in any of the them the information which we have in our files and which we will gladly place at the disposal of this conference.

THE WEEK Here at Home

Fuel Supplies

FOUR

"The heads of our technical departments are here carrying with them the information which we have in our files and which we will gladly place at the disposal of this conference.

"You may rest assured that in tional Health Conference being held by the President's Interdepartmental Committee to Coordinate Health and Welfare Activities any of the efforts which you make for betterment in the health care of the people of this country you have our whole-hearted cooperation. We shall be most glad and

The statement came as a welcome surprise to most of the non-medical delegates representing labor, farmers' groups and other lay organizations interested in medical care from the public's point of view. It had been generally believed here that the national health

"You may rest assured that in any of the efforts which you make view. It had been generally befor betterment in the health care of the people of this country you have our whole-hearted cooperation. We shall be most glad and most happy to give our services to be of help to you in that respect.

New Buildings

Dr Bishop assured the conference that the program and the recommendations presented yesterday were not final but were open to Technical Committee on Medical Care calling for additional expenditures of $850 000 000 a year for a Technical Committee on Medical program outlined yesterday at the conference by the government's Technical Committee on Medical Care, calling for additional expenditures of $850,000,000 a year for a ten-year period, half to be contributed by the American Medical Asmental committee, we accept."

Dr Abell's statement followed a plea for "a spirit of cooperation Care calling for additional expenditures of $850,000,000 a year for a ten-year period, half to be contributed by the American Medical Association.

"On behalf of the interdepartditures of $850.000.000 a year for a

The statement came as a welcome surprise to most of the non-medical delegates, representing labor farmers' groups and other lay organizations interested in medical care from the public's point of

Car Loadings

Before calling on the first scheduled speaker, Dr Bishop recognized mulated in our bureaus through the years that have passed since the organization of the American Dr Abell who spoke as follows:

"The officials of the American Medical Association come to this meeting at the express instructions of its House of Delegates. We come not imbued with a controversial spirit but with a determination to

"The heads of our technical departments are here carrying with and constructive service" offered by Dr F L Bishop executive secretary of the interdepartmental committee, who presided at this morning's session them the information which we have in our files and which we will gladly place at the disposal of this conference.

SPOTLIGHTING THE NEWS

Dr Abell's statement followed a plea for "a spirit of cooperation and constructive service" offered not imbued with a controversial spirit, but with a determination to give this conference our very best thought, our experience and the information which has been accumulated in our bureaus through the years by Dr F L Bishop executive secretary of the interdepartmental committee who presided at this suggestions and amendments.

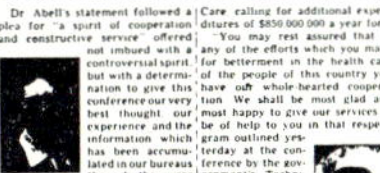

Dr Bishop assured the conference that the program and the recommendations presented yesterday were not final but were open to

Before calling on the first scheduled speaker Dr Bishop recognized Dr Abell, who spoke as follows:

"The officials of the American Medical Association come to this meeting at the express instructions medical delegates, representing labor farmers' group and other lay organizations interested in medical care from the public's point of view. It had been generally believed here that the national health pro- of its House of Delegates. We come not imbued with a controversial spirit but with a determination to give this conference our very best thought, our experience and the information which has been accu- have in our files and which we will gladly place at the disposal of this

"You may rest assured that in any of the efforts which you make for betterment in the health care of the people of this country you have our whole-hearted cooperation. We shall be most glad and most happy to give our services to Care, calling for additional expen- be of help to you in that respect.

"On behalf of the interdepart- Technical Committee on Medical

Care calling for additional expenditures of $850 000 000 a year for a

"You may rest assured that in any of the efforts which you make for betterment in the health care of the people of this country you have our whole-hearted cooperation. We shall be most glad and most happy to give our services to be of help to you in that respect gram outlined yesterday at the conference by the government's Technical Committee on Medical Care, calling for additional expenditures for a ten-year period, to be contributed by the American Med-

"On behalf of the interdepartmental committee, we accept."

The statement came as a welcome surprise to most of the non-medical delegates representing labor, farmers' groups and other lay organizations interested in medical care from the public's point of

The statement came as a welcome surprise to most of the non-medical delegates representing labor, farmers' groups and other lay organizations interested in medical care from the public's point of view. It had been generally be- You may rest astional Health Conference being held by the President's Committee to Coordinate Health and Welfare Activities heard this morning a dramatic statement by Dr Irvin Abell, president of

"The heads of our technical departments are here, carrying with them the information which we efforts which you make for betterment in health care of the people lieved here that the national health view It had been generally be- The statement came as a welcome surprise to most of the non-medical delegates, representing la-

EXAMPLE 142

"If you take any vital editorial and transfer it from normal type size and normal measure on page six or eight to a bigger type size across two columns on page one, a field study of watching people (not asking them, but watching them) would show that that editorial had something like twenty-five times as good a chance of being read."

For more on front-page editorials, see Chapter 5 in Part II of this book. And note the front-page editorial in Example 184.

When the lines of newspaper mastheads are left in the forms for several editions, some of the lines are likely to "thicken up" under repeated stereotyping pressure. And unless such lines are promptly replaced by new ones, they become increasingly difficult to read and mar the appearance of the editorial page as a whole.

When newspapers are printed from flatbed presses and masthead lines are left in the forms for several issues, some of the lines are likely to become ink-encrusted as well as worn or battered.

This writer often has urged newspaper makeup men to see to it that several sets of masthead lines are available at all times—that several recasts of each line be made and put aside each time a masthead is reset—and that a new set of lines be put into use every few issues or as soon as any of the lines fail to print clearly.

That still is good counsel, but the *Washington* (D. C.) *Post* goes it at least one better. The *Post* has its masthead lines *electrotyped*—and thus is able to run through many editions without resetting or replacing the lines.

The date line, of course, is outside of the electro—just below it—and can be changed as desired without interfering with any of the standing lines.

In most newspapers, editorial pages are left-hand pages, but some papers present them as front pages of second sections or as back pages. Many larger city papers present them on left-hand pages, with feature pages to the right of them.

Feature Pages

Many newspaper editors believe that attractive feature pages are decided assets to a paper. Some editors, particularly in smaller cities and towns, are convinced that attractive feature pages are more in-

MONDAY, MAR. 4, 1946

New York World-Telegram

SECOND SECTION

Tito Dictatorship

By Wm. Philip Simms

Simms

SHOWCASTING—Tricky Trade

At left, William Liebling and Audrey Wood read the script of a play, hoping that it may be one of those rare prizes, a hit. At the right, Julie Hayden and Eddie Dowling in a scene from "The Glass Menagerie."

Laurette Taylor—casting her as Amanda Wingfield is called a stroke of genius.

Even Experts Can Guess Wrong on Possible Hits

First of a Series

By DOUGLAS GILBERT

World-Telegram Staff Writer.

If you have a play in your trunk—and almost everyone has—there it is likely to stay. Unknown playwrights have little chance of getting a reading. The reason is more practical than stupid. Only one in a thousand amateur scripts are worthy and producers just haven't time to look for that needle.

Can't Be Analyzed.

Was Already Dead.

Now Has Success.

Kept Plugging.

Tomorrow: A Tricky Business.

Short Cut to Wealth

By Robert C. Ruark

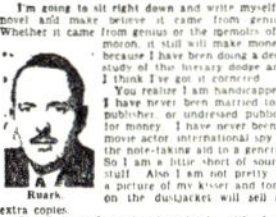

Ruark

The Plain People

By Thomas L. Stokes

Stokes

Charity at Home

By Frederick C. Othman

Othman

Navy Vets' Film Idea Makes Dull Study Fun

Four Films Possible.

Just Advertising.

Everybody Pleased.

METROPOLITAN MOVIES

"My husband had no excuse not to send me to Florida this year. He's making good money, my health is bad and, besides, I've already come."

3 More GI Writers Quit Army's Paper

EXAMPLE 143

The Sun

FRIDAY, MARCH 15, 1946.
NEW YORK.

23

THE SUN DIAL By H. I. Phillips

Pettigrew the Penguin on 'Silent Drama.'

Dear feathered friends

Todays topic is the silent drama and i dont mean the movies i mean the legitimate theater where the boys and girls talk low and keep the whole plot in confidence and a guy has to be a lip reader to know what is happening behind the footlights and this is what accounts for all those people you see in the theater today with those curious gadgets strapped over their ears period new paragraph

* * *

These theatergoers who are all wired for sound with dry batteries in their vests are not deaf at all they are just smart patrons of the drama who long ago gave up hope that the actors would start talking clearly and have made up their minds to use all the devices of science and sound engineers so as to get their moneys worth in the theater and personally i never go to a showhouse that i do not see a dozen or two of my friends with these new aids to hearing affixed to their domes and when i express surprise to find out they are deaf they fix me with a cold look and say quotes i am not deaf in fact my hearing is 100 per cent but 100 per cent hearing is no good in the american theater any more end quotes period new paragraph

* * *

Personally i think the lunts get such raves purely because they are among the few actors in the theater who can be heard without ear trumpets although alfred has a habit of turning his back on the cash customers holding his fist in front of his face and talking to his knuckles and even maurice evans gets pretty confidential in spots and i could name plenty of others who think the best lines in the show should be put over without using the larynx and in truckline cafe i never heard one word the leading lady said all evening so i thought the show was good period new paragraph

* * *

It cant be that all modern actors are born with quiet zone signs in their mouths so i guess the trouble must be with the directors and my belief is that these directors are not interested in making money in the theater but have their dough invested in these new electric gadgets for the deaf and i talked with a big manufacturer of these devices the other day and he said the biggest aid to his business was the modern actor youre for ear trumpets with every ticket.

Pettigrew.

Manhattan Speaks.

("City to ask 10 per cent tax on hotel bills."—News item.)

Oh, come and live a while with us,
A while in Gotham live;
We'll see you get a hotel room
And give and give and give!

The soul of hospitality—
That's us the whole world knows;
We'll put a welcome on the mat,
And you'll pay through the nose!

"Leo Durocher Trial Postponed Again."—*Headline.*

* * *

When that trial is finally held the most-used line will certainly be "Now let me refresh your recollection . . ."

Charles P. Gross, chairman of the New York Board of Transportation, says New York is dirtier than Paris, Moscow, Copenhagen and Brussels all put together. This is an understatement. New York is dirtier than all the towns of Tunisia rolled into one. But they were that way when Mr. O'Dwyer got 'em. You can't clean streets by microphone.

"I have an antique wooden fan that I will swop for a balsam pillow. Conn. M904."—*Yankee Magazine.*

* * *

Down with the strenuous life!

Can You Remember—

Away back when anybody with fair eyesight could tell the difference between a $5,000 one-family house and a $125 chicken coop?

I hear they'll make a sequel to "Lost Weekend" titled "Long Time, No Seagram!" says Herb Shriner.

The alacrity with which the restaurants of America took away the basket of bread and rolls set a new high for swift motion. It went over with the speed of light.

An old friend, Aaron Apsel, has just passed on back home. A man of dignity, standing and influence, he was so beloved that nobody ever spoke of him except as "Happy" Apsel. And at the services the officiating clergyman endowed him with an epitaph for which many of the earth's great would be glad to settle "A millionaire in friendships."

THESE DAYS By George E. Sokolsky

The Loan Agreement.

When Joseph P. Kennedy suggested that the United States make Great Britain a grant-in-aid rather than a loan, he bespoke honesty of purpose, for by no stretch of the imagination, even of politicians, is it possible to call the current transaction between these countries a loan.

For a loan involves an absolute assurance of a return. The lender assumes no risk at all. He takes into account the ability of the borrower to meet his obligations and should he find it inadequate or doubtful, he does not make the loan. He demands security to eliminate risk. The required security depends upon the degree of certainty of the ability of the borrower to repay. The lender wants not only a return of his money but a reward for its use by the borrower. This is interest. If the borrower's credit is poor, he charges a higher interest because whereas he invites no risk, an element of doubt has entered into the transaction. If the borrower's credit is good, the interest charge is likely to be less.

Lender Must Have Money.

But it is essential that the lender shall have the money to lend. That is altogether uncertain in this particular instance, for the lender, the United States, is heavily in debt, actually has to pay higher interest for the money it borrows from its own people than it is charging the British borrower. As a matter of fact, when Secretary of the Treasury Vinson was asked at a Senate committee hearing to elaborate what interest he thought the American government would have to pay to borrow the money to lend to the British, he did not answer. And when asked if some one else in the Treasury would discuss this subject, he said, "No."

All this makes this loan operation exceedingly unbusinesslike. In fact, the loan takes on the appearance of a grant-in-aid while being advertised as a loan. A curious document was issued by Fred M. Vinson, James F. Byrnes, Henry A. Wallace, M. S. Eccles, William McC. Martin Jr.—all of the National Advisory Council on International Monetary and Financial Problems—in which the point is made, in favor of the loan, that

". . . Such a situation has already arisen, for instance, with reference to railroad equipment, machine tools, power and transmission equipment, and certain types of general industrial machinery. This is also true for some of the metals, heavy chemicals, synthetic rubber, and other industrial materials. Similarly, we have quantities of cotton, tobacco and other agricultural products which are surplus to domestic needs. It is fortunate that this excess productive capacity is for many items which are most urgently needed by the war-devastated countries."

Shortage of Commodities.

Now, none of this is true. In fact, this country is frightfully short of these commodities. We are so short of railroad equipment that although the war has been over for months, it is still impossible to restore normal civilian transportation or to move agricultural products with essential rapidity. In spite of this lack of equipment, carloadings in the week of March 2 this year were only one per cent below a year ago when we were at war, which explains why transportation is so difficult.

As for machine tools, power and transmission equipment and industrial machinery, the shortages are so critical that the capital or consumers goods for which the entire country is weeping cannot be provided.

As for steel, the shortage is so keen that buyers practically stand on line to get their quotas. I recently tried to help a veteran who wanted to start a business of his own and bumped up personally and sharply against the shortage. Yet, this week, the American steel industry will produce 1,473,000 tons as compared with 1,731,000 tons a year ago.

I wonder if these great authorities would like to list the products of which there is an excess in this country or which we could afford to export right now. I should like to see some evidence of the excess, for instance, in cotton in the United States this week or last week or next week, in view of the shortage in shirts, underwear, cotton goods. Apparently this false argument is the best these men can do.

TODAY IN WASHINGTON By David Lawrence

World Crises Often Have Simple Solutions.

Washington, March 15.—The American people will have to get used to frequent crises in world affairs, and to the devious ways of power politics.

The assumption of the man on the street is that when two powerful nations happen to differ and there are big headlines about it in the press, it is an occasion for alarm or apprehension and that war is in the offing.

Actually, the situation precipitated by Russia is the direct result of the entrance of the United States into European affairs as pledged in the famous Yalta Conference in 1945. When the United States Government, through the action of the late President Roosevelt, promised to underwrite the peace of Europe and to engage in separate agreements with Britain and Russia relative to the setting up of new Governments in the Balkans and the Near East, this country acquired responsibilities it never before had to discharge.

Roosevelt's Aims.

The late President felt that, in the interest of preventing another world war, American participation in European matters was imperative. He hoped, of course, that the power politics of a Big Three setup would be superseded by the proceedings of the United Nations, but, unfortunately, Russia's insistence on the exercise of a veto power in the Security Council threw the whole problem back on the Big Three.

So today Great Britain, the United States and Russia are engaged in a long-range discussion on how to readjust the power of the world. The British have specific interests in preserving their empire and its lifeline to India through southern Europe and the Suez Canal. The Russians feel their newly won power and prestige and see no reason why Russia should not dominate Europe and the approaches to her territory in Asia.

Hitler had hoped to dominate Europe and failed. He thought Britain the real barrier to Germany's ambitions, and he hoped to put Russia out of the way as he fought. But when Hitler's efforts failed, this left Russia and Britain to struggle for the mastery of Europe.

America, as the single mediating influence without any direct interest in European territory, can perhaps hold the scales even. But many of the Soviet's actions are inscrutable and the United States Government is finding it increasingly difficult to reconcile Russia's professed interest in the peaceful methods of the United Nations Organization with the troop movements that always seem to precede her use of military pressure upon sovereign nations.

The reason why the Red Armies aren't being withdrawn on time from Iran probably is related to the Russian desire to place her troops strategically on the Turkish border so as to coerce Turkey. It is the Dardanelles and the Mediterranean which Russia is aiming at, rather than domination of Iran alone.

Russia Seeks Territory.

Russia wants control of as much territory and resources as she can get. She knows Britain today is powerless to stop her. Hence Moscow is quick to accuse Britain of being desirous of lining up America on the side of the British. That is why Churchill's speech was so bitterly denounced by the controlled press of Russia. A comparison of what Churchill really said about Russia with what Secretary Byrnes said in his address in New York a few days earlier indicates that the two men issued much the same warning about Russia's aggressive tendencies. Byrnes wasn't attacked by Moscow, though it is significant an effort is being made inside the United States—possibly traceable to certain left-wingers—to undermine the Secretary by putting out frequent rumors about his resignation which are without foundation.

Russia plays a peculiar game, but the American people will have to get accustomed to the Russian propaganda methods and the use of force and pressure against weaker countries.

Sooner or later the opportunity to deny Russia things she most needs will come to the United States Government as a trading point. There isn't a remote chance Russia will ever get the atom bomb secret from us. She will find it increasingly difficult to rehabilitate her own country, because she will have alienated the American people, who could be very helpful to her. Russia is losing friends inside America very rapidly and it may be that before long she will come to realize it and execute a complete reversal. Such somersaults also are to be expected as part of the devices of the communistic school of thought.

MINE OPERATORS ASK LEWIS TO MAKE CONTRACT

His Discourse on Health and Medical Service Called Filibuster.

KEEPS PAY DEMANDS SECRET

Owners Insist He 'Get Down to Business'—'Don't Stay,' Is His Retort to Them.

Washington, March 15 (A. P.).—John L. Lewis pressed a war of nerves today in his negotiations for a new wage contract for his 400,000 soft coal miners.

The chief of the United Mine Workers still refused to tip his hand on what specific demands he wants operators to meet, but he insisted on more talk about what he he calls unsatisfactory health and safety conditions prevailing in the industry. Operators called the extended discourse a filibuster.

Charles O'Neill, chairman of the Bituminous Coal Operators Negotiation Committee, said that Lewis, without any actual bargaining, had consumed 20 per cent of the time available for negotiating a contract before the April 1 dead line on the present agreement.

O'Neill Demands Action.

Asking Lewis to "get down to business and make a contract," O'Neill deplored what he termed the repetition of the same speeches by various district presidents.

Lewis reported: "That the operators consider it repetitious and boresome is a matter of no damned consequence to us at all."

"If you don't like it, don't stay," he told operators present.

Lewis said that the discussion of health and medical service available to miners was germane to his demand for creation of a miner's health and welfare fund by the operators.

He insisted "the terrible conditions in the mining industry" described by the succession of district presidents were proper matters for discussion of the national wage conference.

"We expect you to join in reform, whether you like it or whether you don't like it," he said.

Threatens April 1 Strike.

The mine leader has threatened to call a strike April 1 if a new contract has not been signed or an agreement reached to extend the present one.

The wage conference of operators and miners opened Tuesday and the U. M. W. has held the floor ever since for presentation of Lewis's arguments in support of the nine general demands. The operators plan to reply when he completes his case.

The verbal clash between the union leader and the operator chairman occurred late yesterday. It climaxed a day of speechmaking and the reading by Lewis of "an indictment" in which he said the industry "had made dead" 28,000 mine workers in the last fourteen years. He accused the industry of having "violently mangled, crushed and shattered the bodies" of 1,004,000 other mine workers.

VOTE CANVASS SERVES PURPOSE

San Diego, March 15 (A. P.).—Two world war II veterans—Kenneth Fountain and Ralph M. Shuck—volunteered to make a house to house canvass to register voters.

Armed with the registration books they started out, returning at intervals to the County Registrar of Voters' office for more books. Yesterday they brought their filled books in again.

"Do you want new ones?" asked Deputy Registrar Howard Gollohen.

"No, thank you," the veterans replied happily. "We accomplished our purpose—we both found houses to rent."

JEWS IN GALILEE CALL FOR STRIKE

Jerusalem, March 15 (A. P.).—Jewish settlers throughout most of Galilee called for a four-hour protest strike today in sympathy with a group of their countrymen who were prevented by British troops from establishing a new settlement near Birya.

The area where the new settlement was marked out was in the hands of British troops, and reinforcements were reported speeding by truck to Birya to prevent the building of the projected new village, which has not been officially approved by the British.

About 5,000 Jews were estimated to have been involved in the case yesterday. Scores of settlers were detained for a few hours and then released. Today another 1,200 Galileans converged on the area to start again.

Big 'I' in English.

English is the only language that capitalizes "I" in writing. Many languages capitalize "you."

GIRL IS MISSING

Madison, Wis., March 15 (A. P.).—Police Chief William McCormick said today that he had asked the authorities in several Mid-Western States to aid in a search for Suzanne Froedtert, 16-year-old daughter of a wealthy Milwaukee grain and malting company executive, who disappeared from Edgewood Academy, a girls' school here, last Monday.

The girl, a first-year student at the college, was seen last on Monday afternoon by a truck driver who told the police he had given her a short ride from the school before declining her request to drive her to the Madison downtown area.

Her parents, Mr and Mrs. Kurtis R. Froedtert, are vacationing in Florida.

A school official said no disciplinary action had been taken against Miss Froedtert but that she had been notified early Monday that the academy authorities planned to consult her parents concerning a disciplinary matter, the nature of which was not disclosed.

EXAMPLE 144

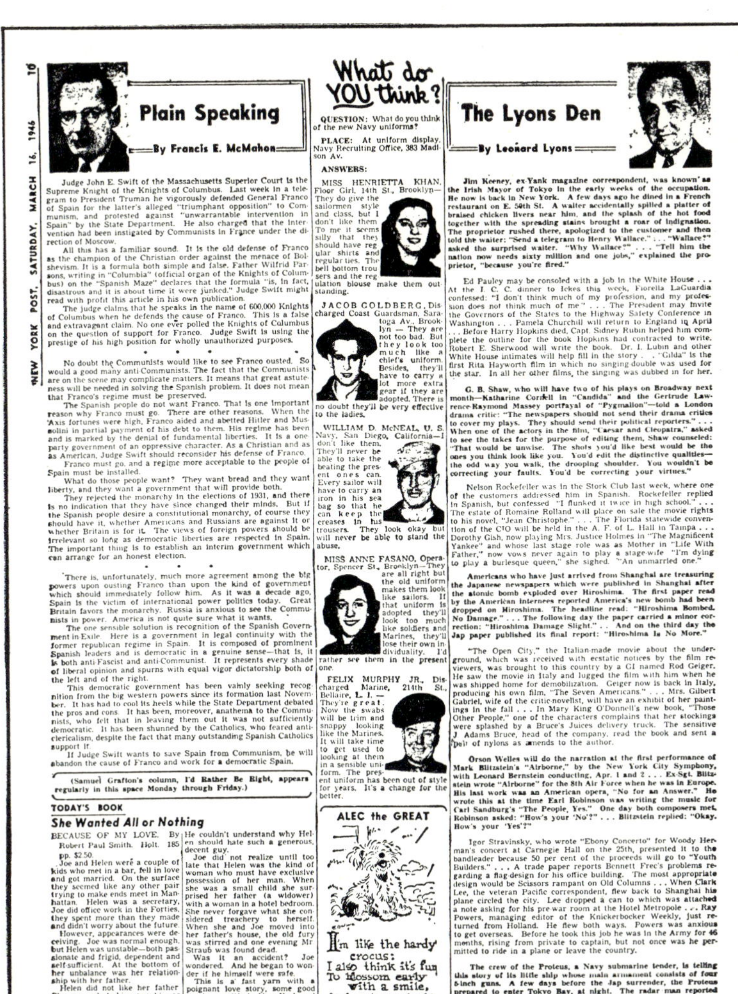

NEW YORK POST, SATURDAY, MARCH 16, 1946 10

Plain Speaking

By Francis E. McMahon

Judge John E. Swift of the Massachusetts Superior Court is the Supreme Knight of the Knights of Columbus. Last week in a telegram to President Truman he vigorously defended General Franco of Spain for the latter's alleged "triumphant opposition" to Communism, and protested against "unwarrantable intervention in Spain" by the State Department. He also charged that the intervention had been instigated by Communists in France under the direction of Moscow.

All this has a familiar sound. It is the old defense of Franco as the champion of the Christian order against the menace of Bolshevism. It is a formula both simple and false. Father Wilfrid Parsons, writing in "Columbia" (official organ of the Knights of Columbus) on the "Spanish Maze" declares that the formula "is, in fact, disastrous and it is about time it were junked." Judge Swift might read with profit this article in his own publication.

The judge claims that he speaks in the name of 600,000 Knights of Columbus when he defends the cause of Franco. This is a false and extravagant claim. No one ever polled the Knights of Columbus on the question of support for Franco. Judge Swift is using the prestige of his high position for wholly unauthorized purposes.

• • •

No doubt the Communists would like to see Franco ousted. So would a good many anti-Communists. The fact that the Communists are on the scene may complicate matters. It means that great astuteness will be needed in solving the Spanish problem. It does not mean that Franco's regime must be preserved.

The Spanish people do not want Franco. That is one important reason why Franco must go. There are other reasons. When the Axis fortunes were high, Franco aided and abetted Hitler and Mussolini in partial payment of his debt to them. His regime has been and is marked by the denial of fundamental liberties. It is a one-party government of an oppressive character. As a Christian and as as American, Judge Swift should reconsider his defense of Franco.

Franco must go, and a regime more acceptable to the people of Spain must be installed.

What do those people want? They want bread and they want liberty, and they want a government that will provide both.

They rejected the monarchy in the elections of 1931, and there is no indication that they have since changed their minds. But if the Spanish people desire a constitutional monarchy, of course they should have it, whether Americans and Russians are against it or whether Britain is for it. The views of foreign powers should be irrelevant so long as democratic liberties are respected in Spain. The important thing is to establish an interim government which can arrange for an honest election.

• • •

There is, unfortunately, much more agreement among the big powers upon ousting Franco than upon the kind of government which should immediately follow him. As it was a decade ago, Spain is the victim of international power politics today. Great Britain favors the monarchy. Russia is anxious to see the Communists in power. America is not quite sure what it wants.

The one sensible solution is recognition of the Spanish Government-in-Exile. Here is a government in legal continuity with the former republican regime in Spain. It is composed of prominent Spanish leaders and is democratic in a genuine sense—that is, it is both anti-Fascist and anti-Communist. It represents every shade of liberal opinion and spurns with equal vigor dictatorship both of the left and of the right.

This democratic government has been vainly seeking recognition from the big western powers since its formation last November. It has had to cool its heels while the State Department debated the pros and cons. It has been, moreover, anathema to the Communists, who felt that in leaving them out it was not sufficiently democratic. It has been shunned by the Catholics, who feared anti-clericalism, despite the fact that many outstanding Spanish Catholics support it.

If Judge Swift wants to save Spain from Communism, he will abandon the cause of Franco and work for a democratic Spain.

(Samuel Grafton's column, I'd Rather Be Right, appears regularly in this space Monday through Friday.)

TODAY'S BOOK

She Wanted All or Nothing

BECAUSE OF MY LOVE. By Robert Paul Smith. Holt. 185 pp. $2.50.

Joe and Helen were a couple of kids who met in a bar, fell in love and got married. On the surface they seemed like any other pair trying to make ends meet in Manhattan. Helen was a secretary, Joe did office work in the Forties, they spent more than they made and didn't worry about the future.

However, appearances were deceiving. Joe was normal enough, but Helen was unstable—both passionate and frigid, dependent and self-sufficient. At the bottom of her unbalance was her relationship with her father.

Helen did not like her father. She was rude to him, saw him as seldom as possible, was upset when he invited Joe and her to live with him. Joe on the other hand was crazy about Mr. Straub. He couldn't understand why Helen should hate such a generous, decent guy.

Joe did not realize until too late that Helen was the kind of woman who must have exclusive possession of her man. When she was a small child she surprised her father (a widower) with a woman in a hotel bedroom. She never forgave what she considered treachery to herself. When she and Joe moved into her father's house, the old fury was stirred and one evening Mr Straub was found dead.

Was it an accident? Joe wondered. And he began to wonder if he himself were safe.

This is a fast yarn with a poignant love story, some good touches on life in New York and real suspense. The psychology is sound and unobtrusive. Recommended.

—MARTHA MacGREGOR.

What do YOU think?

QUESTION: What do you think of the new Navy uniforms?

PLACE: At uniform display, Navy Recruiting Office, 383 Madison Av.

ANSWERS:

MISS HENRIETTA KHAN, Floor Girl, 14th St., Brooklyn—They do give the sailormen style and class, but I don't like them. To me it seems silly that they should have regular shirts and regular ties. The bell bottom trousers and the regulation blouse make them outstanding.

JACOB GOLDBERG, Discharged Coast Guardsman, Saratoga Av., Brooklyn — They are not too bad. But they look too much like a chief's uniform. Besides, they'll have to carry a lot more extra gear if they are adopted. There is no doubt they'll be very effective to the ladies.

WILLIAM D. McNEAL, U. S. Navy, San Diego, California—I don't like them. They'll never be able to take the beating the present ones can. Every sailor will have to carry an iron in his sea bag so that he can keep the creases in his trousers. They look okay but will never be able to stand the abuse.

MISS ANNE FASANO, Operator, Spencer St., Brooklyn—They are all right but the old uniform makes them look like sailors. If that uniform is adopted they'll look too much like soldiers and Marines, they'll lose their own individuality. I'd rather see them in the present one.

FELIX MURPHY JR., Discharged Marine, 214th St., Bellaire, L. I. — They're great. Now the swabs will be trim and snappy looking like the Marines. It will take time to get used to looking at them in a sensible uniform. The present uniform has been out of style for years. It's a change for the better.

ALEC the GREAT

I'm like the hardy crocus:
I also think it's fun
To blossom early with a smile,
And welcome back the sun!
R.D.

The Lyons Den

By Leonard Lyons

Jim Keeney, ex-Yank magazine correspondent, was known as the Irish Mayor of Tokyo in the early weeks of the occupation. He now is back in New York. A few days ago he dined in a French restaurant on E. 50th St. A waiter accidentally spilled a platter of braised chicken livers near him, and the splash of the hot food together with the spreading stains brought a roar of indignation. The proprietor rushed there, apologized to the customer and then told the waiter: "Send a telegram to Henry Wallace." . . . "Wallace?" asked the surprised waiter. "Why Wallace?" . . . "Tell him the nation now needs sixty million and one jobs," explained the proprietor, "because you're fired."

Ed Pauley may be consoled with a job in the White House . . . At the I. C. C. dinner to Ickes this week, Fiorella LaGuardia confessed: "I don't think much of my profession, and my profession does not think much of me" . . . The President may invite the Governors of the States to the Highway Safety Conference in Washington . . . Pamela Churchill will return to England in April . . . Before Harry Hopkins died, Capt. Sidney Rubin helped him complete the outline for the book Hopkins had contracted to write. Robert E. Sherwood will write the book. Dr. I. Lubin and other White House intimates will help fill in the story . . . "Gilda" is the first Rita Hayworth film in which no singing double was used for the star. In all her other films, the singing was dubbed in for her.

G. B. Shaw, who will have two of his plays on Broadway next month—Katharine Cornell in "Candida" and the Gertrude Lawrence-Raymond Massey portrayal of "Pygmalion"—told a London drama critic: "The newspapers should not send their drama critics to cover my plays. They should send their political reporters." . . . When one of the actors in the film, "Caesar and Cleopatra," asked to see the takes for the purpose of editing them, Shaw counseled: "That would be unwise. The shots you'd like best would be the ones you think look like you. You'd edit the distinctive qualities—the odd way you walk, the drooping shoulder. You wouldn't be correcting your faults. You'd be correcting your virtues."

Nelson Rockefeller was in the Stork Club last week, where one of the customers addressed him in Spanish. Rockefeller replied in Spanish, but confessed "I flunked it twice in high school." . . . The estate of Romaine Rolland will place on sale the movie rights to his novel, "Jean Christophe." . . . The Florida statewide convention of the CIO will be held in the A. F. of L. Hall in Tampa . . . Dorothy Gish, now playing Mrs. Justice Holmes in "The Magnificent Yankee" and whose last stage role was as Mother in "Life With Father," now vows never again to play a stage-wife. "I'm dying to play a burlesque queen," she sighed. "An unmarried one."

Americans who have just arrived from Shanghai are treasuring the Japanese newspapers which were published in Shanghai after the atomic bomb exploded over Hiroshima. The first paper read by the American internees reported America's new bomb had been dropped on Hiroshima. The headline read: "Hiroshima Bombed. No Damage." . . . The following day the paper carried a minor correction: "Hiroshima Damage Slight." . . And on the third day the Jap paper published its final report: "Hiroshima Is No More."

"The Open City," the Italian-made movie about the underground, which was received with ecstatic notices by the film reviewers, was brought to this country by a GI named Rod Geiger. He saw the movie in Italy and lugged the film with him when he was shipped home for demobilization. Geiger now is back in Italy, producing his own film, "The Seven Americans." . . . Mrs. Gilbert Gabriel, wife of the critic-novelist, will have an exhibit of her paintings in the fall . . . In Mary King O'Donnell's new book, "Those Other People," one of the characters complains that her stockings were splashed by a Bruce's Juices delivery truck. The sensitive J. Adams Bruce, head of the company, read the book and sent a pair of nylons as amends to the author.

Orson Welles will do the narration at the first performance of Mark Blitzstein's "Airborne," by the New York City Symphony, with Leonard Bernstein conducting, Apr. 1 and 2 . . . Ex-Sgt. Blitzstein wrote "Airborne" for the 8th Air Force when he was in Europe. His last work was an American opera, "No for an Answer." He wrote this at the time Earl Robinson was writing the music for Carl Sandburg's "The People, Yes." One day both composers met. Robinson asked: "How's your 'No'?" . . . Blitzstein replied: "Okay. How's your 'Yes'?"

Igor Stravinsky, who wrote "Ebony Concerto" for Woody Herman's concert at Carnegie Hall on the 25th, presented it to the bandleader because 50 per cent of the proceeds will go to "Youth Builders." . . . A trade paper reports Bennett Frec's problems regarding a flag-design for his office building. The most appropriate design would be Scissors rampant on Old Columns . . . When Clark Lee, the veteran Pacific correspondent, flew back to Shanghai his plane circled the city. Lee dropped a can to which was attached a note asking for his pre-war room at the Hotel Metropole . . . Ray Powers, managing editor of the Knickerbocker Weekly, just returned from Holland. He flew both ways. Powers was anxious to get overseas. Before he took this job he was in the Army for 46 months, rising from private to captain, but not once was he permitted to ride in a plane or leave the country.

The crew of the Proteus, a Navy submarine tender, is telling this story of its little ship whose main armament consists of four 5-inch guns. A few days before the Jap surrender, the Proteus prepared to enter Tokyo Bay, at night. The radar man reported that he had a radar contact. The Proteus' skipper ordered his signalman to send the challenging message: "Identify yourself or we will open fire." Back came the reply from the target: "This is the U. S. S. New Jersey. Don't scratch our paint."

EXAMPLE 145

terest arousing than what they consider good editorial pages. Some, again, maintain that a compromise measure has proved more satisfactory in their particular fields—the combination editorial and feature page.

It is not the purpose here to discuss the case for or against the running or not running of editorial or feature pages or combinations of the two. Different localities, of course, suggest different treatments.

Each editor should know, or should make it his concern to find out, which is best in his particular case.

Some papers run feature pages opposite their editorial pages; others run them as the front pages of second sections; others as back pages, and others in other positions.

Of course the term "feature pages" applies to many different kinds of pages—pages made up entirely or nearly so of pictures and accompanying legends; pages presenting human-interest or fiction stories; pages carrying special articles, and perhaps current-event cartoons; pages containing signed columns, and so on.

Example 143 shows how the *New York World-Telegram* has presented a feature page, as the front page of a second section.

Note that, while five regular-width columns have been used at the right, two wider columns have been presented at the left. Note, also, that, while five column rules have been used on the page, strips of white have been employed, instead of rules, to separate the wider columns of the four signed and pictured columnists. No advertising is carried.

Example 144 shows how the *New York Sun* has featured leading columnists on the front page of a second section.

The five columns at the right are regular-width columns separated by column rules, particularly because the *Sun* often runs advertising at the right on such pages, but the features at the left are presented in two wider columns separated by white space.

The *New York Post*, a five-column tabloid newspaper, has presented signed columns and other features as suggested by Example 145.

Note that the signed features are presented in double-width columns at the left and right, with a question-and-answer column with five half-column pictures, followed by some illustrated verse, separating the wider columns.

Woman's and Society Pages

Although many women long since have become interested in the newspaper as a whole, rather than in any one part of it, many metropolitan papers continue to run pages of particular interest to women—supposedly of more interest to women than to men. And many such papers give their woman's pages lighter treatments as to type and pictures than they ordinarily give their other pages, with the exception of society pages.

In fact, many papers that run pages of particular interest to women make no distinction between woman's pages and society pages, but run one or more "mixed" pages. In this group are many smaller dailies that cannot spare the space for the two separate and distinct pages, as well as most of the weeklies that attempt to present pages of particular interest to women.

To repeat, many metropolitan papers run pages of particular interest to women. And they run those pages, executives of those papers would be quick to explain, if they thought it necessary, because of the undoubted interest of many readers in them, and because important advertisers are desirous of appearing on those pages—more desirous, in many instances, than they are of appearing on other pages.

For studies of newspaper reading continue to show, as previously pointed out in this chapter, that women in general read more advertising than men in general, and spend more money on advertised products and services.

Some newspaper executives have expressed the opinion that women readers should be given much more consideration throughout the paper than many newspapers now give them—not merely on woman's and society pages but on virtually all pages.

In speaking at the school of journalism at Montana State University in the spring of 1944, Alexander Warden, business manager of the *Great Falls* (Mont.) *Tribune-Leader*, who is quoted more fully in Chapter 1 of Part II of this book, had the following to say about women readers and woman's pages:

"Men editors are patterning the news for men readers. Yet there are as many women readers of a paper as men. Probably the women spend more time with the paper, both because they have more time and because they study the advertisements for their buying needs also.

"Most publishers have considered themselves extremely progressive, if not verging on left-wingers, if they have recognized their women readers with an atrocity known as the woman's page, filled with a strange conglomeration of boiler-plate serial stories, fashions, recipes, and advice to the lovelorn. Most of it is trash, and women recognize it as such. Season this dish with a picture of the president of some uplift league and 10,000 women readers are supposed to give thanks.

"This isn't what they want. They want the whole paper to talk to them, too."

Some of the many Linotype faces (available in various sizes) particularly appropriate for heads on woman's pages and society pages —comparatively light faces—are shown here:

18-point Bodoni

Some Newspapers Are Easier to Read Th

18-point Bodoni Italic

Some Newspapers Are Easier to Read Th

18-point Bodoni Book

Some Newspapers Are Easier to Read Than

18-point Bodoni Book Italic

Some Newspapers Are Easier to Read Than

18-point Caslon Old Face

Some Newspapers Are Easier to Read Than Ot

18-point Caslon Old Face Italic

Some Newspapers Are Easier to Read Than Ot

18-point Caslon Italic

Some Newspapers Are Easier to Rea

18-point Century Expanded

Some Newspapers Are Easier to Read

18-point Century Expanded Italic

Some Newspapers Are Easier to Read

18-point Cheltenham

Some Newspapers Are Easier to Read Tha

18-point Cheltenham Italic

Some Newspapers Are Easier to Read Tha

18-point Cheltenham Condensed

Some Newspapers Are Easier to Read Than Oth

18-point Cloister

Some Newspapers Are Easier to Read Than Ot

18-point Cloister Italic

Some Newspapers Are Easier to Read Than Ot

18-point Erbar Light Condensed

Some Newspapers Are Easier to Read Than Others an

18-point Garamond

Some Newspapers Are Easier to Read Than O

18-point Garamond Italic

Some Newspapers Are Easier to Read Than O

18-point Garamond Bold No. 3

Some Newspapers Are Easier to Read T

18-point Garamond Bold No. 3 Italic

Some Newspapers Are Easier to Read T

18-point Garamond No. 3

Some Newspapers Are Easier to Read Than

18-point Garamond No. 3 Italic

Some Newspapers Are Easier to Read Than

18-point Granjon

Some Newspapers Are Easier to Read Than Oth

18-point Granjon Italic

Some Newspapers Are Easier to Read Than Oth

18-point Memphis Light

Some Newspapers Are Easier to Read

18-point Memphis Medium

Some Newspapers Are Easier to Rea

18-point Memphis Medium Italic

Some Newspapers Are Easier to Rea

18-point Spartan Medium

Some Newspapers Are Easier to Read T

18-point Spartan Medium Italic

Some Newspapers Are Easier to Read T

Although the smaller sizes of some of these faces—sizes below 12 point in some instances, below 10 and 8 point in others—would be too light to show up well in newspapers, the larger sizes of all of the faces often can be used to advantage on pages where the light or comparatively light touch is desirable.

Sports Pages

Next to a big crime or scandal story, as an interest arouser and circulation builder, runs the feeling in many newspaper offices in large cities, comes live sports news.

So firmly convinced of the drawing power of sports news are many editors of large-city papers that they often give such news prominent treatment on front pages. Some large-city dailies run two or three or more sports pages in each issue. The sports departments of several such papers enjoy more freedom than many other departments of the same papers. They are allowed more by-lines, often operate their own copy desks, set and follow rules of their own as to headlines and story treatments, and plan the makeup of their own pages. Often, too, they are given a much freer hand in the employment of "art" than are the planners of the general-news pages.

Before World War II many illustrations on the sports pages of many newspapers were given complicated treatments—treatments that called for the cutting away or mortising of certain portions of halftones and line-cuts to accommodate fitted-in headlines, legends or body matter, and that often involved the setting of type run-arounds. The run-arounds were used above and below and sometimes at the side of comparatively small portions of illustrations that extended from the main bodies of illustrations into adjoining columns consisting almost entirely of type lines.

But the newsprint, zinc and manpower shortages of World War II caused many newspapers to give up many of those treatments, and now the illustrations on sports pages of most newspapers are no more complicated than those on most of the other pages. Simplicity has taken the place of "trickiness."

Many sports-page editors employ rather heavy italics for heads over leading stories—an appropriate enough treatment if no more than a few such heads are used on a page, as rather heavy italics can suggest strength and action—qualities often written up and pictured on sports pages.

Quite a number of evening dailies that feature late baseball, football and racing news on their front pages, present such news in type faces different from and usually heavier than those used for regular news heads. Such news usually is presented in double-column lines toward the upper left of the page—a position of prominence that does not interfere with the presentation of the most important news of the day where readers are accustomed to looking for it—at the upper right of the page.

Some evening dailies that go to press after baseball games have started but have not been completed, not only present the scores as they stand at press time but prepare to present later scores as the word comes in, and without delaying press runs more than a few seconds, by using what are known as baseball matrices and punches. The matrices provide white figures on 12-point black squares, as well as black squares into which figures later can be punched by hand.

To illustrate, Example 146 shows the inning-by-inning score of a game between St. Louis and Brooklyn teams up to the end of the seventh inning.

ST. LOUIS
BROOKLYN

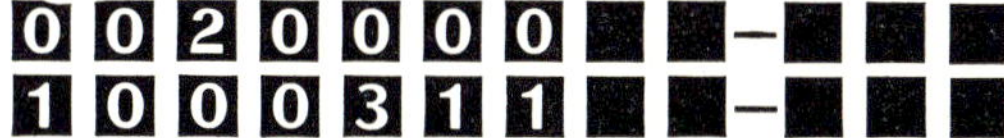

EXAMPLE 146

Note that blank squares have been provided for the punching in of eighth- and ninth-inning scores as the word comes in, as well as blanks for the total runs, hits and errors. The type face is 12-point Metroblack No. 2, which gets along well with the white figures and letters in the black squares.

When the scores for the eighth inning become known in the cityroom, the word is quickly passed to the pressroom, the press is stopped long enough—usually no more than a few seconds—for figures to be impressed, by means of small punches and a hammer, into the eighth-inning blanks on the stereo plate—and the press run is resumed.

Of course, in the case of weeklies or other papers printed direct from type, the figures can be punched into the blanks on the slugs.

When the ninth-inning scores become known, and the total runs, hits and errors, the same sort of procedure as that already described is repeated in the pressroom, until the final results of the game are shown, and without any resetting or substitution of slug lines, or re-casting of stereo plates, having been necessary—and with very little delaying of the press run. See Example 147.

ST. LOUIS	0	0	2	0	0	0	0	3	3	–8	10	0
BROOKLYN	1	0	0	0	3	1	1	1	0	–7	9	3

EXAMPLE 147

Some papers also make use of black squares and figure punches to present late racing news on front pages, the figures denoting the numbers of the horses winning certain races. Other papers, however, which not only wish to feature racing news and inning-by-inning baseball news, but important general news as well, after they have gone to press, make use of fudge blocks, or fudges.

Fudges are easily handled mechanical devices with curved upper surfaces, designed to receive slugs or hand type, and to be fastened to press cylinders to be printed from in place of blocked-out portions of stereo plates.

While one set of fudges is being used on a press, other sets can be made ready with later news and quickly substituted.

Some large evening dailies, on Saturday afternoons in the fall, concentrate a dozen or so editorial workers and operators or compositors about one or more telegraph instruments near Linotypes or type cases in the composing room, preparing fudges to present up-to-the-minute football results. Sometimes as many as two dozen fudges are kept moving from the composing room to the pressroom and back again, from one edition to another, until the "final final" is out.

To allow for the curved printing surface of the fudge blocks, the slugs used in them are thicker at the top than at the bottom, or the slugs or hand types used are supplemented with tapered leading material. Special slugs for use in fudges are cast in special molds—fudge molds—which provide the desired taper.

Poster Bodoni is a strong face for the featuring of football, baseball or other last-minute news in fudges, as suggested by Example 148.

AMERICAN LEAGUE

AT DETROIT										R	H	E
CHICAGO	0	0	0	0	2	0	0	0	0–	2	4	1
DETROIT	0	0	0	0	0	1	1	0	1–	3	7	0

EXAMPLE 148

During the baseball world series in 1945, the *New York World-Telegram* played up the games prominently on front pages, as it had been accustomed to doing for years, even though other and possibly much more significant news was breaking at the same time.

Example 149 shows how the *World-Telegram* played up a world's-series game October 3, 1945, in an eight-column box above its nameplate, and with much of columns one, two and three given over to a story of and the box score of the game, even though 60,000 striking waterfront workers had clamped a strike on the port of New York that very afternoon.

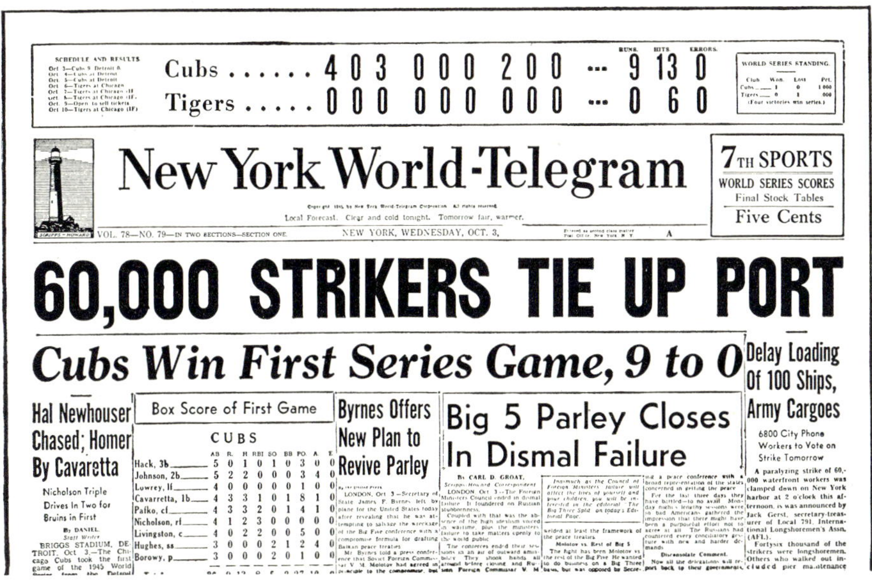

SCHEDULE AND RESULTS
Oct 3—Cubs 9 Detroit 0
Oct 4—Cubs at Detroit
Oct 5—Cubs at Detroit
Oct 6—Tigers at Chicago
Oct 7—Tigers at Chicago (If)
Oct 8—Tigers at Chicago (IF)
Oct 9—Open to sell tickets
Oct 10—Tigers at Chicago (IF)

					RUNS	HITS	ERRORS
Cubs	4 0 3	0 0 0	2 0 0	---	9	13	0
Tigers	0 0 0	0 0 0	0 0 0	---	0	6	0

WORLD SERIES STANDING

Club	Won	Lost	Pct.
Cubs	1	0	1 000
Tigers	0	1	.000

(Four victories win series.)

New York World-Telegram

Local Forecast. Clear and cold tonight. Tomorrow fair, warmer.

VOL. 78—NO. 79—IN TWO SECTIONS—SECTION ONE. NEW YORK, WEDNESDAY, OCT. 3.

7TH SPORTS
WORLD SERIES SCORES
Final Stock Tables
Five Cents

60,000 STRIKERS TIE UP PORT

Cubs Win First Series Game, 9 to 0

Hal Newhouser Chased; Homer By Cavaretta

Nicholson Triple Drives In Two for Bruins in First

By DANIEL
Staff Writer

BRIGGS STADIUM, DETROIT, Oct 3.—The Chicago Cubs took the first game of the 1945 World

Box Score of First Game

CUBS

	AB	R.	H	RBI	SO	BB	PO.	A.	E
Hack, 3b	5	0	1	0	1	0	3	0	0
Johnson, 2b	5	2	2	0	0	0	3	4	0
Lowrey, lf	4	0	0	0	0	0	1	0	0
Cavarretta, 1b	4	3	3	1	0	1	8	1	0
Pafko, cf	4	3	3	2	0	1	4	1	0
Nicholson, rf	4	1	2	3	0	0	0	0	0
Livingston, c	4	0	2	2	0	0	5	0	0
Hughes, ss	3	0	0	0	2	1	2	4	0
Borowy, p	3	0	0	0	2	0	1	0	0

Byrnes Offers New Plan to Revive Parley

LONDON, Oct 3.—Secretary of State James F. Byrnes left by plane for the United States today after revealing that he was attempting to salvage the wreckage of the Big Five conference with a compromise formula for drafting Balkan peace treaties.

Mr. Byrnes told a press conference that Soviet Foreign Commissar V. M. Molotov had agreed in principle to the compromise, but

Big 5 Parley Closes In Dismal Failure

By CARL D. GROAT,
Scripps-Howard Correspondent

LONDON, Oct 3.—The Foreign Ministers Council ended in dismal failure. It foundered on Russian stubbornness.

Coupled with that was the absence of the high idealism voiced in wartime, plus the ministers' failure to take matters openly to the world public.

The conferees ended their sessions in an air of outward amiability. They shook hands all around before closing and Russian Foreign Commissar V. M.

Inasmuch as the Council of Foreign Ministers' failure will affect the lives of yourself and your children, you will be interested in the editorial "The Big Three Split" on today's Editorial Page.

welded at least the framework of the peace treaties.

Molotov vs. Rest of Big 5

The fight has been Molotov vs the rest of the Big Five. He wanted to do business on a Big Three basis, but was opposed by Secre-

ing a peace conference with a broad representation of the states concerned in getting the peace.

For the last three days they have battled—to no avail. Monday night's lengthy sessions were so bad Americans gathered the impression that there might have been a purposeful effort not to agree at all. The Russians had countered every conciliatory gesture with new and harder demands.

Disconsolate Comment.

Now all the delegations will report back to their governments,

Delay Loading Of 100 Ships, Army Cargoes

6800 City Phone Workers to Vote on Strike Tomorrow

A paralyzing strike of 60,000 waterfront workers was clamped down on New York harbor at 2 o'clock this afternoon, is was announced by Jack Gerst, secretary-treasurer of Local 791, International Longshoremen's Assn. (AFL).

Fortysix thousand of the strikers were longshoremen. Others who walked out included pier maintenance

EXAMPLE 149

The strike story, however, was given a strong play in a banner line and a column-eight drop just below the nameplate.

Financial Pages

Most weekly newspapers, as well as many small dailies, present their financial news about the same as they do any other sort of news on inside pages. That is, they give it little if any special typographic treatment. The same column width followed for the general-news columns is employed and the same sort of head and body faces are used. But many large-city dailies devote one or several pages in each issue to financial news, and usually present their stock and bond tabulations in wider columns and in smaller type sizes than those regularly employed for the general-news columns. Many a daily that uses a 7½- or 8-point face for its general-news columns presents its stock and bond and other tabulations in a 6- or 5½- or even a 5-point face.

While, of course, the smaller size is harder to read than the larger (assuming that both sizes are in the same type family), the use of the smaller is justified by the considerations that it makes possible the presentation of more lines of information to the page or issue, and that the average reader is put to comparatively little inconvenience by the smaller size, as he is interested in no more than a few of the lines in any one table—the same sort of reasoning applied to the classified-advertising pages.

Some eight-column papers present their stock and bond tables in four double columns to the page; others run six columns to the page, and still others convert the six inside columns of a page into three double columns, or into four columns each about one and one-half times the width of a regular column, with a regular-width column on either side of the tabular matter. And the body lines of those regular-width columns, which present news stories of a financial nature, are in the same type face and size used in the general-news columns.

Example 150 shows a stock table with body lines in 6-point Bell Gothic, Two-Letter, on a 7-point body.

Example 151 shows a stock table with body lines in 5-point Ionic No. 5 with Bold Face No. 2 on a 6-point body.

And Example 152 shows a stock table with body lines in 5½-point Excelsior with Gothic No. 3 on a 6-point body.

◆		**A**						
84¼	61½	Abbot Lab 2a..	11	70	70¾	69	69	—1
19	10	ACF-Brill Mot.	9	10⅝	10⅝	10	10	— ½
50	30½	Acme Stl 1.55e	7	39	39½	38½	38⅝	— ⅜
24¾	13¾	Adams Ex .20e.	28	15¼	15¼	13⅞	14	— ¾
68½	44¼	Adams-Milis 2e	2	50	50	49½	49½	+1¼
41¾	24⅝	Addrso-M 1.10e	4	27	28⅛	27	28⅛	+1⅝
20⅜	10	Admirl Crp ⅛e	2	11	11	10⅝	10⅝	+ ⅛
59¾	38	Air Reduct 1a.	43	41½	42¼	39⅝	39¾	— ⅛
12¼	5	Alaska Juneau..	25	6	6	5½	5½	— ⅛
51¾	29	Aldens Inc 1.20	13	32¼	32⅞	31	31	— ½
103	95½	Ald Inc pf 4¼.	z210	96	96	95½	95½	— ½
8¼	3⅝	Alleghany Corp.	200	4	4	3¾	3¾	— ¼
69¼	33¾	Alleghany pf...	20	36½	37	33¾	34¼	—1⅝
82	55	Alleghany pr pf	2	55	55	55	55	— ½
61⅛	38	Alleg Lud Stl 2	27	42¾	42¾	40	40½	— ½
212¼	157	Al Chm & Dye 6	11	161	163	159	159	—1
29½	19	Allied Kid 1a..	4	20⅞	21	19	19	—1½
39	29½	Allied Mills 1e.	4	31	31½	31	31	+ ¼
◆		**B**						
38⅞	19⅝	Bald Loco ½e.	46	22¼	22¾	20¼	20¼	—1⅜
30¼	12¼	Balt & Ohio...	151	14⅛	14⅜	12¼	12¾	— ¾
47¼	19¼	Balt & Ohio pf.	18	22	22	19¼	20¼	—1
30	14½	Bangor & Ar...	3	15	15½	14¾	14¾	— ¼
88½	68	Ban & Ar pf 5.	z170	71	71	68	69	—1½
64¼	36¾	Barber Asph 1.	18	52¼	52¾	50	50	—1
41½	26⅞	Barker Bros 1a.	7	30¾	32	29⅞	29⅞	+ ⅛
31	21	Barnsdall Oil 1.	31	23	23⅝	22¼	22½	— ¼
39¾	20½	Bath Ir W 3½e	14	21⅜	21½	20¾	20⅞	+ ¼
63½	40½	Bayuk Cig 1½e	1	45	45	45	45	.....
73	46½	Beat Fds 1.40a.	2	49½	50¼	49½	50¼	+1¼
110	104	Beck Sh pf 4¾	z50	105¾	106	105¾	106	+1
30⅞	12¾	Beech Airc 1g.	22	15⅝	16	14⅞	14⅞	— ⅝
43	35	Beech Creek 2.	z10	35	35	35	35	—2½
28¾	15½	Beld-Hem .80.	3	16½	16½	15⅞	16	+ ⅛
35½	18⅞	Bell Airc 1e...	22	21⅜	21⅜	19⅝	20	— ½
37	18¾	Bell & Howll ½	6	21½	21½	20⅜	20⅜	+ ⅜
◆		**C**						
58	54	Calif P pf 2½.	z10	54⅜	54⅜	54⅜	54⅜	.....
7½	3	Callahan Z-Ld..	24	3⅝	3⅝	3½	3½	.....
12¾	6⅝	Calum & H .15c	16	7¼	7¼	7	7	— ⅛
40⅜	22	Campb Wy ¾e.	8	22½	23	22½	22⅝	+ ⅛
18	13	Can Dr GA .15e	12	15	15	14	14	— ¾
22⅞	13	Canad Pac 1¼e	104	14	14¼	13⅛	13¼	— ⅜
73¾	55¾	Cannon M 2e..	1	58½	58½	58½	58½	+2½
21¼	12¼	Capital AA .40g	5	13	13	12¼	12¼	— ½
137	112	Caro C & O 5..	z70	112	112	112	112	—3
61½	39	Carpenter S 2e.	7	41⅞	42½	40	40	— ⅛
34	16	Carrier Corp...	36	17⅞	18½	17½	17½	— ⅛
60	39¾	Carrier Cp pf 2.	5	44	44	42⅞	42⅞	+3⅛
10⅜	6⅝	Carrs & G .20a	16	7	7	7	7	+ ⅜
55	34¾	Case JI 2e....	9	37¾	37¾	36	36	—1

EXAMPLE 150

Some papers sometimes present four of the "column and one-half" columns above or below three double columns, or present regular-width columns above or below some of the columns wider than 12 picas. Certain minor tabulations are run in the form of four narrower columns in the width of three regular columns, or are doubled up,

◆		**A**						
84¼	61½	Abbot Lab 2a....	11	70	70¾	69	69	—1
19	10	ACF-Brill Mot....	9	10⅝	10⅝	10	10	— ½
50	30½	Acme Stl 1.55e...	7	39	39½	38½	38⅝	— ⅜
24¾	13¾	Adams Ex .20e...	28	15¼	15¼	13⅞	14	— ¾
68½	44¼	Adams-Milis 2e...	2	50	50	49½	49½	+1¼
41¾	24⅝	Addreso-M 1.10e..	4	27	28⅛	27	28⅛	+1⅝
20⅜	10	Admirl Crp ⅛e...	2	11	11	10⅝	10⅝	+ ⅛
59¾	38	Air Reduct 1a....	43	41½	42¼	39⅝	39¾	— ⅛
12¼	5	Alaska Juneau....	25	6	6	5½	5½	— ⅛
51¾	29	Aldens Inc 1.20..	13	32¼	32⅞	31	31	— ½
103	95½	Ald Inc pf 4¼....	z210	96	96	95½	95½	— ½
8¼	3⅝	Alleghany Corp...	200	4	4	3¾	3¾	— ¼
69¼	33¾	Alleghany pf.....	20	36½	37	33¾	34¼	—1⅝
82	55	Alleghany pr pf..	2	55	55	55	55	— ½
61⅛	38	Alleg Lud Stl 2...	27	42¾	42¾	40	40½	— ½
212¼	157	Al Chm & Dye 6..	11	161	163	159	159	—1
29½	19	Allied Kid 1a....	4	20⅞	21	19	19	—1½
39	29½	Allied Mills 1e....	4	31	31½	31	31	+ ¼
◆		**B**						
38⅞	19⅝	Bald Loco ½e....	46	22¼	22¾	20¼	20¼	—1⅜
30¼	12¼	Balt & Ohio.....	151	14⅛	14⅜	12¼	12¾	— ¾
47¼	19¼	Balt & Ohio pf...	18	22	22	19¼	20¼	—1
30	14½	Bangor & Ar.....	3	15	15½	14¾	14¾	— ¼
88½	68	Ban & Ar pf 5....	z170	71	71	68	69	—1½
64¼	36¾	Barber Asph 1...	18	52¼	52¾	50	50	—1
41½	26⅞	Barker Bros 1a...	7	30¾	32	29⅞	29⅞	+ ⅛
31	21	Barnsdall Oil 1...	31	23	23⅝	22¼	22½	— ¼
39¾	20½	Bath Ir W 3½e...	14	21⅜	21½	20¾	20⅞	+ ¼
63½	40½	Bayuk Cig 1½e...	1	45	45	45	45	.....
73	46½	Beat Fds 1.40a...	2	49½	50¼	49½	50¼	+1¼
110	104	Beck Sh pf 4¾...	z50	105¾	106	105¾	106	+1
30⅞	12¾	Beech Airc 1g....	22	15⅝	16	14⅞	14⅞	— ⅝
43	35	Beech Creek 2....	z10	35	35	35	35	—2½
28¾	15½	Beld-Hem .80....	3	16½	16½	15⅞	16	+ ⅛
35½	18⅞	Bell Airc 1e......	22	21⅜	21⅜	19⅝	20	— ½
37	18¾	Bell & Howell ½.	6	21½	21½	20⅜	20⅜	+ ⅜
◆		**C**						
58	54	Calif P pf 2½....	z10	54⅜	54⅜	54⅜	54⅜	.....
7½	3	Callahan Z-Ld...	24	3⅝	3⅝	3½	3½	.....
12¾	6⅝	Calum & H .15c..	16	7¼	7¼	7	7	— ⅛
40⅜	22	Campb Wy ¾e...	8	22½	23	22½	22⅝	+ ⅛
18	13	Can Dry GA .15e.	12	15	15	14	14	— ¾
22⅞	13	Canad Pac 1¼e..	104	14	14¼	13⅛	13¼	— ⅜
73¾	55¾	Cannon M 2e....	1	58½	58½	58½	58½	+2½
21¼	12¼	Capital AA .40g..	5	13	13	12¼	12¼	— ½
137	112	Caro C & O 5....	z70	112	112	112	112	—3
61½	39	Carpenter S 2e...	7	41⅞	42½	40	40	— ⅛
34	16	Carrier Corp.....	36	17⅞	18½	17½	17½	— ⅛
60	39¾	Carrier Cp pf 2...	5	44	44	42⅞	42⅞	+3⅛
10⅜	6⅝	Carriers & G .20a	16	7	7	7	7	+ ⅜
55	34¾	Case JI 2e........	9	37¾	37¾	36	36	—1

EXAMPLE 151

with two half-column widths to the column. Some papers present two or three double columns of tabular matter to the left on their financial pages, with four or two columns of advertising at the right; or two or four columns of tabular matter each about one and one-half times the width of a regular column, to the left, with five or two columns of advertising to the right.

Some papers employ head dresses for their financial pages different from those used on their general-news pages, and run banners at the tops of most of their financial pages to relieve the physical monotony

◆		A						
84¼	61½	Abbot Lab 2a.	11	70	70¾	69	69	—1
19	10	ACF-Brill Mot	9	10⅝	10⅝	10	10	— ½
50	30½	Acme Stl 1.55e	7	39	39½	38½	38⅝	— ⅜
24¾	13¾	Adams Ex .20e	28	15¼	15¼	13⅞	14	— ¾
68½	44¼	Adams-Milis 2e	2	50	50	49½	49½	+1¼
41¾	24⅝	Addro-M 1.10e	4	27	28⅛	27	28⅛	+1⅝
20⅜	10	Admirl Crp ⅛e	2	11	11	10⅝	10⅝	+ ⅛
59¾	38	Air Reduct 1a.	43	41½	42¼	39⅝	39¾	— ⅛
12¼	5	Alaska Juneau	25	6	6	5½	5½	— ⅛
51¾	29	Aldens Inc 1.20	13	32¼	32⅞	31	31	— ½
103	95½	Ald Inc pf 4¼.	z210	96	96	95½	95½	— ½
8¼	3⅝	Alleghny Corp	200	4	4	3¾	3¾	— ¼
69¼	33¾	Alleghany pf..	20	36½	37	33¾	34¼	—1⅝
82	55	Alleghny pr pf	2	55	55	55	55	— ½
61⅛	38	Alleg Lud Stl 2	27	42¾	42¾	40	40½	— ½
212¼	157	Al Cm & Dye 6	11	161	163	159	159	—1
29½	19	Allied Kid 1a.	4	20⅞	21	19	19	—1½
39	29½	Allied Mills 1e	4	31	31½	31	31	+ ¼
◆		B						
38⅞	19⅝	Bald Loco ½e.	46	22¼	22¾	20¼	20¼	—1⅜
30¼	12¼	Balt & Ohio..	151	14⅛	14⅜	12¼	12¾	— ¾
47¼	19¼	Balt & Oh pf..	18	22	22	19¼	20¼	—1
30	14½	Bangor & Ar..	3	15	15½	14¾	14¾	— ¼
88½	68	Ban & Ar pf 5	z170	71	71	68	69	—1½
64¼	36¾	Barber Asph 1	18	52¼	52¾	50	50	—1
41½	26⅞	Barker Bros 1a	7	30¾	32	29⅞	29⅞	+ ⅛
31	21	Barnsdall Oil 1	31	23	23⅝	22¼	22½	— ¼
39¾	20½	Bath Ir W 3½e	14	21⅜	21½	20¾	20⅞	+ ¼
63½	40½	Bayuk Cg 1½e	1	45	45	45	45	.....
73	46½	Beat Fds 1.40a	2	49½	50¼	49½	50¼	+1¼
110	104	Beck Sh pf 4¾	z50	105¾	106	105¾	106	+1
30⅞	12¾	Beech Airc 1g	22	15⅝	16	14⅞	14⅞	— ⅝
43	35	Beech Creek 2	z10	35	35	35	35	—2½
28¾	15½	Beld-Hem .80..	3	16½	16½	15⅞	16	+ ⅛
35½	18⅞	Bell Airc 1e...	22	21⅜	21⅜	19⅝	20	— ½
37	18¾	Bell & Hwll ½	6	21½	21½	20⅜	20⅜	+ ⅜
◆		C						
58	54	Calif P pf 2½.	z10	54⅜	54⅜	54⅜	54⅜	.....
7½	3	Callahan Z-Ld	24	3⅝	3⅝	3½	3½	.....
12¾	6⅝	Calm & H .15c	16	7¼	7¼	7	7	— ⅛
40⅜	22	Campb Wy ¾e	8	22½	23	22½	22⅝	+ ⅛
18	13	Cn Dr GA .15e	12	15	15	14	14	— ¾
22⅞	13	Canad Pa 1¼e	104	14	14¼	13⅛	13¼	— ⅜
73¾	55¾	Cannon M 2e.	1	58½	58½	58½	58½	+2½
21¼	12¼	Capitl AA .40g	5	13	13	12¼	12¼	— ½
137	112	Caro C & O 5.	z70	112	112	112	112	—3
61½	39	Carpenter S 2e	7	41⅞	42½	40	40	— ⅛
34	16	Carrier Corp..	36	17⅞	18½	17½	17½	— ⅛
60	39¾	Carrier Cp pf 2	5	44	44	42⅞	42⅞	+3⅛
10⅜	6⅝	Carrs & G .20a	16	7	7	7	7	+ ⅜
55	34¾	Case JI 2e....	9	37¾	37¾	36	36	—1

EXAMPLE 152

of the many small tabular lines, and some papers make use of charts and occasional pictures of people to break up the pages.

It would be possible to illustrate here various effective column-width treatments of financial tables, but the chief variations already referred to should suffice to suggest the various possibilities.

Many large-city dailies make use of nameplates on their leading financial pages (although some of those dailies gave up that practice during World War II because of newsprint shortages), and some papers occasionally present pertinent editorials on such pages.

Some newspapers confine advertising on their financial pages to certain kinds and sizes of type faces, as well as to certain kinds and sizes of rules or borders, comparatively light in weight, to tone in with the comparative lightness, physically, of the news and feature matter on such pages.

Radio Pages

While some newspapers publish little radio news, other papers, particularly large-city papers, maintain regular radio departments, run radio programs in all editions, and sometimes devote a full page or more to radio news and features.

Today's Radio Programs

WMCA—570Kc.
WEAF—660Kc.
WOR—710Kc.
WJZ—770Kc.
WNYC—830Kc.
WABC—880Kc.
WINS—1010Kc.
WHN—1050Kc.
WNEW—1130Kc.
WLIB—1190Kc.
WOV—1280Kc.
WEVD—1330Kc.
WBYN—1430Kc.
WQXR—1560Kc.
WWRL—1600Kc.

Tonight's News

6:00—WEAF, WOR, WJZ, WABC, WMCA, WQXR
6:30—WOR, WNEW, WHN, WMCA
6:45—WEAF, WJZ, WABC, WNYC
7:00—WOR, WMCA, WHN, WQXR
7:15—WEAF, WMCA
7:30—WMCA, WNEW, WNYC
7:45—WEAF
8:00—WOR, WMCA, WQXR, WJZ
8:45—WEVD
9:00—WOR, WMCA, WNEW, WQXR, WEVD, WHN
9:30—WNEW
10:00—WJZ, WMCA
10:30—WMCA, WHN, WNEW
10:45—WHN, WQXR
11:00—WEAF, WOR, WJZ, WABC, WMCA, WHN, WEVD
11:15—WEAF, WOR
11:30—WNEW, WEVD
12:00—WEAF, WABC, WMCA, WQXR

3:00—WEAF—Life Can be Beautiful
WOR—Martha Deane
WJZ—Ladies, Be Seated
WABC—Cinderella, Inc.
WQXR—News; Request Program
3:15—WEAF—Ma Perkins
3:30—WEAF—Pepper Young's Family
WOR—News; Rambling with Gambling
WJZ—Meet Me in Manhattan
WABC—Winner Take All
WEVD—Mrs. E. Leibowitz, Talk
3:45—WEAF—Right to Happiness
WEVD—Morris Asofsky, Talk
WNYC—News
4:00—WEAF—Backstage Wife
WOR—Better Half Matinee
WJZ—Jack Berch Show
WABC—House Party
WNYC—Four Strings At Four
WNEW—Fun At Four
WEVD—Melodic Gems
4:15—WEAF—Stella Dallas
WJZ—Lum 'n Abner
WABC—Inner Sanctum
WMCA—News; Music Hall
WNYC—That Reminds Me—Pru Devon
WNEW—Magic of Music
WHN—Books on Trial
WQXR—News; Symphony Hall
10:45—WMCA—Music by Americans
WHN—Sports Final
11:00—WEAF—News, Kenneth Banghart
WOR—News, VanDeventer
WJZ—News
WABC—News, Charles Collingwood
WMCA—News; The Bandbox
WHN—Newsreel Theater
WQXR—News; Hour of Symphony
11:10—WABC—News, George Bryan
11:30—WEAF—The Doodlesockers
WOR—Weather; Griff Williams Orchestra
WJZ—Talk; Eliot Lawrence Orchestra
WABC—Eileen Farrell
WMCA—South of the Border
12:00—WEAF—News; Music (to 1:01)
WOR—News; Music (to 5:45)
WJZ—News; Music (to 5:45)
WABC—News; Music (to 2:00)
WMCA—News; Music (to 7:00)
WNEW—Milkman's Matinee (to 6:00)

Tomorrow Morning

7:00—WEAF—News; Music
WOR—News; Music
WJZ—News; Music
WABC—Arthur Godfrey
WMCA—News; Music
WNYC—Sunrise Symphony
WNEW—Anything Goes
WHN—Music; News
WEVD—Morning Serenade
WQXR—News; Morning Parade
7:30—WEAF—News, Charles F. McCarthy
WMCA—Melody Caravan
WEVD—News
WQXR—Breakfast Symphony
7:45—WEAF—Bob Smith Show

EXAMPLE 153

Many of the smaller papers that run radio departments present their radio programs and other radio news in the same sort of head and body faces used for the general-news columns, but the larger dailies that present the programs of several radio stations in each issue run the programs in 6-, 5½- or even 5-point faces—the same faces, in many cases, employed for tabular lines on the financial pages and for body lines on the classified-advertising pages.

Example 153 suggests one effective way of presenting radio programs in a double-column measure, with display lines in Memphis Light and body lines in 5-point Excelsior on a 5½-point body.

And Example 154 suggests another way of treating radio tables, with display in Spartan Medium and body lines in 5-point Bold Face No. 2 on a 5½-point body.

A.M.	WEAF 660k	WOR 710k	WJZ 770k	WABC 880k
Noon	Eternal Light: Drama	The Show Shop:	F. H. La Guardia....	Invitation to Learn:
12:15	Chronicle of Dead	Walter Preston	12:25, news..........	Point Counter Point
12:30	Today's Concert:	Special Assignment	Sunday Strings:	Yours Sincerely:
12:45	Clarence Fuhrman	News, Melvin Elliott	Ruggiero Ricci....	FromN.Y.&London
1:00	News, Ed Herlihy..	'The Wigglesworths'	Johnny Thompson..	People's Platform:
1:15	Sunday Matinee....	Opportunity, U. S. A.	Orson Welles........	Is Wallace Right?
1:30	Chicago Roundtable:	Singing Sweethearts	Sammy Kaye's	Lyman Bryson......
1:45	Must Men Fight?	Jimmy Farrell, songs	Serenade; news...	Howard K. Smith...
2:00	Robert Merrill,	Private Showing:	Warriors of Peace:	Report from Campus:
2:15	Frank Black Orch.	Walter Hampden	ArmySpec'lServices	The Vet. in Education
2:30	Raymond Massey:	News, G. C. Putnam	Sunday Vespers: Dr.	Weekly News Review
2:45	Nino Ventura.....	Vet Wants to Know	Paul Scherer......	" " ......
3:00	Carmen Cavallaro's	Quiz of Two Cities,	Danger,Dr.Danfield,	Stars in Afternoon:
3:15	Orch.; Max Hill...	N. Y. and Chicago	drama,MichaelDunn	Dinah Shore, Frank
3:30	One Man's Family,	Vera Holly Sings	Hollywood Present..	Sinatra; Bob Hawk,
3:45	dramatic sketch...	" "	Samuel Pettengill...	Jimmy Durante,
4:00	National Hour:	Mysterious Traveler,	Stump the Authors,	Hoagy Carmichael,
4:15	'Report to Now'...	mystery-drama	quiz: Sidney Mason	Dick Haymes,others
4:30	America United: Rep.	True Detective	Right Down Your	Anne Jamison,
4:45	Mike Munroney	Mysteries	Alley, sports quiz	Robert Shanley...
5:00	N. B. C. Symphony:	The Shadow, drama	Allen Prescott's	Patrice Munsel:
5:15	Frank Black;	" "	Party	Frank Parker.....
5:30	Sibelius's Second	Quick as a Flash,	David Harding—	Jean Sablon, songs..
5:45	Symphony	quiz: Ken Roberts	Counterspy, drama	William L. Shirer...

EXAMPLE 154

Many papers feature on their radio pages, often in boxes or box effects employing fairly large body lines and prominent heads, the leading items on current or future radio programs.

Many papers with Sunday editions present in those editions detailed radio programs for the week to come, for the benefit of "Sunday-only" patrons, even though each day's program will be repeated in that day's editions to follow.

Magazine and Book Sections

The nature of magazine and book sections suggests "bookish" treatments for such sections, particularly when they are presented in tabloid form, as most of them now are, especially in Sunday editions of metropolitan newspapers.

Although many newspapers issuing such sections run five 12-pica columns on most of the pages, in many instances the leading pages (devoid of advertising) are presented in wider columns separated by strips of white space, rather than column rules. However, on the five-column pages carrying advertising, column rules usually are employed, for display lines in advertisements placed side by side and not separated by column rules often "run into" and, at first glance, seem to form parts of, display lines in neighboring advertisements.

The rear pages of some magazine sections make use of both strips of white and column rules—strips of white to separate columns of story matter from each other, and a column rule or two to separate stories from advertisements, or columns of advertisements from each other.

The larger sizes of many book faces and other comparatively light faces can be effectively employed for heads in magazine and book sections. But book faces should not be used for the regular body matter if such sections are printed from stereotypes on coarse-fibered newsprint and on high-speed presses—for reasons previously mentioned, particularly in Chapters 4 and 5 of Part I.

Many newspapers are now presenting their magazine sections in gravure and colorgravure. In fact, as pointed out in a later chapter in this book, color is coming to play an increasingly important part in virtually all sections of a newspaper.

Among the many type faces that can be used effectively for heads in magazine and book sections are many of those shown in Chapters 5, 16 and 17, particularly in Chapter 16, of Part I.

17

Display Advertising

It is not the purpose of this chapter to attempt an exhaustive discussion of the designing of newspaper advertisements, which is a well-nigh limitless subject, and one over which the newspapers themselves exercise only limited control, as many advertisements come to them already made up in the form of plates or stereotype matrices. It is the purpose, however, to point out some of the things required of advertisers by some of our better looking newspapers, to present a few examples of physically faulty advertisements contrasted with others much more attractive looking, and to make other suggestions concerning the physical treatment of advertising in newspapers.

Many years ago it was customary for many newspapers in this country to run advertising on their front pages. At present, though, most of our newspapers decline to sell space in their show windows—in any event not more than a few "filler" lines at the bottom of columns. And properly so, it seems to this writer.

After all, a newspaper is supposed to be a *news*paper first, and an advertising medium secondarily, even though it usually is the advertising that pays the paper's bills and accounts for its profits.

Certain it is that advertising can disfigure the appearance of a front page, as may be seen by a glance at some of the front pages of the comparatively few American newspapers that continue to sell front-page display space.

Two or three generations ago the front pages of many of our newspapers were regarded more as front covers than front pages—more as wrappers to protect inner pages from the elements—and in some instances advertising space could be purchased on front pages at a fifth of the price charged for the same amount of space on certain inside pages of the same papers.

Some newspapers in the past printed some of their pages several hours or even days in advance of other pages, to speed up publication when the closing pages were ready to be printed. Some papers, most of them four-page papers, printed pages one and four in advance—and ran most or much of their advertising on those pages because that advertising was ready to be run before the items of latest news were.

In the 150th anniversary number of the *London* (England) *Times* appeared a story with the following statements on printing practices in the *Times* plant back in 1785: "Newspaper compositors were generally employed from 6 A.M. to 8 P.M. preparing two of the small four folio pages, and from 6 P.M. to 5 A.M. on the inner two pages containing the news. The first or outer forme was worked off by pressmen during the setting of the two inner pages."

Two or three generations ago, though, advertisers in our metropolitan papers were encouraged not to "break" column rules, and not to call for large display types—chiefly for mechanical reasons. However, many advertisers in those days planned their advertisements to "jump over" the column rules, and secured display effects by the employment of built-up (composite) lines of the small body type.

For twenty years or so following 1846 many of our larger papers were printed on type-revolving presses. And as pages of papers using such presses (before the Linotype and the general adoption of stereotype plates) were made up in turtles (curved forerunners of the chases of today) and the turtles were applied to and rotated with certain cylinders of the presses, the column rules played an important part in holding the thousands of pieces of hand type in the rotating forms. Those column rules were thicker near the top than at the bottom, to allow for the curved printing surface of the form, with the top of the rules tapered up to a hairline. And the curved printing surface made it impossible to use regular large types for display in the forms, hence the building up of display lines from the flexible body units. In the days of turtles, newspaper pages were printed sidewise, rather than lengthwise, as from curved stereotype plates of today.

Example 155, which shows a fragment of an advertisement from the *Brooklyn Daily Eagle* of Sunday, January 25, 1880, is typical of many newspaper advertisements of half a century and more ago in this country.

Notice the "jumped" column rule and the built-up (composite) display lines!

That advertisement appeared on the front page, the advertising bargain page, of the *Eagle*, and the advertiser filled two columns with his sales arguments—columns 25¼ inches deep. Incidentally, he employed several other built-up lines in the course of his ode to dry goods.

"Rates for advertising," ran a statement under the *Eagle* masthead of that day, "solid agate measurement, each insertion, per line: First page, 10 cents; second or fourth page, 20 cents; local and commercial

DRY GOODS, &c. | DRY GOODS, &c.

UNDERWEAR. | UNDERWEAR.

UNDERWEAR

TO-MORROW MORNING AT 9:30 WE BEGIN A FURTHER GREAT SALE OF LADIES' UNDERWEAR, INFANTS' AND CHILDREN'S DRESSES. LADIES' AND MISSES' CORSETS. WE OFFER ONE GREAT COMBINATION LOT OF EIGHT THOUSAND LADIES' CHEMISES, NIGHTDRESSES, SKIRTS, DRAWERS, CORSET COVERS, TOILET SACQUES. THREE THOUSAND CHILDREN'S SHORT DRESSES, SIX THOUSAND INFANTS' LONG SLIPS, FIVE HUNDRED PAIRS OF CAMBRIC PILLOW SHAMS, TWO THOUSAND LADIES' AND MISSES' CORSETS. ALL AT THE UNIFORM PRICE OF

98 CENTS

LADIES WILL FIND THAT THIS SALE IS NOT CONDUCTED AFTER THE MANNER OF AN ENORMOUS GRAB BAG OUT OF WHICH SOME SECURE PRIZES AND OTHERS OBTAIN INFERIOR GOODS. NOT A SINGLE ARTICLE IS OFFERED AT THIS SALE WHICH IS NOT WORTH FULLY ONE DOLLAR.

EXAMPLE 155

notices, third or fourth page, 50 cents; amusements, 20 cents. Personals, marriage and death notices, one dollar for each insertion, when not exceeding six lines. Religious notices, 50 cents for each insertion. No deviation from these rates. Cash in advance in all cases."

It is interesting to observe that advertising rates for pages two, three and four were at least twice as high as the front-page rate, in some instances five times as high; and that the rate for personals, marriage and death notices was higher than the front-page rate.

The *Eagle* of that day (and the *Eagle* then claimed "a larger circulation than any other evening newspaper published in the United States") consisted of four pages of nine columns each, with columns about 13½ picas wide. Front-page columns, as already stated, were 25¼ inches deep, while columns on other pages were 26¾ inches.

On the front page of the *Eagle* of January 25, 1880, appeared three columns of agate "reading matter" headed "Colonial Politics" and "Miscellaneous Items," and a poem 186 lines long on "New Hampshire," by Edna Dean Proctor, with an accompanying editorial note stating that the poem "was pronounced by Mr. Whittier, while in Boston last week, as one of the grandest poems produced in this country." Another long poem was presented on the editorial page.

Before type-revolving presses were adopted by newspapers, several of those papers had been accustomed to running many illustrations in their advertising columns, along with comparatively large types.

"Before the type-revolving cylinder press made its appearance," states James Melvin Lee in his *History of American Journalism*, "many of the newspapers were so profusely illustrated that they resembled catalogues, rather than newspapers. Some of the more fastidious sheets seriously objected to the use of these cuts which gave such a black appearance to the newspaper, and charged extra for their insertion, even though no extra mechanical labor was involved."

But with the adoption of such presses, display types were abandoned for the built-up (composite) lines previously referred to, and comparatively few illustrations were used. As those that were used had to be given special treatment to make them agree with the curved printing surface of the forms (see Chapter 14 of Part I), higher rates were charged for advertisements with pictures, and for the "breaking" of column rules. Hence, comparatively few pictures were used and comparatively few column rules "broken" in some papers for several years—habits that persisted for some time even after over-all stereotyping had been adopted by the papers.

Our most attractive and influential newspapers of today have definite typographic standards for their advertising columns, and advertisers ordering space in those papers must comply with those standards or the papers will change the displays to meet their requirements.

In some instances the changing of advertisements has been quite expensive to the newspapers doing the changing, but they have willingly borne the expense for the more satisfactory printing results that have followed.

A growing number of influential newspapers will not permit the use of comparatively heavy borders round comparatively small advertisements. For single- and double-column advertisements in those papers, solid-black borders can be no wider than 6 points, nor can a solid-black border wider than 8 points be used for even a full-page advertisement. If an advertiser wishes to use a solid border wider than the sizes adopted as standard, his wider solid blacks are toned down by the use of a screen.

Other points insisted on for the advertising columns by newspapers with high typographic standards are as follows:

Type faces or lettering the widest strokes of which are more than 12 points must be Ben Dayed.

Black reverse cuts are prohibited, other than those of trademarks no more than ¾ of an inch in diameter.

Advertising halftones must be 65-line screen or coarser.

Single-column or smaller illustrations preferably should be in the form of line-cuts, which, when properly designed, are less likely to fill in, and usually show up better in newspapers than would small halftones.

Vignetted halftones usually are unsatisfactory, for the reason stated in Chapter 14 of Part I.

Advertisements ordered for pages in certain sections (amusements, financial, and so on) must be set in the same style as other advertisements in such sections.

In 1942 Harry L. Gage, Linotype vice-president, wrote a booklet entitled *For More Effective Advertising, Don't Screen Type!*

To demonstrate the soundness of that advice, the booklet (printed from stereo plates on newsprint) presented six pairs of type panels—the first of each pair consisting of certain type faces popular with advertisers for body matter, and the second of each pair showing what happened to those same faces when treated with screens or presented in the form of reverse plates.

The booklet stated, in part:

"The studies in readability of type in which Linotype has been collaborating with Dr. Matthew Luckiesh and Frank K. Moss have shown that type is most readable when printed in black ink on white paper. We recognize letter forms through their contrast against the background on which they appear.

"When type is printed on gray or colored paper, we know that it loses some of its legibility through loss of contrast against its background. If you try to read in the dwindling twilight, the page becomes increasingly difficult to read as the amount of light decreases.

"When a screen, or pattern of fine black dots, is thrown across the entire surface of a block of type, the effect on the readers' eyes is identical with the adverse conditions of gray paper or diminishing illumination. The screen becomes a partial black-out and the type becomes less readable."

Three pairs of test panels (1, 2 and 3) showed the effects of screens laid directly over type. One pair (4 and 5) showed the result of reversing type, to print white on black, with a screen added to break up the solid black. Another pair (6) showed an unmodified reverse plate, white on black.

"These six pairs of panels," Mr. Gage stated, "were prepared for these tests with the co-operation of a large metropolitan newspaper. The type matter is typical of the descriptive paragraphs in retail advertising. It is set in 10-point faces selected to give the *best possible* results with the screened treatments. If some of the wiry, delicate book types, sometimes favored by advertisers, had been used, the loss of readability would have been even more pronounced. . . .

"The losses of readability under the varying conditions are shown in detail on the following pages. The plain type is rated as 100% for comparative purposes. (Newsprint would actually measure about 75% as against a pure white surface.) But since all the test panels were printed on newsprint, the comparative losses in readability remain the same and the percentages of loss, from 18% to 38%, are directly compared with the plain type.

"With such direct losses of readability, the advertiser makes it difficult in that degree for his readers to get the message that has been veiled by a screen. Why black-out type when its selling job is so vital? The moral is obvious—*Don't screen type!*

"When type is reversed, white on black, the results are similarly unfortunate. Panel 6 is reversed but *not* screened. This panel, as printed in the test sheets, showed a certain mottling, due to texture of paper and press blankets. . . . Panel 6 showed a loss of 27% against the plain type.

"On Panel 4 a fairly coarse screen was used and the readability loss was 38%. It is apparent that the white dots interfere with the white details of the type characters. Thus there is a double loss of legibility —first, the background contrast is diminished; second, the letter forms themselves are distorted and obscured by the dots of the screen.

"On Panel 5 a finer screen was used in reverse. Here the loss in readability was 31%, obviously too great a handicap for an intelligent advertiser to inflict upon his readers. These tests are potent evidence against reversed plates of any kind when body type is to be printed. And they show that screened reverse plates are the least readable of any treatment of type.

"With this simple and obvious demonstration of losses of readability, the wise advertiser will not permit any art director, layout man or copy-writer to hold that masses of screen enhance the effectiveness of advertisements. When he realizes that such treatments seriously handicap the reader, he will insist that types be permitted to do their work cleanly and clearly on simple paper. . . .

"Today's selling calls for the utmost effectiveness in advertising. *Don't screen type!*"

But at the end of that booklet appeared this note: "The findings in this booklet should not be construed as inimical to the treatment of full feature pages carrying a high-light halftone screen over the entire page. The finer screen, while reducing contrast somewhat, does not necessarily produce adverse effects, on properly selected types."

Example 156 presents a reduced showing of a display advertisement with many faults. Yet the advertisement was typical of many display advertisements appearing in many newspapers not so particular as they might be about advertising typographic standards.

The four least important elements in the advertisement (but the four most prominently treated) were the four borders. All of them were too heavy. The lower border was not designed for newspaper use. Although the type faces themselves were heavy, the borders, still heavier, distracted attention from the types—from the messages the types were supposed to convey. The funereal border about the three men in the illustration suggested that they may have been discussing a

THE ORDINARY NEWSPAPER

FINAL CLEARANCE OF SUITS AND OVERCOATS

$49.50

Large black type, screaming for attention, trying to plow its way through to the front position results in other advertisers adopting the same tactics with the final result that each one neutralizes the effect of the other and the resultfulness of advertising, collectively and individually is seriously impaired. There are approximately the same number of words in this block of copy as in the one on the opposite page under the same heading.

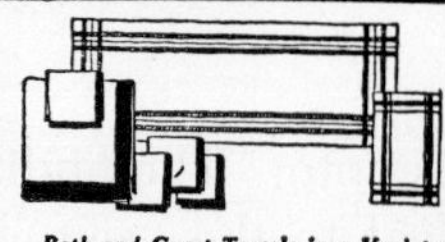

***Bath and Guest Towels in a Variety of Patterns*—Cramped, disorderly stores are not frequented by customers whose patronage is most sought after and neither do advertisements that convey this impression get favorable attention from the majority of readers. $1.35 Pr.**

***Handkerchiefs of Finest Irish Linen, Colored and Plain*—Building a fence around every item in an advertisement makes it difficult and confusing for the reader to follow through the sequence of the advertisement in a comfortable and intelligent manner. $3.75 Doz.**

***Imported Handbags in all the Latest Designs*—A store that would place difficulties in the way of its customer's movements from one department to another would be hard to imagine but this very thing is done in advertisements arranged like this. $12.00.**

COLORFUL
R U G S
FROM THE ORIENT
$15.95

White space is frequently more effective in the body of a department store advertisement than rules and boxes.

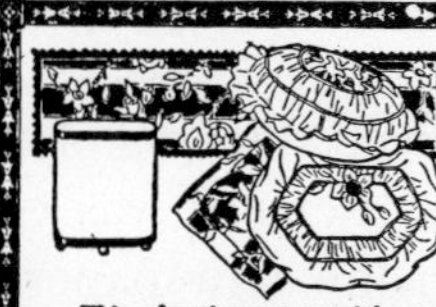

Large Assortment of Fancy Silk Sofa Cushions

$7.50

This advertisement certainly would not be considered easier and quicker to set and make-up than the one shown on the opposite page yet a great deal of bad typography is laid to lack of time.

THE
LANCASTER
KITCHEN CABINET
$42.50

It is better to place the spacing around the copy rather than to open it up too much by leading between the lines.

EXAMPLE 156

THE DISTINGUISHED NEWSPAPER

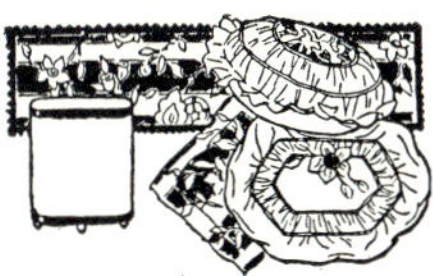

Large Assortment of Fancy Silk Sofa Cushions

Broad aisles of white space in the advertisement compare with the spacious passageways throughout the well arranged department store. They make "visualized shopping" trips easy, comfortable and pleasant . . $3.75

Imported Handbags in all the Latest Designs

Merchandise is grouped in an orderly and related manner in the store and the same practice should be very strictly adhered to in the typographic treatment of a department store announcement. . . . $12.00

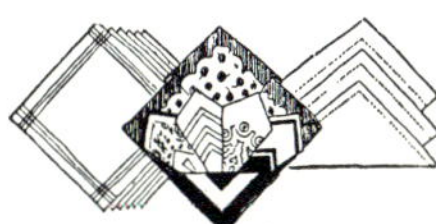

Handkerchiefs of Finest Irish Linen, Colored and Plain

The simplicity of this layout suggests good taste—refinement. It is more in the form of a polite invitation to read rather than an abrupt demand for attention. . . $3.75

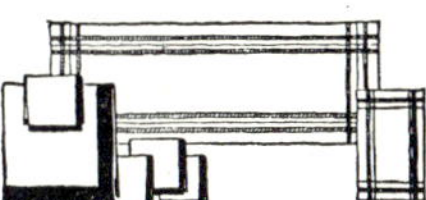

Bath and Guest Towels in a Variety of Patterns

Using a smaller type size for all text and display lines gives us as much emphasis and a great deal more dignity and saves much time in setting and making-up $1.35

Final Clearance of Suits and Overcoats

$49.50

. . . Here is the main entrance,—the wide swinging doors welcoming the advertising shopper to its inviting display of offerings in print. This, the main feature, is intended to serve the double purpose of attracting attention to the advertisement as a whole and of selling the merchandise offered under this heading. It stands out by itself yet it is not barricaded from the rest of the group for which it serves as a focal point

Men's Department—Second Floor

Colorful Rugs from the Orient

$15.95

The department store advertisement should correctly reflect the atmosphere of the store so far as type, copy and illustration can do so. It *is* the store, brought into the reader's home.

The Lancaster Kitchen Cabinet

$42.50

Just as the show windows attract attention of passersby so must the advertisement attract and interest the passing eye of the reader travelling through the pages of the paper.

EXAMPLE 157

death in the family of one of them. The condensed bold face used for the larger body lines was not designed to be used in masses, and, used that way, was difficult to read. The smaller lines in the three horizontal panels were too cramped, and the heavy and fancy vertical borders between the three units of the panel actually served as barriers to the gaze of the reader. They made it difficult for him to shift from one unit to another.

The whole advertisement was too crowded. It did not make sufficient use of the important element of white space. Moreover, its unattractive, commonplace appearance suggested that the store behind it was commonplace and probably offered commonplace goods at questionable prices.

Notice how much more attractively the same items were treated in Example 157.

Observe the restrained borders, and that fewer of them were used; that the main headlines were closely associated with the main illustration—not separated from it by attention-distracting rules; that all type lines, both heads and body matter, were attractive and easy to read, with price figures that stood out unmistakably, but harmoniously; that white space was judiciously employed throughout.

The advertisement was dignified, confidence inspiring. It suggested that the store behind it was a high-class institution.

An important consideration to the newspaper is that that simple, dignified and effective advertisement required for its composition and makeup only a small fraction of the time required to set and put together the commonplace and less effective advertisement suggested by Example 156.

In February, 1945, the *Times-Herald* of Washington, D. C., put into effect for its advertising columns certain regulations designed to improve the effectiveness of those columns and to enhance the readability of the *Times-Herald* as a whole. The regulations were based on the results of personal interviews conducted by a Washington advertising firm with 654 Washington homemakers—94.9% of whom said they found advertisements in lighter type faces more readable than advertisements in heavier faces.

A story in *Editor & Publisher* for June 6, 1945, contained the following statements about the *Times-Herald* survey and its advertising regulations:

"Convinced that lighter type faces coupled with judicious use of white space make a more readable newspaper and increase the reader attention given to individual advertisements, the *Washington* (D.C.) *Times-Herald* has been requiring advertisers to conform to this thinking, with a success that is reflected in a recent readership survey. Some merchants were fearful that their customary black advertisements would lose 'punch' when cleaned up, but 654 personal interviews conducted by Kal, Ehrlich & Merrick, Washington advertising firm, with capital homemakers show that 94.9% of them find the lighter ads more readable.

"The housewives, carefully selected to represent a population cross-section of the city and its suburbs, were asked three questions pertaining specifically to grocery advertising. In reply 85.3% asserted that they regularly read the *Times-Herald* before shopping for food products, and 4.4% said 'sometimes.' . . .

"In addition to being asked which type, light or black, ads they prefer, the women were also requested to check which of twenty-two ads, eleven of each kind, they found the more readable. Consistently, they indicated the lighter ads, giving no black one more than 6.4%. Typical comments were: 'Clean type is so fresh-looking!' and 'The lighter version is easier to read and neater' and 'Already noticed the new type and had remarked how much cleaner it was.'

"Results of the survey are reported in a brochure which also contains examples of the display type available to *Times-Herald* advertisers and reproductions of commendatory letters from eleven of the local merchants who expressed their appreciation of the newly enforced system.

"For some time the newspaper, in an effort to maintain a high standard of typographical excellence, has stated in its national rate card: 'The right to Ben Day or modify heavy blacks, background, borders or reversed type, to conform with the *Times-Herald* rules, is expressly reserved,' but not until February, 1945, did it begin enforcement.

"Space limitations have created a 'tighter' appearance, the *Times-Herald* explains, and consequently many advertisers, in an effort to gain visibility and dominance, have resorted to stronger layouts and type. However, it continues, instead they defeated their purpose, and consequently the paper has stepped in and arbitrarily required lighter, cleaner ads.

"Previous efforts in this direction, but put on a voluntary basis, had failed, since not enough advertisers fell into line, so that the no-compromise stand was necessitated. It applies equally to every type of advertising and every advertiser. As a result, the paper adds, the *Times-Herald* has lost a few accounts which demanded black advertisements, but 'this has been more than offset by an increased use of the paper by advertisers who prefer light copy.'"

Not many years ago some of the largest advertisers in the way of food stores made mistakes in advertising. They went in for meaningless arrays of heavy and black rules—as heavy and as black as the newspapers running the advertisements would tolerate. But the more successful of such stores have abandoned the use of many and heavy rules—either because they themselves recognized the advisability of doing it, or because the more particular newspapers declined to accept their offerings in their original forms—and are now presenting more attractive and more effective advertisements.

In 1945, in a booklet by Harry L. Gage entitled *What Makes Your Advertising Pull?* the Linotype Company reproduced and discussed seven differently treated food-store advertisements that had appeared in a certain newspaper, with various degrees of success. Some of the advertisements, as the booklet pointed out, were much more successful than others. The simpler, less complicated ones—the advertisements with fewer and lighter rules, fewer reverse plates, and with more white space—were much more effective than the heavier and more complicated treatments.

At the beginning of the booklet Mr. Gage stated:

"All the answers to the all-important question of pulling power represent every factor in modern selling. Product, location, suitability to market, reputation, service—all these familiar points come in for study if we seek what's back of an effective advertisement.

"But if all the basic factors are *equal*, it is still true that one ad may be read by more people than another. Why? Usually the answer is copy (the advertising message), plus layout (the plan on paper), plus perhaps the attraction of illustration.

"Further simplified, however, to the point that copy, as a selling message, is boiled down to the limit, and illustration is only incidental, is that class of advertising known as 'food-store.' Other lines, notably drug and hardware stores, sometimes employ the same style, but food-store ads have become a nationwide feature of our newspapers. If we can determine what makes them readable, we have some indication of value for other fields as well.

"An excellent opportunity to make comparisons, based on scientific studies, has come with the investigations of newspaper readership conducted by the Advertising Research Foundation."

The booklet reproduced seven food-store ads from one issue of a daily paper in a Midwest city of moderate size. The extent to which men and women read those ads was accurately determined, and the booklet analyzed those readership values in terms of advertising planning and type arrangement.

"The seven examples," Mr. Gage continued, "show that any effort to add a note of 'originality' hurt the readership values.

"A turned and twisted panel of type used more space for one less item and didn't increase readership.

"Too many cuts brought confusion, rather than interest.

"Heavy and elaborate borders cut down effective selling space and didn't pull more readers.

"Type blocks packed into a surrounding border-illustration added only distraction.

" 'Reversed' type, photo-engraved to make white letters on a black ground, featured the *least* effective ad of the seven.

"Extra-black type likewise failed to produce higher values.

"All these 'stunts'—so frequently sought by planners of ads—are known by top-flight advertising designers and typesetters to be more hazardous than valuable. Here are simple demonstrations, all in one paper on the same day, giving a basis of comparison that must afford convincing proof that simple type arrangement makes for high readership of the ad."

Only 12% of the men readers of the paper in which the seven advertisements appeared, and only 31% of the women, read the least effective of the seven advertisements—one that included more than a half dozen reverse plates, closely packed type lines, a heavy wavy rule in one of its sections, and a heavily boxed section set into the main layout on an angle. As the booklet pointed out, that least effective of the seven displays, compared with the most effective of the seven, showed a relative *loss* of pulling power of 43% for the men and of 40% for the women.

The critical comment that accompanied the worst of the seven ran, in part, as follows:

"Even in its half-scale reproduction here this ad is so 'noisy' in its use of blacks that it loses pulling power. It is a typical example of *over-emphasis*, the blaring of all the instruments in the band that drowns out the music in sheer noise.

"Ad planners sometimes attempt the method employed here to make 'reverse cuts.' . . . They believe, mistakenly, that the contrasts thus afforded add interest. Then they feel the need for extra-black, heavy borders and the blackest types the printer can supply. . . .

"When sheer blackness adds up to confusion, readership must suffer.

"We can only point to this . . . ad as an example of what to avoid. It is wasteful of space and effort. As a finished ad, it would be exceedingly difficult to correct, if necessary, particularly the items photo-engraved in reverse. And its noisy discord obviously doesn't get readership."

That "all display is no display" is just as true in the advertising columns of a newspaper as in its news and feature columns.

Place an unusually black advertisement among several considerably lighter ones and the heavy display, of course, will dominate the page—whether or not that display will be easy to read.

Many newspaper advertisers call for heavy typographic treatments. Naturally, they want their displays to stand out among others on a page. But many such advertisers fail to realize that other users of space on the same page want their statements to stand out, also, and that they plan to bring about that result by means of typographic treatments just as heavy as, or even heavier than, others on the page.

Such thinking often results in pages of black blotches that fight among themselves for attention without any one of them getting as much of it as its planner expected to attract—blotches that not only spoil the looks of pages but that abuse the eyesight of the reader and make it difficult for him, the potential buyer of the things advertised, to concentrate on any of the statements of any of the advertisers.

Some advertisers who now call for heavy typographic treatments would be willing to tone down their displays were it not that they feel compelled to use them in self-defense—to keep from being "out-shouted" by adjacent and competing displays. And that is why certain progressive newspapers have established definite typographic standards for their advertising pages—standards which, by setting definite limits on the degrees of blackness that may be employed by any advertiser, assure fair treatment for all users of space, and that make for much more attractive and readable pages.

Of course blackness is a comparative term. A rule or decorative border that would be too heavy, or a type face that would be too large or too black, for a comparatively small advertisement, would not necessarily be objectionable in a comparatively large display. Heavy rules and borders and large or heavy type faces were made to be used in large areas and to be generously treated with white space. But when large and black units are jammed into small areas, unsightliness is bound to result.

Some advertisers, however, are shrewd enough, even when using space in newspapers that permit advertisers to employ unusually heavy display, to plan their advertisements to stand out in a group of heavy ones. And such advertisements are made to stand out, not by the use of heavy faces but by the employment of light faces and the judicious use of white space.

To some extent the subject or subjects (as well as the size) of an advertisement should dictate the sort of type and other physical treatment the advertisement should be given. While it is easily possible to go to extremes in such matters—sometimes to ridiculous extremes—some subjects naturally call for lighter treatments, some for heavier, than others.

Advertisements uninteresting in themselves tend to make the paper as a whole uninteresting. In this class fall advertisements kept standing from issue to issue—kept standing so long, through so many issues, that they become too familiar to too many readers to be interesting to them. Besides, the practice of letting advertisements stand from issue to issue often results in unsightly displays after the first few runnings—unsightliness caused by broken, battered or worn type faces, cuts, rules or borders, or improperly cleaned forms, with consequently impaired printing qualities.

Many papers long since have declined to run displays merely reading "Compliments of a Friend," on the ground that such displays cannot be interesting to many readers. Besides, such displays smatter of charity.

Rules and borders enclosing advertisements should be carefully joined at the corners. Some rules and borders were designed to be mitered—to be trimmed at an angle of forty-five degrees at the points at which they are to be joined—not merely put together without mitering. Often otherwise attractive layouts are spoiled by carelessly "joined" rules or borders.

Some advertisers are always on the hunt for the unusual in type faces, and from time to time break into newspaper print with faces that have no other virtue than that of novelty—if novelty be a virtue—and that cannot, because of their physical characteristics, be used effectively in newspaper advertising. But more experienced newspaper advertisers do not employ a face merely because it seems unusual. It has to be considerably more than that. It has to be a face that, in addition to intrinsic merit, will stand up well in the stereotyping department and that will print clearly and do a good selling job despite the handicaps imposed by coarse-fibered newsprint, soupy news ink, high-speed presses, and little if any make-ready.

Some of the many Linotype faces (available in various sizes) that can be used effectively in newspaper advertising, in addition to the faces shown in Chapters 5 and 16 of Part I, are:

18-point Antique No. 1

Some Newspapers Are Easier to Read

18-point Antique No. 1 Italic

Some Newspapers Are Easier to Read

18-point Caledonia Bold

Some Newspapers Are Easier to Read

18-point Garamond Bold

Some Newspapers Are Easier to Read Th

18-point Garamond Bold Italic

Some Newspapers Are Easier to Read Th

18-point Garamond Bold No. 3

Some Newspapers Are Easier to Read T

18-point Garamond Bold No. 3 Italic

Some Newspapers Are Easier to Read T

18-point Memphis Extra Bold

Some Newspapers Are Easier to

18-point Memphis Extra Bold Italic

Some Newspapers Are Easier to

18-point Memphis Extra Bold Condensed

Some Newspapers Are Easier to Read Than Ot

18-point Poster Bodoni Compressed

Some Newspapers Are Easier to Read Than Others and

18-point Pabst Extra Bold

Some Newspapers Are Easier

18-point Pabst Extra Bold Italic

Some Newspapers Are Easier

18-point Pabst Extra Bold Condensed

Some Newspapers Are Easier to Read

18-point Pabst Extra Bold Condensed Italic

Some Newspapers Are Easier to Read

18-point Vulcan Bold

Some Newspapers Are Easier to

18-point Vulcan Bold Italic

Some Newspapers Are Easier to

Years ago many space buyers felt that right-hand pages were more to be desired than left-hand for advertisements because readers, in turning the pages from front to back, would be more likely to see the pages at the right before the ones at the left, and, consequently, many advertisers used to request positions on right-hand pages.

That sort of reasoning may have been sound years ago, but it is not so sound today, for studies of many newspapers in many parts of the country through several years have shown that advertisements on left-hand pages have just about the same chance of being read as advertisements of equal size and general attractiveness on right-hand pages.

Perhaps the fact that so many advertisers called for right-hand pages had much to do with that "balancing of left and right" by necessitating the exclusion of more and more important news and interesting feature stories from right-hand pages, to provide space for more and more advertising at the right, to a point where many readers more interested ordinarily in news and feature stories than in advertising came to look for preferred reading matter on left-hand pages—but could not easily fail to see and to read much of the advertising on those same pages.

At any rate, studies of many newspapers in recent years show that left-hand pages can be just about as effective for advertisers as right-hand pages.

Advertising in larger city dailies usually is sold by the agate line; in smaller city dailies and weeklies by the column inch.

18

Placing Display Advertisements

A NEWSPAPER PAGE on which display advertising is pyramided to the right can be much more attractive as a whole, as well as more considerate of the reader and more effective for advertisers, than a page on which advertisements are scattered in helter-skelter fashion. A page with its advertising pyramided, not only makes possible the running of news or feature stories or departments at the top of the page, where readers are accustomed to looking for important stories or departments, but it helps the reader to concentrate on the items in which he is most interested at the moment—"reading matter" or advertising, as the case may be. On a helter-skelter page the various stories and advertisements keep interrupting and diverting his attention, often to his annoyance and to the disadvantage of all the units. Moreover, the stories on such a page, even important stories, appear to be little more than fillers.

Example 158 presents a reduced showing of an advertising page on which four advertisements have been pyramided upward to the right.

Note the orderly arrangement of the advertisements and stories, and that the largest advertisement was in the lower-right corner. And be sure to note that, although fully two-thirds of the page was given over to advertising, the tops of all eight columns presented news stories.

Equally graphic, but in a negative way, would that page have been had the two larger displays been given the top-of-page position sometimes requested by advertisers, with the two smaller displays and the news stories and pictures placed below the four advertisements—a re-arrangement that would not be acceptable to newspapers in this country with high typographic standards.

Had the larger displays been placed at the top of the page, with the stories and pictures below them and the two smaller displays, the page would have been unorganized, chaotic. It would have been confused and confusing. The re-arrangement (disarrangement) would have tended to pull the reader's attention in too many different direc-

42 NEW YORK HERALD TRIBUNE, SUNDAY, FEBRUARY 17, 1916

Joan Bixler Fiancee Of F. D. Guernsey, Tennis Champion

Donald Bixlers' Daughter; Officer Was Decorated Twice With 8th Air Force

Mr. and Mrs. Donald S. Bixler, of Garden City, L. I., have announced the engagement of their daughter, Miss Joan Bartlett Bixler, to Mr. Frank D. Guernsey jr., former major in the A. A. F., decorated twice with the 8th Air Force, son of Mr. and Mrs. Frank D. Guernsey, of Orlando, Fla. Miss Bixler was graduated from Cherry Valley School and Edgewood Park, '43, where she was president of her class.

Mr. Guernsey is a graduate of Rice Institute, '40. He was operations officer of the 339th Fighter Group and received the Air Medal with four clusters and the Distinguished Flying Cross. With Mr. W. D. McNeill he is national indoor tennis doubles champion, and last month won the Florida state singles championship. He was the national intercollegiate singles champion in 1938 and 1939.

Grace Kathryn Crane, Capt. Richards to Wed

Officer, Son of Clergyman, Served With 26th Division

Mr. and Mrs. Wilbur Hyde Crane, of 1711 Newkirk Avenue, Brooklyn, announce the engagement of their daughter, Miss Grace Kathryn Crane, to Captain Donald Kirtland Richards, on terminal leave after serving with the 26th (Yankee) Division overseas, son of the Rev. Parke Richards and Mrs. Richards, of Lawrenceville, N. J. Miss Crane is a graduate of Berkeley Institute, attended the Young School and is a member of the Brooklyn Junior League and Daughters of 1812.

Captain Richards is a graduate of Lawrenceville School and Princeton University.

Simister—Wray

Mr. and Mrs. James B. Wray, of Montclair, N. J., and Shelter Island, N. Y., announce the engagement of their daughter, Miss Betty Jane Wray, to Mr. Frederic W. Simister, son of Mr. and Mrs. Frederic P. Simister, of East Orange, N. J. Miss Wray attends the Parsons School of Design. Mr. Simister was recently discharged from the Navy after twenty-seven months in the Pacific. He is continuing his studies at Wake Forest College.

Shinners—McConnell

Mrs. William P. McConnell, of 22 Riverside Drive, announces the engagement of her daughter, Miss Mary Donn McConnell, to Mr. James E. Shinners, son of Mr. and Mrs. Joseph J. Shinners, of Milwaukee. Miss McConnell is a daughter of the late William P. McConnell. She attended Barnard School for Girls and was graduated from Trinity College, Washington. Mr. Shinners, a graduate of Marquette University, attended Georgetown Law School.

Hall—Eichhorn

Mr. and Mrs. William Alois Eichhorn, of South Orange, N. J., announce the engagement of their daughter, Miss Rita Wismar Eichhorn, to Mr. Warren Smith Hall jr., son of Mr. and Mrs. Warren Smith Hall, of Montclair, N. J. Miss Eichhorn was graduated from Columbia High School, Maplewood, N. J., and the Melissa Mills School, New York; her fiance from Stevens Institute of Technology, '29. He served in the Army eighteen months.

Morford—Brenneis

Mr. and Mrs. August F. Brenneis, of 491 Eighth Avenue, Brooklyn, and West End, N. J., announce the engagement of their daughter, Margaret Brenneis, to Mr. Courtney William Morford, son of Mrs. Cornelius M. Morford, of Toledo, Iowa, and the late Dr. Morford. Miss Brenneis attended Berkeley Institute, Wells College and Katharine Gibbs School. Mr. Morford received the B. S. degree from Coe College and M. S. from Iowa State. He was honorably discharged recently from the Army after serving in the China-India-Burma theater.

Pauley—Cotton

Mr. and Mrs. W. M. Cotton, of Poundridge, N. Y., and 1050 Park Avenue, announce the engagement of their daughter, Miss Barbara Anne Cotton, to Mr. Robert Reinhold Pauley, son of Mrs. Grace Pauley, of Noroton, Conn., and Mr. Edward M. Pauley, of New Canaan.

Fiances Served in Army Air Forces and Navy

Miss Joan Bartlett Bixler (Delar) — Miss Mary Walker Bell (Jay Te Winburn)

Engaged to Ex-Navy Man

Mary Walker Bell Will Be Wed to Chapin Coit, of Buffalo

Mr. and Mrs. Harold Corey Bell, of 115 East Fifty-third Street and Peconic, L. I., announce the engagement of their daughter, Miss Mary Walker Bell, to Mr. Chapin Coit, son of Mrs. J. Chapin Coit, of Buffalo, and the late George Coit, of Buffalo and Santa Monica, Calif.

Miss Bell attended Kent Place School, Summit, N. J., and the Parsons School. Mr. Coit attended Nichols School, Buffalo, and Cheshire Academy and was discharged recently from the Navy.

Marie J. C. Whitman, Of Marine Corps, Samuel Myer to Wed

Harold Cutler Whitmans' Daughter; Her Fiance in 82d Airborne Division

Mr. and Mrs. Harold Cutler Whitman, of Bedford Village, N. Y., announce the engagement of Mr. Whitman's daughter, Miss Marie Josepha Claire Whitman, to Mr. Samuel Clarendon Myer, A. U. S., son of Mrs. Madaline Edwards Myer, of Santa Barbara, Calif., and of Major Albert J. Myer, of Wiscasset, Me. Miss Whitman attended Ethel Walker School and is serving in the Marine Corps Women's Reserve.

Lieutenant Myer attended St. Paul's School and was graduated from Princeton University, '43. He served overseas with the 17th Airborne Division and is now stationed at Fort Bragg, N. C., with the 82d Airborne Division.

Walter—Ficke

Announcement has been made by Mr. and Mrs. Theodore F. Ficke jr., of Bay Ridge, Brooklyn, of the engagement of their daughter, Miss Ruth Claire Ficke, to Mr. Charles Richard Walter, son of Mrs. Charles Walter, of Chicago.

Miss Hull, an Ex-Wave, Charles Dennis Engaged

Fiance of Brooklyn Girl Was Army Officer in South Pacific

Mr. and Mrs. Lawrence Cameron Hull jr., of 257 Hicks Street, Brooklyn, announce the engagement of their daughter, Miss Margaret Callender Simmons Hull, to Mr. Charles Cheney Dennis, son of Mr. and Mrs. Rodney Gove Dennis, of 1105 Park Avenue. A graduate of Packer Collegiate Institute, Miss Hull attended Barnard College, enlisted in the Waves in 1942, was in the first group of radio trainees at the University of Wisconsin and was discharged in December as a petty officer, first class.

Mr. Dennis is a graduate of Ken School, attended Yale University, and has just completed his terminal leave as a lieutenant in the Army after two years in the South Pacific.

Rothacker—Cooper

Mr. and Mrs. W. Stanfield Cooper, of Manhasset, L. I., announce the engagement of their daughter, Miss Jean Frances Cooper, to Mr. Douglas Dustin Rothacker, son of Mr. Douglas D. Rothacker, of Great Neck, L. I., and Mrs. Margaret T. Rothacker, of Manhasset and Evanston, Ill. Miss Cooper is attending Wells College. Mr. Rothacker, a graduate of Phillips Exeter, attended Yale.

"A room of distinction, featuring the cuisine and wines that are making the Embassy famous the world over."
Bill Miller's Embassy

MILGRIM

Long Life Ahead for the SHORT JACKET SUIT

Take a pastel tweed windbreaker jacket . . . highlight it with black hairline patterning . . . set it off against a soft black skirt . . . and you have a headline fashion for Spring. Also in our short jacket series, a brief box jacket suit of the same fabric combination. Jacket in white wine, light blue, pink. Skirt black. 100% wool. 10-18. $35

SALYMIL SUITS—FOURTH FLOOR

MILGRIM 6 WEST 57TH STREET

Carriage trade never speaks loudly

RITZ CARLTON

The very élite quietly insist on quality in every thing surrounding them—especially beauty preparations, the most distinctive of which is made-to-order face powder, formulated by experts to cater to milady's every color-whim or fancy.

Charles of the Ritz

its bow news by Bally

IN POLISHED BLACK SUIT PUMPS

foot-flattering new versions of bows . . . created by Bally of Switzerland to lend piquant interest to suit pumps . . . all in fine black calfskin that glows with a soft patina . . . detailed with typically fine Swiss craftsmanship.

top: heart-shaped bow with a whipstitched corded edge, pair 21.85

below: stitched butterfly bow on a closed-back pump, pair 23.00

Altman shoe fashions, second floor
also at our East Orange and White Plains shops

B. ALTMAN & CO. Fifth Avenue New York

EXAMPLE 158

tions, and the stories and pictures would have been little more than fillers.

Had the larger advertisements been set in heavier type faces and enclosed with heavier rules, as such advertisements often are treated in some newspapers, the page would have appeared decidedly top-heavy and even less attractive.

It is well for advertisers to bear in mind (and perhaps for publishers to remind them, diplomatically, from time to time) that an attractive advertisement on an attractively arranged page can be more effective for all concerned than a good-looking advertisement on an unattractive page—the sort that often results when demands for isolated positions have been complied with. Every advertisement is affected in some way "by the company it keeps."

Not only do many metropolitan newspapers and some smaller papers follow the pyramid plan, but several alert advertisers, recognizing the effectiveness of the plan, follow it themselves for many of their displays.

Example 159, a reduced showing of a page with all of the advertising on it from the same store, suggests the way in which several large New York stores often present advertisements in newspapers—attractively, effectively pyramided to the right.

Example 160 suggests another treatment of the same idea.

Note that, on both pages, the tops of five columns have been left open for news stories and pictures.

Such advertisers are shrewd enough to appreciate that space on a page attractively arranged as a whole can be much more effective for them than on a page of the helter-skelter kind. And they appreciate, too, that stories or departments at the top of a page can be attention arresting to many a reader who, were there no such matter there, would be inclined to turn the page without more than glancing at the advertising on it, but who, being stopped by those stories or departments, may look over the advertisements too before directing his attention to other pages.

Moreover, when an advertiser does his own pyramiding, he is in a position to give each unit of the pyramid the treatment it seems to call for in relation to its other units—the degrees of display and white space that will cause it to stand out on its own, yet any border or other typographic treatment that will cause it to tie in well with the whole. And he has the assurance, within certain reasonable limits set up by

12 NEW YORK WORLD-TELEGRAM, TUESDAY, MARCH 5, 1946

Ask United Nations To Found University

By Science Service.

LONDON, March 1.—A World University is advocated from several quarters, who have communicated their suggestions to the Secretary of the United Nations Educational, Scientific and Cultural Organization.

The Colombian delegation was among the first to ask for a University of the United Nations in order to encourage scientific research and higher education both in technical science and in other branches of human knowledge.

The International Committee for a World University Alliance of New York, created to promote the establishment of a world university, has submitted a scheme for a World University charter.

Dr. Maxwell Garnett, formerly of the League of Nations Union, suggested creation of an international university established mainly for research workers qualified in a number of fields.

Dr. Hugh Trowbridge (U. S. A.) proposed the establishment of a United Nations University in realization of Article 62 of the charter. At the same time he suggested the creation of degrees for the United Nations, a program of study, means for promoting the scheme and a method for the selection of candidates for this university.

These proposals have been referred for further study to special committees.

West Indian Cherry Is Rich in Vitamin

By Science Service Medical Writer.

WASHINGTON, March 5.—A new very rich source of anti-scurvy vitamin C has been discovered in the West Indian cherry. Reporting their discovery in Science, Dr. Conrado F. Asenjo and Dr. Ana Freire de Guzman of the School of Topical Medicine at San Juan, Puerto Rico, state that this is "one of the richest if not the richest edible fruit source" of the vitamin so far described in scientific literature.

These cherries supply about 34 times as much vitamin C as oranges, it appears from the analyses of the Puerto Rican scientists which give the average vitamin C content of 100 gm of edible cherries as 1,707 mg. One cherry, it seems, would supply four or more times the amount of vitamin C recommended by nutrition authorities for the day's ration of this vitamin.

These cherries, commonly called acerola in Spanish, grow on small trees native to tropical and subtropical America. They are fleshy, bright red when ripe and have what the scientists call "an agreeably acid taste." About six of them would weigh one ounce.

Botanists will recognize these cherries under the name, Malpighia punicifolia L., and will know that in spite of their common name, West Indian cherry, they are only distantly related to the cherry family.

Shot in Harlem Fight

Oliver Richardson, 16 of 135 W 117th St., was shot in the left forearm last night during the course of a fight with two men, police reported. Richardson, who was treated for the superficial wound at Sydenham Hospital, told police he was attacked on Fifth Ave between 116th and 117th Streets by the two men, one of whom drew a revolver and fired at him

Reds Bar Mukden Door After Press Invasion

By the Associated Press

TIENTSIN, March 5.—Russians, surprised at seeing 22 uninvited foreign news correspondents roaming Soviet-held Manchuria, have recovered—and barred the door. Now they're stopping trains to Mukden to search them for foreigners.

Only surprise could have enabled the coup which brought the first on-the-scene stories of Soviet activities, in the opinion of the first group of newsmen to return. For Soviet hospitality cooled after the first startled week.

Undoubtedly any more foreigners apearing in Russian-held territory will be in for a rough time unless they have proper Soviet-approved credentials—especially when Soviet officers hear what the boys have been writing about.

They Just Boarded a Train.

(Stories have covered shipping of Jap war prisoners to Siberia; dismantling and removal of Manchurian industrial plants; full-dress military maneuvers of the Red Army outside Dairen.)

The first wave of eight Americans and one British writer had grown weary of red tape which kept them out of Manchuria. They wanted to cover what they considered a legitimate news story within the jurisdiction of Lt. Gen. Albert C. Wedemeyer, U. S. commander in the China theater, which includes Manchuria.

So they entrained for Mukden. Russians in Mukden still were suffering from that first shock when another group of a dozen correspondents arrived by the same expedient. A French newsman turned up later, alone.

The first group found the Russians guarding the city with submachine guns. The Soviets put the newsmen in the Intourist Hotel and said it would be dangerous outside. The correspondents fumed until eventually the Russians said they could roam. Certain factories, however, remained banned.

The second wave registered at the Intourist without incident and proceeded to look over the city.

The first wave meanwhile decided to go to Changchun, the capital. The Mukden commandant strongly urged them not to go. They went, by night. That was a week ago, and they haven't been heard from since, except indirectly. Chinese sources said they were detained at first, but later freed.

A Machine-gun Sendoff.

Three newsmen wandered to Dairen. The Dairen commandant was not happy about this. He said, in effect, that they were standing (uninvited) on Soviet soil. They went back to Mukden, some Russian guards going along for the ride.

From Mukden they entrained back to Chinhsien. They got a rousing sendoff—a Soviet guard stopped their Chinese truck en route to the train by firing a submachine-gun burst over their heads. But when he found the foreigners were leaving—not entering—Mukden he became quite cheery, and even provided an escort.

He didn't want them to miss their train.

To Wed Austrian

Acme Newspictures

Wac Cpl. Ottilie Schmakal (above), Vienna-born girl from Astoria, L. I., is one of the first three Americans granted permission to marry Austrians by Gen. Mark Clark. She will wed her childhood sweetheart, Dr. Frederick Blodi, Vienna ophthalmologist.

YOUR RED CROSS MUST CARRY ON GIVE GENEROUSLY

EXAMPLE 159

NEW YORK HERALD TRIBUNE, SUNDAY, MARCH 10, 1946

Collins Slated For Surrogate's Post Tomorrow

Death of Medalie Delayed Appointment by Dewey; Tammany Split on Issue

Justice William T. Collins, of the Supreme Court, is slated to be appointed Surrogate of New York County tomorrow by Governor Thomas E. Dewey as the interim successor of the late James A. Foley.

The appointment of Justice Collins, a Democrat, was recommended by the Association of the Bar of the City of New York and by distinguished lawyers of the two major parties. During the last illness of Surrogate Foley, Justice Collins acted as surrogate at the request of Mr. Foley.

The dominant faction in Tammany Hall, headed by Clarence H. Neal jr. and Bert Stand, favored the appointment of Justice Louis A. Valente, of the Supreme Court, as the interim Surrogate, and their followers threatened a primary fight in the event that Justice Collins is a candidate.

Loughlin Backs Collins

This opposition to Justice Collins is not shared by Edward V. Loughlin, leader of Tammany Hall, and friends of the justice and prospective Surrogate are relying on Mr. Loughlin to win over the anti-Collins group in his organization.

Justice Collins, who has ten years to serve as a member of the State Supreme Court, must resign as justice before he may be sworn in as Surrogate. This, it was learned, he is prepared to do, confident of carrying his own party's primary as well as the Republican, where he will have the organization's backing.

"A contest in the Tammany primary over the nomination for Surrogate would mean an all-out primary fight among the Democrats, as Justice Collins has many friends among the Tammany district leaders as well as with the rank and file of the organization.

These Democratic friends of Justice Collins, according to several of their number, would put up their own slate for Assemblyman, State Senators and a justice of the City Court to be nominated in the primary in September. The City Court justice to be chosen in the general election in November will succeed Justice Joseph W. Keller, who will retire on Dec. 31 because of the age limit.

Supporters of Justice Collins in the Democratic party asserted that he has fallen heir to the numerous and influential friends of the late Surrogate Foley and that these would serve him in excellent stead in the event of a primary contest.

Party Leaders Fear Strife

Leading Democrats in the state, aware of the possibility of a primary contest over the nomination for Surrogate here, were reported to be planning to use their influence to avert any party strife this year, when a United States Senator, a Governor and other state officers are to be elected.

Governor Dewey was prepared to send the nomination of Justice Collins as Surrogate to the Senate last week, but delayed acting because of the death of Associate Judge George Z. Medalie, of the Court of Appeals. No successor to Judge Medalie, a Republican, will be chosen for some time.

The appointment of Justice Collins as Surrogate and his resignation as a Supreme Court justice will give Governor Dewey an additional judicial appointment. It is expected that he will name a Republican to the Supreme Court to serve as successor to Justice Collins. The term of this appointment, like that of Justice Collins as Surrogate, would be until Dec. 31. Nominations for justice of the Supreme Court are made in judicial conventions.

Slated for Surrogate

Justice William T. Collins

Rail Man Cites U. S. Aid To Competitive Carriers

Tells Wage Boards Rate Rise Must Be Held to Minimum

CHICAGO, March 9 (AP).—A. F. Cleveland, of Washington, vice-president of traffic of the Association of American Railroads, asserted today that the future of the railroad industry is jeopardized by what he termed government subsidization of competitive carriers.

Mr. Cleveland appeared before combined arbitration boards hearing wage increase demands of operating and non-operating railway brotherhoods.

"Any increase in rates, which of coursee would affect directly the ability of the railroads to meet competition, must be held to the lowest possible level," Mr. Cleveland declared.

He testified that railroads have lost large traffic volume to water carriers and added that the loss was occasioned directly by expenditure of government funds to improve and maintain channels, harbor and terminal facilities. He added that railroads are losing passenger and rail volume to the air lines, whose "air terminal facilities are provided largely at public expense without any investment therein by the air lines."

Mr. Cleveland charged that motor trucks travel over Federal and state highways at what he called a relatively small proportionate share of the cost.

The brotherhoods had presented witnesses to support their demands, all of whom generally testified that railroad workers suffer pay inequalities with other industries.

Edge Deplores 'Hysteria' Over Housing Problem

Says Recent Demands Have Proved To Be Unsound

TRENTON, N. J., March 9 (AP).—Calling for "calm business consideration" and no "hysteria" concerning the existing housing problem, Governor Walter E. Edge said today that housing for veterans is a "shining example" of the American trait "to do the right thing and do it quickly" and thereby cause "unnecessary trouble without accomplishing their objective."

In a statement the Governor said:

"Housing for veterans is a shining example of such action. No sane citizen questions the existing emergency and the necessity for prompt solution. It must be realized, however, after the many ill advised and unsuccessful efforts to construct houses over night that lack of deliberation and co-operation among all the organizations and officials necessary to bring about this result simply emphasizes that haste makes waste.

"It must now be fully realized that the insistent demands of a few months ago for a special legislative session were without merit.

"Temporary housing is now in the process of fulfillment through the only practical method of transferring units already constructed for war purposes to peace-time requirements. At first the Federal government had little to offer in this direction. As far as New Jersey is concerned, after weeks of negotiation, one small development in West Trenton was provided and immediately accepted by the state. Now, through more recent negotiations, it seems quite possible that other cantonments in New Jersey will be made available in the near future."

Mrs. Borotra Is Sought With 3 as Gestapo Spies

France Names Tennis Star's Wife as Agent

PARIS, March 9 (UP).—Warrants have been issued for the arrest of three women—one the wife of tennis star Jean Borotra—and one man who allegedly were members of a gang of Gestapo agents in France during the occupation.

Mrs. Beatrice Borotra, whose husband served as Vichy commissioner of sports, was said to be in hiding in Switzerland. Others for whom warrants were issued were Russian Princess Olga Galitzin, Countess Hildegarde von Seckendorf and Philippe de Dellune, alias De Pacheco.

The four were charged with acting as agents for Count Guy de Glebe de Marcheret, who called himself "Count de Montreuil" and was chief of the Gestapo service at Paris. He was arrested last year.

jay Thorpe
24 WEST 57

THE HAT . . . towering felt cloche, banded with sparkle, from our custom order collection. 55.

jay Thorpe

THE SHOES . . . soaring black suede platform pumps by La Valle, studded with a double row of nailheads. 22.95

This with That*

Key words with Jay Thorpe. In fact, *our credo.* We believe that the well dressed woman is the woman whose ensemble is as integrated as her daily schedule. And it is toward this harmony of costume that Jay Thorpe has dedicated itself for over a quarter of a century.

THE SUIT . . . Regency inspired, from our collection of custom made originals. Forstmann gabardine or soft wool in black, gray, ginger or navy. Sizes 12 to 18. 155.

JAY THORPE—THIRD FLOOR

*Reg. U. S. Pat. Off.

EXAMPLE 160

8 NEW YORK WORLD-TELEGRAM, WEDNESDAY, FEBRUARY 13, 1946

Albany Bill Backs New Market Here

Special to the World-Telegram.

ALBANY, Feb. 13.—A bill to create a three-member market authority for New York City as part of Mayor William O'Dwyer's administration program was introduced under bi-partisan sponsorship yesterday.

The authority would be empowered to establish and operate a wholesale produce market on the site of the present Washington Market. Former Mayor La Guardia bitterly opposed the authority plan for this project. The O'Dwyer-backed measure would allow the authority to finance operation with a $60,000,000 bond issue.

Owing to confusion of procedure, action on a proposed amendment to create a new judicial district for Queens, Nassau and Suffolk counties was put off for a week.

Truck Victim Dies

Special to the World-Telegram

JERSEY CITY, Feb. 13.—Struck by a truck on Ocean Ave. Saturday, Mrs. Anna Graziano, 80, of 489 Ocean Ave. here, died yesterday in Jersey City Medical Center.

Women Suit the Men, Tailors Told

By EDWARD J. MOWERY,
World-Telegram Staff Writer.

You fellows just out of service: Don't fuss around if you can't get reet pleats, slouch pockets or elbow macaroni lapels in your first suit of civvies (if you can find one)!

Be philosophical! Because, no matter how you fool yourself, it's the wife or girl friend who influences the cut of your haberdashery!

Thus was the expert opinion expressed today by Mrs. Ed Reed, of Portland, Oreg., one of the 300 members of the Merchant Tailors & Designers Assn. of America, holding their annual style conclave at the Hotel Roosevelt. The custom clothiers have been so busy taking care of veterans' needs that they didn't even have time to design those dazzling, new dinner jackets for their annual dinner. But listen to Mrs. Reed.

"Boys out of uniform want clothes as unmilitary in cut as possible. I don't blame them! But no matter how much they fume over a style, they won't buy to please themselves! No, sir! The little woman at home will give them the OK or dissent."

Mrs. Reed, a tall, pleasant, middle-aged widow, who took over a thriving business five years ago at the death of her husband, jarred a cluster of fellow tailors with this one:

"I advise every custom tailor in this country to have a woman in his salesroom! Women influence the cut of men's clothes at least 80 per cent! The men can't win! I know. If the wife isn't too critical the daughter is. I pass on every suit before it leaves my shop. I'm ahead of the wives. Get it? That's why even my severest doubters had to call me for suggestions before taking their suits home for the once-over."

Mrs. Reed, with a luxurious sense of humor, said a woman in a tailor shop wouldn't rub the cash customers the wrong way if she were discreet, dignified and conservative.

"The older man doesn't care about his suit until the women criticize it. The tailor shop woman shouldn't be a bleached, theatrical blonde! Neither should she go into fitting rooms. I never did. But women know style. And they can make suggestions. Ahem."

She said there was little hope for the guy whose wife was "fat and floppy." Why should he care how he dresses? But the 20-to-30-year group is very style conscious."

Middle-age does what to a man's appearance?

"Makes it better, as a rule," she asserted. "But the 60-to-70 bunch—the upper executive bracket—you have to camouflage them if they don't watch their diets."

Mrs. Reed, whose annual business soon will top $70,000, hesitated before singling out the nation's consistently best-dressed male.

"I'd say Ralph Bellamy (the movie guy)." She paused. "He's always in colorful good style. And who makes up Mr. Bellamy's largest audience?"

Aw . . . you can't win, fellows!

Cops Hunt Stolen Blasting Caps

The police bomb squad early today was looking for three boxes of electric blasting caps reported missing from a locked magazine of a construction company at 15 E. 91st St.

Each of the boxes, police said, contained 50 caps. Even without dynamite, it was asserted, the caps would injure anyone who set them off by hammering.

17,000 Servicemen To Debark Today

Nearly 17,000 service personnel were expected to reach four U. S. ports today on 30 transport vessels, the Associated Press reported.

Robbed Dealer Shot in Foot

In an effort to block the escape of two bandits from his Brooklyn stationery store, Meyer Singer, 61, of 156 E. 54th St., Bklyn., was shot in the right foot last night.

The thugs entered the store at 99 E. 54th St., Bklyn., with guns, took $30 from the cash register and started to leave. Mr. Singer told police of the Empire Blvd. station he leaped after them. One shot him in the foot, the other hit him on the head with his revolver. Both escaped.

STERN'S

Young

YOUNG DEBONAIRS HALF PEPLUM DRESS

25.00

. . . Half a peplum is better than none . . . just for fun. "Young Charm's" version . . . young yet sophisticated . . . free and easy sleeves cuffed with color . . . squared off shoulders . . . Grey, navy or black with kelly cuffs. Shocking and beige with black cuffs. 9, 11, 13, 15. Young Debonairs, Third Floor.

YOUNG DEBONAIRS GO-GETTING GABARDINE SUIT

48.95

Our collector's item suit . . . butter-smooth wool gabardine you love . . . shined up for spring with brass. Pure and simple . . . with newer than ever deep-set sleeves . . . up and coming collar . . . flanged interest, whipstitched for detail . . . buttoned and belted briskly in brass. Black. 9, 11, 13, 15. Young Debonairs, Third Floor.

STORE HOURS
THURSDAY
11 A. M. TO 8 P. M.

IT'S GLENWEAR'S "FIDDLESTICKS" BLOUSE

2.70

Glenwear's dashing bow blouse . . . like the swashbuckling shirts the gypsy fiddlers of old sported. The perfect soft touch for the trim lines of tailored suits and skirts . . . the elegant bow has drawn hemstitched detail . . . the fabric is suds-happy rayon crepe. White, pink, blue maize. 32 to 38. Blouses, Street Floor.

EVE ARLINGTON'S CROSSTOWN RAYON GABARDINE

14.95

We've netted a well turned shirtwaist collar . . . smoothly set raglan sleeves, deep well pockets and the fullest center pleat under which peep mock tortoise shell buttons to match the big handsome one on the bodice front. Tailored to perfection . . . it's a wonderful background for accessories. Pink, aqua or blue with simulated alligator belt. 12 to 20. Budget Dresses, Third Floor.

Stern's

STERN BROS., 41 W. 42nd ST., N. Y. 18 • LO 5-6000

EXAMPLE 161

NEW YORK WORLD-TELEGRAM, WEDNESDAY, FEBRUARY 13, 1946

Find Mold to Aid Tuberculosis Fight

By the Associated Press.

WASHINGTON, Feb. 13.—Another step in the hunt for a weapon against tuberculosis is described today in Science, official journal of the American Assn. for the Advancement of Science.

Drs. Isadore E. Gerber and Milton Gross of the Hudson County Tuberculosis Hospital at Jersey City report that a mold derived substance, they called mycocidin, had rendered active tuberculosis germs—taken from human beings—powerless to produce the disease in guinea pigs.

The doctors offered no statements as to any possibilities of using the substance in the treatment of tuberculosis in human beings. They said they still are working toward isolating and purifying the active principle.

Seat of His Worries

By the United Press.

PITTSFIELD, Mass., Feb. 13.—During his 28 years as water inspector Frank A. Shepardson estimates that he was bitten more than 20 times by vicious dogs.

War's Scars Concern Pythians Anew

"You know the story of Damon and Pythias? That's where our lodge got its name, away back during the Civil War," Milton Gelman said.

"Since then our knights have had their busiest times after wars, promoting the brotherhood idea, and we certainly have our work cut out for us this year. Our birthday gathering will be a new starting point."

Mr. Gelman, chairman of the Knights of Pythias Committee to Combat Intolerance was referring to the meeting in Pythian Temple Feb. 19 when the Grand Lodge of the State of New York, representing 280 lodges and 54,000 members, will celebrate its 82nd anniversary.

Lively Animosities.

"There never was a war that didn't end with lively animosities between groups. Certainly this last war's aftermath is no exception," he pointed out. "Our keynote this year is brotherhood. Right now we consider that the most important word in the vocabulary. Our meeting will highlight Brotherhood Week."

"Brotherhood was the dominant idea when President Lincoln approved the lodge's name and aims, and, through his sympathetic help, gave it a great boost. Then the order was new and members few—earnest men who undertook to warm up the brotherhood idea between North and South as well as between individuals.

Incorporated by Congress.

"Ours was the first order ever incorporated by Act of Congress. There were big-hearted men in high places then, just as there are today. We remember that Gen. Grant told Gen. Lee not to let his men surrender their wagons and horses or anything that could be used on the land."

A proposed undertaking that Mr. Gelman hopes will be approved at the anniversary gathering is the establishment of several $1000 college scholarships for high school girls and boys.

"The best way to eliminate misunderstandings is to educate the young," he asserted. "Because girls are becoming increasingly vocal we think it's high time for us to extend some of our benefits to them as well as to boys. Our summer camp all these years has been for boys only. This year we'd like to start one for girls.

Why Not Girls, Too.

"Why not? Our home for the sick and aged at Ogdensburg is for both sexes and when we help a veteran or any member we certainly include his wife and children if he is a family man.

"A Pythian lodge," he explained, "will stake a young member to get married, to furnish a home or start a small business. One lodge of young unmarried men has thousands of dollars in a rehabilitation fund. These boys are now staking other veterans and are helping them to find jobs."

Speakers at the anniversary program will include former Sen. Guy M. Gillette, Justice Ferdinand Pecora, Attorney General Nathaniel L. Goldstein, Justice Francis E. Rivers and Prof. Robert O'Donnell.

Minority Power Hit at GOP Dinner

By the Associated Press.

GETTYSBURG, Pa., Feb. 13.—Two world wars have been fought to guarantee the American way of life, says Pennsylvania's Secretary of Internal Affairs William S. Livengood Jr., but it is now endangered by the gross ineptitude, political ambition and deliberate destructiveness of small minorities.

He told the Adams County Republican Committee at a Lincoln Day dinner here last night that government by and for groups, rather than by and for all the people, has brought about our present unhappy conditions.

Vivisection Bills Die in N. Y. Senate

Special to the World-Telegram.

ALBANY, Feb. 13.—Two antivivisection bills sponsored by Sen. Richard A. Di Constanzo (R., Manhattan) apparently were without prospect of revival today following rejection of the measures by the Senate Codes Committee.

Sen. Di Constanzo himself said he would make no further effort to push the bills, and there can be no further consideration in the Senate unless a new bill is introduced.

The bill applied specifically to the use of dogs for medical research purposes, and a companion measure in the Assembly Codes Committee is expected to be killed also.

3 Join Banking Board

Special to the World-Telegram.

ALBANY, Feb. 13.—John Foster Dulles of New York City and two others from the metropolitan area were among those confirmed by the Senate yesterday as members of the State Banking Board. The others were F. Abbot Goodhue, Hewlett, L. I., and George L. Harrison, New York.

EXAMPLE 162

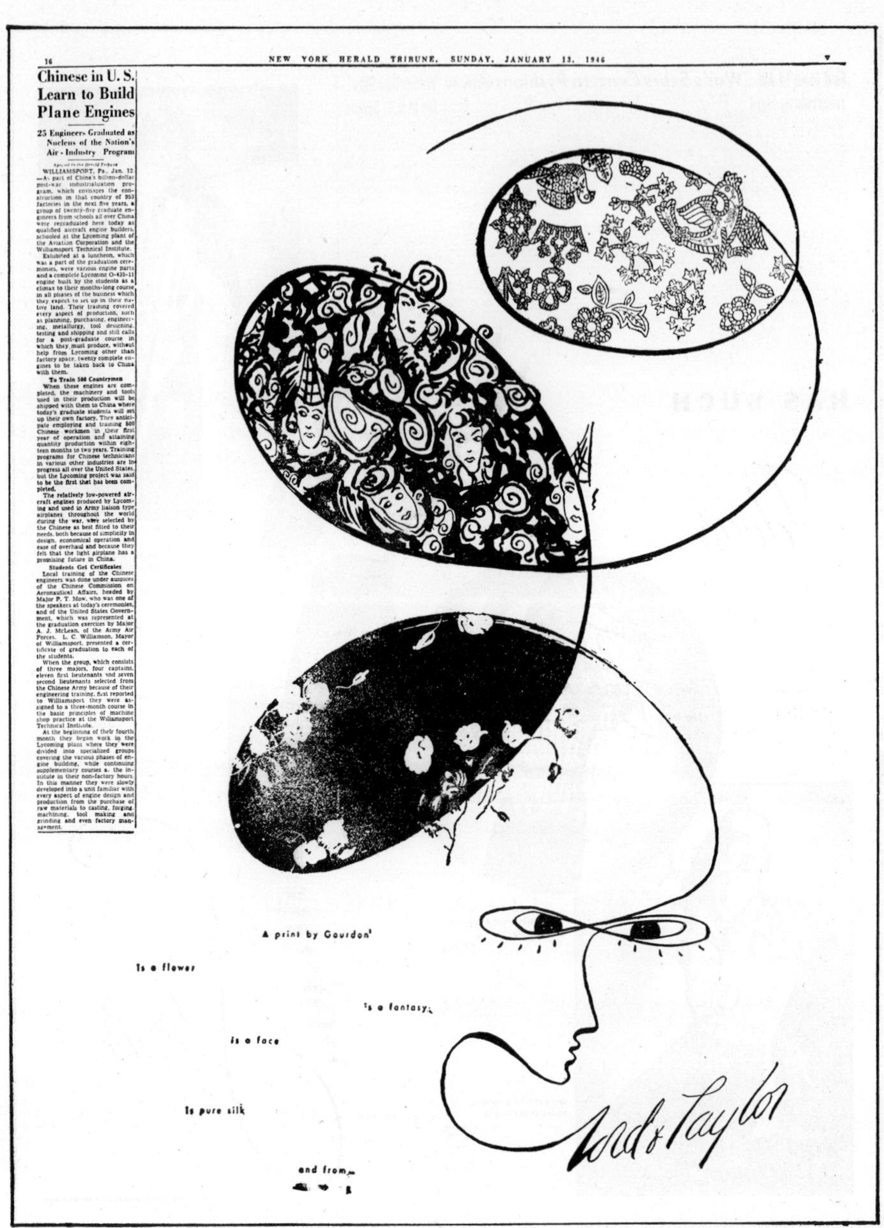

16 NEW YORK HERALD TRIBUNE, SUNDAY, JANUARY 13, 1946

Chinese in U. S. Learn to Build Plane Engines

25 Engineers Graduated as Nucleus of the Nation's Air-Industry Program

Special to the Herald Tribune

WILLIAMSPORT, Pa., Jan. 12.—As part of China's billion-dollar post-war industrialization program, which envisages the construction in that country of 953 factories in the next five years, a group of twenty-five graduate engineers from schools all over China were regraduated here today as qualified aircraft engine builders, schooled at the Lycoming plant of the Aviation Corporation and the Williamsport Technical Institute.

Exhibited at a luncheon, which was a part of the graduation ceremonies, were various engine parts and a complete Lycoming O-435-11 engine built by the students as a climax to their months-long course in all phases of the business which they expect to set up in their native land. Their training covered every aspect of production, such as planning, purchasing, engineering, metallurgy, tool designing, testing and shipping and still calls for a post-graduate course in which they must produce, without help from Lycoming other than factory space, twenty complete engines to be taken back to China with them.

To Train 500 Countrymen

When these engines are completed, the machinery and tools used in their production will be shipped with them to China where today's graduate students will set up their own factory. They anticipate employing and training 500 Chinese workmen in their first year of operation and attaining quantity production within eighteen months to two years. Training programs for Chinese technicians in various other industries are in progress all over the United States, but the Lycoming project was said to be the first that has been completed.

The relatively low-powered aircraft engines produced by Lycoming and used in Army liaison type airplanes throughout the world during the war, were selected by the Chinese as best fitted to their needs, both because of simplicity in design, economical operation and ease of overhaul and because they felt that the light airplane has a promising future in China.

Students Get Certificates

Local training of the Chinese engineers was done under auspices of the Chinese Commission on Aeronautical Affairs, headed by Major P. T. Mow, who was one of the speakers at today's ceremonies, and of the United States Government, which was represented at the graduation exercizes by Major A. J. McLean, of the Army Air Forces. L. C. Williamson, Mayor of Williamsport, presented a certificate of graduation to each of the students.

When the group, which consists of three majors, four captains, eleven first lieutenants and seven second lieutenants selected from the Chinese Army because of their engineering training, first reported to Williamsport they were assigned to a three-month course in the basic principles of machine shop practice at the Williamsport Technical Institute.

At the beginning of their fourth month they began work in the Lycoming plant where they were divided into specialized groups covering the various phases of engine building, while continuing supplementary courses at the institute in their non-factory hours. In this manner they were slowly developed into a unit familiar with every aspect of engine design and production from the purchase of raw materials to casting, forging, machining, tool making and grinding and even factory management.

EXAMPLE 163

the paper in which he runs the pyramid, that its size and shape will preclude the possibility of any other large and perhaps clashing advertisement's being run on the same page.

Of course small displays from other advertisers can be, and often are, run on the same page, and in fairness to all concerned, at the discretion of the paper's advertising department. But the pyramiding advertiser knows that, ordinarily, a fairly large pyramid has a good chance of being the only advertising on a page, and that, in any event, no other fairly large advertisement will be run beside it.

Occasionally, when advertisers run pyramids on facing pages, they pyramid their displays upward to the left of left-hand pages, and upward to the right on right-hand pages, as suggested by Examples 161 and 162.

Note that the tops of five columns on each of the pages were left open for news stories.

Some advertisers are so "sold" on the idea of having news stories appear on the same pages with their displays, that they purposely "leave holes" for stories in what otherwise would be full-page advertisements, as suggested by Examples 163 and 164.

Yet note that both advertisers thought enough of the value of white space to see to it that generous areas of white were provided to separate the news stories from their own statements. The stories on both pages could have run several inches deeper without actually "hurting" the advertisements had the advertisers cared to economize on space, but they evidently preferred the larger areas of white.

A page that must carry several fairly large advertisements and several or more smaller ones presents a different problem. Such a page suggests a compromise with the pyramid plan.

Example 165 presents a reduced showing of an effectively arranged page with two displays three columns wide, two two columns wide and three single-column advertisements.

It will be observed that the four larger displays were pyramided to the right, and that the three single-column advertisements were used to fill out column one.

The page as a whole was much more attractive than it would have been had the advertisements been scattered in helter-skelter fashion.

Observe that all seven of the displays were "next to reading mat-

8 NEW YORK HERALD TRIBUNE, SUNDAY, OCTOBER 14, 1945

GIVE MORE THAN THANKS—NEW YORK NATIONAL WAR FUND

O.P.A. Expected

(Continued from page one)

delegated to the task of making their plans public.

It is generally agreed among O. W. M. R. officials that there will be no formal announcement of the new wage-price policy, but that one will be held in the background to be used in settling labor disputes as they arise. This policy is expected to allow for the wage and price rises proposed by the Commerce Secretary.

The government's immediate policy, according to these officials, will be to allow wages to rise at a greater rate than prices. Where increases of over 15 or 20 per cent are granted, they said, industry will have to absorb all the increase above the allowable level. Mr. Wallace said he did not believe the 30 per cent increase sought by labor could be granted.

The O. P. A. has been operating on the theory that its most important job, in carrying out the stabilization program, is to keep prices down to as near their pre-war levels as possible. This policy will now give way, it is believed, to prevention of temporary un-controlled inflation, which would make the deflationary period more acute.

The downward trend in earnings, when it becomes a reality, O. W. M. R. officials believe, will affect first such items as textiles and foods, with reconversion items—radios, refrigerators, automobiles and other commodities not manufactured during the war—being the last to be affected. The one thing that is not expected to feel deflation for some time is housing. It is generally agreed, and here controls will be instituted. These controls, however, are expected to be far less drastic than those proposed by Chester Bowles, Price Administrator.

Dissatisfaction with the slowness of the O. W. M. R.'s action in completing its new wage-price policy, which has prevented the quick settlement of most strikes, is considered certain to bring about reorganization of that agency. The Administration is said to feel that these strikes will make the deflation more acute by retarding industrial reconversion.

Asked to Railroad Celebration

HANNIBAL, Mo., Oct. 13 (AP).—President Truman heads a list of prominent citizens invited to the Oct. 25 tenth anniversary celebration of the sponsoring of the Burlington Railroad's Mark Twain Zephyr. Others invited include Charles G. Dawes, former Vice-President; Ralph Budd, Burlington Railroad president; the Iowa, Illinois and Missouri Governors; Mark Twain's granddaughter, Nina Gabrilowitsch, who sponsored the train at the 1935 ceremonies, and mayors and chambers of commerce presidents of cities along the train's route.

EXAMPLE 164

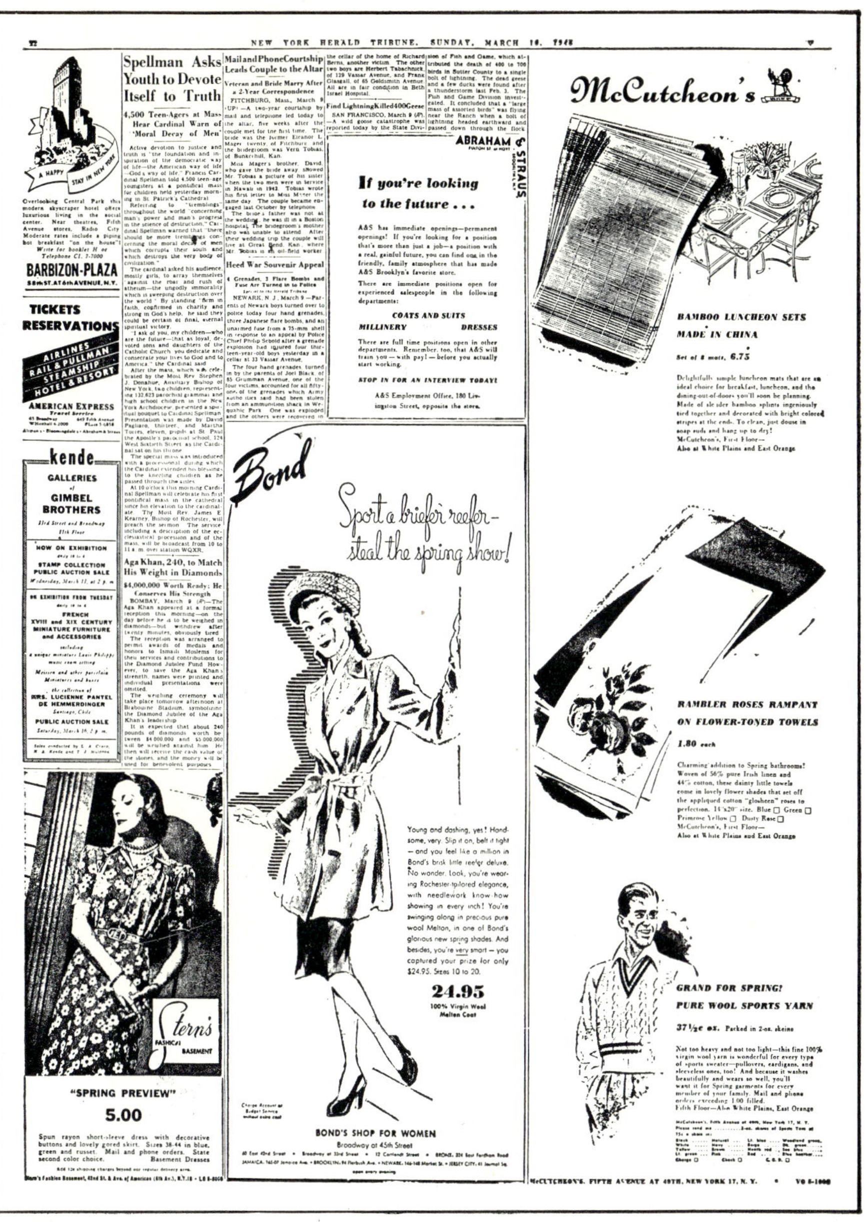

72 NEW YORK HERALD TRIBUNE, SUNDAY, MARCH 10, 1946

A HAPPY STAY IN NEW YORK

Overlooking Central Park this modern skyscraper hotel offers luxurious living in the social center. Near theatres, Fifth Avenue stores, Radio City. Moderate rates include a piping hot breakfast "on the house"! *Write for booklet H or Telephone CI. 7-7000*

BARBIZON-PLAZA

58th ST. AT 6th AVENUE, N.Y.

TICKETS RESERVATIONS

AIRLINES RAIL & PULLMAN STEAMSHIP HOTEL & RESORT

AMERICAN EXPRESS *Travel Service*

kende GALLERIES of GIMBEL BROTHERS

33rd Street and Broadway 11th Floor

NOW ON EXHIBITION

STAMP COLLECTION PUBLIC AUCTION SALE *Wednesday, March 13, at 2 p. m.*

ON EXHIBITION FROM TUESDAY

FRENCH XVIII and XIX CENTURY MINIATURE FURNITURE and ACCESSORIES

including a unique miniature Louis Philippe music room setting

Meissen and other porcelain Miniatures and boxes

the collection of MRS. LUCIENNE PANTEL DE HEMMERDINGER *Santiago, Chile*

PUBLIC AUCTION SALE *Saturday, March 16, 2 p. m.*

Sales conducted by L. A. Craco, H. A. Kende and T. J. Muldoon

Spellman Asks Youth to Devote Itself to Truth

4,500 Teen-Agers at Mass Hear Cardinal Warn of 'Moral Decay of Men'

Active devotion to justice and truth is "the foundation and inspiration of the democratic way of life—the American way of life—God's way of life," Francis Cardinal Spellman told 4,500 teen-age youngsters at a pontifical mass for children held yesterday morning in St. Patrick's Cathedral.

Referring to "tremblings" throughout the world "concerning man's power and man's progress in the science of destruction," Cardinal Spellman warned that "there should be more tremblings concerning the moral decay of men which corrupts their souls and which destroys the very body of civilization."

The cardinal asked his audience, mostly girls, to array themselves "against the roar and rush of atheism—the ungodly immorality which is sweeping destruction over the world." By standing "firm in faith, confirmed in charity and strong in God's help," he said they could be certain of final, eternal spiritual victory.

"I ask of you, my children—who are the future—that as loyal, devoted sons and daughters of the Catholic Church you dedicate and consecrate your lives to God and to America," the Cardinal said.

After the mass, which was celebrated by the Most Rev. Stephen J. Donahue, Auxiliary Bishop of New York, two children, representing 132,623 parochial grammar and high school children in the New York Archdiocese, presented a spiritual bouquet to Cardinal Spellman. Presentation was made by David Pagliaro, thirteen, and Martha Torres, eleven, pupils at St. Paul the Apostle's parochial school, 124 West Sixtieth Street, as the Cardinal sat on his throne.

The special mass was introduced with a processional during which the Cardinal extended his blessings to the kneeling children as he passed through the aisles.

At 10 o'clock this morning Cardinal Spellman will celebrate his first pontifical mass in the cathedral since his elevation to the cardinalate. The Most Rev. James E. Kearney, Bishop of Rochester, will preach the sermon. The service, including a description of the ecclesiastical procession and of the mass, will be broadcast from 10 to 11 a. m. over station WQXR.

Aga Khan, 240, to Match His Weight in Diamonds

$4,000,000 Worth Ready; He Conserves His Strength

BOMBAY, March 9 (AP).—The Aga Khan appeared at a formal reception this morning—on the day before he is to be weighed in diamonds—but withdrew after twenty minutes, obviously tired.

The reception was arranged to permit awards of medals and honors to Ismaili Moslems for their services and contributions to the Diamond Jubilee Fund. However, to save the Aga Khan's strength, names were printed and individual presentations were omitted.

The weighing ceremony will take place tomorrow afternoon at Brabourne Stadium, symbolizing the Diamond Jubilee of the Aga Khan's leadership.

It is expected that about 240 pounds of diamonds worth between $4,000,000 and $5,000,000 will be weighed against him. He then will receive the cash value of the stones, and the money will be used for benevolent purposes.

Mail and Phone Courtship Leads Couple to the Altar

Veteran and Bride Marry After a 2-Year Correspondence

FITCHBURG, Mass., March 9 (UP).—A two-year courtship by mail and telephone led today to the altar, five weeks after the couple met for the first time. The bride was the former Eleanor L. Mager, twenty, of Fitchburg, and the bridegroom was Vern Tobias, of Bunkerhill, Kan.

Miss Mager's brother, David, who gave the bride away, showed Mr. Tobias a picture of his sister when the two men were in service in Hawaii in 1943. Tobias wrote his first letter to Miss Mager the same day. The couple became engaged last October by telephone.

The bride's father was not at the wedding; he was ill in a Boston hospital. The bridegroom's mother also was unable to attend. After their wedding trip the couple will live at Great Bend, Kan., where Mr. Tobias is an oil-field worker.

Heed War Souvenir Appeal

4 Grenades, 3 Flare Bombs and Fuse Are Turned in to Police

Special to the Herald Tribune

NEWARK, N. J., March 9.—Parents of Newark boys turned over to police today four hand grenades, three Japanese flare bombs, and an unarmed fuse from a 75-mm. shell in response to an appeal by Police Chief Philip Sebold after a grenade explosion had injured four thirteen-year-old boys yesterday in a cellar at 33 Vassar Avenue.

The four hand grenades turned in by the parents of Joel Black, of 85 Grumman Avenue, one of the four victims, accounted for all fifty-one of the grenades which Army authorities said had been stolen from an ammunition shack in Weequahic Park. One was exploded and the others were recovered in the cellar of the home of Richard Berns, another victim. The other two boys are Herbert Tabachnick, of 129 Vassar Avenue, and Frank Glasgall, of 65 Goldsmith Avenue. All are in fair condition in Beth Israel Hospital.

Find Lightning Killed 400 Geese

SAN FRANCISCO, March 9 (AP).—A wild goose catastrophe was reported today by the State Division of Fish and Game, which attributed the death of 400 to 700 birds in Sutter County to a single bolt of lightning. The dead geese and a few ducks were found after a thunderstorm last Feb. 3. The Fish and Game Division investigated. It concluded that a "large mass of assorted birds" was flying near the Ranch when a bolt of lightning headed earthward and passed down through the flock.

ABRAHAM & STRAUS

If you're looking to the future . . .

A&S has immediate openings—permanent openings! If you're looking for a position that's more than just a job—a position with a real, gainful future, you can find one in the friendly, family atmosphere that has made A&S Brooklyn's favorite store.

There are immediate positions open for experienced salespeople in the following departments:

COATS AND SUITS

MILLINERY DRESSES

There are full time positions open in other departments. Remember, too, that A&S will train you—with pay!—before you actually start working.

STOP IN FOR AN INTERVIEW TODAY!

A&S Employment Office, 180 Livingston Street, opposite the store.

Bond

Sport a briefer reefer—steal the spring show!

Young and dashing, yes! Handsome, very. Slip it on, belt it tight—and you feel like a million in Bond's brisk little reefer deluxe. No wonder. Look, you're wearing Rochester-tailored elegance, with needlework know-how showing in every inch! You're swinging along in precious pure wool Melton, in one of Bond's glorious new spring shades. And besides, you're very smart—you captured your prize for only $24.95. Sizes 10 to 20.

24.95

100% Virgin Wool Melton Coat

Charge Account or Budget Service without extra cost

BOND'S SHOP FOR WOMEN

Broadway at 45th Street

60 East 42nd Street • Broadway at 33rd Street • 12 Cortlandt Street • BRONX, 324 East Fordham Road

JAMAICA, 165-07 Jamaica Ave. • BROOKLYN, 94 Flatbush Ave. • NEWARK, 146-148 Market St. • JERSEY CITY, 41 Journal Sq.

open every evening

Stern's FASHION BASEMENT

"SPRING PREVIEW"

5.00

Spun rayon short-sleeve dress with decorative buttons and lovely gored skirt. Sizes 38-44 in blue, green and russet. Mail and phone orders. State second color choice. Basement Dresses

Add 12c shipping charges beyond our regular delivery area.

Stern's Fashion Basement, 42nd St. & Ave. of Americas (6th Av.), N.Y.18 • LO 5-8000

McCutcheon's

BAMBOO LUNCHEON SETS

MADE IN CHINA

Set of 8 mats, 6.75

Delightfully simple luncheon mats that are an ideal choice for breakfast, luncheon, and the dining-out-of-doors you'll soon be planning. Made of slender bamboo splints ingeniously tied together and decorated with bright colored stripes at the ends. To clean, just douse in soap suds and hang up to dry! McCutcheon's, First Floor—Also at White Plains and East Orange

RAMBLER ROSES RAMPANT ON FLOWER-TONED TOWELS

1.80 each

Charming addition to Spring bathrooms! Woven of 56% pure Irish linen and 44% cotton, these dainty little towels come in lovely flower shades that set off the appliqued cotton "glosheen" roses to perfection. 14"x20" size. Blue ☐ Green ☐ Primrose Yellow ☐ Dusty Rose ☐ McCutcheon's, First Floor—Also at White Plains and East Orange

GRAND FOR SPRING!

PURE WOOL SPORTS YARN

37½c oz. Packed in 2-oz. skeins

Not too heavy and not too light—this fine 100% virgin wool yarn is wonderful for every type of sports sweater—pullovers, cardigans, and sleeveless ones, too! And because it washes beautifully and wears so well, you'll want it for Spring garments for every member of your family. Mail and phone orders exceeding 1.00 filled. Fifth Floor—Also White Plains, East Orange

McCutcheon's, Fifth Avenue at 49th, New York 17, N. Y.

Please send me ....2-oz. skeins of Sports Yarn at 75c a skein in:

Charge ☐ Check ☐ C.O.D. ☐

McCUTCHEON'S, FIFTH AVENUE AT 49TH, NEW YORK 17, N. Y. • VO 5-1000

EXAMPLE 165

46 NEW YORK HERALD TRIBUNE, SUNDAY, MARCH 10, 1946

FIFTH AVE. AT 38TH ST., NEW YORK 18, N. Y. • WI. 7-9800
GREENWICH, EAST ORANGE, CLEVELAND, BRIDGEPORT

Franklin Simon

Wool Suit-Dress Exclusive

Decidedly spring-like manners excite our newest wool suit dress exclusive, with twin bows making it look very wee-waisted. Beige, aqua, grey or seafoam green all wool by American Woolen Co. Sizes 12 to 20. Misses' Dresses, Fourth Floor

17.95

MAIL AND PHONE ORDERS FILLED

FIFTH AVE. AT 38TH ST., NEW YORK 18, N. Y. • WI. 7-9800
GREENWICH, EAST ORANGE, CLEVELAND, BRIDGEPORT

Franklin Simon

Kay Dunhill interprets a classic

... giving it lots of crisply feminine line! It's all done with stripes on a fly-front silhouette in grey, copen or lime with white. A rayon fabric by Verney. Sizes 12 to 20. Kay Dunhill Shop, Second Floor.

7.50

Miss Grantham Wed To Mr. Auchincloss, Congressman's Son

New Yorker, Who Was With O.W.I. in London, Marries Art Museum Aid Here

Miss Evelyn Grantham, daughter of Mr. and Mrs. James Grantham, of Evanston, Ill., was married yesterday afternoon to Mr. J. Douglas Auchincloss, of New York, son of Representative James C. Auchincloss and Mrs. Auchincloss, of Rumson, N. J. The ceremony was performed in Christ Church, Methodist, Park Avenue and Sixtieth Street.

The bride was given in marriage by her father. Her cousin, Mrs. Charles Wolcott, of New York, was her attendant. Mr. James C. Auchincloss was best man for his son. Ushers were Mr. Gordon Auchincloss 2d, brother of the bridegroom, and Mr. Nicholas B. Samstag. A reception took place at the home of Mr. Auchincloss's uncle and aunt, Mr. and Mrs. Reginald Auchincloss, 16 East Eighty-ninth Street.

Mrs. Auchincloss was graduated from Radcliffe College and is in the publications department of the Metropolitan Museum of Art. Mr. Auchincloss was graduated from Groton School in 1932 and attended Yale in the class of 1936. He was with the O. W. I. in London for two years, and is on the staff of "Time." He is a grandson of the late Mr. and Mrs. Edgar S. Auchincloss and of Mrs. Welcome T. Alexander. His great-grandfather was Samuel Sloan. His father represents the 3d New Jersey District in Congress.

The couple will live in New York.

J. Douglas Auchincloss and Museum Aid Wed

Arthur Steiner

Daughter of Mr. and Mrs. James Grantham, of Evanston, Ill., married to New Yorker, Yale '36, in Christ Church, Methodist, yesterday

Mary Peace Hazard Wed in Rhode Island To James S. Douglas

Son of Lewis W. Douglases, of New York, Served as Lieutenant in the Army

PROVIDENCE, March 9.—Miss Mary Peace Hazard, daughter of Mr. and Mrs. Frederick Rowland Hazard, of Saunderstown, R. I., was married today to Mr. James Stuart Douglas, former Army lieutenant, son of Mr. and Mrs. Lewis W. Douglas, of New York. The wedding took place in the Church of the Ascension, Wakefield, the rector, the Rev. John Wyatt, officiating, assisted by the Rev. John Crocker, headmaster of Groton School, where the bridegroom was graduated before attending Amherst.

Mrs. E. Sheldon Potter, sister of the bride, was matron of honor, and Miss Sharman Douglas, sister of the bridegroom; the Misses Sally Ann Atwater, Jane Campbell, Deborah Hunt, of Providence, and Rhonda Reed, Geneva, N. Y., were bridesmaids. They wore light blue tulle gowns and carried spring flowers.

Mr. Lewis W. Douglas jr. was best man for his brother. Ushers were Mr. Robert Baldridge, Washington; Dr. Edmund Goodman, Mr. Moulton Sawin, of New York, Mr. E. Sheldon Potter, Mr. Charles Michael Hazard, brother of the bride, and Lieutenant (j. g.) John Zinsser.

The bride was graduated from Lincoln School here and from Pine Manor Junior College. The bridegroom's father, formerly a Representative in Congress from Arizona and later Director of the Budget, is president of the Mutual Life Insurance Company and chairman of the board of Memorial Hospital. The couple will live in Sonoita, Ariz., after a trip to Bermuda.

Mrs. Truman to Attend Ball

Special to the Herald Tribune

WASHINGTON, March 9.—Mrs. Truman and Miss Margaret Truman will be special guests March 13 at the Congressional fashion show and cotton ball to be given at the Shoreham Hotel by the state societies of Tennessee, North Carolina and Mississippi.

Births

RAND—Mr. and Mrs. Edward Henry Rand (nee Carol Barrsky) are happy to announce the birth of daughter Laura Susan, at the Methodist Hospital, Sunday, March 3.

Engagements

HALPERT—KLEIN—Mr. and Mrs. Samuel Klein, of 137 Riverside Drive, N. Y. C., announce the engagement of their daughter, Anita, to Lt. Leonard S. Halpert, son of Mr. and Mrs. David Halpert, of Brookline, Mass.

Marriages

EGERT—FISCHEL—Mr. and Mrs. Alvin N. Fischel, New York and Westport, announce the marriage today of their daughter, Phyllis Joy, to Mr. Arthur E. Egert, son of Mr. and Mrs. Harry Egert, New York.

MURCEK—CHAMBERLAIN—On March 4, at the Rectory of St. Paul's Roman Catholic Church, Jacksonville, Florida, Judith, daughter of Mrs. Chamberlain and the late Will Hurst Chamberlain, of Chappaqua, N. Y., to Edward J. Murcek, U. S. N. R., son of Mr. and Mrs. John Murcek, of Chicago.

Virginia Hull Brown Wed To W. A. Prendergast 3d

Lawson H. Browns' Daughter; Husband in Navy 4 Years

Special to the Herald Tribune

MAHWAH, N. J., March 9.—Miss Virginia Hull Brown, daughter of Mr. and Mrs. Lawson Hull Brown, of Mahwah, formerly of Brooklyn, was married this afternoon in the Ramapo Reformed Church to Mr. William A. Prendergast 3d, gunner's mate, second class, U. S. N., son of Mr. and Mrs. Thomas Hull Prendergast, also of Mahwah, formerly of Brooklyn. The Rev. Clarence Howard, the pastor, officiated. A reception took place at the Ridgewood Woman's Club.

The bride was given in marriage by her father. She was attended by her sisters, Mrs. Charles Edwin Miller and Mrs. John Lee Bogdanoff. Linda Ruth Miller was flower girl for her aunt. Mr. Carl Hamlin, U. S. N., was best man. Mr. Charles Edwin Miller and Mr. John Lee Bogdanoff were ushers.

Mrs. Prendergast is a graduate of Packer Collegiate Institute and Southern Seminary and Junior College and was a nurses' aide at Samaritan Hospital, Suffern, N. Y., during the war. Her father was formerly secretary to the late Brooklyn Borough President Raymond V. Ingersoll.

Mr. Prendergast attended Cornell. In service four years, he has just returned from the Pacific. He is a grandson of Mr. William A. Prendergast, former Comptroller of the City of New York and former chairman of the New York State Public Service Commission, and Mrs. Prendergast, of New York.

The couple will live in Norfolk, Va., for the present.

Elizabeth Wilson Married

Wed in Washington to Lt. Francis Netherwood, D. F. C., Air Medal

Special to the Herald Tribune

WASHINGTON, March 9.—Miss Elizabeth Bailey Wilson, daughter of Mr. and Mrs. Harry Franklin Wilson, of Little Rock, Ark., was married today to Lieutenant Francis B. Netherwood, A. A. F., son of Mrs. Douglas B. Netherwood, of Washington, and the late Brigadier General Netherwood. Chaplain Ivan Gonser officiated at the Netherwood home.

The bride was given in marriage by Brigadier General Edgar P. Sorensen, U. S. A. Mrs. Seth Lithicum was her attendant. Mr. William D. Netherwood was his brother's best man. Ushers were Major David Brown and Captain Edward Ablitt, of the British Army, and Lieutenant Louis Avrami, A. A. F.

The couple will live in Washington. Lieutenant Netherwood, recently in the Pacific, is stationed at Bolling Field. He flew thirty-five missions over Japan and has the Distinguished Flying Cross, Air Medal, Purple Heart and his unit a Presidential citation. The bride has been with the State Department.

Mrs. Roosevelt To Be Guest

WASHINGTON, March 9.—Mrs. Franklin D. Roosevelt will be guest of honor at a luncheon March 14 at the Mayflower Hotel given by the Women's National Press Club and in the evening at a dinner sponsored by the Women's Joint Congressional Committee. Mrs. Truman, Miss Margaret Truman and Mrs. Woodrow Wilson will be special guests at the dinner. Senator Tom Connally will introduce Mrs. Roosevelt, who will speak. Another speaker will be Secretary of Commerce Henry A. Wallace. The Marine Band will play.

Harriet Shay Married

Bride of Charles W. Gillen, of New Canaan, Conn.

Special to the Herald Tribune

FAIRFIELD, Conn., March 9.—Miss Harriet A. Shay, daughter of Mr. and Mrs. James L. Shay, of Fairfield, was married today at Hickory Dell Farm, her parents' home to Mr. Charles W. Gillen, of New Canaan, Conn. A reception followed. The bride was given in marriage by her father. Her sister, Mrs. William J. McKeon, was her attendant, and Mr. Harold W. Gillen was best man for his brother. Mr. Gillen is a partner of Gillen & Co., members of the New York Stock Exchange.

U.S. Official's Daughter to Wed

Special to the Herald Tribune

WASHINGTON, March 9.—The Comptroller General of the United States, Lindsay Carter Warren, and Mrs. Warren announce the engagement of their daughter, Miss Emily Carter Warren, to Mr. Dudley Mitchell Jones jr., recently an Army captain overseas, son of Mr. Dudley M. Jones, of Lynchburg, Va., and the late Mrs. Celia Howell Jones. The wedding is planned for March 30. Miss Warren attended St. Mary's School, Raleigh, N. C., and is vice-president of the North Carolina Society of Washington. Mr. Jones attended Augusta Military Academy.

Son to Lt., Mrs. Ollendorf

A son, Richard Ollendorf, was born to Lieutenant Gerald Ollendorf, U. S. N. R. Medical Corps, stationed in New Orleans, and Mrs. Ollendorf on March 6 at St. Vincent's Hospital, New York. Mrs. Ollendorf (Juanita Penichet) is the daughter of Dr. and Mrs. Waldo Penichet, of Havana, Cuba, and New York.

RITZ-CARLTON

"Keeping up with the Joneses"—

"The Joneses"—recognized everywhere for their beauty and chic—have been loyal devotees of made-to-order face powder. Year after year there are many more thousands that "keep up with them"—learning what they know—that there is nothing in beautifiers so strongly personal, so unregimented, as face powder blended to their individual order.

Charles of the Ritz
RITZ-CARLTON NEW YORK

McCutcheon's

Sheer Perfection

A wonderful spun-sugar confection to froth from the front of your new Spring suit! Fashioned of finest quality Swiss organdy and lovely Swiss embroidery, and frosted with ripples of Val-type lace at the convertible neckline. In the permanent-finish, edelweiss-white organdy that is so much longer-wearing than it appears. Sizes 32 to 38.

29.95

Second Floo

McCutcheon's, Fifth Ave. at 49th, New York 17 • VO 5-1000

Our Squirrels look like wild Mink

Know that pale new blondish mink? That's wild mink, and so wonderful we knew you'd want your little squirrel jacket to be just that color. So we had *our* squirrel skins blended the color of wild mink by those famous Windsor Fur Dyers. Then we worked them into this cardigan and a little scalloped short coat. Either goes over suits or evening gowns—keeps on going from Easter to Christmas. $300. Young Marylin Furs, Second Floor.

Russeks

Subject to 20% Federal Excise Tax

FIFTH AVENUE AT 36th ST., NEW YORK 18 • FULTON AND BRIDGE STS., BROOKLYN 1

EXAMPLE 166

ter," and that, although the advertisements appeared in all of the eight columns, the tops of four consecutive columns presented stories.

When a page must carry several fairly large displays, again the compromise-pyramid plan often can be followed to advantage, as suggested by Example 166, with columns one and two and seven and eight filled with advertising, as well as the lower parts of columns three, four, five and six, and with stories and a picture in four consecutive columns at the top of the page.

The orderly, easy-to-follow arrangement of both "reading matter" and advertisements treats both advertising and news stories fairly. And it treats readers fairly. It helps them to concentrate on one group or the other, and on one group at a time. They are not obliged to shift attention from story to advertisement and advertisement to story, over and over, to find the items of interest to themselves on the page.

Advertising is important, of course. But so is news. And so, decidedly, are readers, who read in direct ratio as the reading is made easy for them, and who skip when concentration is made difficult.

The newspaper page that must present a dozen or so fairly small and no large advertisements presents still another problem. The pyramid plan, or even a compromise-pyramid plan, could not be followed effectively, as the following of either would result in the "burying" of too many of the advertisements. Such a page—particularly a five- or six-column page—calls for the "well," or magazine, form of makeup for the reading-matter columns, with the advertisements placed in vertical rows to the left and right.

For a discussion of dummies for pages containing advertising, see Chapter 15 of Part I.

19

Theatrical Advertising

Type was made to read—even in theatrical-advertising columns. But many a potential reader of such columns in many a newspaper probably has wondered if many theatrical advertisers are aware of that. Many of them seem not to be. In fact, many of them seem to work on the theory that the chief business of types should be to "out-shout" competitors and only secondarily to convey any messages of their own.

At any rate the theatrical-advertising columns of many a newspaper offer an affront to the eyesight of the potential reader. He looks there to find certain information—and is met with a welter of bold-face types, blotches of grotesque lettering, smashing reverse plates and brutal borders that make it difficult for him to find what he seeks. The sort of ballyhoo—of drum-pounding and ear-splitting yelling—greets him there that would assail his ears in a street of side-shows at Coney Island—unless the newspaper comes to his rescue by obliging theatrical advertisers to meet certain reasonable typographic standards, at least in certain sections of theatrical-advertising pages.

Example 167, a reduced showing of a theatrical-advertising page from a high-class metropolitan daily, presents many advertisements that are hard to read, along with many that are much easier to read.

Most of the displays in columns three to eight, in which theatrical advertisers beat their tom-toms unrestrainedly and attempt to "out-shout" each other, are difficult to read.

Observe the many reverse plates, the grotesque lettering, the many lines set entirely in capitals, the many unusually small type lines. And then try to get from those displays the information you would be likely to want about the plays advertised.

Then glance at the lower half of columns one and two, where the newspaper has obliged advertisers to conform to a certain typographic standard for the convenience of readers. Note how the alphabetical listing helps the reader to find the name of the play or plays he wants to know more about; how the uniformly restrained treatments of all

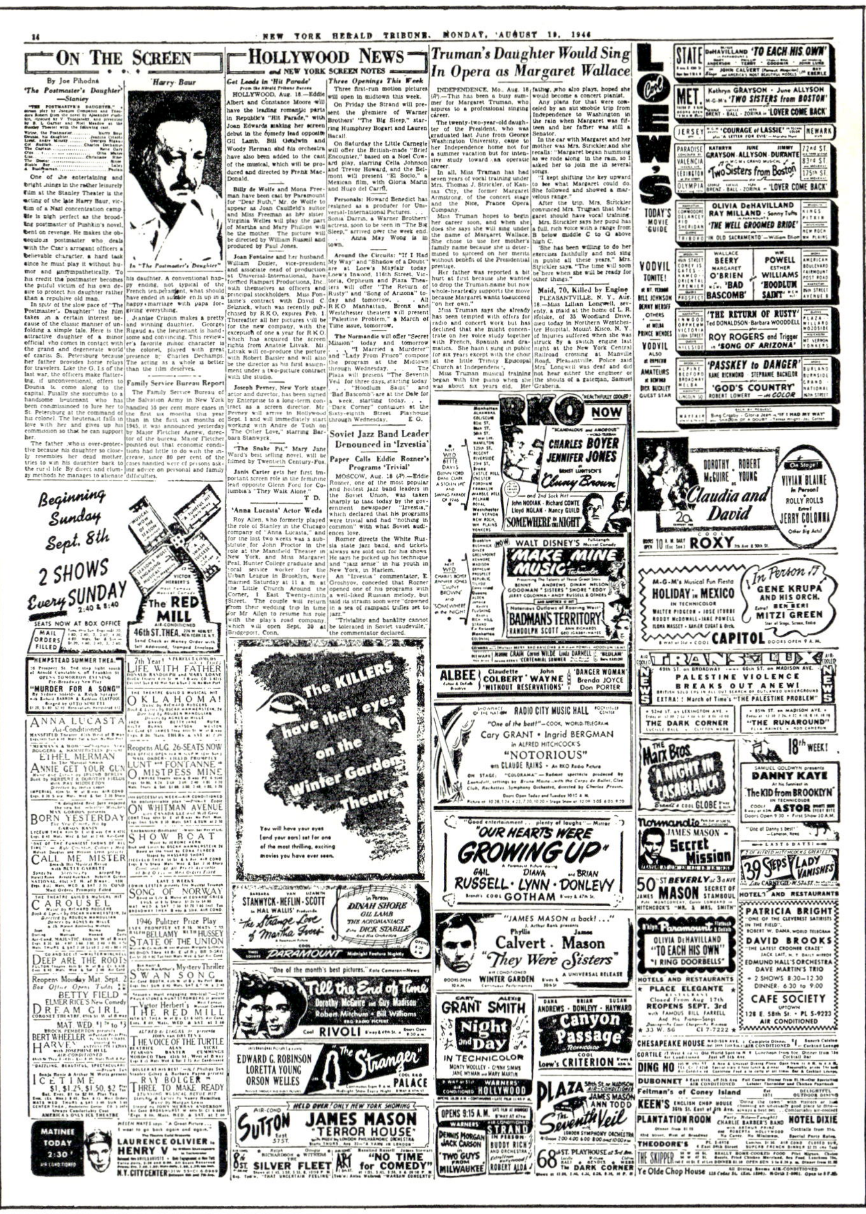

14 · NEW YORK HERALD TRIBUNE, MONDAY, AUGUST 19, 1946

ON THE SCREEN

By Joe Pihodna

'The Postmaster's Daughter'—Stanley

"THE POSTMASTER'S DAUGHTER," a screen play by Jacques Companeez and Theodore Robert from the novel by Alexander Pushkin, directed by V. Tourjansky, and presented by B. L. Garner and Noel Meadow at the Stanley Theater with the following cast:

Virine, the Postmaster ... Harry Baur
Dounia, his daughter ... Jeanine Crispin
Lieut. Andre Minsky ... Georges Rigaud
Col. Radtich ... Charles Dechamps
The Captain ... Rene Dary
Olga ... Gina Manes
Lisa ... Christiane Ribes
The Doctor ... Ginner
Stable Boy ... Labry
A Bus[s]man ... Paulais

One of the entertaining and bright things in the rather leisurely film at the Stanley Theater is the acting of the late Harry Baur, victim of a Nazi concentration camp. He is nigh perfect as the brooding postmaster of Pushkin's novel, bent on revenge. He makes the obsequious postmaster who deals with the Czar's arrogant officers a believable character, a hard task since he must play it without humor and unsympathetically. To his credit the postmaster becomes the pitiful victim of his own desire to protect his daughter rather than a repulsive old man.

In spite of the slow pace of "The Postmaster's Daughter" the film takes on a certain interest because of the classic manner of unfolding a simple tale. Here is the attractive daughter of a minor official who comes in contact with the grand and degenerate world of czarist St. Petersburg because her father provides horse relays for travelers. Like the G. I.s of the last war, the officers make flattering, if unconventional, offers to Dounia to come along to the capital. Finally she succumbs to a handsome lieutenant who has been commissinoed to lure her to St. Petersburg at the command of his colonel. The lieutenant falls in love with her and gives up his commission so that he can support her.

The father, who is over-protective because his daughter so closely resembles her dead mother, tries to win his daughter back to the rural life. By direct and clumsy methods he manages to alienate his daufhter. A conventional happy ending, not typical of the French temperament, what should have ended in suicide ends up in a happy marriage with papa forgiving everything.

Jeanine Crispin makes a pretty and winning daughter. Georges Rigaud as the lieutenant is handsome and convincing. This reviewer's favorite minor character is the colonel, played with great presence by Charles Dechamps. The acting as a whole is better than the film deserves.

Harry Baur

In "The Postmaster's Daughter"

Family Service Bureau Report

The Family Service Bureau of the Salvation Army in New York handled 55 per cent more cases in the first six months this year than in the first six months of 1945, it was announced yesterday by Major Fletcher Agnew, director of the bureau. Major Fletcher pointed out that economic conditions had little to do with the increase, since 80 per cent of the cases handled were of persons asking advice on personal and family difficulties.

HOLLYWOOD NEWS and NEW YORK SCREEN NOTES

Get Leads in 'Hit Parade'

From the Herald Tribune Bureau

HOLLYWOOD, Aug. 18.—Eddie Albert and Constance Moore will have the leading romantic parts in Republic's "Hit Parade," with Joan Edwards making her screen debut in the comedy lead opposite Gil Lamb. Bill Goodwin and Woody Herman and his orchestra have also been added to the cast of the musical, which will be produced and directed by Frank MacDonald.

Billy de Wolfe and Mona Freeman have been cast by Paramount for "Dear Ruth," Mr. de Wolfe to appear as Joan Caulfield's suitor and Miss Freeman as her sister. Virginia Welles will play the part of Martha and Mary Phillips will be the mother. The picture will be directed by William Russell and produced by Paul Jones.

Joan Fontaine and her husband, William Dozier, vice-president and associate head of production at Universal-International, have formed Rampart Productions, Inc., with themselves as officers and principal stockholders. Miss Fontaine's contract with David C. Selznick, which was recently purchased by R K O, expires Feb. 1. Thereafter all her pictures will be for the new company, with the exception of one a year for R K O, which has acquired the screen rights from Anatole Litvak. Mr. Litvak will co-produce the picture with Robert Bassler and will also be the director as his first assignment under a two-picture contract with the studio.

Joseph Pevney, New York stage actor and director, has been signed by Enterprise to a long-term contract as a screen director. Mr. Pevney will arrive in Hollywood Sept. 1 and will immediately start working with Andre de Toth on "The Other Love," starring Barbara Stanwyck.

"The Snake Pit," Mary Jane Ward's best selling novel, will be filmed by Twentieth Century-Fox.

Janis Carter gets her first important screen role in the feminine lead opposite Glenn Ford for Columbia's "They Walk Alone."

T. D.

'Anna Lucasta' Actor Weds

Roy Allen, who formerly played the role of Stanley in the Chicago company of "Anna Lucasta," and for the last two weeks was a substitute for John Proctor in the role at the Mansfield Theater in New York, and Miss Margaret Peal, Hunter College graduate and social service worker for the Urban League in Brooklyn, were married Saturday at 11 a. m. at the Little Church Around the Corner, 1 East Twenty-ninth Street. The couple will return from their wedding trip in time for Mr. Allen to resume his role with the play's road company, which will open Sept. 30 at Bridgeport, Conn.

Three Openings This Week

Three first-run motion pictures will open in midtown this week.

On Friday the Strand will present the premiere of Warner Brothers' "The Big Sleep," starring Humphrey Bogart and Lauren Bacall.

On Saturday the Little Carnegie will offer the British-made "Brief Encounter," based on a Noel Coward play, starring Celia Johnson and Trevor Howard, and the Belmont will present "El Socio," a Mexican film, with Gloria Marin and Hugo del Carril.

Personals: Howard Benedict has resigned as a producer for Universal-International Pictures. . . Sonia Darrin, a Warner Brothers' actress, soon to be seen in "The Big Sleep," arrived over the week end. . . . Anna May Wong is in town.

Around the Circuits: "If I Had My Way" and "Shadow of a Doubt" are at Loew's Mayfair today. Loew's Inwood, 116th Street, Victoria, Orpheum and Plaza Theaters will offer "The Return of Rusty" and "Song of Arizona" today and tomorrow. . . . All R K O Manhattan, Bronx and Westchester theaters will present "Palestine Problem," a March of Time issue, tomorrow.

The Normandie will offer "Secret Mission" today and tomorrow. . . . "I Married a Murderer" and "Lady From Frisco" compose the program at the Midtown through Wednesday. . . . The Plaza will present "The Seventh Veil" for three days, starting today. . . . "Hoodlum Saint" and "Bad Bascomb" are at the Dale for a week, starting today. . . . "Dark Corner" continues at the Sixty-eighth Street Playhouse through Wednesday.

E. G.

Soviet Jazz Band Leader Denounced in 'Izvestia'

Paper Calls Eddie Rozner's Programs 'Trivial'

MOSCOW, Aug. 18 (AP).—Eddie Rozner, one of the most popular and hottest jazz band leaders in the Soviet Union, was taken sharply to task today by the government newspaper "Izvestia," which declared that his programs were trivial and had "nothing in common" with what Soviet audiences love.

Rozner directs the White Russia state jazz band, and tickets always are sold out for his shows. He says he picked up his technique and "jazz sense" in his youth in New York, in Harlem.

An "Izvestia" commentator, E. Groshyov, conceded that Rozner opened one of his programs with a well-liked Russian melody, but said its strains soon were "drowned in a sea of rampant trifles set to jazz."

"Triviality and banality cannot be tolerated in Soviet vaudeville," the commentator declared.

Truman's Daughter Would Sing In Opera as Margaret Wallace

INDEPENDENCE, Mo., Aug. 18 (AP).—This has been a busy summer for Margaret Truman, who aspires to a professional singing career.

The twenty-two-year-old daughter of the President, who was graduated last June from George Washington University, came to her Independence home not for a summer vacation but for intensive study toward an operatic career.

In all, Miss Truman has had seven years of vocal training under Mrs. Thomas J. Strickler, of Kansas City, the former Margaret Armstrong, of the concert stage and the Nice, France Opera Company.

Miss Truman hopes to begin her career soon, and when she does she says she will sing under the name of Margaret Wallace. She chose to use her mother's family name because she is determined to succeed on her merits without benefit of the Presidential prestige.

Her father was reported a bit hurt at first because she wanted to drop the Truman name but now whole-heartedly supports the move because Margaret wants to succeed "on her own."

Miss Truman says she already has been tempted with offers for radio and concert work but has declined that she might concentrate on her voice study together with French, Spanish and dramatics. She hasn't sung in public for six years except with the choir at the little Trinity Episcopal Church at Independence.

Miss Truman musical training began with the piano when she was about six years old. Her father, who also plays, hoped she would become a concert pianist.

Any plans for that were canceled by an automobile trip from Independence to Washington in the rain when Margaret was fifteen and her father was still a Senator.

In the car with Margaret and her mother was Mrs. Strickler and she recalls: "Margaret began humming as we rode along in the rain, so I asked her to join me in several songs.

"I kept shifting the key upward to see what Margaret could do. She followed and showed a marvelous range."

After the trip, Mrs. Strickler convinced Mrs. Truman that Margaret should have vocal training.

Mrs. Strickler says her pupil has a full, rich voice with a range from B below middle C to G above high C.

"She has been willing to do her exercises faithfully and not sing in public all these years," Mrs. Strickler says. "The time will soon be here when she will be ready for other things."

Maid, 70, Killed by Engine

PLEASANTVILLE, N. Y., Aug. 18.—Miss Lillian Longwell, seventy, a maid at the home of L. R. Holske, of 35 Woodland Drive, died today in Northern Westchester Hospital, Mount Kisco, N. Y., of injuries suffered when she was struck by a switch engine last night at the New York Central Railroad crossing at Manville Road, Pleasantville. Police said Mrs. Longwell was deaf and did not hear either the engineer or the shouts of a gateman, Samuel Graberia.

EXAMPLE 167

displays in that section keep some of the displays from overpowering others and making it difficult for the reader.

As previously stated, the page suggested by Example 167 was taken from a high-class metropolitan daily. Many papers less considerate of readers do not run listings such as those at the left on that page, to offset the objectionable features of unrestrained displays, but leave the reader to grope his way through the jungles of the tom-tom beaters with no compass to guide him and no magnifying glass to help him save the only pair of eyes he can ever have.

20

Classified Advertising

To the newspaper reader in quest of employment, a house, an apartment, a place to board, a used car, or any one of scores of other things, the contents of a paper's classified-advertising section can be more interesting than front-page news. But the reader not consciously on the hunt for something he believes the classified pages may help him find is inclined to skip those pages entirely, even though he may take the time at least to skim the headlines and glance at the pictures on most of the other pages. (Reference is made to the average edition of the average daily or weekly; not to large Sunday and special editions, complete sections of which are passed up by readers who lack the time or inclination, or both, to look at more than a few of the several sections.)

And one reason why the classified pages are passed up by the casual reader is that there is little on them to catch his eye. In appearance they are among the least attractive pages in a paper.

Naturally enough, a multiplicity of small items unrelieved by any considerable amount of display or decorative or illustrative material makes for a monotonous-looking and unattractive page.

Many publishers, of course, realize this, and have adopted various devices to brighten up their classified sections. To attract the casual reader to the small-ad columns, some publishers run current-event cartoons or comic strips or crossword puzzles on their classified pages. Some offer prizes to the readers who find the most misspelled words on such pages—words purposely misspelled to encourage a careful reading of all lines. Some sprinkle such columns with names and addresses of individuals reprinted from city directories or telephone books, with prizes for the ones who find their names and addresses in the columns. Some run letters of commendation from satisfied users of space on such pages. Some encourage their advertisers to use certain forms of display type in their messages. (During World War II, however, and for a time afterward, when newsprint had to be conserved in many newspaper plants, some papers temporarily prohibited the use of display lines in classified, and other papers limited the number and point sizes of such lines in any one advertisement. In fact, many of our larger dailies temporarily limited the number of agate lines—taken up by display or body matter or both—in any one advertisement. Those papers did so that more advertisers, many of whom could not be accommodated on other pages, because of newsprint shortages, could run at least something on classified pages. Many papers, also, as pointed out in more detail later in this chapter, started running more columns on their classified pages.)

Many of our dailies now set the body matter of their classified-advertising columns in 5-point faces, solid, or in 5½-point faces on a 5-point body, which gives them fourteen lines to the inch and, consequently, more income than they would receive at the same rate from lines in larger point sizes and leaded, or from the 5½-point leaded, or even cast on its own body size, 5½ point.

Some newspapers present their classified advertisements with all lines starting flush at the left, except second lines, which are indented one em or so, and other papers present first lines flush at the left, with following lines uniformly indented. The first words in both treatments usually are set in roman or bold-face capitals or bold-face capitals and lower-case.

Some papers, but not so many as formerly, start classified advertisements with two-line initial letters.

Smaller city dailies and weeklies usually present their classified advertisements in larger faces—often in 6-, 7- and even 8-point faces—often in the same sizes used for regular news and feature body matter.

Newspapers that use display faces in classified advertisements can secure attractive effects by using various sizes of faces such as Spartan Light, Spartan Medium, Metrothin No. 2, Metrolite No. 2, Memphis Light or Erbar Light Condensed for display. The comparative lightness of those faces makes it possible to present many lines in them on a page without giving it a decidedly spotty appearance—a condition that would make it difficult for the reader to concentrate on individual advertisements and that would make the page as a whole unattractive physically.

In all three of the classified examples that follow, body lines are in 5½-point Excelsior with Bold Face No. 2 set solid.

Clerical Position

VETERAN, ABOUT 21
Midtown firm, 5-day week.
Write stating details. Y 99 Herald Tribune

Clerk—Young

UNDER 30, GOOD HANDWRITING
Pleasant Phone Voice,
Experience Unnecessary (Vet preferred)
Pleasant Working Conditions

BREYER ICE CREAM, INC.

34 St. & Queens Blvd., L. I. City

CLERK, age 22-28, old estab. concern. Must be accurate and have elementary knowledge of bookkeeping. Salary $40 to start. Write stating qualifications. D 681 Herald Tribune.

CLERK, shipping and receiving room, National Magazine; 35 hrs., 5 day week. Salary $108 month. Apply 250 Park av., 12th fl. Morning interviews.

CLERKS, 1-8 a. m., under 40 years, bank $45. Wilman Agency, 11 John st.

CLERKS, many 22-38 yrs., bank, $35-40 Wilman Agency, 11 John st.

CLERKS, 6-2 a. m. or 12-8 a. m., Bank, $2,100. WILMAN AGENCY, 11 John st.

Compositor Stone Hand

Must know book work imposition. Steady, over-scale pay. Box HT 324, 113 W. 42.

CORRESPONDENT

Permanent opening for good typist with flair for letter writing. Five-day week. 166 West 35th st.

MACY'S

Cost-Reduction Engineer

with time-study experience to head small department; man we are looking for will be an industrial or a mechanical engineer with at least 5 years in time study and whose over-all experience involves work in standard costs and cost reduction over period of about 12 to 15 years. Kindly send us resume to include your experience, education, salary requirements, etc. Box HT 309, 113 W. 42d st.

September Openings

FOR STENOGRAPHERS
Good pay. Convenient hours. Excellent transportation—pleasant office surroundings. Permanent position for the person who can qualify for Travel and Financial Departments.
Apply any weekday 9-3, Personnel Dept., 5th floor.

AMERICAN EXPRESS CO.

65 Broadway

HOUSEWIVES

Permanent Openings as saleswomen on part-time schedules allows time for household duties, avoid rush hour commuting.
work 11 A. M.—4:30 P. M.
or 12 Noon—5:30 P. M.
later only on Thursday
FIVE DAY WEEK
no experience necessary
166 WEST 35TH ST.

MACY'S

High School Graduates

If you wish to become associated with an old established text book publishing company, please write stating why & in what capacity you feel qualified. We offer permanent, congenial employment 35 hrs. per week to serious minded, courteous and ambitious young high school graduates. TR 136 Herald Tribune.

MAKE money fast. Sell Christmas, Everyday cards, Notes, Gift Wrappings, Stationery. Bonus. Special offers. Write for sample 21 card Christmas box on approval and free 50 for $1.00 cards. Comm. Call-write Hedenkamp, 343 Broadway, Dept. E-202.

College Graduates

Outstanding, interested in aptitude testing, fellowships now available with the Johnson O'Connor Research Foundation. $85 a month. Call RE 7-5530.

RE-EDUCATION PROGRAM in Conn. psychiatric hospital. College or undergrads may obtain practical experience, maintenance & salary. Five day week. Mon. thru Fri., 10-6. 58 E. 65th st.

EXAMPLE 168

In Example 168 Metrothin No. 2 has been used for display.

Example 169 shows the use of Spartan Medium for display.

And Example 170 shows the use of Memphis Light for display.

Although some of our newspapers have long been presenting nine columns on their classified pages, many other papers changed from eight to nine columns during World War II, prompted by newsprint and other war shortages and the desire for more income from fewer pages.

In November of 1943 the *Richmond* (Calif.) *Independent* started running most of its classified on ten-column pages.

Clerical Position

VETERAN, ABOUT 21
Midtown firm, 5-day week.
Write stating details. Y 99 Herald Tribune

Clerk—Young

UNDER 30, GOOD HANDWRITING
Pleasant Phone Voice,
Experience Unnecessary (Vet preferred)
Pleasant Working Conditions

BREYER ICE CREAM, INC.

34 St. & Queens Blvd., L. I. City

CLERK, age 22-28, old estab. concern. Must be accurate and have elementary knowledge of bookkeeping. Salary $40 to start. Write stating qualifications. D 681 Herald Tribune.

CLERK, shipping and receiving room, National Magazine; 35 hrs., 5 day week. Salary $108 month. Apply 250 Park av., 12th fl. Morning interviews.

CLERKS, 1-8 a. m., under 40 years, bank $45. Wilman Agency, 11 John st.

CLERKS, many 22-38 yrs., bank, $35-40 Wilman Agency, 11 John st.

CLERKS, 6-2 a. m. or 12-8 a. m., Bank, $2,100. WILMAN AGENCY, 11 John st.

Compositor Stone Hand

Must know book work imposition. Steady, over-scale pay. Box HT 324, 113 W. 42.

CORRESPONDENT

Permanent opening for good typist with flair for letter writing. Five-day week. 166 West 35th st.

MACY'S

Cost-Reduction Engineer

with time-study experience to head small department; man we are looking for will be an industrial or a mechanical engineer with at least 5 years in time study and whose over-all experience involves work in standard costs and cost reduction over period of about 12 to 15 years. Kindly send us resume to include your experience, education, salary requirements, etc. Box HT 309, 113 W. 42d st.

September Openings

FOR STENOGRAPHERS
Good pay. Convenient hours. Excellent transportation—pleasant office surroundings. Permanent position for the person who can qualify for Travel and Financial Departments.
Apply any weekday 9-3, Personnel Dept., 5th floor.

AMERICAN EXPRESS CO.

65 Broadway

HOUSEWIVES

Permanent Openings as saleswomen on part-time schedules allows time for household duties, avoid rush hour commuting.
work 11 A. M.—4:30 P. M.
or 12 Noon—5:30 P. M.
later only on Thursday
FIVE DAY WEEK
no experience necessary
166 WEST 35TH ST.

MACY'S

High School Graduates

If you wish to become associated with an old established text book publishing company, please write stating why & in what capacity you feel qualified. We offer permanent, congenial employment 35 hrs. per week to serious minded, courteous and ambitious young high school graduates. TR 136 Herald Tribune.

MAKE money fast. Sell Christmas, Everyday cards, Notes, Gift Wrappings, Stationery. Bonus. Special offers. Write for sample 21 card Christmas box on approval and free 50 for $1.00 cards. Comm. Call-write Hedenkamp, 343 Broadway, Dept. E-202.

College Graduates

Outstanding, interested in aptitude testing, fellowships now available with the Johnson O'Connor Research Foundation. $85 a month. Call RE 7-5530.

RE-EDUCATION PROGRAM in Conn. psychiatric hospital. College or undergrads may obtain practical experience, maintenance & salary. Five day week. Mon. thru Fri., 10-6. 58 E. 65th st.

EXAMPLE 169

A representative issue of the *Independent* showed two ten-column classified pages and a third page runover of five of the narrow columns alongside four regular-width news columns.

Several months before the switch to ten-column pages, the *Independent* changed its classified treatment from 8-point Ionic No. 5 set 12 picas wide to 6-point Ionic No. 5 set 10½ picas wide. But in November of 1943 it changed to 5½-point Ionic No. 5 set 9½ picas wide, to hold its classified to three pages.

Several five-column tabloids are now running six columns on their classified pages.

In March of 1944 the *Brooklyn Eagle* changed its classified pages

Clerical Position

VETERAN, ABOUT 21
Midtown firm, 5-day week.
Write stating details. Y 99 Herald Tribune

Clerk—Young

UNDER 30, GOOD HANDWRITING
Pleasant Phone Voice,
Experience Unnecessary (Vet preferred)
Pleasant Working Conditions

BREYER ICE CREAM, INC.
34 St. & Queens Blvd., L. I. City

CLERK, age 22-28, old estab. concern. Must be accurate and have elementary knowledge of bookkeeping. Salary $40 to start. Write stating qualifications. D 681 Herald Tribune.

CLERK, shipping and receiving room, National Magazine; 35 hrs., 5 day week. Salary $108 month. Apply 250 Park av., 12th fl. Morning interviews.

CLERKS, 1-8 a. m., under 40 years, bank $45. Wilman Agency, 11 John st.

CLERKS, many 22-38 yrs., bank, $35-40 Wilman Agency, 11 John st.

CLERKS, 6-2 a. m. or 12-8 a. m., Bank, $2,100. WILMAN AGENCY, 11 John st.

Compositor Stone Hand

Must know book work imposition. Steady, over-scale pay. Box HT 324, 113 W. 42.

CORRESPONDENT

Permanent opening for good typist with flair for letter writing. Five-day week. 166 West 35th st.

MACY'S

Cost-Reduction Engineer

with time-study experience to head small department; man we are looking for will be an industrial or a mechanical engineer with at least 5 years in time study and whose over-all experience involves work in standard costs and cost reduction over period of about 12 to 15 years. Kindly send us resume to include your experience, education, salary requirements, etc. Box HT 309, 113 W. 42d st.

September Openings

FOR STENOGRAPHERS
Good pay. Convenient hours. Excellent transportation—pleasant office surroundings. Permanent position for the person who can qualify for Travel and Financial Departments.
Apply any weekday 9-3, Personnel Dept., 5th floor.

AMERICAN EXPRESS CO.
65 Broadway

HOUSEWIVES

Permanent Openings as saleswomen on part-time schedules allows time for household duties, avoid rush hour commuting.
work 11 A. M.—4:30 P. M.
or 12 Noon—5:30 P. M.
later only on Thursday
FIVE DAY WEEK
no experience necessary
166 WEST 35TH ST.

MACY'S

High School Graduates

If you wish to become associated with an old established text book publishing company, please write stating why & in what capacity you feel qualified. We offer permanent, congenial employment 35 hrs. per week to serious minded, courteous and ambitious young high school graduates. TR 136 Herald Tribune.

MAKE money fast. Sell Christmas, Everyday cards, Notes, Gift Wrappings, Stationery. Bonus. Special offers. Write for sample 21 card Christmas box on approval and free 50 for $1.00 cards. Comm. Call-write Hedenkamp, 343 Broadway, Dept. E-202.

College Graduates

Outstanding, interested in aptitude testing, fellowships now available with the Johnson O'Connor Research Foundation. $85 a month. Call RE 7-5530.

RE-EDUCATION PROGRAM in Conn. psychiatric hospital. College or undergrads may obtain practical experience, maintenance & salary. Five day week. Mon. thru Fri., 10-6. 58 E. 65th st.

EXAMPLE 170

from eight to nine columns, with results that have been typical of those experienced by many other papers that have made the same sort of changes.

The *Eagle*, which had been using 5½-point Ionic No. 5 set solid, switched from eight 12-pica columns and 4-point column rules to nine columns each 10 picas and 8 points wide and 3-point column rules.

"And," as Stephen J. Lambert, *Eagle* mechanical superintendent, informed this writer shortly after the change was made, "we now get at least one and a half more columns of advertising on each classified page and in some instances as much as one and three-quarter columns. Where more display ads are used, we gain somewhat less space, but always at least a column and a half to the page."

George Barthelme, *Eagle* classified manager, said that what used to make five pages of classified in the old makeup can now be held to four pages in a Sunday edition, for an increase in classified revenue of about twenty-five per cent.

Any carry-overs from the nine-column to eight-column pages usually are handled in one of two ways. If a comparatively small amount of the nine-column matter is carried over, it is run vertically on an eight-column page and leaded on both sides to fill the wider column or columns. If considerable nine-column matter is carried over, it is evened up horizontally, in nine columns across the lower part of a page, with news or feature matter evened up across eight columns above it.

The *Los Angeles Times* found that some advertisers were more than anxious to buy the narrow strips left open when some of the narrower classified columns were run full depth on pages with wider columns, as suggested by Example 171.

That narrow advertisement ran the full depth of the page and consisted of more than a hundred well-leaded 10-point lines separated here and there by conspicuous black dots.

At least once that narrow strip (about a third of a column in width) was used by an advertiser to present a line of 42-point display complemented by smaller display, to be read sidewise from the top to the bottom of a page.

Example 172 suggests how the *Minneapolis Morning Tribune* used its strip of "extra space" to call attention to its own want ads.

Many newspapers that have been using 5½-point faces for their classified columns have found it possible to get considerably more lines on a page—and increased income—without changing to smaller faces or adding an extra column, but simply by adopting short descending letters for their 5½-point faces (g, j, p, q and y) and casting them on a 5-point body.

Consider the case of a certain publisher who made that sort of change.

He had been setting his classified in 5½-point Excelsior, solid, and getting 305 lines to the column, with eight columns to the page. He adopted short descenders, had the lines cast on a 5-point body, and picked up thirty lines to the column, or 240 to the page.

At twenty-one cents a line, the rate that publisher continued to

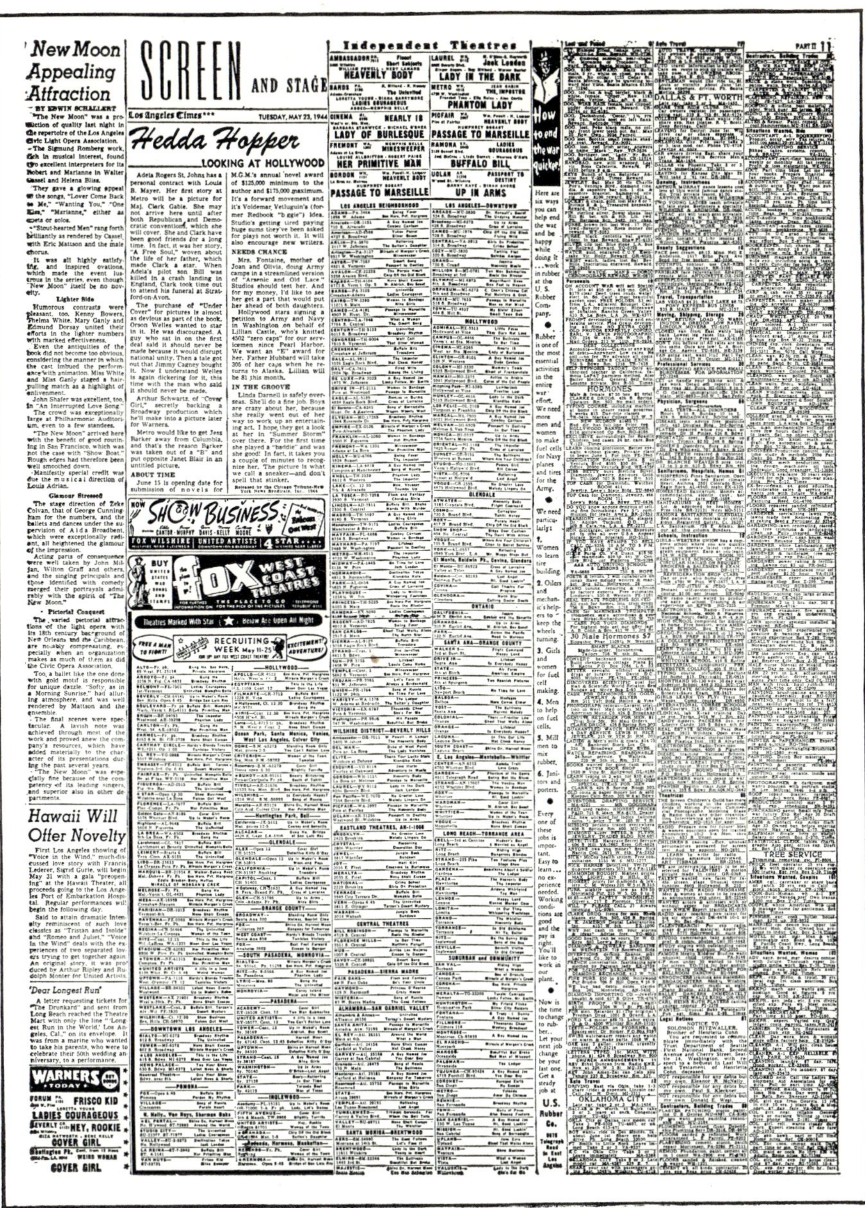

'New Moon' Appealing Attraction

BY EDWIN SCHALLERT

"The New Moon" was a production of quality last night in the repertoire of the Los Angeles Civic Light Opera Association.

The Sigmund Romberg work, rich in musical interest, found two excellent interpreters for its Robert and Marianne in Walter Cassel and Helena Bliss.

They gave a glowing appeal to the songs, "Lover Come Back to Me," "Wanting You," "One Kiss," "Marianne," either as duets or solos.

"Stout-hearted Men" rang forth brilliantly as rendered by Cassel with Eric Mattson and the male chorus.

It was all highly satisfying, and inspired ovations, which made the event lustrous in the series, even though "New Moon" itself be no novelty.

Lighter Side

Humorous contrasts were pleasant, too. Kenny Bowers, Thelma White, Mary Ganly and Edmund Dorsay united their efforts in the lighter numbers with marked effectiveness.

Even the antiquities of the book did not become too obvious, considering the manner in which the cast imbued the performance with animation. Miss White and Miss Ganly staged a hair-pulling match as a highlight of enlivenment.

John Shafer was excellent, too, in "An Interrupted Love Song."

The crowd was exceptionally large at Philharmonic Auditorium, even to a few standees.

"The New Moon" arrived here with the benefit of good routining in San Francisco, which was not the case with "Show Boat." Rough edges had therefore been well smoothed down.

Manifestly special credit was due the musical direction of Louis Adrian.

Glamour Stressed

The stage direction of Zeke Colvan, that of George Cunningham for the numbers, and the ballets and dances under the supervision of Aida Broadbent, which were exceptionally radiant, all heightened the glamour of the impression.

Acting parts of consequence were well taken by John Miljan, Wilton Graff and others, and the singing principals and those identified with comedy merged their portrayals admirably with the spirit of "The New Moon."

Pictorial Conquest

The varied pictorial attractions of the light opera with its 18th century background of New Orleans and the Caribbean, are notably compensating, especially when an organization makes as much of them as did the Civic Opera Association.

Too, a ballet like the one done with gold motif is responsible for unique dazzle. "Softly, as in a Morning Sunrise," had alluring atmosphere, and was well rendered by Mattson and the ensemble.

The final scenes were spectacular. A lavish note was achieved through most of the work and proved anew the company's resources, which have added materially to the character of its presentations during the past several years.

"The New Moon" was especially fine because of the competency of its leading singers, and superior also in other departments.

Hawaii Will Offer Novelty

First Los Angeles showing of "Voice in the Wind," much-discussed love story with Francis Lederer, Sigrid Gurie, will begin May 31 with a gala "preopening" at the Hawaii Theater, all proceeds going to the Los Angeles Port of Embarkation Hospital. Regular performances will begin the following day.

Said to attain dramatic intensity reminiscent of such love classics as "Tristan and Isolde" and "Romeo and Juliet," "Voice in the Wind" deals with the experiences of two separated lovers trying to get together again. An original story, it was produced by Arthur Ripley and Rudolph Monter for United Artists.

'Dear Longest Run'

A letter requesting tickets for "The Drunkard" and sent from Long Beach reached the Theatre Mart with only the line "'Longest Run in the World,' Los Angeles, Cal.," on its envelope. It was from a marine who wanted to take his parents, who were to celebrate their 50th wedding anniversary, to a performance.

SCREEN AND STAGE

Los Angeles Times — TUESDAY, MAY 23, 1944

Hedda Hopper — LOOKING AT HOLLYWOOD

Adela Rogers St. Johns has a personal contract with Louis B. Mayer. Her first story at Metro will be a picture for Maj. Clark Gable. She may not arrive here until after both Republican and Democratic conventions, which she will cover. She and Clark have been good friends for a long time. In fact, it was her story, "A Free Soul," woven about the life of her father, which made Clark a star. When Adela's pilot son Bill was killed in a crash landing in England, Clark took time out to attend his funeral at Stratford-on-Avon.

The purchase of "Under Cover" for pictures is almost as devious as part of the book. Orson Welles wanted to star in it. He was discouraged. A guy who sat in on the first deal said it should never be made because it would disrupt national unity. Then a tale got out that Jimmy Cagney bought it. Now I understand Welles is again dickering for it, this time with the man who said it should never be made.

Arthur Schwartz, of "Cover Girl," secretly backing a Broadway production which he'll make into a picture later for Warners.

Metro would like to get Jess Barker away from Columbia, and that's the reason Barker was taken out of a "B" and put opposite Janet Blair in an untitled picture.

ABOUT TIME

June 15 is opening date for submission of novels for M.G.M.'s annual novel award of $125,000 minimum to the author and $175,000 maximum. It's a forward movement and it's Voldemar Vetluguin's (former Redbook "biggie") idea. Studio's getting tired paying huge sums they've been asked for plays not worth it. It will also encourage new writers.

NEEDS CHANCE

Mrs. Fontaine, mother of Joan and Olivia, doing Army camps in a streamlined version of "Arsenic and Old Lace." Studios should test her. And for my money, I'd like to see her get a part that would put her ahead of both daughters.

Hollywood stars signing a petition to Army and Navy in Washington on behalf of Lillian Castle, who's knitted 4502 "zero caps" for our servicemen since Pearl Harbor. We want an "E" award for her. Father Hubbard will take 305 of her caps when he returns to Alaska. Lillian will be 81 this month.

IN THE GROOVE

Linda Darnell is safely overseas. She'll do a fine job. Boys are crazy about her, because she really went out of her way to work up an entertaining act. I hope they get a look at her in "Summer Storm" over there. For the first time she played a "baddie" and was she good! In fact, it takes you a couple of minutes to recognize her. The picture is what we call a sneaker—and don't spell that stinker.

Released by the Chicago Tribune-New York News Syndicate, Inc., 1944

Independent Theatres

HEAVENLY BODY — LADY IN THE DARK — PHANTOM LADY — LADIES COURAGEOUS — NEARLY 18 — LADY OF BURLESQUE — PASSAGE TO MARSEILLE — MINESWEEPER — HER PRIMITIVE MAN — BUFFALO BILL — PASSAGE TO MARSEILLE — UP IN ARMS

LOS ANGELES NEIGHBORHOOD — LOS ANGELES—DOWNTOWN — HOLLYWOOD — GLENDALE — SANTA ANA—ORANGE COUNTY — ONTARIO — LONG BEACH—TORRANCE AREA — SUBURBAN and COUNTY — CENTRAL THEATRES — EASTLAND THEATRES — SANTA MONICA—BRENTWOOD — PASADENA — INGLEWOOD

PART II 11

HORMONES — 30 Male Hormones 57 — TREE SERVICE — OKLAHOMA CITY

EXAMPLE 171

MINNEAPOLIS MORNING TRIBUNE
12 ★ Sat., May 11, 1946

RATE VERDICT AIDS STATE

Officials Hail Ruling Upholding ICC Order

Decision of a three-judge federal court in Utica, N. Y., was hailed Friday as a "Minnesota victory" that will give the state's manufacturers a 10 per cent reduction in freight rates.

George B. Sjoselius, assistant state attorney general, declared the decision will put Minnesota manufacturers in a much better position to compete for markets now held by eastern industry.

Attorney General J. A. A. Burnquist appeared in opposition to a petition of nine northeastern states to set aside an interstate commerce commission order raising class railroad freight rates 10 per cent in the north and east and lowering them an equal amount in the south and west.

The court dismissed the petition and also dissolved a temporary injunction granted last December which prevented the ICC from putting the rate changes into effect.

Sjoselius said Burnquist is participating in President Truman's safety conference at Washington and is appearing in opposition to a railroad petition for a blanket 25 per cent increase in freight rates.

U. S. EYES PLAN FOR NEXT CROP

Bureau Promises Immediate Action

WASHINGTON — (AP) -- The agriculture department will draft its policies for the next grain crop year during the next two weeks and expects to let farmers, millers and the grain trade know those plans promptly

Robert Shields, director of the department's production and marketing administration, reported this Friday to a conference of grain trade representatives and government officials, called by senators from Oklahoma Kansas, Texas, Colorado and Nebraska.

He said he was unable to say now what plans would be developed.

Between now and July 1 the government wants to obtain 90,000,000 bushels of wheat and 35,000,000 bushels of corn for export to feed the starving of other lands, he told the conference.

He was unable to say whether any shortages in these amounts would be taken from the new crop.

Nor was he able to tell the conference now, he said, whether the department would continue into the new crop season its order requiring 80 per cent flour extraction from wheat

J. Monroe Johnson, director of the office of defense transportation, asserted the nation faces the most serious transportation condition in history because of the coal strike.

Wheat may have to be piled on the ground, he said, until it can be transported, but he promised it eventually would be moved.

Herman Fakler, vice president of the Millers National federation, declared it is vital that mills and elevators know promptly the policies for the new wheat crop. Under present operations, he said, mills are running out of flour, and there may be no wheat for flour during June and part of July.

Implement Price Increase Granted

WASHINGTON—(AP)— A 10 per cent increase in the manufacturers' price on farm equipment, to cover increases in wage and material costs, was approved by the OPA Friday

For farmers, OPA said, the result will be a price rise averaging approximately 3 per cent

SCHOOL LAND VOTE SET

ST. JAMES, MINN—(AP)—The St. James school district will vote May 21 on a proposal for purchase of land for creation of a new athletic field.

C. J. MOFFATT, B. F. MOFFATT
Brothers in M and St. L. service 108 years

★ ★ ★ ★

Brothers Mark 108 Years' Work

Two brothers, veterans of a combined total of nearly 108 years in the employ of the Minneapolis & St. Louis railway, were honored Friday by their associates at a testimonial luncheon at Minneapolis Athletic club.

They are Bruce F. Moffatt, Minneapolis, executive representative of the road, and Cady J. Moffatt, Marshalltown, Iowa, general agent.

Born at Iola, Kan., they entered the employ of the old Iowa Central railroad, one of the predecessor roads of M & St L., at Marshalltown, as accounting department clerks in 1892

H M Ward, vice president, traffic, presided at the luncheon and presented testimonial scrolls to the Moffatt brothers on behalf of L. C Sprague, president, and other officials of the line.

FHA SETS UP VET STUDENT HOUSING

Three N. W. States Given Allocations

CHICAGO (AP)- The Federal public housing authority Friday announced allocations of emergency housing units for student war veterans and their families at colleges and universities in North and South Dakota and Minnesota.

They were: Minnesota — St John's university, Collegeville, 38, Moorhead State Teachers college, Moorhead, 10, St Cloud State Teachers college, St. Cloud, 13, Winona State Teachers college, Winona, 7.

North Dakota - State Teachers college, Dickinson, 8, N D. Agricultural college, Fargo 30, University of North Dakota, Grand Forks, 16, State Teachers college, Minot, 10.

South Dakota—Northern State Teachers college, Aberdeen, 4, S D. State College, Brookings 29, University of South Dakota, Vermillion, 8.

Johnson Asks End of Long Mine Strike

DULUTH — (AP) — State Labor Conciliator Leonard Johnson met here Friday with agents of 11 mining companies, 25 local officers of the CIO United Steelworkers and representatives of a dozen Iron Range communities in a renewed effort to settle the strike which has halted operations at independent mines since Feb. 8.

FAITHFUL PUP SHARES HIS MASTERS' DEATH

GALESBURG, ILL.—(AP) — Junior, a small black pup of doubtful ancestry, inconsolable since his young masters were killed by a hit-and-run driver Wednesday night, was struck and killed by a hit-and-run driver Friday.

His masters were the Crouch brothers, Teddy and Edwin, 12 and 8 years old.

HOUSING COST RULE SET UP

Dividing Line Is $6,500 in Dakotas

SIOUX FALLS S D —(AP)—The dividing line on low cost housing in North and South Dakota has been set at $6,500 by the federal housing administration, N. I Blegen, district director for the two-state area said Friday.

A previous figure of $5,500 proposed by the FHA and the national housing administration was protested by the district office as "not in conformity with building costs in this area."

The new order, retroactive to May 1, imposes a rule that half of the new homes must be built to sell under $6,500.

A veteran's application in his own name will be authorized regardless of quota but his application will be charged against the quota.

A dividing line of $50 was established on rentals for the Dakotas. This means at least half of the new houses built for rental must rent below that figure.

S. D. HOLDS STATE MEN FOR LARCENY

One Also Charged in Deadly Assault

ABERDEEN, S. D. —(AP)— Two Minnesota men, reported by police to have more than $500 worth of clothing and household appliances in their car, were charged Friday with grand larceny and one of them with assault with a dangerous weapon.

State's Attorney Vernon Williams filed the assault and larceny charges against Erwin Ekren, 33, Princeton, Minn., and a larceny charge against Vern Hall, 41, St. Paul.

Ekren, who said he was a circus laborer, was accused of striking Dean Byerson, department store manager, with a knife when the pair was taken into custody Thursday.

Police listed articles in the car as including 13 pairs of trousers, nine ladies suits and several dresses, which they said the men admitted taking from Aberdeen stores.

RESORT SCHOOL GRADUATES VETS

North Central Course Completed by 32

Thirty-two veterans trained in resort work and management were graduated Friday night at North Central school of agriculture, Grand Rapids, Minn., following a five-week course.

Selected by United States employment service, the group studied game and fish laws, conservation, first aid and water safety and methods of repair and upkeep of resort property.

University of Minnesota staff members at the school co-operated with state department of conservation, Minnesota Resorts association, Arrowhead association and Red Cross in conducting classes. The course was financed by veterans administration.

Students Combine Music, Fun at U. Festival Contest

By GEORGE GATES
Minneapolis Tribune Staff Writer

Making music was just part of the fun for some 2,000 teenagers who gathered at University of Minnesota Friday for the state east-central area high school contest and festival.

The students performed in their best manner, but quickly scattered after the contests to look over the campus and visit the loop. It was the first such contest held since 1942, so they made the most of it.

One of the largest delegations on hand from out of the city was the band and chorus from Benson, Minn., high school. Plan of the program was for all instrumental competition to be Friday, with the voice competition Saturday.

"We decided to bring them all down at once," Earl Prall, band director, said. "Arrangements were made to let the chorus appear today too."

The group left Benson at 6 a m.—three busloads of them. Within ten minutes after the band finished playing "Morning, Noon and Night in Vienna" for the judges the young musicians were off "to see the town."

Prall, who has been band director in Benson for ten years, stayed behind to pack up the music after cautioning his flock not to miss the bus going home.

Benson was one of the schools winning an "A" rating for bands.

Others winning "A's" were St. Cloud, Elbow Lake, Howard Lake, Excelsior, St. Peter, Roosevelt and Edison of Minneapolis and Cretin, St. Paul. Roosevelt's orchestra also was rated "A".

Soloists from these schools also got top ratings: Cretin, French horn and tuba; Grove City, piccolo; Excelsior, bassoon and bass clarinet; Benson, tenor vocal and baritone horn; Robbinsdale, trombone; Buffalo trombone; Columbia Heights, violin; Edison, trumpet.

BE SURE TO READ TODAYS WANT ADS

OBITUARIES AND FUNERALS

BOATS

ELMER N. OLSON CO.

CHAMPION OUTBOARD MOTORS CO.

Outboard Motor Repairing

W. O. ANDERSON SALES

Steel - Aluminum

ALUMINUM

Industrial Products Co.
St. Paul, Minn.

EMERGENCY DIESEL POWER

Cummins Diesel Engines

HOT WATER HEATERS

PLASTIC PAINT SPRAY

STEEL
Gruman Iron & Steel Co.

STAR-JOURNAL AND TRIBUNE WANT AD RATES

CALL AT 8111

AIR COMPRESSORS

BRIGGS STRATTON ENG.

LIVESTOCK & FARM EQUIPMENT

MILK COOLERS
NEW VICTOR COOLERS
with G. E. motor and compressor, 4-6-8 can size for immediate delivery.

NORMAN
APPLIANCE COMPANY
1204 East Lake DU 3393
LARGEST APPLIANCE STORE IN NW.

BABY CHICKS, POULTRY

BROODER HOUSES
MADE IN SECTIONS

HIAWATHA LBR. CO.

MAURICE SCANLAN & CO.

DOGS, BIRDS, PETS & SUPPLIES

DOG SHOW

NEW LOCATION

POSITIONS WANTED—MEN

HELP WANTED—MEN

Engineers
FIRST CLASS
and
Mechanics
Wanted

NEW MIDWEST PLANT
Offers
GOOD OPPORTUNITIES
to the Right Men
STEADY WORK
GOOD FUTURE
Write or Call
Peter J. Schweitzer, Inc.
Fiber Division
Windom, Minnesota

SALESMEN AND SOLICITORS

SALESMAN

EDUCATION

MEN AND WOMEN TRAIN NOW

National Radio School

For details come in, write, or call BR 2588
Entire 2nd floor Phoenix Bldg
60 S. 4th St., Mpls. 1

AIRLINE STEWARDESS!

100% Placement Record

McConnell Schools, Inc.

BE AN AIRLINE

Earn A Good Salary

Midwestern Schools

WOMEN
Airlines Need You
Be an Airlines Specialist
EARN A GOOD SALARY

CENTRAL RADIO SCHOOLS, INC

Hinck Flying Service

Switchboard School

The K. Switchboard School

TRAFFIC MANAGEMENT

Investigate Diesel

Tractor Training Service

Business Colleges

MEDICAL TECHNICIAN TRAINING

LEARN SHORTHAND

Dancing, Music, Dramatic

Learn Latest Dances!

HELP WANTED—WOMEN

HELP WANTED — WOMEN

IDEAL CAREER
For Girls 16 to 30

Openings for Floor or Counter Girls. Permanent positions at good salary plus a liberal bonus plan. Neat uniforms are furnished and laundered by the company. Experience is not necessary. We train you. If you are ambitious you may advance to a key position in a nationally known Cafeteria. Don't wonder if this is for you—It Is For You—if you do something about it tomorrow. Ask Cashier for Miss Stinson, Personnel Manager.

FORUM CAFETERIA
36 South 7th Street

Household & Domestic

AIRLINES
NEED MEN

AS TRANSPORTATION AND OPERATION AGENTS

WE NOW OFFER a complete training — Airlines approved. (Some communications training included.)

BETTER THAN AVERAGE SALARIES
FAST PROMOTION

VETERANS—A life long career in an interesting and fascinating field. Train under the GI Bill of Rights.

The only school in Minneapolis equipped to give this type of training. Must be high school graduate to qualify. Not a correspondence course, you learn by doing.

E.R.T.I.
(SPECIALIZING IN AIRLINES TRAINING)
2933 Hennepin Ave.,
Mpls., Minn.
PL. 2426

DePonti Aviation Co., Inc.
Wold-Chamberlain Field
Minneapolis, Minn.
ANNOUNCES
the opening of an
AIRPLANE & ENGINE MECHANICS COURSE
Offering refresher training for veterans under the G.I. Bill. Classes now in progress. Prepare now for a career in aviation!
For Further Information Call DU. 8374, Mpls.; NE. 4191, St. Paul

The Dayton Company

SALESPEOPLE	NON-SELLING
Housewares	Elevator Opr.
Notions	Pen Bookkeepers
Women's Dresses	Receiving Cashiers
Silverware	Waitresses
Stationery	Typists
Hosiery	Clericals
China and Glassware	Cashier Wrappers

Positions available on 5½ day basis with other advantages consisting of Paid Vacations, Hospitalization, Sick Benefits, Credit Union for Savings, Retirement Plan Program, Employes' Cafeteria and Discount Privileges.

APPLY EMPLOYMENT OFFICE
8TH FLOOR

United Garment Mfg. Co.
Has Opening for
POWER MACHINE OPERATORS
to sew on sportswear in a new, modern factory. Top wages, steady work. Experience not necessary. Good pay while learning. Many workers' benefits. Paid holidays and vacations. Apply—
400 FIRST AV. N.—4TH FL.

EXAMPLE 172

charge, the increased revenue from a page amounted to $50.40. From six classified pages, the number usually run by that paper, the increase amounted to more than $300 every day.

The only expense of the change was the cost of two mold liners and about fifty matrices for each of twenty typesetting machines.

"And so," as that publisher later put it, "for a total expenditure of about $160, I am picking up more than $300 every day, and no longer have to risk offending advertisers by keeping out any classified lines in excess of the six pages we at present regard as our standard."

Some newspapers use column rules on bodies of different thicknesses—on 1-, 3- and 6-point bodies—when justifying different combinations of the narrower and regular-width columns on run-over pages. To illustrate, when one 12-pica column is used alongside seven or eight 10½-pica columns, 1-point column rules are used on the page; when four of the wider and four of the narrower columns are presented on a page, 6-point column rules are used, and when seven wider and one narrower columns are arranged side by side, 3-point column rules are employed.

One of the liveliest classified departments run by weekly newspapers in this country is run by the *Star News* of Medford, Wis. That paper nearly always runs more than a full page of classified, and sometimes presents the small ads on as many as three pages. (Incidentally, the *Star News* has built up an "amusement section" that sometimes presents as many as two pages of advertisements from restaurants, theaters and other amusement places in a single issue—especially just before New Year, Easter, Thanksgiving and other holidays.)

Some newspapers, instead of, or in addition to, running classified advertisements in a main classified section, confine some of the advertisements to certain categories and group them on other pages.

For instance, some papers run on their sports pages classified groups headed "Dogs and Pets," "Boat Directory," "Used Cars," and so on; on society pages, groups headed "Where to Dine," "Entertainment," and so on; on feature pages, groups headed "The Stamp Mart" (about postage stamps for collectors, about coins, curios and auctions), "Camera Exchange," and so on; in book sections, "The Book Mart" (about books, manuscripts, autographs, bookplates, auctions), and so on; on general-news pages, groups headed "Public Notices," "Lost and Found," "Births, Marriages, Deaths," "Announcements" of various kinds, and so on.

In a book entitled *Getting and Keeping Classified Advertising*, by Morton J. A. McDonald, a classified-advertising manager of much experience, appeared the following statements, in his chapter on typography:

"The type dress, then, of the classified section is a matter of prime importance to the reader, to the advertiser, and of course to the publisher. Yet of all the problems connected with this department of the newspaper, not one receives less, or so little, thought. . . . It has been proved that the majority of those who read the want-ad pages are past thirty years of age, and to them legibility is a deciding factor in the papers they read. . . . Many newspapers suffer from poor printing, and this fault is aggravated by the use of small type faces. Press blankets fail to give proper compression, the quality of ink is often only fair to middling, and finally, those papers employing the dry-mat system subject their type forms to excessive pressure in the process of molding, with the result that the delicate surfaces of finely cut letters are flattened or broken off. . . . For those who desire to save space, obtain ease of handling, and yet escape the optical defects of the smaller types, some of the newer faces such as Ionic should be considered. These newcomers, retaining the form of the roman letter, have been cut, in accordance with scientific principles, with a maximum of white space within the character, giving greater legibility and the illusion of larger size."

During World War II and for some time following the war, as previously explained, many newspapers tightened up their classified pages, as well as other pages, because of newsprint shortages.

But with the relaxing of newsprint restrictions, many papers planned to go back to opened-up treatments of their classified and other pages; to go back to larger and more generously leaded body faces on all of their pages, and back to fewer columns on their classified pages.

For they realized that the easier they made it for readers to read, the more likely they would be to read and keep on reading their papers.

21

Gravure, Offset and Color

MUCH PROGRESS has been made in recent years in the gravure and colorgravure branches of printing, and more and more newspapers and advertisers are coming to employ gravure and colorgravure.

While it is not the purpose here to describe in detail how gravure printing is done, it is the purpose to point out the kinds of type faces, kinds of artwork, kind of paper, and colors of ink, that have proved successful in gravure printing.

And this writer can think of no more authoritative or compact way of accomplishing this purpose than to present extracts from an article in *Printers' Ink Monthly* entitled "Taking the Mystery Out of Rotogravure"—an article prepared by that publication with the assistance of gravure experts with the Kimberly-Clark Corporation, Art Gravure Corporation, Neo Gravure Corporation, Alco Gravure, Inc., the *New York Times*, and the *Chicago Tribune*. And here are the extracts:

"Intaglio, gravure, rotogravure, photogravure—all are one and the same thing. The basic process involves printing from a copper surface on which the design or picture has been depressed by etching. The term 'intaglio' is the general term describing all processes of this kind, the word itself meaning 'incised or counter-sunk.' Sheet-feed gravure is different from other gravure in only one respect—the job is printed on single sheets, rather than on a web. With the web rotary press, rolls of paper are used.

"There are three basic methods of printing: (A) Relief, or raised surface, to which the term 'printing' is commonly applied; (B) Planographic, or surface, which takes in lithography and offset; (C) Intaglio, or subsurface, which takes in all forms of gravure.

"Although different screens are available, it is probable that ninety-nine per cent of rotogravure work is done with 150-line screen.

"In rotogravure the tendency is for type matter to reproduce more softly than in letterpress printing. This is an important point to bear in mind when selecting type faces for rotogravure reproduction. It is also essential to give thought to the fact that the fine screen used is likely to break up letters that have delicate curlicues. Moreover, the screen accentuates the heavier lines.

"Don't use a thick-and-thin type face, especially in the smaller sizes. Select strong, even-weight type.

"Don't use large blocks of small-size type—6 point, for example.

"Don't use smaller than 10 point where type is to be surprinted over a tinted background.

"Don't use smaller than 10 or 12 point if the type is to be in reverse —white on a dark background.

"Don't use a design background for reverse type.

"Don't use reverse type on a light or varying background.

"Headings and captions should be set in type, actual size, and perfect press proofs attached with library paste in the spaces allowed.

"Type matter for advertisements should be set actual size, but the press proofs should be attached to the layout only when it is possible to locate them in exactly the correct position. Otherwise, type proofs should be sent separately. [When no change in size is desired, the type should be proved on transparent film.]

"To eliminate the shadows cast by the edges of paper proofs that are pasted to the layout, it is advisable to run a thin line of Chinese white around each edge.

"Pen-and-ink drawings, dry-brush work and oil paintings reproduce excellently when a generous range of tone values is used. A charcoal drawing does not reproduce so well, because it usually lacks that range of tone. With oil paintings it is necessary to consider that the brush marks may be exaggerated, because rotogravure printing picks up every detail. Also, where the work is in color, the photographic print supplied for copy should be made from a color-separation negative in order to retain original tone values.

"In brief, one of the chief values of the process is that it is capable of reproducing a full gradation of tones, holding fine details in the deepest shadows as well as in the middle tones and higher lights. Consequently, to use line may mean losing one of the principal advantages of rotogravure.

"Wash drawings are good, especially the poster type, where the tints are blocked in quickly and not worked over too much. A muddy or streaky wash is exaggerated in the process. Opaque colors are usually better than transparent, for brush marks and drying lines do not show so plainly.

"Pen drawings with a technique that produces fine gradation of tone values lend themselves well to rotogravure. Dry-brush work frequently makes attractive rotogravure, particularly when a generous range of tone values is used.

"The reproduction of photographs is, of course, one of rotogravure's strongest points. In fact, it is claimed for it that it more closely approximates photographic originals than any other method of printed reproduction. There is no doubt that photographs are the best sources of illustration.

"Photographs should be selected with care. Photographs that are contrasty, chalky or flat, lacking detail in the highlights and having heavy shadows also lacking detail are unsatisfactory. Photographs that are brilliant and sharp, containing full tones, with the point of highlights pure white, are preferable to prints that are flat, because rotogravure softens.

"Avoid photographic prints with a rough egg-shell or linen finish. When the photographic print has a rough surface, the surface may reproduce and give a grainy appearance in the final result.

"Do not greatly enlarge or reduce a photograph. Good judgment will indicate the proper limits, after examining the print closely.

"Soft-focus photographs can be handled, and sometimes the results are exceedingly good. However, more often the details are likely to be further softened by the thin ink that is used, which has a tendency to spread slightly when it reaches the paper. Consequently, if a picture is used the details of which are already soft, and if these details are further softened by the process, a blurry reproduction may result. However, if a part of the picture is diffused to center attention on the part to be emphasized, the process will turn in an excellent job.

"As to paper stock, a super-calendered slack size—a paper that has great absorptive power and capacity, so that the thin liquid ink used may spread slightly without showing through on the opposite side—affords the best results. The ink used is much more fluid than ordinary printers' ink, being about the consistency of thick soup.

"Ink of any color may be employed in gravure, but experience has demonstrated that the best results, particularly in newspaper rotogravure, are obtained with brown, green and black."

In answer to certain questions from this writer having to do with colorgravure, J. Thomson Willing, then of the Gravure Service Corporation, New York City, replied as follows:

"In quantity production of pictorial color copy, there have been two great problems—register and clarity of tone when one wet color was superimposed on a previous color still wet. But these problems have been solved, and often now it is impossible without analysis to determine whether more than one color has been used on a certain spot. A speed that makes for the almost simultaneous imposing of one color on another stops all 'out of register.'

"Color photography of copy gives an exact determination of the quantity of each ingredient of the three primary colors—blue, red, yellow—thus making it possible to secure a non-variable facsimile of copy.

"There are three possible forms of copy available for colorgravure. Photography, oil paintings or water-color renderings. Each of these has definite advantages for special uses.

"Color photography is beyond all question the best method of rendering textures, textiles or factual objects and packages. A color photograph will show the purchaser of the advertised product what he is to get as nothing else can.

"Oil paintings can give fine results, as the brush technique can be effectively retained, especially if the painting has been done in a high key of color.

"Water-color copy gives brilliant effects with surety. It is desirable that color designs be complete, and not provided in separate units to be assembled. Assembling in a gravure plant, though possible, is difficult. When text type is to be used, it can be flashed onto a surface. It must not be pasted on a color surface, but clean black proofs of it supplied. A few special colors, such as emerald green and magenta, are to be avoided, but otherwise it is easy to get a full range of rich, glowing color in gravure."

(As improvements in color photography are constantly being made, with developments in gravure keeping pace, readers particularly interested in this phase of newspaper designing should check with gravure specialists on latest developments.)

Offset-Printed Newspapers

In recent years several newspapers—most of them weeklies and small dailies—have given up letterpress printing (the kind employed by most newspapers) in favor of offset printing. They have done this chiefly because, in the words of an offset enthusiast, "pictures can be produced in large numbers more readily and economically by offset lithography than by photo-engraving and letterpress."

However, as the same fundamental principles of makeup that apply to newspapers printed by letterpress apply as well to papers printed by offset, it seems inadvisable to take the space here to explain either process or to discuss the merits of one against the other.

The point to be emphasized here is that the same fundamental principles of makeup apply to either process—letterpress or offset.

Comics

Little if anything can be done to make attractive pages—attractive physically—of pages filled or nearly filled with comic strips. The strips often vary decidedly in weight from unit to unit within the same strips, and even more so from one strip to another. Usually the strips clash with each other and the other units of composition on a page, to the physical disadvantage of the page as a whole.

However, comic pages have been found by many newspapers to be circulation builders and holders and so are run as a matter of course.

Usually such pages are run toward the end of a paper, but some newspapers run comics as "brighteners" on feature, sports, classified-advertising and other pages, and many newspapers present entire sections of comics in color.

During World War II, when zinc and newsprint saving became a necessity in many newspaper plants, many comic strips that previously had been presented across five columns were shrunk to four columns. That shrinkage, coupled with the fact that the drawers of such strips nearly always present their dialogues or descriptions entirely in capitals, rather than in capitals and lower-case, made the strips even harder to read than before.

Whether or not this is a blessing to humanity depends on the point of view. At any rate, many of the strips are hard indeed on the eyes of the many people—young, middle-aged and old—who read or attempt to read them.

Since the middle of September, 1946, the *St. Louis Post-Dispatch* has been running comic sections of unusual brilliance as to color, and with excellent register, on a new gravure press.

When this writer asked Charles J. Hentschell, production manager of the *Post-Dispatch*, for a brief explanation, he and Alex Primm of the production department responded with these statements:

"Our process begins with the making of flat casts from the stereotype mats furnished by advertisers and the comic syndicates.

"Once these casts are made, they are sent to the engraving room, where transparent cellophane proofs are pulled. These proofs are then sent to the rotogravure department, where they are used in printing the carbon tissue. The usual rotogravure process then follows.

"The *Post-Dispatch* makes some comics itself and in those cases the process varies in that the Ben Day is laid directly on glass, which is then used in printing the carbon tissue. By not laying the Ben Day on zinc, the necessity of etching and pulling proofs is avoided.

"At this time the comics are being printed on roto news stock, a thirty-four-pound paper, only because regular newsprint, thirty-two-pound paper, is not available. Some comics have been printed on the latter stock and experienced pressmen had difficulty distinguishing between the two. We know, therefore, that regular newsprint will do a satisfactory job.

"The roto comics have such brilliancy because the vehicle carrying the pigment evaporates when the printed web passes through steam-heated dryers, leaving all the pigment on *top* of the paper."

At least a few small dailies that are not equipped to run comics in full color in their own plants give their strips a background of color by using tint blocks. The comic pages of those papers are printed in black on white in the usual way, but the main bodies of the comics are given "pink" backgrounds by additional impressions made from coarse-grained Ben Day tint blocks and the use of red ink.

The *New Orleans Item* and perhaps other newspapers have found that some of their local advertisers are more than anxious to run advertisements between certain comic strips—preferably immediately above or below strips that are particularly popular locally—and at rates that attract many extra dollars of revenue to the papers annually. *Extra dollars* because such pages previously had brought in no advertising revenue and because the advertisers who use them continue, in many instances, to run the same amount of advertising as before on other pages in the same papers.

Example 173, a fragment of a page containing sixteen comic strips each four columns wide, with fifteen accompanying advertisements, shows how such advertising has been handled on a comic page by the *New Orleans Item*, which also has run advertisements of similar size and appearance between time tables on its radio pages.

EXAMPLE 173

Of course many advertisers employ comic strips of their own—many in color—in newspapers to publicize their products, and many national advertisers, appreciating the wide popularity of colored comics, issue specially prepared comic papers of their own for distribution through dealers.

Run-of-Paper Color

More and more newspapers are going in for more and more color printing, not only for Sunday issues but weekday issues as well.

In 1934 newspapers in this country ran forty times as much run-of-paper color as they did in 1930. And that decided increase in R-O-P color was independent of the comic, gravure and magazine or special-section color advertising run.

By the summer of 1934 more than 500 daily or Sunday newspapers in this country (in forty states and the District of Columbia) were offering advertisers run-of-paper color, but comparatively few of those papers were actually running any.

Today many papers are offering, and even more are getting ready to offer, advertisers "full-color" treatments in their regular advertising columns.

An article in the *Wall Street Journal* for May 22, 1945, contained these statements:

"Printing-equipment makers, in whatever time they have free from war work, are designing a four-color rainbow that promises to lead to a postwar pot of gold.

"They have made color printing commonplace in the editorial and advertising pages of the monthly and weekly magazines and Sunday supplements. Now they plan to put color on a daily basis and sell it to the newspapers. . . .

"Color has been used since 1900 on newsprint stock in Hearst's *American Weekly* and in the Sunday comics. But only in the last dozen years has it been developed beyond the front-page headline stage. Some half dozen metropolitan dailies have used it in editorial and advertising pages, and the *Chicago Tribune* has been able to take a news photograph in four colors in the afternoon and have it on the press by midnight."

Newspaper Wrappers

Many a newspaper that looks attractive or fairly attractive when it comes off the press, and is fairly easy to read, is decidedly otherwise when it reaches a subscriber by mail. Some papers sent out as singles—individually wrapped—are rolled so tightly in the mail-room that it is difficult for the receiver to unwrap them without tearing, and have become so crumpled that it is difficult for him to flatten them out and to keep them from rolling up as he attempts to read them. And a too-liberal use of paste in the mail-room often results in the mutilation of newspapers.

A friend of this writer's, an exchange editor who receives scores of newspapers by mail weekly, and who has to look them over quickly if at all, declines to unwrap some of the papers received.

"It isn't that they couldn't be valuable to us," he once told this writer. "They could be. But the harder they make it for us to let them prove it, the less chance they get to do it. Some of them have been squeezed and twisted so much in the mailing that any receiver would have to have more time and patience than we have to be willing to fight his way through their wrinkles and creases."

While sympathizing with that editor's point of view, this writer remarked: "But an exchange editor with many papers to choose from is hardly to be compared with a person who receives, say, only one paper by mail, and his favorite one, at that."

"True enough," the editor replied. "That person would read that paper, or attempt to do so, no matter how handicapped. But he wouldn't thank its editor or staff members for making it difficult. He would though, you can be sure, whether or not he ever told them so, appreciate their making it easier to read."

Many singles are wrapped in cut-up sections of exchanges—surely no good advertisement for the papers inside. Others are mailed out, neatly enough, perhaps, in remnants of blank newsprint.

But printed wrappers can be much more effective, in an advertising way, and newspaper publishers should be interested in advertising their commodities all the way from the mail-room to the home or office of the person or firm receiving copies by mail.

Certain rulings have been made as to the kind and amount of printing that legally may be employed on newspaper wrappers, but there is room enough within those rulings for many publishers to improve the effectiveness of their wrappers.

In response to a letter addressed by this writer to the Postmaster General, Washington, D. C., the following statements were received from the Post Office Department as this chapter was being written:

". . . With reference to the item which you wish to include in your manuscript on newspaper makeup, regarding newspaper wrappers, you are informed that while this office is not unaware of the desire of publishers to dress up the wrappers of their publications, it is not contemplated that under Section 552, Postal Laws and Regulations, the envelopes or wrappers, etc., used by publishers in mailing copies of their publications at the second-class rates of postage shall contain other information than the following:

" 'The name and address of the person to whom the matter shall be sent, index figures of subscription book, either printed or written, the printed title of the publication and the place of its publication, the printed or written name and address without addition of advertisement of the publisher or sender, or both, and written or printed words or figures, or both, indicating the date on which the subscription to such matter will end, the correction of any typographical error, a mark, except by written or printed words, to designate a word or passage to which it is desired to call attention; the words "sample copy" when the matter is sent as such, the words "marked copy" when the matter contains a marked item or article.' "

Surely, the newspaper that is well written and edited, attractively set, made up and printed, when sent out in a single wrapper, deserves a well-worded and attractively printed wrapper—one that both protects and reflects the superior product it contains.

22

School Papers

This writer has talked at many conventions of scholastic press associations on school-paper makeup, has analyzed hundreds of school papers, and has illustrated and discussed many "before" and "after" pages of school papers in the "Newspaper Makeup" department of the *Linotype News.*

It would be possible to illustrate and discuss many of those "before" and "after" pages here, as well as many other pages from school papers, but such illustrations and discussions probably would be superfluous in this book.

For many of the makeup principles that apply to newspapers of general circulation, and particularly to tabloids of general circulation, apply as well to school papers, most of which are tabloid in size.

However, some school papers have several advantages in the way of makeup over papers of general circulation, and so are in a position to turn out even better looking products.

As most school publications have comparatively small circulations, they need not employ stereotyping and can be, as most of them are, printed direct from type on flatbed presses.

Many school papers, because of their comparatively small circulations, can afford to use grades of paper considerably better than newsprint—another advantage.

Such papers, printing, as has been stated, direct from type on flatbed presses, on smoother surfaced paper, can use effectively halftones with finer screens than the 55- or 65-line screens used by newspapers employing stereotyping. The school papers can use effectively 85-, 100- or even finer line screens, which make for better reproductions of pictures on the better paper, particularly when the halftones are given the better make-ready possible when stereotyping is not employed.

Such school papers sometimes can use to advantage for body matter certain book faces the finer lines of which would not stand up well under the tremendous pressure of modern stereotyping and would not print clearly on coarse-fibered newsprint.

However, as the editors of most school papers want their publications to look more like *newspapers* than *magazines*, it is better usually to avoid "bookish" treatments and to employ for body matter one or more of the latest and best *newspaper* body faces.

Among the most appropriate body faces for school papers are those shown and discussed in Chapter 6 of Part I of this book.

And among the most appropriate head faces for school papers are those shown and discussed in Chapters 5 and 16 of Part I.

Among the chief faults of the less attractive school papers are:

Inappropriate nameplates. Often the nameplates are so heavy that they overshadow even the largest heads over the most important stories on front pages. Some school-paper nameplates, in addition to being unattractive, are made difficult to read by incorporating background drawings of school buildings, association emblems, and so on. Simpler, clearer nameplates usually are more appropriate and more effective.

Too many different kinds of type faces, and particularly unrelated faces, which do not get along well together.

Too many headlines entirely in capitals, which are harder to read than lines set in capitals and lower-case.

And too many rules and dashes, and the wrong kinds of rules and dashes. (See Chapter 10 in Part I of this book.)

As previously stated in this chapter, some school papers have several advantages in the way of makeup over papers of general circulation, and so are in a position to turn out even better looking products. And some school papers are attractive indeed.

But many school papers are set, made up and printed in small print shops with limited equipment; in shops that do not have and cannot reasonably supply, at the prices charged, some of the latest and best type faces that school editors would like to use.

Naturally, type faces cost money, and it would be unreasonable for school editors to ask the owners of small shops to add one or several new fonts of type unless the owners are specially compensated for the additions, or feel that they can use the new faces to advantage on other forms of printing as well as on the school papers.

23

Influences of World War II

World War II, with its shortages of newsprint, zinc and other newspaper-production materials, and consequent restrictions on the use of them imposed by the government, brought about marked changes in the makeup of many newspapers in this and other countries.

Hundreds of papers that, up to the war, had persisted in employing complicated and space-wasting heads of several decks over leading news stories abandoned such treatments in favor of simplified flush-left heads.

While many of those die-hards may have adopted the simpler heads reluctantly, as a temporary expedient to save newsprint, they must soon have discovered that such heads are easier to write, easier to set and easier to read, and probably would not think of returning to the outmoded heads formerly employed.

Many papers, to save newsprint, tightened up their pages in various ways.

Some papers went back, temporarily, to smaller body faces, employed less leading between lines, reduced full-width running heads to narrower measures, adopted column rules on narrower bodies, and ran more and narrower columns on their classified-advertising pages.

Some papers printed fewer pages to the issue. Some started using lighter weight newsprint. Some changed from eight-, seven- or six-column pages to five-column formats for some or all of their issues. Many went out of business altogether.

In 1942 alone, sixty-three papers in this country that had been appearing as dailies suspended publication altogether or became weeklies or semi-weeklies. Of those sixty-three, thirty-four announced that they were suspending operations permanently, and four that they were closing "for the duration." Nineteen became weeklies, and six became semi-weeklies.

Many papers not only restricted advertisers to less space in an issue but increased advertising rates. Others accepted certain kinds of advertising for split runs only, or for certain editions only, and sold the same space in other editions to other advertisers, to accommodate as many applicants for space as they could.

In the meantime, gasoline rationing, blackouts and other restrictions were confining more and more people to their homes and thus making for more and more readers of newspapers, as many listeners could not get from their radios as much news as they wanted. Circulations kept climbing—soaring.

So much so that many newspapers and magazines requested the original purchasers of copies to share them with other people who otherwise would be unable to obtain copies.

Magazines, also, of course, were affected by restrictions. Many of them, too, were forced to run fewer pages or to reduce page sizes. Some of the more popular magazines were obliged to decline many millions of dollars in advertising.

Some of that advertising went automatically to radio stations or to newspapers that could manage to handle it.

After Pearl Harbor, many newspaper executives asked how space could be saved in their papers without sacrificing too much in the way of attractiveness and legibility.

This writer replied with a list of space-savers—many of them only emergency measures, to be abandoned as soon as possible—that later were reprinted in a widely distributed booklet entitled *How Many Sacred Cows Are You Feeding?*

Each time, in replying to requests for space-savers, this writer stated:

"The first savings, of course, should be made in the editorial rooms by the cutting down of any over-written stories and the elimination of any inconsequential items.

"To conserve space, something, of course, must be given up, but that something should not be legibility.

"For what good would it do the reader to be served with more lines of type—more words of reading matter—if he would not be able to read them, or want to read them, because of the strain on his eyes?

"The average newspaper reader reads only part of a paper—not all of it—and is much less interested in more stories in an issue than in easy reading of the stories he happens to read."

Several of the space-savers suggested by this writer, as previously stated, were intended only as emergency measures, and were accepted as such, but others are just as applicable to newspaper-publishing conditions of today as they were to conditions in the war days, and are repeated at the end of this chapter.

After the War Production Board had issued its Limitation Order L-240, the News-Journal Newspapers of Wilmington, Del., with the assistance of the National Newspaper Promotion Association, wrote to sixty newspapers in the United States and Canada in January of 1943 and asked what those papers were doing about it.

From replies received W. Murray Metten, promotion manager of the News-Journal Newspapers, compiled a report entitled *An Early Survey of the Newsprint Situation.*

Among the "obvious curtailments" being made by replying newspapers were:

"Reduction of complimentary mailing copies.

"Cutting of departmental checking and office copies.

"Reduction of 'free lists' and more strict supervision of free copies released both for official and unofficial accommodation of advertisers and others.

"Elimination of copies spoiled in printing.

"Elimination of all returns. Some papers have adopted this policy. Others report they have filed notice to go on a non-return basis in April and May. Managements advise they are allowing returns in cases of emergency such as severe bad weather and unusual news breaks.

"Sample copies discontinued.

"Greater effort being made to watch the handling of newsprint from the paper mills and railways to pressrooms to reduce damage to a minimum.

"Cutting down of time allowed renewals to pay.

"Cutting of tear pages to an absolute minimum.

"Discontinuance of all printing of outside circulars, even though the copy has been used in the paper.

"Reduction of reprint pages for promotional purposes.

"Conserving on editorial-page space by doing away with a leaded slug, giving an opportunity for additional features.

"Cutting roll widths from 68½ to 68 without reducing 6-point column rules, by undercutting plate in stereotype room and shifting the press lockups.

"Using larger rolls by cutting into press floor, thereby saving on spoils by less pasting, less number of cars to handle as well as cores.

"Cutting of comics to four columns.

"Elimination of serial stories.

"Reduction of Sunday comics to tab size.

"Cartoons taken off comic pages and distributed through paper wherever room.

"Sports. Reduction of space by one and one-half and even two pages, these totaling in several cases as much as fifty per cent. This applies daily.

"Running of three sport pages Sunday, instead of four and five.

"Elimination of all bowling scores.

"Elimination of racing returns and entries.

"Tightening up of editorial ratio to advertising.

"Shortening of all news stories wherever possible.

"Cutting down on the amount of space devoted to heads.

"Use of smaller cuts.

"Cutting down of main news section by Sunday papers.

"Run-overs from front pages not carried unless it is absolutely necessary.

"Closer editing of wire dispatches, as well as local stories.

"Avoidance of six- and eight-column streamers on inside pages.

"Punctuation and abbreviation rules overhauled.

"Elimination of crossword puzzles, horoscopes, bridge articles, personality charts, beauty and charm features.

"Reduction of special background articles.

"Handling of features as 'optional' that formerly ran as 'must.'

"Elimination of editorial cartoons.

"Reduction in editorial content on business-review pages, as well as building, farm and similar advertising pages.

"Cutting down of recipes on food pages.

"Elimination of camera features.

"Elimination of feature pages and picture pages.

"Reduction of volume of stock quotations.

"Reduction of volume of financial news.

"Elimination of the movie-review page which gives news of the week ahead.

"Cutting to half a page of zinc on first-section page of drama news, instead of using full page of zinc.

"Strict elimination of 'readers' and major as well as minor publicity releases that come under the head of advertiser co-operation.

"Elimination entirely of Saturday church page.

"Judiciously reducing size of promotion copy.

"Study of each promotion ad to be sure it is worthy.

"Promotion material pushed into magazine and roto where space is available.

"Space budget allotted to departments for promotion purposes.

"Cutting of society pages generally. Some report a fifty per cent cut.

"Reduction of the size of heads in the society and woman's pages.

"Reduction of two-column cuts to one column.

"Elimination of cutlines by tying pictures directly in with stories wherever practical.

"Elimination of art on wedding announcements.

"Reduction of out-of-town society news."

Among the "unusual programs" being followed by some of the replying newspapers were:

"Discontinuance entirely of engagement notices and pictures. Advertising charge made for engagement notices.

"Reduction of pressroom waste by careful skiving of roll-edges to avoid press breaks when roll is running. Also careful culling of printed waste.

"Rate increases in local and national advertising with rates based in some cases on space quota used monthly. Expected not only to increase revenue in spite of some falling off in linage but also to reduce newsprint consumption.

"Drastic reductions and eliminations made in number of proofs furnished advertisers.

"Taking off eight-column running head, which includes the dateline, and putting this in one column, thus gaining about two inches per page.

"Running of paper down to last few layers and using more paper off rolls which are damaged.

"Sending of damaged paper back to be re-wound. What is desirable is the paper and not the filing of the claim.

"Long lists of names, etc., set in 6-point instead of 8-point body type.

"Reduction of size of paper from 68 to 66½ by the use of 4-point column rules.

"Reduction in size of heads and elimination of decks and dashes on inside pages.

"On classified pages a reduction in number of classifications and size heads between items.

"Reduction in number of editions.

"Drastic reduction in number of Monday and Saturday papers.

"Newsprint curtailment affords opportune time to institute rigid censorship of medical advertising.

"Trimming of 'edge' spots on paper and using them even with torn spot.

"Have mills ship newsprint from 31.5 to 31.8 basis weight.

"Discontinuance of Sunday rotogravure."

Some papers, to save newsprint, reduced their Saturday editions from what had been twelve- up to sixteen-page papers down to eight pages. They called them "V" editions—the "V" being, of course, for "Victory."

Many papers increased their subscription rates or the prices of copies on the newsstands.

In 1943 one small-town paper announced:

"From the present time on, we do not care for the so-called country correspondents. Time was when these people were courted no end, but no longer is the correspondence item worth its space. However, worthwhile bits of news, such as are classed as legitimate news, are welcomed with all particulars concerning same contained therein.

"*Adieu* to the kitten lingo, the big ironing and so on and so on, and the sneak punch of the correspondent. They are gone forever from our columns."

In 1943, also, to save zinc and newsprint, many comic strips that formerly had been made five columns wide were reduced to four columns.

In that same year—1943—in line with the War Production Board's order to reduce the consumption of zinc in photo-engraving, one association of publishers adopted the following rules for retail advertisers:

"1. No type will be engraved. (Except when the sizes to be made are over 72 points—1 inch—on the face.) A great deal of zinc is needlessly used when type is engraved from a reproduction proof, or double-printed on an illustration or background.

"When outside typographer's setting is used and a mat of this composition is not furnished, the advertisement will be reset in nearest matching type faces available and cuts of illustrations only will be made.

"Hand lettering from advertisers for which engraving must be made will be restricted to ten per cent of the area of the entire advertisement.

"2. No Ben Day or reverse cuts will be made of any type areas. Thousands of square inches of zinc are consumed annually for this purpose.

"3. No fancy borders, panels, or mortised areas for type will be engraved. All newspapers stock a large number of 1-, 2-, 3-, 4-, 6- and 12-point type rules in both plain and fancy patterns as well as light Ben Day and reverse tone rules.

"Consult the type books issued by the different newspapers for selections. A wide variety of unusual borders and panels can be readily created with these stock materials of which all newspapers have an adequate supply.

"4. Signature cuts will be made as individual units and are limited to one size for each column width. The remaking of new signature cuts in slightly different forms and sizes will not be permitted.

"5. Backgrounds on merchandise must be confined to the immediate overall area of the illustration.

"6. Cuts remade because of change in drawing detail will be charged for at cost. All unused or killed engravings will be charged for at cost. Have all drawings checked before ordering cuts.

"It is believed that these regulations will not interfere with retail-advertising routine, as under them the size and number of merchandise illustrations remain normal. This program is necessitated by current wartime restrictions affecting the conservation of strategic materials. The regulations will be modified in line with government directives.

"Advertising copy suggestions:

"1. Supply all copy complete with art work. Type and cuts can be more accurately fitted when copy for both is received together and such practice will act to reduce the demand for make-overs for any reason.

"2. Have your copy and art work in as early as possible. An early flow of drawings will make possible larger and fuller engraving-room 'flats' and this will make for an automatic reduction in zinc used by avoiding the waste of incompletely filled stripping glasses.

"There will be no restriction on the use of mats, electrotypes, zinc or copper plates when they are furnished by the advertiser. Newspapers are permitted to keep old engravings, provided that there is the possibility of their re-use within a reasonable length of time.

"Advertisers can materially aid in the conservation if they will notify newspapers in advance of publication whenever an engraving is likely to be repeated or used by more than one newspaper, so that exchanges can be arranged."

At least one newspaper, the *Chicago Daily News*, appeared from December 23, 1943, until January 3, 1944, without any advertising at all, except death and legal notices, church bulletins and amusement copy.

"This was the only course available, the *News* explained," according to a story in the *Publishers' Auxiliary* for January 1, 1944, "after it decided not to restrict advertising copy materially during October, November and December. Instead, it elected to let advertisers maintain all important and necessary schedules up to Christmas week and then to clamp down drastically for the remainder of the year.

"Beginning with the issue of Monday, January 3, the daily explained in a published announcement to advertisers, 'advertising will again be accepted for that date and all subsequent publishing days in 1944.' "

Newsprint and other shortages in certain other countries during World War II were more severe, of course, than in the United States and Canada. Many Latin American papers had to get along with considerably less newsprint than before. Newspapers in Great Britain, New Zealand and Australia suffered unusually severe newsprint cuts, and were obliged to trim their issues accordingly. Many a paper that had been appearing before the war with sixteen or more pages to an issue had to trim down to four pages. Many papers that formerly ran classified advertising on front pages, started running news there instead. Some of them made the change even before World War II.

A representative instance of that change is afforded by the *Daily Telegraph* of London.

Example 174 presents a reduced showing of the front page of that paper of April 4, 1939.

And Example 175 suggests how, soon after, the *Telegraph* began displaying news on its front page.

Of course we know that in enemy-dominated countries *news*papers as such ceased to exist at all, except for certain underground publications, usually quite small, that managed to carry on in various ways and forms, and more or less regularly, in spite of the enemy.

On the other hand, many "governments in exile" or groups of away-from-home sympathizers with the causes of invaded countries, issued newspapers from "outside" countries. Many such papers were printed in England.

Moreover, many units of our armed forces operating at home or abroad published newspapers of their own—literally hundreds of papers. Perhaps the best known of these was the tabloid *Stars and Stripes.* That paper, revived from World War I, was issued in many editions from many points abroad. *Yank,* a service publication in magazine form, also was issued in many editions from many points.

It may be interesting to some readers of this book to consider here some of the "blackout touches" employed by certain London papers in the war days.

In February, 1942, this writer stated:

"Because of newsprint and other shortages and restrictions, the London papers run fewer pages now than they did before the war, although most of the papers seem not to have reduced their page sizes.

"Several London papers have used the 'V-for-Victory' symbol in various ways, usually alongside front-page ears or in editorial-page mastheads, and at least one London paper—the *Daily Mirror*—has employed the 'V' with some of its 'continued lines' used in connection with jumped stories. The 'continued lines' reproduced here [see Example 176] were used with a story started on page one of the *Daily Mirror* of last July 23 and jumped to the back page.

"Several London journals seem to run blackout boxes regularly, or at least did up to July, 1941, judging by papers that lay on this writer's desk when these words were being put down.

"The *News of the World* of last July 27 carried its blackout box [upper right in Example 176] at the bottom of column four on its eight-column front page. The London edition of the *People* of the same date carried its box [upper left] near the top of column seven on its eight-column back page. And the *Daily Express* of last July 23 presented its

The Daily Telegraph and Morning Post, April 4, 1939.

OUR POSITION CLEAR—*The Premier*

The Daily Telegraph and Morning Post

TO-DAY'S WEATHER: Rain; bright intervals later

BROADCASTING: Page Eight

No. 26,158 Daily Telegraph / 52,029 Morning Post

LONDON, TUESDAY, APRIL 4, 1939

LONDON LATE EDITION

ONE PENNY

BIRTHS, MARRIAGES and DEATHS

BIRTHS

MARRIAGES

SILVER WEDDING

DEATHS

DEATHS

(Continued on next column)

PERSONAL

DEATHS

IN MEMORIAM

ON ACTIVE SERVICE

PERSONAL

CONCERTS, &c.

GIORGIO CIOMPI

DANCING

CLUB ANNOUNCEMENTS

HELLENIC TRAVELLERS' CLUB MEDITERRANEAN CRUISE, FROM 22 GUINEAS.

REMOVALS & STORAGE

MOTOR CAR HIRE SERVICE

POSTAGE STAMPS

GARDENING

PERSONAL

TOURS, CRUISES, &c.

A Change of Scenery . . .
A Change of Companions .
A Change All Round .

HOLIDAY IN FRANCE THIS YEAR!

Paris . . Mentone, Nice and Corsica . Biarritz . . St. Malo by Train or Motor-Coach from £4 · 5 · 6

The "favourable" franc means a luxury holiday at an economical cost.

FRENCH HOTEL PLAN

BOOK YOUR HOLIDAYS WITH LUNNS

DEVON AND CORNWALL MOTORING

"TRAVEL 1939" 308 PAGES, FULLY ILLUSTRATED, IS A COMPLETE GUIDE TO HOLIDAYS AT HOME OR ABROAD.—POST FREE FROM SIR HENRY LUNN, LTD.,

EXCLUSIVE HOLIDAYS.

SPRING SKI-ING.

SUMMER HOLIDAYS.

SUMMER SKI-SCHOOL.

OCEAN VOYAGE to JAMAICA

FYFFES LINE

1,000 MILES up the AMAZON

BOOTH LINE

AMERICAN PRESIDENT LINES

CALIFORNIA AND BACK IN 35 DAYS. £108.10 ALL INCLUSIVE.

AMERICAN EXPRESS

LEISURELY MOTORING TOURS!

EASTER HOLIDAYS ABROAD

BATTERSBY & SONS

HOLIDAYS by CARGO LINERS

WAINWRIGHT BROS. & CO. LTD.

CRUISES to GREEK ISLANDS

U.S.A. & CANADA £27.5.0

J. W. KEARSLEY & CO.

U.S.A. & CANADA £27.5.0 Ret.

CONVOYS LTD.

Daily Telegraph and Morning Post *All the Real News*

SPECIALISTS NEEDED IN TERRITORIALS Page 17

Page 17

TOURS, CRUISES, &c.

"That's the Ticket!" For EASTER

GET YOUR TICKETS IN ADVANCE AT COOKS

THOS. COOK & SON LTD., BERKELEY-STREET, LONDON, W.1.

Meet Spring half way . . . . go now by AIR FRANCE!

FOLLOW THE ROYAL LEAD—VISIT U.S.A. & CANADA

DEAN & DAWSON, Ltd.

ORKNEY and SHETLAND

Inclusive Tours—3-12 days £3 10s. to £12.

RED LINE

WEST INDIES!

HOLIDAYS on HORSEBACK.

CENTROPA

CRUISES, VOYAGES & TOURS

J. D. HEWETT & CO.

UNITED STATES and CANADA

GREYHOUND LINES

SEA-GOING for EASTER

BATTERSBY & SONS

SEVENTEEN CRUISES

ORIENT LINE

AIR SERVICES

EASTER GIFTS

FULL INDEX TO CLASSIFIED ADVERTISEMENTS ON PAGE 22

EXAMPLE 174

THE DAILY TELEGRAPH AND MORNING POST, May 6, 1939.

The Daily Telegraph

NO. 26,185 SATURDAY, MAY 6, 1939 Morning Post LATE LONDON EDITION ONE PENNY

HITLER CONFERS ON POLAND

SEVEN-HOUR TALK WITH VON RIBBENTROP

DANZIG LEADERS AT BERCHTESGADEN

COL. BECK'S SPEECH REGARDED AS NO BASIS FOR NEGOTIATION

Herr Hitler was in conference for seven hours at Berchtesgaden yesterday with Herr von Ribbentrop, his Foreign Minister, on the declaration made by Col. Beck, the Polish Foreign Minister, in which he rejected Germany's demands for one-sided concessions on Danzig, but offered to negotiate on a basis of equality.

Herr Foerster, Gauleiter of Danzig, and Herr Greiser, President of the Senate in the Free City, were present, states our Munich correspondent, although this was officially denied in Berlin. During the day Msgr. Orsenigo, Papal Nuncio to Germany, flew from Berlin to take leave of the Fuehrer before relinquishing his post.

At 11.50 p.m. Herr von Ribbentrop left by train for Italy to meet Count Ciano, the Italian Foreign Minister.

Official quarters in Germany remained silent on Col. Beck's speech last night, but it is clear, states our Berlin Correspondent, that it is regarded as no basis for further negotiations.

The British Government yesterday decided on its reply to the Soviet proposals for an alliance. M. Molotoff, the Russian Premier, who has succeeded M. Litvinoff as Foreign Commissar, is expected to make an important statement of policy on May 25.

BERLIN TALK OF DANZIG PLEBISCITE

CROWDS HAIL COL. BECK

CALLED TO BALCONY LAST NIGHT

"TIME FOR FINESSE IS PAST"

COL. BECK SPEAKING IN WARSAW

A telegraphed picture of Col. Beck, Polish Foreign Minister, during his address in Warsaw.

SOVIET PREMIER TO MAKE A STATEMENT ON POLICY

NO CRISIS IN MOSCOW OVER THE FALL OF LITVINOFF

AMERICA TO-DAY

FREE SUPPLEMENT ON MONDAY

STATE DRIVE TO ROYAL SHOW

WINDSOR CEREMONY

DEATH OF SIR H. STONOR

SERVED FIVE MONARCHS

PAPAL NUNCIO SEES FUEHRER

PLANE AT HIS DISPOSAL

GERMAN ENVOYS RETURN

LORD COLEBROOKE'S WILL

HITLER MEETS HIS EXPERTS

DANZIG LEADERS THERE

ALL-NIGHT HUNT FOR INJURED AIRMAN

Trapped In Wreckage Of 'Plane

COMPANION'S LONG TREK FOR AID

NAVY RESERVISTS WITH THE KING

IN ESCORTING CRUISERS

POTEMKIN LEAVES TURKEY

RECALLED BY MOSCOW

CONCERT ANNOUNCEMENTS

AILEEN MARSON

ACTRESS DIES AFTER BIRTH OF TWINS

KING & QUEEN SAIL FOR CANADA AND U.S. TO-DAY

FAREWELL PARTY AT PALACE

WHERE TO SEE THE DEPARTURE

ANOTHER LINER FOR THE RETURN

CANADA'S MESSAGE

News Summary: Other Pages

EXAMPLE 175

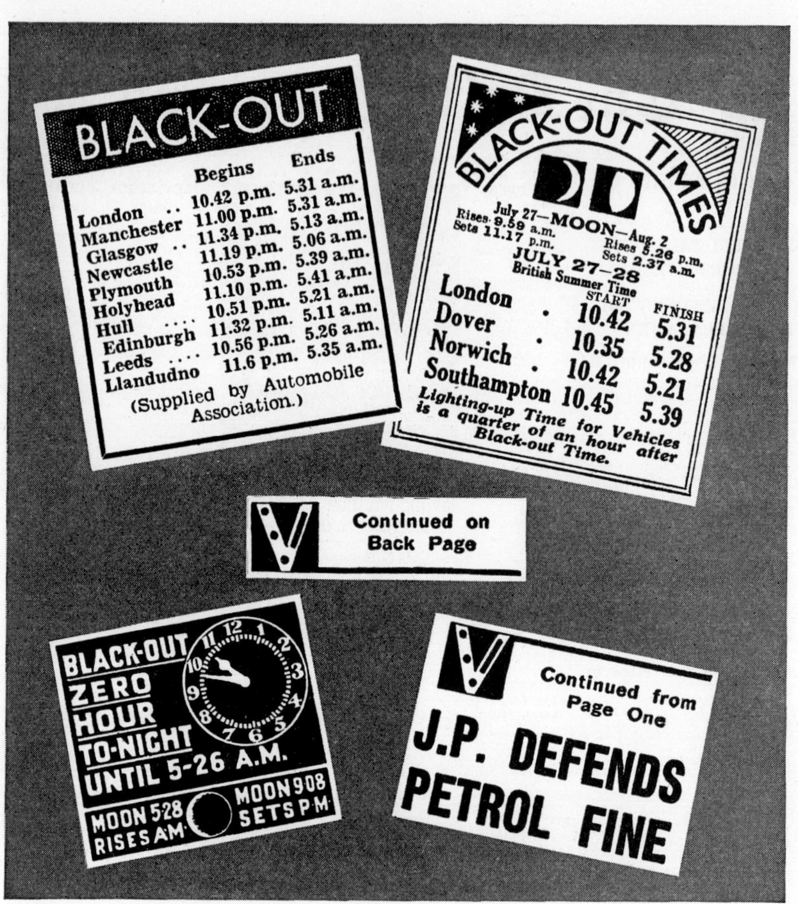

BLACK-OUT

	Begins	Ends
London ..	10.42 p.m.	5.31 a.m.
Manchester	11.00 p.m.	5.31 a.m.
Glasgow ..	11.34 p.m.	5.13 a.m.
Newcastle	11.19 p.m.	5.06 a.m.
Plymouth	10.53 p.m.	5.39 a.m.
Holyhead	11.10 p.m.	5.41 a.m.
Hull	10.51 p.m.	5.21 a.m.
Edinburgh	11.32 p.m.	5.11 a.m.
Leeds	10.56 p.m.	5.26 a.m.
Llandudno	11.6 p.m.	5.35 a.m.

(Supplied by Automobile Association.)

BLACK-OUT TIMES

July 27—MOON—Aug. 2
Rises 9.59 a.m. Sets 11.17 p.m. Rises 5.26 p.m. Sets 2.37 a.m.

JULY 27–28
British Summer Time

	START	FINISH
London .	10.42	5.31
Dover .	10.35	5.28
Norwich .	10.42	5.21
Southampton	10.45	5.39

Lighting-up Time for Vehicles is a quarter of an hour after Black-out Time.

Continued on Back Page

BLACK-OUT ZERO HOUR TO-NIGHT UNTIL 5-26 A.M.
MOON 5·28 RISES A.M. MOON 9·08 SETS P.M.

Continued from Page One

J.P. DEFENDS PETROL FINE

New Moon To-mrw.
MOONRISE 5.28 a.m.
MOONSET 9.8 p.m.
BLACK-OUT
London 10.48 p.m. to 5.26 a.m.
Birmingham 10.59 p.m. to 5.29 a.m.
Bristol 10.58 p.m. to 5.36 a.m.
Liverpool 11.10 p.m. to 5.29 a.m.
Newcastle 11.26 p.m. to 5.0 a.m.
Glasgow 11.41 p.m. to 5.6 a.m.
Penzance 11.4 p.m. to 5.54 a.m.

EXAMPLE 176

blackout information in the form of a reverse plate [lower left] alongside the left ear on its front page. But perhaps the oddest blackout treatment of all, to an American, was the tall and thin one employed by the *Daily Mirror* of last July 23, when it printed its box, in addition to certain radio-program information, in the gutter between its pages two and seven." See cut at bottom in Example 176.

In December, 1945, this writer stated:

"Now that the war is over, even though newsprint continues to be restricted, many newspaper executives are thinking about letting the light shine through their papers again.

"They are thinking about restoring the leading they gave up during the war in the effort to squeeze more lines into fewer pages. They are thinking about new and more attractive head dresses; about larger and generously leaded body faces; about wider shouldered column rules or more white space between columns, and about less shrinkage from stereotype matrices. Some of them are even thinking about giving up the nine-column idea for classified pages and going back to eight columns in larger and more legible types.

"These are facts brought out in letters being received by this department from many newspaper editors and publishers.

"Early in 1943, when newspaper-production materials had become quite restricted, this department offered many specific suggestions as to how space could be conserved in newspapers—suggestions that later were reprinted in a widely distributed booklet entitled *How Many Sacred Cows Are You Feeding?*

"Several of those suggestions were intended only as emergency measures, and were accepted as such, but others are just as applicable to newspaper-publishing conditions of today . . . as they were to conditions in the war days.

"So this department states again, as it stated three years ago, that space can be conserved—

"By limiting all news heads to two decks at most—even heads over most important stories.

"By holding most news and feature heads to single decks.

"By reducing any three-line heads over brief stories to two lines or even single lines.

"By eliminating jim dashes in favor of white space.

"By employing fewer overlines with cuts, or doing away with them altogether, and by using briefer cut legends. . . .

"By simplifying mastheads on editorial pages. (Some mastheads are displayed more than need be, and some contain many lines that . . . might well be eliminated.)

"By eliminating superfluous advertising cutoff rules. (Unless advertisers are billed for space from ad cutoff to ad cutoff, all such cutoffs should be done away with in connection with advertisements having full-width self-containing rules or borders, or full-width top and bottom rules or borders of their own. Instead of such superfluous cutoffs, use, in each instance, from 3 to 6 points of white space.)

"To repeat, these suggestions are just as sound today as they were three years ago.

"One good thing the war did was to compel or induce many more newspapers to adopt simplified flush-left heads in place of space-wasting, hard-to-write, hard-to-set and hard-to-read heads of the sort many journals had been using eighty years or more.

"Even when newsprint restrictions have been eliminated altogether, newspapers that adopted simplified flush-left heads as a war measure should not give them up, but keep on using them. In fact, it is hard to believe that any publishers who changed from the old to the new would think of going back. . . .

"Today it is safe to say that most of our newspapers, and surely most of our outstandingly successful newspapers, are employing heads of the sort pioneered and long advocated by the *Linotype News.*

"Shortly after V-E day, the Wright Company, Inc., of New York City, a distributor of newsprint, issued a booklet that reproduced the front pages of one hundred of 'America's topflight newspapers,' issued on V-E day, 'to present the general-news coverage from the standpoint of typography, layout and appearance.'

"And fifty-nine of those one hundred newspapers employed flush-left heads.

"Of the fifty-nine, the heads of twenty-three were chiefly in members of the Bodoni family, the heads of twenty-two chiefly in sans serifs, and the heads of fourteen in various other faces.

"While the hundred pages illustrated were from newspapers published in only seventeen states, in the East, Middle West and South, it is the belief of this department that a nation-wide survey at present would show that considerably more than fifty-nine per cent of our newspapers, both large and small, are employing flush-left heads.

"And well they might, for there is nothing faddish about flush-left heads. They are not a passing fancy, but are basically and functionally sound. They are easier to write, easier to set and easier to read than the old-fashioned kind. And they save valuable space and help to hold down production costs all along the line."

PART II

1

Modern Comment

IN THE BOOK *Newspaper Makeup*, first published in the spring of 1936 by Harper & Brothers, this writer stated:

"While . . . many newspapers have changed body faces for the better since 1926, comparatively few papers have made their head dresses as attractive, legible and otherwise effective as they could be, and in a practical way.

"This is rather remarkable—that many newspapers that have grasped the opportunity to improve the appearance of their body matter have neglected to enhance the attractiveness of their headlines, particularly when, in many cases, they could do so at a fraction of the cost involved in the changing of body fonts. . . .

"Many newspapers continue to use headline faces dating from before the Civil War—faces the selection and use of which were dictated by economic conditions that do not apply to the same degree today—and that are just as unattractive now and as hard to read as they were then."

But since the spring of 1936 many North American newspapers have improved their head dresses and made other changes for the better.

The extent of the changes made in two brief years was pointed out by this writer in the magazine *Typography* of London, England, in the spring of 1938:

"Less than two years ago there were fewer than half a dozen modernly planned, physically attractive and easy-to-read daily newspapers published in North America. . . .

"But in less than two years many papers in North America have undergone decided changes for the better. They have abandoned the use of outmoded and clashing display faces, have simplified their headlines, have adopted larger and more legible body faces, and have discarded needless dashes and other typographic superfluities in favor of a more generous employment of white space.

"More than that, several papers have abandoned archaic and no-longer-adequate forms of news and editorial writing in favor of modern and much more appropriate forms. A growing number of papers, in addition to using simplified heads and larger body types, are presenting front-page summations of the leading news and feature stories throughout the papers, and are departmentalizing much of the news.

"For years, of course, we have had sports pages, society pages, financial and other pages; but more and more papers are now departmentalizing local news, crime news, labor news, news of industry, news of agriculture, and so on, without, of course, withholding from their front pages outstandingly important news in any category!"

So many newspapers are now using sensible flush-left heads, and so many others are in the course of changing to them, that the old and complicated heads of many decks that are hard to write, hard to set, hard to read, and much more expensive to produce, promise soon to become museum items.

Expertly planned flush-left heads are easier to write, easier to set and easier to read—much easier than the antiquated staggered, crosslined, pyramided or hanging-indented heads that waste space, time and money, and distort language into often-incomprehensible journalese.

The big idea behind the flush-left heads, with no evening up at the right, is to free the headline writer from artificial barriers to expression; to release him from the meticulous unit counting required for exactly staggered, crosslined, pyramided or hanging-indented heads; to help him to write heads naturally, conversationally. And the extra white space at the ends or beginnings of the lines provides a contrast that helps the heads to stand out—that enhances readability.

Some newspapers, naturally, are doing a better job with these modern heads than other papers. Some such heads are not as effective as they could be. Some type faces are more effective than others, and some combinations of faces are better than other combinations.

While many different type families can be and are being used to advantage on certain modern newspaper pages, the most popular and effective type faces at present for general-news heads are the sans serifs, as represented by members of the Erbar, Metro and Spartan families; the square serifs, as represented by members of the Memphis family, and the moderns, as represented by members of the Bodoni family. (See many of the examples that follow.)

The flush-left idea is basically sound, and well-planned flush-left heads can be much more effective than the complicated and wasteful heads they are replacing.

In an editorial published in March, 1938, this writer stated:

"Our campaign for better makeup experienced slow going at first, as we knew it would. Newspaper habits are tenacious—absurdly and expensively tenacious.

"We knew that many papers, at least at first, would resent any 'fundamental' changes of makeup. We knew that many of them would keep on presenting stories as they did a generation or two before, and for no better reason than the ridiculous one that they were used to presenting them that way. We knew that even many of the papers which, on their editorial pages, applauded changes for the better in other fields, and urged their readers to keep up to date, would continue to express that very approbation and advice, however inconsistently, in archaic type treatments. We appreciated these things—and proceeded to point a repeating pea-shooter at the drowsy giant of journalism."

The weekly publishers and the school editors were the first to listen and to act.

Shortly after the *Linotype News* began presenting and campaigning for simplified flush-left heads, some twenty or more weekly papers and school publications began to adopt them. In less than a year, at least seventy-five weekly papers and school publications had begun to use them. (For details, see the next chapter.)

It was several years before the big dailies began to try them out. But now hundreds and hundreds of newspapers—large and small—are employing such heads to advantage.

The editors and publishers of these now modernly dressed papers realize that reading habits have undergone marked changes in recent years; that the radio, the moving picture, the sprightly weekly news digests, the news-picture magazines, the automobile, and a great many other things, now compete for the average reader's leisure time, and that he is quick to appreciate attractiveness and enhanced legibility in his newspapers.

And they realize, too—these alert editors and publishers—that the better modern forms of news presentation not only please readers but save time and money in the editorial end by simplifying head writing, save time and money in the mechanical departments by simplifying and speeding up head setting and makeup, and exert a tonic effect on, and instill a feeling of pride in, staff members.

In that editorial published in March, 1938, previously referred to, this writer concluded:

"Things are happening in journalism—happening for the better—and the *Linotype News* is gratified that its pea-shooting activities of nearly ten years ago have developed into big-gun barrages that are blasting the bunk out of makeup and helping so materially to make the newspaper of today really representative of today—for readers of today—not of a hundred years ago, or even a dozen years ago."

In 1940 the *Oklahoma Publisher*, issued by the Oklahoma Press Association, presented an editorial, and later a feature article entitled "Streamlining," which called attention to many changes going on in the world, and to the reactions of many of our newspapers to them.

The editorial stated, in part:

"Wherever we turn today, we see improvements. New trends and new habits are being formed. Buses are made roomier. Railroads are abandoning their old iron horses for *de luxe* streamliners. Airlines are adding greater speed to travel. Neon signs replaced bulbs . . . and now comes fluorescent lighting. Steel has taken the place of wood—even into our bedrooms. The transition in other fields has been equally as great. Time marches on!

"But what about newspapers?

"Fortunately for most of us, all newspapers haven't been sleeping. Many have modernized their dress. New, larger and more readable type faces have been adopted here and there, month by month. Some publishers have constantly experimented. It is all a healthy sign."

The feature article included these statements:

"Front pages are being stripped to the bare essentials. Going are the boxes, dingbats, logotypes, initial capitals and other ornaments.

"Fewer type families appear on a page. Inverted-pyramid heads give way to flush heads. Sans-serif types, more legible types, more white space are gaining prominence. Newspapers, like the skating lady, suggest motion, an easy skimming abreast of fast-moving events in a changing world.

"This is one of the responses of live newspaper publishers to a new psychological order. They realize that when he settles down to the front page, the reader wants action and is in no mood to contemplate the engraved intricacies of fancy furbelows. But he is interested in the new, easy-to-comprehend makeup and is grateful for its clarity and the greater ease with which it enables him to read. The streamlined newspaper lowers reader resistance.

"One of its outstanding features and the one on which all who use streamlining agree is the flush-left head, which with one great sweep picks newspaper makeup out of the Spanish War period and sets it on the doorstep of tomorrow, eliminating the drop line, the hanging indention or inverted pyramid.

"The majority of editors using this form report that it is easier to write.

"Publishers using the new makeup report that expenses, too, are streamlined in the process. No more expensive replacement of easily broken initial letters and ornaments. No longer do makeup men, whose time is valuable, spend a large percentage of it among panels and boxed rules. With the flush-left head, no tedious juggling of matrices for centering is necessary.

"Advertising agencies almost invariably mention modern typography when listing factors which influence them in the choice of newspapers."

In 1942 an editorial in the *Publishers' Auxiliary* included the following statements:

"We once attended a press meeting where the judges in the annual newspaper contest supplemented their report of the prize-winning papers with this comment:

" 'The judges feel that this annual exhibit will have failed in its purpose if it fails to bring home to publishers of the weeklies and smaller dailies in particular the undeniable fact that their newspaper is judged by its readers as much by its appearance as by its contents.

" 'It costs little more to publish a newspaper that is dressed up. Too many publishers are more interested in their own personal appearance than in the appearance of their newspaper. Yet they overlook the fact that one is synonymous with the other. In the average small town or city the newspaper is the man and the man is the newspaper. One is judged by the other, and the publisher should have pride enough in good impression to see that it makes a good impression. Its appearance has much to do with selling its news and advertising.

" 'A newsy, well-dressed-up newspaper is half sold to the advertiser. If it looks the part, the advertiser will picture to himself that he likes to be seen in it. If it is printed from out-of-date type, poorly arranged, poorly printed, the advertiser will feel that he doesn't want to be seen in it, for he will conclude that it can't possibly have appeal to readers of intelligence and discrimination.

" 'Publishers must realize that the people have become educated to better looking homes inside and out, to more stylish clothing, to better looking automobiles, and so on. Likewise, their tastes are accustomed to better looking newspapers. Publishers should remember that their front page, for instance, is their own window. Merchants spend thousands of dollars for attractive show windows, but so many publishers appear to overlook this vital fact, and they continue to put out papers that look little better than they did twenty years ago.

" 'Many publishers have seen the light, and they are publishing newspapers that are attractive in appearance as well as interesting in contents.

" 'There is no question as to the success of the smaller city dailies which use news pictures. Ninety-nine per cent of suburban and rural readers want news pictures.

" 'While it may be true that everybody, so to speak, may take that particular newspaper in its community, it will not be one for which they have any great respect. This is not theory. We know that this is an actual fact.'

"We were reminded of that statement the other day when there came to our desk an issue of a country weekly which certainly needed some 'dressing up.' The printing was dim and gray, probably due to the self-evident fact that the type from which it was printed was badly worn; the front-page makeup can best be described as having been 'done with a shovel'; the headlines were poorly written and all set in exactly the same size type; and in general it was about as good (or bad) an example of down-at-the-heels, shiftless newspaper production as we have seen in many a year.

"So it wasn't much of a surprise to find that the volume of local advertising was very, very small, and that the circulation of the paper was less than 400—in a town of 1700 population! It was also easy to understand why the publisher of this paper was able to charge only one dollar a year for it.

"To the publisher of such a paper—and fortunately the number of them is becoming smaller every year—we recommend a reading and a rereading of the above statement of the newspaper contest judges. And one sentence in it we'd like to underline:

" '*It costs little more to publish a newspaper that is dressed up.*' "

In 1943 the Linotype Company engaged the research and statistical division of Dun & Bradstreet, Inc., to interview executives of many hundreds of newspapers—large and small, both dailies and weeklies—on the outlook for newspapers after World War II. Also interviewed were executives of printing plants, advertising agencies, and representatives of other branches of the graphic arts.

Many and varied were the questions asked, and many and diverse the answers received.

One of the questions asked executives of 1470 dailies called for additional comments on the outlook of the daily newspaper business generally during the decade immediately following World War II, and the replies, with few exceptions, constituted "a symphony of optimism."

Part of that "symphony" ran as follows:

"Newspapers have a big job ahead to maintain their leadership, but they will rise to the challenge. Newspapers will be stronger than at any time in their history after the war.

"Flexibility of newspapers, their timeliness and local appeal, will be strong selling points. Reading habits are at an all-time high level. This interest will be retained in the postwar period, especially by those papers alert to public needs and wants.

"Tomorrow's newspapers will contain more factual reporting, less sensationalism, more pictures, more color advertising and better styling. They will be compact, streamlined, highly illustrated, things of beauty—unlike any newspapers now published. Color developments and a thorough study of sales problems will produce advertisements with appeal and punch.

"Dramatic competitors, such as magazines and radio, will force overdue mechanical improvements. The whole field of electrical devices is virtually untouched in newspaper production. There is a possibility of stereotyping departments being eliminated and printing direct from photographic plates on new streamlined offset-type presses, to assure a printed page and color work to compete with magazine reproductions."

For a week in the spring of 1944 Alexander Warden, business manager of the *Great Falls* (Mont.) *Tribune-Leader*, served as guest lecturer in the school of journalism at Montana State University.

In one of his talks, Mr. Warden asked: "What will be the successful newspaper of the morrow? How will it differ in format, aim and execution from the traditional pattern which has, in my humble estimate, lagged badly in the speeding field of communication?"

A condensation of Mr. Warden's answers to those questions follows:

"Perhaps as good a starting point as any is the axiomatic fifteen minutes which is the national average for a reader to spend with his newspaper. In the cities, the hurrying reader spends less than this; in the rural districts the time is a little longer.

"Since the time that our reader will spend is but a small fraction of that necessary for a word-for-word reading of the entire content, isn't it important that the format, or style, or pattern, of our newspaper should aim to help him over as much ground as possible in the allotted time?

"If this is true, then why not a well-leaded body type that he can read easily, upper- and lower-case heads that he can digest at a glance, more picture stories, less eye-confusing ornaments and gimcracks that make no more sense than telephone-pad doodlings? Less stories that start on page one and break inside.

"Type and arrangement should be for ease and celerity of reading, rather than evidence of the disordered mind of a dyspeptic makeup editor.

"Concentrate on news and local or area features which your readers can't get from any other source. Here is the great insurance for survival and success. Cultivate that part of the field where the product can be exclusively yours. Material that the fiction, news and trade magazines and the radio can't and won't have. In a word, your local and area news, the news in which the people of your community are always bound to have enough interest so that you will always have eager readership.

"On page one of my newspaper of tomorrow, world and national news is going to have to give up its long-time position priority. Why? Because, by the time it gets into the reader's hands on the printed page, the stuff is cold potatoes. Hours before, radio newscasts have made it known to the reader; commentators have interpreted it over the air *ad nauseam.* It simply no longer rates the banner play that it gets today in our own and most every other newspaper.

"Let's grant that the visual appeal is stronger than the auditory. Let's grant, further, that people want to read in detail what they have heard over the air. We'll give it to them, but not with a fanfare that pretends that here is something they have known nothing about until the paper came. The Yanks win the world series in the early afternoon, mountain time. Millions have followed the play-by-play over their radios. For those who couldn't, a succession of evening newscasts have laid down their barrages. Then we, as a morning newspaper, arrive on the front porch, sixteen hours later, with a 120-point banner line across the top of the page naively pretending that we are the first with glad tidings that the Yanks have done it again.

"This just doesn't make sense. Elsewhere in the same issue, buried on inside pages below the fold, are dozens of items of genuine interest to our reader, about his own area, that are real news to him, coming to him in his home newspaper for the first time. News he doesn't get from any other source. If we aren't burying our own light under a bushel, I don't know what to call it.

"Why do we keep doing this? Most of the reason is a hide-bound tradition dating back to the days before radio, when the spot-news realm was the exclusive domain of the newspaper. Now, as then, the makeup editor was either the telegraph editor or sitting next to the incoming flow of wire news. There were, and are, so many thousand words carried on the wire. Early pages close. Page one is left open for possible breaks, local or wire. Nine times out of ten there are no important local spot breaks. So the leads of the wire are plastered all over the front window of the paper as the main dish for the reader, irrespective of his appetite.

"For several years now we have belonged to the Bureau of Advertising of the American Newspaper Publishers' Association. This bureau has what is known as the *Continuing Study of Newspaper Reading.* They make reader surveys to find what news, what advertising, are getting the consumer's attention. Their system of sample interviews by trained and competent field investigators, over an expertly picked cross section of the community, permits them to come up with the answers by talking to 400 people only, whether the work is done in New York, Seattle or Great Falls.

"In addition to the published findings on a particular paper, which are circulated through all bureau members, they compile a confidential file for the publisher of the particular paper surveyed. In this file, unidentified of course as to source, are included all the frank critical comments that individual readers have made, particularly as to what is wrong with the paper.

"This is a revealing truth session for any publisher, and our own faces deepened into several of the redder shades.

"Some of our sacred cows got pretty rough handling; some of the things we had been giving a very light touch were found to be of intense interest.

"Our own survey was made in October, 1941, but we still consider the information as gospel and keep going over it to avoid straying away from the reader and along the primrose path of our own notions.

"I have studied scores of these reports on other papers, large and small, particularly the findings on the ten best read stories of the issue among men and women. There are seldom more than two or three that appear in both lists. When they do, there is no correlation in their rank in the two lists.

"Men editors are patterning the news for men readers. Yet there are as many women readers of a paper as men. Probably the women spend more time with the paper, both because they have more time and because they study the advertisements for their buying needs also.

"Time after time I have seen these studies come up without a single page-one story included among the ten best read by women. Yet the makeup editor has filled 160 inches of page one with banner lines and heads heralding what he considers the important news of the day.

"Most publishers have considered themselves extremely progressive, if not verging on left-wingers, if they have recognized their women readers with an atrocity known as the woman's page, filled with a strange conglomeration of boiler-plate serial stories, fashions, recipes and advice to the lovelorn. Most of it is trash, and women recognize it as such. Season this dish with a picture of the president of some uplift league and 10,000 women readers are supposed to give thanks.

"This isn't what they want. They want the whole paper to talk to them, too. They want local stories with human interest. A war story with a local angle in two sticks is worth two columns about the Russian front. In my tomorrow's paper, I hope that makeup editors won't be able to ignore the woman reader.

"I shall play wire-photo pictures up, because these come to the reader first in the paper, or will at least until television takes over. Radio may have taken the bloom off the spot news, but the news pictures of it are still hot.

"In talking about news, I include pictures as a most essential part of news itself. By this I don't mean the pans of prominent citizens and groups of solemn-visaged convention delegates, but pictures that tell a news story in themselves without more than caption help. I mean giving your own field the same news-picture story treatment that *Life* is giving the world.

"Tomorrow's reporter will use a camera or he won't get a job. Many of his assignments will be covered with a captioned picture, instead of half a column of type. Incidentally, we have found in our own limited experience that a gathering or event of most any kind is better pleased with a picture than all the story you can write into type.

"Pictures of happenings in your own area don't get to your reader from any other source. The cost? With your own engraving plant and photographic facilities, and using half a dozen local pictures every day, your square or column inch of cuts will be less than the cost of the same area of printed type. You'll save enough in composition to pay for your art.

"Features? Use them with discretion, for seasoning or garnishing; not for main courses. Let the crossword puzzle addicts go buy a book; likewise the bridge addicts. Loan libraries cater to every fiction taste. Cookbooks are a dime a dozen.

"Instead of competing with specialists in their own fields, where the newspaper looks bad as an amateur, let the newspaper specialize in its own field, that of news. Let the newspaper give the reader as much as possible of what it knows he wants, news of his own bailiwick, and forget columns of extraneous matter which might get by.

"One feature I do want in tomorrow's newspaper is comics. I want a full page of them, and I want the best comics there are on the market, even if this doubles or triples the cost.

"If the 100,000,000 people in this country who read and like comics are wrong, then I'll be wrong along with them. More Americans read comic strips than anything else; four out of five adults who buy newspapers read them.

"I think tomorrow's newspaper is going to have lots more color; color of a sort approximating the great strides that have been made in magazine color in recent years. The problem of quick-drying inks and kind of paper is more difficult than that in magazines, but it will be solved and merchandise advertised will be the more attractive because of its appearance in natural color tones.

"A publisher will have to be highly alert in carrying the torch for his own community. This has always been acknowledged important, but practiced too seldom. I think it will be more so in the future. The *Pelican Press Messenger* of the Louisiana Press Association puts it this way, 'Promote your own community—without it you wouldn't exist.' I can recommend this as opposed to the feeling of too many publishers that the community owes them a living. They say that their paper should be 'supported.' Perhaps, but this matter of support is a mutual one. A paper will get support in about the same ratio it gives support."

At a convention of the New York State Publishers' Association, at Syracuse University, September 11, 1944, John S. Knight, widely known editor and publisher of several metropolitan dailies and at that time president of the American Society of Newspaper Editors, told the assembled newspaper people that the demand for newspapers after World War II would depend on how interesting and attractive their publishers made them.

"There is no particular difficulty these days in selling all the papers which your restricted newsprint quota permits you to print," stated Mr. Knight, and he continued, in part, as follows:

"Circulations which would normally jump by leaps and bounds are now frozen at a given level.

"The same thing is true of advertising. Each and every one of you is refusing advertising because you do not have enough newsprint with which to serve both your readers and advertisers. As good newspaper publishers, you are alertly aware that the reader comes first.

"Therefore, a tremendous volume of newspaper advertising is being forced into other media and they have not been slow to advantage themselves of the situation.

"The challenge is, will you get it back after V-day?

"Well, gentlemen, I should say the answer to that challenge lies in the product which you produce after V-day.

"Are you prepared to repackage your product, to keep it constantly modern, to see that it is a step ahead of competing media in meeting the tastes and preferences of a new generation of customers?

"In my humble opinion, the day of the dull, stodgy newspaper is nearing an end. Popular newspapers will have the call and by using the term 'popular,' I am not implying that they must be either cheap or sensational.

"But they can be typed attractively, have eye appeal, be easy to read.

"As far-sighted business men, you realize that these times are no true indication of business in the future. After V-day, your solicitors will again be pounding the streets for advertising, and the circulation department will be fighting for orders.

"When that day comes, the newspapers will have to stand on their own feet and sell the product on merit. During the war, a large amount of advertising has been diverted to other media. How will you go about getting it back?

"Personally, I have always been impatient with publishers who gather at convention time, assemble in a mutual friend's room and, over a few drinks of Scotch, spend their time deploring the inroads being made by radio. Well, radio is here to stay, and television is just around the corner.

"You can denounce them and any other media all you like, but in the final analysis you can get the business only by proving to the advertiser that his copy will get results in your paper.

"The radio people have done a smooth job of selling and we have gone at it like plumbers at a grand piano.

"The old fundamental rules of journalism still hold good, but don't cling long to an outmoded formula when the public is expecting a new model.

"Take a leaf from the manufacturers who constantly repackage their products to make them more and more attractive."

When, in the fall of 1945, Paul C. Smith, editor and general manager of the *San Francisco Chronicle*, returned to the *Chronicle* after nearly four years in our Marines and the Navy, he was interviewed for *Editor & Publisher* by Campbell Watson.

In three paragraphs in that story Mr. Smith stated:

"Publishing today is the collection, processing and dissemination of information and not merely the business of printing a paper.

"The newspaper, of course, remains first and foremost. It is the keystone of the structure. But it should assemble about it whatever vehicles of collection and dissemination are needed—radio, television, FM, facsimile, documentary film or whatever aids are available.

"That, of course, is a view for the long pull, over a period of time."

January 14, 1946, at a meeting in Chicago of the Newspaper Advertising Executives' Association, Erwin D. Canham, editor of the *Christian Science Monitor*, stated:

"We are approaching the halfway point of the twentieth century. During the last forty-six years, or thereabouts, newspapers have gone through a significant series of changes—changes which give us some clear indications of their future trends. Before this century, American newspapers had relatively limited circulations, and an equally limited formula of contents. For the most part, their prevailing news formula was brief coverage of local happenings, largely drawn from police records; partisan reporting of politics; a few columns of telegraphic news, mainly from Washington unless a major disaster like the Johnstown flood held attention, and a smattering of news from Europe or other continents."

He continued, in part, as follows:

"In the 1890's and the early years of this century the formula was changed fundamentally by the publishers who discovered the mass-circulation possibilities of sensation: of what Arthur Robb called the formula of 'Wealth, Women, and War.' This trend greatly changed American journalism. Emphasis on politics dwindled, there was little interest in crusading for social betterment or the control of corruption in government. There was little interest in the real news, as contrasted with the sensation, of the outside world. Those were the days in which the murder story dominated the American front page.

"The coming of the first World War modified this trend. There was more attention on world affairs, newspapers and press associations built up their staffs abroad and in this country, and there was a growing interest in significant news. Of course, there was still much emphasis on the kind of news that had been so prominent at the turn of the century. And through the unrestrained and unrealistic decade of the 1920's this emphasis continued. It was an era of newspaper sensation. Nearly everybody was concerned with making money and spending it. Remember 'Daddy Browning,' the Hall-Mills case, and all the other sensations which dominated the front pages of many newspapers. Remember the birth of the tabloids, and their early excesses. In a word, newspapers reflected the face of America and marched to the tempo of the times.

"But with the coming of the depression and its deepening in the early 1930's, newspapers were among the first voices in America to realize that they had been too shallow. The murder stories which have been national sensations since 1931 have been extremely few, although we have had plenty of murders. Instead, newspapers turned to serious and challenging facts: to the grave national problem of the depression, to the efforts of government to cope with the situation, and to the world tension and unrest which led to the second World War. Throughout the war, newspaper coverage was almost entirely serious, and today the major news emphasis is on such problems as industrial unrest, even though an occasional crime sensation briefly brings back the old days.

"Through all this, we can see an evident trend. American newspapers, from being provincial, narrow, and intensely partisan sheets fifty years ago, and after passing through a sensation-ridden era of yellow journalism, have now settled down in the main to being alert, vigorous, conscientious purveyors of news, of news interpretation, of opinion, and of entertainment. This is not to say that we have attained an ideal state, and can rest easy. Far from it. There is plenty wrong with American newspapers—plenty we must do if we are to retain the confidence of the public and survive—but it is only historical accuracy for us to recognize the distance we have come and the improvements we have made.

"During this same period, two other big things happened to American newspapers. First, they became more and more expensive to operate, until a tendency to consolidate has wiped out direct newspaper competition in more than fifty per cent of American cities. Second, we have acquired a competitor in the dissemination of news, comment, and entertainment: the radio.

"For the last twenty years, the most frequent prophecy about newspapers was that the radio would drive us out of business, as an advertising medium and as a disseminator of news. What is the situation today? For a number of reasons, some of them relevant and some of them not, newspapers are in a stronger fundamental position than they have been for many years. Newspapers are in a position today to do a far better job than they have ever done before. And radio today faces a technological revolution the consequences of which are very uncertain indeed. I am confident, of course, that radio will surmount the problems it now faces and will emerge stronger than ever. But it is certainly noteworthy that newspapers, which so many so-called experts were counting down and out ten and fifteen years ago, are throbbing with power, eagerness, and confidence, while radio is looking ahead with no little apprehension at the rough spots that must be traversed in the emergence and application of frequency modulation and television. The position may well be reversed in the next five or ten years: I am simply calling to your attention the striking situation of today.

"The gloomy prophets have also been fooled about the effect of newspaper consolidations and monopoly towns. I am not defending consolidations or monopolies. But the effect has been very different from that anticipated. The monopoly newspaper, far from becoming arrogant and overbearing in its community, ruthlessly refusing to publish the news of unpopular minorities, is far more at the mercy of pressure groups than competitive newspapers are. The monopoly newspaper has been forced more and more into the position of a public utility, where it has to serve the whole community. This is not necessarily a good thing at all. It takes away a newspaper's color, its ability to take a strongly partisan position and get away with it. Most editors of my acquaintance would by far prefer to work on a competitive newspaper than on a monopoly newspaper, for they are convinced that the competition actually brings more freedom. This paradox has fooled all the prophets.

"And the newspaper prophets of the immediate prewar days have been fooled, too. I am sure that if you had asked me to deliver this paper in early 1942, it would have been stupendously inaccurate today. We have gone through nearly four years of wartime censorship. This followed nine years of strongly centralized national government. We have experienced severe raw-materials shortages, of newsprint and other supplies. We have had rigid governmental rationing. We have had even more difficult manpower shortages and regulations. Our advertisers have had few commodities to sell. Government was their best customer. We have experienced the rising power of labor. Now, five years ago I would have told you that these perils and trials would leave deep scars upon American newspapers. I would have said that many of us would have perished. I would have said that censorship, and the spread of propaganda through such an agency as O.W.I.

would have tainted and weakened us. And there were plenty of gloomy prophets who said all this and more. But has it come about?

"No. American newspapers have survived censorship, have survived rationing, have survived the rigid governmental controls of wartime, and emerged strong and free and eager to go ahead. That is not prophecy. That is history.

"And this history encourages me to set down a few fundamentals about American newspapers, which is as near to prophecy as I shall get:

"First. Dissemination and interpretation of news through the printed word are here to stay. There will, thank goodness, be plenty of improvements in our technique of reproduction and distribution of the printed word. But there is and will be a fundamental need for our kind of job.

"Second. Our future progress, while necessarily linked to the inescapable element of reader-interest, will have to be increasingly responsible in order to retain reader-confidence. We are not in the relatively carefree eras of the '90's or the 1920's. We are in Month Six of the Atomic Age. And the doctrine of newspaper responsibility must cover a lot of territory.

"In the light of these two fundamentals, let us discuss the technical changes which we can all see coming. We know, of course, that the dissemination of spot news can be done much more quickly by radio than by newspapers. But the radio must struggle with the frailties of the spoken word and of the human ear. And how often our newspaper switchboards are clogged with calls from radio listeners who have either heard something wrong or won't believe their ears.

"However, mere publication of spot news in newspapers is not enough, and most newspapers have acted on that assumption for some time. The news must be clarified, explained, interpreted and integrated with other news. The commentators do that on the radio, too. But people still demand the printed word. They still can't quite depend on what they hear.

"Also, today's news is increasingly complicated. Therefore newspaper writers must be increasingly expert. They must be specialists in various subjects. Big news stories of the world can no longer be covered by a bright boy just off the police beat. It takes a good man to explain to the lay reader the workings of the atomic bomb.

"Manifestly, there will be many technical improvements in the production and distribution of newspapers. We all know that superb full-color work is on our door-step and will come along fast. With the use of color on the news and editorial side, there will be much more careful makeup, classification and arrangement of news. As the emphasis on spot news lessens, the number of daily editions will become fewer, and the care with which the remaining editions are prepared will become greater.

"Therefore, newspapers will trend in the direction of daily news magazines. Extensive use of color, fine printing, careful makeup, are all steps we can foresee not so very far ahead. There might well be daily magazine supplements distributed by wire-photo. Indeed, that is the way I would expect national newspapers to come about—as supplements to existing newspapers, rather than as competing publications circulating every day over the entire country, or large parts of it.

"That opens up the question of nationally distributed newspapers. Doubtless improved methods of distributing the paper, up to the point of instantaneous distribution, would improve the value of such a newspaper. But I cannot see that it could ever supplant the local newspaper. It could never carry the same volume or impact of local advertising or local news. It could never serve the local community in the same way. I believe there is ample room for the nationally or internationally circulated newspaper and the local newspaper, just as there is room for radio and newspaper side by side.

"I do not see yet the day when facsimile will supplement the centrally produced newspaper. Meantime, of course, newspapers all over the country are in on the ground floor in seeking channels for frequency-modulation radio, with resultant television and facsimile.

"Realistically, what one can foresee is a period of great uncertainty and a certain amount of shirt-losing in the newer radio field. If newspapers go ahead with the improvement of their product technically and in its content, if they meet the public's demand to know why things are happening and what they mean, I believe we can go forward into stronger and stronger positions.

"But there must be much more than technique in the newspaper of the future. There must be a continually enlarging sense of responsibility.

"We must be increasingly careful about our facts. Too many readers are distrustful of newspapers. They are cynical. They don't think we tell the whole story. They think we are reckless and careless.

Well, sometimes we are. And that isn't good enough. The first job of a newspaper is to inform its readers accurately and fully, without fear of consequences."

September 30, 1946, the first seminar of the American Press Institute was opened at Columbia University. In attendance were twenty-five managing editors and news editors from leading United States dailies from coast to coast.

Sevellon Brown, editor and publisher of the *Providence* (R. I.) *Journal* and the *Evening Bulletin*, who originated the idea for the Institute and induced thirty-seven publishers to underwrite the experiment for a two-year trial, made the opening address.

"Under the auspices and sanctions of the trustees of this great university, we gather here as skilled and experienced newspaper men selected from every section of the country," stated Mr. Brown. "We are here to pioneer for American journalism—indeed, I hope for world journalism—in an experiment in professional education on a high level. Through clinical, self-driven study, it is our high purpose to make ourselves and the newspapers we represent of greater service and effectiveness in performing the vital function of a free press in a democracy."

Mr. Brown continued, in part:

"We are here because we recognize the tremendous social responsibilities which are ours, responsibilities of a scope and complexity scarcely dreamed of by newspaper men a short generation ago.

"No intelligent man can approach with other than courage and humility the responsibility for providing the basic, primary source of information for 140,000,000 Americans of the significant day-to-day happenings in community, state, nation and world. If this Institute is to succeed, it must be the living symbol of a newborn determination of publishers, editors and reporters of newspapers to strive unceasingly to improve themselves that they may fulfill their obligations with increasing effectiveness in this critical period of human history.

"It is not too much to say that responsibility for the survival of our way of life, based on human liberty and the dignity of the individual, rests as heavily upon the shoulders of editors and reporters as upon any professional group. It cannot be too often recalled that the very impetus for the spectacular flowering of cultural and material progress in our Western World came from the painfully won victories of centuries for freedom of thought and expression. One has only to travel about the world to know that the great majority of its inhabitants, still living under varying degrees of intellectual serfdom, continue to struggle as they have for ages on the ragged edge of bare subsistence.

"We know that every great human achievement, spiritual or material, is the result of the free, uninhibited collaboration of many minds. We know that the only way to truth is through the free and unlimited association of ideas and information, and that what seems a great truth today may be replaced with a very different one tomorrow. We know that the genius who makes a great discovery in physical science, or develops a great new principle in social science, bases his work on the labors of untold thousands who preceded him, and depends upon innumerable thousands more to test his discovery and bring it to practical application for you and me. When the flow of ideas and information is blocked, human progress and creativeness languishes.

"The very core of the sources of current information in our democratic world is the news-gathering activity of our daily press and the world-wide news-collecting instrumentalities which it supports. So long as we are fired by ever-glowing zeal to get the news, whatever the difficulties or obstacles, and to present it honestly, objectively and understandably, however complex or controversial the subject matter may be, we may have faith in the survival of this creative way of life.

"But it would be foolhardy to minimize the moral hazards which confront us. The atom bomb and the rocket-propelled missile may be the particular products of war which make our flesh creep. But the war brought to infamous fruition other weapons just as deadly. I refer to the psychological weapons by which a Goebbels, manipulating the instruments of mass communication, and assisted by secret police in every city block and crossroads community, took control of the minds of virtually an entire people, and drove it to mass madness.

"These techniques, using the new science of mass psychology to short circuit the processes of rational public decision and drive men to hysterical mass action, are available to unscrupulous cabals and pressure groups throughout the world. They may be, and are, used with diabolical cunning, even in lands where the press and other instruments of mass communication appear to be, or actually are, free. In these troubled times, men are vulnerable to these psychological devices. Men without food and shelter have little patience with deliberative processes. In such times, skillful appeals to fear, prejudice and hatred are shockingly effective.

"Even the discoveries and inventions in the field of communications have made the news man's responsibilities immeasurably greater. The words of the head of a great power are almost instantaneously delivered to every part of the globe. News of an act of violence, attributed to an antagonistic power, whether rightly or falsely, may bring the world to the brink of war in a matter of hours. The tempo of events, both domestic and foreign, has been fantastically quickened.

"We know that sound public opinion can be nourished only by full disclosure, by reporting all of the significant facts, statements and conflicting opinions. It is the great moral strength of soundly functioning democracy that public action is motivated by informed conviction, not by passion or servility. We were not afraid, even while at war, to print fully the rantings of Hitler. A fully informed people could not be corrupted by them. His ravings exposed his viciousness when read by an enlightened people.

"But the task of full disclosure, in this headlong flow of complex events, is enormous. We must guard vigilantly against incomplete and misleading reports. This swift flood-stream of news may motivate social, political and economic action of incalculable consequences; action which may bring war or peace, prosperity or depression, weal or woe. Yet we cannot withhold the news. It is not our lordly function to tell the public only what we deem to be 'safe' or 'good' for it to know. In a democracy, such power cannot be delegated to any group; it is the first step toward tyranny and stagnation.

"But we must recognize that in our effort to report all significant news fully, we run the risk in this fantastically complicated world of creating mere confusion. There are limits to the number of impressions which may be made upon the human mind in a given time. Unless we brilliantly improve our skills and techniques, we face what may be described as a crisis of meaninglessness. Innumerable brief reports presented without perspective or background can only drive the reader into a mental fog.

"What answers to our problem we can find, therefore, must lie in the organization of newspapers and news services to bring into effective use a high degree of specialization of our talents. It is not enough that a reporter report exactly what he sees or hears. Unless he understands what he sees or hears, his report will be meaningless or misleading. We must lift our sights as to what is news, and exercise increasingly astute and responsible selectivity in deciding what is the significant news of each day. It may create only confusion to report minor and unimportant changes in a given situation day after day, but in every important situation there comes a day which calls for a clear and comprehensive report with intelligent perspective.

"We are well past the day when events considered news were primarily those involving novelty, shock, violence or conflict. We are engaged in writing, editing and interpreting news reports from direct contacts in remote parts of the earth; reports that must cope with the enigmas of Soviet Russia, with the mysteries of India, with the contradictions of revolutionary China. Moreover, the news is compounded of the facts and speculations of science, of the dogmas of religious belief, of all the social, economic and political concernments of mankind.

"It is manifest that the intellect of a single reporter or editor cannot span that range. We must organize staffs of experts with penetrating knowledge of a wide range of specific fields, as well as the highest skills in effective journalistic technique; experts who never passively accept the outgivings of pressure groups and special pleaders, but who aggressively seek out the whole meaning of the news event.

"It is facing this responsibility that we come here in the dual role of experienced newspaper men and of students, to make more adequate our understanding of social, political and economic problems, more skillful our use of techniques, and, above all else, more acute our professional consciousness."

At the forty-third annual convention of the Advertising Federation of America, in Boston, May 26, 1947, Louis B. Seltzer, editor of the *Cleveland Press*, said that regional newspapers covering large sections of the country are possible for the United States within the next five to twenty-five years.

According to the *New York Herald Tribune*, "Mr. Seltzer said that perhaps a half dozen great newspapers, resembling the national dailies of England, will blanket the country with circulations far greater than any in the country today. He mentioned New York, Chicago, San Francisco and 'somewhere' in the Southwest and Northwest as possible locations for the dailies. Newspapers serving communities will have to be closer to their localities than in the past when the regional sheets arrive, he said."

2

Parade of Progress—Typographic

Before the first number of the *Linotype News* was issued, in July, 1922, it was decided that each number should contain news and feature stories, pictures, and technical articles, all having to do with printing and publishing, and that each number should present a different type dress.

Naturally enough, the dresses of early numbers suggested the formats of long-established and outstandingly successful American newspapers, so that readers in all sections of North America could study at close range the typographic treatments that had figured in those successes.

That plan was followed several years, seemingly to the interest and advantage of a steadily growing list of readers, when it was decided that a new program might well be followed.

Why, it was reasoned, continue to show type dresses merely because such dresses were employed by successful papers? Had those dresses helped to make those papers successful, or had the papers been successful in spite of them?

Many of the dresses that had been shown, admittedly, had not been particularly good; many had employed certain treatments that even then had seemed outmoded, and nearly all of them could have been better.

Why help to perpetuate certain type treatments that had never had any good reason for being, and others that long since had lost any effectiveness they may have had?

So why not, it was asked, turn that publication into a typographic laboratory? Why not use it for experimental purposes? Why not present by means of it many different and, if possible, more effective typographic treatments?

The new program was launched in September, 1928.

With the thought that such a campaign should be begun with something decidedly out of the ordinary, the September, 1928, issue

The Modern Newspaper You Like to Read

The Linotype News

This Issue More Than Seventy Thousand

Volume VII | The Machine That Lasts | Brooklyn, New York, September, 1928 | The Service That Lasts | Number Two

Isn't This Page Attractive and Easy to Read?

Why Should Front Pages Be Restricted to Narrow Columns?

It is the ambition of many newspaper publishers to have a front page decidedly different from other papers; a front page of distinction, outstandingly attractive in appearance, tangibly individual, and decidedly easy to read.

This page is an experiment in that direction. It is different, is attractive, has character, is easy to read.

Its wider columns make possible the displaying of prominent headings over stories to be emphasized, without the use of three or four column headlines. One of these single column headings has almost as much attention value as a double column heading over narrower columns. The wider lines of larger body type make the page inviting and easy on the eyes.

The whole page has a lively airy appearance. There is no feeling of crowding. All lines have been given a chance "to breathe."

Yet, although there are only six columns here, as against the customary eight, there are only about five stories fewer on this front page than ordinarily appear on an eight column front page. And those that do, appear, appear prominently. There is less chance of a story "getting lost" on the page—being overlooked—as all stories are given prominent treatment—even the briefer ones.

These columns are sixteen picas wide, with an extra shoulder of white space on either side of the column rules. The body lines are 8 Point Ionic No. 5 on nine point body, with some of the lines extra leaded. The head dress is in 18, 24 and 30 Point Bodoni Bold and 14 and 24 Point Bodoni Bold Italic. No heading is entirely in capitals. Capitals and lower case, which are easier to read, are used throughout.

As the deepest headings here consist of only six lines—two decks—a saving in depth is made over the main news headings used by many newspapers—assuming, of course, that two such decks ordinarily are sufficient, which may or may not seem the case to editors accustomed to more decks.

Against these good features, however, are some that are not so good from a mechanical standpoint.

Stories continued from such a front page to inside pages would have to be set in two different measures, and stories transferred bodily would have to be reset. These are important objections, to be sure.

Whether or not they overshadow the good points of this six column front page is something for editors and publishers to give earnest consideration.

Of course it is not even intimated here that advertising pages be set in wider columns, as that would tend to disrupt the standard widths followed by advertisers.

This treatment is suggested only for the front page, and is frankly an experiment. It has good points, and points that are not so good.

At any rate, it should prove an interesting experiment—one that many editors and publishers will be glad to study carefully, and may care to comment on.

Patterson of Chicago Plans To Erect 22 Story Building

Capt. Joseph Medill Patterson of the Chicago Tribune plans to build a twenty-two story shop and office building on the southeast corner of LaSalle Street and Wacker Drive. The site, fronting sixty feet on Wacker Drive by 100 feet on LaSalle Street, was acquired about three and a half years ago.

South Carolinians at Linotype Factory

Members of the South Carolina Press Association pictured in front of Mergenthaler headquarters, just before enjoying luncheon as guests of the Company

Editors Have Royal Good Time On Recent Visit to New York

When eighty-five members and friends of the South Carolina Press Association reached New York City, July 26, they began an unusually interesting round of activities.

The accompanying illustration pictures the party in front of the Linotype factory in Brooklyn.

Friday morning, July 27, the South Carolinians were guests of the Mergenthaler Linotype Company on a sightseeing trip round the city. Special permission had been secured to take the sightseers through Central Park. Then the buses went along Riverside Drive, down Broadway to the Battery, through the East Side, and over the river to the Linotype factory, where luncheon was served. Norman Dodge, Mergenthaler president, welcomed the visitors.

Then the Linotype buses took the newspaper people to Coney Island and brought them back to the Roxy Theater.

At Coney they were guests at Luna Park of Barron Collier. In the evening they were entertained at a shore dinner at Feltman's, Coney Island, by the American Type Founders Company, with W. A. Parker, assistant secretary, presiding.

All officers were reelected at the business meeting: B. H. Peace, president; W W Harris, Clinton, vice-president; C. O. Hearson, Spartanburg, second vice-president, August Kohn, Columbia, treasurer; H. C Booker, Columbia, secretary; Dr. E. O. Watson, Columbia, chaplain. Members of the executive committee are Thomas R Waring, Charleston; J. A. Latimer, Williston; F. D West, Abbeville; Allison Lee, Laurens; A. W Huckle, Rock Hill; J E. Norment, Darlington; McDavid Horton, Columbia.

The newspaper people left New York for the Southland on the S. S. Cherokee, Saturday, July 28.

National Labor Committee Sends Linotype to Palestine

Another Linotype is en route to Palestine—a Model 14 equipped to compose type in Hebrew and English.

The machine was purchased by the National Labor Committee for the Organized Jewish Workers in Palestine, with headquarters in New York City, and was sent as a gift to the Hebrew labor daily in Palestine, Davar

The purchase price of this Linotype was raised from various labor organizations in the United States affiliated with the National Labor Committee. The largest contribution was made by the Hebrew Typographical Union, Local 83, of New York City, and by individuals in the organization, to the amount of $600.

"The Davar," says Isaac Hamlin, secretary of the National Labor Committee, "is the only labor daily in the entire Orient, and has a circulation not only in Palestine but in other parts of the world, including America. The organizations in sympathy with the achievements of the General Federation of Labor in Palestine are particularly proud to send this Linotype as a gift from the Jewish labor movement in the United States."

Melville Stone Busy On 80th Birthday

Gets Scores of Telegrams from Friends in All Walks of Life

Melville E Stone, whose position as general manager of the Associated Press for more than a quarter of a century brought him into personal contact with monarchs, statesmen, educators, inventors, actors, artists and literary persons throughout the world, celebrated his eightieth birthday anniversary August 22 at his summer home at Woodstock, Vt.

It was not an idle day for Mr. Stone, for, in addition to keeping up his lifelong habit of reading newspapers, he was called on to open scores of telegrams. The telegrams were messages of congratulation from prominent persons, but the one which he prized most, he said, was from his former associates. It was sent on behalf of the members, officials and employees of the Associated Press, by Kent Cooper, Mr Stone's successor as general manager, and was distributed over the Associated Press wires, preceded by a news item.

"The business of sending news dispatches gathered from all quarters of the globe over the wires of the Associated Press," the news item said, "was momentarily halted today for a message of another kind—a salutation to Melville E Stone, counselor and former general manager, on the occasion of his eightieth birthday"

Seated amid newspapers and books in his study, and surrounded by autographed portraits of celebrities whom he numbered among his friends, Mr Stone recalled to visitors some of the vast strides made in the transmission of news since he helped organize the Associated Press On his walls hung portraits of the last Czar of Russia, whom he once interviewed, Joseph Jefferson, President McKinley Eugene Field, Henry Irving, Caruso, the King of Siam, Cardinal Gibbons, Viscountess Astor, Clemenceau, Ibsen, Joffre, Roosevelt and Cleveland

"I have lived from lightning rod to radio," said Mr Stone "I have again and again seen electricity expedite the business of news gatherings. Geniuses in electricity have played an important part in my life

"Professor Morse, inventor of the telegraph, was a neighbor of my uncle at Binghamton, N Y Cyrus W Field, who laid the first cable across the Atlantic, was a distant relative of mine. Dr Alexander Graham Bell once told me he wished to be remembered not as the inventor of the telephone but as the inventor of a system of communication between deaf mutes I met Helmholtz and Hertz, from whose work wireless and radio were born Thomas A. Edison and I are close friends, and I knew William Marconi well. Within my eighty years these men made and changed history with their discoveries and inventions."

Mr. Stone was born at Hudson, Ill., August 22, 1848, the son of a Methodist clergyman, who preached from a covered wagon before he settled in Chicago in 1860. It was not until he had engaged at first in the machine shop business and later in the banking business that Mr Stone began newspaper work When he established the Chicago Daily News, in 1875, as a one cent evening paper, he found there was a scarcity of pennies. He remedied the situation by obtaining several barrels of pennies from the Philadelphia mint and putting them into circulation. His ingenuity also evidenced itself when he induced the government to establish the first fast mail train, and when he interested himself in promoting the Linotype before it was generally used.

Mr. Stone's career is summarized in his book, "Fifty Years a Journalist."

38 Languages in Circular Produced on the Linotype

The International Press, New York City, Gregory Weinstein, proprietor, recently composed and printed in forty-two different languages a circular descriptive of a thirteen month calendar.

This calendar plan, states the circular, which presents in color a graphic illustration of the purposed calendar, "is being submitted to the governments of all the leading nations, principal universities, the special 'calendar reform' committee of the League of Nations, and the Pope, with the hope that it may expedite the solution of this one world problem"

Of the forty-two languages printed on the circular, states Mr Weinstein, "thirty-eight were composed on the Linotype"

Record to Move To New Quarters By November 15

Philadelphia Paper to Occupy Modern Building on North Broad

By November 15 the Philadelphia Record, purchased in June by J. David Stern, publisher, and his associates, expects to be operating in a modern nine story building on North Broad Street, with floor space of 200,000 square feet.

Twelve units of super-speed presses, two double sextuples, are now being built for installation in the basement of the new home. The circulation department, to be on the first floor, will be equipped with the latest devices to convey papers speedily to a loading platform and a fleet of delivery trucks.

The North Broad Street building is a fine modern structure well lighted on three sides. Its exterior of white tile makes it one of the finest looking business buildings in Philadelphia

At first the Record will occupy the first three floors and basement, with the upper six floors given over to other offices. As the paper grows, the upper floors will be taken over by various departments of the Record.

That the paper is destined to grow is evidenced by the personality and activities of its publisher. J. David Stern is a man of abundant energy and with a long string of accomplishments to his credit in the publishing world.

A native of Philadelphia, he is thoroughly familiar with local conditions. Added to this is a background of national newspaper experience. He has worked on or directed newspapers in the East, the Middle West and the Northwest. And he is a young man, at that—only forty-two—an aggressive young man with his feet firmly treading solid ground but with his mind directed toward higher things. He is ambitious to make the success of the Record his outstanding accomplishment

Stern was born in Philadelphia April 1, 1886, was graduated from the William Penn Charter School in 1902, University of Pennsylvania College in 1906, and University of Pennsylvania Law School in 1909

Even in his school days he was active in newspaper work, as managing editor of the Pennsylvanian.

With his school days behind him, and despite his training in the law, and his admission to the Pennsylvania bar, he plunged immediately into newspaper work—his life work.

As a lad of twenty-three he began as a cub reporter with the Philadelphia Public Ledger And right here an interesting side story comes to light. On the Ledger at that time Henry M Eaton was city editor—the same Eaton now identified with the Whaley-Eaton Service of Washington, D C, and—but wait a minute As a cub reporter Stern was inspired by the high principles and editorial abilities of Eaton, and stated—at least told himself—that an ambition of his was some day to be publisher of a metropolitan newspaper and to have associated with him that same Henry M Eaton And that ambition has been realized, as Eaton now is director of the editorial department of the Philadelphia Record

After Stern had worked a while as a cub with the Ledger, he got on as a reporter with the Philadelphia North American Then he served as reporter with the Philadelphia Bulletin, and later as advertising solicitor with the Philadelphia Record.

Wanderlust took him to the Northwest, where he soon secured a place with the Seattle Post-Intelligencer as marine editor covering news of the waterfront Later he served as advertising manager of the Seattle Star

(Continued on page three)

Linotype Aboard Battleship Works Well in Any Climate

That the Linotype is operated successfully under virtually all conditions of weather is substantiated again—this time by Edward W Quielisch, first class printer aboard the U. S. S. California, Linotype equipped

"On a tropical cruise one time," says Quielisch, "it was so hot in the print shop that the printers had to strip to trunks, and use these for clothing At this time I was the operator, and perspiration was excessive Two weeks later I was operating the same machine wearing an overcoat We were on the Hudson River, and the print shop was as cold as the outside air.

"When differences of temperature, of operators that differ from one who knows just enough to cast a line to one who sets 5,000 ems an hour, of the vibration of the ship when it is cruising to that of firing a broadside, are taken into consideration, then one may really wonder why the Linotype stands up. It does, however, for the California's machine is used twenty-four hours daily while the fleet is engaged in mimic warfare

"The California, the flagship of the battle fleet, requires its Linotype to print all the 'secret and confidential' orders of the Commander-in-Chief, a daily newspaper (at sea), a weekly newspaper, and a routine printing of menus, programs and office forms for the Commander-in-Chief, together with the numerous blank forms and booklets used by the ship."

Its Paper From Cornstalks —Covers From Cottonseeds

A book now being issued by the Rae D Henkle Company, 45 Fourth Avenue, New York City, should be of interest to many printers and publishers because of its paper and binding The book, "Farm Products in Industry," by George M Rommel, is said to be the first book to be printed on paper made from cornstalks, and with covers made from cottonseed hulls

For Better Looking Papers

Roy W Howard

Every Line in This Issue Was Set on the Linotype

As usual, every line in this issue of THE LINOTYPE NEWS, with the exception of two large lines in two display advertisements, is a Linotype line. All lines were produced the Linotype way—body matter, heads, advertisements, rules, borders, ornaments

See page four, "Makeup of This Issue"

The Brooklyn Standard-Union Adds Nine New Linotypes

When, recently, Paul Block purchased the Brooklyn Standard-Union, he at once set in motion a program for increased efficiency in various departments, and immediately ordered nine new Linotypes.

These nine new machines—a Model 26 and eight Model 8s—were in operation when the formal announcement of the purchase of the paper appeared in print.

Mr Block, who also controls the Newark Star-Eagle, the Toledo Blade, the Duluth Herald, and the Pittsburg Post-Gazette, operates more than seventy Linotypes

Wilmington Every Evening Adds Five New Linotypes

Five new Linotypes have been installed in the new home of the Wilmington (Del) Every Evening, published by William F Metten The new machines are a Model 21 Display Linotype a Model 8 and three Model 14s

This latest installation gives the Every Evening thirteen Linotypes—a Model 21 seven Model 8s and five Model 14s

Later we plan to publish an illustrated story about the Every Evening

New York Training School Equipped With 7 Linotypes

Playing a leading part in the School for Machine Training, 240 West Fortieth Street, New York City, which opened this month, are seven Linotypes

The School for Machine Training is a joint project of the Printers' League, the Publishers' Association of New York, Typographical Union No 6, and the Board of Education Those eligible to attend are apprentices in their fifth year in the composing room.

Thirty-three Years Old

In August the Weekly Chronicle of Dunnville, Ont, rounded out thirty-three years of publication The issue of August 3 devoted an entire page to Chronicle history, with a picture of the Model 14 Linotype, and a writeup of Linotype Ionic in which the paper is set

Roy Howard Says Better Printing Wins Advertising

Scripps-Howard Official Indicates New Trend in Typography

By Roy W. Howard
Chairman of the Board
Scripps-Howard Newspapers
Reprinted from the "Book of Art Printing"

Never in the history of American newspaper making has there been the demand for, or appreciation of, good printing that exists today. This appreciation, which unfortunately has not as yet extended to the entire newspaper making craft, is happily evidencing a tendency to increase and spread rapidly Competitive conditions and a new public demand are the guarantees that the improvement will continue.

Until comparatively recently the printing end of newspaper production was regarded simply as a very necessary operation in the production It was not thought of seriously as a factor in meeting competitive conditions The paper had to be printed. If it could be printed legibly well and good But emphasis by an enterprising publisher upon the importance of really good printing was viewed with much the same disdain that would focus upon a pair of spats in a western mining camp. Consideration centered almost entirely on what was presented in a news, editorial and advertising way Very little consideration was devoted to the actual visual characteristics of the presentation. As a result there has been, until very recently, little or no improvement in the printing and the appearance of the average daily newspaper As a matter of fact, with the speeding up of presses to meet competitive conditions, there has been, in many instances, distinct deterioration in the quality of the printing in the finished product

More recently, however, there have been signs of the development of an appreciation of the tangible value to a newspaper of good printing Several causes have contributed to this For one thing, America has become a nation of eyeglass wearers. With the increase of the newspaper reading habit to a point where it has become almost universal, has come a demand for printing clear enough to banish eye strain New and better type faces, particularly in body type, have produced good will and circulation increases that were not known to exist

But possibly even more important than this has come the tardy realization by newspaper publishers of the existence of an appreciation by the public of the graphic arts as distinguished from the printing business Candor compels the admission that the credit for this awakening interest in good printing is chiefly attributable to American magazines which, taken as a whole, in their printing as well as their editorial contents, are far superior to any periodicals published anywhere else in the world

To resort to a paraphrase, "beauty has brought its own reward" Improvement in printing of both text and illustrations has made possible not only great advance in the editorial appeal of magazines, but it has also made possible a much broader reader appeal in magazine advertising This result is so definite that it is common knowledge among big national advertising agencies that many manufacturers of commodities which would obtain a quicker and more certain reader appeal and merchandising response through newspaper advertising, are spending large amounts of their appropriations in magazine media because of the greater appeal made to the advertisers' own eye by the more attractive line of copy possible in magazine advertising

With considerable alacrity now that the move (long overdue) has actually started, a number of the most progressive American newspapers are freeing themselves from the terrible typographical habits acquired, first during the days of the Spanish-American War and more recently revived during the days of the World War

Eight column banner lines—even two, three or four of them to a page—bold Gothic type in two and three column heads over ten line stories, and other typographical monstrosities are giving way to sane composition and a recognition of the fact that headlines

(Continued on page three)

Calgary Albertan Plans to Enter Its Fine New Home Early in November

Early in November the Calgary (Alberta) Albertan expects to occupy its fine new home at Ninth Avenue and Second Street West, Calgary. The building is to be occupied exclusively by the various departments of the Albertan Publishing Company. It will cover ground space measuring 75 by 120 feet, and, will cost, when completed, apart from all equipment, approximately $200,000.

Contrary to the custom followed in the construction of many newspaper offices, the pressroom of the new Albertan building will be located not in the basement but on the main floor. The basement will be occupied by the press foundations, the boiler and transformer rooms, and extensive storage space for newsprint, inks, and so forth.

That portion of the main floor facing Ninth Avenue is to accommodate the business and private offices of the company. Here will be located the offices of the president, general manager and advertising manager. The plans provide for two entrances to the business office, one from Ninth Avenue and the other from Second Street. Both entrances are to be faced in Tyndal stone.

In the business office, which is to be finished in oak, besides the private offices above mentioned, will be the circulation, display and classified advertising and accounting departments. The business office will be separated by a soundproof wall from the pressroom.

The second floor of the new building will be given over entirely to the various editorial departments, and the newspaper composing and stereo rooms. Private offices are to be provided for the managing editor, editorial writer, sporting editor and social editor, while the telegraph editor, city editor and reporters will be accommodated in a large room adjoining these offices. Ample provision is made for that necessary adjunct of the newspaper office—a well stocked reference library.

Canadian press operators will have their room on this floor next to the general editorial room.

The remaining portion of this floor has been assigned to the composing and stereo rooms, where provision is made for the eventual installation of eighteen Linotypes and other equipment The floor of this department will be capable of sustaining a weight of 500 pounds per square foot. Ingenious systems of ventilation and lighting feature the equipment of this floor.

At the rear of the third floor will be the commercial printing department. Toward the front of the third floor will be the editorial office of the Western Farmer, the new farm magazine, the first issue of which is to be published on November 10.

Specially provided for the use of executive meetings of local organizations, a large community room is to be located on the third floor. This will also be used as a general conference or board room.

Adjoining the community room the plans call for an uptodate and completely equipped radio studio, designed according to the latest radio engineering principles. This will include a radio room, a reception room and a broadcasting chamber The latter room is to be soundproof, and visitors will be able to view the artists broadcasting without in any way interfering with the performance

The roof slab is to be built strong enough to serve as a floor, if it is decided at a future date to add a story to the building. For the time being, the roof will be of tar and gravel, guaranteed for twenty years.

Editor Regretfully Bids Farewell to Two Old Linotypes Replaced by New

"More sentiment attaches to a piece of machine than one might believe at first thought," declared the Bowling Green (Ohio) Sentinel-Tribune editorially in July "The Sentinel-Tribune has just installed two new Linotypes to take the place of two old ones They will do better work than the latter One of the old ones has been here longer than the manager, who came in the plant twenty-nine years ago It was here early in 1898, nearly three years before the editor became a member of the force It was here before the foreman began his first lessons at the case The other is nearly as old

"One's mind runs back to the days through which these machines have passed, and the character of the work which they have done during those years; and it is not without a heart throb that we see them passing out of our doors never to return, doomed to the scrap heap to which Mergenthaler will consign them They are companions to whom we must say 'farewell' They have been coworkers whose wonderful mechanism has seldom failed to deliver their tasks. They are the means through which, in the last analysis, the bread and butter of this paper's personnel has come Like one's heart, they have been the pulsating organ of the newspaper system

"What stories they could tell were they able to speak The history of the community the heartaches the joys, the hopes, the fears, of individuals would be related. They would tell of men and women joyously welcomed at birth, of their cunning chatter of their school triumphs, of their marriage—of their deaths They would conjure up the past of the pioneer, the future as seen by local prophets. They would people a village with the new born, and present a vast cemetery filled with those whose obituaries they have related They would express the eager expectations that accompany those setting out to do life's work, rejoice over their success, and sometimes mourn over their defeats. They would tell of self denials and of personal ambitions They would remind us of the lonely strangers stricken by misfortune, and the erring ones caught in the toils of their own misconduct They would bring back to mind political and moral fights with words that might appear blistering now The one would tell the tale of the Spanish-American War and both would join in relating how our boys in khaki learned the life of camp and field and fought valiantly 'over there'

"Through these machines has passed the news of the city, the county the state, the nation, the world but they will relate them no more Their task is done—well done And for them we shall say with regret that printer's word which signifies completion of the day's work, 'Thirty'"

EXAMPLE 177

was presented with a front page that disregarded tradition. Yet it was not a "wild page." In fact, it was quite conservative, but considerably different from other current front pages.

At that, there was at least an echo from the past about it (for it presented six wide instead of eight regular-width columns), as many front pages many years ago made use of wide columns. See Example 177.

The columns of that page were 16 picas wide, with an extra shoulder of white space on either side of each column rule. Body lines were in 8-point Ionic No. 5 on a 9-point body, with some of the lines extra leaded. (The news matter of most American dailies at that time was set in 7 point or smaller, and that 8-on-9 was flying in the face of Tradition with a capital T.) The head dress was in capitals and lowercase (with no line entirely in capitals) of 30-, 24- and 18-point Bodoni Bold, and 24- and 14-point Bodoni Bold Italic. (Many dailies at that time were setting most of their heads in condensed capitals, and employing unrelated type faces in their head dresses.) The cut legends were in 10-point Antique No. 1 Italic. Ten-point Bodoni Bold Italic would have been more consistent and fully as effective, if not more so.

In a story at the top of column one on that page—a story headed "Isn't This Page Attractive and Easy to Read? Why Should Front Pages Be Restricted to Narrow Columns?" this writer stated, in part:

"It is the ambition of many newspaper publishers to have a front page decidedly different from other papers; a front page of distinction, outstandingly attractive in appearance, tangibly individual, and decidedly easy to read.

"This page is an experiment in that direction. It is different, is attractive, has character, is easy to read.

"Its wider columns make possible the displaying of prominent headings over stories to be emphasized, without the use of three- or four-column headlines. One of these single-column heads has almost as much attention value as a double-column head over narrower columns. The wider lines of larger body type make the page inviting and easy on the eyes.

"The whole page has a lively, airy appearance. There is no feeling of crowding. All lines have been given a chance 'to breathe.'

"There is less chance of a story's 'getting lost' on the page—being overlooked—as all stories are given prominent treatment—even the briefer ones.

"As the deepest heads here consist of only six lines—two decks—a saving in depth is made over the main news heads used by many newspapers.

"Against these good features, however, are some that are not so good from a mechanical standpoint.

"Stories continued from such a front page to inside pages would have to be set in two different measures, and stories transferred bodily would have to be reset. These are important objections, to be sure.

"Of course it is not even intimated here that advertising pages be set in wider columns, as that would tend to disrupt the standard widths followed by advertisers."

Three months later, in December, 1928, the *Morning Telegraph* of New York City came out with an out-of-the-ordinary format, designed by Heyworth Campbell of New York City. See Example 178.

That and many subsequent issues of the *Morning Telegraph* appeared with six wider columns to each page; with simplified flush-left heads in members of the Bodoni family and limited to two decks; with second decks in italic; with white space between decks, instead of jim dashes; with triangular ornaments between some of the items; with shoulders of white space between columns, instead of column rules, and with upright display initials at the beginnings of lines here and there in nearly all stories run.

The *Morning Telegraph* continues to use flush-left heads, but for several years now has been presenting eight columns on most of its pages, although it continues to run much of its racing news in lines four columns wide.

Example 179 presents a reduced showing of a more recent front page from the *Morning Telegraph*. (Note, among other things, that column rules are now employed in place of strips of white between columns.)

Early in 1929 the *Linotype News*, appreciating the possibilities of flush-left-head treatments, began to present many different versions of flush-left heads, and has been demonstrating their advantages ever since.

Some of those heads have been presented with cutoff rules in place of jim dashes; many with centered dashes; some with flush-left dashes, and many with nothing but white space between and below decks. And

The MORNING TELEGRAPH

America's Oldest, Authoritative Newspaper of Recreation, Theatre and Sports

TUESDAY, DECEMBER 4, 1928 — TEN CENTS *in Greater New York, 15¢ elsewhere*

Founded in 1836

FINAL
Complete

WEATHER FORECAST
TUESDAY—Partly cloudy and colder.

VOLUME NO. 112 — NUMBER 157

PUBLISHERS' NOTICE.

The Morning Telegraph

Telephone Columbus 9667

NEW YORK, TUESDAY, DECEMBER 4, 1928

The Old Lady Shows Her Medals

THE MORNING TELEGRAPH appears this morning in its new type and dress, a refreshing combination prepared by artist typographers from selected materials. Frankly, we like it immensely, and we hope that you also will not only [illegible] new ownership plan for the diverting Old Lady who has been in town since 1836.

With the discarding of her old and unfashionable garments, she discarded all of her old and unfashionable ideas. The Morning Telegraph—almost a centenarian—will devote its new and invigorated existence to the competent reporting and contemplation of the pleasurable side of life. Clean sports, good drama and music, intelligent films, and fine living will be its program and aim.

THESE five are stimulating events, worthy in every sense of thoughtful attention. News is flexible and elastic, and the measure of it which directs homicide and politics to the front page works as logically in recreative reporting.

The Morning Telegraph will, therefore, content itself with the upbuilding of these gifts to life, believing that clean sport is as thrilling as crime, that the theater involves more human drama in a day than reaches the combined front pages of the regular journals in a week, and that motion pictures are entertaining and educational and, finally, that fine living is the heritage and obligation of every man.

WE appear in new type and dress to improve our looks, but more important is the birth of a personality in journalism, a vigorous spirit that will come through and go beyond the type which is but its symbol. Six columns on a page are essentially no more to be desired than eight, or seven, but they suggest breadth and freedom and those are the very things for which this newspaper will strive.

The pages are cast now into unalterable form, but The Morning Telegraph is not. It will devote itself to things desired, but will not follow mawkishly in their wake. A staff selected because of peculiar ability individually to carry out the program has been at work and will continue. The paper will augment this regular company with guest writers in each department. Already in sports and in drama outside writers have reported events which might be expected from the staff. This has produced intensely interesting results and has inspired the regular reporters.

HERE, then, is your first copy of The Morning Telegraph new in face and form and ambition, lively heir to the rich heritage which came with it, and deeply conscious that the task before it is as difficult as it is challenging.

Crow's Nest Wins Grayline Purse

Regenerated Man of War Colt Beats Marlboro—Lincoln Plaut Third.

by **Perry Johnson**

Flying Torch Sets Pace

Weather Ideal

Turf Elite Drawn to Coffroth Cup

Purse Draws Many

Many Entered

All-Eastern Eleven Chosen

Even the Best Minds Had Nothing to Do With These Selections.

by **James R. Harrison**

Snagged at Ends

DOWN IN FRONT

by **Richards Vidmer**

Gone But Not Forgotten.

The Eastern Enigma

Ring, Alma Mater!

Under the Old Chicago Bridge

Mr. Cozy Dolan Handed Technical K. O. in One of the Worst Fights Ever Seen.

by **Westbrook Pegler**

RING'S *Side*

Simply Explaining the Strange Phenomenon of the Real Reasons Impelling a Young Fellow to Go Back to Work Again.

by **Ring Lardner.**

PREFACE

What? No Reporter?

May Be Necessary

LEAVE GARDEN

No More Thrills Than a Hearth Fire, but the Fun Is Sure to Start if You Depart

by **Lois Long**

NOWHERE LITTLE NEARER NOWHERE

Six-Day Athletes With Caged Squirrel Complex Hold Pace Marked by Few Cash Sprints.

by **Joseph Gordon**

Standing of the Teams

EXAMPLE 178

The MORNING TELEGRAPH

America's Authority on Motion Pictures, Theater and Turf

The Weather Cloudy, Occasional Light Rain

Complete ★★★

VOL. 148. NO. 71 — 3 2 1 — NEW YORK, TUESDAY, SEPTEMBER 24, 1946 — *Price* **25** *Cents*

Cassis and True North One-Two at Belmont

News Round-Up
By UNITED PRESS

FOREIGN:

Tanks Patrol Palestine

Endorses Truman Policy

Rush Troops to South Iran

Bevin-Molotov Confer

Communication Restored

NATIONAL:

Seek Cause of Market Break

Asks Report on Troops

Sees Anti-Lynch Group

Fight Socialized Medicine

BASEBALL RESULTS

NATIONAL LEAGUE

AMERICAN LEAGUE

Last 'A' Marathon at 'Gansett Today

Dodgers Down Phillies, 6-1

Stage 5-Run Rally in 8th; Still Trail by Half As Cardinals Beat Cubs.

by Ira Seebacher

Injury May Keep Blanchard on Bench

Recordings Next On Petrillo List

Reconciliation Reported

Actor-Producer-Magician Orson Welles and his glamorous wife, Rita Hayworth, have become reconciled, their studio announced yesterday. Welles flew East Sunday to pinch hit as a speaker for former Secretary of Commerce Henry Wallace after celebrating the reconciliation in a weekend round of night spots with his wife. He is scheduled to address a rally at Providence, R. I., tonight.

Wondrous Happenings In Postwar Hollywood

Freud Reigns, Prices Soar, Salaries Climb and Black Market Flourishes

by Frederick C. Othman

Pre-B'way Television Test Of Plays Has Possibilities

by Jack Gaver

Marquest Topweight

Only Five Defy Rugged Racer at Two Miles, 70 Yds.

by Evan Shipman

Rain Threatening

Suffolk Horsemen Must Get Licenses

Hollywood *in* Review

by Carl Schroeder

Stars at Belmont

Jockey Basil James was the riding star at Belmont Park's opening yesterday, riding Cassis to a head victory in the Fall Highweight Handicap and completing a double with Rico Monte in the nightcap.

Juveniles Top Jersey Stage

El Mono and Lighthouse Head Fleet 2-Year Olds At Atlantic City Today.

by Jack Carpenter

Ellendale Likely Choice

Md. Board to Hear Dope Case Thursday

Mudlarks Are Set for Field Day at Hawthorne Track

by Teddy Cox

Buzfuz Finishes Third In Fall Highweight 'Cap

I Will Takes Secondary Feature Before 22,880 Opening-Day Fans

by Bob Horwood

Jerome Lures Bulky Field

Assault Is Conspicuous Absentee From Feature At Belmont Park Today.

Remainder of Field

22,880 See Opening

Brilliant Rush

Narragansett Dope Case Is Postponed

Detroit's Leading Rider Now Here

Racing Today

(Eastern Daylight Time)

EXAMPLE 179

many different type faces have been presented in such heads—old-style faces, modern faces, square-serif and sans-serif faces.

Example 180, a reduced showing of a front page of February, 1929, represents the first attempt of the *Linotype News* at flush-left heads. The idea was suggested by F. T. Denman, then a member of the Linotype organization, but now an executive with an advertising agency.

Looked at now, that page seems crude, and Mr. Denman would be the first to admit it; but it was a commendable pioneering effort and played an important part in the evolution of modern heads.

Even when that page was being put together, it was realized that it was not a thing of beauty. But it was different, and it had good features.

In the story at the top of column one on that page—a story headed "New Style of Heads Designed to Give Subject of Story at First Glance," this writer stated, in part:

"Yes, they are different—decidedly different—the main news heads used in this issue. . . .

"They are designed to announce the subject of the story at a glance, with the 'key words' emphasized. They save valuable space. They simplify the work of the copy desk. They can be easily handled in the composing room. They attract the attention of readers and save time for them.

"For many years newspapers have been presenting multiple-deck heads over their main news stories. Some papers employ six or more decks. This treatment, repeated over and over for years by papers in all parts of North America, has become a habit. New papers have grown accustomed to following the patterns of older ones. They have adopted multiple-deck news heads as a matter of course. Other papers were doing it—successful papers—so it seemed the right thing for the new ones to do. And so, while radical changes have taken place in all other departments of newspaper work, virtually no changes have occurred in the physical treatment of news heads.

"Alert editors and publishers wouldn't think of following antiquated methods in certain phases of their work. They know that better methods have been discovered. But even the most progressive papers—papers that employ the latest and best methods in all other departments—continue to handle heads of main news stories the way they handled them many years ago.

"Reading habits have undergone marked changes in recent years.

The Modern Newspaper You Like to Read

The Linotype News

This Issue More Than Seventy Thousand

Volume VII | *The Machine That Lasts* | Brooklyn, New York, February, 1929 | *The Service That Lasts* | Number Four

NEW Style of HEADS Designed to give Subject of Story at First Glance

They attract attention; save valuable space; are easy to write and to compose; effect savings all along the line.

Yes, they are different—decidedly different—the main news heads used in this issue of THE LINOTYPE NEWS.

They are designed to announce the subject of the story at a glance, with the "key words" emphasized. They save valuable space. They simplify the work of the copy desk. They can be easily handled in the composing room. They attract the attention of readers and save time for them.

For many years newspapers have been presenting multiple decked heads over their main news stories. Some papers employ six or more decks. This treatment, repeated over and over for years by papers in all parts of North America, has become a habit. New papers have grown accustomed to following the patterns of older ones. They have adopted multiple decked news heads as a matter of course. Other papers were doing it—successful papers—so it seemed the right thing for the new ones to do. And so, while radical changes have taken place in all other departments of newspaper work, virtually no changes have occurred in the physical treatment of news heads.

Alert editors and publishers wouldn't think of following antiquated methods in certain phases of their work. They know that better methods have been discovered. But even the most progressive papers—papers that employ the latest and best methods in all other departments—continue to handle heads of main news stories the way they handled them many years ago.

Reading Habits Have Changed

Reading habits have undergone marked changes in recent years. Advertisers have been quick to note this and to take advantage of it. The modern newspaper reader has little leisure. He doesn't read—he glimpses. Clever advertisers tell their stories in brief eyefuls. And so should clever editors.

The main news heads used here present the "high spots" in a single deck. A brief italicised paragraph immediately below sums up the story. The reader can tell at a glance whether or not he cares to read the story. He is not obliged to wade through several decks to make such a decision.

Of course the particular type treatment used here is not the ultimate in modern news-head presentation. We have purposely used type faces that are available in many newspaper plants, rather than certain other faces. The weight of the larger condensed faces used in these heads is about uniform with the weight of the smaller expanded faces used. The "color" is fairly even throughout and the lines of the headings hold together well. This would not have been the case had smaller sizes of Cheltenham Bold been used in conjunction with the larger sizes. The contrasts in weight between the larger and smaller lines would have been too pronounced and the lines of the heads would not have held together so well. But the thing we wish to stress here is not the using of these particular faces in preference to certain others, but the serious consideration of this head plan—a single deck head with important words emphasized, followed by a brief summing up paragraph.

These heads attract attention. They give the reader the gist of the story in a single eyeful.

Space Saving Important

They save valuable space—from two to three or more inches to each head. And space is a newspaper's stock in trade—the commodity it has to sell—with circulation, of course. The space saved can be utilized for the running of additional stories or to accommodate more advertising. The saving on a dozen heads will amount to a column or more; on the heads throughout a paper, perhaps a page or even several pages, with resultant savings all along the line.

These heads simplify the work of the copy desk, by doing away with tedious letter counting and line fitting. They obviate the necessity of stringing the head along—even padding it—through several decks. The head writer simply puts down in three or four or five lines the high spots of the story. A glance at his style sheet lets him know at once just what faces and sizes should present the lines. And the writing of the summing up paragraph calls for no letter counting or line fitting whatsoever. He simply lets it run as it will.

These heads can be easily handled in the composing room. The head copy is passed to one machine for certain lines. Those lines and the copy are passed to another machine or machines. When the head reaches the makeup bank, it is already assembled and ready to be dropped in the form.

The head plan suggested here should be seriously studied by editors and publishers. It is a radical departure, to be sure. But many radical changes in other fields have been made in recent years and have proved advantageous.

See page four, "Makeup of This Issue."

In other issues of THE LINOTYPE NEWS we shall present similar head treatments in other type faces.

Chicago Tribune Promotes Several of Its Executives

W. E. Macfarlane is now business manager of the Chicago Tribune, and W. E. Donahue is advertising manager.

Mr. Macfarlane had served for seventeen years as manager of the classified advertising department of the Tribune. Prior to his latest promotion he was advertising manager. E. M. Antrim is now assistant business manager.

Mr. Donahue has been with the Tribune since 1904. He is well fitted for the position as advertising manager, as for fifteen years he has been at the head of the paper's local and financial display advertising.

D. F. McMahon, who for twenty years with the Tribune has been manager of the automotive advertising, western advertising manager, and manager of national advertising, has taken Mr. Donahue's place. Clyde S. Benham becomes manager of national advertising.

Linotype Company Again Wins Prize On Safety Record

THE MERGENTHALER LINOTYPE COMPANY has been awarded a bronze plaque for its excellent safety record in the fourth annual accident prevention campaign of the Associated Industries of New York State, Inc.

This is in keeping with the showing made last spring by the makers of the LINOTYPE, when the Associated Industries gave the MERGENTHALER organization a safety rating of 99.49 per cent, declared it the group winner in class one in its accident prevention campaign, and presented it with a certificate of merit.

The plaque carries these statements: "Fourth Annual Accident Prevention Campaign of Associated Industries of New York State, Inc.—1928 Group Winner. Awarded to the management and employees of MERGENTHALER LINOTYPE COMPANY for their service to humanity in achieving this splendid safety record. Banish the cruel; admonish the thoughtless; educate the careless. For it is written that the careful worker shall live long and prosper."

This Issue, as Usual, Composed on Linotype

As usual, every line in this issue of THE LINOTYPE NEWS, with the exception of one large line in one display advertisement, is a Linotype line. All lines were produced the Linotype way—body matter, heads, advertisements, rules, borders, ornaments.

See page four, "Makeup of This Issue."

40 Languages Simplified by 100 Scholars to Speed Printing

Important work directed by Dr. Harold H. Bender, professor of Indo-Germanic philology at Princeton University. Mergenthaler Linotype Company cooperating. Makes possible printing of scholarly works at lowered costs. Will affect writing practices in many countries.

"Forty languages of Europe and Asia have been simplified by a group of nearly one hundred scholars to facilitate the mechanical setting of type, it was announced in Princeton, N. J., February 2, by Dr. Harold H. Bender, professor of Indo-Germanic philology at Princeton University, who directed the survey just completed," ran a story in the New York Times February 3.

"Professor Bender's recommendations have been adopted in their entirety by the European and American divisions of the Mergenthaler Linotype Company, at whose request the survey was conducted. It is expected that not only commercial printing will be benefited, but it will make possible, by reducing manufacturing costs, the production of many scholarly works. By the elimination of some characters and the simplification of others, this linguistic 'house-cleaning' will make it possible to supply all the characters needed in the ordinary printing of these languages, even for scholarly editions and many philological publications.

"Professor Bender's recommendations cover all the Scandinavian, Romance and Continental Germanic languages, and most of the Balto-Slavic, as well as Albanian, Basque, Estonian, Finnish, Hungarian and Welsh in Europe, Urdu in India, and Tagalog in the Philippine Islands. In addition to the forty languages, many dialects and variations were studied. Professor Bender and his assistants consulted hundreds of grammars and dictionaries and read thousands of pages in books, magazines and newspapers.

"For each language there were three phases of the investigation: historic, phonetic and conventional. The practical results consist mainly in the selection of the best usage, and in simplification of symbols, accents, and diacritical marks. Under the old scholarly system in Lithuania, for instance, fourteen different forms of the letter 'e' were required. That number has been reduced to three for ordinary purposes.

"Professor Bender said today that scholars, pressed by the tremendous expense involved in printing under the old system, had been gradually discovering that it was not necessary to preserve all the details of diacritical marks that have been handed down by tradition. Such distinctions have no linguistic value, he added, and can interest only the paleographer, who does not need them in printed books.

"It is expected that by this simplification in printed matter the written languages will be changed in the countries affected. In providing a romanization of Urdu, Professor Bender and his assistants found it necessary to devise a new system which would accommodate itself to the various systems now in use and provide for the symbols used in writing Hindu, Arabic, and Persian."

Gannett Group Adds Brooklyn Eagle

Frank E. Tripp becomes acting publisher. Herbert F. Gunnison remains as chairman of board. Harris M. Crist is managing editor. Arthur Howe, editor, remains.

The Brooklyn Daily Eagle was purchased January 8 by Frank E. Gannett, owner of fifteen other newspapers, all of which save two are published in New York state. The purchase was made from those who have been in active charge of the management of the Eagle under Herbert F. Gunnison, president and publisher.

Frank E. Tripp, vice-president of the Gannett newspapers, becomes acting publisher, and announces that no changes are contemplated in the personnel of the various departments.

Negotiations for the purchase of the Eagle were in progress for several weeks. The news of the sale was published on page one of the Eagle January 8. The new owner said, in part:

"The history of the Brooklyn Daily Eagle is a challenge to those who would control its future, and no one is more sensible of the responsibility which this record imposes than I, now that I have become the controlling owner.

"The borough of Brooklyn and the city of New York are fortunate not only in that the Brooklyn Daily Eagle is one of the outstanding newspapers of the country but also because it has been one of the strongest factors working for the best development of the city and its own community. Nothing shall be done under my ownership that will change this situation; rather I shall strive to improve and strengthen its work."

Gunnison Chairman of Board

Herbert F. Gunnison, who has been associated with the Eagle for forty-six years, will remain as chairman of the board of trustees. Raymond M. Gunnison, vice-president, has gone South for a holiday, and will announce his business plans later. Harris M. Crist is to continue as managing editor. Arthur Howe, who has been with the Eagle thirty-six years, and has been editor since 1915, remains with the Eagle.

Herbert F. Gunnison said: "In turning over control of the Eagle to Mr.

port of all the communities he has served as a publisher. In welcoming him Brooklyn will find that the Eagle under his management will not only continue to devote itself to protecting and promoting the best interests of Brooklyn but that its field of useful endeavor will be greatly enlarged."

Some Eagle History

The Brooklyn Eagle and Kings County Democrat, as it was first called, was started October 26, 1841, by a group of Brooklyn politicians as a party organ.

(Continued on page three)

Mutual Association Builds Homes for Chicago Tribune Employees and Earns $262,000

Medill Building and Loan Association, beginning in 1922 with $1,000,000, now capitalized at $5,000,000. Two hundred and thirty members have bought homes, and 1,130 others are buying stock valued at $3,129,400 and paying seven per cent.

Six years ago a little group of executives and department heads of the Chicago Tribune became enthusiastic over the "own your own home" idea.

After considerable discussion and investigation the Medill Building and Loan

Lino-Set Papers Win in Illinois

Again Linotype set papers won virtually all of the prizes in the latest front page contest put on by the Illinois Press Association.

The Harvard Herald was first among Illinois weeklies, with the Tri-County Press, Polo, second, and the Aledo Times-Record third. In the daily class the Bloomington Pantagraph was first; Moline Dispatch, second, and Decatur Herald, third. The Danville Commercial-News, the Sterling Gazette, the Centralia Sentinel, and the Antioch News were given honorable mention. Weeklies receiving honorable mention were the Mendota Reporter, Iroquois Times, Carmi Tribune-Times, Wheaton Progressive, Crystal Lake Herald, Rantoul Press, Graville Mercury-Independent, Jersey County News, Tazewell County Reporter, Rushville Times, and Sparta News-Plaindealer.

Ad Club Honors CURTIS on Saturday Evening Post's 200th Birthday

Publishing and business leaders present, with Charles M. Schwab as main speaker. Honor guest sketches history of publication founded by Franklin. Editor Lorimer began at $1,000 a year.

Leaders in the publishing and business world joined in paying tribute to Cyrus H. K. Curtis December 19, at a luncheon given by the Advertising Club of New York, in commemoration of the 200th anniversary of the founding of the Saturday Evening Post, of which Mr. Curtis is the publisher.

Charles M. Schwab was the principal speaker.

Mr. Schwab described Mr. Curtis as

the history of the Saturday Evening Post from its founding by Benjamin Franklin, in 1728, to the present. He told how he bought the magazine in 1897 for $1,000 after the heirs of the former owner had decided it wasn't worth while to put up the money to get out the next week's issue.

George Horace Lorimer, editor of the Post, was hired by Mr. Curtis as a young man at $1,000 a year. The publisher insisted that Lorimer was primarily responsible for the magazine's success.

Adolph S. Ochs, publisher of the New York Times, said great praise was due the Curtis publications for the high standards they had set in the field of journalism. Other speakers were H. H. Charles, a former president of the Advertising Club; Stanley R. Latshaw, president of the Butterick Publishing Company; Ivy Lee, public relations counsel; Stanley B. Resor, president of the J. Walter Thompson Company, and Louis Wiley, business manager of the New York Times. Mr. Wiley spoke of the commendation due Mr. Curtis for his leadership against fraudulent and objectionable advertising.

Others among those present included Ogden Reid, president and editor of the New York Herald Tribune; Julian S. Mason, editor of the New York Evening Post; John F. Bresnahan, business manager of the New York World; Hugh Burke, eastern representative of the Public Ledger Company; James Wright Brown, president of Editor and Publisher; Philip S. Collins, vice-president and treasurer of the Curtis Publishing Company; George Ethridge, Frederic W. Hume, public relations counsel; Charles C. Green, president of the Green Advertising Agency; William H. Johns, president of Batten, Barton, Durstine & Osborn; John Martin, general manager of the Curtis-Martin Newspapers, Inc.; E. V. Thompson, New York manager of the Curtis Publishing Company; C. C. Younggreen, president of the International Advertising Association; Walter Strong, publisher of the Chicago Daily News, and Colver Gordon, vice-president of the Outdoor Advertising Agency.

Gilbert T. Hodges, president of the Advertising Club, presided.

Messages regretting their inability to attend were received from Bruce Barton, Arthur Brisbane, Mr. Lorimer, and Ralph Pulitzer, editor and publisher of the New York World.

New Headquarters for National Editorial Ass'n

The headquarters of the National Editorial Association has been moved from 621-622 Merchants' National Bank building, St. Paul, to 1501 University Avenue, St. Paul.

"The association will now have ample room, and will be in better position than ever to look after the affairs of the association," says H. C. Hotaling, executive secretary. "The new office is midway between St. Paul and Minneapolis, at a favored spot."

Says Lino Metal Feeders Worth Weight in Gold

In ordering four additional ingot casting molds for his Linotype metal feeders, Erskine M. Brooks, general manager of the Masonic Home Journal, Louisville, Ky., declared:

"When it comes to efficiency, Linotype metal feeders are worth their weight in gold. Our production has increased nearly two galleys per day on each of our Linotypes."

Declares Lino Is Salvation Of Country Publisher

"A great majority of the country publishers today are Linotype users," recently stated W. A. Brundage, president of the Northeast Texas Press Association, "and this machine has been the salvation of the country publisher. The Linotype has undoubtedly saved the country press, and has made it what it is today."

Manuscripts of Great Value Missing

Six costly works disappear from International Press Exhibition at Cologne, Germany. Americans requested to be on lookout for them.

Word comes from Dr. A. Ruppel, director of the City Library and of the Gutenberg Museum at Mayence, Germany, that several valuable manuscripts are missing from the International Press Exhibition at Cologne.

"In case you are in a position to give useful information or hints leading to the recovery of the lost volumes," says Dr. Ruppel, "we request you to notify the police headquarters at Cologne, or

for pictures. Richly illustrated (water-colored pen and ink designs): 80 in the Old Testament; 19 in the New Testament; initials ornamented with small men and angels. The illustration on page 2, opposite the beginning of the text, comprises a whole page. The text is arranged in double column. Ink: brown having turned yellowish; paper also has turned yellowish. Manuscript II 64 of the City Library of Mayence. Owned formerly: By the Capuchin Convent at Mayence. Stamp: as above. (Description by Rud. Kautzsch, "Centralblatt fur Bibliothekwesen"; vol. XII, 1895; pages 61, 62).

3) *Psalterium, liturgical.* Manuscript of the 15th century (letters from 12 to 14 mm high). Parchment; small 2° (about 220 x 320 mm). Binding supposedly in smooth brown leather (of recent times). Manuscript II 141 of the City Library of Mayence. Stamp: as above.

4) *Evangelium Johannis cum glossis* (incomplete). Vol XII. Parchment. Small 4°. Binding supposedly in white leather having turned yellow. Manuscript II 15 of the City Library of Mayence. Stamp: as above.

5) Sammelband, Latin. Manuscript from the beginning of the 14th century (in the fourth place a German manuscript). At the beginning: Sermones dominicales; at the end: Regula B. Augustini exposita. Authors: Anselmus, Augustinus, Bernardus, Dionysius, Gregorius, Hugo, Petrus Lombardus, Seneca, and others. Paper (?). (Small) 4°. Manuscript 195 of the City Library of Mayence. Stamp: as above. Binding as in the preceding number.

6) *Sammelband*, 13th century. Contents: 1) Gregorius papa, Moralia. At the end: anno MCCXXV.VI.Kal.Jul. . . . . quem scribi fecit prepositus Otto.—2) Augustinus, Exhortationes de iustitia.—3) Passio Sancti Eutropii. Together; 145 pages. Parchment. (Small) 4°. Binding supposedly as Nos. 4 and 5. Manuscript II 7 of the City of Mayence. Former owner: "Monast. Sti. Mauritii in Hallis ordin. canonicor. regular". Stamp: as above.

Chicago Op Quits Keyboard To Dig for Indian Gold

"On the west bank of the Kankakee River, about ten miles from the city of Kankakee, Ill., is located a tract of land which is all that is left of a 100 acre farm," ran a story in the C. D. N. Circle, house publication of the Chicago Daily News.

"The family that owned the farm at that time made a good living on it, but the mother had a reputation for baking fine cookies. The reputation of her cookies spread to various tribes of Indians that infested that part of the country, and she had hundreds of customers among them. On the last visit of an old Indian chieftain, waving his hand toward a hill back of the old farm house, he said: 'Dear woman, if you had all the gold that is in that hill, you could shoe all your horses with silver, and you would never have to do any more baking or work.'

"This story has been handed down to the descendants of this woman, of whom Louis W. Kurth, Linotype operator of the Daily News, is one. Some time ago, Louis and his cousin, Walter Ruff, secured a lease on this ten acre tract, and started to dig for this gold a few weeks ago. They dug up crudely squared boulders, arrow heads, colored beads, and roughly carved ornaments of personal adornment. After digging a few feet more they came upon a slab with a rough looking cross upon it. That gave them more encouragement and they dug about four feet deeper. They unearthed a large quantity of broken glass and more arrow heads, then called it a day. Kurth is now organizing a company for exploration purposes, and is determined to get to the bottom of this hill. As soon as the frost is out of the ground, next spring, he will start a steam shovel on the entire hill."

Dayton Journal and Herald Installs 6 New Linotypes

The Burkam-Herrick Publishing Company, Dayton, Ohio, which publishes the Journal (morning) and Herald (evening), made a replacement in its Linotype battery recently, involving the purchase of six new Linotypes—five Model 8s and a Model 26.

Messrs. Burkam and Herrick are the owners of the two dailies, which are managed by Ralph Jones. Arza Millard is superintendent of the day side, and Jesse Pigman of the night.

FIRE in Lawrence Eagle-Tribune Brings QUICK LINOTYPE SERVICE

Six of the new Linotypes in the temporary plant

When, Wednesday, November 28, fire broke out in the Eagle-Tribune building in Lawrence, Mass., the Mergenthaler Linotype Company was right on the job prepared to render all possible service, and played an

day afternoon Mr. Flynn telephoned us specifications for six Linotypes, and the order was at once transmitted to Brooklyn.

"Although this was the eve of Thanksgiving, with a holiday scheduled for next day at the factory, Mergenthaler executives and employees worked that night and next day to get the shipment through. And they got it through.

"In addition to this, through certain officials of the Eastern Steamship Company, freight handlers were arranged for, and the entire shipment was placed on a boat Thanksgiving night and landed

rence at nine o'clock Sunday morning. To do this it was necessary for the express company to open the car at Lawrence on Sunday, and furnish a special truck for the delivery. This arrangement was made through C. H. Emery of Boston, general manager for the American Express in New England, and Mr. Balfour's office at the Grand Central Terminal in New York City."

"All of the concerns occupying the first three floors of the easterly half of the building were completely put out of business," stated the Evening Tribune the

(Continued on page ten)

Million Line Gain Celebrated in Special Edition of St. Louis Star

35,000 separate display ads carried. Circulation gain of 13,000. Linotypes and octuple press added.

"While this progress edition of the St. Louis Star is dedicated primarily to the civic and industrial progress of Greater St. Louis, it might not be inappropriate to mention the progress of the Star itself during the year since it published a similar edition," declared the St. Louis Star, November 1, 1928.

[February 4, 1929, the Star announced the installation of nine new Linotypes.]

"In this progress is found the promise of greater things for the advancement of St. Louis. That progress divides itself logically into three classes:

"First, circulation and reader influence. The readers of the Star have shown

Chapman Co. of Huntington, W. Va., Works Fast on Marshall College Sports Extra

Gets football special to stadium less than five minutes after end of game, with three-fourths of crowd still present. Special wire from field speeds play by play account to Linotypes and presses.

Less than five minutes after the timekeeper's gun signalled the close of the Marshall-Wesleyan football game at Huntington, W. Va., last Thanksgiving Day, newsboys were selling "sport extras" of the Parthenon containing the final score and a play by play account of the game, at the various entrances to the

Country Papers Must Audit Says Ole Buck

Advertisers have right to know what they are buying. Fifty Nebraska papers already have been audited, with twenty-five on waiting list. Trade surveys being developed.

By Ole Buck, Field Manager Nebraska Press Association

Certified audits of country newspaper subscription lists will answer the demand for service on the part of advertisers. Country publishers in Nebraska have recognized the need and demand for this service, and those who have joined the ranks of audited circulations have already found that it pays in direct dividends.

Advertisers have the same right to know what they are buying as any other customer. Dealers in other commodities must deliver what is claimed or lose patronage. No grocer can sell a short dozen or pound and not be called upon

way, the decks were cleared for action and the real, serious work of auditing was started. To date about fifty Nebraska newspapers have been audited. Half that many more have orders on file, and new recruits are being added constantly.

As far as the publisher is concerned, the audit requires no effort on his part. He merely signifies a desire for the service and the auditor does the rest. A professional auditor is employed, a man who has a reputation and professional standing of his own to maintain. He goes in just as a bank examiner or post-office inspector does. All records and information must be turned over to him without reservation. He proceeds to

(Continued on page three)

Editor Saves Child From Burning Hotel

Arthur M. Herndon, editor and advertising manager of the Hazard (Ky.) Herald, proved himself a hero when fire destroyed a Hazard hotel, recently. He was in his room on the third floor when the fire was discovered. In rushing down the stairs he found a child on the second floor screaming for her mother. He seized the child and escaped with her just as the stairway between the first and second floors collapsed. The child's mother was later rescued from a fourth story window. Mr. Herndon lost all of his personal belongings except the apparel he was wearing. He is a well known Kentucky and Tennessee newspaper man. Before connecting with the Hazard Herald he was with the Clarksville (Tenn.) Leaf-Chronicle, and the News-Banner of Murfreesboro, Tenn.

Lord Buys Prize Lamb At Dollar a Pound

J. M. Lord, publisher of the News at Willow Lake, S. D., was the lucky bidder for the grand champion lamb sold at auction at the American Royal Exposition at Kansas City in December.

The fact that this lamb came from the vicinity of Willow Lake prompted Mr. Lord to bid him up to one dollar a pound, live weight, and the bidding was one of the high spots of the entire show at Kansas City.

Mr. Lord had the lamb dressed and hung up in a local market, where many people admired the carcass and wanted to buy portions of it. However, Mr. Lord had other plans, and the News force had a Christmas dinner in which the champion lamb featured, and there was none to spare.

475 Columns of Advertising In Regular Issue of News

The largest regular edition ever issued by the Chicago Daily News, one of eighty pages, was issued in November. There were five sections, and they contained 409.96 columns of display advertising and 35.23 columns of classified, a total of 475.19 columns—more advertising than had ever been printed before in a single issue of the News in one day.

But a week later seventy-two pages were printed with a total of 397 columns of display advertising and thirty-six columns of classified, or a total of 433 columns.

San Francisco Bulletin Now Using Linotype Ionic

November 12 the San Francisco Bulletin came out in a new dress of Linotype Ionic. "With today's editions," stated the Bulletin, in a story headed "Bulletin Made Easier to Read by New Type," "the Bulletin has changed the type in which the body of the paper is printed, and has achieved thereby a distinct gain in legibility and clearness."

280,000 Impressions From Linotype Slugs

The Nittany Printing & Publishing Company, State College, Pa., operating a Model 8 and a Model 14, recently printed a folder direct from slugs to the extent of 280,000 impressions.

EXAMPLE 180

Advertisers have been quick to note this and to take advantage of it. The modern newspaper reader has little leisure. He doesn't read—he glimpses. Clever advertisers tell their stories in brief eyefuls. And so should clever editors.

"The main news heads used here present the 'high spots' in a single deck. A brief italicized paragraph immediately below sums up the story. The reader can tell at a glance whether or not he cares to read the story. He is not obliged to wade through several decks to make such a decision.

"Of course the particular type treatment used here is not the ultimate in modern-news-head presentation. We have purposely used type faces that are available in many newspaper plants, rather than certain other faces.

"The thing we wish to stress here is not the using of these particular faces in preference to certain others, but the serious consideration of this head plan—a single-deck head with important words emphasized, followed by a brief summing-up paragraph.

"These heads attract attention. They give the reader the gist of the story in a single eyeful.

"They save valuable space—from 2 to 3 or more inches to each head. And space is a newspaper's stock in trade—the commodity it has to sell—with circulation, of course. The space saved can be utilized for the running of additional stories or to accommodate more advertising. The saving on a dozen heads will amount to a column or more; on the heads throughout a paper, perhaps a page or even several pages, with resultant savings all along the line.

"These heads simplify the work of the copy desk by doing away with tedious letter counting and line fitting. They obviate the necessity of stringing the head along—even padding it—through several decks. The head-writer simply puts down in three or four or five lines the high spots of the story. And the writing of the summing-up paragraph calls for no letter counting or line fitting whatsoever. He simply lets it run as it will.

"The head plan suggested here is a radical departure, to be sure. But many radical changes in other fields have been made in recent years and have proved advantageous."

A somewhat simpler and cleaner looking presentation of the same general idea was introduced on the front page of the number for April,

The Modern Newspaper You Like to Read

The Linotype News

This Issue More Than Seventy Thousand

Volume VII — The Machine That Lasts — Brooklyn, New York, April, 1929 — The Service That Lasts — Number Five

Big Time Planned for N. E. A.

Yellowstone Park to be visited. Frontier Day; buffalo roundup; Indian sun dance. Party to be limited to 400. Reservation should be made early.

BY H. C. HOTALING
Executive Secretary
National Editorial Association

Those who attend the forty-fourth annual convention of the National Editorial Association, in Wyoming, this year, will have an opportunity to see a feature of the old West that they probably never will be able to witness again, in a buffalo roundup that will be staged at Roosevelt Camp on July 29.

Champion Bike Racer Is Linotype Operator

Franco Georgetti, Linotype operator and bicycle racer

Newspaper System for West Virginia Legislature

L. F. Reed, clerk of house of delegates at Charleston, institutes efficient system for publishing of daily record.

Fine One for San Antonio

A fine modern business home is being completed for the San Antonio Express and Evening News. The building, of Bedford limestone, will occupy 188 feet on Third Street and 144 feet on Avenue E. On inner walls will be murals in colors, telling, in sequence, of the making of a newspaper. Cold water will be piped to the far corners of the building, and the air will be washed and cooled. The floors will be quiet, and all rooms well lighted. A story will be published in a future issue of The Linotype News, telling, in detail, about this fine new newspaper home

Tramp Printer of Other Days Now Famous Artist

John T. Nolf of Grand Detour, Ill., wins two prizes with canvas entitled "Two Boys Plowing."

Contest

Turn to page two and read about the "How I Did It" contest to be conducted by The Linotype News.

Oriental Press Established at Princeton

3,000 Oriental and Occidental manuscripts in Garrett collection to be published, as well as many other manuscripts in other famous collections. Fund of $100,000 already raised. Six Linotypes to be used to compose fifteen different Oriental languages.

Lino Set Papers in Indiana Contest Win All Prizes

Newcastle Courier, Delphi Journal and Versailles Republican win loving cups. Several other papers receive honorable mention.

This Issue, as Usual, Composed on Linotype

Fifty Years with New Orleans Times-Picayune

Herman J. Seiferth presented with $2,000 purse on golden anniversary. Many notables gather to honor him.

Lino Set Papers in Wisconsin Show Win Most Prizes

Algoma Record-Herald declared leading weekly in state. One hundred and twelve newspapers participate in various contests.

Sets Big String of Mixed Matter on Model 26 Lino

C. Austin Edee of Lincoln Star sets 2615 lines of body matter and display heads in regular shift of eight hours.

C. A. Edee

Large Sum Raised By Boxing Meets

S. F. Stock Exchange Installs Linotypes

W. J. Sullivan with Dubuque Paper Fifty Years

Makeup foreman with Telegraph Herald presented with watch and $50 in gold by publishers and fellow workers on his half century anniversary.

Chicago J. of C. Insures Employees

Ukrainian Language Composed on Linotype

Scripps Succeeds Booth As Detroit News Head

Knight of 90 Keys Plies Trade In Many Cities of the World

C. J. Smith Receives State Appointment

Illinois State Journal Building Fine New Home

Calls Model 26 Best Head Machine

Some High Scores Rolled Up At Bowling Congress at Toledo

(Continued on page two)

(Continued on page eight)

EXAMPLE 181

1929. Members of the Bodoni family were used for heads. See Example 181.

But that February front page had stirred up a lot of interest, and already several newspapers—but no big metropolitan dailies—had tried out the suggested head plan.

In the leading editorial in the number for April, 1929, this writer stated, in part:

"That new-style head plan suggested in the February issue . . . came in for a lot of comment—and considerable emulation.

"Some people didn't like the heads, and frankly said so. But others did like them, or at least appreciated some of their merits, and put the plan to work for themselves.

"At this writing we are sure that at least eleven papers are trying out the plan. Perhaps others are experimenting with it, too.

"The eleven papers referred to are: *Park Falls* (Wis.) *Leader; Palo Alto* (Iowa) *Reporter; Tiger Cub* of Hastings, Neb.; *Valley Irrigator* of Newell, S. D.; *Burlingame* (Kan.) *Enterprise-Chronicle; Adair County Democrat,* Stilwell, Okla.; *De Smet* (S. D.) *News; Warren* (Ill.) *Sentinel-Leader; Dickey County Leader* of Ellendale, N. D.; *Auburn* (Wash.) *Globe-Republican,* and *Millersburg* (Pa.) *Sentinel.*

"Various type faces are used by these eleven papers, and of course the results vary. One of the most attractive papers headed the new way (and there are several attractive ones) is the *Auburn* (Wash.) *Globe-Republican.* It does not use different sizes of the same or related faces in a head, but sets all three of its main lines in the same size, 30-point Bodoni. The summing-up paragraph is in 14-point Bodoni Italic."

One reader of the *Linotype News* wrote that "I do not like the new style of heads. They look as if they were dug out of some backwoods weeklies of thirty or forty years ago, and I hardly think they will prove popular."

But readers of the *Park Falls* (Wis.) *Leader,* one of the eleven papers previously referred to, did like the *Leader's* new treatment. A story in the *Leader,* a week after it introduced its new heads, included these statements: "During the past week a great many have expressed approval of the new head system. Business men of the city were first to express their approval, and the *Leader* received some warm compliments on the change."

By June, 1929, the new head plan had been considerably improved, as suggested by Example 182.

The Linotype News

The Modern Newspaper You Like to Read

This Issue More Than Seventy Thousand

Volume VII | The Machine That Lasts | Brooklyn, New York, June, 1929 | The Service That Lasts | Number Six

Toronto Star Has 36 Linos In New Home

Paper occupies first five stories and three basement levels of twenty-three story Star building. Straight line production plan followed. Fred West, superintendent, employs novel means of lifting Linotypes.

Fine One for Toronto

New home of Toronto Star

All Plans Now Complete for N. E. A. Trip

Business sessions to be held at Cheyenne from July 20 to 23, followed by tour of Wyoming and Yellowstone Park. Many unusual entertainment features on program. Last call for reservations.

By H. C. Hotaling

Alabama Press In New York City

A feature of the recent trip of the Alabama Press Association was a sightseeing trip about Manhattan and Brooklyn as guests of the Mergenthaler Linotype Company. Two large buses conveyed the visitors to various points of interest. Luncheon was served in the main dining room of Linotype headquarters, in Brooklyn, and some of the guests accepted the Company's invitation to inspect the Linotype factory. The accompanying illustration pictures the visitors in front of Mergenthaler headquarters

Ole Buck Writes About Associations

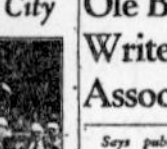

Says publishers should take press organizations seriously, and give them adequate support. Declares publishing is not profession but business.

By Ole Buck

Five Firms Order Eighty Linotypes

Chicago Daily News orders 27; MacFadden, 21; San Antonio Express, 17; New York American, 8, and Vail-Ballow, 7.

Star of "Broadway Melody" Meets a Model 26 Linotype

Lino Set Papers Win 7 Prizes In Minnesota

Dawson Sentinel and Minnesota Mascot place first in six and seven column divisions of front page makeup contest. Other papers make good showings.

Twenty of "Fifty Books of Year" Were Composed on the Linotype

By Paul A. Bennett

Jury's Task Unenviable

Caslon Leads Preferred Types

Linotype Scores New Record

Printers to Play Ball and Golf At Indianapolis

Nineteenth annual tournament of Union Printers' Baseball and Golf Association to be held in Hoosier metropolis August 23 to 30. Teams from eleven cities to play ball. Golfers may enter golf tourney from any city.

This Issue, as Usual, Composed on Linotype

Twenty Printers Buy Lowe Plant in Nashville

N. E. A. Research Department Gives Statistics on Incomes of Weeklies

Rountree of Montgomery Advertiser Proved Hero in Alabama Flood

Uses Chicago Tribune as Substitute for Prayer Rug

Memphis Press-Scimitar Adds Linotype, More Ionic

More Than Satisfied with His Display Linotypes

Advertises "Blue Streak" With Sky Writing

Dean Williams Writes Book On Press Congress of World

West Virginia Group Re-elects Tetrick President for Eighth Time

EXAMPLE 182

It had been simplified, "cleaned up." There was no mixing of different sizes or widths in first decks.

In an editorial in that issue, this writer stated, in part:

"All main news heads have been limited to one display deck and a summing-up second bank, as before, but we have kept all three of the display lines in each such head in the same size of the same type face. This simplifies the writing and casting of the headlines, and, we believe, enhances the attractiveness of the heads and of pages.

"Only three fonts were used for the two different main news heads—the larger in 30-point Cloister Bold, with summing-up bank in 10-point Cloister Bold Italic; the smaller in 24-point Cloister Bold, with summing-up bank in 10-Cloister Bold Italic. Other news and feature heads in this issue are in 14- and 24-point Cloister Bold Italic.

"We repeat here what we have stated before: That these new-style heads attract attention, save valuable space, are easy to write and to compose, and effect savings all along the line. They do away with tedious letter counting and line fitting. All three of the display lines in main news heads are set flush to run as they will, and the writing and setting of the summing-up banks are just as easy—the lines are started flush, and a bank is not limited to any certain number of lines.

"That these new-style heads appeal to editors and publishers is shown by the fact that already at least twenty papers are trying out the new heads. In addition to the eleven papers mentioned in our April issue, these nine other papers are trying out the heads:

"*La Farge* (Wis.) *Enterprise; Massillon* (Ohio) *Guide; Grantsburg* (Wis.) *Journal of Burnett County; Roosevelt Crimson* of Roosevelt High School, Oakland, Calif.; *Miller County Autogram* of Tuscumbia, Mo.; *Daily Ontario* of Belleville, Ont.; *Woodville* (Wis.) *Times; Spring Valley* (Wis.) *Sun,* and *Pocahontas* (Iowa) *Democrat.*"

By September, 1929, the point size and display value of second decks had been increased, as suggested by Example 183, with heads in Poster Bodoni, Poster Bodoni Italic and Bodoni Bold. Note, though, that only four heads on that page had as many as two decks. The twenty other heads, including the single-liners in the two boxes, were held to single decks. Advanced simplification!

The number for April, 1930, came out with a front page with simplified flush-left heads in Metroblack, and with an editorial given a four-column-wide display. See Example 184.

Turn to Page Three—
"How I Did It"

The Linotype News

This Issue More Than
Seventy Thousand

Volume VIII — *The Machine That Lasts* — **Brooklyn, New York, September, 1929** — *The Service That Lasts* — Number One

The Pittsburgh Press Now Operates Battery Of Forty-six Linotypes

Five new Model 25s recently added. Sixteen Linotypes are used for "ad" composition. Box formation of news machines speeds up production

N. E. A.

Pictured here are Past President Erwin Funk and President Lem Hall nobly supporting the adequate western sun protectors bestowed on them by the welcoming committee at Cheyenne

Pennsylvania Publishers to Audit Papers

New set up of association to be presented at next convention. Bryan gives pointers on advertising

N. E. A.

George B. Dolliver, co-publisher of the Battle Creek (Mich.) Moon-Journal, and newly elected vice-president of the N. E. A., is pictured here scanning a friendly valley in quest of buffaloes to photograph

Graphic Arts Courses at New York U.

Six classes this fall to teach type setting, printing design, layout, and history of graphic arts

Fifty-four Linotypes Operated in New Home Of Chicago Daily News

Recent order called for twenty-seven new machines—twenty-one Model 8s, five Model 14s and one Model 22. Twenty Linotypes used in adroom

MacFadden Buys New Haven Times-Union

Lino Set Papers Lead the Field In West Texas

The Providence Journal Now 100 Years Old

N. Y. Times and N. Y. American Add Linotypes

Says Linotype Has Contributed Most

Chas. Henricks Opens Auxiliary Plant

All Plants in State Soon Will Have Linos

This Issue, as Usual, Linotype Composed

Donnelley Building Wins High Praise

Clinton Herald Gives Readers Gift of Ionic

Nash Tells of Work Of German Printers

Linos Helped Build Home of Fallon Eagle

Rearranged Ad Room Speeds Production

Stamford Advocate Passes Century Mark

Enthusiastic About Lino Metal Feeder

WLS Radio Station Guarantees Its Ads

Digs Up Another Copy Of Marble 'Newspaper'

When the Flood Came Lino Service Served

EXAMPLE 183

The Linotype News

Volume VIII — Brooklyn, New York, April, 1930 — Number Seven

N. E. A. to Meet In Milwaukee June 16 to 18

To Visit Dells and Enjoy Steamboat Trip on Great Lakes — Reservations Should Be Made Early—Pfister Hotel to Be Headquarters

Milwaukee is making plans for the entertainment of members of the National Editorial Association, from June 16 to 18. Walter Dunlap is chairman of the local committee. Headquarters have been established at the Pfister Hotel, which has ample convention hall facilities, and, with other hotels in the immediate vicinity, will be able to take care of all who attend the convention. It is thought that the attendance will be the largest in many years.

Following the annual meeting, a special train will take the party to Kilbourn, where there will be an opportunity to view the Dells of the Wisconsin, nationally known for their scenic beauty. A steamboat will take the party for a trip through the winding canyons and gorges that the river for centuries has been cutting through the cliffs that rise from eighty to 100 feet above its waters.

The next step will be to Madison, the capital of the state, a city filled with interest and abounding with historic lore. More than 1,000 Indian mounds are to be found on the grounds of the Wisconsin State Hospital. Madison, itself, with its beautiful lakes, furnishes many delightful drives. The night will be spent at Madison, with headquarters at the Loraine Hotel, where the party will be guests at an evening banquet.

To Be Guests of Governor

Friday morning, June 20, the special train will leave for Kohler, where the entire party will be the guests of Gov. Walter J. Kohler.

Following the banquet and welcome by Governor Kohler, the party will take electric cars for Sheboygan. There one of the steamships of the Goodrich Steamship Company, the Alabama, will be boarded for a trip into Door County, the great tourist section. Dinner will be served on the boat, which will arrive in Sturgeon Bay the next morning.

At night the boat will be boarded at Ephraim, in the midst of a cherryland where 4,000 acres of the hillside are covered with cherry trees.

Sunday morning will find the editorial boat at Mackinac. Here there will be more to enjoy, and then, at noon, the trip will be onward to the Soo, where the most optimistic will be amazed at the immensity of the freight traffic through that great inland water channel.

Monday forenoon will be spent at the Soo, where there will be a chance to step upon Canadian soil.

Leaving Monday noon, the boat will proceed to Manitowoc, Wis., where the editors will inspect the plant of the Hamilton Manufacturing Company. A visit will also be made to an aluminum factory.

Then the trip homeward will be started, arriving in Milwaukee early Wednesday morning, so that those desiring to take trains for home can do so.

Cost of Trip Very Low

The boat trip, covering five nights on board and all meals not otherwise provided, will amount to just $50, or $15 less than the regular fare, with a few extra meals thrown in. The rail trip covering the journey to the Dells, to Madison, the return to Milwaukee and on to Kohler will cost about $6, or $4.50 less than the regular fare. On that part of the outing there will be a number of banquets and dinners as arranged by Wisconsin hosts.

The capacity of the steamship is

(Continued on page eight)

Daily Gleaner Of Kingston Has 14 Linos

Jamaica Paper Nearly Hundred Years Old Has Been Operating Mergenthalers Twenty-two Years —Managing Director Is Alert Executive

Twenty-two years ago the Daily Gleaner of Kingston, Jamaica, decided that it had set up its pages quite long enough by hand, and that the time had come to adopt the modern method of newspaper composition. Accordingly, three Linotypes were installed. Those were the days of the old high base machines, and the plant consisted of two Model 5s and one Model 4.

As happens whenever new ideas are put into practice, there were many Jeremiahs who declared the venture was doomed to failure—"the Linotype was too complicated to be practical in Jamaica; it had to be kept in a glass house; it required an almost uncanny degree of skill to operate," and so forth. But the Gleaner was not deterred by these opinions. It went straight ahead, and found from actual experience that the Linotype is a far less difficult machine to handle than was at first thought; and as for the impossibility of securing local skill to operate, that also turned out to be nothing of a problem at all.

With that experience, when the time came for improving its equipment—and the Gleaner is always improving, always doing something to make this department or that department a little more efficient—another Linotype was installed. Then later on another and another, until today the battery in the news composing room alone numbers nine, with five other Linotypes in the advertising department and the commercial printing plant. The Linotype equipment consists of seven Model 14s, five Model 8s and two Model 5s.

The accompanying picture shows some of the Linotypes in the news composing room, all electrically heated. The room has a high ceiling, is amply lighted, and is so well ventilated that it is actually the coolest part of the whole establishment.

What has happened in Linotype expansion is an indication of what has been happening in all other departments of the Gleaner's business. The management of the company is characterized by a policy of aggres-

(Continued on page three)

Its Classified, Too, Now Set in Ionic No. 5

"With today's issue of the Telegram," declared the Superior (Wis.) Telegram, March 18, "one more change is made in typographical makeup for the sake of the 100,000 readers of the Telegram.

"A new type face is being used in the classified department and in all places where a smaller type face is indicated. This type is the famous Ionic No. 5, designed by the Linotype Company to give greatest legibility.

"Two months ago the Telegram changed over its larger body type face, giving a bigger and more easily read type face to its readers. The change today is in line with the Telegram's policy of making the paper as attractive and easily read as possible, and completes the change in body type.

"Read the classified page and note the extreme readability of the type. It is achieved through a better designed type face, approved by optometrists the world over."

Linotype Sets Encouraging Pace In City of Auckland, New Zealand

"In the various issues of The Linotype News which I have received, I have noticed that little mention is made, in the general news and school notes, of places beyond the confines of the United States and Canada," writes John F. McDermott, Linotype instructor at Seddon Memorial Technical College, Auckland, New Zealand. "I have concluded that it is no fault of yours that such is the case—but that it could be accounted for by the fact that many like myself have failed to acquaint you of what is going on in other parts.

"Although New Zealand is an unknown quantity to perhaps millions, you are no doubt well aware that its million and a half inhabitants are a very up to date and progressive people, and such papers as the Auckland Star and New Zealand Herald (published in the city of Auckland—population 200,000) claim a place in the front rank of the world's best.

"The Auckland Star has a battery of thirty Linotypes, Winkler equipment in the stereo department, and four rotary presses. The circulation approximates nigh on the 50,000 mark. The issues run from twenty to thirty-two pages, according to display advertisements offering, and on Saturdays, with magazine section added, up to fifty-six pages.

"I might go on indefinitely giving items of general information relative to this 'outpost of civilization,' but I think I have, for the present, said enough on that score.

"I will now turn my attention to the matter of educational facilities provided for printers by the New Zealand Education Department. Schools of printing are in operation at Auckland (North Island), and Christchurch (South Island). The Christchurch school was started some time in advance of the one at Auckland. Just over five years ago Linotype instruction was added to the existing class at Christchurch.

"In 1925, compositors', letterpress machinists', and Linotypists' classes were opened at the Seddon Memorial Technical College at Auckland, the equipment comprising three Model 1 Linotypes and six dummy keyboards. This equipment has been added to and now consists of six Linotypes, two complete power driven Linotype keyboards and six dummy keyboards. I have obtained very satisfactory results during my five years as instructor.

"I have noted a request over your leader columns for samples of machine composition, and I am enclosing one that I set up several years ago. I leave it to you to pass judgment after noting particulars typewritten."

The specimen referred to was an ingenious tint block for checks composed of Linotype border units.

"Personally," continues Mr. McDermott, "I subscribe to your motto: 'The Linotype Way is the Only Way.'"

Typographic Sanity

AN EDITORIAL

AFTER AN ORGY of tangled type design, a weary printing industry is shaking its head and asking, "Whither are we bound?"

The descent was easy; from black to blacker, from fanciful to grotesque, from freaky to freakier, the very depths have been plumbed; but when the tastes of printer, customer, reader are all thoroughly debauched, when the ultimate in blackness, in illegibility, in riotous disorder has been achieved—

—Then to seek the return to regions of calm, ordered sanity; to reaccustom our ink sated, jazz jaded senses to a normal scale of values; this is labor—and this is the path that lies just ahead of the users of type.

The present wave of reaction against the excesses of the past few years has been inevitable. Throughout this mad era, the Linotype organization has pleaded for moderation; for the guiding hand of good taste and good sense in the laudable quest for freshness of expression. In the face of insistent demands from many of its customers for surrender to the vagaries of the moment, it has strived to maintain its policy of typographic sincerity and to issue only type faces of lasting worth.

It would have been a simple matter for the Company to design and cut matrices that would sell. It took far more vision to refuse to issue worthless types merely for profit, and instead to present only those faces which are fundamentally sound in design and character, and which will be a credit to the publisher who uses them.

This policy is not new with Linotype. It goes back to the very beginning of the Company's typographic activity. It has been restated and reiterated frequently in many Linotype publications during the last fifteen years. It is summarized and reviewed again in the current issue of *The Linotype Magazine*, now being mailed, which will reach you shortly. Read this issue carefully. We believe it will be well worth your time, in this crucial period of typographic tribulation.

Press Readers Praise Linotype Ionic No. 5

March 3 the Atlantic City (N. J.) Press stated: "Over 100,000 readers of the Press and the Evening Union, with their gross circulation of around 45,000, are sitting as a jury today to determine the accuracy of the newspapers' claim that they are now among the easiest to read newspapers obtainable.

"Readers have eyes for which newspapers expecting to be read should show the utmost consideration. Hence the effort which the Press-Union papers make beginning today. . . Most of the type in the whole plant, from the smallest to the largest faces, has been thrown out to make room for a new family of type which experts say is the easiest to read in existence, and therefore the best for the human eye. It is the Ionic No. 5, as trade names go, and with it the Press hopes to make itself easy to read for all members of the family, young and old, and in any place from the bounding trolley car to poorly lighted rooms."

Next day, March 4, the Union declared: "The easier to read, more attractive Press has made a hit.

"Eye glasses came off and eyebrows went up yesterday when this paper appeared at the breakfast table in the new typographical dress, and without exception there was praise for Ionic No. 5, the latest spring style in newspaper print.

"The new, clearer type received the warmest praise from persons with imperfect sight, eye specialists and oculists. Bankers, merchants, professional men and a whole cross section of the population of Atlantic City joined in congratulating the Press for giving its readers a paper unexcelled in legibility by even the most carefully printed magazines."

Then followed statements of enthusiastic approval from half a hundred readers of the Press.

Dean Williams Named Head of Missouri U.

Dr. Walter Williams, dean of the school of journalism of the University of Missouri, has been elected president of the university. He will continue his relationship with the school of journalism, retaining the title of dean of the school. Prof. Frank L. Martin, who has been a member of the faculty of the school of journalism since its organization, in 1908, has been made associate dean.

Tourneys at Pittsburgh August 24 to 30

The twentieth annual tournament of the Union Printers' International Baseball League and Golf Association will be held at Pittsburgh, August 24 to 30, inclusive.

The Hotel Webster Hall has been selected as headquarters by the Pittsburgh Typographical Athletic Association.

St. Louis Star Buys Site for New Plant

Property on which a new plant will be erected for the St. Louis Star has been acquired at Twelfth Boulevard and Washington Avenue, St. Louis. The present building, at Twelfth Boulevard and Olive Street, opposite the Post-Dispatch, was bought by the Union Electric Light and Power Company. As the Star's lease does not expire for almost three years, there is ample time in which to have a new plant constructed.

Two Prague Reporters Pass Through Chicago

Jerry Formanek and Charles Tulka, each twenty-four years old, a pair of happy go lucky newspaper reporters from Prague, Czechoslovakia, were visitors in Chicago in February. They are traveling around the world.

More Than 40 Papers Added To Ionic List

Forty-three Other Publications Either Should Have Been Listed in the March Issue or Since Have Adopted Easy to Read Type Face—List Nears 1900

In connection with the running, in the March number of The Linotype News, of a list of more than 1800 newspapers using Linotype Ionic No. 5, we ran this statement: "If the names of any Ionic set papers you know about do not appear on this list, we shall appreciate your writing us about them."

As was to have been expected, in a list so large, several omissions and other errors occurred.

As we go to press with this issue of The Linotype News, the names of at least forty-three more newspapers should be added to the ever growing list of Ionic users. The names of some of these papers were omitted by mistake from our previous listing. Other papers among these forty-three have added Ionic since that March listing appeared.

Here are the forty-three:

Athens (Ala.) Alabama Courier
Clinton (Ark.) Democrat
Dierks (Ark.) Banner
Hope (Ark.) News
Van Buren (Ark.) Press-Argus
Gonzales (Calif.) Tribune
Placentia (Calif.) Courier
Roseville (Calif.) Press
Ocala (Fla.) Daily Banner
Lihue (Hawaii) Garden Island
Louisville (Ky.) Times
Sturgis (Ky.) News
Nashua (Mont.) Independent
Albion (Neb.) Argus
Atlantic City (N. J.) Press-Union
Beverly (N. J.) Banner
Keyport (N. J.) Weekly.
Newark (N. J.) Star-Eagle
Plainfield (N. J.) Courier-News
Bayville (N. Y.) Times
Geneseo (N. Y.) Livingston County Leader
Glen Cove (N. Y.) Echo
Glen Cove (N. Y.) Record
Peekskill (N. Y.) Star
Nunda (N. Y.) News
Oyster Bay (N. Y.) News
Bryson City (N. C.) Times
Oxford (N. C.) Public Ledger
Reidsville (N. C.) Review
Leedey (Okla.) Times
Madill (Okla.) Record
Coudersport (Pa.) Potter Enterprise
Millersville (Pa.) Eastern Farmer
Nanty-Glo (Pa.) Journal
Nazareth (Pa.) Item
Alpena (S. D.) Journal
Hitchcock (S. D.) News-Leader
Bruceton (Tenn.) Twin City Times
Sequin (Texas) Bulletin
Bowling Green (Va.) Caroline Progress
Harrisonburg (Va.) News-Record
Luray (Va.) Courier
Webster Springs (W. Va.) Republican

This Issue, as Usual, Linotype Composed

This issue of The Linotype News, as usual, was composed entirely on the Linotype, with the exception of a few large display headings in some of the advertisements. All other lines—body matter, heads, advertisements, rules, borders, ornaments—were produced the Linotype way.

See page four, "Makeup of This Issue."

Shaffer Establishes Lecture Course at Yale

John C. Shaffer, publisher of the Chicago Evening Post and a number of other newspapers, has established at the Yale divinity school a foundation the income from which will be used to support a lecture course on "The Life, Character and Teachings of Jesus."

The foundation is in memory of his son, Kent Shaffer, a Yale graduate, who died in 1925.

Daily News of New York Has Model Plant

Move from Old to New Quarters Made in Record Time—Ingenious Models Used in Laying Out Departments—Thirty Linotypes Operated

One of the largest moving jobs in New York in recent years was accomplished over a weekend when the New York Daily News moved from its downtown plant to its fine new $10,000,000 home on East Forty-second Street.

J. W. Barnhart

The new home is L-shaped, with a thirty-six story tower and a horizontal arm nine stories high. That horizontal section was built for the use of the publication, and has been equipped with $1,250,000 worth of new machinery and furniture. The tower structure forms an office building.

The executive offices of the News are on the eighth floor of the nine story wing.

In the ninth floor space occupied by Liberty a suite of offices has been provided for Capt. J. M. Patterson, editor of the News. Col. Robert R. McCormick, editor of the Chicago Tribune, will occupy offices on the twenty-first floor of the main building, where his paper will maintain its New York headquarters.

Private offices of Roy C. Holliss, general manager; Clarence Worden, assistant to Mr. Holliss; John W. Barnhart, business manager, and F. M. Flynn, assistant to Mr. Barnhart, are grouped at one end of the eighth floor, with a private reception room.

Frank Hause is managing editor; Harvey Duell is city editor.

The Linotypes were moved intact, packed in specially constructed steel crates. They were lowered out of third story windows of the downtown plant, and shipped uptown without being disassembled. Rubber tires placed on the floor of the moving trucks deadened road shocks.

Equipment from the engraving shop was carried to the new building in the same manner. This material was hoisted out of fifth story windows. The majority of the typesetting machinery was not moved until the latest moment possible. Edward J. Duffy, mechanical superintendent, directed the work.

Thirty Linotypes are now in operation on the sixth floor of the new building, and room for the erection of twelve more is provided. Thirteen new makeup tables have replaced old ones. The new tables are marked by the absence of all overhead accessory racks. Slugs, leads, and rules are kept in spaces below the working level.

The composing room extends across the width of the "L" and the light coming through great plate-glass windows is supplemented by banks of Cooper-Hewitt daylight lamps.

Several departures in composing room equipment are evident in the News plant. The most novel of these is a copy marking desk resembling a regular editorial copy desk. It is near the ad foreman's table and is used for marking type and layout indications on advertising copy. From six to twelve markers are on duty at one time. The head marker sits in the center and passes out copy much as the head of a city room copy desk. The second interesting arrangement is the location of a telegraph instrument on the composing room floor for receiving late racing and sports results and late news flashes.

Separate locker and wash rooms are provided for each mechanical department. Automatic ventilation carries off all fumes from all mechanical departments.

The fifth floor is reserved entirely for paper storage. There 8,440 tons can be stored. Rolls are delivered at street level, conveyed on a gravity roller track to a special elevator which lifts them to their storage space. There they are carried on trucks to their proper places. The trucks lift the rolls to a three high tier themselves. A second elevator drops the paper to the reel room. Together with space available on other floors, 30,000 square feet can be devoted to paper storage.

The huge pressroom, with space for seventy-six units of straightline presses, is housed on the extra sized third floor. That room is twenty-four feet high and has an area of 30,458 square feet. These measure-

(Continued on page five)

Printing Engineers Recommend Adoption of Definite Standards

April 4, as a prelude to the fiftieth anniversary meeting of the American Society of Mechanical Engineers, the printing industries division of the society held an all day meeting in the auditorium of the Westinghouse Lighting Institute, Grand Central Palace, New York City. Edward Pierce Hulse, president of Crittenden & Hulse, was general chairman. The chairman for the afternoon session was John Clyde Oswald, managing director of the New York Employing Printers' Association. J. W. Rockefeller, Jr., engineer with the Edgar C. Ruwe Company, presided at the evening session.

The first speech of the afternoon was by Samuel P. Weston, specialist in newspaper buildings and mechanical layouts, and dealt with "Engineering Research and the Publishing Industry." Mr. Weston said that engineering and research service is worthy of more definite consideration by the printing and publishing industry. He pointed out that engineering research had been responsible for the application of the sequence theory of plant layout to newspaper plants.

The second speaker was Hadar Ortman, director of operation and finance for the Meredith Publishing Company, Des Moines, Iowa. His subject was "Printing Plant Operation Without Alibis—Is It Possible?" His recommendations for the improvement of printing plant operation were as follows: Train each job holder in his tasks; adopt standards for materials and supplies; place definite responsibility on every worker; use specialists when necessary; functionalize certain operations, such as material handling and cleaning of presses; use controls—production follow up, quality checking, and cost analysis.

Samuel G. Hibben, manager of the commercial engineering department of the Westinghouse Lamp Company, Bloomfield, N. J., spoke interestingly on "The Engineering of Light in a Printing Plant." The last speaker of the afternoon was H. R. Lewis, general manager of the W. B. Conkey Company, Hammond, Ind. He discussed "Production Engineering in the Printing Plant."

Those who addressed the evening session were W. L. Churchill, engineer-economist, on "The Printing Engineer and Printing Profit"; Howard Chapman, and Ernest A. Barvoets, vice-president of the J. B. Lyon Company, Albany, on that modern plant, and O. J. Hutchinson, superintendent of the mechanical division of the MacLean Publishing Company, Toronto, on "The Printing Plant Engineer and His Profitable Work."

EXAMPLE 184

By that time many more newspapers—but no metropolitan dailies—had adopted flush-left heads, among them the *Livermore* (Calif.) *Herald*. M. R. Henry of that paper had written this writer, in part, as follows:

"Immediately upon adopting this head, there was a favorable reaction on the part of our readers, who noticed the change to a far greater degree than we had anticipated. We find that the head-writer's job is now a real joy, instead of being a nerve-racking task, as it had been previously. The time in writing heads has been cut fifty per cent, and the composition time about thirty-three and a third per cent."

The number for November, 1930, came out with the front page suggested by Example 185.

That front page (which was suggested by F. T. Denman) threw front-page traditions to the winds and made its own rules as it went along. It presented its main stories under alternating dark and light display lines ranging from six to two columns in width and each followed by a single-column single-deck drop in a smaller size of the same dark or light type face. And an editorial was displayed in a double-column box at the upper left of the page.

"Certain principles that have grown up round newspaper makeup through the years, and to many newspaper men have become almost sacred, were deliberately set aside," this writer stated editorially. "The typographic slate was rubbed clean of any hampering 'must nots,' and the building of the page proceeded along lines of its own.

"Those four display lines at the top of the page were planned to present four important stories prominently—more prominently than would be possible with single-column or even double-column heads. The chief display in each head is presented horizontally and without interruption. Each drop from each display line appears at the right—a point easily and naturally reached by the reader accustomed to reading from left to right. The eyes do not have to travel back and forth several times to comprehend the gist of the statements displayed. Jim dashes, so long considered necessary by many makeup men, have been omitted altogether. Only one drop is used with each display line. No head consists of more than two decks.

"The main editorial in this issue begins at the top of the front page, to the left, in a two-column box. Its raised position gives it more prominence than it would have below the nameplate.

BROOKLYN, NOVEMBER, 1930

THE LINOTYPE NEWS

When Selling Regains Its Courage

AN EDITORIAL by MERLE THORPE

In "Nation's Business," Official Magazine of the United States Chamber of Commerce

IS OUR vaunted American selling only a fair-weather phenomenon? Has it no stamina? Does it cave in, crumple up and take the count at the first blow?

It would seem so.

For years the world has watched with amazement, not unmixed with envy, the selling forces of America in action. We have modestly acknowledged the applause. We knew we were good.

And we were. American selling was hard-hitting, tireless, resourceful, enthusiastic. It not only created demands but it helped buyers to find the means to satisfy those demands. It raised standards of living overnight, and in the joy of accomplishment it sang as it worked.

Came the stock-market squall of last October. Hesitation. Overcaution. Pessimism.

(Continued on page three)

Twenty-three Linotypes in New Home of San Francisco News

New Twelve Unit, Three Folder High Speed Press in Operation—Most Other Equipment Also Is Right Up to Present Minute

SAN FRANCISCO.—Completion of the News Building in the heart of this city's downtown shopping district gives the News, a Scripps-Howard paper, one of the finest publishing plants in the United States. Purchase of the building was necessary to provide much needed floor space for the rapidly growing News.

The steel frame and concrete structure is six stories high. It has a seventy-five foot frontage at 812 Mission Street, near Fourth Street, and a depth of 175 feet to Jessie Street.

During the last quarter century the News has been housed in a plant in this city's light industrial district. As additional space was needed, annexes were constructed. Last fall the last available adjoining space was built upon. The space gained was not sufficient for the needed expansion, so plans for a new building were ordered.

After plans had been drawn and work was about to start, W. N. Burkhardt, editor, and J. L. Cauthorn, business manager, purchased the modern building that had been occupied about four years by the Bulletin, which ceased publication August 28, 1929.

The building was entirely remodeled and refinished to suit the News plan of publication. The move from the old structure to the new was made without missing or even delaying a single edition.

The basement of the new building is used for storing paper, for heating equipment and for two huge electric control panel rooms.

On the main floor is the business office. The display advertising department is on a mezzanine floor above the business office. The mail rooms and the pressrooms are on the main floor in the rear of the business office.

The editor's office, editorial rooms, library, art, photo and engraving rooms adjoin on the second floor. The national advertising department, the composing room and the stereotyping department are on the third floor. The business manager's offices, the classified advertising and the circulation departments are on the fourth floor.

(Continued on page five)

Kansas City Star Completes Half Century of Service

Much Civic Betterment Brought About by Paper Founded by William R. Nelson—Many Famous Men Got Training with It

KANSAS CITY, Mo.—The Star of this city reached its fiftieth birthday September 18 and celebrated the occasion by mailing to every subscriber a duplicate of the first copy of the Star, issued September 18, 1880. Originally a four page, six day paper, the Star now publishes evening, morning and Sunday editions. The daily editions frequently exceed forty pages, and the Sunday, 100 pages.

GEORGE B. LONGAN

Only one small press was required to print the entire circulation fifty years ago; today, thirty-six press units of the high speed type are used.

Fewer than 10,000 papers were sold or distributed at first. The circulation today finds the combined evening and morning editions close to 600,000, and the Sunday edition exceeds 300,000. More than twice as much newsprint is used in a day now as was used in an entire year a half century ago. Incidentally, the Star installed entirely new press equipment within the last two years at a cost of approximately one million dollars. The average number of persons on the payroll fifty years ago was thirty-two. The small army required to produce and distribute the Star now totals 7,000 in all departments.

It is interesting to note that whereas originally two men set the advertisements, at present sixty to eighty men are required.

Forty-four Linotypes Operated

The Star's big composing room has forty-four Linotypes, and there is a force day and night of 250 employees.

William Rockhill Nelson founded the Star. From the first, according to Henry J. Haskell, Nelson "made the Star an intensely human publication. It did not slight important news. But, in addition, it featured news of interest to the home—house planning, gardens, interior decorating, cooking,

(Continued on page two)

Buffalo Evening News Enters Fifty-first Year

Special Section Put Out on Golden Anniversary Set in 8 Point Linotype Textype—Many Headlines in Linotype Cloister

BUFFALO, N. Y.—Observing the fiftieth anniversary of its establishment as a daily, the Evening News of this city issued a golden anniversary edition Saturday, October 11, which served not only as a history of the publication but also traced the progress of Buffalo.

Typographically different from its usual editions, the anniversary supplement was prepared in 8 Point Linotype Textype for body matter. Headlines up to and including eighteen point were set in Linotype Cloister. The composition and makeup were supervised by William Obenaur, superintendent of the composing room. Because many readers would want to save the edition, a special grade of paper was used.

The Evening News is an outgrowth of the Sunday News of this city, launched in 1873 by John B. Adams and Edward H. Butler. Mr. Butler had been connected with the Le Roy Gazette, Scranton Times and Scranton Free Press. October 10, 1880, this announcement appeared in the Sunday News: "We are satisfied, after a thorough canvass of the field, that Buffalo needs a bright, wide awake, sparkling evening paper, and with tomorrow we shall commence the publication of the Buffalo Evening News."

Not long ago the Evening News established its own radio station. Its powers of expansion have been tested to the utmost in the last sixteen years. During that period, in buildings and equipment alone, the plant of the News has been nearly doubled in size. Whereas in its first few years the paper consumed only 1300 pounds of newsprint daily, the present figure is 150,000 pounds. At one time a half unit press was employed. Now thirty press units are used. Thirty Linotypes are operated.

Among the veterans with the paper are Jerry Smith, formerly composing room foreman but now proofreader, fifty years with the paper; Frank Davis, former circulation manager, now in charge of collections, forty-six years; Louis Konrad, superintendent of News building, forty-five years; John W. Rosenbach, mechanical superintendent and production manager, forty-four years, and Julius Ritter, formerly composing room foreman but now in charge of the copycutting desk in the composing room.

When Mr. Rosenbach first came to the News it was printed four pages at a time by a four cylinder press powered by a little steam engine. His first job was to learn to run this engine. The first Linotype installed by the paper, in 1892, was operated by a belt that ran from a shafting that in turn was powered by a steam engine.

An amusing reminiscence of Mr. Davis concerns the first automobile truck that carried copies of the paper. It had no reverse gears and could not be backed. "If it was desired to turn the thing around in a hurry, a couple of men would lift the rear and carry it to the desired angle."

New Building for New York Telegram

West Street Structure to Cost Million and Half and to House Another Million and Half in New Equipment Throughout

Architect's drawing of new home for the New York Telegram

Because its circulation and advertising linage have been increasing with amazing rapidity since purchase by Scripps-Howard, in 1927, the New York Telegram has under construction a new $1,500,000 building in West Street, between Park Place and Barclay Street. The building, constructed of steel and concrete and modern in design, will rise six to ten stories and cover half a block.

ROY W. HOWARD

An additional $1,500,000 will go into new equipment. There will be sixteen units of press equipment in the new building, to be run in conjunction with twelve units in the Telegram's west side plant, at Thirty-fourth Street and Tenth Avenue, and sixteen units in its east side plant, at 305 East Forty-fifth Street. On the east side the Telegram has stereotyping, fudge and circulation departments. By means of its auxiliary plants the paper improves its coverage, particularly on items like up to the minute sporting results.

Three floors and a basement, comprising an area of approximately 100,000 square feet, will be occupied by the Telegram in its West Street plant. The basement will be used for paper storage. The street floor will be devoted to press equipment and the circulation department. This floor will be designed with a view to facilitating fast delivery of printed papers from presses to trucks. Papers will be carried to the delivery room by a conveyor system, with a haul of less than fifteen feet. This room will take practically the whole front on West Street, about 180 feet.

The composing, stereotype, and engraving rooms will be on the second floor. According to the Scripps-Howard News, the composing department "will contain all new and augmented machinery for the setting of type in all its branches."

In the stereotype department "new automatic equipment will cast the plates for the presses, these plates being automatically dropped to the pressroom floor, directly underneath.

"New equipment will make possible the sending of press plates to the west side plant quicker than the present system of sending mats, thereby insuring faster delivery of papers in the Pennsylvania, Times Square, and upper west side districts."

The editorial and advertising departments will be on the third floor of the Telegram's new building.

Stone Retires After 50 Years with Chicago News

Cousin of Melville Stone Has Trained Many Newspaper Executives and Has Perfected Several Inventions for Newspaper Use

Fifty years ago a husky youth of twenty-five stepped into the plant of a struggling young newspaper. He fired the boiler, operated the steam engine and ran the press. With two helpers he got out the entire edition. Today, a virile man of seventy-five, he sits in an office from which he is in touch with hundreds of workmen, while roaring presses near by turn out every minute more papers than a whole day's issue amounted to when he began his labors.

IRVING I. STONE

This romance of personal loyalty and achievement coupled with modern industry centers about Irving I. Stone, mechanical superintendent of the Chicago Daily News, who entered the employ of the paper August 13, 1880, and has been with it ever since. His completion of half a century of unique and distinguished service is marked by his retirement from active duty "with

(Continued on page two)

'Journalism Best University'—Finley

But N. Y. Times Editor Also Advises Newspaper Aspirants to Study Shorthand and Typewriting

"If a young man has a strong inclination to be a journalist and a manifest aptitude, he should turn his whole effort toward preparing for this vocation and then stick to it."

So declared John H. Finley, editor of the New York Times, in a radio talk in a vocational guidance series.

"And the preparation should not be a narrow one," continued Mr. Finley. "There is no occupation that demands a broader basic preparation or that gives one a better opportunity to develop oneself through the vocation in which he does, or tries to do, his share of the world's work and earns his living.

"It is the best university in the world in which to study and make the most of oneself, as well as the most influential university in which to teach, if indeed one is fitted to gather or interpret the news by which the world is made new every morning. In order to do this, and be this, a journalist must know the past 'like a book,' for without a knowledge of the past one cannot know the significance of what is coming up in the present. The journalist is the historian of the present tense, but the present grows out of the past. All the past is indeed in the present, if one has the discernment to see it.

"And the journalist must be able to tell what he knows. This means that he must know the meaning of words and not only their meaning but their 'mass' impressions when put into cold type. To be a master of words, one must be a student of words and a lover of words. If it be true that 'words are the daughters of men,' while deeds are 'the sons of heaven,' it is to be remembered that it is by the daughters of men that the sons of heaven get born. 'All the good or bad that gets done in this world is done by words.' It is through words that the individual enters into the race mind. It is through words that he makes his own life useful to the world.

"One cannot be too broadly informed for this vocation. Nothing is wasted. All is grist that comes to the journalist's mill. I have often spoken of the greatest of managing editors within my knowledge, who, when the tomb of Tut-Ankh-Amen was opened, was prepared to enter with the archeologist; who, when Einstein announced his theory, had some notion of what the great physicist was saying in his formulas, and who, when the discovery of a new planet was reported, was able to follow the astronomer's computations. Baseball championships and presidential election figures were also within his range. Nothing in the universe was foreign to his interest. My point is that one who looks forward to journalism should first of all have a foundation wide enough to take in the world and strong enough to support a structure as high as human thought can go.

"This will seem an exclusive sort of invitation to the vocation of journalist, but it should invite only the best. The first obligation of a man is to find a vocation which 'puts him on his mettle by challenging his skill.'

"To this rather idealistic advice, I should add this practical suggestion: Learn stenography and typewriting. They will stand you in better stead than the 'case' which has now given way to the Linotype."

Now Is Time to Modernize

This Issue, As Usual, Linotype Composed

This issue of The Linotype News, as usual, was composed entirely on the Linotype, with the exception of a few large display headings in some of the advertisements. All other lines—body matter, heads, advertisements, rules, borders, ornaments—were produced the Linotype way.

See page four, "Makeup of This Issue."

Linotype Set Paper Wins in Iowa Contest

IOWA CITY, Iowa.—The Bremer County Independent and Waverly Republican, Waverly, Iowa, Linotype composed, was declared the best weekly newspaper in Iowa and awarded a silver cup at the fall newspaper conference here. The paper scored ninety-five out of a possible 100 points, receiving a perfect score in nine of the eleven classifications. The score sheet included such points as use of headlines, coverage of territory, front page makeup, number and kind of cuts used, editorial page, farm page, advertising makeup, and so forth. J. F. Grawe is editor and publisher of the prize winning paper.

Post-Dispatch Has Fine Auxiliary Plant

ST. LOUIS.—An auxiliary publishing plant housing rotogravure and printing equipment has been established by the Post-Dispatch, at an investment of about $500,000, to provide outlying districts with earlier delivery of papers. Floor space in the new plant amounts to 55,000 square feet. The new plant, which also has eight units of presses, is three and a half miles from the central plant.

So States Col. McCormick of Chicago Tribune in Talk on "How To Bring Back Good Business"

Speaking on "How to Bring Back Good Business," at a luncheon of the Kiwanis Club at the Hotel Sherman, Chicago, recently, Col. Robert R. McCormick, editor and publisher of the Chicago Tribune, drew a pointed parallel between conditions today and those that existed in 1893.

"I hardly think you will find a manufacturer today who will say that his factory is ideal in theory and perfect in equipment," said Colonel McCormick. "I am frank to say ours is not and has not been. And we are acting upon that theory. In New York, where we publish a newspaper, we have only just completed an entirely new building, somewhat along the line of and certainly analogous to the Tribune Tower and plant in Chicago.

"We bought a new garage, bringing the garage something like three-quarters of a mile nearer to the newspaper plant than the old garage, and bought it on very satisfactory terms.

"Here we have acquired another piece of real estate, some 400 by 600 feet in extent. We have installed paper handling machinery. We are just completing the installation of a new printing press which, the manufacturer assures us, is at least twenty-five per cent more efficient than our old equipment, and, assuming that is correct and assuming that now is the most opportune time to buy machinery, we intend to fit up the Tribune throughout with new press equipment.

"The English newspapers are far ahead of the American newspapers in the quality of the paper they print on. Just how they make that paper, we don't know, but we are going to send over and find out. In the meantime we are improving the product by every method known to us. We are also trying to develop color printing in the daily papers."

F. E. Wilder Appointed Chairman of Pan-Graphic Cooperation Committee

The appointment has been announced by the printing industries division of the American Society of Mechanical Engineers of Floyd E. Wilder as chairman of the committee on Pan-Graphic Cooperation. This committee will keep in touch with the score or more of national and international organizations connected with all branches of the printing industry, and will work out plans of cooperation wherever possible.

In 1907 Mr. Wilder went into the plant of P. F. Collier & Son Company as assistant superintendent, later being made superintendent, and then director of production and assistant to the president. For several years he had been with Hearst publications, engaged in consulting and research work on mechanical production. Mr. Wilder has had a long connection with the mechanical side of printing and has designed several machines used in the industry. He was the first vice-president of the New York Club of Printing House Craftsmen, and its second president. He has also taken a prominent part in employers' organizations, serving as secretary of the Employing Printers' Association for three years, and as president of the Printers' League. He is a member of the A. S. M. E.

Edward Pierce Hulse, chairman of the printing industries division, announces that the plans for cooperation of all printing organizations in the second conference of the technical experts in the printing industry will be worked out through Mr. Wilder.

The second conference, originally scheduled for November 18 and 19 at Washington, D. C., has been postponed until February or March. Many of those who were to make laboratory demonstrations of modern processes or exhibits of the latest mechanical appliances have expressed the desire for more time, to include the most recent devices.

At this conference papers will be presented discussing technical and engineering developments in printing, to be accompanied by laboratory demonstrations and working exhibits of the latest devices and machinery. These will include machines effecting precision methods, the pre-makeready appliances, air conditioning apparatus, chromium plating, etc.

Milton A. McRae Passes On

Was Counselor and Guide of Scores of Men in Big Organization He Helped to Found Years Ago

"Starting in the typical American boy fashion—literally sweeping out a newspaper business office, a score of which he was one day to dominate—Colonel McRae moved steadily to the top of his profession, and twenty-five years ago enjoyed (and the word is used literally) one of the widest acquaintances of any newspaper man in America," stated the New York Telegram editorially, October 13, referring to the passing of Col. Milton A. McRae, co-founder with E. W. Scripps of the Scripps-McRae (now Scripps-Howard) newspapers.

"The antitheses of each other, the late E. W. Scripps and Colonel McRae formed a perfect partnership. The former devoted his life to editorial policies formulated in the interests of the masses, but was less democratic in dealing with the individual. . .

"Colonel McRae, on the other hand, loved to mingle in terms of personal intimacy with his friends and associates, and had a genius for locating and extolling their individual strengths and virtues.

"Ever an optimist and a great believer in the asset value of youth in journalism, Colonel McRae was for twenty-five years following his retirement the chief friend, counselor and guide of scores of men in the organization he had helped to found. . . .

"He was urbane, a cultured gentleman, a traveled and well informed man. Yet none of this describes the personal charm of the man, his stimulating personality, which was a spark that set fire to the imagination of scores whom he delighted to call 'his boys.'

"Milton McRae directly did much to make American journalism better and cleaner for his having been an important factor in it. His indirect contribution through the inspiration he furnished and the courage he inspired in 'his boys' has proved great and in the years to come will prove even greater."

New Auxiliary Plant For Chicago News

The Chicago Daily News has begun the construction of an auxiliary printing plant to facilitate the distribution of papers to the south and southwest sides. The structure, which will represent an investment of more than $500,000, will be at West Fifty-sixth Street and the tracks of the Baltimore and Ohio Railroad, just east of Oakley Avenue. It will be three stories high and will contain 15,700 square feet of floor space. The plant will contain fifteen press units capable of printing 40,000 eighty page papers an hour, and will make it possible for residents of the south and southwest sides to obtain their copies of the Daily News many minutes ahead of existing delivery schedules.

Copley Gives Hospital More Than $2,000,000

AURORA, Ill.—Col. Ira C. Copley, publisher of the Beacon-News of this city and of other papers in Illinois and California, has given to the Aurora Hospital Association a building fund of $1,000,000, a site valued at $150,000 and endowment of $1,295,000. The gifts are pursuant to an agreement entered into in 1927. Announcement of the gifts was made by G. A. Anderson, president of the Aurora Hospital Association.

Linotype Set Paper Wins in Louisiana

BASTROP, La.—The Morehouse Enterprise, composed the Linotype way here, has been awarded the loving cup offered by the Monroe (La.) Morning World to the paper adjudged the outstanding weekly in northern Louisiana. C. G. Scott is publisher of the Monroe Enterprise, and Isaac Chapman is editor.

Mayborn Now B. M. Of Baltimore Papers

BALTIMORE.—Ward C. Mayborn, publisher of the Temple (Texas) Telegram and formerly business manager of the Houston (Texas) Press, has been appointed business manager of the News and American of this city, according to an announcement by Col. Frank Knox, general manager of Hearst newspapers.

Mr. Mayborn succeeds Norman H. Hill, who has been transferred to the Detroit Times as business manager. For more than thirty years Mr. Mayborn was with Scripps-Howard newspapers in various capacities. For some time he was general manager of the southwest group of Scripps-Howard papers. When that position was abolished in January, 1928, he became business manager of the Houston Press. In 1929 he resigned from the Scripps-Howard syndicate to devote his time to the management of the Temple Telegram, which he purchased in October of that year. He has left his son in charge of the Temple paper.

Cincinnati Post To Improve Plant

CINCINNATI.—The Post of this city plans improvements to its plant aggregating $600,000. An additional story will be added, and the second floor will be remodeled to give more space to the composing room and stereotyping departments. New press units will be installed.

News Syndicate, N. Y., Adds Six Linotypes

Six Linotypes—five Model 8s and a Model 21 display machine—have been added by the News Syndicate Company, Inc., 220 East Forty-second Street, New York City.

Experts to Discuss Presses

Noted Engineers to Take Part in Program Scheduled by A. S. M. E. for December 2 to 5

One of the most helpful meetings for printing press owners, operators and designers will be, it is expected, the symposium on the engineering and operating features of flat bed cylinder presses planned by the American Society of Mechanical Engineers. At the annual meeting of the society in New York from December 2 to 5, the printing industries division will have morning and afternoon sessions on Friday, December 5, in the main auditorium of the Engineering Societies Building, 29 West Thirty-ninth Street. There will be addresses by officials and engineers of five leading makers of this type of press. All interested are invited.

Edward Pierce Hulse, who heads the division of printing engineers, announces that the meeting has been planned by Fred S. English, who will be the chairman. The presiding officer for the morning session will be Ernest F. Trotter, managing editor of Printing, New York City, and the afternoon session will be presided over by M. C. Robbins, president of the American Printer, New York City.

"Some Problems in Standardization" will be discussed by Fred S. English, chief engineer, Babcock Printing Press Manufacturing Company, New London, Conn.

"Design of the New Harris Automatic Two Color Flat Bed Press," by Alfred S. Harris, vice-president in charge of engineering, Harris-Seybold-Potter Company, Cleveland.

"Sizes and Tolerances for Metal Fits," by C. R. Reiman, special investigation department, Kelly press division, American Type Founders Company, Elizabeth, N. J.

"Design of the Miller Simplex Automatic Two Revolution Cylinder Press," by A. W. Barrett, vice-president and general works manager, Miller Printing Machinery Company, Pittsburgh.

"Forces in Connection with the Reciprocating Beds of Flat Bed Cylinder Printing Presses," by B. D. Stevens, first vice-president and chief engineer, and H. E. Golber, research engineer, Miehle Printing Press and Manufacturing Company, Chicago.

A report, "Progress in Printing," will be presented by title by Winfield S. Huson, chairman of the progress report committee of the printing industries division. There will be a brief talk on "Safety Measures in Printing Plants" by H. W. Mowery, New York, chairman of the A. S. M. E. safety committee.

Following each session there will be ample time for discussion from the floor. Preprints of the five papers and the progress report may be obtained from the A. S. M. E. by anyone desiring to prepare written discussion.

Salem News Rounds Out 50 Years of Service

SALEM, Mass.—The Evening News of this city recently celebrated its fiftieth anniversary. John B. Tivnan, managing editor, as a newsboy, carried the first issue of the paper, and has served it ever since. Not only has Mr. Tivnan served here and in other communities reached by the Evening News but he has also acted in an official capacity for the commonwealth. Beginning in 1895 he served fifteen years as overseer of the poor. He was chosen a member of the trustees of Plummer Farm School in 1896, and was chairman of that body many years. He organized the anti-tuberculosis committee of this city and was its first chairman. In 1901 he was appointed a trustee of the state farm at Bridgewater and state infirmary at Tewksbury, serving as chairman of the commission to study the need of state hospitals for causes of nervous breakdown. Governor McCall appointed him a member of the commission on mental diseases in 1916. During the World War he was a member of the local fuel board, chairman of the Red Cross emergency committee, and vice-president of the war chest association. Besides being managing editor of the News, he is a director in several corporations and societies.

Butte Daily Post Has Fine Composing Room

BUTTE, Mont.—No expense has been spared in the rearranging of the Daily Post composing room by J. H. Dickey, Jr., general manager of the big company's chain of papers. Today the Post has one of the finest and most up to date printing plants in this section. Mr. Dickey is a stickler for progress and economy in the print shop. Pat Geraghty, head of the mechanical department, who made a tour of inspection of the mechanical departments of some of the larger papers in the East, supervised all installations and changes in the Post composing room. Included in the equipment are ten Linotypes equipped with Linotype metal feeders. James H. Daly, machinist, has the battery working fine.

Chicago Post Runs 2,280 Column Tax List

The delinquent tax list set in the composing room of the Chicago Evening Post and appearing in that publication ran 2,280 columns. There was close to 25,000,000 ems of type. It provided work in a dull season for operators on three shifts. The Post is anticipating running a special assessment list that will run approximately 200 pages.

EXAMPLE 185

"The three secondary display lines above the center fold make it possible to display three other stories prominently on the page.

"Although the display lines alternate from dark to light, the faces used are all members of the same type family, and the dark and light lines get along well together. In fact, the difference in weight between those lines keeps them from being confused with each other in the reading. Each presents its message without clashing with the others. And the rules with corners to the right help to guide the eyes to the drops of the respective display lines."

Note that the date-line matter, instead of being presented under the nameplate, was boxed off by itself just above the editorial at the upper left of the page.

The heads on that page were in various sizes of Metroblack and Metrothin.

The next two issues presented other versions of the same general idea, before the plan was dropped in favor of other modern developments.

Makeups such as that suggested by Example 185 could be effectively employed by some papers. In fact, several papers tried it out, and readers seemed to like it. But such treatments could hardly be employed to advantage by papers issuing several editions daily, as the treatments are a bit too complicated to permit of frequent and speedy rearrangements of the display units. Too many resettings of heads would be called for for stories shifted from one position to another on front pages or from front to inside pages.

In the meantime, many other papers had adopted the flush-left-head idea, but most of those papers were weeklies or school papers. As stated before, in less than a year, at least seventy-five weekly newspapers and school publications had begun to use them.

The first big daily of general circulation to adopt them was the *Cleveland News*, in 1934.

Writing about the new makeup of that paper, in September, 1934, this writer stated, in part:

"Simplified heads—easy to write, easy to set, easy to read—are now being used by the *Cleveland News*, Earle Martin, editor.

"Most of the heads are set flush at the left and permitted to run as they will, with no evening up at the right, mostly in Bodoni Bold and Bodoni Bold Italic, and only one or two of the most important stories on a front page are given more than one deck. When subordinate decks are used, the lines of them, too, are lined up toward the left, usually with the lines indented, and permitted to run as they will.

" 'Our new heads,' Mr. Martin informed this writer, 'are just naturally written, with no effort made to count the characters this side of certain maximum counts. They speed up the work of the copy-desk, and can be handled speedily in the composing room.

" 'They attracted an immediate favorable response.' "

A little later, though, Mr. Martin began presenting nearly all of his heads—even most of those over important front-page stories—in single decks set flush at the left, and he gave his front-page date line unusual treatment by employing, in place of a pair of rules, a single rule below the date line, and a tapered dash above it.

"The *News*," Mr. Martin informed this writer, "changed its body type from 7 point on a 7½-point slug to 7-on-8, and later to 7-on-8½, at a cost of 1¼ inches per column. We gladly gave it away to get white back of that black. Whenever you get enough white you get a good page. Since surveys show that only one reader in ten reads anything below the display bank of the headline, the *News* greatly simplified its headline style by dropping the extra banks. Besides simplifying the appearance of the paper, adding to its attractiveness and encouraging the reader, this change resulted in a saving of from two to two and a half columns of space daily. This, in turn, more than offset the opening up of the pages by extra leading.

"In its new dress the first page of the *News* is as irregular as nature can make it. Every one of those chunks of irregular white lifts the page. White patches will help any page. It affords sharp contrasts. The left-flush-headline idea automatically forces the reader into the white.

"We are trying to make the headlines as nearly like conversation as we can. The big thing is that you can tell the story simply and naturally."

Later Mr. Martin, who since has died, presented another argument in favor of simplified heads for news stories by comparing the amount of space occupied by heads in the upper half of a representative front page of the *Cleveland News*, with the head displacement in a like area in another paper—and a conservative metropolitan daily, at that.

"In the other paper," said Mr. Martin, "the nameplate, date-line matter and headlines above the fold on a representative front page occupy 51 column inches, while the display elements in a like area in the *Cleveland News* occupy only 33 column inches.

"Here is an important saving of 18 column inches on the upper half of a front page, and our left-flush-and-bankless display attracts more attention and is easier to read.

"On the lower half of our front page, we present considerably more heads than does the other paper, a treatment that lends color and interest to that often-neglected part of a page. And yet we run considerably more body lines on a page—the lines that readers really read."

The *Linotype News* continued to experiment with head treatments, and in March, 1935, presented the front page suggested by Example 186.

Note the secondary banner, below the fold, an unusual treatment, with three double-column pyramided drops, for contrast with the flush-left heads on the page. Most of the heads were in Memphis Bold or Memphis Bold Italic, and most of the jim dashes were presented flush at the left, with the first dash of each pair shorter than the second dash.

The number for October, 1935, presented the front page suggested by Example 187.

Most of the heads on that page and in that issue were in Erbar Light Condensed, Metrolite No. 2 and Metrolite No. 2 Italic—faces that since have been adopted by many newspapers for head dresses. Most of the news body lines were in 7-point Paragon on an 8-point body, but a news-story lead, the editorials and a feature column were in 8-point Paragon on a 9-point body.

Note that while all of the heads but one on that page were presented flush at the left, the display lines dropping from the picture in column six were pyramided, to keep them and some of the lines of an adjacent head from seeming to run into each other.

Another metropolitan daily of general circulation to adopt the flush-left-head idea was the *Seattle Star*, in November, 1935.

Earle Martin presented a showing of the *Star's* front page of November 8, 1935, in his *Cleveland News* of November 22, 1935, with the following comment:

"The *Seattle Star* is the latest metropolitan paper to join the easy-

21 Lino Set Books Among 1935 Fifty (See Pages Five and Six)

The Linotype News

21 Lino Set Books Among 1935 Fifty (See Pages Five and Six)

VOLUME XIII — BROOKLYN, MARCH, 1935 — NUMBER FOUR

The Brooklyn Daily Eagle Puts In Twenty-four New Model 8 Linos

New York Journal Installs All-Purpose Linotype and Adopts Erbar for Heads

Big Plant's New A-P-L Equipped to Cast Large Banner Lines, Advertising Display

The New York Journal, which, with the New York American, has added twenty-one new Linotypes in the last year—eleven Model 25 mixer machines and ten Model 8s—has installed an All-Purpose Linotype with many display fonts and is now appearing with banner lines and advertising display lines produced on the A-P-L.

Many Journal news heads are now being presented in 24, 34, 42, 48 and 72 point Erbar Light Condensed—the 24, 34 and 42 point sizes being produced on both the A-P-L and Model 21 Display Linotypes—and the larger sizes on the A-P-L.

In the case of two deck heads, Erbar Light Condensed is used for first decks, and 14 point Metrolite No. 2 for second decks.

Among the other A-P-L faces being used by the Journal for news banners or advertising display lines are 96 point Erbar Bold Condensed, 72 point Cheltenham Bold Condensed and 96 and 120 point Cheltenham Bold Extra Condensed.

Among the large advertising figures being cast on the Journal's All-Purpose Linotype are figures in 96 and 120 point Metrolite No. 2; 96 and 120 point Metrothin No. 2, and 72, 96 and 120 point Memphis Bold.

The Journal and American now operate 115 Linotypes, including four Model 21 display machines and the new All-Purpose.

Man Trades Dog For Oil Well—Well!

WICHITA, Kan.—When a man trades a dog for an oil well, that's news. And when the oil well proves highly profitable, that should be front page news.

Some time ago, Robert Richards, Sunday editor of the Wichita Beacon, swapped a Scottie pup for some oil royalty rights that seem likely to bring him something like $10,000, as a well that the rights cover is said to be producing 100 barrels of oil daily.

Lino Users Win in Ohio

Capture Most Prizes At Latest Meeting Of Buckeye Press

COLUMBUS, Ohio.—Linotype users won nearly all of the honors in the various newspaper contests concluded at the meeting of the Buckeye Press Association here in January.

First place was awarded the Logan Republican for front page and other makeup, with honorable mention going to the Morrow County Sentinel of Mount Gilead, and the Holmes County Farmer-Hub of Millersburg. Paul G. Mohler of Berea was the judge.

In the contest for the best showing and treatment of community farm news by county seat papers, first prize was won by the Morrow County Sentinel, and honorable mention by the Georgetown News-Democrat, and the Eaton Register-Herald. In the division for non-county seat papers first prize went to the Wadsworth Banner-Press, and honorable mention to the Delta Atlas, and the Bethel Journal. Dusty Miller of Wilmington was the judge.

In the contest for advertising composition and display, first prize went to the Freeport Press, and honorable mention to the Greenfield Republican, the Delta Atlas, and the Wadsworth Banner-Press. Orrin R. Taylor of Archbold was the judge.

In the editorial page contest, the Greenfield Republican ranked first, with honorable mention to Wadsworth Banner-Press, the Freeport Press, and the Delta Atlas. Raymond Durbin of McConnelsville was the judge.

In the community service contest, the Wadsworth Banner-Press came in first, and the Pemberville Leader received honorable mention. E. F. Broderick of the Willoughby News-Herald was the judge.

Fred E. Huls, editor and publisher of the Logan Republican,

(Continued on page 2)

21 Lino Set Books Among 1935 Fifty

In the 1935 Fifty Books exhibition of the American Institute of Graphic Arts, there are twenty-one Linotype set books — a generous proportion, and a tribute by their sixteen designers and fourteen printers to the quality of Linotype faces. This year the linotyped volumes are in excellent company, for twenty of the books are hand set, and the nine remaining were produced by other machine composition.

Janson was the preferred Linotype face this year, being used on eight books. Baskerville followed with its use on five; two books were in Caslon Old Face, two more in Estienne; with Granjon, Cloister, Original Old Style and Scotch each being used for one volume. The volume on which Granjon was used (the Grabhorn printed Bibliography of the Writings of Edgar A. Poe) had an almost equal amount of composition in foundry Garamond, yet so cleverly were the two faces mixed that only an expert could detect the distinction.

Fourteen different printing organizations produced the twenty-one linotyped books, R. R. Donnelley Sons & Company leading the group with four books; two books each being printed by the Grabhorn Press, the Harbor Press and the Walpole Printing Office, with nine other printers each being responsible for a volume.

William A. Kittredge led the designers of the Linotype set books with three to his credit; three others had two each: John S. Fass, Edwin and Robert Grabhorn, and Fred Anthoensen; with the twelve remaining books each coming from a different designer's hand.

On pages five and six of this issue, title pages of the linotyped volumes are reproduced and discussed.

Another Texas Paper Now Using Excelsior

PARIS, Texas.—Five fonts of 7½ point Excelsior No. 1 with Bold Face No. 2 have been installed by the Morning News here, A. G. Mayse, publisher, for a change of body dress.

Many Join In Tribute To A. E. G.

More Than 1,000 at Washington Banquet To Public Printer—Now Col. Giegengack

WASHINGTON, D. C. — More than 1,000 representatives of various branches of the graphic arts, legislators and government officials attended the testimonial dinner to the Hon. A. E. Giegengack at the Wardman Park Hotel, Saturday evening, March 2. Many delegations were present from other cities.

The dinner was sponsored by the employees of the Government Printing Office, with a score of graphic arts organizations co-operating.

The Hon. J. Walter Lambeth, vice chairman of the joint committee on printing and chairman of the committee on printing of the House of Representatives, presided as toastmaster.

Among the speakers was the Hon. William V. Gregory, representative from Kentucky, who apprised the guest of honor that Gov. Ruby Laffoon had made him a Kentucky colonel.

Other addresses were made by Sen. Duncan U. Fletcher of Florida; Edward F. McGrady, assistant secretary of Labor; William Green, president of the American Federation of Labor; Major George L. Berry, president of the International Printing Pressmen and Assistants' Union of North America, and John J. Deviny, executive vice president, United Typothetae of America.

Dr. George C. Havenner was committee chairman in charge.

Colonel Giegengack also was presented resolutions from the Government Printing Office American Legion Post, No. 33, in which the post welcomed the new executive as its head and expressed confidence in his leadership.

Other guests of honor included Mrs. M. C. Giegengack, mother of the public printer; his wife; Alvin W. Hall, director of the Bureau of Engraving and Printing; Harry B. Mitchell, president of the Civil Service Commission, and Representative Robert F. Rich of Pennsylvania.

In making the principal address, Senator Fletcher, who has been a member of the joint committee on printing in congress twenty-six

(Continued on page 2)

Typos Endorse Printing Plan

Endorsement of the proposed program to increase the consumption of printing through the co-operative effort of all allied organizations in the graphic arts industries was expressed in a resolution recently voted by the Typographers' Association of New York.

The resolution stated that the organization "unanimously endorses this plan and pledges its assistance to co-operate with all other allied industries to aid in the intelligent and economical furtherance of this plan for increased printing consumption."

Beloit News In New Dress

Wisconsin Paper Adopts Excelsior And Changes Heads To Bodoni Bold

BELOIT, Wis.—The Daily News here, which recently installed four Linotypes—two Model 8s and two Model 14s—and adopted Linotype Excelsior in several sizes, as well as several display sizes of Bodoni Bold and Bodoni Bold Italic, is now appearing with a new body dress in Excelsior and with heads in capitals and lower case of Bodoni Bold and Bodoni Bold Italic.

The new head dress replaced a dress that had involved the use of several different and unrelated faces, including heavy condensed Gothic capitals, Century Bold, Cheltenham Bold Italic and other faces.

A preliminary announcement in the Daily News prepared readers for the change with the statements:

"The body type that will appear in the Daily News Monday is the newest and it is also the best and most readable type ever produced for newspaper use. Your eyes will recognize the great improvement the Daily News is making in adopting it.

"The new Daily News head letter type style will be just as greatly improved. The new heads do not march rigidly in stiff capital letters like so many soldiers on pa-

(Continued on page 2)

Big Time Planned For N. E. A.

Several State Groups To Help Celebrate Golden Anniversary In New Orleans

By HARRY B. RUTLEDGE
Managing Director
National Editorial Association

At the invitation of *The Linotype News*, I'm going to let you in on the plans for our golden jubilee celebration at New Orleans May 4 to 12. It's going to be a great party, with the greatest attendance of newspaper publishers and printing shop proprietors in the history of this half century old trade association.

And here's why:

The National Editorial Association, founded fifty years ago this year, has achieved a new peak in membership as a result of its expanded services and the realization among publishers that co-operation is essential to cope with their pressing problems. In recent months several state press associations have voted to affiliate directly with the national association, bringing nearer the objective of making a national association of state associations for the common good of all.

In the light of this awakened interest, the fiftieth anniversary of the National Editorial Association is assuming an unusual importance throughout the country.

State press associations of Louisiana, Florida, Alabama, Mississippi and Arkansas have already voted to hold a joint meeting at New Orleans on Saturday, May 4, as an unprecedented inaugural to the national meeting.

The several hundred winners of the N. E. A. national newspaper contests, started ten years ago, have been invited to hold a reunion during the convention.

Arrangements are being made, also, for a gala reunion of Prof. John H. Casey's weekly newspaper elevens.

Winners of this year's newspaper contests will be announced and trophies and certificates will be awarded.

As Kenneth F. Baldridge, president of the N. E. A., has pointed out, Louisiana is front page news these days, and the convention at its metropolis offers a timely op-

(Continued on page 2)

Enterprising Paper Modernizes Its Plant To Be Prepared for Better Business Ahead

The Brooklyn Daily Eagle has completed the installation of twenty-four new Model 8 Linotypes, and has added several display series of matrices for the setting of news heads and advertising, in addition to the more than fifty fonts of Linotype Ionic No. 5 that accompanied the new machines.

The twenty-four new Model 8s, which replaced a like number of older models, were installed a few at a time, to avoid interfering with production schedules, and the closing of editions proceeded as usual in the Eagle's busy composing room.

Fifty-two multiple magazine Linotypes are now operated by the Eagle—forty in its news composing room, and twelve in its commercial printing department, the Eagle Press. The two batteries include thirty-four Model 8s, seven Model 9s (four magazine mixers), seven Model 25s and a Model 26 (mixers), a Model 12, a Model 14, and a Model 20 Display Linotype.

Each of the new machines carried a font of 7 point Ionic No. 5 with Bold Face No. 2, the Eagle's news body face, and each machine, with one or two exceptions, also carried a font of 5½ point Ionic No. 5 with Bold Face No. 2 for classified ads and financial tables. Other Ionic fonts in the installation were 5½, 6½ and 7 point Ionic No. 5 with Italic, and 9 point Ionic No. 5 with Bold Face No. 2.

Many Display Faces Included

Among the faces for news heads and advertising included in the installation were 8 and 10 point Century Expanded with Italic; 10 point Century Expanded with Century Bold; 8 and 10 point Bodoni Bold with Italic; 8, 12 and 14 point Poster Bodoni with Italic; 8, 10 and 12 point Metroblack with Metrolite, and 8, 10, 12 and 14 point Memphis Bold with Memphis Light.

Business has been going along merrily with the Eagle, with a decided pickup in advertising, but that paper is preparing its big plant for even better business in the days ahead.

Last year its total weekday advertising linage, not including Sundays, amounted to 12,300,955 lines.

M. Preston Goodfellow is president and publisher of the Eagle;

(Continued on page 2)

Excelsior Easy on Eyes

Many Readers of Winnipeg Free Press Congratulate Paper On New Body Face

WINNIPEG.—Immediately following the installation of Linotype Excelsior by the Free Press of this city—twenty-five fonts of three different point sizes—and the appearance of the Free Press in its new dress, letters of commendation began to pour in to that paper.

"I am ninety-three years of age, so my eyes are a little dim," wrote one man, in a letter published in the Free Press. "Of late I have found the reading of the Free Press a little difficult. But the new type is fine; can read it readily without eye strain."

Another stated: "I am an old man over eighty-five years of age, still able to read without glasses the ordinary print of the newspaper, but I notice there is no strain on my eyes as I read your paper today."

A seventy-three year old youngster had this to say: "I had noticed that, even with glasses, I could not see the print as clearly as I used to. But this new type—ah, boy! I can read it very easily, even without glasses in a good light."

But the letters of appreciation came not from the aged alone. Scores of letters of commendation came from middle aged and young readers.

Another man stated: "Our chief engineer says that it is almost the difference between having a paper and not having one."

(Continued on page 2)

More-Advertising and More-Printing Plans Shaping Up

Mackey Addresses Virginia Publishers on Movement to Attract More Newspaper Advertising

LYNCHBURG, Va. — Speaking about the movement to attract more advertising to newspapers, at the mid-winter meeting of the Virginia Press Association here in January, Joseph T. Mackey, executive vice president and treasurer of the Mergenthaler Linotype Company, stated:

It has been well said that "in the war against Reality man has but one weapon—Imagination." Certainly you will agree that for some years past we have been engaged in a great war—a war against economic depression.

To date I have had sufficient experience with it to make me realize that such a war has existed and still exists, but I have refused to acknowledge a sense of defeat. From the beginning of it I have been of the firm belief that the situation is one that calls for co-operative, practical and constructive effort, and so I have been using my imagination and such other weapons as are at my command in an effort to contribute my mite toward improving the general situation and, in particular, the situation in our own joint field of endeavor.

I realized that, individually, none of us could do much about improving general conditions, but I have long held to the view that if we could get the thousands of newspapers from Maine to California to instill in the minds of the public, day after day and week after week, sane ideas looking to the improvement of purchasing power, that something worth while might be accomplished. I have felt an improvement in general purchasing power might more readily be accomplished by directing reader attention to advertising appearing in the newspapers than through any other medium. Such action would help the millions to help themselves.

Probably one of the most vexatious questions confronting you, and one which undoubtedly gives rise to misunderstandings, is the matter of gratuitous news space in connection with advertised products. Is it not conceivable that this problem—for I take it that it is a problem—might be solved by the proposal made for general advertising of the newspapers' advertising columns?

According to Babson

In a summation of the important place of the newspaper in our present civilization, Roger W. Babson, industrialist, economist and business adviser, recently said:

> Few people realize to what extent the newspapers, by their popular appeal, help to release the energies that make news. Through the efforts of the press, old industries will expand and new industries will be nurtured into growth. American and Canadian newspapers will play a tremendous part in this march toward economic and political greatness.

Many concerns curtailed their ad-

(Turn to last page, No. 1)

Pine Bluff Commercial Adds All-Purpose

PINE BLUFF, Ark.—The Commercial of this city has installed an All-Purpose Linotype equipped with, among other faces, 18 and 36 point Pabst Extra Bold Italic; 60, 72, 96 and 120 point Pabst Extra Bold; 72, 96 and 120 point Erbar Bold Condensed, and 60 and 72 point Metrolite No. 2.

The new machine is being used to produce news banners and other news heads, advertising display lines, and display composition for a wide range of commercial printing.

The Linotype News Lino Set Throughout

All lines of composition in this issue of *The Linotype News* were composed the Linotype way, even the banner lines on this page and the banners and other big display lines on other pages. Most of the body matter is in 7½ point Excelsior No. 1 with Bold Face No. 2 cast on an 8½ point body.

See "Makeup of This Issue," on page four.

French Newspaper Installs Excelsior

THREE RIVERS, Que.—Le Nouvelliste of this city has installed four fonts of Excelsior—three fonts of 8 point Excelsior No. 2 with Bold Face No. 2, and one font of 8 point Excelsior No. 2 with Italic—for a change of body dress.

Campaign to Increase Consumption of Printing Explained to New York Employing Printers

Representing the National Printing Equipment Association, Inc., Joseph T. Mackey, chairman of a special printing-plan committee appointed by that organization, spoke before the New York Employing Printers' Association February 18 on "A Plan to Increase the Consumption of Printing."

After having explained what already had been done by the N. P. E. A. and other organizations and individuals to get the more-printing movement started, Mr. Mackey stated:

"When our committee considered the size of the job ahead it was deemed premature to attempt the formation of a completely developed program. We recognized the need for study and enlightenment toward which five preliminary steps should be taken:

"First: To invite co-operation and preliminary suggestions from all the interested organizations.

"Second: To organize committees representing the major groups of the industries to pass upon the preliminary outline of scope and purpose, and to underwrite the cost of survey and organization.

"Third: To make a survey of the printing industry, particularly of its selling methods and problems; its present and potential markets.

"Fourth: To formulate, from the results of the survey, a statement of achievable objectives; a program for accomplishing these purposes; and a budget of estimated cost over the full period to be covered by the program.

"Fifth: To present the plan and budget to the participating organizations with a statement of the support in funds and effort that would be required from each.

Announcement Mailed Last Fall

"The first of these steps has been taken and is the only action taken thus far. It consisted of the mailing of an announcement under date of November 24, 1934, to every known organization of master printers, printer-publishers and craftsmen and to all members of the National Printing Equipment Association. . . .

"We proposed that all the printers' organizations make the proposed campaign the subject of a special meeting for all those affiliated with their membership and that non-members be invited to the discussion. It was suggested that the meetings should be devoted to every phase of the problem of increasing the use of printing; that their purpose should be frankly clinical—to inquire into today's conditions—to define the major obstacles in selling printing—and to discuss the means which might be organized to overcome them.

"We asked that the results of all such meetings be summarized and

(Turn to last page, No. 2)

14 Excelsior Fonts For Trenton Times

TRENTON, N. J.—Fourteen fonts of 7½ point Excelsior No. 1 with Bold Face No. 2 have been installed by the Trenton Times, and are now being used for new body dresses for the Trenton Evening Times, the Trenton State Gazette, and the Sunday Times-Advertiser.

The change to the new face was made, as stated in the Evening Times when the new dress was introduced, after months of research and experimentation.

Included in the installation were 375 wide range spacebands.

Don A. Johnson, promotion manager of the papers, has received many compliments on the improved appearance and easier to read qualities of all three papers since Excelsior was adopted.

Mechanical Conference In Detroit May 27-29

As we go to press, the information reaches us that the ninth mechanical conference of the American Newspaper Publishers' Association will be held in Detroit Monday, Tuesday and Wednesday, May 27 to 29, with the Hotel Statler as headquarters.

For additional information about the conference, see the preliminary story on page nine headed "Wines Invites Conference Ideas."

Mr. Wines wants the conference to center round practical ideas and invites members to co-operate.

Means for Adoption of Ad Plan Considered by Industries Meeting in New York City

At a dinner tendered by Joseph T. Mackey, executive vice president and treasurer of the Mergenthaler Linotype Company, at the Engineers' Club, New York City, Tuesday evening, January 29, representatives of printers' and publishers' supply houses, service organizations and advertising agen- favorable interest in the plan to increase the volume of newspaper advertising by advertising the advantages of such advertising.

Figures were presented concerning the number of newspaper publishers who already had expressed favorable interest in the plan (more than 1,800 such publishers), and various ways in which the plan might be put definitely and successfully into effect were considered from various points of view.

In opening the discussion, Mr. Mackey stated:

"I assume you have each received a copy of the portfolio containing the open letter I addressed and mailed in October, 1934, to the newspaper publishers of the United States, suggesting a promotional campaign to safeguard and increase advertising; also of the bulletin issued and distributed to the same body in November last, analyzing and reporting on the first 1,068 replies received on the proposition. There was also recently sent to you a copy of the talk I had the privilege of making at the mid-winter meeting of the Virginia Press Association at Lynchburg January 9.

Bulletin Explains Preliminary Plan

"These papers tell the present day status of the matter in so far as I have had to do with it personally. You will observe that there is apparently a substantial interest in the subject on the part of the trade. It seems timely to me, therefore, to call together for an informal discussion a representative cross section group of the entire industry serving the publishers, large and small, to consider what future action should be taken.

"Two questions arise in my mind: (1) whether, in view of the interest manifested by so large a number of publishers in the proposal outlined, you are now willing to undertake to determine the interest of that part of the industry with which you are associated? and (2) if the proposal as presented does not meet with its or your approval, what are the further steps to be taken to develop a plan that will most effectively meet the needs of the situation? I think we should now work toward a general trade planning group.

Mr. Mackey's Observation at Chicago

"Before entering upon my discussion this evening, I should like to call attention to an observation

(Turn to last page, No. 3)

EXAMPLE 186

The LINOTYPE Legibility Group (See Page 12)

The Linotype News

The LINOTYPE Legibility Group (See Page 12)

VOLUME XIV — CHICAGO, OCTOBER, 1935 — NUMBER TWO

MORE THAN 3,400 PAPERS NOW USING IONIC AND EXCELSIOR

Fred'k Wagner Now Publisher Of Call-Bulletin

Succeeds Robert P. Holliday With San Francisco Daily; Was V.P., Coast Manager Of Paul Block & Associates

Frederick Wagner, for thirty-three years associated with newspapers on the Pacific Coast, has succeeded Robert P Holliday as publisher of the San Francisco Call-Bulletin.

Mr. Wagner went to the Call-Bulletin from Paul Block & Associates, national advertising representatives, with whom he was vice president and Pacific Coast manager.

In 1902 Mr. Wagner started his newspaper career as an office boy with the Seattle Post-Intelligencer, and in 1904 joined the staff of the Seattle Times which he served twelve years.

In 1916 he resigned as automobile editor, and joined the Los Angeles Evening Express in the same capacity. He was promoted to national advertising manager of that paper, and then successively became business manager and general manager. In 1931, when the Los Angeles Herald purchased the Express, Mr. Wagner joined the Paul Block organization.

Mr. Holliday will make his home in northern California. "I have known Mr. Wagner for many years," Mr. Holliday said. "I know that he is a competent newspaper man and a great asset to the publishing business in San Francisco, and he has my very best wishes. As for my personal plans, for a long time I have looked forward to an extended rest after twenty-five years of continuous service in the newspaper business. I have always had an extensive interest in the California National Guard, and will now have more time to devote to it."

Lincoln Star Adopts Erbar and Memphis

LINCOLN, Neb.—The Star of this city, which recently adopted 7½ point Excelsior No. 1 with Bold Face No. 2 for a new body dress, has since come out with a new head dress making use of Erbar Light Condensed in the 24, 34 and 42 point sizes, 12 point Memphis Light with Memphis Bold, and 8 point Memphis Bold with Memphis Bold Italic.

Twelve point Memphis Bold is used for cut overlines, and 8 point Memphis Bold Italic for cut legends.

Frank D. Throop is publisher and general manager of the Star, and J. E. Lawrence is editor.

New S. F. Publisher

Frederick Wagner

Excelsior Now Used By Atlanta Journal

New Dress Proving Popular With Old and Young Alike, Who Find It Easy on Eyes

ATLANTA.—"With a pride that cannot well be concealed from any eye, the Atlanta Journal appears today in a bright new type dress—a larger, clearer face which is a joint triumph of art and science."

Thus began a front page story in the Journal here in August, following the installation by that paper of nineteen fonts of 8 point Excelsior No. 2—eighteen of them with Bold Face No. 2, and one with Italic and Small Caps.

News body matter is now appearing in the Journal in 8 point Excelsior on an 8¼ point body twelve picas wide, and editorial matter in 8 point Excelsior on a 10 point body fifteen picas wide.

"Excelsior," the Journal's front page story continued, "has characteristics tailored perfectly for the newspaper it will clothe. Well fitted letters flow into one another, set off artistically by a uniform distribution of white space within and around each letter.

"The days of the ox-cart are over, but if you had an ox-cart, and went home in it every evening, the chances are you could peruse the Journal comfortably without undergoing any extraordinary optical gymnastics. Certainly you will find it convenient and pleasing to read on the street car or in your automobile."

Editorially, in the same issue, the Journal stated:

"Psychology, as well as optics, contributes much to these improvements, for the one great purpose of type is to produce impressions that will be clear and pleasing to the eye and to the mind back of the eye. The keenest wit or the loveliest

(Continued on page two)

Tampa Tribune in New Home; Makes Move in Record Time

TAMPA.—The Morning Tribune of this city, of which S. E. Thomas is publisher; J. S. Mims, general manager, and R. W. Simpson, managing editor, is now in a new and up to date home. The composing room equipment, including eighteen Linotypes, was moved and installed in the new building in less than four hours, so that no edition deadline was missed, and the quality of production was not affected.

J. S. Mims

Thirty-five extra helpers, under the direction of Clifford Alves, composing room foreman; W. E. Spain, machinist; P. W. Pressby, head electrician, and Sam Black, stereotype foreman, moved the machines from a fourth floor location to the street and on a low truck to the new home. The octuple press had been moved and installed previously.

The Tribune's new plant has 30,000 square feet of floor space. All mechanical departments are on the ground floor, and the executive, advertising, and news offices are on the second floor. Each department has ample room for expansion, having twenty per cent more floor space than before. Departments are arranged in a "straight line assembly" system for efficiency.

The building is of modern architectural design, emphasizing simplicity without decoration. The main entrance is of black glass and white metal, while the building is constructed of brick, steel and stucco, and is air conditioned throughout.

The comfort of employees was placed next to efficiency in requirements of the building. Floors in the mechanical departments are of wood block to make soft walking surfaces. Spring steel chairs are used in the composing room, and all lighting was designed to minimize eye strain. Each mechanical department has its own shower and locker rooms.

Part of the Tribune's Linotype department is shown in an accompanying picture.

One section of the Tampa Tribune's Linotype department

Sixty Newspapers in Drive To Secure More Advertising

Another plan to build up volume of advertising in newspapers was launched September 1, with sixty newspapers in thirty-eight cities in the United States participating by running in their papers the first of a series of display advertisements, each to carry the slogan: "Newspaper advertising is point-of-shopping advertising."

This campaign, introduced by the Chicago Tribune, is open to all papers desiring to participate. The series consists of twenty advertisements designed to reaffirm the selling power of the newspaper as a primary medium. The largest advertisement measures three columns by 175 lines. The campaign has been planned for small units of space, so that every paper can use it easily and inexpensively.

Canadian newspapers also have become interested in the idea. Arthur Partridge of the Canadian Daily Newspapers Association has arranged to purchase a set of electros. From these, mats will be made and distributed to all association members on request.

All newspapers co-operating in the campaign will receive a supply of gummed stickers to be applied to letters and direct mail promotional matter sent to advertisers and agencies. The stickers bear the keynote slogan of the campaign.

Any newspaper may obtain proofs of the advertisements, together with an outline of the plan, upon request to Chesser M. Campbell, advertising manager of the Chicago Tribune. The cost of the twenty electros is thirty-five dollars.

"Behind this campaign, which is open to all newspapers," ran a story in Editor & Publisher August 17, "is the underlying thought that before individual newspapers can materially increase their volume of national advertising, there must come from manufacturers and their agencies a greater total volume of advertising intended for newspapers."

Mr. Campbell of the Chicago Tribune emphasized to Editor & Publisher that "the campaign is not designed primarily to sell newspaper advertising to the man on the street.

(Continued on page twelve)

Panama Daily Praises A-P-L

Panama, one of the eighteen foreign countries to know the value of the All-Purpose Linotype, praises the A-P-L.

The Panama American, combining an English and Spanish edition in one newspaper, added an All-Purpose Linotype last year, and all concerned praise it for its output. Nelson Rounsevell, principal owner and president, calls it a life-saver. V. J. Matthews, chief of work, says it saves the day when it comes to catching the mails, that for advertisements coming in near closing time the machine beats any other known method of getting copy into type. Chester O. Olive, business manager, who does not take chances on machinery, is proud of his installation.

The All-Purpose Linotype was erected by Jose Domenech, following a few written suggestions made by the Foreign Department of the Mergenthaler Linotype Company when the machine was shipped. Mr Domenech had never seen such a machine before, but he handled the erection rapidly and satisfactorily in every way. The operator, Julio Diaz A., an enterprising young man, also without previous knowledge of the A-P-L., is said to be doing wonders in the way of production.

Although that A-P-L already is equipped with a generous selection of faces up to 144 point, further faces are being considered. Not only is the machine used for all the banner lines and ordinary headlines and display lines, but it turns out a lot of the display lines for the large run of commercial work done by the Panama American.

In the American plant, in addition to the All-Purpose, are seven keyboard Linotypes, including a new style Model 14.

The Linotype News Lino Set Throughout

All lines of composition in this issue of The Linotype News were composed the Linotype way, even the banner lines and the largest lines in display advertisements. Most of the body matter is in the 7 point size of the new Linotype Paragon with Paragon Bold on an 8 point body, with some of the lines extra leaded.

See "Makeup of This Issue," on page four, and the side by side showing of the five faces in the Linotype Legibility Group, on page twelve.

Craftsman Curry International Leader

CINCINNATI.—John B. Curry of Boston was elected president of the International Association of Printing House Craftsmen at the organization's annual convention here August 28. He succeeds Thomas E. Cordis of San Francisco.

Clark R. Long, Washington, D. C., was elected first vice president; George Marshall, Toronto, second vice president, and John M. Callahan, Cincinnati, third vice president. Mark A. Mullee, Newark, was re-elected treasurer, and L. M. Augustine, Baltimore, was re-elected secretary.

The 1936 meeting will be held in Minneapolis.

Completes 55 Years At Helm of Gazette

WATERTOWN, Wis.—James W. Moore, who this summer entered his eightieth year, has been publisher of the Gazette here fifty-five years.

Polish Daily News Adds Four Linotypes

DETROIT.—Four Linotypes, including a Two-in-One Model 14, have been added by the Polish Daily News of this city.

Proud of Excelsior Says Denver News

Paper's Readers Also Praise Easy to Read Body Face; Seventeen Fonts Installed

DENVER.—"Our New Easy-to-Read Type—First Issue."

With these words printed in red diagonally across the front page, the Denver Rocky Mountain News announced that it had installed seventeen fonts of 7½ point Excelsior No. 1 with Bold Face No. 2, and that it was presenting its new and easy-to-read face on an 8½ point body.

"We Are Proud of Our New Type—A Modern Newspaper Advance," ran a head over a front page story that included comparative showings of body matter faces used by the paper in 1915 and in 1025, alongside a specimen of its new Excelsior.

"I am tempted to use superlatives when speaking of your new type," declared J. C. Bloom, secretary-treasurer of the Colorado State Optometrical Association, in the second issue of the News using the Excelsior dress. He continued: "Excelsior type—naturally, I speak from the viewpoint of one whose business it is to study ways of relieving eyestrain—is easy to read, it endows every word with proper significance, and it stands out strongly. I should say it is the ideal newspaper type."

Dr. John M. Foster, one of Denver's foremost eye, ear, nose and throat specialists, thanked the News for performing a public service. "The eye travels quickly from one letter to another," he said. "It is easier to catch the meaning—the eye doesn't stumble."

Said Thomas Patterson Campbell, instructor at the Colorado School of Mines, and grandson of Thomas Patterson, late publisher of the News: "I noticed it the minute I opened my morning paper. The

(Continued on page two)

G. P. O. to Erect Annex Building And Warehouse

Plan Getting Under Way To Modernize Big Layout May Involve an Expenditure Of Close to Six Millions

WASHINGTON, D. C.—The Government Printing Office, headed by Col. A. E. Giegengack, is soon to have a new annex building and a warehouse as part of a modernization program authorized by the government and that will involve an expenditure of close to six million dollars.

Attention was first called to the overcrowded conditions in the Government Printing Office, and to the need for annex buildings to take the place of several old structures, as far back as 1913.

Immediately upon taking the oath of office, July 2, 1934, Colonel Giegengack inspected all of the structures occupied by the Government Printing Office and came to the conclusion that the greatest need, and the one to which he should devote untiring efforts, was the securing of an appropriation to replace the old group of buildings on H Street, one of which was a seventy-nine year old structure that had been reported as unsafe by both federal and district officials.

Not only is it the plan of Colonel Giegengack to replace those old buildings with a modern eight story annex, but he proposes to acquire certain lands opposite the present Government Printing Office on which to build a warehouse, into which railroad tracks will be laid, for the unloading of paper and other printing supplies.

At present it requires the services of twenty-eight trucks to haul paper from the railroad terminals to the Government Printing Office, and to deliver the finished product to congress, the executive departments and the several independent government establishments in the District of Columbia.

The work of the Government Printing Office has so increased in the last two years that paper shipments are received at an average

(Continued on page three)

Adds Wide Measure 8 And Nine Kendalls

LOS ANGELES.—A new Forty-two Pica Model 8 with considerable extra equipment has been installed by Parker, Stone & Baird, large legal printing firm here.

Kendall metal feeders for the nine Linotypes the firm now has, and a 1,000 pound remelting furnace and water cooled molds were also installed.

Six Excelsior Fonts For Orange Courier

ORANGE, N. J.—Six fonts of 7½ point Excelsior No. 1 with Bold Face No. 2 have been installed by the Daily Courier of this city for a change of body dress.

N. E. A. Is Out to Increase Its Membership to 6,000

By R. H. PRITCHARD
President
National Editorial Association

The decision of the Supreme Court affecting the N. R. A. and its codes, coming as suddenly as it did, left the N. E. A. as well as many other associations temporarily without much reserve cash for immediate operating expenses, since the association practically carried the code burden since December, 1934, and had advanced to it more than $12,000 of strictly association funds. This was felt necessary by the officers of the association and the leaders in the industry in order to still continue to defend our establishments in whatever relationship might be necessary in connection with the code.

Definite action was taken by the N. E. A. convention in New Orleans in May on this phase of association activity that would have made it possible to work out a new financial arrangement, had the Supreme Court decision not come so suddenly.

Immediately after that action, President Kenneth F. Baldridge, Managing Director Harry B. Rutledge, Bruce R. McCoy, president of Newspaper Association Managers, and our entire board of directors started working on plans for a solution to our problems. Since July 1, I have given my entire time to association activity, and have invested in association work several hundred dollars of my own money. Managing Director Rutledge has done likewise. During this short period of time a plan under which the gradual liquidation of outstanding code expenses of both the national and regional code authorities may be brought about has been approved, and this basis of taking care of that phase of our activity has been practically assured. The immediate outstanding obligations of the association have been underwritten, and we are now ready to go forward with our program for the year.

We ask every N. E. A. member and every other publisher to give full consideration to the program that has been outlined. We believe the N. E. A. in the next twelve months should have a membership of at least 6,000 publishers. That's the goal during the year, and one of the most important phases of our activity. In a short time complete plans will be announced for an active membership campaign that is to be launched. Through an increase in our membership our services can be increased. Our strength, of course, will be increased through a larger membership. Our financial status will become stronger and every activity of the association more assured.

During the last year I have visited many state associations and other publishers' groups in many sections of the country. I have found among all of them a deep interest in the National Editorial Association. I ask in beginning my year as president of the organization that these friends of the association who are not now members lend their active support through a membership in the organization. This action on their part will show not only their appreciation for what the N. E. A. has done for them in the past, but also their active support and aid in its future program of development and service to them.

(Continued on page two)

Veteran

John Walker Ross at his desk

Associates Honor John W. Ross, Fifty Years With New Orleans States

John Walker Ross, who celebrated his fiftieth anniversary with the New Orleans Daily States back in June, was the guest of honor at a banquet given by the Times-Picayune Publishing Company, owners of the Daily States.

Mr. Ross ascended the journalistic ladder from proofreader to editor, serving under three owners. He began his newspaper career as a proofreader in 1885, at the age of seventeen. Shortly after, he became a reporter. In 1892 he was made city editor, and in 1909 was named managing editor by the late Col. Robert Ewing. On the death of Colonel Ewing, in 1931, Captain Ross was made publisher of the New Orleans Daily States, and remained in that position until the paper was purchased from the Ewing estate by the Times-Picayune Publishing Company, July 18, 1933, when the New Orleans Daily States was moved into the Times-Picayune building. Captain Ross was named editor and managing editor, positions he still holds.

On his fiftieth anniversary Captain Ross received many letters of congratulation from national leaders, including President Roosevelt, Vice President Garner, and many important newspaper men in the South.

Puts in 18 Fonts Of Excelsior

MONTREAL.—Eighteen fonts of Linotype Excelsior have been installed by the Gazette of this city for a change of body dress.

The installation consisted of sixteen fonts of 7 point Excelsior No. 1 with Bold Face No. 2; one font of 7 point Excelsior No. 1 with Italic and Small Caps, and one font of 8 point Excelsior No. 1 with Bold Face No. 2.

The 7 point size is being used for the general news columns, and the 8 point for editorials and certain features and for leads of important news stories.

New Manhattan Firm Installs Two Linos

The Manhattan Linotyping Company, Inc., of New York City, a new trade composition concern at 228 East Forty-fifth Street, with Robert Schneider as president, and George J. Reuter as treasurer, has installed two Linotypes, sixteen extra full length magazines and many fonts of matrices.

Among the Linotype faces in the installation are fonts of 6 and 8 point Old Style No. 1 with Italic and Small Caps; 8, 10 and 12 point Cloister Bold with Italic; 8, 10, 12 and 14 point Memphis Light with Bold; 18 point Memphis Bold; 6 and 12 point Gothic No. 31-A with No. 32-A; 6 and 12 point Gothic No. 31-B with No. 32-B; 6 point Gothic No. 31 with No. 32, and 12 point Gothic No. 31-C with No. 32-C.

Hall Enlarges Paper For Better Business

ALEXANDER CITY, Ala.—To be prepared for the improved business conditions and increased demand for advertising space which the Outlook of this city is expecting this fall and winter, that paper has enlarged its page size from six to seven columns.

E. C. Hall, editor of the Outlook, says that that paper is the forty-eighth weekly in Alabama to adopt the larger page size.

A. J. Tagley, Aged 75, With Paper 50 Years

GRAND FORKS, N. D.—When A. J. Tagley celebrated his fiftieth anniversary with the Grand Forks Herald, recently, a special edition was printed in his honor.

Mr. Tagley was born in Wisconsin seventy-five years ago, and first became connected with printing in Jackson, Minn.

Leading Metropolitan Dailies and Smaller Newspapers, as Well, Now Setting Their Body Matter In These Easy to Read Type Faces

As we go to press, more than 3,400 newspapers in thirty-six countries are using Ionic No. 5 and Excelsior for body matter. More than 2,700 papers—large and small—are using Ionic No. 5, and more than 750 papers—large and small—are using Excelsior.

Ionic and Excelsior are two of the five newspaper body faces in the Linotype Legibility Group, which also includes Textype, Paragon and Opticon, the latter two faces only recently introduced. (See the side by side showings of these five faces on page twelve.)

Ionic No. 5 is being used by more than 2,400 newspapers in all forty-eight of the states of this country. New York state leads the list with 204 Ionic users, followed by California with 142; Texas, 139; Pennsylvania, 131; Ohio, 130; Illinois, 94; Oklahoma, 92; Missouri, 85; Minnesota, 82; Michigan, 75; Kansas, 74; Iowa, 72; Indiana, 70; New Jersey, 67, and Arkansas, 52—to name only those states with fifty or more users each.

But in each of eighteen other states there are twenty-five or more users, and in only five of the forty-eight states are there less than ten users of Ionic No. 5 in each.

One hundred and fifty-one newspapers in nine provinces in Canada are Ionic users, and more than 125 papers in Alaska, Australia, Belgium, Brazil, Denmark, England, Finland, France, Hawaii, Holland, Newfoundland, Norway, Rumania, Scotland and Spain are setting their body matter in Ionic.

Excelsior Going Strong

Linotype Excelsior, which was introduced only four years ago, in the midst of the depression, and was designed to meet the conditions imposed by dry mat stereotyping, with its tremendous pressure, and to print well on high speed presses with rubber rollers, is now used by more than 560 newspapers in forty-five states in this country, and by nearly 200 other papers in thirty-five foreign countries.

California heads the list of Excelsior set papers in the United States, with 56 users, followed by Missouri and Pennsylvania with 33 each; Texas with 31; Kansas, 26; Wisconsin, 22; Minnesota, 21, and Illinois, 20—to name only those states with twenty or more Excelsior users each.

Forty-four newspapers in nine provinces in Canada are Excelsior set, and Excelsior is being used for body matter by nearly 150 more papers in Alaska, Algeria, Australia, Belgium, China, Colombia, Cuba, Denmark, Ecuador, El Salvador, England, Finland, France, Guatemala, Hawaii, Holland, India, Ireland, Italy, Jamaica, Newfoundland, New Zealand, Norway, Philippine Islands, Porto Rico, Portugal, Scotland, Spain, Sweden, Turkey, Union of South Africa, Venezuela, Wales and Yugoslavia.

Textype is also widely used abroad.

Again we suggest: See the side by side showing of the five newspaper body matter faces in the Linotype Legibility Group—Ionic No. 5, Excelsior, Textype, Paragon and Opticon—on page twelve.

Two Norfolk Papers Change to Paragon

The Virginian-Pilot Also Adopts New Head Dress In Linotype Bodoni Bold

NORFOLK, Va.—After exhaustive experimentation with different body and head faces, the Norfolk Virginian-Pilot and the Norfolk Ledger-Dispatch came out September 9 with news body matter in 7 point Linotype Paragon on an 8-point body, and the Virginian-Pilot appeared with a new nameplate and a new head dress in the bold branch of the Linotype Bodoni family.

"We are highly pleased with the change," says P. S. Huber, president of Norfolk Newspapers, Inc., publishing the two papers. "The readability of the papers has been tremendously improved, and the new body type has met with general favor."

L. I. Jaffe, editor of the Virginian-Pilot; Winder R. Harris, managing editor; Douglas Gordon, editor of the Ledger-Dispatch; Keville Glennan, managing editor, and other executives of the two papers also are highly pleased with the new dresses.

Referring, in a front page story, to the 7 point Linotype Paragon adopted for body matter for both papers, the Virginian-Pilot stated:

"The changes, made after the most careful study and deliberation, accomplish the twofold purpose of

(Continued on page two)

Prized Turkish Books Composed on Model 8

ANKARA, Turkey.—Several valuable books in Turkish have been composed in recent weeks on a Model 8 Linotype in the plant of Koyhocasi here.

"One of these," Bay Ozman Fevzi of Istanbul informs The Linotype News, "is 'Turk Hukuku Tarihi,' which means the 'History of the Turkish Law.' It was set from an original text that is very rare, and dates from 1087. Another is 'Asafname,' also set from a rare text, and containing the advices of a very instructed Vezir to Sultan Soliman the Magnificent."

Los Angeles Times Operating In Handsome New Building

LOS ANGELES.—Facing on the new Los Angeles civic center, where white towered buildings are rising in what promises to be one of the architectural showplaces of the Pacific Coast, is the new white limestone building which has been the home of the Los Angeles Times since July.

In appearance the Times home is one building, with a high and a low part, but in reality it consists of two structures separated by a six inch earthquake joint. A similar earthquake joint separates the Times building and the Times-Mirror Printing and Binding House. The latter plant, built several years ago, houses the Times engraving facilities in addition to its own job department equipment.

In the main entrance lobby, on the first floor, is a cast aluminum globe five and a half feet in diameter, and on the walls are Hugo Ballin murals, one of which depicts the printing of a newspaper, and another the gathering of the news.

Also on the first floor are the travel and resort bureaus, classified and subscription counter, cashier, classified department, composing room, stereotype department, black and white pressroom, color pressroom, and loading concourse.

The second floor has the local and national display departments, statistical department, mechanical superintendent's office, promotion department, main telephone exchange, multigraph department and stock

(Continued on page twelve)

Fine new home of the Los Angeles Times

EXAMPLE 187

to-read school. It has just adopted a new system of typography similar to that employed by the *Cleveland News.*

"Mr. R. L. Brink, the editor, says: 'The new headline dress of the *Seattle Star* is vastly more legible and practicable. The Bodoni family of type surely rings the bell for lasting grace and ease of reading.'"

August 31, 1936, the *Los Angeles Times* adopted flush-left heads, most of them in the Erbar and Metro families, and presented its news body matter in 8-point Paragon on a 9-point body.

Shortly after the appearance of the *Los Angeles Times* in its new dress, Frank Rospaw, publisher of the *Placentia* (Calif.) *Courier* and at that time president of the California Newspaper Publishers' Association, stated in his "Orange Peals" column in the *California Publisher,* organ of the association:

"There is a lesson for all California publishers in the action of the *Times.* . . . If it can entirely redesign its format, make a more readable product, and sell it, surely smaller newspapers can clean up their products. Throw away the old condensed head letters, buy or use some of the open faces now in the shop, get larger body type, whiten up all the pages. Give readers a new, readable product."

Many other publishers followed Mr. Rospaw's advice.

In the meantime, the *Linotype News* continued its experiments, and in September, 1936, presented the front page suggested by Example 188.

Note the unusual display treatment above the fold, without benefit of illustrations on that part of the page. The heads were in Bodoni Bold, Bodoni Bold Italic and Bodoni Bold Condensed.

Early in April of 1937 the typographic laboratory co-operated with editorial executives of the *New York Evening Journal* in the working out of many front pages built along the line of vertical makeup, a treatment made public by the *Journal* in May of 1937, and soon tried out by several other Hearst papers.

The *Linotype News* for May-June, 1937, presented a version of the vertical idea, and the next issue of the same publication presented still another version. See Example 189.

That sort of makeup was based on the thought that many people, particularly New Yorkers, while reading newspapers on trains, street

Newspapers Everywhere Are Sprucing Up

The Linotype News

Newspapers Everywhere Are Sprucing Up

VOLUME XV — BROOKLYN, SEPTEMBER, 1936 — NUMBER TWO

Boston Evening Transcript Changes to Ionic

N.E.A. Out To Enhance Effectiveness

Reorganization Program Calls for More Members And Increased Income; Many Active Committees

CHICAGO.—As a part of the new program to make the National Editorial Association more responsive to modern needs, the services of outstanding weekly and daily publishers in the United States are to be enlisted for the association's 1936-37 committees, it is announced by Clayton Rand, president.

In the decentralization move, each committee will be headed by a director as its chairman, with publishers throughout the nation assisting as committeemen.

Because of the primary importance of new members in the rebuilding of the national association, President Rand has assigned Director Howard W. Palmer, editor of the Greenwich (Conn.) Press and president of the Connecticut Editorial Association, as chairman of this committee, with Director Raymond Howard, publisher of the Madison Press at London, Ohio, as assistant chairman.

More Sustaining Memberships Needed

"We shall have to convert more five dollar individual memberships into twenty-five dollar sustaining ones during the coming year," said President Rand. "The National Editorial Association cannot render its larger service on a five dollar per membership basis. Many loyal editor-publishers should be in the twenty-five dollar sustaining minimum column permanently.

"I appeal to your business and professional sportsmanship to give us your substantial support as well as your verbal co-operation."

The legislative committee is headed by Robert H. Pritchard, publisher of the Weston (W. Va.) Democrat and immediate past president of the national association. Because of Mr. Pritchard's nearness to Washington, he expects to devote a generous part of his time to national legislative affairs in co-operation with William L. Daley, manager of the Washington office.

Chairman of the finance commit-

(Continued on page eight)

Likens Blue Streak to Speedy Streamline Train

Hackensack Paper Using Larger Ionic

Bergen Evening Record Lauds Reading Quality Of 7 Point on 8 Body; Puts in Nineteen Fonts

HACKENSACK, N. J.—Nineteen fonts of 7 point Ionic No. 5 with Bold Face No. 2 were installed by the Bergen Evening Record here in August for a new body dress. An 8 point body is used for the new type.

"Even the casual reader and the person who takes but scant interest in the technicalities of newspaper publication will observe how easily the new type is read," ran a story in the first issue in the new dress. "It was originally designed to overcome eye fatigue and impaired vision of newspaper readers, particularly those with eye defects and those of advanced years.

"With the improvement of technical equipment in newspaper plants there has been a steady progress in readability of type faces. Two considerations have led to alterations in the design of type: readability and reduction of eye strain, and technical requirements of the mechanical department.

"Thus a type must be easily read, and at the same time it must be so designed that there are no small openings to fill up and smudge; there must be no fine lines or serifs to break down in stereotyping, electrotyping, or printing; the lower case should be fairly large in relation to the capitals, and the individual letters must be full, round and well proportioned.

"The new Bergen Evening Record body type is a product of the Mergenthaler Linotype Company, which has been a leader in many developments in typography."

Elizabeth Journal Installs 2 New 8s

ELIZABETH, N. J.—The Daily Journal of this city has added two Blue Streak Model 8s equipped with 5½ and 6¾ point Ionic No. 5 with Bold Face No. 2.

Fifteen Linotypes are now operated by the Daily Journal—thirteen Model 8s and two Model 25s.

Charlotte Observer Adds Four-Magazine 8

CHARLOTTE, N. C.—The Charlotte Observer has added a Four-Magazine Model 8 equipped with a Margach metal feeder and fonts of 5½ and 7 point Excelsior No. 1 with Bold Face No. 2; 14 point Metroblack with Metrolite, and 28 and 42 point Erbar Light Condensed.

Twelve Linotypes are now operated by the Observer.

Texas Ad Draws South Sea Order

GRAPEVINE, Texas.—That it pays to advertise in the Sun of this community was demonstrated in July when one of the Sun's advertisers received an order from Pitcairn Island, an isolated spot in the south Pacific made famous by stories by Charles Nordhoff and James Norman Hall.

Roy Clark of Pitcairn is a regular reader of the Sun. When he saw a local merchant's advertisement of files and shaving soap, necessities that cannot be purchased on Pitcairn Island, he ordered some.

The Sun believes that "this is a record for sales made through a weekly newspaper. Anyway, we are going to claim that honor until we are cited to one of greater distance."

W. E. Keeling is editor of the Sun.

Evening News of Paterson, N. J. Installs 2 Blue Streak Model 8s

PATERSON, N. J.—The Paterson Evening News, Harry B. Haines, publisher, has added two Blue Streak Model 8 Linotypes.

Included in the matrix equipment were three fonts of 8 point No. 2 with Bold Face No. 1, and one font each of 6 point No. 2 with Bold Face No. 1; 12 point Century Bold with Italic, and 10 point DeVinne with Antique No. 3.

When the two new machines were installed, the two obsolete typesetting machines they displaced were scrapped on the premises, as shown in the accompanying picture. The man at the right, directing the scrapping, is D. B. Watson, mechanical superintendent of the Evening News.

Eleven Linotypes are now operated by that paper.

Superintendent Watson directs the scrapping of the obsolete machines displaced by Blue Streaks

Scranton Republican Now Appearing With Its Body Matter Set in Excelsior

Annenberg Now Owner Of Inquirer

Well Known Publisher Pays Fifteen Million For Philadelphia Paper; No Change in Policies

PHILADELPHIA.—"It is a pleasure to announce that I have bought the Philadelphia Inquirer," stated M. L. Annenberg in a two column box at the top of the front page of the Inquirer here August 6.

Mr. Annenberg, who is publisher of the New York Morning Telegraph, the Miami Beach Tribune, Running Horse, Radio Guide, Racing Form and other publications paid $15,000,000 for the Inquirer and its real estate.

Mr. Annenberg entered journalism in the circulation department of the Chicago Examiner, and in four years was circulation manager of that paper. Later he went to Milwaukee and became agent in that city for all Chicago papers.

When Arthur Brisbane bought the Evening Wisconsin, the Free Press and the Daily News, they were merged into the Wisconsin News, and Mr. Annenberg was made publisher. In 1919 the News joined the Hearst organization.

In 1920 Mr. Annenberg was made circulation director of all Hearst publications, with offices in New York, and became president of the New York Daily Mirror. He retained his own interests, however, and by 1926 these had grown so large that he resigned from the Hearst organization to devote his full time to his own properties.

Mr. Annenberg announced that there would be no change in the editorial policies of the Inquirer, and invited the entire personnel of the paper to remain.

Austin Newspapers In New Building

AUSTIN, Texas.—In a 150 page special edition July 19 the American and the Statesman of this city announced that a modern new three story home had been completed for those papers.

The new building, constructed with Texas limestone, is ninety-two by 128 feet. The newspaper offices and plant occupy the ground floor and basement. The business offices, editorial and news rooms and composing room are on the ground floor, with the pressroom and space for newsprint storage in the basement. Two new presses, with a capacity of 35,000 to 40,000 thirty-two page papers an hour, have been installed.

The new building is soundproofed throughout, and has plenty of daylight, as it has open space on all four sides.

In addition to telling about the new newspaper home and about the work involved in issuing the papers, the special carried many stories about the Texas centennial, the history of Texas, and other features.

Louis N. Goldberg is business manager of the American and the Statesman, and John H. Keen is advertising manager. Ray E. Lee is managing editor of the American, and Charles E. Green holds that position on the Statesman staff.

Nine Linotypes are operated by the American and the Statesman—five Model 14s and four Model 8s.

W. F. Thompson is superintendent and night foreman. Ed Davenport is day foreman. Willard Dyer is machinist.

Baltimore Firm Adds 42 Pica 8

BALTIMORE.—The Baltimore Linotype Composition Company has added a Forty-two Pica Two-in-One Blue Streak Model 8 with a self-quadder.

Included in the matrix equipment are fonts of 8, 10, 12 and 14 point Memphis Light and Bold; 8 and 12 point Caslon No. 3 with Italic and Small Caps; 18 point Caslon No. 3, and 24 point Metroblack No. 2.

The San Jose Mercury-Herald Installs 20 Fonts of Paragon

SAN JOSE, Calif.—Twenty fonts of Linotype Paragon and four fonts in the Linotype Bodoni family have been installed by the Mercury-Herald of this city for a new body and head dress.

The installation included fifteen fonts of 8 point Paragon with Paragon Bold, one font of 8 point Paragon with Italic, two fonts of 6 point Paragon with Paragon Bold, and two fonts of 10 point Paragon with Paragon Bold. For headlines the Mercury-Herald installed fonts of 24 and 30 point Bodoni Bold Condensed, 18 point Bodoni Bold and 14 point Bodoni Bold with Italic.

Before the installation, the paper announced the changes in a series of advertisements stressing the fact that "eyes are your most precious possession," and pointing out that the adoption of new type was the Mercury-Herald's contribution toward relieving eyestrain. The first issue in the new type carried a front page announcement under an eight column streamer.

J. O. Hayes is president of the Mercury-Herald Company, and E. A. Hayes is vice president. Frank L. Baker is business manager, and Harold Hayes is assistant business manager.

Eighteen Linotypes are operated by the paper.

Edwin Musser is composing room foreman, and Otis Whiting is head machinist.

Knoxville Men Buy Journal

Lotspeich Is President; Clagett Is V. P., Editor; No Change in Personnel

KNOXVILLE.—With announcement of the purchase of the Knoxville Journal by a group of local business men including Roy N. Lotspeich, Ira A. Watson, R. H. Clagett and Robert R. Spillman, that paper enters a new era in its history, which has covered more than a century.

At a meeting of the stockholders Mr. Lotspeich was elected president and treasurer; Mr. Clagett, executive vice president; Mr. Watson, vice president, and Mr. Spillman, secretary.

Mr. Lotspeich is president of the Appalachian Mills Company. Mr. Watson is a prominent merchant of Knoxville and is associated with Mr. Lotspeich in various business enterprises. Mr. Spillman is vice president and secretary of the Appalachian Mills Company and director of the Home Federal Savings and Loan Association.

Clagett Continues as Editor

Mr. Clagett, who has been editor and general manager of the Journal since 1928, continues in that position. He is a native of Centerville, Tenn., and has been in newspaper

(Continued on page eight)

Grit Now Using Two Blue Streaks

WILLIAMSPORT, Pa.—Two Blue Streak Model 8s equipped with self-quadders have been added by Grit of this city.

Included in the matrix equipment are fonts of 5½ point No. 1 with Clarendon No. 1; 6 and 8 point Scotch with Italic and Small Caps; 8 point Old Style No. 1 with Antique No. 1, and 8 and 10 point Bodoni Book with Italic and Small Caps.

Eight Linotypes are now operated by Grit.

Scripps-Howard Names Davis to Denver Post

DENVER.—Forrest Davis, until recently a general staff writer for the Scripps-Howard newspapers, has been appointed editor of the Rocky Mountain News here to succeed Charles E. Lounsbury, who had been editor of the News five years.

Mr. Davis formerly was a member of the staffs of the New York World-Telegram and the New York Daily News. In addition to his work as reporter, commentator and critic, Mr. Davis has published two books and contributed to magazines.

Mr. Davis has announced the appointment of Larry L. Sisk, formerly managing editor of the Fort Worth Press and the Toledo News-Bee, as managing editor. Mr. Sisk has also been on the staff of the United Press and on Mid-Western newspapers.

Mr. Lounsbury has been granted an extended leave of absence.

Thirty-four Linos, Two New 27s, In New Home of Adelaide Paper

ADELAIDE, South Australia.—With the completion of a handsome modern four story building at the rear of the offices in Waymouth Street, the Advertiser Newspapers, Ltd., has installed the latest in printing equipment, including, among other things, a new newspaper press and two Model 27 Display Linotypes, the first to be installed in this part of the world. The paper now operates thirty-four Linotypes, including the two new display machines.

The new press, similar to one recently installed by the Chicago Tribune, has a capacity of 120,000 twenty-four page papers an hour.

The handsome new building occupies an "island" position with natural light and roadways on all four sides. Soundproofing treatment has been applied throughout. In the composing, stereotyping and other workrooms, mercury vapor lamps are employed.

Bridge Connects Buildings

A bridge between the old building and the new plant gives the editorial department easy access to the composing room, on the first floor of the new building.

The basement contains the autoreels, the paper store, a pneumatic tube power plant, an air compression unit and a water circulating system for cooling the metal castings used on the press cylinders.

The circulation department, loading docks, the stereoplate casting department and the pressroom occupy the ground floor. A gallery enables the public to inspect the whole of the mechanical operations on the ground floor.

A mezzanine floor is used for the publishing department, engineering workshop equipment and a general supplies store.

The composing room and the editorial and advertising departments are connected with a pneumatic tube system for the carrying of advertisements and news copy to a central station in the composing room, whence it is distributed to the Linotype operators. Part of this tube system runs to the telegraph department at the general post office, to expedite delivery of press telegrams to the Advertiser sub-editors' room.

The top floor of the building provides adequate space for the general printing department.

News Goes Through Fast

In the new building, putting the news into the paper is a swift procedure made possible by up to date equipment.

After the news and advertising matter has been set in type by the Linotype operators, it is arranged in flat formes. From these formes matrices are moulded in the stereo section and sent to the plate casting department, on the ground floor, by means of a vertical spill. For the production of the metal casts a pot containing eight tons of metal, kept at a temperature of 600 degrees by electrical heating elements, is used. Attached to this pot are two casting mechanisms, each of which will cast two fifty pound plates a minute ready for the press.

The semi-cylindrical reproductions of the pages are securely locked in the printing press by quick acting locks. The press itself is set in motion by two 250 horsepower motors. Each unit of the press, and there are six, is capable of producing sixteen pages of a complete newspaper. Two sets of folders collate the sheets from the different units and count out the papers.

Progressive Penn Daily Puts in Eighteen Fonts And Is Now Presenting News Matter in 7½ on 8

SCRANTON, Pa.—"A triumph of visual engineering" is the description given by the Republican here to its new dress of 7½ point Excelsior on an 8 point body.

Eighteen fonts of Excelsior have been installed by the Republican—twelve fonts of 7½ point Excelsior No. 1 with Bold Face No. 2; four fonts of 5½ point Excelsior No. 1 with Bold Face No. 2, and one font each of 8 point Excelsior No. 1 with Bold Face No. 2, and 9 point Excelsior with Bold Face No. 2.

"In its creation, art and science were partners," ran the story about Excelsior, which continued: "The change is of double significance. The Republican helps itself with a better looking product, and it helps its readers by lightening the optical task involved in absorbing news.

"Yet it is more than a change in the mechanics of newspaper publishing and an improvement in the art of reading. It is a definite contribution to the beauty of language.

"The English language is a priceless inheritance, and the Republican conception of the line of true enterprise is . . . , through constantly improving typography, to emphasize the power, the vividness and the virility of those words.

"In this philosophy the Republican for months has devoted much study to the selection of a type that would reduce eye strain to a minimum, and the new face and size adopted richly reward the study, experiment and expense invested in the quest."

Frank D. Schroth is editor and publisher of the Republican.

Albany News, Press Undergo Changes

ALBANY, N. Y.—The home of the Evening News and the Knickerbocker Press of this city is being given an extensive remodeling and redecorating.

The building is to have a new facade, of black glass trimmed with aluminum. White stucco will be used above the first floor. A modernistic neon sign will carry the name of the company.

An entrance through doors of hollow aluminum will open to a wide first floor vestibule. A steel stairway with bronze rails will lead from this to a decorative lobby from which all parts of the plant will be easily reached. Linoleum floors and redecorated interiors will further improve the building.

The changes are being made as part of a re-organization planned by A. J. McDonald, who has been general manager of the papers since May 1. The staffs of the Evening News and the Knickerbocker Press are being separated and segregated to opposite sides of the building. New personnel has been added to round out the newly created units and groups.

One of the new positions is that of advertising manager of the Evening News. Louis D. Young, formerly of the Syracuse Herald, was chosen by Mr. McDonald for that position.

John A. Burke, production manager of the Gannett newspapers, is supervising and directing the physical changes in the plant.

The Linotype News Lino Set Throughout

All lines of composition in this issue of The Linotype News were composed the Linotype way, even the largest lines in display advertisements. Most of the body matter is in the 7 point size of the new Linotype Opticon with Opticon Bold on an 8½ point body, with some of the lines extra leaded.

See "Makeup of This Issue," on page four.

Calmly Sleeping Puppy Nearly Bites Want Ad

ASHLAND, Ky.—Unusually quick results were obtained from a classified advertisement placed with the Daily Independent here for the return of a white and black pup.

Bill Rise, Linotype operator setting up ad copy, found the missing pet—asleep under the keyboard of his Linotype.

La Porte Herald-Argus, In Introducing Readers To Its New Models 8, 14, Calls Them Last Word

LA PORTE, Ind.—"What the streamline train is to land transportation, the Queen Mary and the Normandie to sea travel, the giant American Clipper planes and the Hindenburg to aviation—that's what the new Blue Streak Linotype is to printing," ran a front page story in the Daily Herald-Argus of this city August 7.

The story continued: "The Herald-Argus proudly announces today the installation of two new Blue Streak Linotypes—a Model 8 to serve both its job printing and newspaper departments, and a Model 14 to amplify its equipment for producing a better newspaper typographically.

"The new Blue Streaks are the last word in typesetting machinery! Just as the Herald, forerunner of the Herald-Argus, was the first newspaper in La Porte County to install a Linotype—just thirty-five years ago—so the Herald-Argus is the first Hoosier newspaper to reap the benefits of remarkable typography made possible by the new Blue Streak."

The new Model 14 is equipped with a self-quadder, a Mohr Lino-Saw and a Kendall metal feeder. Matrix equipment includes display sizes of Pabst Extra Bold Condensed and Metroblack No. 2.

The accompanying picture shows H. A. Lindgren, president of the La Porte Printing Company and general manager of the Herald-Argus, at the keyboard of the new Model 14. A story in the Herald-Argus told

(Continued on page eight)

Ohio Newspaper Praises Excelsior

NEWARK, Ohio.—"Civilized man required 5,000 years to produce a form of printing in which legibility does not interfere with the complete transfer of complex thought," ran a story in the Advocate here July 20.

"The Newark Advocate," the story continued, "today presents to its readers one of the latest and most satisfactory products of that procession of centuries. Excelsior body type, in which the Advocate presents its news and features today for the first time, is as new as tomorrow, as crisp and clear as church chimes across the snow."

C. W. Spencer is president of the Advocate Printing Company, issuing the Advocate.

Morristown Paper Adds Blue Streaks

MORRISTOWN, N. J.—Two Blue Streak Model 8s have been installed by the Daily Record and Jerseyman of this city, Norman B. Tomlinson, editor and publisher.

On the new machines are fonts of 7½ point Ionic No. 5 with Bold Face No. 2; 5½ point Ionic No. 5 with Bold Face No. 2; 10 point Century Expanded with Cheltenham Bold; 12 point Bodoni Bold with Italic, and 18 point Bodoni Bold.

Three Model 8s and a Model 26 are now operated by the Daily Record and Jerseyman.

Chooses Eight Point Size With One Point Leading To Enhance Legibility Of Its News Body Matter

BOSTON.—"New Clear Cut Type Adopted by Transcript," ran a front page headline in the Evening Transcript of this city July 27, on a story announcing that that paper had adopted a new body dress of 8 point Ionic No. 5 on a 9 point body.

"Vision Experts Hail New Type in Transcript," ran a headline the next day, and the following day a headline stated that "Ad Men Praise the Transcript's New Ionic Type."

The stories included comments by twenty-five men and women, all of whom were enthusiastic in their praise of the new dress. John E. Corbett, chairman of the Massachusetts board of registration in optometry, stated: "The style and size of the new type increases the normal reading speed by about seventy-five per cent, and will retard the development of eye strain, and be somewhat in the nature of a blessing to those who are already handicapped by defective vision."

Professor Copeland Praises It

Prof. Charles Townsend Copeland, one of Harvard's most distinguished men of letters, declared that "valuable as the Transcript was in its old print, it will be doubly valuable in its new."

Myron E. Pierce, attorney, stated: "It will make life a lot pleasanter for your many devoted readers. In these critical times when we scan the papers eagerly for accurate information and sound comment on public affairs, it will be a real pleasure to read the Transcript."

A letter from L. W. Munro of Doremus & Company stated: "This agency was fortunate in having one of its clients represented in your first issue to have this new format, and I believe that, as a result, the attention value of the advertisement was enhanced about 100 per cent."

Perry Walton of the Walton Advertising and Printing Company congratulated the Transcript, and added: "Type is like glass in a window. The clearer it is, the quicker and the deeper is the mental reception of the idea it conveys. If, in addition to this, it has a subtle beauty, so much more effective is its use."

"A great improvement, a fine, clean looking page," was the comment of L. B. Slocum of N. W. Ayer & Son.

Henry B. Humphrey of the H. B. Humphrey Company commented: "When I picked up the Transcript Monday night I noticed at once the fresh appearance of the page. Then I saw the article on the new type and knew why I had been particularly struck with the paper. I think it's a splendid improvement."

George R. Dunham of the Greenleaf Company stated: "The new type is a good bet for the advertiser."

Keeping Pace With Modern Times

Frank Hatch of Batten, Barton, Durstine & Osborn, also welcomed the type change. "I take this type al-

(Continued on page eight)

Offers Up Sheep Before New Lino

ISTANBUL, Turkey.—Just before a recently installed Model 8 Linotype was started on its career of usefulness in the plant of the Ulka Printing Office here a sheep was sacrificed before the machine as a thanks offering to Allah.

Later the same day the sheep was roasted and Bay Mehmed Faruk Gurtanca, proprietor, served it at a banquet to friends and visitors who called to see the new machine in operation.

Davenport Daily Times, Fifty, Publishes 172 Page Special

DAVENPORT, Iowa.—Forty-two thousand copies were printed of the 172 page special issued by the Daily Times here in July to celebrate its fiftieth anniversary and the centennial of the city.

The difficulties that confronted carriers in distributing the papers were illustrated in a humorous drawing on the front page showing a carrier trying to figure out how to deliver a stack of papers so high he could not see over it.

Each copy weighed nearly three pounds, and the carriers could take only about twenty papers on each trip, although nearly all of them had one or two assistants each. Some of the parents helped their boys by driving automobiles for them. To express appreciation for the work of the carriers, the Times entertained them at a dinner and theater party after the edition had been distributed.

Copies of the special mailed outside of the city were sent in a striking wrapper that had two sets of rules printed in red and blue on each side. Several special advertisements were printed in blue, red and yellow.

E. P. Adler, publisher of the Times, and members of the staff received many compliments on the big edition.

Mr. Adler is president of the Lee Newspaper Syndicate, of which the Daily Times is a member. The organization was founded by A. W. Lee, who purchased the Ottumwa Courier in 1890. The Davenport Times was the second paper in the group, and Mr. Adler, who had been business manager of the Courier, became publisher of the Times when it was purchased by Mr. Lee.

The Lee group today includes, in addition to the Davenport Times and the Ottumwa Courier: the Davenport Democrat and Leader, the Muscatine Journal, the Mason City Globe-Gazette and Times, the Madison (Wis.) State Journal, the La Crosse (Wis.) Tribune and Leader-Press, the Hannibal (Mo.) Courier-Post, the Kewanee (Ill.) Star-Courier, and the Lincoln (Neb.) Star.

After Mr. Lee's death, in 1907, Mr. Adler was named president, and James F. Powell, who had succeeded Mr. Adler as business manager of the Ottumwa Courier, was made vice president. Mr. Powell died in 1928, and Frank D. Throop, publisher of the Lincoln Star, succeeded him as vice president. Lee P. Loomis, business manager of the Mason City Globe-Gazette, was named secretary.

(Continued on page eight)

EXAMPLE 188

THE LINOTYPE NEWS

July-August 1937
VOL. XVI—NO. 1

Many Plants Install MANY LINOTYPES

Many large installations of Linotypes and of faces in the Linotype legibility group have been made on both sides of the Atlantic since the latest previous issue of The Linotype News.

Thirty Linotypes have been installed by Allied Newspapers, Ltd., Manchester, England.

Twenty-five Linotypes—five of them with teletypesetter attachments—by the Glasgow Herald.

Seventeen Linotypes by the Western Morning News of Plymouth, England.

Seventeen by the Chronicle of Newcastle, England.

Sixteen by the Journal of Aberdeen, Scotland.

Eleven by the Guardian of Nottingham, England.

Five Linotypes by the News of Norfolk, England.

The Christian Science Monitor, Boston, which issues seven editions daily, each individually planned for a particular geographical section, and which have to be put together quickly, has ordered four Blue Streak Linotypes—three Model 8s and a Model 29 mixer.

Four Blue Streak Linotypes—a Two-in-One Four Magazine Model 29, two other Model 29s and a Model 30 with a six-mold disk—have been installed by the Houston Chronicle.

Three Linotypes—two Model 14s and a Model 22—have been added by the Toronto Evening Telegram.

Two Forty-two Pica Blue Streak Model 8s with self-quadders have been added by Benjamin H. Tyrrel, Inc., New York City. Thirteen Linotypes are now operated by that concern.

Shortly after the installation of a Forty-two Pica Model 8, a Model 25 was added by the Gotham Typographers, Inc., New York City. Forty-four fonts of matrices, twenty-seven full length magazines, twenty split magazines, four matrix cabinets and two magazine racks also have been installed.

Twenty-four fonts of Linotype Excelsior have been installed by the Youngstown (Ohio) Vindicator and Telegram—twenty-one fonts of 7 point Excelsior with Bold Face No. 2, and one font each of 7 point Excelsior with Italic and Small Caps; 10 point Excelsior with Bold Face No. 2, and 12 point Excelsior with Bold Face No. 2.

Twenty-four fonts of 7½ point Linotype Ionic No. 5—twenty-three fonts with Bold Face No. 2, and one font with Italic and Small Caps—have been installed by the Buffalo Evening News.

Twenty-four fonts of 7 point Linotype Excelsior with Bold Face No. 2 have been installed by the Cleveland Plain Dealer.

Twenty-two fonts of 5½ point Linotype Excelsior with Bold Face No. 2 have been added by the Louisville (Ky.) Courier-Journal and Times.

Sixteen fonts of 7½ point Ionic No. 5 with Bold Face No. 2 have been installed by the Portland (Maine) Press-Herald and Express and Telegram.

Thirteen fonts of 7 point Excelsior with Bold Face No. 2 have been installed by the Wilkes-Barre (Pa.) Times-Leader.

Thirteen fonts of 7½ point Opticon with Bold Face No. 2 have been installed by the Worcester Post.

Twelve fonts of 7 point Ionic No. 5 with Bold Face No. 2, and ten fonts of the 5½ point size, have been installed by the Providence (R.I.) Star-Tribune.

Linotype Users Win Most Prizes At N. E. A. Meet

Attract 24 Honors Out of Possible 36 In 12 Classifications

DETROIT.—Twenty of the twenty-nine papers that won prizes at the annual convention of the National Editorial Association here in July were Linotype users. The twenty Linotype users won twenty-four of the thirty-six prizes. Certificates provided by the Mergenthaler Linotype Company were presented to all winners.

First prize in the general excellence contest for dailies of more than 3,500 circulation was won by the Morristown (N. J.) Record. The Ada (Okla.) Evening News won second, and the Bellefontaine (Ohio) Daily Examiner, third. In the division for dailies of less than 3,500 circulation the Chelsea (Mass.) Record won first; the Montrose (Colo.) Press, second, and the Crookston (Minn.) Times, third.

The Park Region Echo of Alexandria, Minn., won first in general excellence for weeklies with circulations of more than 1,000. The New Canaan (Conn.) Advertiser was second, and the Hillsboro (Ore.) Argus, third. In the division for weeklies of less than 1,000 circulation the Claremont (Calif.) Courier placed first; the Heron Lake (Minn.) News, second, and the Chadwick (Ill.) Review, third.

The New Canaan (Conn.) Advertiser won first in the best editorial page contest. The Detroit Lakes (Minn.) Record was second, and the Hillsboro (Ore.) Argus, third.

The Morristown (N. J.) Record won first in the newspaper production contest for dailies, the Norman (Okla.) Transcript placed second, and the Ada (Okla.) News, third. In the weekly division of the same contest the Montclair (N. J.) Times won first; the Archbold (Ohio) Buckeye, second, and the Barrington (Ill.) Review, third.

The International Falls (Minn.) Daily Journal won first in the most outstanding edition contest for dailies. The Ada (Okla.) News placed second, and the Seminole (Okla.) Producer, third. First place in the most outstanding edition contest for weeklies was won by the Matawan (N. J.) Journal. The Crystal Lake (Ill.) Herald placed second, and the Peninsula Enterprise, Accomac, Va., third.

For the best use of illustrative material the Sheldon (Iowa) Mail won first; the Storm Lake (Iowa) Pilot-Tribune, second, and the Sheldon (Iowa) Sun, third.

The Greenwich (Conn.) Press won first in the job printing exhibit contest. The Claremont (Calif.) Courier placed second, and the Norman (Okla.) Transcript, third.

The Mitchell (Neb.) Index won first in the community service contest for weeklies. The Worthington (Minn.) Globe ranked second, and the Crawford County Press, Prairie du Chien, Wis., third.

The Linotype News Lino Set Throughout

As usual, all lines of composition in this issue of The Linotype News were composed the Linotype way, even the big heads and the largest lines in display advertisements.

Most of the body matter is in 7½ point Excelsior with Bold Face No. 2 on a 9 point body, with some of the lines extra leaded, and most of the heads are in the new Erbar Medium Condensed.

See "Makeup of This Issue," on page four.

Chelsea Evening Record Adopts New Head Dress

CHELSEA, Mass.—The Evening Record here has adopted a new head dress, using various sizes of Metromedium No. 2, set flush at the left in caps and lower case.

H. D. Hancock, general manager, states, "Many favorable comments were made by readers to the effect that the new style made for easier reading. It 'opened up' the front page considerably and changed its appearance a good deal."

The Record won first in the general excellence contest for dailies of less than 3,500 circulation at the recent convention of the National Editorial Association in Detroit.

Cheyenne Paper Installs Two Blue Streak Linos

CHEYENNE, Wyo.—Two Blue Streak Linotypes—a Model 30 and a Model 14—have been installed by the Wyoming State Tribune-Leader of this city.

Both of the new machines carry duplex display equipment for casting two-letter 18 and 24 point matrices. Matrix equipment includes various sizes of Erbar Bold Condensed, Garamond Bold and Italic, Gothic No. 16 with Cheltenham Bold, Pabst Extra Bold Condensed with Italic, Metromedium No. 2 with Italic, and advertising figures.

Alfred G. Hill is president of the Tribune Publishing Company John Charles Thompson is editor. The advertising department is managed by Lester A. Walker, with Cal Owen in charge of national advertising. R. R. Olbaugh directs the Wyoming Stockman-Farmer, which is published by the same organization.

Ty L. Hopgood is mechanical superintendent.

Mr. Hill came to this city from Fort Collins, Colo. He formerly was with the Philadelphia Public Ledger, and later on the Washington staff of the United Press.

Martinsville Bulletin Puts in Two Blue Streaks

MARTINSVILLE, Va. — Two Linotypes equipped with Kendall metal feeders—a Blue Streak Model 14 and a Four-Magazine Model 8—have been added by the Martinsville Daily Bulletin and Morning Post.

Included in the matrix equipment are fonts of 7½ point Excelsior with Bold Face No. 2; 10 point Excelsior with Memphis Bold; 14 point Memphis Light and Bold; 18 point Memphis Medium with Italic; 18 and 30 point Memphis Bold Advertising Figures; 24 point Erbar Light Condensed, and 24 and 30 point Gothic No. 13.

Norfolk Papers to Have Fine Modern Building

NORFOLK, Va.—Work is progressing rapidly on a modern new building for Norfolk Newspapers, Inc., publishing the Ledger-Dispatch and the Virginian-Pilot of this city, which will be ready for occupancy next fall.

The building will be in two sections, with a connecting wing between them. The four story front section, measuring seventy-five by 111 feet, will house the editorial and business departments and executive offices, while the mechanical plant will be in the rear part, a two story structure 106 by 126 feet. The total depth will be nearly 231 feet.

Both sections will be of reinforced concrete construction. The imposing four story front section will be in semi-classic design with finish in Indiana limestone, while the rear section and the connecting wing will be faced with brick.

A handsome lobby twenty by thirteen feet will greet visitors on the first floor of the front section, back of which will be the main public offices, cashier's office, and circulation and classified advertising departments. Advertising offices of the Ledger-Dispatch will occupy the east part of the first floor, and those of the Virginian-Pilot the west part.

News rooms of both papers will be on the second floor, with a soundproof room for news service teletypes convenient to news offices of both papers. On that floor also will be photographic dark rooms and engraving rooms.

Executive Offices To Be on Third Floor

Offices of executives and editorial writers will be on the third floor, together with the morgue, the accounting department and the record vault. On that floor will be the offices of S. L. Slover, chairman of the board of Norfolk Newspapers, Inc.; Paul S. Huber, president; Frederick Lewis and W. S. Wilkinson, vice presidents, and H. S. Lewis, secretary-treasurer.

The fourth floor will provide for future expansion.

The first floor of the mechanical plant will house the pressroom, mailing room, paper storage room and boiler room. Two sextuple presses and double octuple presses, with a total capacity of 100,000 twenty-four page papers an hour, will be installed.

The composing room will be on the second floor of the mechanical plant. Space will be provided for thirty-five Linotypes. The stereotyping department will occupy space on both the first and second floors.

The heating system will be of the automatic downfeed, gravity return, low pressure steam type, burning oil, with radiators hidden behind ornamental grills throughout the building, and zone controlled for temperature. In the mechanical plant the humidity also will be controlled.

Indirect lighting will be used in all the offices, with direct lighting in the mechanical departments.

How the fine new home of Norfolk Newspapers, Inc., will look

F. S. Murphy Now Heads Hartford Times

Began as Errand Boy With That Newspaper Thirty-nine Years Ago

HARTFORD, Conn. — Francis S. Murphy, former general manager of the Times of this city, has been named head of that paper and its radio station, to succeed the late John F. Rolfe.

Mr. Murphy has been with the Times since 1898, when he became an errand boy. He has worked in various departments, and has been a stockholder since the paper was incorporated, in 1909. He was elected secretary at that time, also, and was holding that position when the paper was purchased by Frank E. Gannett, in 1928. He was then promoted to business manager and advertising director, and in December, 1935, became general manager.

Among Mr. Murphy's achievements are a successful campaign for the modernization of houses and buildings of greater Hartford, and the Times highway safety campaign, which has attained national importance.

In 1907 Mr. Murphy married Iva P. Marsh of Hartford. They have one son, Warner Murphy.

Charles C. Hemenway, editor of the Times, was named a director to succeed Mr. Rolfe. He also became assistant secretary. Mr. Hemenway joined the staff in 1920, as an editorial writer, and became, successively, managing editor, associate editor, and editor.

David R. Daniel was promoted from local advertising manager to business manager. Mr. Daniel, a native of Hartford, has, like Mr. Murphy, worked for no other newspaper or business.

Alex G. Berglund, former local advertising solicitor, has been made local advertising manager.

Linotype Set Papers Lead Field in Maine

ORONO, Maine.—All but one of the papers that won prizes at the annual meeting of the Maine Press Association, held here June 25 and 26, are Linotype users. The winners were awarded certificates presented through the association by the Mergenthaler Linotype Company.

The Houlton Pioneer-Times won the awards for the best front page and for best general makeup in the division for weeklies with circulations of more than 1,800. The Rumford Falls Times won the prize for the best handling of display advertising in that division, and the Brunswick Record for the best classified advertising columns.

The Boothbay Register, Boothbay Harbor, which has its body matter set in Linotype Ionic No. 5, won the best front page and the best general makeup awards in the class for weeklies with circulations of less than 1,800. The certificate for the best handling of display advertising went to the Guilford Register, and the Piscataquis Observer won the award for the best classified advertising columns.

Four Weeklies Win Rhame Certificates

MARION, Va.—At the convention of the Virginia Press Association held here July 23 and 24, C. C. Rhame certificates of award were presented to four Virginia weeklies, first prize winners in the association's latest better newspaper contest.

To the Farmville Herald went the certificate for the best front page. The Eastern Shore News of Onancock received the award for best general makeup; the Peninsula Enterprise of Accomac the certificate for best advertising display, and the Pittsylvania Tribune, Chatham, the certificate for best press work.

Judges were Josiah P. Rowe, Jr., manager of the Fredericksburg Free Lance-Star; W. C. Stouffer, managing editor of the Roanoke World-News, and Ellis Loveless, assistant business manager of the Norfolk Virginian-Pilot and Ledger-Dispatch. Mr. Rowe announced the awards and presented the certificates.

Loomis Succeeds Clayton T. Rand As N. E. A. Head

W. H. Conrad Is V. P., With McCoy and Abels New Board Members

DETROIT.—At the meeting of the National Editorial Association here in July, W. W. Loomis, publisher of the La Grange (Ill.) Citizen, was elected president to succeed Clayton T. Rand, publisher of the Gulfport (Miss.) Guide.

William H. Conrad, publisher of the Taylor County Star-News, Medford, Wis., was elected vice president, and Walter H. Crim, editor of the Salem (Ind.) Republican-Leader, was re-elected treasurer.

Major Bruce McCoy, field manager of the Louisiana Press Association, and Edwin F. Abels, publisher of the Douglas County Republican, Lawrence, Kan., were elected to the board of directors. Other members of the board are Roy A. Brown, San Rafael, Calif.; R. B. Howard, London, Ohio; Howard W. Palmer, Greenwich, Conn.; R. C. Stitser, Winnemucca, Nev., and Mr. Rand.

Lino, Press Play Requiem For Paris, Mo., Editor

PARIS, Mo.—A clacking Linotype and a whirring press played the requiem for Tom V. Bodine, who died July 29, after having presided over the Paris Mercury fifty years.

Mr. Bodine was a prominent democrat, known for his militant political editorials.

He confided to a relative two weeks before his death that he thought he would soon die, and said, "After my death I want to be taken to the newspaper office with the presses and the new Linotype all running."

J. A. Kautz Has Owned Kokomo Tribune 50 Years

KOKOMO, Ind.—John Arthur Kautz recently celebrated his fiftieth anniversary as owner and publisher of the Tribune of this city.

With H. E. McMonigal of Wabash, he purchased the paper from Benjamin B. Johnson in May, 1887, and took over the entire ownership and control ten years later.

The Tribune was founded in 1850. The Kokomo Dispatch, founded in 1870, was consolidated with the Tribune in 1930.

Oakland Tribune Adopts Up to Date Type Dress

OAKLAND, Calif.—"TNT—Timely Newspaper Typography" is the description given by the Tribune here to its new head dress, using Erbar Light Condensed for main heads and Metroblack No. 2 for second decks and smaller heads.

A Blue Streak Model 30 Linotype with a self-quadder and a six-pocket mold disk was installed preceding the change to the new head dress.

Heads are now set flush at the left and jim dashes have been eliminated. Heads are limited to single decks, except at the top of columns. Second decks there are indented twelve points.

Memphis Bold, Memphis Medium and Memphis Light have been installed for use on the society page, in heads, for cut overlines and cut legends. Memphis Light is used for cut legends in other parts of the paper.

Attention compelling colored posters featuring the letters "TNT" and "Timely Newspaper Typography" were printed to publicize the change in dress. Sample copies were distributed bearing red flyers telling about the new dress.

J. R. Knowland is president, publisher and editor of the Tribune. J. R. Knowland, Jr., and William F. Knowland are assistant publishers. Bruno A. Forsterer is secretary-treasurer and general manager.

A. L. Lengel is production manager. Charles Bramhall is superintendent, and C. F. Kenney is head machinist.

Linotype in Window Attracts Crowds to Sale

MILWAUKEE.—When, last spring, Gimbel Brothers' department store here put on a big sale, it had a large circular printed for it by the Wisconsin News Publishing Company, and had one of that company's Linotypes in operation in a store window.

Paul Utsler of the Milwaukee Sentinel operated the machine, which was referred to by the store, on an accompanying card, "as the throbbing heart of the printing industry."

The circular, which consisted of forty-four newspaper size pages, was the largest ever issued by the store, and probably the largest ever printed in Wisconsin.

The accompanying picture shows Mr. Utsler operating the machine, in a corner display window, with spectators watching him from two streets.

This Linotype and its operator, Paul Utsler, in store window, drew many to the big sale

C. H. Wrightson Tells Customers About His A-P-L

Boston Typographer Describes Facilities Of His Modern Plant

BOSTON.—"Gone are the limitations of size," ran an announcement from Cecil H. Wrightson, Inc., of this city, stating that a new All-Purpose Linotype had been installed by that firm.

"You can now get typesetting," the announcement continued, "in a size range of 5 point to 144 point, with a printing surface that is precision finished to keep press make-ready time down to a minimum, cast in easy to handle, economical all-slug type that meets the high standards of Cecil H. Wrightson, Inc., quality."

The announcement was sent out on a mailing piece on which were shown specimens of type faces available on the A-P-L. Several other attractive mailing pieces have been sent out also publicizing the type faces available to Wrightson customers. Among the faces mentioned were Electra, Baskerville, Benedictine, Bodoni, Bookman, Caslon, Garamond, Memphis and Cloister.

New Lino, Many Fonts For Pittsburgh Firm

PITTSBURGH. — Pfeuffer & Dibert of this city has installed a Two-in-One Blue Streak Model 14, five extra magazines, and several fonts of matrices.

Included in the matrix equipment were fonts of 12 and 18 point Memphis Extra Bold with Italic; 14 and 18 point Bodoni Bold with Italic; 18 point Erbar Light Condensed with Erbar Bold Condensed; 24 point Bodoni Bold; 24 point Bodoni Bold Italic; 24 point Memphis Extra Bold, and 28 point Erbar Bold Condensed.

Four Linotypes are now operated by that company.

Mechanical Conference At Birmingham, Alabama

BIRMINGHAM. — The first mechanical conference to be staged by the Southern Newspaper Publishers' Association will be held here September 20 and 21. Frederick K. Forstall of the New Orleans Times-Picayune and States is chairman of the committee on arrangements.

EXAMPLE 189

cars, buses or other conveyances, as well as many people while reading them at home, do it with their papers folded vertically.

To such readers, any heads, illustrations, picture legends or double-width body lines that straddle the vertical halves are annoyances, as such things make it necessary for those readers to keep turning pages back and forth, over and over, to follow such items.

Note that the nameplate in Example 189 was presented flush at the left (as also was the nameplate for the last page of the same issue); that no item was permitted to straddle the vertical half, and that the body lines of six of the leading stories were two columns wide.

The double-column body lines at the upper right were set in 12-point Excelsior leaded 2 points, and the other double-column body lines on the page were set in 9-point Excelsior on an 11-point body. Heads were in Erbar Medium Condensed and Metromedium No. 2.

The center column rule—a dividing rule—was somewhat heavier than the other column rules, and the same sort of rule treatment was carried out on all other pages of the same issue, except on the editorial page, where a full pica of white space, instead of a rule, was used between columns. Each inside page carried two sets of running heads and folios—one flush at the left, the other flush at the right.

Just how far a newspaper publisher or advertising manager would care to follow that vertical-half idea on the advertising pages would be "something else again." Surely neither executive would want to encourage an advertiser to hold down an eight-, seven-, six- or five-column display to four columns.

In the meantime, the typographic laboratory continued to turn out many other modern pages, as suggested by Examples 190 through 203.

In Example 190 the heads were in Bodoni Bold, Bodoni Bold Italic, Bodoni Bold Condensed and Poster Bodoni, with body matter in 7-point Ionic No. 5 with Bold Face No. 2 on an 8-point body.

A stronger page, which employed various sizes of the same head faces, and with body matter in 7½-point Excelsior with Bold Face No. 2 on an 8-point body, is suggested by Example 191.

And a stronger page still, with the eight-column line in 60-point Poster Bodoni, is suggested by Example 192.

In Example 193 the heads were in various sizes of Erbar Light Condensed, Metromedium No. 2, Metromedium No. 2 Italic and Memphis Medium Italic.

Weather Forecast
By U. S. Weather Bureau
Partly Cloudy, Slightly Warmer
Tonight and Tomorrow

The Modern Newspaper

NIGHT EDITION
Long Island News on Page 2

VOL. I, No. 1 — NEW YORK CITY, THURSDAY EVENING, THIS YEAR — PRICE FIVE CENTS

Sixty-three Local Men Capture Seven Prizes In State Tournament

Wall Street Tickers Lag Two Hours Behind As Purchasing Orders Pour in, Boost Prices

Will Have Plenty

Pretty and youthful Miss Joana Doran probably will never know the pangs of hungers, as an uncle has willed her thirty-six millions

Public Buying Boosts Market

Wall Street Tickers Lag Two Hours Behind As Prices Leap Ahead

Prices Leap Ahead As Market Mounts

Wall Street Tickers Lag Two Hours Behind

INDEX

Amusements	16
Bob Quillen	6
Brain Teaser	14
Bridge	15
Christian Science Lecture	8
Church News	5
Comics	14 and 15
Crossword Puzzle	13
Dr. Brady	15
Editorial	6
Edgar Guest	Page 1, 2d Section
Helen Worth	4
Jimmy Wood's Sportopics	10
John A. Heffernan	6
Long Island News	2
Lost and Found, Personals	2
Novel	15
Obituaries	7
Radio	14
Real Estate	13
Society	4
Sports	10 and 11
Theaters	16
Wants Ads	12 and 13
Washington	Page 1, 2d Section
Willie Willis	15

Public Buying Again Rushing Stock Market

Wall Street Tickers Lag Two Hours Behind As Purchasing Orders Pour in, Boost Prices

Prices Leap Ahead As Market Mounts To All-Time High

Thousands of Readers Applaud Our Splendid New Type Dress

Will Have Plenty

Pretty and youthful Miss Joana Doran probably will never know the pangs of hungers, as an uncle has willed her thirty-six millions

Public Buying Boosts Market

Wall Street Tickers Lag Two Hours Behind As Prices Leap Ahead

Prices Leap Ahead As Market Mounts

Public Buying Again Rushing Stock Market

Wall Street Tickers Lag Two Hours Behind As Purchasing Orders Pour in, Boost Prices

Prices Leap Ahead As Market Mounts To All-Time High

Wall Street Tickers Lag Two Hours Behind

Twenty-seven Local Men Capture Eighteen Prizes In National Tournament

Public Buying Boosts Market

Wall Street Tickers Lag Two Hours Behind As Prices Leap Ahead

Prices Leap Ahead As Market Mounts

Will Have Plenty

Pretty and youthful Miss Joana Doran probably will never know the pangs of hungers, as an uncle has willed her thirty-six millions

Public Buying Boosts Market

Wall Street Tickers Lag Two Hours Behind As Prices Leap Ahead

Wall Street Tickers Lag Two Hours Behind

Thousands of Readers Applaud Our Splendid New Type Dress

Wall Street Tickers Lag Two Hours Behind As Purchasing Orders Pour in, Boost Prices

Prices Leap Ahead As Market Mounts

WIRE BRIEFS

Wall Street Tickers

Lag Two Hours Behind

Wall Street Tickers

Lag Two Hours Behind

EXAMPLE 190

Weather Forecast
By U. S. Weather Bureau
Partly Cloudy, Slightly Warmer Tonight and Tomorrow

The Modern Newspaper

NIGHT EDITION
Long Island News on Page 2
★ ★ ★ ★

VOL. I, No. 1 — NEW YORK CITY, THURSDAY EVENING, THIS YEAR — PRICE FIVE CENTS

Nation Smiling Again as Prosperity Nears

People in All Sections of Country Becoming Optimistic

Governors of All of Our Forty-eight States Announce Holidays, and With No Speeches

Will Have Plenty

Pretty and youthful Miss Joana Doe probably will never know the pangs of hunger, as an uncle has willed her thirty millions

Public Buying Again Rushing Stock Market

Wall Street Tickers Lag Two Hours Behind As Purchasing Orders Pour in, Boost Prices

Will Have Plenty

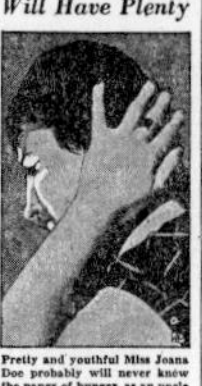

Pretty and youthful Miss Joana Doe probably will never know the pangs of hunger, as an uncle has willed her thirty millions

Public Buying Again Rushing Stock Market

Wall Street Tickers Lag Two Hours Behind As Purchasing Orders Pour in, Boost Prices

Will Have Plenty

Pretty and youthful Miss Joana Doe probably will never know the pangs of hunger, as an uncle has willed her thirty millions

Public Buying Again Rushing Stock Market

Wall Street Tickers Lag Two Hours Behind As Purchasing Orders Pour in, Boost Prices

Will Have Plenty

Pretty and youthful Miss Joana Doe probably will never know the pangs of hunger, as an uncle has willed her thirty millions

Public Buying Again Rushing Stock Market

Wall Street Tickers Lag Two Hours Behind As Purchasing Orders Pour in, Boost Prices

Public Buying Boosts Market

Wall Street Tickers Lag Two Hours Behind As Prices Leap Ahead

Prices Leap Ahead As Market Mounts To All-Time High

Prices Leap Ahead As Market Mounts

Thousands of Readers Applaud Our Splendid New Type Dress

Weather

For North, South, East, West and all points between: Perfectly glorious weather today, tomorrow, next Tuesday and for a whole flock of days to come after. Winds will be of the zephyr sort, stirring pleasantly through fields, through factory and office windows and up and down city streets. So put away your umbrella, little Susan, or exchange it for a parasol.

Station	High	Low	Rainfall
Asheville	86	58	.00
Atlanta	88	66	.00
Augusta	90	70	.00
Charleston	88	74	.00
Charlotte	88	66	.00
Columbia	92	70	.16
Denver	78	58	.28
Detroit	88	68	.00
Galveston	88	80	.00
Greensboro	84	64	.00
Greenville	92	65	.00
Jacksonville	92	74	.00
Key West	90	78	.00
Little Rock	90	72	.00
Los Angeles	78	62	.00
Memphis	86	76	.00
Miami	84	78	.00
Mlps-Stp.	92	68	.14
Mobile	90	76	.00
Mt. Mitchell	66	50	.00
New York	82	68	.00
Raleigh	86	70	.00
San Antonio	92	76	.00
San Francisco	64	50	.00
Spartanburg	92	66	.00
Washington	86	66	.00

(Other Weather Data on Page 9)

Wall Street Tickers Lag Two Hours Behind

The timing of the message is regarded here as more significant than anything in it, for until the beginning of this week's Anglo-French celebrations there had been an almost complete lack of contact between the British Government Foreign Minister, to discuss the European situation. It is scarcely

EXAMPLE 191

Weather Forecast
By U. S. Weather Bureau
Partly Cloudy, Slightly Warmer Tonight and Tomorrow

The Modern Newspaper

NIGHT EDITION
Long Island News on Page 2
★ ★ ★ ★

VOL. 1, No. 1 — NEW YORK CITY, THURSDAY EVENING, THIS YEAR — PRICE FIVE CENTS

Nation Smiles as Prosperity Nears

People in All Sections of Country Becoming Optimistic

Governors of All of Our Forty-eight States Announce Holidays, and With No Speeches

Will Have Plenty

Pretty and youthful Miss Joann Doe probably will never know the pangs of hunger, as an uncle has willed her thirty millions

Public Buying Boosts Market

Wall Street Tickers Lag Two Hours Behind As Prices Leap Ahead

James J. Hines, the Tammany district leader charged with being a member of the Arthur (Dutch Schultz) Flegenheimer gang in the policy racket, won a victory in Supreme Court yesterday when Justice Ferdinand Pecora granted the most important items in his demand for a bill of particulars from District Attorney Thomas E. Dewey.

Under the decision of Justice Pecora, Mr. Dewey received a choice of two courses, one of which he must elect in five days. He must choose between limiting his case against the Tammany leader to evidence that Hines entered an agreement with Schultz to "influence, intimidate and bribe judicial officers," or, if he intends to offer evidence that Hines actually carried out such an agreement, he must name the judicial officers—construed generally to mean judges.

Terms Binding in Trial

Whichever course Mr. Dewey follows will be binding upon him in the trial now scheduled to begin Aug. 15. Justice Pecora suggested in his decision that the point was puzzling because Mr. Dewey's office has, up to now, taken both positions.

At the time of Hines's arrest an information filed with the court charged that "James J. Hines did influence and intimidate judicial officers." Subsequently the indictment charged merely that Hines, Schultz and other dead or missing members of the Schultz gang "conferred and discussed plans to influence, intimidate and bribe judicial

Weather

For North, South, East, West and all points between: Perfectly glorious weather today, tomorrow, next Tuesday and for a whole flock of days to come after. Winds will be of the zephyr sort, stirring pleasantly through fields, through factory and office windows and up and down city streets. So put away your umbrella, little Susan, or exchange it for a parasol.

Station	High	Low	Rainfall
Asheville	86	58	.00
Atlanta	88	66	.00
Augusta	90	70	.00
Charleston	88	74	.00
Charlotte	88	66	.00
Columbia	92	70	.16
Denver	78	58	.28
Detroit	88	68	.00
Galveston	88	80	.00
Greensboro	84	64	.00
Greenville	92	65	.00
Jacksonville	92	74	.00
Key West	90	78	.00
Little Rock	90	72	.00
Los Angeles	78	62	.00
Memphis	86	76	.00
Miami	84	76	.00
Mlps-Stp.	93	68	.14
Mobile	90	76	.00
Mt. Mitchell	66	50	.00
New York	83	68	.00
Raleigh	86	70	.00
San Antonio	92	76	.00
San Francisco	64	50	.00
Spartanburg	92	66	.00
Washington	86	66	.00

(Other Weather Data on Page 2)

Public Buying Again Rushing Stock Market

Wall Street Tickers Lag Two Hours Behind As Purchasing Orders Pour in, Boost Prices

WASHINGTON, August 9.—The National Health Conference being held by the President's Interdepartmental Committee to Coordinate Health and Welfare Activities heard this morning a dramatic statement by Dr. Irvin Abell, president the American Medical Association, assuring the conference of organized medicine's "wholehearted cooperation in any of the efforts which you make for betterment in health care of the people of this country."

Court Explains Stand

The statement came as a welcome surprise to most of the non-medical delegates, representing labor, farmers' groups and other lay organizations interested in medical care from the public's point of view. It had been generally believed here that the national health program outlined yesterday at the conference by the government's Technical Committee on Medical Care, calling for additional expenditures of $850,000,000 a year for a ten-year period, half to be contributed by the Federal Government, would meet as its chief obstacle determined opofficers" and "agreed" to do so, for which Hines, the indictment continued received from "the Dutchman a first payment of $1,000 in cash."

The information was verified by Assistant District Attorney Charles P. Grimes. In view of it, Justice Pecora said, "there is a strong probability that, upon the trial, the people will seek to prove the actual influencing, bribing and intimidating of judicial and other public officers by the defendant Hines, as acts done in furtherance of the conspiracy charged in the indictment."

Prices Leap Ahead As Market Mounts To All-Time High

Dr. Abell's statement followed a plea for "a spirit of cooperation and constructive service" offered by Dr. F. L. Bishop, executive secretary of the interdepartmental committee, who presided at this morning's session.

Will Have Plenty

Pretty and youthful Miss Joann Doe probably will never know the pangs of hunger, as an uncle has willed her thirty millions

Public Buying Boosts Market

Wall Street Tickers Lag Two Hours Behind As Prices Leap Ahead

Prices Leap Ahead As Market Mounts

Public Buying Again Rushing Stock Market

Wall Street Tickers Lag Two Hours Behind As Purchasing Orders Pour in, Boost Prices

Prices Leap Ahead As Market Mounts To All-Time High

Thousands of Readers Applaud Our Splendid New Type Dress

Will Have Plenty

Pretty and youthful Miss Joann Doe probably will never know the pangs of hunger, as an uncle has willed her thirty millions

Public Buying Boosts Market

Wall Street Tickers Lag Two Hours Behind As Prices Leap Ahead

Prices Leap Ahead As Market Mounts

Prices Leap Ahead As Market Mounts

Wall Street Tickers Lag Two Hours Behind

Prices Leap Ahead As Market Mounts

Public Buying Again Rushing Stock Market

Wall Street Tickers Lag Two Hours Behind As Purchasing Orders Pour in, Boost Prices

Prices Leap Ahead As Market Mounts To All-Time High

Prices Leap Ahead As Market Mounts

Wall Street Tickers Lag Two Hours Behind

Will Have Plenty

Pretty and youthful Miss Joann Doe probably will never know the pangs of hunger, as an uncle has willed her thirty millions

Public Buying Boosts Market

Wall Street Tickers Lag Two Hours Behind As Prices Leap Ahead

Prices Leap Ahead As Market Mounts

Prices Leap Ahead As Market Mounts

Public Buying Again Rushing Stock Market

Wall Street Tickers Lag Two Hours Behind As Purchasing Orders Pour in, Boost Prices

Timing Held Significant

Prices Leap Ahead As Market Mounts

Wall Street Tickers Lag Two Hours Behind

EXAMPLE 192

NIGHT FINAL SPORTS

The Modern Paper

NIGHT FINAL SPORTS

VOL. I, No. 1 — NEW YORK CITY, THURSDAY EVENING, THIS YEAR — PRICE FIVE CENTS

Everybody, Everything Leaps Ahead as Industry Shifts Into High

Uncle Rip, 99, Casts Aside Crutches—Breaks Dash Record

Seventeen Men Leap 196 Feet In Seven Jumps

Then They Turn Round And Turn Cartwheels Quickly Out of Town

WASHINGTON, August 9—The National Health Conference being held by the President's Interdepartmental Committee to Coordinate Health and Welfare Activities heard this morning a dramatic statement by Dr. Irvin Abell, president the American Medical Association, assuring the conference of organized medicine's "wholehearted cooperation in any of the efforts which you make for betterment in health care of the people of this country."

To Star in Important Picture

HOME-TOWN BOY — HOME-TOWN GIRL

John Doe and Joana Roe, both of this city, have been officially informed by the Super-Super Studios of Hollywood that they will be given the leading roles in the picture of the century, "Whistling With the Hurricane," which will go into production next December, and be released early next year. The life stories of this home-town boy and girl who made good appear in our society pages today

Seventeen Men Leap 196 Feet In Seven Jumps

Then They Turn Round And Turn Cartwheels Quickly Out of Town

Faith, Hope and Charity Take Brisk Walk

Presented here is a candid camera shot made by our official photographer overseas, and shot across the briny by telepathy, of Three Gentlemen of Verona (or is one of them the Merchant of Venice?) out for a morning stroll along the Rialto. The central figure appears a bit concerned about something. Perhaps he is hoping for news new come from Padua, and hoping Portia will arrive in time

Seventeen Men Leap 196 Feet In Seven Jumps

Then They Turn Round And Turn Cartwheels Quickly Out of Town

Seventeen Men Leap 196 Feet

Then Turn Cartwheels Quickly Out of Town

Seventeen Men Leap 196 Feet

Then Turn Cartwheels Quickly Out of Town

Factories Are Humming, Workers Also, As Humming Birds Besiege Our Cities

Then They Turn Round And Turn Cartwheels Quickly Out of Town

Seventy-seven Lively Kangaroos Hop From Here to Breakfast

Then They Hop Again, As Folks Wonder Why And Ask Who Cares?

Twenty-seven Boys Run Eighteen Miles

But Clear Creek Runs From Here to Podunk

Twenty-seven Boys Run Eighteen Miles

Twenty-seven Boys Run Eighteen Miles

Twenty-seven Boys Run Eighteen Miles

Twenty-seven Boys Run Eighteen Miles

Twenty-seven Boys Run Eighteen Miles

Thirty-nine Girls Hurry 1,462 Yards

Thirty-nine Girls Hurry 1,462 Yards

Seventy-seven Lively Kangaroos Hop From Here to Breakfast

Thirty-nine Girls Hurry 1,462 Yards

Seventy-seven Lively Kangaroos Hop From Here to Breakfast

Twenty-seven Boys Run Sixteen Miles

Thirty-nine Girls Hurry 1,462 Yards

Boys Turn Cartwheels Quickly Out of Town

Boys Turn Cartwheels Quickly Out of Town

The Weather

For North, South, East, West and all points between: Perfectly glorious weather today, tomorrow, next Tuesday and a whole flock of days to follow.

(Weather Data on Page 8)

EXAMPLE 193

On the page suggested by Example 194 the heads were in various sizes of Erbar Medium Condensed, Metroblack No. 2, Metromedium No. 2 and Metromedium No. 2 Italic, with body lines in 7½-point Ionic No. 5 with Bold Face No. 2 on a 9-point body. Second decks of all single-column two-deck heads were in 12-point Metroblack No. 2. (Three pairs of heads on that page were "bumped," as the publisher for whom the page was made up wanted to keep on using some of his heads that way.)

In Example 195 most of the heads were in Erbar Medium Condensed, Metromedium No. 2 and Metromedium No. 2 Italic, but the eight-column lines were in 72-point Erbar Light Condensed and 48-point Memphis Medium Italic. (Another pair of "bumped" heads.)

A much stronger page, with heads in Erbar Bold Condensed, Metroblack No. 2 and Metroblack No. 2 Italic, is suggested by Example 196. (Another pair of "bumped" heads.)

In Example 197 the heads were in various sizes of Memphis Medium, Memphis Medium Condensed and Memphis Bold. The latter face was used for most of the second decks and for cut legends. Body matter was in 7½-point Ionic No. 5 with Bold Face No. 2 on a 9-point body. (Three more pairs of "bumped" heads.)

The heads in Example 198, a stronger page, were in various sizes of Memphis Bold, Memphis Bold Italic and Memphis Bold Condensed. Body matter was in 8-point Opticon with Bold Face No. 2 on a 9-point body.

An even stronger front page—one with two banner lines—worked out in the typographic laboratory is suggested by Example 199.

The main banner was in 120-point Franklin Gothic Condensed and the secondary banner in 60-point Franklin Gothic Italic. Top-of-page single-column heads were in 36- and 30-point Ryerson Condensed, with second decks in 14-point Spartan Heavy. Other members of the Ryerson and Spartan families, as well as 30-point Metroblack No. 2, were employed for other heads, and most of the body matter was in 7½-point Ionic No. 5 with Bold Face No. 2 on an 8½-point body. The lead of the main story on the page was in 12-point Ionic No. 5 leaded 2 points, and the body matter of the two-column-wide story in columns two and three was in 10-point Ionic No. 5 leaded 2 points. First words in cut legends were in 10-point Spartan Heavy and following words in 10-point Spartan Medium.

A variation of the same general makeup was employed for the page

NIGHT FINAL
SPORTS

The Modern Paper

NIGHT FINAL
SPORTS

VOL. I, No. 1 — NEW YORK CITY, THURSDAY EVENING, THIS YEAR — PRICE FIVE CENTS

Seventeen Men Leap 196 Yards In Eleven Jumps

Then They Turn Round And Turn Cartwheels Quickly Out of Town

The National Health Conference being held by the President's Interdepartmental Committee to Coordinate Health and Welfare Activities heard this morning a dramatic statement by Dr. Irvin Abell, president the American Medical Association, assuring the conference of organized medicine's "wholehearted cooperation in any of the efforts which you make for betterment in health care of the people of this country."

The statement came as a welcome surprise to most of the non-medical delegates, representing labor, farmers' groups and other lay organizations interested in medical care from the public's point of view. It had been generally believed here that the national health program outlined yesterday at the conference by the government's Technical Committee on Medical Care, calling for additional expenditures of $850,000,000 a year for a ten-year period, half to be contributed by the Federal Government, would meet as its chief obstacle determined opposition from the American Medical Association.

Cooperation Is Asked

Dr Abell's statement followed a plea for "a spirit of cooperation and constructive service" offered by Dr F L Bishop, executive secretary of the interdepartmental committee, who presided at this morning's session

Dr Bishop assured the conference that the program and the recommendations presented yesterday were not final but were open to suggestions and amendments.

Before calling on the first scheduled speaker, Dr Bishop recognized Dr Abell, who spoke as follows:

"The officials of the American Medical Association come to this meeting at the express instructions of its House of Delegates. ..."

Twenty-Seven Lively Acrobats Leap From Here to Breakfast

Then They Commence Another Large Race All Over Once Again

MRS. JONATHAN DOE
'It's News to Me'

Seventeen Men Leap 196 Yards In Eleven Jumps

Then They Turn Round And Turn Cartwheels Quickly Out of Town

Seventeen Men Leap 196 Yards In Eleven Jumps

Then They Turn Round And Turn Cartwheels Quickly Out of Town

Twenty-four Local Youths Run Eight Thousand Miles Without Pausing for Food

Then They Commence Another Large Race All Over Once Again With Big Enthusiasm

EXCELLENT NEW BUILDING IN AMERICA
One of Finest Structures Ever Erected on This Side

Twenty-one Women Prance 2,196 Yards

Then Turn Cartwheels Quickly Out of Country

Twenty-one Women Prance 2,196 Yards

Then Turn Cartwheels Quickly Out of Country

Seventeen Men Leap 196 Yards In Eleven Jumps

Seventeen Men Leap 196 Yards In Eleven Jumps

Seven Local Women Enter Golf Contests

Seven Local Women Enter Golf Contests

Seven Local Women Enter Golf Contests

Twenty-Seven Lively Acrobats Leap From Here to Breakfast

Seven Local Women Enter Golf Contests

Seven Local Women Enter Golf Contests

Seven Local Women Enter Golf Contests

Index of News and Features

FIRST SECTION	Page
Andrew R. Kelley	6
Clubs	13
Comics (two pages)	14, 15
Drama	8
Editorial	6
Ed Sullivan	8
Eve's Rib	7
How to Keep Well	6
Igor Cassini	11
Louis Sobol	7
Mabelle Jennings	7
Marriage Meddlers	11
Martha Blair	11
Merry-Go-Round	6
Music	4
Paul Mallon	7
Peter Carter	11
Society	10
Vagabondia	7
Walter Winchell	8
Woman's Page	12
Your Horoscope	9
$1,000 Name Contest	9

SECOND SECTION	Page
Bill Corum	21
Classified	25, 26, 27
Finance	22, 23
Inquiring Photographer	17
Legal Record	25
Local	17
Night Clubs	21
Picture Page	34
Powerhouse	18
Radio	25
Shively's Analysis	23
Skippy	17
Smilin' Jack	27
Sports	18, 19, 20, 21
U. S. and Us	25
Vincent Flaherty	19

EXAMPLE 194

NIGHT FINAL SPORTS

The Modern Paper

NIGHT FINAL SPORTS

VOL. I, No. 1 — NEW YORK CITY, THURSDAY EVENING, THIS YEAR — PRICE FIVE CENTS

Everybody, Everything Leaps Ahead as Industry Shifts Into High

Uncle Rip, 99, Casts Aside Crutches—Breaks Dash Record

Seventeen Men Leap 196 Feet In Seven Jumps

Then They Turn Round And Turn Cartwheels Quickly Out of Town

WASHINGTON, August 9.—The National Health Conference being held by the President's Interdepartmental Committee to Coordinate Health and Welfare Activities heard this morning a dramatic statement by Dr Irvin Abell, president the American Medical Association, assuring the conference of organized medicine's "wholehearted cooperation in any of the efforts which you make for betterment in health care of the people of this country."

The statement came as a welcome surprise to most of the non-medical delegates, representing labor, farmers' groups and other lay organizations interested in medical care from the public's point of view. It had been generally believed here that the national health program outlined yesterday at the conference by the government's Technical Committee on Medical Care, calling for additional expenditures of $850,000,000 a year for a ten-year period, half to be contributed by the Federal Government, would meet as its chief obstacle determined opposition from the American Medical Association.

Cooperation Is Asked

Dr. Abell's statement followed a plea for "a spirit of cooperation and constructive service" offered by Dr. F. L. Bishop, executive secretary of the interdepartmental committee, who presided at this morning's session.

Dr. Bishop assured the conference that the program and the recommendations presented yesterday were not final but were open to suggestions and amendments.

Before calling on the first scheduled speaker, Dr. Bishop recognized Dr. Abell, who spoke as follows:

"The officials of the American Medical Association come to this meeting at the express instructions of its House of Delegates. We come not imbued with a controversial spirit, but with a determination to give to this conference our best thought, our experience, and the information which has been accumulated in our bureaus through the years that have passed since the organization of the American Medical Association.

To Star in Important Picture

HOME-TOWN BOY — HOME-TOWN GIRL

John Doe and Joana Roe, both of this city, have been officially informed by the Super-Super Studios of Hollywood that they will be given the leading roles in the picture of the century, "Whistling With the Hurricane," which will go into production next December, and be released early next year. The life stories of this home-town boy and girl who made good appear in our society pages today

Seventeen Men Leap 196 Feet

Then Turn Cartwheels Quickly Out of Town

Before calling on the first scheduled speaker, Dr. Bishop recognized Dr. Abell, who spoke as follows:

"The officials of the American Medical Association come to this meeting at the express instructions of its House of Delegates. We come not imbued with a controversial spirit, but with a determination to give to this conference our best thought, our experience, and the information which has been accumulated in our bureaus through the years that have passed since the organization of the American Medical Association.

"The heads of our technical denot imbued with a controversial spirit, but with a determination to

Seventeen Men Leap 196 Feet

Then Turn Cartwheels Quickly Out of Town

Dr. Abell's statement followed a plea for "a spirit of cooperation and constructive service" offered by Dr. F. L. Bishop, executive secretary of the interdepartmental committee, who presided at this morning's session.

"On behalf of the interdepartwhole-hearted cooperation. We shall be most glad and most happy Medical Association come to this to give our services to be of help to you in that respect."

Josephine Roche, chairman of the Federal Government, would meet as its chief obstacle determined opposition from the American Mediinterdepartmental committee, responded:

Twenty-seven Boys Run Eighteen Miles

Twenty-seven Boys Run Eighteen Miles

Seventy-seven Lively Kangaroos Hop From Here to Breakfast

Boys Turn Cartwheels Quickly Out of Town

Seventeen Men Leap 196 Feet In Seven Jumps

Then They Turn Round And Turn Cartwheels Quickly Out of Town

Twenty-seven Boys Run Eighteen Miles

Thirty-nine Girls Hurry 1,462 Yards

Thirty-nine Girls Hurry 1,462 Yards

Faith, Hope and Charity Take Brisk Walk

Presented here is a candid camera shot made by our official photographer overseas, and shot across the briny by telepathy, of Three Gentlemen of Verona (or is one of them the Merchant of Venice?) out for a morning stroll along the Rialto. The central figure appears a bit concerned about something. Perhaps he is hoping for news new come from Padua, and hoping Portia will arrive in time

Factories Are Humming, Workers Also, As Humming Birds Besiege Our Cities

Seventy-seven Lively Kangaroos Hop From Here to Breakfast

Twenty-seven Boys Run Eighteen Miles

But Clear Creek Runs From Here to Podunk

Thirty-nine Girls Hurry 1,462 Yards

Seventy-seven Lively Kangaroos Hop From Here to Breakfast

Then They Turn Round And Turn Cartwheels Quickly Out of Town

Then They Hop Again, As Folks Wonder Why And Ask Who Cares?

Cooperation Is Asked

Twenty-seven Boys Run Sixteen Miles

Thirty-nine Girls Hurry 1,462 Yards

Seventeen Men Leap 196 Feet In Seven Jumps

Then They Turn Round And Turn Cartwheels Quickly Out of Town

Timing Held Significant

Twenty-seven Boys Run Eighteen Miles

Boys Turn Cartwheels Quickly Out of Town

"The heads of our technical departments are here, carrying with them the information which we have in our files and which we of the efforts which you make for gladly place at the disposal of this conference.

The Weather

For North, South, East, West and all points between: Perfectly glorious weather today, tomorrow, next Tuesday and a whole flock of days to follow.

(Weather Data on Page 8)

EXAMPLE 195

NIGHT FINAL SPORTS

The Modern Paper

NIGHT FINAL SPORTS

VOL. I, No. 1 — NEW YORK CITY, THURSDAY EVENING, THIS YEAR — PRICE FIVE CENTS

Nation Smiling Again as Prosperity Nears

Fourteen Men Leap 196 Feet In Three Jumps

Then They Turn Round And Turn Cartwheels Quickly Out of Town

WASHINGTON, August 9.—The National Health Conference being held by the President's Interdepartmental Committee to Coordinate Health and Welfare Activities heard this morning a dramatic statement by Dr. Irvin Abell, president of the American Medical Association, assuring the conference of organized medicine's "wholehearted cooperation in any of the efforts which you make for betterment in health care of the people of this country."

Cooperation Is Asked

Terms Binding in Trial

Twenty-seven Boys Run Eighteen Miles

Boys Turn Cartwheels Quickly Out of Town

To Star in Important Picture

HOME-TOWN BOY — HOME-TOWN GIRL

John Doe and Joana Roe, both of this city, have been officially informed by the Super-Super Studios of Hollywood that they will be given the leading roles in the picture of the century, "Whistling With the Hurricane," which will go into production next December, and be released early next year. The life stories of this home-town boy and girl who made good appear in our society pages today

Fourteen Men Leap 196 Feet

Then Turn Cartwheels Quickly Out of Town

Fourteen Men Leap 196 Feet

Then Turn Cartwheels Quickly Out of Town

Twenty-seven Boys Run Eighteen Miles

Twenty-seven Boys Run Eighteen Miles

Twenty-six Lively Kangaroos Hop From Here to Breakfast

Fourteen Men Leap 196 Feet In Three Jumps

Then They Turn Round And Turn Cartwheels Quickly Out of Town

Cooperation Is Asked

Twenty-seven Boys Run Eighteen Miles

Thirty-nine Girls Hurry 1,642 Yards

Thirty-nine Girls Hurry 1,462 Yards

Faith, Hope and Charity Take Brisk Walk

Presented here is a candid camera shot made by our official photographer overseas, and shot across the briny by telepathy, of Three Gentlemen of Verona (or is one of them the Merchant of Venice?) out for a morning stroll along the Rialto. The central figure appears a bit concerned about something. Perhaps he is hoping for news new come from Padua, and hoping Portia will arrive in time

Factories Humming, Workers Also, As Humming Birds Besiege Cities

Twenty-six Lively Kangaroos Hop From Here to Breakfast

Twenty-seven Boys Run Eighteen Miles

But Clear Creek Runs From Here to Podunk

Then They Hop Again, As Folks Wonder Why And Ask Who Cares?

Cooperation Is Asked.

Thirty-nine Girls Hurry 1,642 Yards

Twenty-six Lively Kangaroos Hop From Here to Breakfast

Then They Turn Round And Turn Cartwheels Quickly Out of Town

Twenty-four Boys Run 16 Miles

Thirty-nine Girls Hurry 1,462 Yards

Fourteen Men Leap 196 Feet In Three Jumps

Then They Turn Round And Turn Cartwheels Quickly Out of Town

Cooperation Is Asked

Timing Held Significant

Twenty-seven Boys Run Eighteen Miles

Boys Turn Cartwheels Quickly Out of Town

EXAMPLE 196

NIGHT FINAL
SPORTS

The Modern Paper

NIGHT FINAL
SPORTS

VOL. I, No. 1 — NEW YORK CITY, THURSDAY EVENING, THIS YEAR — PRICE FIVE CENTS

Eighty Local Youths Walk Thirteen Miles Then Wonder Why!

NEW BUILDING IN AMERICA
One of Finest Structures Ever Erected

Capture Nine Firsts, Twenty Other Prizes With Great Energy In Rand City Games

Sixteen Men Enter County Tournament

Capture Nine Firsts, Twenty Other Prizes In Rand City Games

Twenty-four Local Boys Win College Diplomas

Capture Nine Firsts, Twenty Other Prizes In Rand City Games

MRS. JONATHAN DOE
'It's News to Me'

Sixteen Men Enter County Tournament

Capture Nine Firsts, Twenty Other Prizes In Rand City Games

Sixteen Men Enter County Tournament

Capture Nine Firsts, Twenty Other Prizes In Rand City Games

Police Chief Jones Arrests Seventeen

Capture Nine Firsts, Twenty Other Prizes

Police Chief Jones Arrests Seventeen

Captures Nine Firsts, Twenty Other Prizes

Police Chief Jones Arrests Seventeen

Police Chief Jones Arrests Seventeen

Ladley Women Seeking Honor As Hi Debaters

Ladley Women Seeking Honor As Hi Debaters

Police Chief Jones Arrests Seventeen

Twenty-four Local Boys Win College Diplomas

Park's Band Concerts Attract Large Crowds

Park's Band Concerts Attract Large Crowds

Park's Band Concerts Attract Large Crowds

Index of News and Features

FIRST SECTION

	Page
Andrew R. Kelley	8
Clubs	13
Comics (two pages)	14, 15
Drama	8
Editorial	6
Ed Sullivan	8
Eve's Rib	7
How to Keep Well	6
Igor Cassini	11
Louis Sobol	7
Mabelle Jennings	7
Marriage Meddlers	11
Martha Blair	11
Merry-Go-Round	6
Music	4
Paul Mallon	7
Peter Carter	11
Society	10
Vagabondia	7
Walter Winchell	8
Woman's Page	12
Your Horoscope	9
$1,000 Name Contest	9

SECOND SECTION

Bill Corum	21
Classified	25, 26, 27
Finance	22, 23
Inquiring Photographer	17
Legal Record	25
Local	17
Night Clubs	21
Picture Page	24
Powerhouse	18
Radio	25
Shively's Analysis	23
Skippy	17
Smilin' Jack	27
Sports	18, 19, 20, 21
U. S. and Us	25
Vincent Flaherty	19

EXAMPLE 197

NIGHT FINAL SPORTS

The Modern Paper

NIGHT FINAL SPORTS

VOL. I, No. 1 — NEW YORK CITY, THURSDAY EVENING, THIS YEAR — PRICE FIVE CENTS

Eleven Men Try to Win Tournament

Capture Nine Firsts, Twenty Other Prizes In Rand City Games

WASHINGTON, D.C.—The National Health Conference being held by the President's Interdepartmental Committee to Coordinate Health and Welfare Activities heard this morning a dramatic statement by Dr. Irvin Abell, president the American Medical Association, assuring the conference of the organized medicine's "wholehearted cooperation in any of the efforts which you make for betterment in health care of the people of this country."

Cooperation Is Asked

The statement came as a welcome surprise to most of the nonmedical delegates, representing labor, farmers' groups and other lay organizations interested in medical care from the public's point of view. It had been generally believed here that the national health program outlined yesterday at the conference by the government's Technical Committee on Medical Care, calling for additional expenditures of $850,000,000 a year for a ten-year period, half to be contributed by the American Medical Association.

Dr. Abell's statement followed a plea for "a spirit of cooperation and constructive service" offered by Dr. F. L. Bishop, executive secretary of the interdepartmental committee, who presided at this morning's session.

Dr. Bishop assured the conference that the program and the recommendations presented yesterday were not final but were open to suggestions and amendments.

Terms Binding in Trial

Before calling on the first scheduled speaker, Dr. Bishop recognized Dr. Abell, who spoke as follows:

"The officials of the American Medical Association come to this meeting at the express instructions of its House of Delegates. We come not imbued with a controversial spirit, but with a determination to give to this conference our best thought, our experience, and the information which has been accumulated in our bureaus through the years that have passed since the organization of the American Medical Association.

"The heads of our technical departments are here, carrying with them the information which we have in our files and which we gladly place at the disposal of this conference.

"You may rest assured that in any of the efforts which you make for betterment in the health care of the people of this country you have our whole-hearted cooperation. We shall be most glad and most happy to give our services to be of help to you in that respect."

responded:

Cooperation Is Asked

"On behalf of the interdepartmental committee, we accept."

The statement came as a welcome surprise to most of the nonmedical delegates, representing labor, farmers' groups and other lay organizations interested in medical care from the public's point of view. It had been generally believed here that the national health program outlined yesterday at the conference by the government's Technical Committee on Medical Care, calling for additional expenditures of $850,000,000 a year for a ten-year period, half to be contributed by the American Medical Association.

Health and Welfare Activities heard this morning a dramatic statement by Dr. Irvin Abell, president the American Medical Association Committee on Medical Care calling for additional expenditures of $850,000,000 a year

Wins First Prize

Miss Diana Cook, who led all contestants with her display of peonies at the flower show here

Seek 3 Honors As Hi Debaters

Capture Nine Firsts, Twenty Other Prizes

WASHINGTON, D.C.—The National Health Conference being held by the President's Interdepartmental Committee to Coordinate Health and Welfare Activities heard this morning a dramatic statement by Dr. Irvin Abell, president the American Medical Association, assuring the conference of the organized medicine's "wholehearted cooperation in any of the efforts which you make for betterment in health care of the people of this country."

Health and Welfare Activities heard this morning a dramatic statement by Dr Irvin Abell, president the American Medical Association Committee on Medical Care calling for additional expenditures of $850,000,000 a year for a ten-year period, half to be contributed by the Federal Government, would meet as its chief obstacle determined opposition from the American Medical Association.

Ladley Women Seek Honors

"You may rest assured that in any of the efforts which you make for betterment in the health care of the people of this country you have our whole-hearted cooperation. We shall be most glad and most happy to give our services to be of help to you in that respect."

Josephine Roche, chairman of the interdepartmental committee, responded:

"On behalf of the interdepartmental committee, we accept."

The statement came as a welcome surprise to most of the nonmedical delegates, representing labor, farmers' groups and other lay organizations interested in medical care from the public's

Park's Band Concerts Attract Large Crowds

Dr. Abell's statement followed a National Health Conference being held by the President's Interdepartmental Committee to Coordinate, assuring the conference of organized medicine's "wholehearted cooperation in any of the efforts which you make for betterment in health care of the people of this country."

Dr. Bishop assured the conference that the program and the recommendations presented yesterday were not final but were open to plea for "a spirit of cooperation and constructive service" offered by Dr. F. L. Bishop,

Eleven Men Try to Win Tournament

Capture Nine Firsts, Twenty Other Prizes In Rand City Games

WASHINGTON, D.C.—The National Health Conference being held by the President's Interdepartmental Committee to Coordinate Health and Welfare Activities heard this morning a dramatic statement by Dr. Irvin Abell, president the American Medical Association, assuring the conference of the organized medicine's "wholehearted cooperation in any of the efforts which you make for betterment in health care of the people of this country."

The statement came as a welcome surprise to most of the nonmedical delegates, representing labor, farmers' groups and other lay organizations interested in medical care from the public's point of view. It had been generally believed here that the national health program outlined yesterday at the conference by the American Medical Association.

Cooperation Is Asked

Dr. Abell's statement followed government's Technical Committee on Medical Care, calling for additional expenditures of $850,000,000 a year for a ten-year period, half to be contributed by the a plea for "a spirit of cooperation and constructive service" offered by Dr. F. L. Bishop, executive secretary of the interdepartmental committee, who presided at this morning's session.

Dr. Bishop assured the conference that the program and the recommendations presented yesterday were not final but were open to suggestions and amendments.

Before calling on the first scheduled speaker, Dr. Bishop recognized Dr. Abell, who spoke as follows;

Terms Binding in Trial

"The officials of the American Medical Association come to this meeting at the express instructions of its House of Delegates. We come not imbued with a controversial spirit, but with a determination to give to this conference our best thought, our experience, and the information which has been accumulated in our bureaus through the years that have

"The heads of our technical departments are here, carrying with them the information which we have in our files and which we gladly place at the disposal of this conference.

"You may rest assured that in any of the efforts which you make for betterment in the health care of the people of this country you have our whole-hearted cooperation. executive secretary of the inter-

Police Chief Jones Arrests Seventeen

Dr. Abell's statement followed a National Health Conference being held by the President's Interdepartmental Committee to Coordinate, assuring the conference of organized medicine's "wholehearted cooperation in any of the efforts which you make for betterment in health care of the people of this country."

Dr. Bishop assured the conference that the program and the recommendations presented yesterday were not final but were open to plea for "a spirit of cooperation and constructive service" offered by Dr. F. L. Bishop, executive secretary of the interdepartmental committee, who is presiding at this morning's session. point of view. It had been generally believed here that the national health program outlined yesterday at the conference by the government's Technical Committee on Medical Care, calling for additional expenditures of $850,000,000 a year for a ten-year period, half to be contributed by the American Medical Association. for a ten-year period, half to be contributed by the Federal Government, would meet as its chief obstacle determined opposition from the American Medical Association.

Departmental Index

Classified	13, 14, 15
Comics	19
Crossword puzzle	12
Editorial	10
Financial	21
Grain and produce	20
Marian Miller	6
Marine	20
Moving picture news	7
News summary and index	2
Obituary	12
Picture page	5
Radio programs	11
Serial	6
Society	8
Sports news	17, 18
Young Oregonians	19

Maternal Red Hen Adopts 5 Kittens

Josephine Roche, chairman of the interdepartmental committee, responded:

"On behalf of the interdepartmental committee, we accept."

The statement came as a welcome surprise to most of the nonmedical delegates, representing labor, farmers' groups and other lay organizations interested in medical care from the public's point of view. It had been generally believed here that the national health program outlined yesterday at the conference by the government's Technical Committee on Medical Care, calling for additional expenditures of $850,000,000 a year for a ten-year period, half to be contributed by the American Medical Association.

Seek 3 Honors As Hi Debaters

Capture Nine Firsts, Twenty Other Prizes

Health and Welfare Activities heard this morning a dramatic statement by Dr Irvin Abell, president the American Medical Association Committee on Medical Care calling for additional expenditures of $850,000,000 a year for a ten-year period, half to be contributed by the Federal Government, would meet as its chief obstacle determined opposition from the American Medical Association.

Dr. Abell's statement followed a National Health Conference being held by the President's Interdepartmental Committee to Coordinate, assuring the conference of organized medicine's "wholehearted cooperation in any of the efforts which you make for betterment in health care of the people of this country"

Ladley Women Seek Honors

Dr. Bishop assured the conference that the program and the recommendations presented yesterday were not final but were open to plea for "a spirit of cooperation and constructive service" offered by Dr. F. L. Bishop, executive secretary of the interdepartmental committee, who is presiding at this morning's session. tion. We shall be most glad and most happy to give our services to be of help to you in that respect." mination to give to this conference our best thought, our experience, and the information which passed since the organization of the American Medical Association.

Terms Binding in Trial

"The heads of our technical department, and the information which has been accumulated in our bureaus through the years that have partments are here, carrying with them the information which we have in our files and which we gladly place at the disposal of this conference.

"You may rest assured that in any of the efforts which you make for betterment in the health care of the people of this country you have our whole-hearted cooperation. We shall be most glad and

Park's Band Concerts Attract Large Crowds

Josephine Roche, chairman of the interdepartmental committee, most happy to give our services to be of help to you in that respect." responded:

"On behalf of the interdepartmental committee, we accept."

The statement came as a welcome surprise to most of the nonmedical delegates, representing labor, farmers' groups and other lay organizations interested in medical care from the public's point of view. It had been generally believed here that the national health program outlined yesterday at the conference by the government's Technical Committee on Medical Care, calling for

Eleven Men Try to Win Tournament

Capture Nine Firsts, Twenty Other Prizes In Rand City Games

WASHINGTON, D.C.—The National Health Conference being held by the President's Interdepartmental Committee to Coordinate Health and Welfare Activities heard this morning a dramatic statement by Dr. Irvin Abell, president the American Medical Association, assuring the conference of the organized medicine's "wholehearted cooperation in any of the efforts which you make for betterment in health care of the people of this country."

Cooperation Is Asked

The statement came as a welcome surprise to most of the nonmedical delegates, representing labor, farmers' groups and other lay organizations interested in medical care from the public's point of view. It had been generally believed here that the national health program outlined yesterday at the conference by the government's Technical Committee on Medical Care, calling for additional expenditures of $850,000,000 a year for a ten-year period, half to be contributed by the American Medical Association.

Dr. Abell's statement followed a plea for "a spirit of cooperation and constructive service" offered by Dr. F. L. Bishop, executive secretary of the interdepartmental committee, who presided at this morning's session.

Dr Bishop assured the conference that the program and the recommendations presented yesterday were not final but were

Terms Binding in Trial

Before calling on the first scheduled speaker, Dr. Bishop recognized Dr. Abell, who spoke as follows:

"The officials of the American Medical Association come to this meeting at the express instructions of its House of Delegates. We come not imbued with a controversial spirit, but with a determination to give to this conference our best thought, our experience, and the information which presiding at this morning's session. departmental committee, who is presiding at this morning's session. additional expenditures of $850,000,000 a year for a ten-year period, half to be contributed by the American Medical Association. has been accumulated in our bureaus through the years that have passed since the organization of the American Medical Association.

Police Chief Jones Arrests Seventeen

Dr. Abell's statement followed a National Health Conference being held by the President's Interdepartmental Committee to Coordinate, assuring the conference of organized medicine's "wholehearted cooperation in any of the efforts which you make for betterment in health care of the people of this country."

Dr. Bishop assured the conference that the program and the recommendations presented yesterday were not final but were open to plea for "a spirit of cooperation and constructive service" offered by Dr. F. L. Bishop, executive secretary of the interdepartmental committee, who is

Attract Large Crowds

Health and Welfare Activities heard this morning a dramatic statement by Dr. Irvin Abell, president the American Medical Association Committee on Medical Care calling for additional expenditures of $850,000,000 a year for a ten-year period, half to be contributed by the Federal Government, would meet as its chief obstacle determined opposition from the American Medical Association Committee on Medical Care, calling for

Twenty-six Youngsters Win 658 College Degrees

President John Smith of American University, who will deliver the commencement address, and confer degrees at graduation exercises tomorrow afternoon

"The heads of our technical departments are here, carrying with them the information which we have in our files and which we gladly place at the disposal of this conference.

"You may rest assured that in any of the efforts which you make for betterment in the health care of the people of this country you have our whole-hearted cooperation. We shall be most glad and most happy to give our services to be of help to you in that respect."

Josephine Roche, chairman of the interdepartmental committee, responded:

"On behalf of the interdepartmental committee, we accept."

Terms Binding in Trial

The statement came as a welcome surprise to most of the nonmedical delegates, representing labor, farmers' groups and other lay organizations interested in medical care from the public's point of view. It had been generally believed here that the national health program outlined yesterday at the conference by the government's Technical Committee on Medical Care, calling for additional expenditures of $850,000,000 a year for a ten-year period, half to be contributed by the American Medical Association.

Health and Welfare Activities heard this morning a dramatic statement by Dr. Irvin Abell, president the American Medical Association Committee on Medical people of this country."

Cooperation Is Asked

The statement came as a welcal Care calling for additional expenditures of $850,000,000 a year for a ten-year period, half to be contributed by the Federal Government, would meet as its chief obstacle determined opposition from the American Medical Association.

Dr. Abell's statement followed a National Health Conference being held by the President's Interdepartmental Committee to Coordinate, assuring the conference of organized medicine's "wholehearted cooperation in any of the efforts which you make for betterment in health care of the people of this country."

Terms Binding in Trial

Dr Bishop assured the conference that the program and the recommendations presented yesterday were not final but were open to plea for "a spirit of cooperation and constructive service" offered by Dr. F. L. Bishop, executive secretary of the interdepartmental committee, who is presiding at this morning's session. medical care from the public's point of view. It had been generally believed here that the national health program outlined yesterday at the conference by the

Attract Large Crowds

Dr. Abell's statement followed a plea for "a spirit of cooperation and constructive service" offered by Dr. F. L. Bishop, executive secretary of the interdepartmental committee, who presided at this morning's session.

Dr. Bishop assured the conference that the program and the recommendations presented yesterday were not final but were open to suggestions and amendments.

Before calling on the first scheduled speaker, Dr. Bishop recognized Dr. Abell, who spoke as follows:

"The officials of the American Medical Association come to this meeting at the express instructions of its House of Delegates. We come not imbued with a controversial spirit, but with a determination to give to this conference our best thought, our experience, and the information which has been accumulated in our bureaus through the years that have passed since the organization of the American Medical Association.

"You may rest assured that in any of the efforts which you make for betterment in the health care of the people of this country you have our whole-hearted coopera-

Ladley Women Seek Honors

Dr. Abell's statement followed a National Health Conference being held by the President's Interdepartmental Committee to Coordinate, assuring the conference of organized medicine's "wholehearted cooperation in any of the efforts which you make for betterment in health care of the people of this country."

Dr. Bishop assured the conference that the program and the recommendations presented yesterday were not final but were open to plea for "a spirit of cooperation and constructive service" offered by Dr F. L. Bishop, executive secretary of the interdepartmental committee, who is presiding at this morning's session. Association Committee on Medical Care calling for additional expenditures of $850,000,000 a year for a ten-year period, half to be contributed by the Federal Government, would meet as its chief obstacle determined opposition from the American Medical Association statement by Dr Irvin Abell, medical delegates, representing ally believed here that the national health program outlined yesterday at the conference by the government's Technical Committee of the efforts which you make for betterment in health care of the lay organizations interested in

Attract Large Crowds

The statement came as a welcome surprise to most of the nonmedical care from the public's point of view. It had been generally believed here that the national health program outlined yesterday at the conference by the government's Technical Committee on Medical Care, calling for additional expenditures of $850,000,000 a year for a ten-year period, half to be contributed by the American Medical Association.

Dr. Abell's statement followed a plea for "a spirit of cooperation and constructive service" offered by Dr. F. L. Bishop, executive secretary of the interdepartmental committee, who is presiding at this morning's session. Association, assuring the conference of the organized medicine's "wholehearted cooperation in any obstacle determined opposition

Eleven Men Try to Win Tournament

Capture Nine Firsts, Twenty Other Prizes In Rand City Games

WASHINGTON, D.C.—The National Health Conference being held by the President's Interdepartmental Committee to Coordinate Health and Welfare Activities heard this morning a dramatic president the American Medical by Dr F. L. Bishop, executive secretary of the interdepartmental committee, who presided at this morning's session.

Dr Bishop assured the conference that the program and the recommendations presented yesterday were not final but were open to suggestions and amendments.

Before calling on the first scheduled speaker, Dr. Bishop recognized Dr. Abell, who spoke as follows:

Terms Binding in Trial

"The officials of the American Medical Association come to this meeting at the express instructions of its House of Delegates. We come not imbued with a controversial spirit, but with a determination to give to this conference our best thought, our experience, and the information which has been accumulated in our bureaus through the years that have passed since the organization of the American Medical Association.

"The heads of our technical departments are here, carrying with them the information which we have in our files and which we gladly place at the disposal of this conference.

Terms Binding in Trial

"You may rest assured that in any of the efforts which you make for betterment in the health care of the people of this country you have our whole-hearted cooperation. We shall be glad and most happy to give our services to be of help to you in that respect."

Josephine Roche, chairman of the interdepartmental committee, responded.

"On behalf of the interdepartmental committee, we accept."

Cooperation Is Asked

The statement came as a welcome on Medical Care, calling for additional expenditures of $850,000,000 a year for a ten-year period, half to be contributed by the American Medical Association heard this morning a dramatic statement by Dr Irvin Abell, medical care from the public's

Police Chief Jones Arrests Seventeen

Dr. Abell's statement followed a National Health Conference being held by the President's Interdepartmental Committee to Coordinate, assuring the conference of organized medicine's "wholehearted cooperation in any of the efforts which you make for betterment in health care of the people of this country."

Dr. Bishop assured the conference that the program and the recommendations presented yesterday were not final but were open to plea for "a spirit of cooperation and constructive service" offered by Dr. F. L. Bishop, executive secretary of the interdepartmental committee, who is presiding at this morning's session. president the American Medical Association Committee on Medical Care calling for additional ex-

Thirty-six Local Youngsters Win 2,658 College Degrees

The statement came as a welcome surprise to most of the nonmedical delegates, representing labor, farmers' groups and other lay organizations interested in medical care from the public's point of view. It had been generally believed here that the national health program outlined yesterday at the conference by the government's Technical Committee on Medical Care, calling for additional expenditures of $850,000,000 a year for a ten-year period, half to be contributed by the American Medical Association.

Dr. Abell's statement followed a plea for "a spirit of cooperation and constructive service" offered by Dr. F. L. Bishop, executive secretary of the interdepartmental committee, who presided at this morning's session.

Dr. Bishop assured the conference that the program and the recommendations presented yesterday were not final but were open to suggestions and amendments.

Before calling on the first scheduled speaker, Dr. Bishop recognized Dr Abell, who spoke as follows:

"The officials of the American Medical Association come to this meeting at the express instructions of its House of Delegates. We come not imbued with a controversial spirit, but with a determination to give to this conference our best thought, our experience, and the information which has been accumulated in our bureaus through the years that have passed since the organization of the American Medical Association.

"The heads of our technical departments are here, carrying with them the information which we have in our files and which we gladly place at the disposal of this

Thirty-six Local Youngsters Win 2,658 College Degrees

The statement came as a welcome surprise to most of the nonmedical delegates, representing labor, farmers' groups and other lay organizations interested in medical care from the public's point of view. It had been generally believed here that the national health program outlined yesterday at the conference by the government's Technical Committee on Medical Care, calling for additional expenditures of $850,000,000 a year for a ten-year period, half to be contributed by the American Medical Association.

Dr. Abell's statement followed a plea for "a spirit of cooperation and constructive service" offered from the American Medical Asso- by Dr F. L. Bishop, executive secretary of the interdepartmental committee, who presided at this morning's session.

Dr. Bishop assured the conference that the program and the recommendations presented yesterday were not final but were open to suggestions and amendments.

Before calling on the first scheduled speaker, Dr. Bishop recognized Dr. Abell, who spoke as follows:

"The officials of the American Medical Association come to this meeting at the express instructions of its House of Delegates. We come not imbued with a controversial spirit, but with a deter-

Thirty-six Local Youngsters Win 2,658 College Degrees

Before calling on the first scheduled speaker, Dr. Bishop recognized Dr. Abell, who spoke as follows:

"The officials of the American Medical Association come to this meeting at the express instructions of its House of Delegates. We come not imbued with a controversial spirit, but with a determination to give to this conference our best thought, our experience, and the information which has been accumulated in our bureaus through the years that have passed since the organization of the American Medical Association.

"The heads of our technical departments are here, carrying with them the information which we have in our files and which we gladly place at the disposal of this conference.

"You may rest assured that in any of the efforts which you make for betterment in the health care of the people of this country you have our whole-hearted coopera- government's Technical Committee. We shall be most glad and most happy to give our services to be of help to you in that respect."

Josephine Roche, chairman of the interdepartmental committee, responded:

"On behalf of the interdepartmental committee, we accept."

The statement came as a welcome surprise to most of the nonmedical delegates, representing labor, farmers' groups and other lay organizations interested in medical care from the public's point of view. It had been generally believed here that the national health program outlined yesterday at the conference by the government's Technical Committee on Medical Care, calling for additional expenditures of $850,000,000 a year for a ten-year period, half to be contributed by the American Medical Association.

Health and Welfare Activities heard this morning a dramatic statement by Dr. Irvin Abell, president the American Medical

EXAMPLE 198

TODAY'S NEWS TODAY!

The Modern Newspaper

NIGHT FINAL SPORTS

VOL. I, No. I — NEW YORK CITY, THURSDAY EVENING THIS YEAR — PRICE FIVE CENTS

FLOOD WATERS NOW FALLING

Five High-Speed Runners Hurry Onward

Sixteen Clubs To Meet Here Monday Night

Crescent Moon Men To Formulate Plans To Attend State Meet

WASHINGTON, D. C.—The National Health Conference being held now by the President's Interdepartmental Committee to Coordinate Health and Welfare Activities heard this morning a dramatic statement by Dr. John Doe, president of the American Medical Association, assuring the conference of organized medicine's "wholehearted co-operation in any of the efforts which you make for betterment in the health care of the people of this country."

SOMEWHERE the sun is shining ever so brightly and not a cloud flecks the lovely azure of the well-known and highly publicized blue sky from morn to night and from here to somewhere else

Nine Local Youngsters Pass for Tournament

WASHINGTON, D. C.—The National Health Conference being held now by the President's Interdepartmental Committee to Coordinate Health and Welfare Activities heard this morning a dramatic statement by Dr. Irvin Abell, president of the American Medical Association, assuring the conference of the organized medicine's "wholehearted cooperation in any of the efforts which you make for betterment in health care of the people of this country."

The statement came as a welcome surprise to most of the non-medical delegates, representing labor, farmers' groups and other lay organizations interested in medical care from the public's point of view. It had been generally believed here that the national health program outlined yesterday at the conference by the government's Technical Committee on Medical Care, calling for additional expenditures of $850,000,000 a year for a ten-year period, half to be contributed by the American Medical Association.

Dr. Abell's statement followed a plea for "a spirit of co-operation and constructive service" offered by Dr. F. L. Bishop, executive secretary of the interdepartmental committee, who presided at this morning's session.

Dr. Bishop assured the conference that the program and the recommendations presented Wednesday were not final but were open to suggestions and amendments.

"The officials of the American Medical Association come to this meeting at the express instructions of its House of Delegates. We come not imbued with a controversial spirit, but with a determination to give to this conference our best thought, our experience, and the information which has been accumulated in our bureaus through the years that have passed since the organization of the American Medical Association.

Before calling on the first scheduled speaker, Dr. Bishop recognized Dr. Abell, who spoke as follows:

Community Food Suppliers Establishing All-Time Highs

Seven Track Records Set by Royal Business

Wendels Group Sells Property On Parksides

Foundation Transfers Several Small Plots In Down-Town Section

Parisian Milliner Leases Floor Here

Housing Authority Puts Off Bond Sale

Two Investors Acquire Big Apartment Houses

SOMEWHERE the moon was shining ever so brightly and not a cloud flecked the lovely

Big Operators to Figure In Eighteen Local Deals

Jones Is Favored To Defeat Ray Thursday Night

Local Tennis Player Conceded Slight Edge Over State Champion

Part of Rail Plan Rejected by Court

Then They Stop Six Hours Before Stepping Up Ahead Toward Bigger Contracts

WASHINGTON, D. C.—The National Health Conference being held now by the President's Interdepartmental Committee to Coordinate Health and Welfare Activities heard this morning a dramatic statement by Dr Irvin Abell, president of the American Medical Association, assuring the conference of the organized medicine's "wholehearted cooperation in any of the efforts which you make for betterment in health care of the people of this country."

The statement came as a welcome surprise to most of the non-medical delegates, representing labor,

Film Leaders Map Unity in Industry

Party Leaders Decline To Relinquish Options

Check-Cashing Operators Now on Vacation in Old Jail

EXAMPLE 199

suggested by Example 200, which, incidentally, looks shorter than the page suggested by Example 199, because the smaller banner, in medium-width italic capitals and lower-case, appears above the deeper and comparatively more condensed banner, in roman capitals, in the latter illustration.

Top-of-page single-column heads in Example 200 were in 30-point Spartan Black Condensed, with second decks in 14-point Spartan Heavy. Other sizes of Spartan Black Condensed, Spartan Black Condensed Italic and Spartan Black were used for other heads, as well as 36-point Metromedium No. 2 and 36- and 30-point Metromedium No. 2 Italic. Most of the body matter was in 7-point Ionic No. 5 with Bold Face No. 2 on an 8-point body. The lead of the main story was in 12-point Ionic No. 5 leaded 2 points, and the double-column body matter in columns two and three was in 10-point Ionic No. 5 leaded 2 points. Cut legends were given the same sort of treatment as those shown in Example 199.

Two other pages worked out in the typographic laboratory are suggested by Examples 201 and 202.

The five-column spread head in Example 201 was in 60-point Franklin Gothic Italic and other heads on both pages were in members of the Ryerson, Spartan and Metro families. Body matter of both pages was in 7½-point Ionic No. 5 with Bold Face No. 2 on an 8½-point body. And again cut legends were in 10-point Spartan Heavy and Spartan Medium.

The "30" dashes on all pages represented by Examples 190 through 202 might well have been omitted in favor of 12 points of white space, in each instance. When the heads on a page are no smaller than 12 point, it is better to use white space than "30" dashes, which actually compete for attention with following heads and keep the heads from standing out on their own. When, however, heads smaller than 12 point are employed, the dashes, or cutoffs, seem necessary. Without them, in such instances, the reader might be confused into thinking that the smaller heads are merely subheads of preceding stories, rather than heads over other stories.

A simply constructed but highly effective seven-column front page (reproduced from a photostat of a rough paste-up) is suggested by Example 203, which involved the use of only four fonts of display

TODAY'S NEWS TODAY!

The Modern Newspaper

NIGHT FINAL SPORTS

VOL. 1, No. 1 — NEW YORK CITY, THURSDAY EVENING THIS YEAR — PRICE FIVE CENTS

Five High-Speed Runners Hurry Onward

FLOOD WATERS NOW FALLING

Members to See Academy's New Quarters Today

Remodeled Buildings Donated by John Doe Now Ready for Public

SOMEWHERE the sun is shining ever so brightly and not a cloud flecks the lovely azure of the well-known and highly publicized blue sky from morn to night and from here to somewhere else

Sixteen Local Teams To Enter 6 Contests

Captain Cecil Jones of Warhawks Says He Expects His Boys to Win

WASHINGTON, D. C.—The National Health Conference being held now by the President's Interdepartmental Committee to Coordinate Health and Welfare Activities heard this morning a dramatic statement by Dr. Irvin Abell, president of the American Medical Association, assuring the conference of the organized medicine's "wholehearted cooperation in any of the efforts which you make for betterment in health care of the people of this country."

The statement came as a welcome surprise to most of the non-medical delegates, representing labor, farmers' groups and other lay organizations interested in medical care from the public's point of view. It had been generally believed here that the national health program outlined yesterday at the conference by the government's Technical Committee on Medical Care, calling for additional expenditures of $850,000,000 a year for a ten-year period, half to be contributed by the American Medical Association.

Dr. Abell's statement followed a plea for "a spirit of cooperation and constructive service" offered by Dr. F. L. Bishop, executive secretary of the interdepartmental committee, who presided at this morning's session.

Dr. Bishop assured the conference that the program and the recommendations presented Wednesday were not final but were open to suggestions and amendments.

"The officials of the American Medical Association come to this meeting at the express instructions of its House of Delegates. We come not imbued with a controversial spirit, but with a determination to give to this conference our best

Before calling on the first scheduled speaker, Dr. Bishop recognized Dr. Abell, who spoke as follows:

Wendels Group On Parksides Sells Property

Foundation Transfers Several Small Plots In Down-Town Section

Frozen Corned-Beef Hash Saves Points on Tasty Meal

Two Local Farmers Missing 10 Months

Place Your Orders For Coal Right Now

SOMEWHERE the moon was shining ever so brightly and not a cloud flecked the lovely

Eighteen Clubs To Meet Here

Crescent Moon Men To Attend Convention

Wide Aid Pledged

Jones Favored To Defeat Ray Thursday Night

Local Tennis Player Conceded Slight Edge Over State Champion

Mill Sisters Submit Their First Petition

Check-Cashing Operators Go to Jail in Bank Swindle

Twenty Young Men Hike to Jonestown On Main Turnpike

WASHINGTON, D. C.—The National Health Conference being held now by the President's Interdepartmental Committee to Coordinate Health and Welfare Activities heard this morning a dramatic statement by Dr. Irvin Abell, president of the American Medical Association, assuring the conference of the organized medicine's "wholehearted cooperation in any of the efforts which you make for betterment in health care of the people of this country."

The statement came as a welcome surprise to most of the non-medical delegates, representing labor, farmers' groups and other lay organizations interested in medical care from the public's point of view. It had been generally believed here that the national health program outlined yesterday at the conference by the government's Technical Committee on Medical Care, calling for additional expenditures of $850,000,000 a year for a ten-year period, half to be contributed by the

Ladies Chalk Up Third Victory

Track Record Set

Fighting to Rescue Seven Men in Mine

EXAMPLE 200

The Modern Newspaper

NIGHT FINAL
SPORTS

VOL. 1, No. 1 — NEW YORK CITY, THURSDAY EVENING THIS YEAR — PRICE FIVE CENTS

SOMEWHERE the sun is shining ever so brightly and not a cloud flecks the lovely azure of the well-known and highly publicized blue sky from morn to night and from here to somewhere else

Five High-Speed Runners Hurry Onward With Italic

Then They Stop Six Hours Before Stepping Up Ahead Toward Bigger Contracts

Nine Local Youngsters Pass for Tournament

WASHINGTON D C—The National Health Conference being held now by the President's Interdepartmental Committee to Co-ordinate Health and Welfare Activities heard this morning a dramatic statement by Dr. John Doe, president of the American Medical Association, assuring the conference of organized medicine's "wholehearted co-operation in any of the efforts which you make for betterment in the health care of the people of this country."

Dr Doe's statement followed a plea for "a spirit of co-operation and constructive service" offered by Dr F L Bishop executive secretary of the interdepartmental committee, who presided at this morning's session.

Sixteen Clubs To Meet Here Monday Night

Crescent Moon Men To Formulate Plans To Attend State Meet

Wendels Group Sells Property On Parksides

Foundation Transfers Several Small Plots In Down-Town Section

SOMEWHERE the moon was shining ever so brightly and not a cloud flecked the lovely

Jones Is Favored To Defeat Ray Thursday Night

Local Tennis Player Conceded Slight Edge Over State Champion

Women Celebrate Passing of Quota

Gay Ceremonies Mark Attainment of Goal

Housing Authority Puts Off Bond Sale

Parisian Milliner Leases Floor Here

Two Investors Acquire Big Apartment Houses

Film Leaders Map Unity in Industry

Party Leaders Decline To Relinquish Options

Women Collect Record Sum For Many Crippled Children

Check-Cashing Operators Now on Vacation in Old Jail

Community Food Suppliers Establishing All-Time Highs

Part of Rail Plan Rejected by Court

Seven Track Records Set by Royal Business

Big Operators to Figure In Eighteen Local Deals

SOMEWHERE the sun is shining ever so brightly and not a cloud flecks the lovely azure of the well-known and highly publicized blue sky from morn to night and from here to somewhere else

EXAMPLE 201

TODAY'S NEWS TODAY!

The Modern Newspaper

NIGHT FINAL SPORTS

VOL. 1, No. 1 — NEW YORK CITY, THURSDAY EVENING THIS YEAR — PRICE FIVE CENTS

Forty Young Men Run to Bunstown And Miles Beyond

Then They Turn Round And Turn Cartwheels Quickly Out of Town

Members to See Quarters Today

Remodeled Buildings Now Ready for Public

Jones Is Favored To Defeat Ray Thursday Night

Local Tennis Player Conceded Slight Edge Over State Champion

SOMEWHERE the moon was shining ever so brightly and not a cloud flecked the lovely

Cigar Smokers Pay Larger Tax

So Do Many Others And Not Just Maybe

Housing Authority Puts Off Bond Sale

Wendels Group Sells Property On Parksides

Foundation Transfers Several Small Plots In Down-Town Section

Part of Rail Plan Rejected by Court

Women Collect Record Sum In Great Nine-Day Campaign For Many Crippled Children

Community Food Suppliers Establishing All-Time Highs

Speeding in Grains In Large Quantities

SOMEWHERE the moon was shining ever so brightly and not a cloud flecked the lovely

Two Million Dollars And Seventeen Cents Speedily Collected

Film Leaders Map Unity in Industry

Two Investors Acquire Big Apartment Houses

Parisian Milliner Leases Floor Here

Party Leaders Decline To Relinquish Options

Nine Local Youngsters Pass for Tournament

Visiting Fire Laddies Giving Officers Hard Battle in Race

Women Collect Large Sum for Children

SOMEWHERE the sun is shining ever so brightly and not a cloud flecks the lovely azure of the well-known and highly publicized blue sky from morn to night and from here to somewhere else

Check-Cashing Operators Now on Vacation in Old Jail

EXAMPLE 202

Metromedium Attractive

The Modern Newspaper

Metromedium Attractive

20 PAGES — TUESDAY EVENING, THIS YEAR — PRICE 3 CENTS

Adds 2 Model 30s N.Y. Herald Tribune Adopts Bigger Ionic

Installs Seventy Fonts Of 7 and 7½ Point For Body Matter

Rocket Heads Pop Makeup of This Issue

Are Cleaner Looking

Some of the many who inspected in the foreground, Norman White

Newark News Decides on Ionic

Puts in 32 Fonts Of 5½ Point Size

Don Shelley Endorses Id

St. Petersburg Times Introduces Opticon In Special Edition

Florida Newspaper Now Using 13 Fonts Of Easy to Read Face

Not Good Collecting Concerning Antique

California Newspaper Started 3 Years Ago

This Attractive Head Is Set In Metromedium No. 2 Italic

Newark News Decides on Ionic

Puts in 32 Fonts Of 5½ Point Size

Burns and Halliwell New Vice Presidents

Old Swimming Hole They Appreciate It

Early Advertising Wins $100 Prize

Was Established in 1869

Are Cleaner Looking

new Courier-Mail building, with, anaging director, and Sir Edward

N.Y. Herald Tribune Adopts Bigger Ionic

Installs Seventy Fonts Of 7 and 7½ Point

New Model 30 Linotypes

Mergenthaler Listed Among 12 Greatest American Inventors

Scientists in Session In Washington, D. C., Honor Linotype Maker

Praises Blue Streaks Many Short Cuts

This Attractive Head Is Set In Metromedium No. 2 Italic

This Attractive Head Is Set In Metromedium No. 2 Italic

EXAMPLE 203

matrices: 28-point Erbar Light Condensed, 24- and 18-point Metromedium No. 2 Italic and 14-point Metromedium No. 2 with Italic.

In 1937, scores of American newspapers adopted simplified flush-left heads, and in the years since, many hundreds of other papers—large and small—have put such heads to work for themselves and their readers. During World War II, when newsprint and manpower kept getting scarcer and scarcer in many newspaper plants, many hundreds of papers gave up their old-style heads of many decks in favor of simplified flush-left heads, to save paper and production time—and their readers applauded the changes.

The temptation is strong to refer specifically to many of those papers—to illustrate and discuss pages from scores and scores of the most attractive papers among those hundreds—but the temptation must be resisted. Merely to list the papers that have improved their type dresses since the spring of 1936 would require many, many pages.

The flush-left idea had crossed the Atlantic and was being applied advantageously in Norway and other countries.

Writing in the *Linotype News* of October-November, 1937, on the application of flush-left heads in Europe, Joh. B. Mikalson, well-known European typographic publicist and mechanical superintendent of the newspaper *1ste Mai* of Stavanger, Norway, whose paper adopted such heads in the summer of 1937, made the following statements:

"The British periodical *World's Press News* may be said to have led the field in Europe and very much in advance of its time.

"Back in 1929, however, the *Linotype News* pioneered a form for headlines that may be described as the most rational one so far. In the latest competition for the Ayer cup, a modified form of that streamline was awarded first prize.

"This American headline treatment has now been introduced into Norway. It is the labour organ *1ste Mai* of Stavanger that is the pioneer not only in Scandinavia but also for the continent of Europe. *1ste Mai* has carried the American idea through in its entirety.

"The form is still new here, and, as is the case with everything new, many people may perhaps shy at it. But, after considering the great advantages and savings in writing and production that the new form offers, one after the other will undoubtedly take up the Norwegian adaptation of the . . . streamline form. The ingenious part of the Norwegian form is the fact that it is equally suitable for the largest and the smallest newspapers, and equally adaptable for large or small headlines. It is in complete harmony with the present day, being futuristic in the real and original sense of the word. It decorates itself without outside aid. It is the streamline executed in typographic practice."

In a personal interview in the summer of 1939 Mr. Mikalson told this writer that at least fifteen newspapers in his country had adopted the flush-left idea. Since then many other newspapers in Europe have adopted it.

In the spring of 1939, *La Prensa* of Buenos Aires, one of the most conservative, successful and respected newspapers in the world, adopted flush-left heads in members of the Erbar, Metro and Memphis families, and began presenting its news body matter in 7-point Excelsior No. 2.

Examples 204 and 205 present reduced showings of two pages from the redesigned *La Prensa.*

In Example 204 most of the heads were in Erbar Light Condensed and Metromedium No. 2.

In Example 205 the heads were in members of the Memphis family.

Here is a translation from the Spanish employed by the South American magazine *Veritas* in its issue of May 15, 1939, about *La Prensa's* new dress:

"The great Argentine newspaper *La Prensa* has just offered its readers a new proof not only of its constant desire to serve them well but also of its potentiality. *La Prensa* has modernized its makeup, now appearing completely changed in its typographical material, both in the text and in the titles, the change extending also to the distribution of the matter, which is original and extremely attractive.

"After an exhaustive study, the executives of the esteemed contemporary adopted the type faces which in the present-day journalistic world are considered to be the most legible and keep pace with the high level that has today been reached by the graphic arts in this aspect. This superior material was manufactured in the United States of America.

"The worthy contemporary of the Avenida de Mayo adds to its undisputed prestige as an excellent informative and editorial organ that of being at present, typographically, the most modern newspaper published in Spanish.

"*Veritas* is pleased to join in the satisfaction with which its large

8 LA PRENSA — VIERNES 13 DE OCTUBRE DE 1939

La Unión Soviética Habría Enviado Oro Al Gobierno Alemán

Esa noticia causó gran sorpresa en los centros financieros de Londres

NOTA GRAFICA RELACIONADA CON LA PARTICIPACION DE GRAN BRETAÑA EN LA GUERRA

El duque y la duquesa de Gloucester despiden al comandante de las fuerzas expedicionarias británicas, vizconde de Gort, poco antes de la partida de éste a Francia

Un contingente de tropas expedicionarias británicas en Francia

Los reyes británicos se disponen a presenciar los ejercicios de un contingente de reclutas

Un grupo de aviadores británicos se dirige a efectuar un vuelo de adiestramiento

Tropas expedicionarias británicas, en viaje a Francia, provistas de salvavidas para caso de emergencia

En Gran Bretaña no se Efectuarán Elecciones Durante la Guerra

Esta determinación es una consecuencia de la situación actual

Lo que se Dice en Riga

Créese en Berlín que el Discurso no Ofrece Base para Nuevas Discusiones

En vista de ello se estima que el Reich debe ahora efectuar consultas con el gobierno ruso

Critica Violentamente la Prensa de Alemania la Actitud de Chamberlain

Dice que al rechazar las sugestiones de paz demuestra que se propone aniquilar al Reich

Información a la prensa extranjera

Actitud atribuída a Inglaterra

Juicios de un diario oficial

Hitler Especula con la Amenaza Comunista para Imponer su Voluntad a los Países Democráticos

Cree que la raza alemana surgiría airosa de una catástrofe europea

Por Ralph Heinzen, especial para LA PRENSA

El avance hacia el este

La derrota rusa en 1918

Las exigencias soviéticas

Ecos del Pedido de Aviones Hecho En la Unión por Gran Bretaña

Se Anticipa que Italia Participará En las Conversaciones Rusoalemanas

Esas conversaciones, se dice en Berlín, deben realizarse, pues no hay ya esperanzas de paz

Por Joseph W Grigg, hijo, especial para LA PRENSA

Declaraciones Hechas por El Señor Van Zeeland

Circuló una Versión Sobre Un Plan para Crear un Bloque Anticomunista Americano

Donaciones Recibidas en París De las Colonias Francesas

Considérase en Roma que es Firme el Discurso y que Hay Esperanzas de Paz

Se desautoriza que el embajador italiano Bastianini sea portador de proposiciones

EXAMPLE 204

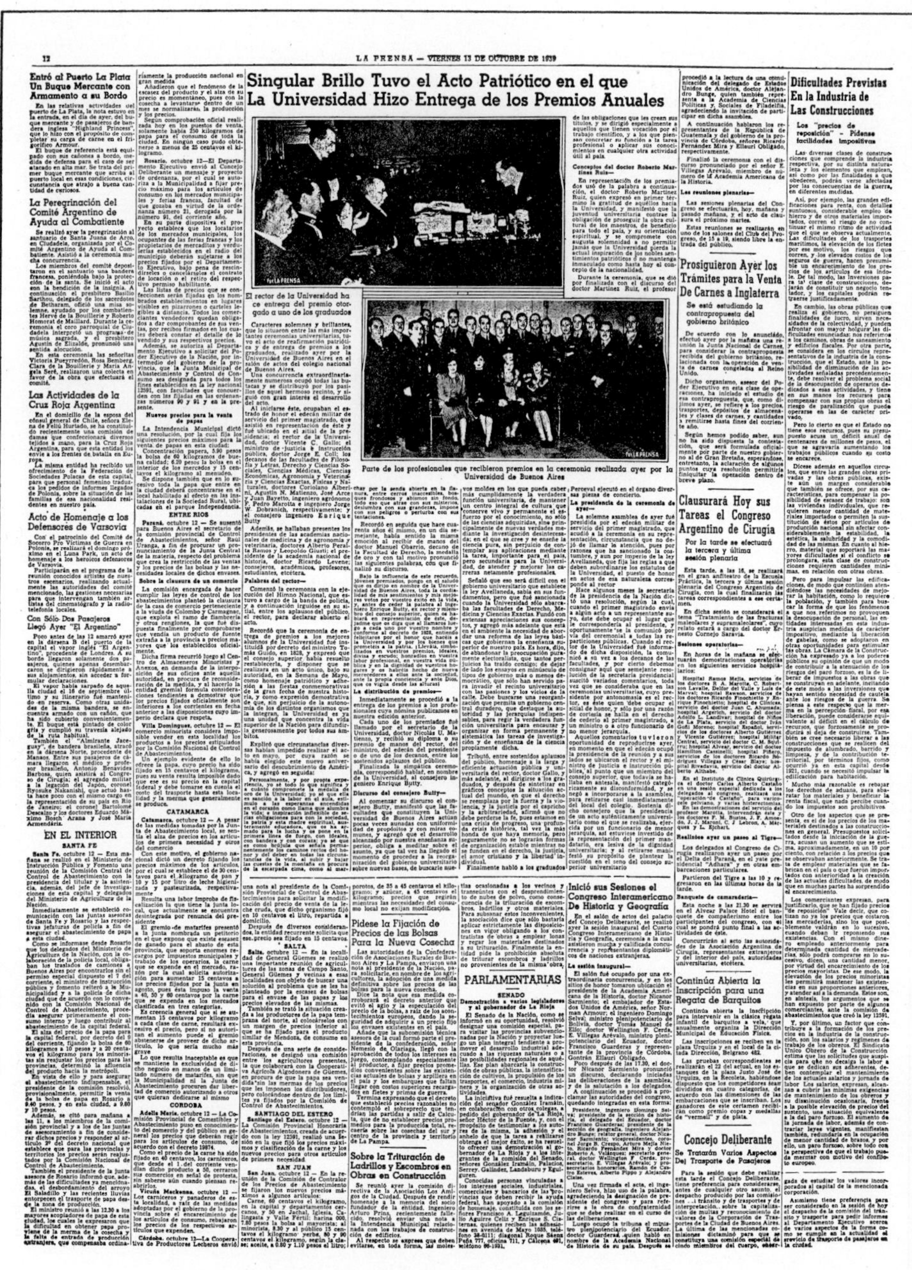

12 LA PRENSA — VIERNES 13 DE OCTUBRE DE 1939

Entró al Puerto La Plata Un Buque Mercante con Armamento a su Bordo

La Peregrinación del Comité Argentino de Ayuda al Combatiente

Las Actividades de la Cruz Roja Argentina

Acto de Homenaje a los Defensores de Varsovia

Con Sólo Dos Pasajeros Llegó Ayer "El Argentino"

EN EL INTERIOR

Singular Brillo Tuvo el Acto Patriótico en el que La Universidad Hizo Entrega de los Premios Anuales

El rector de la Universidad hace entrega del premio otorgado a uno de los graduados

Parte de los profesionales que recibieron premios en la ceremonia realizada ayer por la Universidad de Buenos Aires

Pídese la Fijación de Precios de las Bolsas Para la Nueva Cosecha

Sobre la Trituración de Ladrillos y Escombros en Obras en Construcción

PARLAMENTARIAS

Inició sus Sesiones el Congreso Interamericano De Historia y Geografía

Prosiguieron Ayer los Trámites para la Venta De Carnes a Inglaterra

Se está estudiando la contrapropuesta del gobierno británico

Clausurará Hoy sus Tareas el Congreso Argentino de Cirugía

Por la tarde se efectuará la tercera y última sesión plenaria

Continúa Abierta la Inscripción para una Regata de Barquitos

Concejo Deliberante

Se Tratarán Varios Aspectos Del Transporte de Pasajeros

Dificultades Previstas En la Industria de Las Construcciones

Los "precios de reposición" - Pídense facilidades impositivas

EXAMPLE 205

reading public received the youthful renovation in the dress of the respected grandfather."

Since 1939 many other newspapers in Latin America have adopted flush-left heads and otherwise improved their makeups.

Thus has passed in review a long and important section in the parade of progress in journalism. (However, see, also, many other modern pages in chapters that follow.)

Nearly all of the forward steps clocked in this chapter have had to do chiefly with typography.

Of course, the *content* of a newspaper is of first importance—a point stressed again and again in this volume. Physical appearance is secondary. The reader does not buy a paper, and keep on buying it, merely because it pleases the eye. The best typography cannot make a modern newspaper of one that is behind the times in other important respects.

3

Parade of Progress—In Other Ways

LET'S REVIEW another section in the parade of progress in journalism—a section in which typography plays only a complementary marching role. Let's go back to March 3, 1923, when the *Linotype News* was only eight months old and was producing the type dresses of long-established, successful, but not necessarily well-attired newspapers.

March 3, 1923, the first issue of *Time* magazine appeared.

Soon many people were talking about that publication; some favorably, others not so favorably. Among these latter, naturally, were some newspaper people.

"What a way to write news!" some of them may have scoffed. "Any newspaper man knows that news should be written objectively. The story should tell what happened, and nothing more. No editorializing. No opinions from the writer. Such stuff belongs on the editorial page or in signed departments or columns.

"But what are these people on *Time* doing? They're writing feature stories, short stories, essays! And they call that sort of thing news writing!

"What *Time* ought to have are some people who know all the rules of news writing."

But many lay readers of *Time*—people who knew little or nothing of any rules of news writing—liked the publication.

They liked it because it saved time for them; because it departmentalized the news. They liked its sprightly style. But they liked it best of all for the very thing condemned by some newspaper news writers. They liked the news treatments in *Time* because those treatments often included background explanation, interpretation, even forecasting of events to follow.

Even if and when those readers did not agree with those explanations, interpretations, forecasts, they liked the idea of getting those things right along with the news, in a single story—not the news in one package one day and the editorializing in another several days later.

(It is not the purpose here to argue as to whether or not newspapers should editorialize in news stories. There are some good arguments against their doing so. But that many people seem to like the idea is suggested by the fact that in the N. W. Ayer *Directory of Newspapers and Periodicals* for 1947, *Time* was listed as having an audited circulation of 1,554,323, with a Canadian edition of 97,040, a Latin American edition of 41,172, plus many overseas editions.)

At any rate, *Time* has had a lot to do with the fact that more and more newspapers are departmentalizing more and more of the news.

Our early day papers did that sort of thing, of course; and, through the years, virtually all of our papers have departmentalized certain kinds of news—financial news, society news, sports news, and so on—to the approval of readers.

But *Time* has served to re-emphasize the idea that newspaper readers seem ready and eager for more departmentalizing in their newspapers.

Saturday, December 26, 1931, the *New York Sun* gave its readers an appreciated Christmas present in the form of a week-end review of the week's news, under a five-column head reading "It Happened This Week." (But in 1946 P. A. Dolan, news editor of the *Sun*, informed this writer that "the war and paper shortages compelled its discontinuance.")

Some of the division heads in that department were "In and Near This City," "At the Capital," "For President," "In the Rest of the U. S.," "As to Weather," "The Wide Wide World," "What They Say" (brief quotations from prominent people in the week's news), and "Deaths of a Week."

Several other papers later started presenting week-end reviews of the week's news. Some of those papers gave up the idea during World War II, but later went back to it, to the approval of readers.

The *New York Herald Tribune* has presented a full page in a Sunday issue under an eight-column head reading "History in the Making: A Summary of the Week's News Events," as well as a full page headed "Opinion of the Week"—a page made up of letters from readers, many of them under individual heads two columns wide or wider, along with as many as a half dozen current-events cartoons reprinted from other papers.

April 1, 1935, the *Richmond News Leader* began presenting a front-page digest—not a mere index—of the news in an edition, but that feature was discontinued during World War II. The digest was presented in a high first column headed "Day's News in Digest." Under the subhead "Local" in that column appeared summations of fourteen local stories; under the subhead "Telegraph," summations of eight wire stories; under the subhead "Sports," summations of three stories, and under the subhead "State," a digest of one story.

In August, 1935, the *Atlantic Monthly* carried an article on "The Glut of Occurrences—Today's News and Tomorrow's Newspaper," by Herbert Brucker, then assistant to the dean of the Graduate School of Journalism at Columbia University—an article that aroused much interest when it originally appeared, and again when it was presented in revised form in the *Independent Journal of Columbia University* of October 16, 1936.

Writing about that revised article, in November, 1936, this writer stated, in part:

"Number one of volume four of the *Independent Journal of Columbia University*, which appeared October 16, featured an article by Prof. Herbert Brucker of the journalism staff at Columbia that could be read with profit by every newspaper editor and publisher in America.

"That article, a revision of one by Mr. Brucker that appeared in the *Atlantic Monthly* for August, 1935, shows that it is becoming more and more necessary for newspapers not only to present the news of the day but to familiarize the reader with the background of much of it and to interpret much of it for him, and not in separate stories or editorials on separate pages, but in single attractively written and concise stories.

" 'By publishing this article,' stated Carl W. Ackerman, dean of the Graduate School of Journalism at Columbia, in the *Journal*, 'we seek the interest of educators as well as newspaper men in the necessity for studies of vital changes which are taking place in American journalism.

" 'Later in the academic year the Graduate School of Journalism will prepare an experimental issue of a newspaper giving concrete expression to Professor Brucker's project. The Mergenthaler Linotype Company has offered to print and help circulate this issue as a contribution to the advancement of journalism.' "

That experimental newspaper, called *Gist,* a two-page sheet with an over-all size of 14¾ by 20¼ inches, and with five 15-pica columns to the page, was composed in the typographic laboratory of the *Linotype News,* and widely circulated as a supplement with the number for July-August, 1937. See Examples 206 and 207.

Writing about that supplement, in that July-August issue, this writer stated, in part:

"Another interesting experiment in news writing and makeup is presented in the form of a supplement with this issue . . . That supplement, based on the front and other pages of the *New York Herald Tribune* of March 3, 1937, is a product of students in the Graduate School of Journalism at Columbia University, working under the direction of Herbert Brucker, assistant to Dean Ackerman.

"As Mr. Brucker states, in the explanatory box on page two of the supplement, that front page 'contains summaries of most of the stories which received top headlines throughout the *Herald Tribune* that day. The stories headlined on page one are the same ones displayed in the *Herald Tribune's* front page. . . . Sometimes the standard news-story form has been abandoned in the interests of simplicity, or to avoid repetition. Here and there related background material or interpretative matter has been added.' "

Observe the department heads, and the front-page summations of the leading stories, under "Today's Headlines."

The heads in that supplement were in various sizes of Bodoni Bold, Bodoni Bold Italic, Poster Bodoni and Poster Bodoni Italic, with body matter in 9-point Textype with Bold Face No. 2, and with Italic and Small Caps, on a 10-point body. The explanatory box on page two of the supplement was set in members of the Memphis family.

In the fall of 1937 a book by Mr. Brucker on *The Changing American Newspaper* was published by the Columbia University Press.

In an editorial about that volume, in the *Linotype News* of January, 1938, this writer stated, in part:

"In the book *The Changing American Newspaper,* Herbert Brucker, assistant to the dean of the Graduate School of Journalism of Columbia University, presents many constructive ideas for American newspaper publishers and editors.

"Some of the treatments suggested by Mr. Brucker will be resisted by those newspaper executives who, while appreciating the desirability, even inevitability, of changes of technique in most other fields, con-

Late City Edition of the **3 Cents**

Gist

of Today's News

Vol. 96 No. 32,980 — Copyright 1937 Graduate School of Journalism, Columbia University — **Wednesday, March 3, 1937**

Lewis Wins U. S. Steel Recognition, 40-Hour Week and $5 Minimum Pay

Labor

ORGANIZED LABOR has won formal recognition from the chief unit of the United States Steel Corporation. This epochal step was quietly announced in Pittsburgh last night by Philip Murray, chairman of the Steel Workers' Organizing Committee and chief lieutenant of John L. Lewis in the Committee for Industrial Organization The agreement also provides minimum pay of $5 a day and a forty-hour week, both to take effect March 16. Eight other steel companies signed similar agreements, thereby probably preventing the major strike in the steel industry which many had thought inevitable this spring

News of the agreement elated President Roosevelt and other Administration leaders in Washington Officials of the Navy Department said it cleared the way for construction contracts which had been seriously threatened by the labor restrictions of the Walsh-Healy Act

Unofficial opinion in New York steel circles held that the agreement will necessitate employment of 80,000 to 100,000 more workers in the steel industry at a cost of $100,000,000 a year Prices of finished steel products are expected to increase from $2 to $6 a ton to compensate for the increase On the stock market yesterday U S Steel rose almost $4 a share to 119 and Bethlehem $3 to 97½ Page 2

A five-cent-an-hour salary increase was announced in Los Angeles yesterday by the Douglas Aircraft plant, scene of a sit-down strike which ended Monday with nearly 350 workmen under felony indictments. The pay rise was one-third that asked by the strikers Page 3

A properly-conducted strike "does not constitute duress," Justice Cotillo ruled in a New York County Supreme Court case yesterday, nor does the fact that a union contract has been signed as the result of a strike make his contract void Page 2

National News

SENATOR Arthur H Vandenberg of Michigan endorsed the Wheeler-Bone amendment as a substitute for the President's Supreme Court plan in a nationally-broadcast radio speech last night The amendment would permit Congress to override, by a two-thirds vote after an intervening election, Supreme Court decisions holding laws unconstitutional In endorsing it and in praising the Borah amendment to enlarge state powers on social legislation, Senator Vandenberg became the first orthodox Republican to speak out on the court plan Republicans saw in his action an important indication that conservatives and liberals could join in a workable opposition to the President's proposal.

In the Senate and House debate on the Court continued Senator Hiram Johnson, California Republican, declared that any justice who withdrew under the new retirement bill would lose his self-respect Representative Hatton W Summers, Texas Democrat in reply pled with the justices to do so, saying that thereby they would settle the whole issue Page 5

The Navy appropriation bill for the fiscal year 1937-1938, totaling $526,555,428, was reported to the House of Representatives yesterday as the first of the national defense measures. The money is to be spent for sixty-seven new vessels including two battleships at $60,000,000 each, for aircraft construction and for an increase in Navy personnel to 105,000 Page 5

The Treasury Department reported yesterday for the eight months of the fiscal year ended February 28 a deficit of $2,046,015,287 or $364,389,393 less than that for the same period last year Receipts increased $368,427,542 and expenditures $4,038,149 Page 5

Nine members of the Black Legion, including a former Mayor of Detroit suburb and a Detroit Board of Health inspector were found guilty of a murder conspiracy yesterday They joined more than twenty convicted in Michigan since the Black Legion murder of a WPA worker last May The state's principal witness was Dayton Dean confessed "executioner" of the terror band Page 5

Today's Headlines

Roosevelt comes out for new wage-and-hour laws this session; sends Congress N.R.A. post-mortem urging new regulation of business be more flexible. *Labor, page 3*

Steel's 40-hour week hailed in Washington by Administration leaders; Navy Department holds it clears way for immediate ship construction. *Labor, page 2*

Sit-down strikes close two major parts plants in Detroit serving Ford Motor Co., which is revealed as early C.I.O. objective. One strike settled. *Labor, page 2*

Vandenberg backs Wheeler-Bone Amendment in radio speech attacking Roosevelt's court plan. Sumners implores justices to quit. *National News, page 5*

James Roosevelt may attend coronation of George VI as secretary of American delegation; President says idea is news to him. *Foreign News, page 5*

Niagara Falls Power Co. defies order of state commission to cut use of river water to one-fourth. *Business, page 14*

Mysterious death of four-year-old Queens girl caused by attack in "most brutal murder in 27 years." *Crime, page 9*

S.E.C. charges Germany has secret debt of 2 billion dollars; cautions investors in new bond issue. *Foreign News, page 6*

Two earth tremors were sufficiently pronounced to rattle dishes and sway buildings in the vicinity of Lima and Bellefontaine, Ohio, yesterday Other cities which reported upset furniture and swaying houses were Columbus, Dayton, Zanesville, Springfield, Akron, Toledo, Canton, and Findlay Five states surrounding Ohio felt the shocks but property damage was slight and no injuries were reported Page 5

Foreign News

THE Securities and Exchange Commission in Washington yesterday in effect charged the German Government with maintaining a secret debt of about $2000 million It permitted registration of a $69 million issue of 3% dollar bonds as the only practical means by which American holders of German securities might obtain something of value on their past-due interest claims, but publicly called attention to what it called deficiencies in the German registration statement Page 6.

James Roosevelt, the President's son and new member of his secretariat, may attend the coronation of King George in London as a member of the United States delegation One post is still vacant and it would not surprise the State Department to see him go The President said this was a happy thought, but news to him and his son Page 6

The Fascist Grand Council plunged Italy further into the world armament race at a meeting in Rome lasting until 3 A.M yesterday After listening to Premier Benito Mussolini it passed a resolution providing five lines of action toward further increases in Italian armed forces and economic self-sufficiency In London a responsible report said Germany had tripled her air force in the last year to more than 2000 planes, with comparable increases in mechanizing its army of 830,000 men In Toyko Vice-Admiral Saotake Toyoda, speaking for the government, said no increase in the proposed $342 million five-year naval program was needed because of recently announced British and American naval building plans Page 6

Foreign Secretary Anthony Eden rebuffed German demands for colonies by stating, in a speech in the House of Commons last night, that the Government was not considering any transfer of colonies. Thus he answered Ambassador Joachim von Ribbentrop's undiplomatic speech at Leipzig the previous day Page 6.

The first serious movement by Germany to organize a world-wide resistance to the Communist International was made two weeks ago by establishing a bureau for the purpose in the Hotel Kaiserhof in Berlin, it was revealed yesterday Meanwhile in Prague Dr Kamil Krofta, Foreign Minister declared before Parliamentary committees that Czechoslovakian-Soviet treaty did not make his country an "outpost of Communism in Central Europe," as charged in German newspapers Page 6.

Seven hundred Spanish Fascist troops were surrounded during an attack on the Jamara front, southeast of Madrid, last night, a Government communique reported The attack was said to have been repulsed with heavy losses Page 6. In Paris Niceto Alcala Zamora, who a year ago was President of Spain, was found last night, hard up and trying to make a living as a newspaper man. He refused to identify himself with either faction in the present struggle Page 7

Crime

JOAN MORVAN a four-year-old Queens girl who died Monday, was murdered. Death followed peritonitis caused by a criminal attack, Dr Howard W Neail said after an autopsy yesterday He called it the most brutal murder in his twenty-seven years in the Queens medical examiner's office Page 9

The body of comely Cleo Sprouse, missing Charlottesville, Va., high school girl, was found near the University of Virginia cemetery yesterday by two students. Her head was tied in a chloroform-saturated towel. Page 9.

Two men trying to escape the scene of a Brooklyn hold-up yesterday afternoon made the mistake of commandeering a detective's car One bandit is dead and the other lies under guard at the Kings County Hospital Page 10

Isaac Malester, cafeteria proprietor, was a witness for the defense in the restaurant racket trial yesterday Under skillful questioning by prosecutor Thomas E. Dewey he became a witness for the prosecution Page 9

Harris & Ewing — Associated Press

THEY NEGOTIATED the steel agreement: John L. Lewis (left), head of the Committee for Industrial Organization, and Myron C. Taylor, chairman of the board, U. S. Steel Corporation.

New York City

THIS YEAR'S summer city hall will be Chisholm Manor in College Point Park, Queens, Mayor LaGuardia announced yesterday Page 9

Embezzlement, slipshod financial conditions, and a political spoils system in the Kings County Sheriff's office under previous administrations were reported to the Mayor yesterday by Paul Blanshard, Commissioner of Accounts Page 9

At least 2500 more beds are needed immediately in the city's hospitals to care for tuberculosis patients, Dr Haven Emerson declared yesterday Page 9.

The State

HUGE CAKES of ice rumbled over Niagara Falls last night, jamming the river and threatening the Maid of the Mist steamers. Page 7

In Albany the Federal Child Labor Amendment, already ratified by the Senate, was brought to the floor of the Assembly yesterday afternoon Page 8

Final passage of the Fischel minimum-wage bill for women and minors is scheduled for today in the democratic-controlled Senate Page 8.

The Court of Appeals was asked yesterday to determine whether the Legislature has the right to prohibit alienation-of-affection suits Page 8.

Business

THE New York State Water Power and Control Commission has ordered the Niagara Falls Power Co to cut the amount of water it takes from the Niagara River from 20,000 to 4900 cubic feet a second This became known yesterday when the company announced its refusal to obey, saying that to do so would adversely affect industrial concerns, traction companies, and homes throughout western New York Page 14.

Senator Burton K Wheeler, Montana Democrat, caustically attacked the past practice of New York Stock Exchange Governors in making decisions on securities in which they have an interest, at a Washington railroad investigation yesterday Charles R Gay, "new deal" president of the Exchange, testified how the Exchange is trying to meet criticism of this practice and of its listing of holding securities. Page 13

Harrison Williams, husband of the best-dressed woman in America, was on the witness stand before the Securities and Exchange Commission in Washington yesterday Commission attorneys said Williams' American Cities Power and Light stock rose 250% while its chief asset advanced only 25% Page 13

In Mexico City yesterday President Lazaro Cardenas set up a national petroleum administration, This will put Mexico directly into the oil business in competition with private industry, which includes approximately a $400 million foreign investment. Page 14

Sale of the Gulf States Steel Co. to the Republic Steel Corp was voted at directors' meetings of the two companies yesterday Page 14

Stocks: Steels, rails, and motors were leaders in a bullish but selective market inspired by the announcement of steel wage increases Page 13. **Bonds**: Corporate bonds generally followed the stock rise, but United States government issues fell somewhat. Page 13 **Commodities**: Cotton continued advancing, closing 3 to 16 points higher Wheat was unchanged to ⅛ higher. Page 13. Foreign Exchange was dull and listless Page 14.

Sports

Tennis: George Seewagen upset J Gilbert Hall 6-2, 2-6, 10-8 in the national indoor singles championships here yesterday Herbert Bowman and Frank Parker also advanced Page 15.

Boxing: Max Schmeling arrived on the Berengaria last night with the intention of either fighting James Braddock in June for the heavyweight title or of suing for breach of contract. Page 16.

Hockey: The Detroit Red Wings defeated the Montreal Maroons 7-4 at Montreal yesterday The A.A.U announced it would deny sanction to the Hershey Bears for their scheduled track meet if their hockey team played the disbarred Baltimore Orioles aday Page 15.

Bicycle racing: After a session of wild jamming the team of Thomas and Reboli took undisputed leadership of the six-day race at Madison Square Garden last night. Page 16.

Baseball: Babe Phelps opened training at the Brooklyn Dodger camp with a display of heavy hitting. Mungo and three others hold out. Danning signed with the Giants. Dahlgren signed with the Yankees while seven others hold out. Page 15

Racing: Miss Lizzie won the six-furlong dash at the New Orleans Fair Grounds. Roman Soldier was withdrawn from as contender for the Widener Challenge Cup at Hialeah. Page 16

Basketball: Columbia defeated Yale 41-37 Thomas Jefferson won over Eastern District, 31-26 Poly Prep defeated Trinity 31-16 Page 16.

Golf: Patty Berg won the qualifying medal in the Florida East Coast women's championship yesterday with a 76. Page 15.

Entertainment

Page 11

Books. Somerset Maugham's "Theater" for all its stage glamor and deft craftsmanship, is "plainly make-believe"

Theatre: Barre Lyndon's "The Amazing Dr Clitterhouse" proved to be "a polite and gentlemanly melodrama."

Screen: "Outcast", a medical motion picture, demonstrates that even a good screen idea can grow stale

Music: "Goetterdaemmerung" impressively concluded the Ring cycle at the Metropolitan last night, and the Oratorio Society's Bach Mass in B minor was again acclaimed at Carnegie Hall

Radio. Cleveland Orchestra, WEAF, 1 45 P M Mayor LaGuardia, WMCA, 2 15 Opera "Lucrezia" from Milan, Italy, WJZ, 4 30 Jessica Dragonette, WABC, 9.30 Gladys Swarthout, WEAF, 10.30 Newsboys' hawking contest, WJZ, 11.30

Personal

Page 12

Married. Miss Vera Felicity Story and Henry Latrobe Roosevelt, in Philadelphia yesterday Miss Dorothy Anne Day and Timothy F Crowley, Jr, secretly in Greenwich, Conn., Saturday Mrs Dorothy Campbell, golfer, and Edward L Howe, banker, in Elkton, Md., Monday

Engaged: Miss Vivian Dixon, of New York, to T Dennie Boardman of Boston

Honors. Frederic William Goudy, distinguished type designer, will receive the Ulster-Irish Society medal at a testimonial dinner here March 19.

Deaths: H H Charles, 72, leader in the advertising field, of pneumonia yesterday at his home, 355 Riverside Drive The Rev Warren H Wilson, 69, rural sociology expert, following a mastoid operation yesterday in Presbyterian Hospital.

Weather: Fair and slightly colder today Tomorrow mostly cloudy and warmer

An interesting experiment in news writing and makeup. Explained in the boxed story on page 2.

EXAMPLE 206

2 *The Gist of Today's News* — *Wednesday, March 3, 1937*

Labor — **Labor**

Steel Signs C.I.O. Contract, Reversing Historic Labor Policy

The Setting

From the day in 1795 when South Carolina steel workers were paid $10 a month in bar iron, less $4.50 to the company for board, steel workers in America have struggled to better their lot In 1892 came the bitterly-fought Homestead strike in Western Pennsylvania which Henry C Frick finally broke with the help of Pinkerton men and the National Guard In 1919 the National Committee for Organizing Iron and Steel Workers again sought to organize the rigidly anti-union industry Reprisals by the management and the slowness of public sentiment to see labor's point of view broke that strike too

Last June Philip Murray, first lieutenant of John L Lewis in the Committee for Industrial Organization and chairman of the Steel Workers' Organizing Committee set out to organize the steel industry Supported by a $500,000 war chest raised by the Lewis unions, which have broken away from the more conservative American Federation of Labor, the committee has to date negotiated contracts with about thirty-six small companies employing 30,000 men. More recently its campaign turned against Big Steel—the United States Steel Corporation This, plus recent aggressive C I O activities in the automobile and other industries, led to fears that this spring would see the biggest and bloodiest strike in steel history

What Happened

Day before yesterday Mr Murray and Benjamin F Fairless, president of Carnegie-Illinois, the biggest unit in United States Steel, sat down in an unannounced conference Last night after a three-and-a-half hour continuation of the conference, Mr Murray quietly announced that Carnegie-Illinois had recognized the union as bargaining agent for its members Thus fears of a nation-wide steel strike vanished.

The agreement between Steel's chief unit and the C I O union provides. "1 The corporation recognizes the Steel Workers' Organizing Committee as the collective bargaining agency for those employes who are members of the Amalgamated Association of Iron, Steel and Tin Workers The Corporation will not interfere with the right of its employes to become members of the union. There shall be no discrimination, interference, restraint or coercion because of membership in the union The Steel Workers' Organizing Committee agrees not to intimidate or coerce employes on corporation time or plant property

"2 There shall be an increase in wages of 10 cents an hour on all rates which are at present $4.20 a day, or a minimum for this classification of $5 a day of eight hours

"3. There shall be established an eight-hour day, forty-hour week Time and one-half shall be paid for all overtime

"4 A joint committee shall meet not later than March 10, 1937 for the purpose of effectuating a written agreement on working conditions, application of wage rates, hours, rules and a method for adjudication of disputes

"5 The agreement shall be in force until Feb. 28, 1938"

In New York last night, John L. Lewis issued the following statement. "The settlement is a fine example of an intelligent approach to a great economic problem. It has been made possible by the far-seeing vision and industrial statesmanship of Mr Myron C. Taylor. From time to time over a period of several months, in New York and Washington, Mr Taylor and I have engaged in conversations and negotiations We were each conscious of the great weight of responsibility and the far-reaching consequences attached to our decisions Labor, industry and the nation will be the beneficiaries"

Mr Murray in Pittsburgh said that the agreement "paves the way for the maintenance of peace in the industry, and is in accord with the announced policies of the Committee for Industrial Organization and Steel Workers' Organizing Committee to organize steel workers without resorting to the use of strikes, violence or industrial disturbances. This agreement undoubtedly reflects the definite change in the labor policy of the United States Steel Corporation. We expect organization of the entire steel industry."

Results

The wage-and-hour provisions of the agreement resemble those already announced by twelve other but smaller steel companies. With 120,000 men now added by Carnegie-Illinois, assurance of a $5-a-day minimum is held by 355,000 of the industry's 550,000 workers. The other companies, with the number of men involved, are: Bethlehem, 85,000; Republic, 52,000, National, 20,000; Youngstown Sheet and Tube, 16,000. Inland, 9,000. National Tube, 8,000, Pittsburgh, 7,000, and Sharon, Wheeling, Continental, Otis, and Jones & Laughlin, 25,000

The New York stock market reacted optimistically to the agreement, with its probable end to the strike threat U S. Steel common pushed above 119 a share, a $4 advance, and Bethlehem common followed about $3 to 97½

Unofficial opinion in New York steel circles last night held that a forty-hour week throughout the industry would necessitate employment of from 80,000 to 100,000 more workers while this, plus the rise in basic wage rates, will add more than $100 million to the annual steel payrolls It was strongly indicated that formal announcements of price increases from $3 to $6 would follow before the end of the week The cost of unionizing the industry in other words, will probably be passed on to the consumer It was feared that this may slow down demand at a time when the country's leading industry was gaining real momentum after five or six years of depression.

Washington Is Pleased

Adoption of the forty-hour week in the steel industry was hailed in Washington last night by the Administration as foreshadowing widespread acceptance of the Walsh-Healey Act's labor standards by other large industries

The elation of President Roosevelt and Secretary of Labor Frances Perkins was shared by officials of the Navy Department. Charles Edison, Assistant Secretary of the Navy, prepared to reissue bids for the 25,000,000 tons of steel that the Navy needs to complete six destroyers and six submarines.

Deadlock Ended

Previously the steel companies had refused to bid on the Navy contracts because of the Walsh-Healey Act. This act, which became law September 28, specifies that companies doing business with the government must uphold the Administration's labor standards on any contract of $10,000 or over It provides that workers' wages shall equal the prevailing local rate, that the work week shall not exceed forty hours, that no boys under sixteen or girls under eighteen years of age shall be employed, and that working conditions be healthful

Mr Edison expressed hope that manufacturers in other industries would fall into line with the Walsh-Healey Act's provisions, insuring the Navy the machinery and equipment it needs Miss Perkins defended the government's refusal to exempt the steel industry from the act, saying that to do so would have weakened the Administration drive for better working conditions President Roosevelt, asked whether a recent conference with Myron Taylor, chairman of the United States Steel Corporation, had anything to do with the steel agreement, smiled broadly and said that whenever he and his old friend Mr Taylor got together they always talked about the welfare of the nation

Sit-Down Strikes Close 2 Detroit Plants

Ford Next?

Sit-down strikes closed two major parts plants in Detroit yesterday, but a settlement of one of the disputes was announced last night. Both plants are sources of parts for several automobile manufacturers. They supply some of the requirements of the Ford Motor Company, which has been designated by the United Automobile Workers of America, a C I O Union as one of the next objectives in its organization campaign.

The main plant of the Murray Corporation of America, body manufacturers, was closed when 5,000 of the 6,500 employes struck (union figures) A few hours earlier 2,000 workers of the Motor Products Company had gone on strike, but the company reached agreement with the union by night

The settlement provided immediate evacuation of the plant by strikers, "no discrimination by reason of the sit-down strike" reinstatement of four discharged employes, and a collective bargaining conference between Motor Products and the U.A.W.A.

General Motors

Meanwhile the same union's demand for a national minimum hourly wage was the only point undecided after nearly eleven days of conference with General Motors. Wyndham Mortimer, heading the union negotiations, said last night the union asked "equal pay for equal work, regardless of age, sex, color or locality" A General Motors spokesman said the union was insisting on "a uniform wage rate for all employes regardless of types of work, experience, skill, ability, sex, race or the geographical location in which the work is performed" The negotiators said they were still arguing on principles and had considered no definite figure for a proposed minimum.

The Fisher Body and Chevrolet units of General Motors at Janesville, Wis., closed since Friday by a strike, reopened today returning 2,700 workers to their jobs. Near-capacity operations in General Motors units reopened since the paralyzing strikes ended February 11 were indicated in estimated production of cars and trucks at 123,874, the highest for any week this year and an increase from a revised figure of 108,617 for the preceding week.

More in Detroit

A strike closed the Zenith Carburetor Company, which employs 750, yesterday Strikers demanded a ten-cent hourly wage increase, minimums of 70 cents for men and 55 cents for women, and a forty-hour week.

Sit-down strikers remained in possession of the plants of the Ferro Stamping Manufacturing Company and Timken-Detroit Axle Company The Ferro strikers announced they would defend themselves "against violence and make this factory our graves if necessary" On petition of the companies Circuit Judge Allan Campbell ordered the Ferro strikers to show cause today, and the Timken strikers tomorrow, why an injunction against them should not be issued

The Waiters and Waitresses Union which on Monday called strikes in two of Detroit's F W Woolworth stores, yesterday spread its activities to two of the city's largest restaurants Fifty waitresses and kitchen employes struck at Stauffers' Washington Boulevard Cafe, forcing the management to turn away 250 patrons The strikers demanded $12 for a six-day week, saying their present rate was less than $10 for a forty-eight hour week At the Fisher Building sixty bus girls and boys started a sit-down in the basement concourse cafeteria. They wanted $10 a week, saying they now received $1 15 for a four-and-a-half hour day

Meanwhile 100 sales girls passed the fourth day of their sit-down strike in the downtown Woolworth store, and eleven women clerks remained on strike in another store The other thirty-eight Woolworth stores in the Detroit area continued business as usual. —Associated Press

Other Strike News

Rhode Island Trucks

No serious disorder was reported from Rhode Island yesterday, first day of a strike of 2000 truck drivers Police escorted such trucks as ran. State police, with all leaves canceled, patroled main highways At least a score of trucks were turned back at the state line in Pawtucket

Governor Quinn conferred with Thomas F McMahon, state Director of Labor, to make certain that foodstuffs, fuel, and medicine was kept moving He declared that while "the rights of the strikers must be preserved, the public welfare comes before anything else"

Percy F Arnold, president of the Commercial Haulers of Rhode Island, comprising thirty-five of the state's large trucking concerns, said that granting union demands for a 26 per cent pay rise would mean at least a 15 per cent increase in hauling rates, and that this would require consent of the Interstate Commerce Commission "We might just as well sit tight and rot out of business as accept the union's demands and be driven out in thirty days," he added.
—Associated Press

Pennsylvania Hosiery

Three more hosiery mills in Berks County, Pennsylvania, were closed yesterday by sit-down strikes called in a unionization campaign of the A. F of L. They were: Nolde-Horst Company's main plant in Reading; Reading Maid Company at Hyde Park; and Industrial Hosiery at Shillington. Union official said this brought the totals to ten closed plants, with more than 3000 workers affected.

Roosevelt Offers NRA Study As Basis for New Laws

Not 'Must,' but—

President Roosevelt came out flatly and emphatically yesterday for new wage and hour legislation. He said at a White House press conference that such a statute ought to be enacted and that he hoped it would be before Congress goes home The President warned reporters, however, against quoting him as saying the legislation "must" be passed He said that none of the legislation he has advocated is in the must category so far as he is concerned The term has been used widely in the past to describe bills wanted by the President

The President's move in the midst of his fight for power to name six new justices to the Supreme Court, where NRA with its wage and hour provisions was killed, stirred immediate speculation as to possible effects on that controversy Some Administration supporters have predicted that labor groups would campaign unremittingly for the court reorganization if assured of new federal regulation of working conditions.

Shortly before the President came out for new wage-and-hour legislation he sent to Congress a post-mortem report on NRA which urged that future attempts to regulate business be simpler and more flexible The report was written by the four members of the presidential committee on Industrial Analysis who are not government officers Professor J M Clark of Columbia University, an economist, William H Davis of New York City, a lawyer, George M Harrison of Cincinnati, president of the Brotherhood of Railway Clerks and vice-president of the American Federation of Labor, George H Mead of Dayton, Ohio, manufacturer and former chairman of the Business Advisory Council Other members of the committee are the Secretaries of Agriculture, Commerce, and Labor

Several of the committee findings drew a hot challenge from General Hugh S. Johnson, first NRA head, who said the group was packed with persons inimical to NRA.

NRA Report

A summary of the report compiled by the committee says

"NRA gave jobs to something like 2,000,000 workers by spreading work .

'NRA brought about a large increase in total wage distributions, which was at least partly neutralized by increasing prices Average wage increases were moderate the lowest-paid groups on the whole received the largest increases.

'The moral, and economic value of NRA child-labor provisions is clear The public support given by NRA to the principle of freedom of labor to organize and bargain collectively was of great and probably lasting importance

'It is not possible to answer statistically the question whether NRA did or did not contribute to industrial recovery. NRA attempted to cover more ground, and at greater speed than could possibly be covered effectively.

'Both management and labor went too far, with the result that many impracticable and unenforceable provisions were put into the codes. The apparently simple conception of fixing maximum hours, minimum wages and minimum price provisions developed wholly unexpected degrees of complexity.

'The final NRA policy was, in spirit and intent, quite in harmony with the anti-trust laws.

'NRA's field of action was one in which the public interest is obscure and the conflict of private interests is emphatic.

'Many of the rules made, and which were supposed to have the force of law were wholly devoid of the elements that make a law They were uncertain and too complex to be understood. They did not have the support of that large majority of citizens upon which the enforcement of a law depends, but were such that all who were not in favor of them felt free to resist them.

'Both for legal and for economic reasons, any program similar to that of NRA needs more definite standards than NRA possessed. A minimum wage can be socially beneficial not only as a safeguard to the worker but also as a wage floor for the operation of the competitive system. But in this field code experience developed or implied the need of well-considered standards, which would be even more necessary to a long-run policy.

"If controls of the NRA type are to be tried again, the experience indicates that the attempt should be limited to a few important industries in order that proper standards of investigation and adequate supervision may be maintained."

These Pages . . .

are an experiment Editorially they are the work of students in the Graduate School of Journalism of Columbia University, working under direction of Herbert Brucker, Assistant to the Dean. They have been set in type through courtesy of the Mergenthaler Linotype Company, and are being distributed to friends of the Graduate School of Journalism and as a supplement to The Linotype News.

As will be noted from the format and column width, the practical standards of newspaper work have been put aside deliberately The guiding principle has been a search for a page size and news treatment suited to the needs of the newspaper reader under modern social conditions.

In order to provide ready comparison with standard practice the news published in the New York Herald Tribune of March 3, 1937 was used as a basis. The front page (see over) contains summaries of most of the stories which received top headlines throughout the Herald Tribune that day The stories headlined on page one are the same ones displayed in the Herald Tribune's front page.

This second page is intended to serve as a sample inside page Its news stories are the Herald Tribune or Associated Press stories of March 3, rewritten with condensation primarily in mind Sometimes the standard news story form has been abandoned in the interests of simplicity, or to avoid repetition. Here and there related background material or interpretative matter has been added

Comment and criticism will be welcomed Please address Herbert Brucker, Assistant to the Dean, Graduate School of Journalism Columbia University, New York City

Cotillo Rules Strike Is Not Duress

Justice Salvatore A. Cotillo held in Supreme Court here yesterday that a strike legally called and properly conducted does not constitute duress. He overruled a report of a referee that a strike last fall against Beim, Ivler & Breiter, wholesale dress jobbers of 558 Broadway, was illegal

The case goes back to April 16 last year, when an agreement was signed between the dress company and the Wholesale Dry Goods Employes Union, an A F of L. affiliate Subsequently the union asserted that the employer had broken the agreement by refusing to pay its union employes for Labor Day, when they did not work Ben Golden, arbitrator, favored the union. According to the union the firm refused to abide by this decision, whereupon a strike was called October 12. After two days the firm entered into a new contract with the union.

When later the firm declared that the new contract was invalid, Lorenzo C. Carlino, referee, found that the firm did not voluntarily execute it. Yesterday Justice Cotillo, however, ruled that the firm "may not thus repudiate an agreement entered into to avoid or settle such a strike." He pointed out that the strike may have been ill advised and unnecessary, "but it cannot be said it was illegal or in violation of the then existing agreement. Having thus entered into the agreement and secured all the advantages of its terms until the expiration of the season, it does not appear just or equitable to permit the defendant to now repudiate it."

Douglas Aircraft Grants Pay Increase

Douglas Aircraft in California is a spectacularly successful designer and manufacturer of transports for commercial air lines

Continued at top of next page

The heads on these pages are in the Linotype Bodoni family, with body matter in 9 point Linotype Textype with Bold Face No. 2, and with Italic and Small Capitals, on a 10 point body. The box on this page is in the Linotype Memphis family.

EXAMPLE 207

tinue to write and edit news stories, and to arrange them on pages, as they were taught to do a generation ago.

"Alert newspaper executives, however, will read the book with receptive minds and, conceivably, will be moved to apply at least some of its ideas to their own publications—and to the advantage of themselves and their readers and advertisers. . . .

"Here are a few of the many points made by Mr. Brucker:

" 'Before the war, news tended to be simple and factual. It could be understood by all without help from Walter Lippmann. Today news also springs from involved factors in economics, political science, physics, and so forth—from all the social and exact sciences. To be comprehensible much of this news must be placed against a background of related facts and put into perspective to show its meaning.

" 'The complexity of the news which today's newspaper must cover calls for elaborate newspaper research departments plus a merging of the functions of the copy-reader and rewrite man.

" 'No editor would break up his finance or sports departments and print one story from it on each page throughout the paper. Conversely, if all stories were grouped into categories of related matter the reader could grasp the whole more readily.

" 'The inverted-pyramid form of news story leads to irritating repetition and confusion. Changing the structure of the story so that each item of news is told adequately, but once only, would avoid repetition, allow more dramatic treatment, and encourage condensation of the news.' "

On Labor Day of 1935, the *Minneapolis Star*, which had been purchased in June of the same year by a company headed by John Cowles, one of the sons of the late Gardner Cowles Sr. of the *Des Moines Register* and *Tribune*, adopted a news-writing technique that in four years helped to increase the circulation of the *Star* from some 80,000 to more than 155,000.

On that day Basil L. Walters, then managing editor of the *Des Moines Register* and *Tribune*, was made editor of the *Star*, although he continued to fill the managing editorship in Des Moines. (In May of 1944 Mr. Walters became executive editor of the Knight Newspapers, which publishes papers in several large cities.)

"I realized," Mr. Walters informed this writer in the summer of 1939, "that if we were to get the *Star* from third place to first in the way of circulation in Minneapolis, it would be necessary to adopt a plan of news presentation not generally followed by newspapers.

"The Cowles brothers are great experimenters, and they had some very definite ideas along that line themselves.

"When I got the assignment, I thought back to the days when Dr. George Gallup was making surveys for us in Des Moines. I also happened to drop through Chicago and pick up a bunch of the more modern English newspapers.

"Quite frankly, I combined the English technique with the recommendations of Gallup. We encouraged reporters to write as they talked, and encouraged headline writers to try experiments both in type faces and editorial technique. But, with it all, we tried to put across all the news of the nation, the world and the city, in a very understandable fashion, and stressed accuracy.

"You can see the necessity for the latter, because, naturally, in developing anything new, in order to get effect, it would be very easy to slide into carelessness.

"We found the composing room very co-operative, despite the fact that what we were attempting to do was contrary to many of the things they had been taught since apprenticeship days. In fact, much of the development was due to suggestions from the printers.

"One of the things we developed was what we called traffic through the pages and up and down the pages. Instead of trying to crowd on page one all the news and letting the inside of the paper sink, we tried to make every page inside the paper as interesting as page one.

"I am talking about goals, not accomplishments, as you will understand," Mr. Walters added, "because we still have a long way to go.

"For instance, where it used to be the custom to put all the large heads at the top of the page and to use the smaller heads progressively on down the page, we would put some of the largest heads and some of the best pictures down deep in the page.

"In fact, we practically forgot every rule and started out fresh with experimentation. The idea behind this was to carry the reader's eye through every page in the paper and then carry it up and down the page so that it would travel near by the advertising. The advantage of this method is very much like a merchant having a display window on a busy street. We figured that we would provide the eye traffic near the advertiser's display window on the page. It was then up to the merchant to dress that ad in such a way that it would pull the eye over into it.

"At the time we started with this technique we had a great many small advertisers. We still have them, despite the fact that since then we also have large advertisers. But you can see that this method of bringing eye traffic near the ad down in the page is a particularly beneficial one for the fellow who has a small ad that all too often is buried. We feel that the reason we still have the small advertiser is because this eye traffic near his ad has produced good results for him, and we shall always have him in mind, because small advertisers are just as essential to a newspaper as are the large ones. If we can help a smaller advertiser grow, his ad naturally grows."

It should be explained here that the *Star* guided that eye traffic past small advertisements not by isolating them from each other on a page, not by scattering them, because it followed the plan of pyramiding display advertisements to the right on a page, but by keeping its stories, even brief stories, as interesting as it could, all the way to the bottom of a page.

But let's get back to Mr. Walters and his statements to this writer, in the summer of 1939:

"We went in very heavily for pictures, and, instead of using pictures as filler material, we set up a picture copy desk and scheduled them into the paper exactly as we scheduled news stories into the paper. In case of doubt, we would kick out what we regarded as a five-per-cent-news-interest story or a one-per-cent-reader-interest story and get in a ninety-per-cent-reader-interest picture.

"As a result of our experience here I have the feeling that the greatest opportunity for development of American newspapers, both in holding the reader interest and in getting results for advertisers, lies in a more intelligent use of photographs in conjunction with better written, better edited and better displayed news stories.

"Actually what we have been trying to do is to have our whole paper written with the same ease that the sports pages in many successful newspapers are written."

After some six months in Minneapolis with the *Star*, Mr. Walters returned to Des Moines, but the circulation of the *Star* kept going up and up. By the fall of 1937 the property had become so large that John Cowles decided to establish his home in Minneapolis, and he took Mr. Walters back with him as editor of the *Star*.

One more word from Mr. Walters, uttered in 1939:

"I believe body type is going to get larger in American newspapers, but there will be more white space. You may ask 'What about the increasing white-paper bill?' That will have to be handled by better equipped news rooms which can tell the stories in fewer words. In other words, I believe that high volume of words should give way to make room for proper display of type."

November 20, 1935, the *Evening Star* of Washington, D. C., began presenting brief "background precedes" with important news stories.

The idea behind the idea was that readers probably would welcome brief reviews of events that had preceded and were related to the current news; that such background material would aid readers to get a clearer idea of what had happened and was happening. And readers did welcome the idea.

On the front page of the *Star* for November 20, 1935, "background precedes" were used with several leading stories. Each "precede" was presented in indented italicized lines between the head and the regular body matter of the story it accompanied.

(In the spring of 1946 B. M. McKelway, then associate editor of the *Star*, but since made editor, informed this writer: "The 'background precedes' required, for their preparation, more men than we had available during the war. I am not sure that we shall resume their publication, now that the personnel problem is easing up. On some stories they were very helpful. On others they merely duplicated what was covered in the story itself. Their preparation sometimes required more time than was justified by the results. And I am of the opinion that a well-written news story should in itself contain the necessary amount of background to give the intelligent reader what he needs to have.")

In 1935 the *Wisconsin State Journal*, Madison, Wis., which for several years now has been presenting its heads flush at the left, started running two front-page features designed to direct attention to important news stories on inside pages. One of the features was headed "On the Inside," and the other, "They Say Today." Each occupied 6 or 7 inches in a single-column width, and was illustrated. The "On the Inside" feature included, in addition to a picture, headlines calling attention to news stories on other pages, and a condensed index. The other feature presented, in addition to a picture, brief quotations from people figuring in important news on inside pages.

However, in 1946, Don Anderson, publisher of the *State Journal*, informed this writer: "Both of those features required a certain amount of front-page space, and it required a lot of staff time to prepare them. Consequently, early in the war, when both of those commodities became scarce, we decided to abandon them. There was still a third reason. It frequently held up editions from five to ten minutes to prepare the copy for 'They say Today.' That was another luxury we could not afford during the war. While I think both of those features had a fair reader interest, I still feel they were not important enough to outweigh these other considerations."

September 21 and October 1 of 1936, two Florida newspapers began departmentalizing the news—the *Palm Beach Times* of West Palm Beach, and the *Daytona Beach Morning Journal.*

Through the years, the *Linotype News* has presented thousands on thousands of pictures. From its very beginning, it went in strong for illustrations, and soon began to be referred to by many in the printing and publishing world as "the paper with so many pictures." Many a single issue has carried more than a hundred reproductions of photographs—chiefly of people. (The issue of November-December, 1939—a special issue—carried pictures of more than 400 people.) And that publication has run many an article or story calling attention to the pulling power of pictures.

Newspaper people have long been familiar with that ancient saying, often attributed to the Chinese, that a single picture often tells a clearer and more interesting story than hundreds of words.

Newspaper people, as has been stated, have long been familiar with that saying, and many have professed to believe in it. Yet comparatively few of them have done much about it, except in their gravure and comic sections.

The pulling power of those two sections—the gravure and the comic—should have convinced many more newspaper people than apparently were convinced, that more and more pictures could be used to advantage in other sections of the paper.

Some papers did go in strong for pictures, as witness several statements in this volume; but it took two publications in the magazine field to re-emphasize the fact that many people are intensely interested in pictures, and chiefly in pictures of people.

On November 23, 1936, the first issue of *Life* in its new and livelier form appeared, and in January of 1937 the first number of *Look* was issued.

Both publications went in strong for pictures, and both immediately attracted large and growing circulations. In the N. W. Ayer *Directory of Newspapers and Periodicals* for 1947, *Life* was listed as having an audited circulation of 4,699,688, and *Look* as having an audited circulation of 2,300,592.

The circulation growths of those publications naturally attracted wide attention, and more and more newspapers went in for more and more pictures. The publisher or editor of many a small paper got a candid camera and got busy with it, and many another installed his own "one-man engraving plant."

The influence of those two magazines—of *Life* and *Look*—and, of course, of *Time* continues to be felt in the newspaper world, and that influence has helped to make many a paper livelier, more interesting, more up to date.

(A news story released from New York City in April, 1946, ran as follows: "Time-Life International, division of Time, Inc., revealed here that *Life International* will make its bow July 22, with initial distribution of more than 150,000 copies. This separate edition of *Life* will be fortnightly and is the outgrowth of the military edition of *Life*, sent to the armed forces overseas since 1943 without advertising. Distribution of the new magazine will be everywhere in the world except the United States, Canada, Alaska and Hawaii, which make up *Life's* area. The fortnightly will be the same size as *Life*, and will be a condensation of two weekly issues of the domestic publication. It will be issued in English only.")

March 30, 1937, the *Richmond Times-Dispatch* simplified its head dress, adopted larger and clearer body type, and began departmentalizing much of the news. And readers greeted the changes with enthusiasm.

September 1, 1938, the *San Francisco Chronicle* began departmentalizing much of its news under such heads as "Foreign," "Science," "Education," "Crime," "The Nation," and "Labor's Day."

Paul C. Smith, general manager of the *Chronicle*, in referring to the new makeup, said: "We aim to classify news, to make it accessible and to make the relationship of one event to another more readily discernible."

W. D. Chandler, managing editor, said that he and his associates were delighted with the reception given the departmentalization idea.

European war news was presented under three conspicuously displayed heads—"Summary," "The West" and "War at Sea." At the lower left several stories and a picture were presented under the department head "Religious News."

In July of 1939 the *Baltimore Evening Sun* started grouping related stories under simplified heads.

("What the *Evening Sun* did," Neil H. Swanson, executive editor, informed this writer in 1946, "was to simplify its headlines by eliminating all banks, and then assembling related stories under small labels such as 'Labor,' 'Politics' and 'Foreign Affairs.' The labels cited are merely examples; they were not arbitrary, but changed from day to day as the run of news suggested different groupings. Actually, this device of labels on the grouping of related stories was only a means to an end. That is, it was a first step toward establishing in the makeup of the *Sunpapers* the policy or principle of *integration.* By this word 'integration' we mean simply this: that for the convenience of the reader and the better organization and presentation of the news, we assemble in one place all news dispatches on the same subject, whether it be labor, or economic controls, or events in the Balkans or in China or in England. The use of labels was valuable in training news editors, schedule makers, copy-readers and makeup editors to apply the principle of integration. Once the principle was established and understood, the labels became unnecessary. News in the *Sunpapers* is now grouped, or integrated—that is, stories relating to the same or similar subjects appear in one place in the paper, instead of being scattered; but the labels have disappeared, except on the sports pages of the *Evening Sun.*")

In September of 1939, at the beginning of World War II, the *New York Times* started running a front-page feature headed "War News Summarized." At the end of the war the feature was continued under the head "World News Summarized."

In May of 1944, as previously stated, Basil L. Walters, formerly of the *Minneapolis Star-Journal* and *Tribune,* became executive editor of the Knight Newspapers, which publishes papers in several large cities. His first assignment was at the *Detroit Free Press*, which John S. Knight, head of the Knight Newspapers, purchased in May of 1940.

"The *Free Press*," Mr. Walters informed this writer in 1946, "had been caught with one of the worst white-paper bases in the country when I joined the paper. Mr. Knight, as you will notice by the sample of the paper for May 6, 1943, which I am sending you, had already done considerable modernizing. The problem when I arrived in Detroit—simultaneously with Mr. Knight's return from England, where he served a year as liaison officer in the Bureau of Censorship—was to maintain and continue this modernization in the face of a constantly developing news hole made necessary by the consumption of more and more paper by an increasing circulation.

"We immediately went in for more expansive use of white space. We obtained this white space through better editing. Mr. Knight and I had seen how the English newspapers were holding onto their white space despite the fact that they had been reduced to four pages. We also had observed that the English public actually liked its wartime newspapers, and newsprint rationing was practically the only sort of rationing about which was heard no complaint.

"I am sending you some samples of today's *Free Press* which will show you that we are still holding on to our brevity and our white space.

"One of the most popular things we did was to use 18-point single-line heads over three- and four-line stories. Such stories all too frequently are used under 8-point heads, which Gallup surveys have indicated are not read. Our brief stories under larger one-line heads are the best read material in the paper.

"Our whole news staff and composing room have joined in the spirit of the thing and as a result the Detroit public likes the paper, which it can read very easily and at the same time quickly absorb all of the important news of the world along with an occasional chuckle.

"The entire theory behind our editing technique on the *Free Press* is to make important news interesting—interesting in writing, interesting in content and interesting from a typographical standpoint.

"We still are short on white paper, and during all this time we have been unable to use enough white paper to really try out the circulation strength of the product.

"Another innovation we have put into effect which you may be interested in is eliminating subheads. I have always figured that the subhead had a tendency many times to stop the reader instead of leading him on into the next paragraph. We make use, as you will note, of the asterisk with a couple of bold-face words leading off the following paragraph. We feel this method keeps leading the reader on through the entire story.

"When we purchased the *Chicago Daily News*, in October, 1944, I moved over to Chicago. You can imagine that I was very timid about making changes in that grand old paper. However, we have gradually shortened the stories, being careful always to keep in essential facts and interesting detail.

"At the same time that we have shortened the stories, we have thrown in more white space to make the paper easier to read.

"The circulation response has been steady and certain, as you can determine from the A.B.C. records.

"The Sunday magazine section is easily the most popular section in the *Sunday Free Press*.

"Going back to the *Daily News*, you will note we put a 2-point lead between paragraphs. This was the first change we made on the *Daily News*. We also use the same style of asterisk and bold-face caps in the place of subheads that we use on the *Free Press*.

"The Knight Newspapers are operated as a group and not as a chain, and so each managing editor has complete latitude in building his paper to fit the community in which he operates. Naturally there is a constant exchange of ideas between the managing editors—both through me and between themselves.

"While all four of the Knight Newspapers make generous use of white space, each paper does it in a different way and each paper has a distinct personality."

In the last few years, but especially since the beginning of World War II, many foreign newspapers, particularly in England and Australia, have abandoned the idea of devoting most of the space on their main front pages to classified advertising, and have been featuring there, instead, their main news stories. (See Examples 174 and 175.)

At the New York World's Fair in the spring of 1939 the *New York Herald Tribune*, in co-operation with the Radio Corporation of America, printed a small facsimile newspaper on the fair grounds. The paper was called the *Radio Press*.

A story in the *Herald Tribune* for April 29, 1939, had this to say about that experiment:

"This service, known technically as radio facsimile broadcasting, is now undergoing extensive newspaper testing in Buffalo, St. Louis and in California. Experimental services are now going on in New York City. The *Herald Tribune*-R.C.A. service represents the first newspaper-sponsored test in this area. It represents also the first joint experiment in this medium by unassociated newspaper and broadcasting organizations. . . .

"Each page of the newspaper measures 8½ by 12 inches. With a ½-inch margin all around, the useful area is 7½ by 11 inches. The *Radio Press* will have three columns, each a little wider than the usual newspaper column. They will run parallel to the long side of the sheet. In some of the other experimental work four columns are used, with the rules parallel to the short side of the sheet.

"At the World's Fair exhibit the process actually will not include a wireless transmission. Wire cable will be used to carry the impulses from the scanner to several receivers located at convenient points in the building. The substitution, however, of wireless for the wire lines is easy to make, and the finished product will appear exactly as if it had been transmitted by wireless. . . .

"Facsimile is not a new process. Scientists have been developing it since 1842, when Alexander Bain, an English physicist, created a successful wire system which used pendulums to give synchronization.

"Currently it is being used on a large scale in the transmission of photographs by land line and by radio. The same basic principles apply to this work as apply to home facsimile.

"Successful home radio facsimile, however, is a product of recent years. Besides the R.C.A. equipment to be used at the fair, there are several other systems of accomplishing the same general effect. These, however, use electrolytic action to mark the paper as received.

"The speed of transmission for the fair demonstration is one sheet every twenty minutes."

On May 16, 1939, also on the grounds of the New York World's Fair, the *New York Herald Tribune*, in co-operation with the International Business Machines Corporation, started presenting a visual broadcasting news service that flashed news bulletins on a 4-foot screen in the Business Systems and Insurance Building.

That news service, as a story in *Editor & Publisher* for May 20, 1939, pointed out, "uses I.B.M.'s radiotype machine, operating over an ultra-high-frequency radio wave, enabling the transmission of one hundred words a minute. The words, greatly magnified, are projected on a large Translux screen, similar to those used in motion-picture theaters.

"Opening day's news bulletins were relayed from the *Herald Tribune* offices to I.B.M. headquarters, a mile away, and then relayed from there to the fair by radiotype. . . .

"The radiotype machine is, in effect, a typewriter which operates by radio impulses. It includes an electric writing machine, entirely controlled from the keyboard. Each key, when struck, sends out a separate group of radio impulses, which actuate the corresponding key on any number of receiving machines of a similar nature 'tuned' in on it.

"Unlike television, matter transmitted by the radiotype can be magnified to any size and can be seen accordingly by a greater number of persons at one time. One sending machine is able to furnish an unlimited number of receivers. . . .

"Radiotype communication can be used for any distance, I.B.M. technicians said. The *Herald Tribune* also used it last year at its Forum on Current Problems, to furnish quick copies of the speech of Viscount Halifax, foreign minister of Great Britain, to forum delegates."

In the fall of 1943, the General Electric Company invited executives of leading newspapers to inspect its television equipment and witness several examples of television in action.

Through the co-operation of the *Albany Times-Union* and King Features Syndicate, the audience of about seventy newspaper people saw a "televised newspaper."

January 5, 1944, the *Daily Mail* of London, England, issued the "world's first trans-oceanic newspaper"—a newspaper photographed in London and flown across the Atlantic on microfilm for printing in and distribution from New York City.

In a letter sent in advance to each of some 3000 "influential people in America," the New York representative of the *Daily Mail* stated:

"This is a brief letter to introduce to you the trans-Atlantic edition of the *Daily Mail* of London. It is something entirely new in publishing and I think it will interest you. Just a short time ago, in fact, this first issue was merely typewritten copy 3000 miles away in the capital of Great Britain. Now it is on your desk—a digest of the news which the British people are reading.

"Of course, this trans-Atlantic edition is something of an experiment, but we feel that the magic of microfilm and the speed and range of the modern plane have changed—even revolutionized, perhaps—the science of journalism. This is the first issue and we plan many more. Every week a plane will arrive from England and its pilot will have in his pocket a tiny package of microfilm fresh from Fleet Street. All I do is get them enlarged and printed here and then mail the newspaper to you. I propose to do this every week.

"Why are we doing this?

"Well, we think it will contribute toward closer understanding between the British and American people. That is the one purpose. Of course, as journalists, we are very interested in the technicalities of the project. We are rather proud to inaugurate an entirely new venture in publishing.

"So here is the first issue. I am sending a copy to you with the compliments of the *Daily Mail* and Associated Newspapers, Ltd."

Example 208 presents a reduced showing of the front page of the first issue—an issue of twelve pages 8⅝ by 11 inches in size.

Ionic No. 5 was selected for body matter because that type face was found to photograph and "reproduce" better than certain other body faces.

A story by Lord Rothermere, publisher of the *Mail*, on the front page of the little paper included these statements:

"Today the *Daily Mail* inaugurates a new venture in trans-oceanic publishing. This experiment has one purpose: as a contribution towards the closer understanding of the British and American peoples.

"For the first time in history a great national newspaper in London is setting out to put on the desks of influential people in America an account (in pictures as well as words) of some of the things its readers have been reading in Britain—only two or three days ago.

"On trans-Atlantic aircraft in wartime, every ounce counts. It is impossible to transport publications in bulk after they have been printed. Therefore, this edition, which is a digest of one week's issue of the *Daily Mail*, is set up in England and photographed onto microfilm. The whole issue comes down to the size of a dollar bill. It is then flown to New York, re-enlarged, printed there, and mailed to you.

"With this very great experiment the *Daily Mail* breaks new ground again. For the issue now in your hands is more than a spontaneous messenger of good will from one newspaper in England to the people who shape opinion in America. It is also a pointer to the future:

Daily Mail TRANSATLANTIC EDITION

No. 1. WEEKLY DIGEST. LONDON, WEDNESDAY, JANUARY 5, 1944. Five Cents.

'A VERY GREAT EXPERIMENT'

World's First Transoceanic Newspaper is Born

THE 'MAIL' SPANS ATLANTIC

TO-DAY *The Daily Mail* inaugurates a new venture in transoceanic publishing. This experiment has one purpose as a contribution towards the closer understanding of the British and American peoples.

For the first time in history a great national newspaper in London is setting out to put on the desks of influential people in America an account (in pictures as well as words) of some of the things its readers have been reading in Britain—only two or three days ago.

On Transatlantic aircraft in war-time every ounce counts. It is impossible to transport publications in bulk after they have been printed.

Therefore, this edition, which is a digest of one week's issues of *The Daily Mail*, is set up in England and photographed on to microfilm—the whole issue comes down to the size of a dollar bill. It is then flown to New York, re-enlarged, printed there, and mailed to you.

Perhaps it is particularly fitting that *The Daily Mail* should be the first British newspaper to undertake this task; for the *Daily Mail's* founder, Lord Northcliffe, provided in many ways an impetus to the development of aviation which has become a traditional feature—and a nationally valued feature—of the paper's policy.

With this very great experiment *The Daily Mail* breaks new ground again.

For the issue now in your hands is more than a spontaneous messenger of good will from one newspaper in England to the people who shape opinion in America.

It is also a pointer to the future: a pointer to the exciting possibilities of harnessing together the aeroplane, the camera, and the printing press in the coming Age of Flight.

Rothermere

CROWDED OUT

Train full—no room even for troops on leave. A common scene at a big London terminus. Bulk of our trains are at work mounting the Second Front. No passenger counts to-day. Picture was taken with infra-red (darkness-piercing) plates. Flashlights are forbidden in black-out.

Railroads at Peak Strain Now to Mount Invasion

BRITAIN'S railways are to-day engaged in the most gigantic transport operation in history—the mounting of a full-scale Second Front. Now that Security barriers are down, some of the facts can be told. The travelling public are bluntly warned that at this crucial stage they "just don't count."

Lord Leathers, War Transport Minister, is at work with his staff directing operations day and night. Strict orders have been given to all officials to rate priorities in this order:

1. Troops and war supplies.
2. Mails and other freight.
3. Passenger traffic.

Thousands of passenger trains are engaged day and night moving British and American troops to their destinations. Many more thousands of freight trains are hauling guns, tanks, and munitions of all kinds.

This colossal task is being carried out alongside normal working at a time when the railways are suffering severely from shortage of staff, black-out conditions in the yards at night, and a now waning epidemic of influenza.

All this is being done at the expense of the travelling public. Ordinary passenger trains run packed almost to suffocation. Hundreds run anything from 30 minutes to three hours late.

Passengers, including troops on leave, are deposited at the big London termini in the early

[Turn to Back Page]

RAF RELATIVES GET HOPE FROM AMERICA

One of the most closely studied items of news from America for a long time was the U.S. War Department's announcement that 346 of 581 American airmen missing after the October raid on Schweinfurt are now known to be war prisoners.

This type of information is never given by the British Air Ministry about the great raids made by the R.A.F. at nights. It is common to lose 40 or 50 bombers in these attacks, representing, possibly, 500 men.

Even allowing for the greater safety of making parachute descents in daylight, it is now felt that the proportion of British personnel saved is probably only slightly lower.

WAR DETAINEES FREED

Fifty-six war detainees, including 20 Italians, have just been freed by Home Secretary Herbert Morrison. Only 299 people now remain in custody in Britain as potential menaces to the State.

MILLIONS OF REFUGEES WILL RETURN

SIR HERBERT EMERSON, Britain's High Commissioner for Refugees, told *The Daily Mail* this week that there is every prospect of 18,000,000 civilian refugees being got back to their own homes within a year of the war's end.

Sir Herbert puts Europe's homeless at a figure of 20,000,000, including Germany's slave labour force of men and women.

He declared: "Certainly 90 per cent. of the 20,000,000 will return eventually, and I hope it may be as many as 98 per cent. The difficulty will be to control the first rush back."

Mental Cases, Low in 'Blitz,' Up Again

Mental afflictions, which surprisingly decreased in Britain during the Dunkirk-Blitz era, are showing an up-curve now that life is quieter and safer. In 1942 there were 310 more new cases than there were in 1941. There is still no approach to the pre-war level.

£3,000,000 FILM PLAN

Sir Alexander Korda the producer, announces in London that he is planning to spend £3,000,000 ($12,000,000) making British films when the war ends.

EXAMPLE 208

a pointer to the exciting possibilities of harnessing together the aeroplane, the camera and the printing press in the coming age of flight."

The first issue of the little paper presented news, feature stories and comment, and made use of photographs, cartoons and diagrams, but included no comics, crossword puzzles or advertisements.

For a few weeks, no paid subscriptions were accepted for the trans-Atlantic edition. But soon copies were made available to the many

OVERSEAS AND TRANSATLANTIC

MAIL

WEEKLY EDITION OF THE DAILY MAIL

BRITISH NEWS DIGEST

No. 2,175. 15/- a Year Post Free. LONDON, AUGUST 3-10, 1946. Price 3d.

NEWSVIEWS

A London commentary

UP and down the steps of the Luxembourg Palace, along the bust-adorned galleries, pass the statesmen of 21 nations, engaged in the solemn pretence of taking part in an historic Peace Conference.

The whole thing has a dreamlike unreality, when it should be a dream come true.

For this is the occasion we dreamed of in the darkest days, "the consummation devoutly to be wished." It was the dream of a real Peace Conference, avoiding the mistakes of Versailles, that gave us strength in our desperate resolve.

And now the Peace Conference is here—and no one much cares.

That is the dreadful thought. The Conference is regarded by the world with an almost cynical detachment.

Did not Britain's Foreign Secretary on the eve of the Paris meeting declare: "It is not a Peace Conference." The bluntest Bevinism yet. . . .

Certainly there are no illusions to snare us this time, and that is something. There will be none of the pretty flummery of Vienna in 1815, and none of the delusive idealism of Versailles in 1919.

How different Paris now from then. . . .

Paris in 1919, thronged, eager, agape for a new world, the light of a false dawn over all. Paris was Pisgah, and from it Wilson viewed the Promised Land—a world made safe for democracy.

And Paris now . . . Up and down the steps of the Luxembourg pass the statesmen of 21 nations, and the world hardly notices them.

Powerless

FOR the world—or at least that part of it which is politically undeluded — knows that most of those delegates have no more significance than the statues of long-dead statesmen that adorn the Salle des Séances.

Of the statesmen of the 21 victorious nations now assembled in Paris, many represent the smaller European countries which endured valiantly and made an active contribution to victory. But unfortunately they are not able to make any active contribution to the peace.

It was all very well for Mr. Bevin to tell us that this was the first peace conference where the defeated nations had the right to be heard equally with the victorious nations, but none knows better than he that even among the victorious nations only four have real power at the conference.

The others may speak, yes, they may even by their persuasions gain the two-thirds majority necessary to amend the Big Four's drafts of the five peace treaties.

But when the drafts go back to the Big Four the dominant Powers are not bound to accept the amendments.

Chessboard

BUT if this conference is free of delusive idealism, it also lacks a guiding principle.

It lacks what Talleyrand in 1814 called the *mot d'ordre*. In 1814-15 the *mot d'ordre* was "legitimacy"—that is, restoration of legitimate governments in a Europe that had known the Napoleonic upheaval. It was not, according to our lights, a very lofty principle, but it was a guiding principle, and the Big Four of that day, though they did not carry it through to its limit, were motivated by it in their peace-making at Vienna.

The *mot d'ordre* in 1919 was self-determination, the rights of nations to govern themselves in the ways they thought fit. The guiding principle was liberal democracy.

But today there is no *mot d'ordre*, and there is no Europe any more; only a chessboard of two conflicting ideologies.

And so there is no guiding spiritual motive in this peace-making, but only expediency, and consequently there is no hopeful enthusiasm in the hearts of men.

Yet we cannot shrug our shoulders and turn away from the fact that in Paris now matters of supreme importance to the human race are being decided, and if we do not settle the future now, the future will surely settle us. And as all the Powers should be agreed that the overriding expediency is the survival of the human race, we may have some hopes that a certain amount of horse-sense will be shown at this conference.

But it is hardly a reflection to arouse lofty emotion. . . .

Talleyrand, that brilliant cynic, when he first discovered in Vienna in October 1814 what little progress the Big Four of that day had made in the way of peace-making, observed that they were "too frightened to fight each other, too stupid to agree."

The first part of that observation may safely be made in regard to the Powers in Paris now—and no wonder, with Bikini's footnote to the horrors of Hiroshima and Nagasaki fresh in their memories.

But if the second part of Talleyrand's comment is also applicable to our Big Four, then we have arrived at the ultimate of human stupidity.

The EDITOR to YOU

IN this issue the *Overseas Daily Mail* and the *Transatlantic Daily Mail* are incorporated.

For some time past *The Daily Mail* has been considering ways of extending its service to readers of its weekly editions throughout the world and providing a shop window abroad for British industries, worthy of the goods they offer and in keeping with Britain's great export drive.

Our aim has been to make this combined publication, incorporating the Overseas and Transatlantic editions, a digest of news and pictures of interest to all Britons overseas and to people of every country who are interested in Britain and her products.

Our purpose is to show Britain not only to the Empire but to all countries, and to present a fair and comprehensive picture of the British way of life.

Readers will have noticed that editorial matter has now replaced advertisements in this front page, the back page being reserved for advertisers' announcements. We are grateful to advertisers for their co-operation in this alteration, and we hope that this and other changes will have improved the general attractiveness of the paper, and so made it more worthy of the important rôle of Britain's trade ambassador and a newspaper for the English-speaking world.

May we add a personal note. Much thought has gone into the making of this publication, but no newspaper is so good that it cannot be improved upon. We hope to continue to improve, and in our developments we shall at all times appreciate criticisms and suggestions from readers.

To every one of you, wherever you may be, greetings—and good reading!

Harvest under a 10-mile lake

AFTER the worst summer storms for 19 years many thousands of acres of Britain's harvest lands lie under water. Across the Suffolk plain, between Harleston and Beccles, stretches a ten-mile lake.

The Daily Mail air picture shows a typical scene of devastation. Hay floats on a waste of water. In this district farmers in boats were going to the aid of their cattle marooned on high ground, and water lapped at farmhouse doors.

The river Waveney, shown winding around the little town of Bungay in the picture, burst its banks and spread out into a gigantic lake.

In many other parts of Britain the ripening corn was battered down by downpours of huge hailstones and mashed into the ground by successive waves of storm.

It was estimated that 60 per cent. of Suffolk's barley has been damaged, but much of the corn can be saved.

A vast pall of thundercloud that blacked out London in the middle of a summer afternoon burst in the fiercest storm experienced in the capital since 1927. At its peak five minutes' rain beat down at the rate of 3in. an hour—which happens only once in ten years, say experts.

Lightning leapt around London's buildings; floods immobilised street traffic in the after-office rush-hour and cascaded down into the Underground, swamping the track and holding up some sections of the system until a late hour.

With the downpour came a wind squall at 44 miles an hour which constantly changed direction and had the effect of a whirlwind in some parts of the country. In Streatham, S.W. London, trees were stripped.

EXAMPLE 209

people on this side of the Atlantic who wanted to receive copies regularly.

(August 21, 1946, the trans-Atlantic edition of the *Daily Mail* appeared for the last time as a separate and distinct publication. Earlier in the month that edition had been combined with the larger overseas weekly edition of the *Mail*, and the first issue of the combined editions appeared under the date August 3-10, 1946. For many years the overseas weekly edition had been sent "from London to all parts of the Americas and the British commonwealth of nations.")

Example 209 suggests the front page of the first issue of the combined editions, which consisted of sixteen six-column pages.

August 4, 1944, the *Times* of London distributed copies of its first daily air edition—ten pages 18 by 24¼ inches in size, printed on India paper. See Example 210.

In a story in that first issue, the *Times* stated:

"This copy of the *Times* is one of a limited number printed on India paper, of a weight only one-half of that of the newsprint on which the paper is normally printed.

"From today the *Times* will publish an air edition daily. For the present it will not be on sale in Great Britain. Arrangements have been made for a regular supply to be carried by air to the United States and Canada. They should reach the American eastern seaboard on the second day after the date of publication. Copies will also be transported regularly by air to certain European countries and will be placed on sale.

"It is believed that this is the first occasion on which a full-size daily paper has been printed on India paper by rotary presses, though for several years past a special miniature edition of the *Times Weekly Edition* has been regularly printed on India paper for distribution by air abroad. (Copies of this miniature edition, which is printed by ordinary flatbed process, are not available for distribution through the ordinary trade channels.)

"The paper for the air edition of the *Times* has been specially manufactured for the purpose by James R. Crompton & Bros., Limited, of Elton Paper Mills, Bury, Lancashire. In view of its greater durability, as compared with wartime newsprint, copies of the India-paper edition will be presented to the libraries receiving the *Times* under the Copyright Act. The India-paper edition will to this extent replace the Royal Edition of the *Times*, which was printed on specially durable paper before the war, but had to be suspended when the paper restrictions were imposed."

In commenting on the appearance of the air edition of the *Times* (the body matter of which is set in Times New Roman), the *New York Herald Tribune* stated: "The type stands out with a readable and almost elegant clarity and the photographs and maps have a slick-paper brilliancy."

AIR EDITION

THE TIMES

No. 49,926 LONDON FRIDAY AUGUST 4 1944 PRICE 4d

EXAMPLE 210

April 26, 1945, a story in the *New York Times* written from San Francisco the day before presented these statements:

"In the first experiment of its kind in the history of journalism, the *New York Times* put before delegates and members of the press at the United Nations Conference at breakfast time today a four-page wire-photo edition of the newspaper set in type in New York, 3000 miles away, two hours after midnight.

"Astonished members of delegations picked up their copies, saw '2 A.M. Edition' and looked for the date. It was Wednesday, April 25.

"Newspaper correspondents commented on the postwar possibilities of this new journalistic technique, the page or half-page transmission of daily papers by wire, and discussed its potential effects on newspaper work in this country and abroad.

"This experiment in facsimile reproduction, as an explanatory paragraph in the first number related, was carried out in co-operation with the Associated Press and the *Richmond* (Calif.) *Independent.*

"Similar in appearance to the regular pages of the *New York Times,* except that it contained no advertising matter, the wirephoto edition had thirty-two columns of conference and world news, editorials and war maps. It was distributed without charge at the hotels.

"The four pages were set in type in the composing room of the *New York Times,* in New York. Printer's proofs were taken of each page. The proofs were then cut in half and were transmitted to San Francisco over the wirephoto facilities of the Associated Press, just as photographs have been transmitted for several years.

"At the San Francisco office of the Associated Press, in the Chronicle Building, each negative of a half page of type was developed and a print of it was made.

"A messenger from the publishing plant of the *Richmond Independent,* fifteen miles distant, picked up the prints and hurried with them to his office, where photo-engravers put together the half pages in correct order, photographed the resultant full pages and made zinc engravings. From the engravings 2000 copies of the four-page newspaper were run off on a flatbed letter press in the *Independent's* plant."

Example 211 suggests the front page of one of those facsimile issues of the *Times.*

Copies of the final issue of that facsimile edition of the *Times* were distributed June 27, 1945, to conference delegates and newspaper representatives as they prepared to leave San Francisco. From first to

"All the News That's Fit to Print"

The New York Times.

2 A. M. EDITION (EWT) Transmitted by Associated Press Wirephoto

VOL. XCIV....No. 31,869. NEW YORK, THURSDAY, APRIL 26, 1945. DISTRIBUTED IN SAN FRANCISCO

TRUMAN OPENS WORLD SECURITY PARLEY; RUSSIANS ENCIRCLE BERLIN, CROSS ELBE; 3D NEAR AUSTRIA; BERCHTESGADEN BOMBED

GERMAN SOLDIERS LINE UP TO YIELD TO U.S. FIRST ARMY

In Mortal Fear of Russians, Reich Troops and Civilians Beg Americans for Aid

SOME TRY TO SWIM RIVER

Stream Becomes a Modern 'Jordan' for U. S. Prisoners and a 'Styx' for Foe

AN EXPERIMENT

This special 2 A. M. edition of The New York Times is being distributed daily among delegates to the United Nations conference in San Francisco. It is made possible through the cooperation of The Associated Press and The Richmond Independent, Richmond, California, and is circulated as a public service of The New York Times and its associates in the enterprise and as an experiment in facsimile reproduction of newspapers. Its pages are transmitted photographically each morning from New York over the Wirephoto facilities of the Associated Press and printed on the presses of The Richmond Independent.

BLACK MARKET LAID TO NEW CONCERNS

Illegal Meat Sales Traced by Congress Group to Companies Established Within Year

GERMANS TRAPPED

2 Soviet Armies Merge West of Capital After By-Passing Potsdam

ELBE TOWN SEIZED

Pillau Falls, Ending Nazi Grip on East Prussia —Bruenn Menaced

AMERICANS AND RUSSIANS TIGHTEN GRIP ON THE REICH

3D ARMY 15 MILES FROM AUSTRIAN LINE

RegenCaptured—Battle Rages for Regensburg—3 Forces Drive on German Redoubt

RAF 6-Ton Bombs Score Hits On Hitler's Mountain Chalet

GENERAL ADVANCE MADE ON OKINAWA

Army Troops Retake Kakazu, From Which They Had Been Driven by Japanese

Resources and Security

U. S. and Russia Aware of Their Material Wealth and What It Means to Peace

House Likely to Vote Draft Curb On Combat Use of 18-Year-Olds

First Session Presents a Scene Like Opening of a Great Drama

JUSTICE PUT FIRST

We Will Bow Only to That Tremendous Power, He Tells Delegates

SEES A WORLD TEST

Stettinius, Warren and San Francisco Mayor Welcome Visitors

EXAMPLE 211

last, sixty-four issues had been printed, from 512 half-page wirephoto transmissions.

A story with a San Francisco date line printed in a regular edition of the *Times* for June 28, 1945, included these statements about the facsimile experiment:

"Representatives of the forty-two American consultant organizations at the conference said that they depended largely on the facsimile edition, carrying copies into committee sessions and into meetings of the United States delegation to use in the discussions. Delegates from smaller countries said that only through reading it were they able to keep abreast of detailed happenings in meetings of the 'Big Five' and in many of the committee deliberations.

"A member of the 'Big Five' itself complained that representatives of the major powers might as well open their Nob Hill meeting to the press, inasmuch as every meeting was being reported in detail in the *New York Times* wirephoto edition. On one occasion, Prime Minister Peter Fraser of New Zealand, chairman of the committee on trusteeships, declared that the 'Big Five' paper on trusteeships had not yet reached his committee a week after its text had appeared exclusively in the wirephoto edition, and that the story appearing there was the only knowledge committee members had of the 'Big Five' paper for their discussions.

"Many of the foreign correspondents here used the facsimile edition of the *New York Times* as a guide in their own coverage of the conference. A Far Eastern newspaper man, after trying with difficulty for several days to find out what was going on, reported that he adopted the practice of waiting every morning for the wirephoto edition, then writing 2000 words from it to send to his newspaper.

"As the conference wore on the *New York Times* and its associates in the historic enterprise continued experimentation to improve the technical quality of the facsimile edition. The result was that the issues during the last several weeks attained a high standard of legibility, representing a distinct betterment over those in the early part of the conference.

"Hundreds of delegates and newspaper correspondents collected complete files of the paper. Others, after losing or discarding early copies, began clamoring, often in vain, for replacements of the missing issues. Foreign ministries of many countries sought complete files. So did university and public libraries. West Coast residents, hearing of the publishing experiment, telephoned or wrote asking how they could 'subscribe' for the facsimile edition."

The *New York Post* also issued a special United Nations Conference edition, from April 23 to June 27, 1945. See Example 212.

The San Francisco edition, a sixteen-page tabloid, used the same kinds of head and body types as those employed for the regular edition

Conference Edition

Wednesday
April
25th

New York Post

FOUNDED 1801 • VOLUME 144, NO. 132 • COPYRIGHT, 1945, NEW YORK POST

NEW YORK CITY, WEDNESDAY, APRIL 25, 1945 16 PAGES

5¢ IN NEW YORK CITY AND SUBURBS

10¢ ELSEWHERE IN THE UNITED STATES

SUBWAY BATTLES RAGING UNDER TOTTERING BERLIN

Story on Page 2

PARLEY OPENS TODAY

CONFEREES UNITED ON BASIC AIM

Story on Page 3

3rd Sweeps 28 Miles To Peril Hitler Hideout

Story on Page 2

EXAMPLE 212

in New York. It included everything published in the New York edition except the amusements, sports and comic pages, and in it conference news was played more heavily and conference stories ran somewhat longer than in the regular edition in New York.

Paul A. Tierney, managing editor of the *New York Post*, who served as editor of the conference edition, told this writer in 1946:

"We had two direct teletype lines from New York, one of which terminated in an office in San Francisco and the other at the printing plant of Lederer, Street & Zeus in Berkeley. The *New York Post* coverage of the United Nations Conference, of course, originated in San Francisco and was teletyped back to New York. All the rest of the content of the San Francisco edition, including general news, special articles, columnists, and so forth, was teletyped from New York to Berkeley.

"At San Francisco we took our own photographs for the San Francisco edition. The press run was approximately 5000 daily, of which about 200 were distributed, with the compliments of the *New York Post*, to official delegates. The remainder was placed on sale, at ten cents a copy, at the various hotels and other points where conference interest was concentrated.

"The edition carried New York City date lines on all folios and carried the regular masthead of the *New York Post*. Toward the front of the paper, usually on page two, three, four or five, we carried a small box stating that this was the Conference Edition of the *New York Post* giving the address of the edition's office and the name and address of the printer.

"As far as I know, this was the first time that any paper in the United States published simultaneous editions at points so far apart and for so long a duration. You will note that the conference edition was a complete paper, printed daily at or near the point of distribution, and placed on sale. It was not in any sense a free circular. It carried a moderate amount of national advertising.

"The editorial process of this edition daily required the services of two wire editors in New York and twelve editorial workers at San Francisco, eight of whom were on the staff of the *New York Post*, assigned to the coverage of the conference and four of whom were hired in San Francisco for the necessary period; plus necessary teletype operators at both ends, a small office staff and two circulators."

An article in *Editor & Publisher* for May 5, 1945, by Jerry Walker of the *E. & P.* staff, included these statements:

"Elbert B. M. Wortman, who writes publicity for Finch Telecommunications, Inc., is certain that facsimile on FM broadcasting channels will be gobbled up by the public just as quickly as sets can be produced, and he visions a whole new field of advertising. As for circulation, Wortman believes the time will come when 'space' salesmen will be quoting readership in terms of 'rolls of paper,' for in the consumption of rolls of facsimile paper lies an accurate estimate of the number of facsimile machines in active use.

"The 'radio newspaper,' as the broadcasters see it, will be delivered directly into the home on a facsimile machine which will be made available at 'a moderate price.' Before the war they were being quoted at around seventy-five dollars. They will come on the market at a much lower figure. The machine is about the size of a typewriter and it can be plugged into any FM radio receiver. Even while the owner sleeps, the machine can run on, turning out pages of the newspaper. An 8-by-10-inch sheet filled with headlines, news text, pictures and advertising copy can be transmitted, ready for reading, within ten minutes.

"England's television pioneer, John Logie Baird, has been experimenting with a system by which a whole page of a standard-size newspaper can be transmitted at the rate of twenty-five copies a second, but only for a distance of about thirty miles, until relay stations can be perfected. British interests vision facsimile newspapers and documents between England and Canada, or even eastward over Europe to Alaska.

"Baird's receiving set uses a spool holding a roll of sensitized cinematograph film which is passed continuously in front of a gate upon which is focused the image of the television pictures reproduced on the screen of a cathode-ray tube. The pictures are reproduced at the rate of twenty-five per second and each picture is thus photographed on the moving film.

"For a slant on facsimile's value to advertising, we take you back to Mr. Wortman:

" 'For comic-strip advertising,' he says, 'facsimile would seem to be a natural, and should give that form of selling propaganda a new lease on life. However, inventive minds see in facsimile a chance to develop a whole new editorial and advertising technique of which the first law should be brevity and the second, fast-moving, entertaining copy.

" 'Now for the first time it becomes feasible to sell fashion merchandise over the air. The hitherto-impossible task of holding attention with a word description of what's new in waistlines is now made possible and easy with line sketches, wash drawings and photographs. And this, of course, means that radio becomes truly practical for department stores. Stores, little and big, will be able to use radio to announce their sales specials with pictures, prices, colors, sizes, making a printed and permanent record which the housewife can clip and put in her purse. For this alone, facsimile promises to be a boon to the small-town broadcaster.'

"With almost two years of experimenting in the field of wired facsimile newspapers, officials of Fairchild Publications recognize the potentialities of reproduction by radio for simultaneous publication of a newspaper in distant parts of the country, Circulation Manager Harry Zwirner said this week. In June, 1943, the *Daily News Record* was 'wired' to Los Angeles for distribution during a meeting of the Men's Wear Manufacturing Association, the facilities of Acme News Pictures being used. Later that year the front page of the *Women's Wear Daily* was transmitted over the Soundphoto System to Chicago."

Writing on the same general subject, in *Editor & Publisher* for April 20, 1946, the week before the sixtieth annual convention of the American Newspaper Publishers' Association was held at the Waldorf-Astoria in New York City, and where a demonstration of facsimile was presented in one of the exhibition rooms, Jerry Walker stated:

"If we were a newspaper publisher seeking a permit for an FM station, we would make certain to list a facsimile service as a contemplated part of our programming.

"This writer sat with members of the Federal Communications Commission the other day and saw just about everything the laboratories have developed to date in the way of facsimile machines—equipment intended not only to produce a newspaper-of-the-air but to provide substitutes for some of the present-day means of business communications.

"While all questions put by members of the commission to the designer and his replies were off the record, it can be reported that the general tone of conversation indicated how deeply the commissioners are concerned with the public-service aspects of radio. There was no doubt they had their eyes opened to the many new public-service possibilities of facsimile.

"In this writer's opinion, facsimile is nothing any newspaper publisher should fear. Instead, it is a natural medium for him to adopt. It is not going to make the pressroom obsolete before the next edition, nor before many millions more newspapers are published.

"Indicative of the precincts within which facsimile will be confined for several years are the standards which the commission is about to promulgate, after the members consolidate their opinions on what they have seen the last week. An industry committee has recommended a fundamental standard on the size of the facsimile page—8½ by 11½ inches. This would mean that the newspaper-of-the-air will be a semi-tabloid, four columns wide (or maybe one wide column) and about a half column (standard newspaper measurement) deep.

"Eventually, and even today in some laboratory experiments, facsimile can produce a page almost as large as a standard newspaper page, but machines that are being built are designed to handle the letterhead-size page, which can be transmitted in approximately two minutes by air and four minutes by wire.

"Aside from getting the public interested enough to add facsimile equipment to their radio sets, at maybe eighty or a hundred dollars, the big problem in the 'fax' business today is the special paper required. It is electrolytic and present costs for the cheapest grade run to forty cents for a hundred feet. That means a subscriber might get a hundred pages of a newspaper for forty cents.

"But already the facsimile promoters have ideas to distribute the paper without cost to the set owner. They believe large corporations might be enticed to give rolls of the paper away in return for having their ads either printed on the back of the paper or transmitted by facsimile.

"Whatever the details for distribution, facsimile is a logical 'newspaper baby' and those publishers who can show the commission that they mean to use it as a new or supplemental means of disseminating news and advertising stand a better chance of getting an okay on their FM application than rivals who have had no experience in publishing.

"In the not-too-distant future, facsimile will have an important role in the newspaper's internal business. Copy will be transmitted by the page, rather than by the word on teletype: photographs will be relayed at half the speed of present transmission methods; advertising layouts will come by air, and many business office records in a group operation can be exchanged within a moment.

"One machine has been developed to record a stencil of the original copy, rather than a positive print, and this stencil can be used in an ordinary mimeograph machine to run up to 50,000 copies. Imagine the potentialities of that for distribution of a supplemental newspaper!

"The realm of facsimile invites many dreams. Not too fanciful even at this moment is the thought that some day facsimile may 'free' radio. Once there is a general development of the facsimile newspaper, for instance, any tampering with its content by officialdom would provide a clearcut infringement of the First Amendment. Attempts to interfere with radio programming today do not arouse public opinion to the point of crying aloud against violation of freedom of speech."

At two o'clock eastern daylight-saving time Saturday afternoon, June 22, 1946, Station WGHF, a new frequency-modulation station for sound and facsimile, with studios at 10 East Fortieth Street, New York City, went on the air officially and commercially, as announced a few days before by William G. H. Finch, owner and operator of the station.

A news story in the *New York Herald Tribune* the day of the official opening of the station explained that WGHF had been operating experimentally for several months on a frequency of 99.7 megacycles, and continued:

"It will continue on this frequency in its new daily schedule, which runs from 2 to 5 P.M. and from 6 to 9 P.M. Its radius is approximately sixty miles, covering an area said to contain 75,000 to 100,000 FM receivers.

"Programs on WGHF will emphasize classical music interspersed with special events, news and public-interest programs, Mr. Finch said. Facsimile broadcasts of United Press news and pictures in a four-column, four-page newspaper called *Airpress* will be made at about 1 P.M. and between 5 and 6 P.M. daily, he said. Receipt of the material requires a printing-recording apparatus attached to the receiving set. . . ."

In mid-August of 1946, newsmen in Boston, according to *Editor & Publisher*, "witnessed the first city-to-city transmission of the high-speed microwave facsimile process when messages were sent from New York to the Raytheon Manufacturing Company's plant" in Boston. "The New York terminal point was in the Lincoln Building and the messages were retransmitted from a test circuit of relay stations set up at Lewisboro, N. Y., Oxford, Bristol and Tolland, Conn., Webster and Waban Hill, Mass. The facsimile transmitter and receiver used is known as the Hogan Faximile, invented by John V. L. Hogan, president of Radio Inventions, Inc., which co-operated with Raytheon in conducting the first practical demonstration in history. . . . Microwave is an outgrowth of wartime radar and is not unlike the present wirephoto system, except that it requires no wires; only the relay towers at certain intervals."

But let's return, for a moment, to January 9, 1946, when the *Miami Herald* inaugurated a Clipper edition to be flown daily and Sunday to principal cities in Latin America.

That edition, according to a story by Les Barnhill in *Editor & Publisher* for June 22, 1946, "is a standard-size light-weight version of the regular *Herald*. . . . It is delivered by air on the day of publication to such distant points as Trinidad, 2200 miles from Miami, and Bogota, Colombia, 1500 miles from Miami. To more distant points in central and southern South America, it is delivered on the second day after publication. . . .

"The size of the daily Clipper ranges from fourteen to twenty pages and the Sunday edition from thirty-two to thirty-four pages, plus the comic section and the *American Weekly*. The amount of national advertising governs the size of the editions. All the national advertising printed in the regular *Herald* goes into the Clipper."

August 1, 1946, the European edition of the *New York Herald Tribune*, published in Paris, which for several months had been flying copies regularly to Sweden, Denmark, Norway, Italy, French North Africa and England, began distributing copies by air also to the Netherlands, Eire, Czechoslovakia and Austria.

September 12, 1946, a Raytheon radio telephone, or auto talkie, was tried out in New York City by the *World-Telegram*. A story in that paper explained:

"The two-way communication equipment permits a reporter covering a news story in an automobile to make contact with his office at any time. It also permits the staff writer at the other end of the hookup in the newspaper office to be in contact with the reporter, and the two can carry on conversations.

"The radio telephone, used on U. S. planes during the war, operates on a very high frequency band and its range is the horizon. A longer range is obtainable through contact with relay towers now being developed in this area.

"The *World-Telegram* is the first New York newspaper to be granted the privilege of testing, demonstrating and publicizing the Raytheon radio telephone. Its use in newspaper reporting has been praised because it obviates the necessity of a reporter wasting time seeking regular telephones to contact his city editor after a news story breaks.

"Employing frequency modulation, the equipment is similar to the command sets used on planes during the war and now employed by airlines for plane-to-control-tower conversations. The radiophone is relatively free from static and operates even in areas previously considered dead spots for two-way police radio systems.

"The equipment needed for the reporter's automobile is only a little larger than an ordinary auto radio receiver. It draws about the same current as a standard auto radio receiver and therefore requires no special generator or larger battery. The antenna consists of a small, stiff wire only 18 inches long which is mounted vertically in the center of the automobile roof.

"One transmitter-receiver station covers New York, and Raytheon's location is on the fifty-fourth floor of the Lincoln Building at 60 East Forty-second Street. The equipment is remotely controlled over a leased line from the *World-Telegram* city editor's desk.

"The staff writer in the newspaper office operates his equipment just as he would a regular telephone. He may listen to the reporter phoning in his story, either through a loudspeaker or a telephone headset. Reporters *en route* to the scenes of stories can immediately report fires, accidents or other emergencies encountered and be as close to their editor as if they were beside him.

"Raytheon's radiophones operate at 156 to 162 megacycles and out of the tuning range of conventional shortwave sets. Communication in this band is afforded with maximum reliability at all times, according to Raytheon's engineers. The postwar equipment is now in production and soon newspapers will be able to purchase the mobile sets, the company reported.

"The reporter's radiophone is the same type of equipment recently installed in two racing cars in the annual 500-mile speedway event. Similar systems are being used by a large Chicago trucking concern, in which company officials are in contact with their drivers at all times."

In mid-September of 1946 a picture of a group of New York City newspaper men went through the air in pulse time from downtown New York to a laboratory in New Jersey.

"Simultaneously, from the same transmitter," ran a story in *Editor & Publisher*, "a commentator's voice intoned the dirge of Wall Street, a teletype machine ticked off the latest market quotations, an orchestra played a jolly tune with frequency-modulated clarity, and another teletype machine clattered off copy from press-association wires.

"Thus, a single transmitter developed by engineers of the International Telephone and Telegraph Corporation broadcast facsimile, news copy, voice, FM, and music on a single frequency.

"The full demonstration of the new system, known as pulse-time modulation (PTM), included eight broadcasts of different types emanating from eight studios. All were fused into a single transmission for multiplex broadcasting.

"At the Federal Telecommunications Laboratories, a receiver in combination with a facsimile set or a teletypewriter offered any one of the eight programs desired by simple push-button choice.

"In commercial use, it was explained, a single parabolic antenna atop an office building would pick up the multiplex broadcast from a communications center and the individual services would be distributed where desired—news reports to a radio studio; music to a restaurant; pictures to an advertising agency; stock ticker to a broker's office, and so forth.

"In the immediate field of publishing, it has been forecast that the PTM system might replace the miles of land wires now used in the A.P., U.P., I.N.S. teletype networks. In still another phase of its possible use, PTM might become the means by which a newspaper plant would be the hub of all communications in a given area. . . .

"PTM has been tried and proven in many uses during the war, according to I.T. and T. engineers. They claim it is the answer to the problem of over-crowded broadcast spectrum. As many as 100 stations —if ever any community could support that many—could use a single transmitter and a single frequency for a multitude of programs. One station, if it found it economically wise to do so, could easily send out several different programs at one time.

"PTM is a method of radio communication which involves the transmission of a series of short bursts, or pulses, the waves remaining constant in amplitude and frequency."

October 15, 1946, members of the New York State Society of Newspaper Editors, in convention at Rochester, N. Y., saw photographs snapped, processed and projected on a screen, all within fifteen seconds, at the first public exhibition of a combined camera, processing cabinet and projector developed under wartime secrecy by the Eastman Kodak Company.

According to a story in the *New York Herald Tribune* the next day, "editors entering a room in pairs were photographed at a speed of a ten-thousandth of a second as they passed a flash lamp. Before they reached their seats the photographs were projected on a screen four feet high.

"The completely automatic camera, processing unit and projector uses a special 16-millimeter film which moves along a track inside the light-tight camera, taking the photographs at stated intervals, the company said.

"When a picture is snapped, a few drops of hot chemical solution are squirted on the exposed film, which then is cleared by vacuum. The high temperature of the chemicals, about 140 degrees Fahrenheit, makes it possible to complete processing in about nine seconds.

"The final photographic image is a direct positive picture, which is dried by air pressure after it enters the projection system. The same pressure holds the photograph flat during the immediate projection on a screen."

In the winter of 1946-47, the *New Orleans States* started using a motor truck equipped with a complete set-up for the transmission of pictures by radio and telephone from the scene of action to the newspaper office.

"The new device," according to a story in *Editor & Publisher* for January 4, 1947, "combines the portable Wirephoto sending machine, developed by the Associated Press, and the radiotelephone service installed recently in the *States* contact car by the Southern Bell Telephone Company.

"The use of the radiotelephone is now limited to the vicinity of New Orleans, but the range is being increased by additional facilities being installed in the telephone company's system.

"William H. Fitzpatrick, editor of the *States*, expressed the opinion that the equipment will prove invaluable. Now it is of considerable help on such stories as those developing along the waterfront, he said.

"As soon as the contact car reaches the scene of a news story, the sending machine is plugged into the nearest telephone connection box to be ready for use as soon as the pictures are taken and developed.

"The portable photo laboratory was especially designed by Raymond Frischhertz, superintendent of maintenance for the newspaper.

"Here's an account of a recent demonstration:

"At 10:45 A.M., *States* photographer Jimmy Guillot made a picture of a traveler aboard a steamship moored in the river. While reporter Bill Reid was interviewing the passenger, Guillot went to the truck, developed and printed the photograph.

"Then Guillot signaled the Southern Bell switchboard by pressing a button on the mouthpiece of the radiotelephone in the truck cab. He was connected to the *States* office, and transmitted his picture. The photo was received on a regular Wirephoto receiving set. The electric impulses traveled by radio from the truck to the telephone company station, and by regular wires from there to the *States*.

"When the transmission was completed, Reid called the city desk by radiotelephone and relayed his story to a rewrite man."

A story in the same issue of *Editor & Publisher* included the following about picture transmission from the South Pole:

"Along with radar, walkie-talkie and other war-developed electronic equipment, Acme Telephoto is on its way to Little America with Rear Admiral Richard E. Byrd.

"The latest model Telephoto Trans-ceivers and radio converters will handle all the expedition's picture transmissions and other pictorial communications from the Antarctic to the United States. This is the second peacetime project in which the U. S. Navy is using Acme equipment.

"At the Bikini atomic bomb tests last summer, the Navy used Telephoto machines aboard the *U. S. S. Mt. McKinley* to radio blast pictures back to the United States in time for same-day publication by Pacific Coast newspapers. The same crew of Navy engineers and Telephoto technicians who handled Bikini transmission is in charge.

"At present, the Telephoto Trans-ceivers are aboard the *U. S. S. Mt. Olympus*, flagship and press-radio headquarters of the Byrd expedition. Later this equipment might be transferred to operate from shore radio installations.

"The transmissions from Little America will probably be the longest in radio-Telephoto history. The Navy plans to send pictures directly from the Antarctic to Washington, D. C.—roughly 10,000 miles.

"Depending on atmospheric conditions, the transmissions may go directly to Washington over South America, or around the world the other way—over the North Pole to the U. S."

June 23, 1947, Niles Trammell, president of the National Broadcasting Company, stated in Washington, D. C., according to the Associated Press, that "a new radio communications system has been developed which can send 1,000,000 words a minute. He said the new system, known as Ultrafax, could transmit twenty 50,000-word novels from New York to San Francisco in only sixty seconds.

"Ultrafax was developed by Radio Corporation of America and will be ready for a public showing this summer. Mr. Trammell said that each printed page is treated as a picture, and flashed in rapid succession. At the receiving end the pages are reproduced by a new high-speed process of photography."

How far away and long ago seems April 24, 1704, when John Campbell and B. Green produced the first issue of the *Boston News-Letter!*

How much more diverse, complicated and speeded up are things today in the world of news. But certain typographic treatments in some of today's papers are more complicated than they should be, or need be, and certain simpler and better treatments are considered in the next chapter.

4

Modern Suggestions

THE BASIC PRINCIPLE of modern newspaper makeup, typographically, is simplicity.

The big idea is to present the story as clearly as possible; to strip it of typographic affectations and superfluities; to free it from physical devices that may intrude on the consciousness of the reader—that may get between him and the story itself.

Yet several newspaper executives in recent years, prompted by the commendable desire to improve their makeups, have gone off on the wrong track and have gone in for "precious" typography.

Instead of simplifying, they have complicated. Instead of cleaning up, they have cluttered up. And, of course, the papers are less effective typographically than they were.

Several papers have gone in for heads that are just as affected and complicated as were the heads replaced; for ornamental jim and "30" dashes; for innumerable black dots and other devices of the sort; for many display initial letters; for many consecutive body lines in boldface type, and for heavy or fancy or both heavy and fancy cutoff rules.

Let us consider all of these things. But, first, let us consider the old-style heads of several decks that more and more papers are giving up in favor of sensible flush-left heads, usually limited to two decks at most.

Surely those old-style heads, with their exact and limiting unit counts, were affected, unnatural. Surely they cramped the style and wasted the time of the head-writer. Surely they wasted valuable space in the paper, and valuable time in the composing room. Surely they were largely responsible for the use of words that often meant more to the man at the copy desk than to the man on the street. Surely their squeezed-in or padded-out contents often presented statements that were not borne out by the facts in the stories beneath them—and thus helped to shake reader confidence in the dependability of headlines.

If a headwriter can state exactly the right thing in a line, say, of eleven typographic units, why should he be obliged to discard that line and write a weaker and possibly misleading substitute, to conform to an established count of twelve units to the line? Why should he have to use a seven-letter word when a six-letter word could do a better job? Why should he have to trail a head along through four or more decks—writing, rewriting, counting, recounting, chopping, padding, but mostly padding—when he could write a better head in two decks or even one deck?

Of course, when you come to think of it, those old head forms not only were affected and unnatural; they were absurd.

Yet many newspapers and many newspaper people still cling to them, just as they cling to many other journalistic traditions that never had any sound reasons for being, or long since have outlived their usefulness.

It is only natural that many newspaper men who have been writing old-style heads many years should want to keep on writing heads of that sort, and that they should resent modern flush-left heads.

"What!" we can hear some of those old-timers exclaim. "Those flush-left atrocities! You want me to give up all the head-writing tricks I've learned in twenty years and more—throw away all my experience at head writing—and start all over again, on a par with the greenest cub on the sheet!

"Nothing doing! Not a *thing* doing! Head writing is a trade—a profession—even an art. It takes years of training to master the technique of it. But there's no rhyme or reason to these flush-left things. Any school kid can throw them together!"

Of course any school kid can throw such heads together. So can any newspaper man. And, unfortunately, many such heads *are* thrown together. But not the good ones—the really professional ones.

Good flush-left heads are as carefully planned as were the old-style heads they are replacing. Modern head treatments afford the head-writer more latitude, of course. That is one of the virtues of them. But they have definite rules of their own, and the experienced head-writer is the one best qualified to turn out the most effective modern heads.

After many of our newspapers had abandoned antiquated head forms in favor of modern flush-left heads, a professor of journalism wrote this writer of some difficulty he was having in one of his classes, and asked how to determine the number of typographic units (letters, figures, spaces and punctuation marks) that should or could be employed in the writing of a newspaper headline of a given width.

"The problem," he wrote, "grows out of the fact that I have been teaching a count system in headline writing which some returning students complain doesn't work. They maintain that when they get jobs on newspapers, they have to learn an entirely new count system. The count system I use is the one . . . I learned when I worked for papers using Bodoni and Cheltenham heads. These complaining students are working for papers using some of the modern sans-serif types.

"Thus, the problem which worries me is this: Just how close an approximation is the old rule-of-thumb system of counting heads to the realities of today? Implicit in the problem or its solution is the notion that perhaps a new count system or systems ought to be devised."

This writer replied:

"Specimen sheets of type faces issued by the Linotype Company list the lower-case alphabet lengths of the faces, but this information proves more helpful when applied to body matter than to heads.

"For instance, the knowledge that a certain lower-case alphabet measures 214 points, say, doesn't help a head-writer much when a capital W of the font is as wide as five or six lower-case i's.

"In a sense, the writing of modern heads is more complicated than the writing of heads used to be, but in another sense it is much simpler.

"In the days when most news heads were set in condensed capitals, most of the type characters, as you know, were counted as one unit each, with the wider characters counted as a unit and a half each, and the thinner as a half unit each. But those were the days when newspapers in general followed the practice of presenting heads in exactly staggered or pyramided or hanging-indented decks, rather than in the flush-left form now employed by hundreds of progressive newspapers.

"Today most of the 'normal-width'—not condensed—cap-and-lower-case fonts are laws unto themselves in the way of unit count, because of the variations in width from one character to another.

"For example, two fonts might have exactly the same over-all lower-case alphabet length, and yet the capital W's in one font might be several points wider than those in the other, whereas the lower-case i's of the font with the wider W's might be narrower than the i's in the other.

"It seems rather formidable until we recall that modern flush-left heads do not call for meticulous unit counts, but give the head-writer plenty of freedom from line to line, with the lines running ragged at the right—but not too ragged.

"To me it seems that students might well be made familiar with the fact that the characters in a modern font may vary decidedly in width, one from another, but that no attempt should be made to give the students any rigid rules to follow in that respect.

"A bright student going to work in a certain newspaper plant should be able quickly to qualify himself to write satisfactory heads for that paper. In fact, he could 'learn the unit count' in advance by studying copies of the paper."

Another professor of journalism wrote this writer, about the same time:

"Our large—and small—city dailies around here reject top decks of flush-left heads in which there's a variation of more than two units from line to line.

"My feeling is that by so doing they are going part way back, unnecessarily, to the old days of hamstrung head-writers who were kept altogether too busy obeying meticulous rules that often added nothing to the readability or effectiveness of the heads.

"It seems to me, further, much worse to have, under the so-called free-count system, two-line first decks with eleven units in each line, or thirteen in one and twelve in the other, than thirteen in one and nine and one-half in the other.

"The eleven-and-eleven combination looks stodgy to me, and the even block of white at the right seems inartistic. And the thirteen-and-twelve combination seems, sometimes, to suggest that writer and printer had tried unsuccessfully to make the lines come out even. The thirteen-and-nine-and-one-half, with the long line either at the top or the bottom, pleases me better, since the white space is less studied and it illustrates a fitting of the form to the idea rather than the fitting of the idea to the form."

[NOTE: *But the striving for those longs and shorts can—and usually does—call for an unnatural trimming or padding of units to fit an artificial pattern, and thus sacrifices substance for form.*]

"I didn't mean, of course," our correspondent continued, "that I'd try to bar such heads as the first and second kind referred to, whose defects when not multiplied too often are not too serious; merely, I wouldn't deliberately try for such effects, thereby sacrificing time we thought we were to save under the new plan, to produce effects that are not obviously better."

This writer replied, in part:

"I am glad to learn that large and small dailies in your part of the world *are* presenting their flush-left heads in lines that *do not* vary many units from line to line in the same head.

"Not that I believe that the eleven-eleven combination, or even the thirteen-twelve combination, is greatly to be desired, but that I consider either of them better, usually, than, say, a thirteen-seven combination.

"When the *Linotype News* began pioneering flush-left heads, many of the editors who adopted them seemed at first to think that such heads made unnecessary any head-writing restrictions at all, and many of the heads that resulted were amateurish looking indeed.

"Obviously, when all lines in a flush-left head are short—less than three-quarters of the maximum width—the head is weak looking. When some of the lines are unusually short and others unusually long, the head looks as though it had been thrown together. And yet I agree with you that the unit count of flush-left heads in newspapers should be much less rigid than the old heads they are replacing.

"My own observation has been, however, that newspaper head-writers seem more likely to err on the side of short and careless-looking heads than on the side of fairly full lines of almost the same number of units.

"A flush-left head by itself on a magazine page that merely has to present a title; doesn't have to compete with another head or several heads; doesn't have to sell the story to the hurried reader with fairly strong typography, might well have more variation from line to line.

"But when several or even many flush-left heads are used on a page (as in a newspaper), it seems to me that it is well to keep the heads fairly well filled out—to avoid weakness—and fairly uniform as to unit count—to hold color from head to head of the same general structure."

This exchange of correspondence had an interesting sequel.

Several years later—January 16, 1946—that professor of journalism wrote this writer, in part:

"You may recall that some years ago I wrote you hoping you . . . would back me up in a feeling I had that there was no point in trying to preserve a certain rough balance in [flush-left] headlines of that type. Since you wrote me in hearty-though-courteous disagreement, I have put in three summers writing those heads on the . . . copy desk. I'd like to say that I've changed my mind and am now a little upset by long lines teamed up with short. I found, too, that even a difference of one to two units in a count of eleven or twelve is enough to save considerable time that might be spent striving for a perfect balance—and that any more difference than that just looks a bit sloppy."

Some papers, with the desire to be different, have gone in for heads of the sort illustrated by Example 213.

EIGHTEEN MEN RUSH BACK TO WORK

Hardware Store on Main Street Re-opens Its Doors

EXAMPLE 213

Such treatments, of course (we are not here considering the type faces employed, but the general plan of such heads), are artificial, inhibiting and complicated.

Note that the first deck is slanted down from the right, and that the second deck is slanted down from the left, for typographic "style."

That means, of course, that each succeeding line of each deck must contain fewer type-high units than the line before; that the head-writer must squeeze in or pad out to conform to an unnatural medium of expression; that substance must be sacrificed for form.

Other papers have gone in for heads of the sort illustrated by Example 214.

The second-deck lines have been indented too far from the left; the lines are too short; the face employed is too light to get along well with the face used for the first deck, and those black dots (some typographers call them "cannonballs") not only are superfluous; they actually compete with the headlines by distracting attention from the lines to the dots themselves. The head is affected, artificial, weak looking.

Example 215 suggests a much better handling of the head.

Twenty-one Youths
Prance 2,196 Yards

•

Then They Turn
Round Again

•

EXAMPLE 214

Twenty-one Youths
Prance 2,196 Yards

Then They Turn Round
And Turn Cartwheels
Quickly Out of Town

EXAMPLE 215

Note that a somewhat heavier and more appropriate type face has been used for the second deck; that those second-deck lines (indented only 12 points from the left) are wider and more informative, and that the "cannonballs" have been exchanged for contrasting and non-competing white space. The head is simpler, stronger, more effective than the one suggested by Example 214.

Example 216 suggests another artificial head.

Further Gains
In Steel Output
Seen Indicated

Flow of Orders Reported
as Barely Checked by Re-
affirmation of Prices

EXAMPLE 216

Those ornamental jim dashes are too fancy and competitive for such use, and those second-deck lines have been forced into an unnatural form that calls for the filling out of all lines, even to the extent of padding, and often to the extent of letter-spacing, which weakens the lines and mars the appearance of the head as a whole.

The head suggested by Example 217 has some obvious faults, and others not so obvious.

Of course, two of the lines of the first deck are too short, and give

Sixteen Women to Meet Monday	Sixteen Women To Meet Here Monday Night
Crescent Moon Club to Formulate Plans to Attend State Meeting	Crescent Moon Club To Formulate Plans To Attend State Meet
EXAMPLE 217	EXAMPLE 218

the head a sloppy appearance. And the lines of the second deck have been improperly divided for easy reading.

While it is impossible at times to divide the lines of first decks "according to phrasing," because of the more limited unit count imposed by comparatively large display faces, it usually is possible to divide second-deck lines at the ends of phrases—a treatment that makes for easier reading. (Advertising designers have known for years that display lines should be "broken up for sense" for the quick comprehension of readers; that parts of natural word sequences should not be carried at the ends of preceding lines or at the beginnings of following lines, but that all of the words in a natural sequence should be presented, if possible, in the same line.)

It will be observed in Example 217 that a word ("to") appears at the end of the first line of the second deck that properly belongs at the beginning of the second line of that deck, and that another "to" appears at the end of the second line that properly belongs at the beginning of the third line. Certainly a re-arrangement of those lines would make the deck much easier to read.

Example 218 illustrates those points, with all lines of both decks divided "according to phrasing"; "broken up for sense."

Surely the head suggested by Example 218 is much more effective than the one suggested by Example 217. One represents the sort of flush-left heads that can be thrown together by anyone, and that appear much too often in newspapers whose editors or copy-desk executives have not given the flush-left treatments the study they deserve. The other represents a professionally planned and executed head—one that helps the reader to comprehend quickly the statements displayed.

While, to repeat, the unit counts of flush-left lines in any particular deck might well vary from line to line (for it is that variation that gives the head-writer the freedom to write clearly, naturally, even conversationally), there should not be too much variation from line to line in the same deck.

Lines with too much variation make for sloppy-looking heads. Lines that are too short make for weak-looking heads.

Usually, the lines of a deck should reach at least three-fourths of the way across a given width. And the lines of heads that are to appear at the extreme right on a page might well be full lines, or nearly full, because of the paper margin that will appear at the right of them.

Many newspapers, including several metropolitan dailies, that use capitals and lower-case for heads follow the style of keeping "unimportant words down"—of starting "unimportant" words with lower-case letters—even when such words occur at the beginning of second or following lines in heads.

Perhaps that style is followed "for the sake of consistency," as "unimportant" words are kept down inside of lines. But it is a consistency that makes for unattractive heads.

Example 219 shows a three-line head with second and third lines beginning with lower-case letters—a ragged-looking head. Example 220 presents a resetting of the head, with all lines beginning with capitals. The re-set head has a more finished appearance, and is just as easy to read as the other head.

Sportsmen Ask
for Sanctuary
to Save Birds

EXAMPLE 219

Sportsmen Ask
For Sanctuary
To Save Birds

EXAMPLE 220

In the case of a three-line head with two lines beginning with capitals and one with lower-case, the raggedness sometimes is even more pronounced than that suggested by Example 219.

Example 221 shows a three-line head with first and third lines beginning with capitals, but with the second line beginning with a lower-case letter—a ragged head. But notice how, in Example 222, the use of a capital at the beginning of the second line gets away from that raggedness.

Oil Treatment of Scalp Aids Beauty of Hair	Oil Treatment Of Scalp Aids Beauty of Hair
EXAMPLE 221	EXAMPLE 222

Example 223 shows a three-line head with first and second lines beginning with capitals, but with the third line beginning with a lower-case letter—an unfinished-looking head. But a capital at the beginning of the third line improves the head, as shown in Example 224.

Women's Club To Hear Talk on Dandelions	Women's Club To Hear Talk On Dandelions
EXAMPLE 223	EXAMPLE 224

It is bad form to divide words at the ends of lines in any deck of any head. No metropolitan copy desk would pass a first deck with a divided word, but smaller papers sometimes err in that respect.

It is far from modern to divide words in any decks, yet many big-city papers, as well as many smaller papers, continue to divide words in subordinate decks.

Prominent heads of identical or nearly identical physical structure (particularly top-of-page heads, and, especially, heads with full or nearly full lines) should not be placed side by side. They should be removed from one another sufficiently to obviate clashing.

When two such heads are placed side by side on a page, the reader may think, at first glance, that both heads are parts of the same head, and may read from a line in the first head right into and even through an adjoining line in the second head.

Heads of identical or nearly identical physical treatment placed side by side are referred to in some newspaper offices as "bumped" heads, because they seem to bump into each other. In other offices such heads are called "tombstone" heads, as they seem to suggest tombstones (particularly old-style heads of several decks) and tend to "kill" each other.

A head, of course, is supposed to attract attention to its story. To get the desired attention, the head-writer is supposed to put into the head the outstanding points of the story. The person in charge of the copy desk, or the editor, indicates the type treatment he decides the head should be given. These things are obvious.

But two stories, each prominently headed, can be, and often are, placed on a page to the disadvantage of both stories.

Attention value is enhanced by contrast. When a story, say, with a single-column head is placed beside a box effect or a cut, or beside a story with a double-column head, or beside a story with a much larger head (with the heads in harmoniously related type faces, of course), the heads will not "clash." Each will have its chance for the attention it seems to deserve—and each should be given that chance.

It is not enough that stories be appropriately headed. The work of an expert head-writer can be minimized by a makeup editor or printer who disregards the importance and desirability of contrast.

This writer has seen, in some of our smaller papers, as many as six "tombstones" presented across the top of a page. Of course such pages were far from attractive, and must have been confusing to readers.

Before leaving the subject of "tombstone" heads, however, it is only fair to state that when two flush-left heads of the same or nearly the same physical structure are placed side by side, such heads will not clash with each other to the same degree that old-style heads would—particularly if at least a few units of white space are employed at the end of each line.

Double quotation marks (see Example 225) should not be used in heads, as the shoulders of white below the marks can give a head the appearance of being carelessly spaced—with, apparently, much more space between some words than others. Single quotation marks are better in heads.

But even a single quotation mark, when used at the beginning of a line in a flush-left head of two or more lines, can cause the head to appear ragged.

When a single quotation mark is used at the beginning of any line in a multiple-line flush-left head (and *double* quotes, to repeat, should not be used anywhere in any heads), it is advisable to indent the line or lines without beginning quotes so that the first words of all lines of the head will align vertically with each other, with the quote "thrown off" to the left, as in Example 226.

"Firetrap" Joke
To Park Avenue

EXAMPLE 225

'Firetrap' Joke
To Park Avenue

EXAMPLE 226

Many newspaper editors who would not think of using periods at the ends of first decks of heads continue to use periods at the ends of other decks, as well as at the ends of heads over editorials. They use the periods, some of those editors probably would say, if questioned, "for the sake of consistency," for they sometimes use other punctuation points at the ends of similar heads, such as question marks and exclamation points.

But it seems to this writer that the periods might well be eliminated, as they serve no useful purpose. In the old days, when the wording in a multiple-deck head sometimes ran along from deck to deck for several decks before coming to a full pause, the period undoubtedly had its place in a head; but as heads usually are written today, with each deck self-contained, the reader needs no period at the end of a deck to let him know that he has reached the end.

Periods might well be eliminated from the ends of subheads, too, and from the ends of legends under pictures, as such periods are superfluous, and tend, in the minds of some readers, to date the papers using them as old fashioned, behind the times.

Comparatively few papers now use periods at the ends of nameplates, although that was a common practice in the old days.

5

Modern Pages

THE "NEWSPAPER MAKEUP" DEPARTMENT of the *Linotype News* of May-June, 1937, introduced a series of articles on "The Modern Newspaper."

The first article in that series was illustrated with a reduced showing of the rough paste-up shown here as Example 227.

All heads on the page were in members of the Bodoni type family; most of the heads were given a simplified flush-left treatment, with white space between decks, instead of jim dashes, and the first three columns were designed to suggest how the reader could be given a quick preview of the most important stories in a paper.

The high double column suggested the use of a leading news picture, under the head "In Today's News," followed by summations of the most important news stories in the paper, under the head "Today's Headlines," followed by a leading editorial, under the head "Today's Editorial."

The next column, headed "Inside News," was designed to present the highlights of the most important news or departments on inside pages (not a mere index, but displayed and dramatized summations that could be taken care of almost as quickly as an index), under such heads as "Weather," "Local," "National," "Foreign," "Sports," "Society," "Agriculture," "Industry" and "Finance."

Observe that the body matter in that column was supposed to be indented from the left (1 pica), to give the subheads a better chance to stand out and attract attention.

For emphasis, the heads in the high double column and at the top of the single column next to it were in Poster Bodoni, to harmonize with the Bodoni Bold and Bodoni Bold Italic used for the other heads on the page, and the subheads in the single column were in Poster Bodoni Italic. The body lines in the double column were in 14-point Bodoni Bold generously leaded.

THE MODERN NEWSPAPER

VOL. 1., NO. 1 — NEW YORK CITY, TUESDAY EVENING, THIS YEAR — SINGLE COPY 5 CENTS

IN TODAY'S NEWS

Today The Modern Newspaper makes its first appearance, and it appears with the good will and best wishes of thousands of people in the community it plans to serve—and to the best of its ability.

Today's Headlines

John Doe of New York City, recently indicted on embezzlement charges, shoots self after killing Richard Roe, his accuser. Story on Page 1

Spanish loyalists advance twelve miles beyond Toledo, taking 1,500 prisoners, but sustaining heavy losses. Story on Page 3

John Doe of New York City, recently indicted on embezzlement charges, shoots self after killing Richard Roe, his accuser. Story on Page 1

Spanish loyalists advance twelve miles beyond Toledo, taking 1,500 prisoners, but sustaining heavy losses. Story on Page 3

John Doe of New York City, recently indicted on embezzlement charges, shoots self after killing Richard Roe, his accuser. Story on Page 1

Spanish loyalists advance twelve miles beyond Toledo, taking 1,500 prisoners, but sustaining heavy losses. Story on Page 3

Today's Editorial

Today The Modern Newspaper makes its first appearance, and it appears with the good will and best wishes of thousands of people in the community it plans to serve—and to the best of its ability.

In the last two weeks hundreds of congratulatory messages have come to us from all sections of the state—from state and civic officials, from jurists, educators, business men, housewives, farmers, men and women in all walks of life—even from many school boys and girls.

All of these good friends have wished us well in our new and high venture—that of publishing a modern newspaper in the modern manner—modern in every way—in appearance, in news presentation, in editorial content, in spirit.

In the last two weeks hundreds of congratulatory messages have come to us from all sections of the state—from state and civic officials, from jurists, educators, business men, housewives, farmers, men and women in all walks of life—even from many school boys and girls.

All of these good friends have wished us well in

INSIDE NEWS

Weather

Local

National

Foreign

Sports

Society

Agriculture

Industry

Finance

Insull to Quit As Head Man Of His Plants

Russia Blocks Attempt Britain and Hungary to Please Italy's Dictator By Dismissing Delegat

Jimson Lacks Recovery Idea

Japanese Sending Permanent Naval Force Far Into Hankow

Bank Totals Increase

HARRY E. SHELDON
President of the Allegheny Steel Company, will be the guest of the Brackenridge, Tarentum, Natrona Heights and Harrison township tomorrow in an all-day celebration. All citizens are invited.

Jimson Lacks Recovery Idea

Jury, Headed by Man. Asks Mercy for Morton And Four Companions

Battle at San Sebastian Forces U.S. Staff Home; Rebels Fighting Way In

Insull to Quit As Head Man Of His Plants

Russia Blocks Attempt Britain and Hungary to Please Italy's Dictator By Dismissing Delegat

Jimson Lacks Recovery Idea

Injured Man Kills Self Before Father

Bank Totals Increase

HARRY E. SHELDON
President of the Allegheny Steel Company, will be the guest of the Brackenridge, Tarentum, Natrona Heights and Harrison township tomorrow in an all-day celebration. All citizens are invited.

Jimson Lacks Recovery Idea

Japanese Sending Permanent Naval Force Far Into Hankow

Russia Blocks Attempt Britain and Hungary to Please Italy's Dictator By Dismissing Delegat

$14,000,000 Pledge To City Art Center

EXAMPLE 227

As the smallest heads on the page were in 18 point, even the "30" dashes might well have been omitted in favor of white space.

"To be sure," this writer stated, "this treatment calls for the allotment of about two columns of space on a front page for summations of stories presented in other columns, and at first thought may strike some newspaper executives as wasteful. But readers will commend it, and enthusiastic readers are important assets. Moreover, that editorial displayed right out in front where it cannot very well be missed will

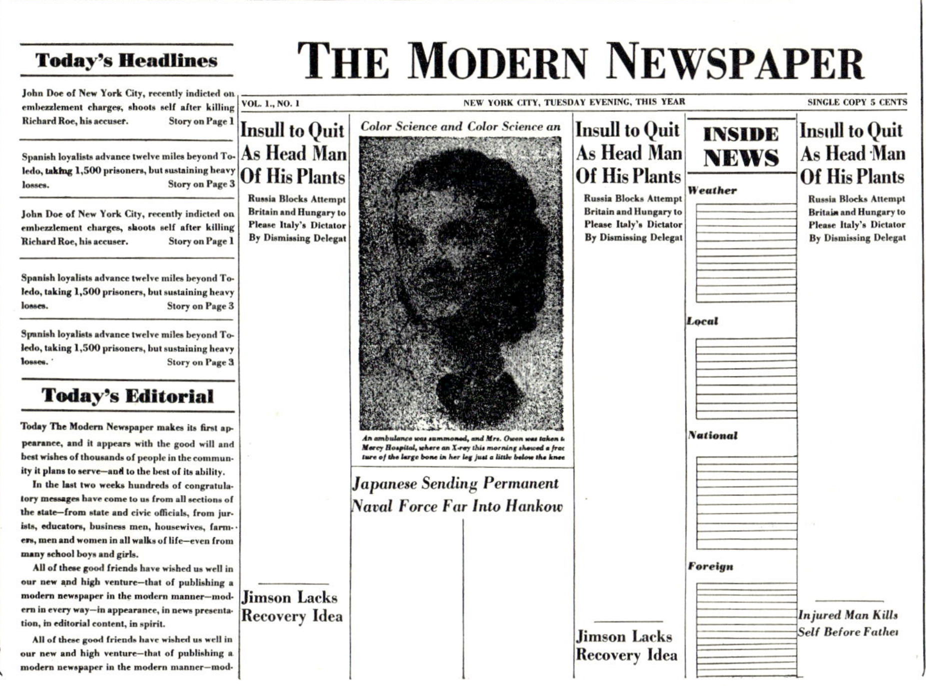

Today's Headlines

John Doe of New York City, recently indicted on embezzlement charges, shoots self after killing Richard Roe, his accuser. Story on Page 1

Spanish loyalists advance twelve miles beyond Toledo, taking 1,500 prisoners, but sustaining heavy losses. Story on Page 3

John Doe of New York City, recently indicted on embezzlement charges, shoots self after killing Richard Roe, his accuser. Story on Page 1

Spanish loyalists advance twelve miles beyond Toledo, taking 1,500 prisoners, but sustaining heavy losses. Story on Page 3

Spanish loyalists advance twelve miles beyond Toledo, taking 1,500 prisoners, but sustaining heavy losses. Story on Page 3

Today's Editorial

Today The Modern Newspaper makes its first appearance, and it appears with the good will and best wishes of thousands of people in the community it plans to serve—and to the best of its ability.

In the last two weeks hundreds of congratulatory messages have come to us from all sections of the state—from state and civic officials, from jurists, educators, business men, housewives, farmers, men and women in all walks of life—even from many school boys and girls.

All of these good friends have wished us well in our new and high venture—that of publishing a modern newspaper in the modern manner—modern in every way—in appearance, in news presentation, in editorial content, in spirit.

All of these good friends have wished us well in our new and high venture—that of publishing a modern newspaper in the modern manner—mod-

THE MODERN NEWSPAPER

VOL. 1., NO. 1 NEW YORK CITY, TUESDAY EVENING, THIS YEAR SINGLE COPY 5 CENTS

Insull to Quit As Head Man Of His Plants

Russia Blocks Attempt Britain and Hungary to Please Italy's Dictator By Dismissing Delegat

Jimson Lacks Recovery Idea

Color Science and Color Science an

An ambulance was summoned, and Mrs. Owen was taken to Mercy Hospital, where an X-ray this morning showed a fracture of the large bone in her leg just a little below the knee

Japanese Sending Permanent Naval Force Far Into Hankow

Insull to Quit As Head Man Of His Plants

Russia Blocks Attempt Britain and Hungary to Please Italy's Dictator By Dismissing Delegat

Jimson Lacks Recovery Idea

INSIDE NEWS

Weather

Local

National

Foreign

Insull to Quit As Head Man Of His Plants

Russia Blocks Attempt Britain and Hungary to Please Italy's Dictator By Dismissing Delegat

Injured Man Kills Self Before Father

EXAMPLE 228

help to make editorial readers of many people who now pay little attention to editorials."

Of course, many variations of that same general plan are possible. The high double column might well lead off with "Today's Headlines" (see Example 228), rather than a news picture, and the rest of the column be devoted to "Today's Editorial," if that much space is required to present the editorial without jumping. And the "Inside News" column can be moved to the right, although, from the point of view of the reader, and he is the one who should be considered, it would be better to keep that "Inside News" column alongside the other "summation" column.

Example 229 presents another treatment of the same general plan.

It will be observed that the high double column started off with "Today's Editorial," followed by "Today's Headlines," and that the "Inside News" appeared in still another column.

Today's Editorial

Today The Modern Newspaper makes its first appearance, and it appears with the good will and best wishes of thousands of people in the community it plans to serve—and to the best of its ability.

In the last two weeks hundreds of congratulatory messages have come to us from all sections of the state—from state and civic officials, from jurists, educators, business men, housewives, farmers, men and women in all walks of life—even from many school boys and girls.

All of these good friends have wished us well in our new and high venture—that of publishing a modern newspaper in the modern manner—modern in every way—in appearance, in news presentation, in editorial content, in spirit.

Today The Modern Newspaper makes its first appearance, and it appears with the good will and best wishes of thousands of people in the community it plans to serve—and to the best of its ability.

In the last two weeks hundreds of congratulatory messages have come to us from all sections of the state—from state and civic officials, from jurists, educators, business men, housewives, farmers, men and women in all walks of life—even from many school boys and girls.

Today's Headlines

John Doe of New York City, recently indicted on embezzlement charges, shoots self after killing Richard Roe, his accuser. Story on Page 1

Spanish loyalists advance twelve miles beyond Toledo, taking 1,500 prisoners, but sustaining heavy losses. Story on Page 3

John Doe of New York City, recently indicted on embezzlement charges, shoots self after killing Richard Roe, his accuser. Story on Page 1

THE MODERN NEWSPAPER

VOL. 1., NO. 1 NEW YORK CITY, TUESDAY EVENING, THIS YEAR SINGLE COPY 5 CENTS

LETTUCE STRIKE GROWING

Insull to Quit As Head Man Of His Plants

Russia Blocks Attempt Britain and Hungary to Please Italy's Dictator By Dismissing Delegat

Jimson Lacks Recovery Idea

INSIDE NEWS

Weather

Local

National

Foreign

Insull to Quit As Head Man Of His Plants

Russia Blocks Attempt Britain and Hungary to Please Italy's Dictator By Dismissing Delegat

Jimson Lacks Recovery Idea

Bank Totals Increase

HARRY E. SHELDON

President of the Allegheny Steel Company, will be the guest of the Brackenridge, Tarentum, Natrona Heights and Harrison township tomorrow in an all-day celebration. All citizens are invited.

Jimson Lacks Recovery Idea

Jury, Headed by Man, Asks Mercy for Morton And Four Companions

Americans Will Quit Capital City for Coast

Insull to Quit As Head Man Of His Plants

Russia Blocks Attempt Britain and Hungary to Please Italy's Dictator By Dismissing Delegat

Russia Blocks Attempt Britain and Hungary to Please Italy's Dictator By Dismissing Delegat

EXAMPLE 229

Note, also, that a six-column line was employed for the first deck of the leading news story. Attention is called to this to point out that this "summation" treatment can be applied to a page without the necessity of limiting main news stories to comparatively small heads. With the single exception that display lines necessarily must be limited to six columns (unless it seems desirable to employ sky-line streamers, or over-banners), the same degrees of display can be employed on pages such as these as on conventional (and considerably less effective) eight-column pages.

Examples 230, 231 and 232, reduced showings of other rough paste-ups, suggest three of the many possible effective variations of the same general plan, with heads in sans-serif and square-serif faces —in Erbar Light Condensed, Metromedium No. 2, Memphis Bold and Memphis Bold Italic.

All body lines in the double columns were in 14-point Metromedium No. 2 leaded 3 points.

Stronger effects could be secured on all three of these sans-serif and square-serif pages by the use of Erbar Medium Condensed in place of Erbar Light Condensed, for most of the heads, and still stronger effects could be secured by the use of Erbar Bold Condensed or Spartan Black Condensed.

Soon after the series on "The Modern Newspaper" was introduced, several newspaper executives in the United States and Canada appreciated the merits of the new plan and put it to work for themselves.

Some of those executives, naturally, did a better job than others, and some of the resultant pages were much more attractive than others, but all of the executives who tried out the plan were enthusiastic about it—and so were their readers and advertisers.

For the consideration of newspaper editors and publishers who were interested in the picture-summations-editorial idea for their front pages, but who hesitated to give over as much space to it as was given over in Examples 227 through 232, the *Linotype News* worked out, in its typographic laboratory, many modern front pages, including those suggested by Examples 233, 234, 235 and 236.

In Example 233 the heads in the last six columns were in 60-, 42-, 34-, 28-, 24- and 18-point Erbar Light Condensed; 24- and 18-point Metromedium No. 2 Italic, and 14-point Metromedium No. 2. Body matter in those columns was in 7½-point Ionic No. 5 on an 8-point body; subheads were in 7½-point Bold Face No. 2, and cut legends were in 8-point Bold Face No. 2.

Heads in the high double column were in 30- and 24-point Memphis Bold, and body matter was in 12-point Ionic No. 5 on a 14-point body.

The use of Erbar Medium Condensed, instead of Erbar Light Condensed, was responsible for the stronger page suggested by Example 234.

IN TODAY'S NEWS

THE MODERN NEWSPAPER

VOL. I., NO. 1 — NEW YORK CITY, TUESDAY EVENING, THIS YEAR — SINGLE COPY 5 CENTS

John Doe of New York City, recently indicted on embezzlement charges, shoots self after killing Richard Roe, his accuser. Story on Page 1

Today's Headlines

John Doe of New York City, recently indicted on embezzlement charges, shoots self after killing Richard Roe, his accuser. Story on Page 1

Spanish loyalists advance twelve miles beyond Toledo, taking 1,500 prisoners, but sustaining heavy losses. Story on Page 3

John Doe of New York City, recently indicted on embezzlement charges, shoots self after killing Richard Roe, his accuser Story on Page 1

Spanish loyalists advance twelve miles beyond Toledo, taking 1,500 prisoners, but sustaining heavy losses, Story on Page 3

John Doe of New York City, recently indicted on embezzlement charges, shoots self after killing Richard Roe, his accuser. Story on Page 1

Spanish loyalists advance twelve miles beyond Toledo, taking 1,500 prisoners, but sustaining heavy losses. Story on Page 3

Today's Editorial

Today The Modern Newspaper makes its appearance, and it appears with the good will and best wishes of thousands of people in the community it plans to serve—and to the best of its ability.

In the last two weeks hundreds of congratulatory messages have come to us from all sections of the state—from state and civic officials, from jurists, educators, business men, housewives, farmers, men and women in all walks of life—even from many school boys and girls.

All of these good friends have wished us well in our new and high venture—that of publishing a modern newspaper in the modern manner—modern in every way—in appearance, in news presentation, in editorial content, in spirit.

In the last two weeks hundreds of congratulatory messages have come to us from all sections of the state—from state and civic officials, from jurists, educators, business men, housewives, farmers, men and women in all walks of life—even from many school boys and girls

All of these good friends have wished us well in

INSIDE NEWS

Weather

Local

National

Foreign

Sports

Society

Agriculture

Industry

Finance

Globe and Mail Will Soon Have New Building

New Equipment Also For Toronto Paper Recently Acquired By C. G. McCullagh

Marshall Newspaper Adds Blue Streak 14

Former Stock Broker

Messrs. Eduard and Baumgartn r at the A-P-L and one of the

Six Blue Streaks For Dunlap Firm

Philadelphia Company Puts in 8s and 25s With Tabular Devices

Former Knight of Case and Road NeRecalls Tramp Through Arkans

Roanoke World-News and Times Add Five Blue Streak Linotypes

The Examiner Of Peterborough In New Home

Many Editors Inspect Blue Streak Model 8 And 42 Page Press In New Ontario Plant

Mrs. Fred Williamson Wins Two Degrees

Panhandle Herald, Guymon Adds Two Blue Streaks

He Joined as Newsboy

Chronicle when the flood cut Attractive new home of the O

3 Linos in New Plant Of Schenectady Sun

Governor Reads Paper Without Glasses Now; City School Head Praises New Type

Mease Finishes 50 Years As Madison Publisher

Chicago Daily News Now Appearin HWith Its Body Matter in Excelsi

EXAMPLE 230

Today's Headlines

John Doe of New York City, recently indicted on embezzlement charges, shoots self after killing Richard Roe, his accuser. Story on Page 1

Spanish loyalists advance twelve miles beyond Toledo, taking 1,500 prisoners, but sustaining heavy losses. Story on Page 3

John Doe of New York City, recently indicted on embezzlement charges, shoots self after killing Richard Roe, his accuser. Story on Page 1

Spanish loyalists advance twelve miles beyond Toledo, taking 1,500 prisoners, but sustaining heavy losses. Story on Page 3

Today's Editorial

Today The Modern Newspaper makes its appearance, and it appears with the good will and best wishes of thousands of people in the community it plans to serve—and to the best of its ability.

In the last two weeks hundreds of congratulatory messages have come to us from all sections of the state—from state and civic officials, from jurists, educators, business men, housewives, farmers, men and women in all walks of life—even from many school boys and girls.

All of these good friends have wished us well in

THE MODERN NEWSPAPER

VOL. 1., NO. 1 — NEW YORK CITY, TUESDAY EVENING, THIS YEAR — SINGLE COPY 5 CENTS

The Union Of Sacramento Puts in Paragon

Governor Reads Paper Without Glasses Now; City School Head Praises New Type

Barnes Printing Company Adds 8, Ten Magazines

Times-Picayune executives and some of the many gifts of flov Messrs. Burns, Siegfriedhe paper's hundredth annivers and Trotter

Australian Daily and Weekly Paper Change Over to Linotype Excelsior

The Union Of Sacramento Puts in Paragon

Governor Reads Paper Without Glasses Now; City School Head Praises New Type

INSIDE NEWS

Weather

Local

National

Foreign

Globe and Mail Will Soon Have New Building

New Equipment Also For Toronto Paper Recently Acquired By C. G. McCullagh

EXAMPLE 231

Today's Editorial

Today The Modern Newspaper makes its appearance, and it appears with the good will and best wishes of thousands of people in the community it plans to serve—and to the best of its ability.

In the last two weeks hundreds of congratulatory messages have come to us from all sections of the state—from state and civic officials, from jurists, educators, business men, housewives, farmers, men and women in all walks of life—even from many school boys and girls.

All of these good friends have wished us well in our new and high venture—that of publishing a modern newspaper in the modern manner—modern in every way—in appearance, in news presentation, in editorial content, in spirit.

All of these good friends have wished us well in our new and high venture—that of publishing a modern newspaper in the modern manner—modern in every way—in appearance, in news presentation, in editorial content, in spirit.

Today's Headlines

John Doe of New York City, recently indicted on embezzlement charges, shoots self after killing Richard Roe, his accuser. Story on Page 1

Spanish loyalists advance twelve miles beyond Toledo, taking 1,500 prisoners, but sustaining heavy losses. Story on Page 3

THE MODERN NEWSPAPER

VOL. 1., NO. 1 — NEW YORK CITY, TUESDAY EVENING, THIS YEAR — SINGLE COPY 5 CENTS

WASHINGTON TIMES AND HERALD ADD 9 MOD

The Union Of Sacramento Puts in Paragon

Governor Reads Paper Without Glasses Now; City School Head Praises New Type

INSIDE NEWS

Weather

Local

National

The Examiner Of Peterborough In New Home

Many Editors Inspect Blue Streak Model 8 And 42 Page Press In New Ontario Plant

Half Century on Paper

Joe T. Cook and three first prizes

Seven Model 8s For Cuneo Plants

Five to Philadelphia, Two to Milwaukee; All With Feeders

Scripps-Howard Buys The Commercial Appeal

The Examiner Of Peterborough In New Home

Many Editors Inspect Blue Streak Model 8 And 42 Page Press In New Ontario Plant

New Equipment Also For Toronto Paper Recently Acquired By C. G. McCullagh

EXAMPLE 232

IN TODAY'S NEWS

John Doe of New York City recently indicted on embezzlement charges, shoots self after killing Richard Roe his accuser Story on Page 1

Today's Headlines

John Doe of New York City, recently indicted on embezzlement charges, shoots self after killing Richard Roe, his accuser Story on Page 1

Spanish loyalists advance twelve miles beyond Toledo, taking 1,500 prisoners but sustaining heavy losses in the mountains Story on Page 3

John Doe of New York City recently indicted on embezzlement charges shoots self after killing Richard Roe, his accuser Story on Page 1

Spanish loyalists advance twelve miles beyond Toledo, taking 1,500 prisoners, but sustaining heavy losses in the mountains Story on Page 3

John Doe of New York City recently indicted on embezzlement charges shoots self after killing Richard Roe his accuser Story on Page 1

Spanish loyalists advance twelve miles beyond Toledo, taking 1,500 prisoners but sustaining heavy losses in the mountains Story on Page 3

Today's Editorial

Today The Modern Newspaper makes its appearance and it appears with the good will and best wishes of thousands of people in the community it plans to serve—and to the best of its ability

In the last two weeks hundreds of congratulatory messages have come to us from all sections of the state—from state and civic officials, from jurists, educators, business men, housewives, farmers, men and women in all walks of life—even from many school boys and girls

All of these good friends have wished us well in our new and high venture—that of publishing a modern newspaper in the modern manner—modern in every way—in appearance in news presentation in editorial content in spirit

In the last two weeks hundreds of congratulatory messages have come to us from all sections of the state—from state and civic officials, from jurists, educators, business men, housewives, farmers, men and women in all walks of life—even from many school boys and girls

All of these good friends have wished us well in our new and high venture—that of publishing a modern newspaper in the modern manner—modern in every way—in appearance, in news presentation, in editorial content in spirit

Today The Modern Newspaper makes its appearance, and it appears with the good will and best wishes of thousands of people in the community it plans to serve—and to the best of its ability

In the last two weeks hundreds of congratulatory messages have come to us from all sections of the state—from state and civic officials, from jurists, educators, business men, housewives, farmers, men and women in all walks of life—even from many school boys and girls

All of these good friends have wished us well in our new and high venture—that of publishing a modern newspaper in the modern manner—modern in every way—in appearance, in news presentation, in editorial content in spirit

Today The Modern Newspaper makes its appearance, and it appears with the good will and best wishes of

The Modern Newspaper

VOL. I, No. 1 NEW YORK CITY, THURSDAY EVENING, THIS YEAR PRICE FIVE CENTS

This Snappy Looking Head Is Set in 42 Point Erbar Light

New Equipment Also For Toronto Paper Recently Acquired By C G. McCullagh

Rochester last night took action to halt reported abuses and alay fears of racketeering in snow cards, token of employment for hundreds of idle, public works officials revealed, in announcing a new issue of special duty slips

The alleged abuses took the form of improper use of cards distributed during the last days of the former Democratic administration and the racketeering fears centered on unconfirmed reports cards were being sold to those for whom they were not intended by persons outside official circles

In the absence of Public Works Commissioner William H Roberts, who is out of the city, departmental aides were cautious in discussing the incident that arose last week when the new administration faced its first major snow removal test. Edwin A Miller superintendent of maintenance, however did say

"There might have been some abuses by unscrupulous persons, for there appeared to be more cards in use last week than were issued. We do not know where the surplus came from, but to avoid any confusion dcided to change the syseree to consider Sibley's demands

'Democrats Blameless'

Miller said former Democratic officials were in no way to blame. He admitted "hearing" reports that cards had been sold by persons outside the city service and said it was an old complaint but concrete evidence of the practice could not be obtained.

Whether the cards were legitimate or improper Miller said, the city did not lose any money. The card, he explained, is merely a ...

Wins First Prize

Miss Diana Cook, who led all contestants with her display of peonies at the flower show here

Seven Blue Streaks For Dunlovy Firm

Philadelphia Company Puts in 31s and 32s With Tabular Devices

Eight Local Women Enter Golf Contest

Mease Finishes 50 Years As Madisonian Publisher

Globe and Mail Will Soon Have New Building

New Equipment Also For Toronto Paper Recently Acquired By C G McCullagh

Eight Local Women Enter Golf Contest

Twenty-seven Children Leave Town for Chicago

Inside Today

Wednesday, April 6

Akron Briefs ... Page 8
Botzum's Column ... Page 11
Case Records ... Page 9
Clapper's Column ... Page 10
Crossword Puzzle ... Page 17
Donald Gray ... Page 9
Editorials ... Page 10
Frying Political Fat ... Page 10
Foreign News ... Page 2
General Johnson ... Page 10
Jimmie Fidler ... Page 6
Letters To The Editor Page 10
Markets ... Page 14
Mrs Ferguson ... Page 10
Mrs. Roosevelt ... Page 9
Pegler's Column ... Page 9
Pyle's Column ... Page 10
News In Pictures ... Page 9
O'Keefe Says ... Page 11
Radio News ... Page 7
Serial ... Page 14
Sermonette ... Page 11
Society and Clubs ... Pages 4-5
Sports ... Pages 12-13-14
Theaters ... Page 6
Want Ads ... Pages 14-15-16
Your Birthday ... Page 17

This Unusually Attractive Head Is Set in Sixty-Point Erbar Light

Visiting Here Today at City Club

John Smith of Omaha, who will speak to local business men today on national affairs

New Equipment Also For Toronto Paper Recently Acquired By C G McCullagh

Mrs. Fred Williams Wins Three Honors

Mrs. Fred Williams Wins Three Honors

Eight Local Women Enter Golf Contest

Rounds Out Ten Years

Mease Finishes 50 Years As Madisonian Publisher

This Attractive New Head Face Is 24 Metromedium No. 2 Italic

This Attractive New Head Face Is 24 Metromedium No. 2 Italic

EXAMPLE 233

IN TODAY'S NEWS

John Doe of New York City, recently indicted on embezzlement charges, shoots self after killing Richard Roe, his accuser Story on Page 1

Today's Headlines

John Doe of New York City, recently indicted on embezzlement charges, shoots self after killing Richard Roe, his accuser Story on Page 1

Spanish loyalists advance twelve miles beyond Toledo, taking 1,500 prisoners, but sustaining heavy losses in the mountains. Story on Page 3

John Doe of New York City, recently indicted on embezzlement charges, shoots self after killing Richard Roe, his accuser Story on Page 1

Spanish loyalists advance twelve miles beyond Toledo, taking 1,500 prisoners, but sustaining heavy losses in the mountains Story on Page 3

John Doe of New York City, recently indicted on embezzlement charges, shoots self after killing Richard Roe, his accuser Story on Page 1

Spanish loyalists advance twelve miles beyond Toledo, taking 1,500 prisoners, but sustaining heavy losses in the mountains Story on Page 3

Today's Editorial

Today The Modern Newspaper makes its appearance, and it appears with the good will and best wishes of thousands of people in the community it plans to serve —and to the best of its ability

In the last two weeks hundreds of congratulatory messages have come to us from all sections of the state —from state and civic officials, from jurists, educators, business men, housewives, farmers, men and women in all walks of life—even from many school boys and girls.

All of these good friends have wished us well in our new and high venture—that of publishing a modern newspaper in the modern manner—modern in every way—in appearance, in news presentation, in editorial content, in spirit.

In the last two weeks hundreds of congratulatory messages have come to us from all sections of the state —from state and civic officials, from jurists, educators, business men, housewives, farmers, men and women in all walks of life—even from many school boys and girls

All of these good friends have wished us well in our new and high venture—that of publishing a modern newspaper in the modern manner—modern in every way—in appearance, in news presentation, in edithousands of people in the community it plans to serve Today The Modern Newspaper makes its appearance, and it appears with the good will and best wishes of thousands of people in the community it plans to serve —and to the best of its ability

In the last two weeks hundreds of congratulatory messages have come to us from all sections of the state —from state and civic officials, from jurists, educators, business men, housewives, farmers, men and women in all walks of life—even from many school boys and girls

All of these good friends have wished us well in our new and high venture—that of publishing a modern newspaper in the modern manner—modern in every way—in appearance, in news presentation, in edi- Today The Modern Newspaper makes its appearance, and it appears with the good will and best wishes of

The Modern Newspaper

VOL. I, No. 1 NEW YORK CITY, THURSDAY EVENING, THIS YEAR PRICE FIVE CENTS

This Snappy Looking Head Is 42 Point Erbar Medium

New Equipment Also For Toronto Paper Recently Acquired By C. G. McCullagh

Rochester last night took action to halt reported abuses and alay fears of racketeering in snow cards, token of employment for hundreds of idle, public works officials revealed, in announcing a new issue of special duty slips.

The alleged abuses took the form of improper use of cards distributed during the last days of the former Democratic administration and the racketeering fears centered on unconfirmed reports cards were being sold to those for whom they were not intended by persons outside official circles

In the absence of Public Works Commissioner William H. Roberts, who is out of the city, departmental aides were cautious in discussing the incident that arose last week when the new administration faced its first major snow removal test. Edwin A. Miller, superintendent of maintenance, however, did say:

"There might have been some abuses by unscrupulous persons, for there appeared to be more cards in use last week than were issued. We do not know where the surplus came from, but to avoid any confusion dcided to change the syseree to consider Sibley's demands

'Democrats Blameless'

Miller said former Democratic officials were in no way to blame. He admitted "hearing" reports that cards had been sold by persons outside the city service and said it was an old complaint but concrete evidence of the practice could not be obtained.

Whether the cards were legitimate or improper, Miller said, the city did not lose any money. The card, he explained, is merely a means of identification for a man getting a job and before he is paid he must work.

Cards, under custom of recent years, are passed out by ward leaders. An old card, now canceled, carried a line for an "authorized" signature, usually that of the ward leader, as well as the signature of either the public safety commissioner or his secretary.

The new card, just issued, is signed by Commissioner Roberts alone.

Democratic headquarters reported last night it had no direct about Dec. 1 the old administration printed cards designed for use before Jan. 1 in event of a storm.

Those were distributed directly to Democratic ward leaders rather than to headquarters because of the short time involved

Report Old Cards Tried

Democratic headquarters spokesman said reports were heard that some Democratic leaders passed out cards last week with instructions to hopeful shovelers "to try them out and see if they work." In several cases, the report reaching headquarters said, the cards were honored and Democrats got jobs.

Unruly scenes Monday night at the Byron St. yards of the DPW, where snow workers received assignments, first drew official attention to the cards, it was said. Not only were too many prospective workers on hand, in comparfsion with the number of cards is-

"We must speak up in unmistakindividuals were reported to have used "bulldozing" tactics on less forceful men to gain possession of the timid men's cards and then to peddle them to friends. Police were called at one stage to maintain order

Wins First Prize

Miss Diana Cook, who led all contestants with her display of peonies at the flower show here

Seven Blue Streaks For Dunlovy Firm

Philadelphia Company Puts in 31s and 32s With Tabular Devices

Cleveland — Col Frank Knox suggested last night a "plain folks" Republican program which would tell business boldly it must renounce all "excessive" tariff schedules tending to increase the cost of living, and then would insist the farmer expect no cash bonuses for crop restriction

Colonel Knox, 1936 vice-presidential candidate of the party which for decades has championed dered DiPasquale held in Monroe latter, Eldon, near Troupsburg Many lives were feared lost in a pre-dawn raid on the government's tariff protection, told a Cleveland the taxes imposed to finance them.

'Deliberately Provocative'

"Protect wage standards, yes! Continue to protect monopoly, no! able terms to those industries which, through excessive tariff schedules, have enjoyed a monoposued, officials said, but also certain ly of the domestic market and thus inordinately increased the cost of living for both farmers and workers.

"The Republican Party could then, with both logic and justice, oppose any project for direct cash subsidies to agriculture

"If this unfair advantage is taken away from industry, the American farmer will readily forego his present demands for direct

Mease Finishes 50 Years As Madisonian Publisher

Sheriff's deputies thought they "had something there" when they found what they thought was a stolen truck loaded with clothing and firearms apparently abandoned near 270 Grosvenor Rd., Brighton, early yesterday.

Besides clothing the truck contained a shotgun, rifle and ammunition. The "loot" was taken to the jail and an investigation launched. It ended when the owner of the U. S. Chamber of Commerce, of the truck, Howard Lieb, Bloomingdale, identified it. He said he night, fits into a revamped system while driving in the country

Eight Local Women Enter Golf Contest

Newark—Sudden flare of an oil associates called his first major political statement since 1936, was on the program of a dinner honoring the recent re-election of Harold H. Burton, Cleveland's Republican brother, Martin, and son of the Earlier, an insurgent communique

This attack was a reprisal for a leaders called today for informal public "criticism or suggestions" beaten during a quarrel and her on Democratic Gov Lehman's budget and tax program

Previously, the party's high command indicated no partisan opposition would be offered to the Govuation of all existing emergency imposts

The Chicago publisher said he had prepared his address to be "deliberately provocative" because he felt widespread discussion was essential in the development of a party sponsor a program which sound program

Globe and Mail Will Soon Have New Building

New Equipment Also For Toronto Paper Recently Acquired By C G. McCullagh

"The real reason I did it was to frighten them the gun was not loaded," investigators quoted the 25-year-old youth.

Donovan told police the assault occurred while the couple were alone in the living room of the girl's home. There was a scuffle, he said, then Miss Leas ran from the room screaming hysterically and bleeding from nose and mouth.

He said he intervened and that Panagiotakos left the house, but returned in a few minutes with a revolver Donovan said he ran a quarter mile to call police after the youth pointed the pistol at him and threatened him. Panagiotakos pulled the trigger, Donovan related, but the gun did not discharge.

Investigators said the youth was extremely jealous of the girl and insisted she remain home and follow the "Greek code." He had forced her to resign a bookkeeping position at her parents' sea food restaurant, police said, because he objected that she "came into contact with other men" The girl presently is unemployed.

Promises Action

Miss Leas, a Roman Catholic, was in the habit of going to church daily, but was forced to give up the practice because of her fiance's objections, police said.

Labor forces of Rochester last night were preparing their offensive to push ratification of the national Child Labor Amendment through the current session of the State Legislature

Announcement by the Catholic Diocese of Rochester that it had launched its drive against ratification by New York State met the reply from the Committee for Industrial Organization, American Federation of Labor and American Labor Party that they would call meetings this week to open their 1938 counter drives.

"We've done our talking," said Abraham D Chatham, CIO Amalgamated leader "Monday we'll be in action."

The legislative committee of the CIO, headed by Hugh Thompson now is drafting plans for the renewed campaign to create public the Board of Education, said he did sentiment in favor of immediate ratification Chatham said

Eight Local Women Enter Golf Contest

Discussion of the Rochester AFL campaign is expected to occupy a major place in Thursday night's regular meeting of the Central Trades and Labor Council.

Michael Reed, Labor Party leader, said illness among members had caused postponement of a special meeting called last week at which the ratification drive was to be speeded by appointment of a legislative committee. Another meeting will be called this week, he said.

Others in Rochester reported ready to fight for ratification are the Monroe County League of Woman Voters, Rabbi Philip S Bernstein of Temple B'rith Kodesh, member of the State Child Labor Committee and the Federation of Churches.

James E. Kittrell, chairman of not know whether the board would

Twenty-seven Children Leave Town for Chicago

Asserting "The people are in no mood right now for any 'I told you so's' ", Colonel Knox suggested the States customs authorities had sealed the coach in which he was a day evening by insurgent bombs. The trucks were belived to have carried troop reinforcements. (One report said 3,000 were killed and a rabbit out with a stick. Martin terday in one of the most intense air battles of the civil war while

Inside Today

Wednesday April 6

Akron Briefs .... Page 8
Botzum's Column .... Page 11
Case Records .... Page 9
Clapper's Column .... Page 10
Crossword Puzzle .... Page 17
Donald Gray .... Page 9
Editorials .... Page 10
Frying Political Fat .... Page 10
Foreign News .... Page 2
General Johnson .... Page 10
Jimmie Fidler .... Page 6
Letters To The Editor Page 10
Markets .... Page 14
Mrs. Ferguson .... Page 10
Mrs. Roosevelt .... Page 9
Pegler's Column .... Page 9
Pyle's Column .... Page 10
News In Pictures .... Page 9
O'Keefe Says .... Page 11
Radio News .... Page 7
Serial .... Page 14
Sermonette .... Page 11
Society and Clubs .... Pages 4-5
Sports .... Pages 12-13-14
Theaters .... Page 6
Want Ads .... Pages 14-15-16
Your Birthday .... Page 17

This Attractive New Head Face Is 24 Metromedium No. 2 Italic

Charged with violating immigration laws because at one time after a felony conviction he traveled in a customs-sealed train coach from Michigan to Buffalo across Canada, a former Rochester resident faces deportation to Italy.

The alien, Giuseppe DiPasquale, 45, of Buffalo, sought his freedom on a writ of habeas corpus returned before Judge Harold P Burke in Federal District Court here yesterday. He won a stay of deportation proceedings until Feb 14 when Judge Burke will hear arguments in the case

U S. Department of Labor authorities had ordered him deported to Italy on a ship sailing Sunday, parked the truck for the night and engaged a room, expecting to conknowledge of snow card uses this year, Spokesmen pointed out that tinue in the morning He said he carried the guns for protection Pending the hearing, however, Judge Burke refused bail and or- County jail

Immigration authorities reported that in 1911 DiPasquale began his long criminal record with a 60-day felony sentence in Erie County In 1915 he was sentenced to Auburn State Penitentiary on a first degree robbery charge but his sentence of 5 years was later commuted by Governor Whitman.

In 1919, records of the immigration authorities showed, DiPasquale was sentenced to serve 38 years for first degree robbery. When he was released in December immigration authorities instituted deportation proceedings. Contending that when DiPasquale traveled from Detroit to Buffalo across Canernor's program calling for expenditures of $385,000,000 and continada he left the country and resimilar bombardment Friday of Salamanca, Gen. Francisco Franco's capital in Western Spain

A report from Zaragoza, Franco's entered illegally at Buffalo, although Canadian and United passenger

THIS ATTENTION-ARRESTING HEADING IS SET IN 42 POINT ERBAR MEDIUM

Visiting Here Today at City Club

John Smith of Omaha, who will speak to local business men today on national affairs

New Equipment Also For Toronto Paper Recently Acquired By C. G. McCullagh

Pale, sandy-haired Gordon Proctor, 42, on trial for his life, sat through his first day in a courtroom yesterday and "wished to heaven it could be my last."

With 11 jurors chosen at adjournment, the lawyers had moved speedily to decide whether the defendant, a truckman, will go to the chair for the slaying of Mrs. Alameda Griffiths, 35, and Ralph E. Hall, 30, her escort the night of Oct. 31 when both were shot.

"I'm tired," he said as guards clamped handcuffs on him for the ride back to the County Jail at the end of the day long session. "The sooner it's over with, the better"

Neatly dressed in a dark blue suit, dark tie and lighter blue shirt, Proctor had watched the proceedings calmly, almost without expression. He sat either with his hands folded in his lap, or leaning back, elbow on the chair arm and hand supporting his chin. He nodded briefly when the defense counsel, George D. Ogden, consulted him on the selection of jurors but seldom spoke

Hits at Monopoly

Whether temporary mental derangement will be the basis of the plea to save Proctor's life appeared to be uncertain late yesterday Ogden said, however he would not attempt to prove "insanity as such."

Prospective jurors were questioned as to prejudices against drinking and "the defendant's relations with a woman not in accordance with accepted social standards" Police had attributed the double slaying to a love triangle.

Hall, an automobile salesman of 50 Spencer St. and Mrs. Griffiths were shot in the driveway of her home at 78 Jefferson Ter

All but witnesses and veniremen were barred from the courtroom yesterday by order of Judge William C Kohlmetz. A large group of spectators who arrived an hour before court opened had been reduced by afternoon to a handful who loitered in the corridor outside

Trial will probably get under way at 11 a m today after selection of two jurors

Liner on Mercy Errand

Return "to a certain and fixed dollar, redeemable in gold;" substitute for the undistributed profits tax a "rational measure aimed only to prevent corporations from accumulating excessive surpluses to avoid taxation," let state and local governments handle relief of unemployment, reduce "waste and public squandering" to solve taxation problems; require union officials to account for finances and set up boards of inquiry in strikes

"If the Republican Party can point the way back to good times the voters will restore our party to power," Colonel Knox said "Unless it can become 'positive' again, its service is ended and the party will die

"In the last campaign, the Republican Party came to be regarded, by millions of workers and farmers as the special representative and spokeman of entrenched to aim at the rabbit His hands

Freezes to Death

"The Republican Party must become again the party of the plain folks of America—the sort of people who gave it life 75 years ago and the same sort of people who kept it in power most of that time"

Colonel Knox said "natural monopolies, such as telephones street cars and electric power must be regulated by law" while "artificial monopolies effected through improper, unsocial methods must be stamped out by enforcement of existing anti-monopoly laws." He placed in another class those industries which, he said, were enjoying a monopoly of the domestic market made possible by excessive tariffs

Colonel Knox charged the prescial security tax receipts" and asserted "the continuance of present government policies leads inevi- Teruel

The government reported 1,500 Celadas about 10 miles from insurgent soldiers were lost there

Mrs. Fred Williams Wins Three Honors

Washington—A Spanish insurwhere it was 32 degrees below zero night before last, came two Malone state troopers yesterday to Rochester's warmer climes to claim a man wanted in Franklin County on a contempt of court charge

Bearing a warrant issued by Judge Carey of Children's Court, Troopers Thomas Hansen and H. J Mayn of Troop B Malone, arrested Martin Bryan Cummings, 40, a lumberjack The troopers rested here after their more than purveyors of the information If it 300-mile ride in a curtained touring car, before starting the return where they lived Eldon was poking

Security Cost High

Out of the frozen north country, gent naval officer is in control of the American tanker Nantucket Chief, seized Jan 18 by insurgent warships, T Monroe Fisher, American vice-consul at Palma, informed the State Department yesterday

The ship is at Palma, Island of Majorca, together with 27 members of the crew who are American citizens, Fisher said in his cable.

The Nantucket Chief's manifest indicates the vessel has a cargo of gasoline and kerosene shipped from a Russian port destined for Barcelona, he added. The tanker was captured off Barcelona

Secretary Hull's information is that the Nantucket Chief, although the property of an American corporation in New York, was chartered to the Spanish Loyalist government.

It is considered doubtful if much can be de done through diplomatic

Insurgent columns led by tanks assailed the government fortification only to be broken and turned back by a withering counterfire declared "retiring" government in-

Eight Local Women Enter Golf Contest

Lawrence, Mass.—His belief that she was failing to live up to the "Greek code" was blamed last night for a Massachusetts Institute of Technology instructor's alleged assault on his pretty fiancee

Paul Panagiotakos, 25, brilliant institute graduate and candidate bail after pleading not guilty in toting, assault with a dangerous weapon and licenseless driving He will be given a hearing next Thursday.

The "Greek code," he told the court, forbids an engaged woman to see or meet other men until after she is married.

Panagiotakos was seized at his home early yesterday after police

Rounds Out Ten Years

Twenty passengers were slightly shaken up when a southbound trolley split a switch at St Paul and Andrews this afternoon

The front trucks of the car, operated by Irvin Gibson, crossed the switch but the rear trucks swerved cut on an East Ave automobile showroom when Supreme Court Justice John VanVoorhis andown Andrews St. The trolley was hauled back on the St Paul St tracks by a traction company truck

Harper Sibley, former president nounced he would appoint a ref- 300 in the 1936 city tax assessment

Mrs. Fred Williams Wins Three Honors

Charged with criminal negligence in Rochester's fourth 1928 traffic fatality, Girard J Dalle, 24, of 1580 Maiden Lane, Greece, pleaded not guilty in City Court yesterday and was granted adjournment until Feb 21 by Judge Frederick J Mix

Police said Dalle's car struck and fatally injured Mrs. Mary Whalen, 63, of 1021 Campbell St., as she was crossing near 123 St. Paul St. after alighting from a bus at 2 p m Friday She died of a fractured skull 40 minutes later in Highland Hospital. She was the third woman fatally hurt in traffic grabbed a gun and with a sweeping

If Junior wants to curry favor with teacher—he'll have to find some other way than through the Christmas gift medium

For gifts to teachers in the Rochester public school system this year again are under the Board of Education's traditional were clumsy with heavy mittens

This doesn't mean that pupils cannot send Christmas greeting cards — if they are inexpensive cards But it does mean that chocolates, fruits and in fact any gift will be decidedly unwelcome

Mease Finishes 50 Years As Madisonian Publisher

Reason for the Board of Education's policy Superintendent James M Spinning told school principals, is obvious Many children can't afford even a few cents contribution—the question of a class collection would embarrass them deeply

However, there is one exception to the otherwise ironclad rule If children make something themselves, such as a desk blotter, teacher may accept it in the spirit offered

But meanwhile, in the best interests of all—teachers, parents, fantry left 400 dead in the vicinity of Villabaja and Tortajada between Celadas and Teruel

Planes carried the war again to

This Attractive New Head Face Is 24 Metromedium No. 2 Italic

Rochester's total of unemployed stood at 18,083 as 1937 neared its end, if figures released yesterday on the voluntary census taken Nov 16 to 20 are correct.

Estimating the charting of jobless as 72 per cent correct, John D Biggers, census administrator, made public the results of the nationwide count which shows the country's jobless number between 7,822,912 and 10,870,000

Rochester's average of unemployment was lower than that of New York State as a whole and that of the other principal cities of the state, the figures reveal.

With a population of 328,132, Rochester, the tabulation revealed, had 12,465 males and 5,618 females totally jobless. Emergency work and part time occupations engaged 11,817 others

Buffalo, with a population of 573,076 had 37,613 out of work, and Syracuse's unemployed numbered 10,541 of the city's 209,326 population Rochester's percentage of jobcent in comparison to the entire state's total of more than 6 per cent

Checking the approximately 12,000 total of state unemployment insurance applications filed here since the beginning of the year against Biggers' figures yesterday, Paul B Smith, Rochester manager of the state unemployment and placement bureau, said the federal count was reasonably accurate.

In explanation the disparity between the two totals, Smith said persons filling out unemployment insurance form primarily are those paper reporter may be compelled to disclose the source of his information, the persons giving it will refuse to supply the reporter with is known in advance that a newswho either are or believe they are in covered employments

For Monroe County, the figures were Population, 423,881; totally unemployed, 19,919 (males, 13,838 females, 6,081), on emergency work, 5,670; partly employed 7,861 New York City numbered 514,446

EXAMPLE 234

IN TODAY'S NEWS

John Doe of New York City, recently indicted on embezzlement charges, shoots self after killing Richard Roe, his accuser. Story on Page 1

Today's Headlines

John Doe of New York City, recently indicted on embezzlement charges, shoots self after killing Richard Roe, his accuser. Story on Page 1

Spanish loyalists advance twelve miles beyond Toledo, taking 1,500 prisoners, but sustaining heavy losses in the mountains. Story on Page 3

John Doe of New York City, recently indicted on embezzlement charges, shoots self after killing Richard Roe, his accuser. Story on Page 1

Spanish loyalists advance twelve miles beyond Toledo, taking 1,500 prisoners, but sustaining heavy losses in the mountains. Story on Page 3

John Doe of New York City, recently indicted on embezzlement charges, shoots self after killing Richard Roe, his accuser. Story on Page 1

Spanish loyalists advance twelve miles beyond Toledo, taking 1,500 prisoners, but sustaining heavy losses in the mountains. Story on Page 3

Today's Editorial

Today The Modern Newspaper makes its appearance, and it appears with the good will and best wishes of thousands of people in the community it plans to serve —and to the best of its ability.

In the last two weeks hundreds of congratulatory messages have come to us from all sections of the state —from state and civic officials, from jurists, educators, business men, housewives, farmers, men and women in all walks of life—even from many school boys and girls.

All of these good friends have wished us well in our new and high venture—that of publishing a modern newspaper in the modern manner—modern in every way—in appearance, in news presentation, in editorial content, in spirit.

In the last two weeks hundreds of congratulatory messages have come to us from all sections of the state —from state and civic officials, from jurists, educators, business men, housewives, farmers, men and women in all walks of life—even from many school boys and girls.

All of these good friends have wished us well in our new and high venture—that of publishing a modern newspaper in the modern manner—modern in every way—in appearance, in news presentation, in editorial content, in spirit.

Today The Modern Newspaper makes its appearance, and it appears with the good will and best wishes of thousands of people in the community it plans to serve —and to the best of its ability.

In the last two weeks hundreds of congratulatory messages have come to us from all sections of the state —from state and civic officials, from jurists, educators, business men, housewives, farmers, men and women in all walks of life—even from many school boys and girls.

All of these good friends have wished us well in our new and high venture—that of publishing a modern newspaper in the modern manner—modern in every

The Modern Newspaper

VOL. I, No. 1 NEW YORK CITY, THURSDAY EVENING, THIS YEAR PRICE FIVE CENTS

Eleven Men Try to Win Tournament

Capture Nine Firsts, Twenty Other Prizes In Rand City Games

Newark—Sudden flare of an oil to halt reposted abuses and alay fears of racketeering in snow cards, token of employment for hundreds of idle, public works officials revealed, in announcing a new issue of special duty slips.

The alleged abuses took the form of improper use of cards distributed during the last days of the former Democratic administration and the racketeering fears centered on unconfirmed reports cards were being sold to those for whom they were not intended by persons outside official circles.

In the absence of Public Works Commissioner William H. Roberts, who is out of the city, departmental aides were cautious in discussing the incident that arose last week when the new administration faced its first major snow removal test. Edwin A. Miller, superintendent of maintenance, however, did say:

"There might have been some abuses by unscrupulous persons, for there appeared to be more cards in use last week than were issued. We do not know where the surplus came from, but to avoid any confusion dcided to change the syseree to consider Sibley's demands.

'Democrats Blameless'

Miller said former Democratic officials were in no way to blame. He admitted "hearing" reports that cards had been sold by persons outside the city service and said it was an old complaint but concrete evidence of the practice could not be obtained.

Whether the cards were legitimate or improper, Miller said, the city did not lose any money. The card, he explained, is merely a means of identification for a man getting a job and before he is paid he must work.

Cards, under custom of recent years, are passed out by ward leaders. An old card, now canceled, carried a line for an "authorized" signature, usually that of the ward leader, as well as the signature of ...

Wins First Prize

Miss Diana Cook, who led all contestants with her display of peonies at the flower show here

Ladley Women Seek Honors As Hi Debaters

Capture Nine Firsts, Twenty Other Prizes In Rand City Games

Ladley Women Seek Honors

Police Chief Jones Arrests Seventeen

Eleven Men Try to Win Tournament

Capture Nine Firsts, Twenty Other Prizes In Rand City Games

Park's Band Concerts Attract Large Crowds

Asserting "The people are in no mood right now for any 'I told you so's'" Colonel Knox suggested the States customs authorities 'had sealed the coach in which he was a day evening by insurgent bombs. The trucks were belived to have carried troop reinforcements. (One

Inside Today

Wednesday, April 6

Akron Briefs..........Page 8
Botzum's Column......Page 11
Case Records.........Page 9
Clapper's Column.....Page 10
Crossword Puzzle.....Page 17
Donald Gray..........Page 9
Editorials...........Page 10
Frying Political Fat..Page 10
Foreign News.........Page 2
General Johnson......Page 10
Jimmie Fidler........Page 6
Letters To The Editor.Page 10
Markets..............Page 14
Mrs. Ferguson........Page 10
Mrs. Roosevelt.......Page 9
Pegler's Column......Page 9
Pyle's Column........Page 10
News In Pictures.....Page 9
O'Keefe Says.........Page 11
Radio News...........Page 7
Serial...............Page 14
Sermonette...........Page 11
Society and Clubs...Pages 4-5
Sports........Pages 12-13-14
Theaters.............Page 6
Want Ads......Pages 14-15-16
Your Birthday........Page 17

Visiting Here Today at City Club

John Smith of Omaha, who will speak to local business men today on national affairs

Twenty-six Local Boys Win College Degrees

Police Chief Jones Arrests Seventeen

Police Chief Jones Arrests Seventeen

Park's Band Concerts Attract Large Crowds

Eleven Men Try to Win Tournament

Capture Nine Firsts, Twenty Other Prizes In Rand City Games

Ladley Women Seek Honors

Twenty-six Local Boys Win College Degrees

Twenty-six Local Boys Win College Degrees

EXAMPLE 235

IN TODAY'S NEWS

John Doe of New York City, recently indicted on embezzlement charges, shoots self after killing Richard Roe, his accuser. Story on Page 1

Today's Headlines

John Doe of New York City, recently indicted on embezzlement charges, shoots self after killing Richard Roe, his accuser. Story on Page 1

Spanish loyalists advance twelve miles beyond Toledo, taking 1,500 prisoners, but sustaining heavy losses in the mountains. Story on Page 3

John Doe of New York City, recently indicted on embezzlement charges, shoots self after killing Richard Roe, his accuser. Story on Page 1

Spanish loyalists advance twelve miles beyond Toledo, taking 1,500 prisoners, but sustaining heavy losses in the mountains. Story on Page 3

John Doe of New York City, recently indicted on embezzlement charges, shoots self after killing Richard Roe, his accuser. Story on Page 1

Spanish loyalists advance twelve miles beyond Toledo, taking 1,500 prisoners, but sustaining heavy losses in the mountains. Story on Page 3

Today's Editorial

Today The Modern Newspaper makes its appearance, and it appears with the good will and best wishes of thousands of people in the community it plans to serve—and to the best of its ability.

In the last two weeks hundreds of congratulatory messages have come to us from all sections of the state—from state and civic officials, from jurists, educators, business men, housewives, farmers, men and women in all walks of life—even from many school boys and girls.

All of these good friends have wished us well in our new and high venture—that of publishing a modern newspaper in the modern manner—modern in every way—in appearance, in news presentation, in editorial content, in spirit.

In the last two weeks hundreds of congratulatory messages have come to us from all sections of the state—from state and civic officials, from jurists, educators, business men, housewives, farmers, men and women in all walks of life—even from many school boys and girls.

All of these good friends have wished us well in our new and high venture—that of publishing a modern newspaper in the modern manner—modern in every way—in appearance, in news presentation, in editorial content, in spirit.

In the last two weeks hundreds of congratulatory messages have come to us from all sections of the state—from state and civic officials, from jurists, educators, business men, housewives, farmers, men and women in all walks of life—even from many school boys and girls.

All of these good friends have wished us well in our new and high venture—that of publishing a modern newspaper in the modern manner—modern in every way—in appearance, in news presentation, in editorial content, in spirit.

Today The Modern Newspaper makes its appearance, and it appears with the good will and best wishes of thousands of people in the community it plans to serve—and to the best of its ability.

In the last two weeks hundreds of congratulatory messages have come to us from all sections of the state—from state and civic officials, from jurists, educators, business men, housewives, farmers, men and women in all walks of life—even from many school boys and girls.

All of these good friends have wished us well in our new and high venture—that of publishing a modern newspaper in the modern manner—modern in every

The Modern Newspaper

VOL. I, No. 1 NEW YORK CITY, THURSDAY EVENING, THIS YEAR PRICE FIVE CENTS

Eleven Men Try to Win Tournament

Capture Nine Firsts, Twenty Other Prizes In Rand City Games

Newark—Sudden flare of an oil to halt reported abuses and alay fears of racketeering in snow cards, token of employment for hundreds of idle, public works officials revealed, in announcing a new issue of special duty slips.

The alleged abuses took the form of improper use of cards distributed during the last days of the former Democratic administration and the racketeering fears centered on unconfirmed reports cards were being sold to those for whom they were not intended by persons outside official circles.

In the absence of Public Works Commissioner William H. Roberts, who is out of the city, departmental aides were cautious in discussing the incident that arose last week when the new administration faced its first major snow removal test. Edwin A. Miller, superintendent of maintenance, however, did say:

"There might have been some abuses by unscrupulous persons, for there appeared to be more cards in use last week than were issued. We do not know where the surplus came from, but to avoid any confusion dcided to change the syseree to consider Sibley's demands.

'Democrats Blameless'

Miller said former Democratic officials were in no way to blame. He admitted "hearing" reports that cards had been sold by persons outside the city service and said it was an old complaint but concrete evidence of the practice could not be obtained.

Whether the cards were legitimate or improper, Miller said, the city did not lose any money. The card, he explained, is merely a means of identification for a man getting a job and before he is paid he must work.

Cards, under custom of recent years, are passed out by ward leaders. An old card, now canceled, carried a line for an "authorized" signature, usually that of the ward leader, as well as the signature of either the public safety commissioner or his secretary.

The new card, just issued, is signed by Commissioner Roberts alone.

Democratic headquarters reported last night it had no direct about Dec. 1 the old administration printed cards designed for use before Jan. 1 in event of a storm.

Those were distributed directly to Democratic ward leaders rather than to headquarters because of the short time involved.

Report Old Cards Tried

Democratic headquarters spokesman said reports were heard that some Democratic leaders passed out cards last week with instructions to hopeful shovelers "to try them out and see if they work." In several cases, the report reaching headquarters said, the cards were honored and Democrats got jobs.

Unruly scenes Monday night at the Byron St. yards of the DPW, where snow workers received assignments, first drew official attention to the cards, it was said. Not only were too many prospective workers on hand, in comparision with the number of cards is-

"We must speak up in unmistak-individuals were reported to have used "bulldozing" tactics on less forceful men to gain possession of the timid men's cards and then to

Police Chief Jones Arrests Seventeen

Sheriff's deputies thought they "had something there" when they found what they thought was a stolen truck loaded with clothing and firearms apparently abandoned near 270 Grosvenor Rd., Brighton, early yesterday.

Besides clothing the truck contained a shotgun, rifle and ammunition. The "loot" was taken to the jail and an investigation launched. It ended when the owner of the U. S. Chamber of Commerce. of the truck, Howard Lieb, Bloomingdale, identified it. He said he night, fits into a revamped system while driving in the country.

Wins First Prize

Miss Diana Cook, who led all contestants with her display of peonies at the flower show here

Ladley Women Seek Honors As Hi Debaters

Capture Nine Firsts, Twenty Other Prizes In Rand City Games

Cleveland — Col. Frank Knox suggested last night a "plain folks" Republican program which would tell business boldly it must renounce all "excessive" tariff schedules tending to increase the cost of living, and then would insist the farmer expect no cash bonuses for crop restriction.

Colonel Knox, 1936 vice-presidential candidate of the party which for decades has championed dered DiPasquale held in Monroe latter, Eldon, near Troupsburg Many lives were feared lost in a pre-dawn raid on the government's tariff protection, told a Cleveland the taxes imposed to finance them.

'Deliberately Provocative'

"Protect wage standards, yes! Continue to protect monopoly, no! able terms to those industries which, through excessive tariff schedules, have enjoyed a monoposued, officials said, but also certain ly of the domestic market and thus inordinately increased the cost of living for both farmers and workers.

"The Republican Party could then, with both logic and justice, oppose any project for direct cash subsidies to agriculture.

"If this unfair advantage is taken away from industry, the American farmer will readily forego his present demands for direct

Ladley Women Seek Honors

Rochester last night took action associates called his first major political statement since 1936, was on the program of a dinner honoring the recent re-election of Harold H. Burton, Cleveland's Republican brother, Martin, and son of the Earlier, an insurgent communique

This attack was a reprisal for a leaders called today for informal public "criticism or suggestions" beaten during a quarrel and her on Democratic Gov. Lehman's budget and tax program.

Previously, the party's high command indicated no partisan opposition would be offered to the Govdistrict court to charges of gunless was slightly more than 5 per uation of all existing emergency imposts.

The Chicago publisher said he had prepared his address to be "deliberately provocative" because peddle them to friends. Police were called at one stage to maintain he felt widespread discussion was essential in the development of a party sponsor a program which sound program.

Twenty-six Local Boys Win College Degrees

Charged with violating immigration laws beeause at one time after a felony conviction he traveled in a customs-sealed train coach from Michigan to Buffalo across Canada, a former Rochester resident faces deportation to Italy.

The alien, Giuseppe DiPasquale, 45, of Buffalo, sought his freedom on a writ of habeas corpus returned before Judge Harold P. Burke in Federal District Court here yesterday. He won a stay of deportation proceedings until Feb. 14 when Judge Burke will hear arguments in the case.

U. S. Department of Labor authorities had ordered him deported to Italy on a ship sailing Sunday. parked the truck for the night and engaged a room, expecting to conknowledge of snow card uses this year. Spokesmen pointed out that tinue in the morning. He said he carried the guns for protection Pending the hearing, however, Judge Burke refused bail and or-County jail.

Immigration authorities reported that in 1911 DiPasquale began his long criminal record with a 60-day felony sentence in Erie County. In 1915 he was sentenced to Auburn State Penitentiary on a first degree robbery charge but his sentence of 5 years was later commuted by Governor Whitman.

In 1919, records of the immigration authorities showed, DiPasquale was sentenced to serve 38 years for first degree robbery. When he was released in December immigration authorities instituted deportation proceedings. Contending that when DiPasquale traveled from Detroit to Buffalo across Canernor's program calling for expenditures of $385,000,000 and contin-ada he left the country and re-similar bombardment. Friday of Salamanca, Gen. Francisco Franco's capital in Western Spain.

A report from Zaragoza, Franco's entered illegally at Buffalo, although Canadian and United passenger.

Eleven Men Try to Win Tournament

Capture Nine Firsts, Twenty Other Prizes In Rand City Games

Lawrence, Mass.—His belief that to frighten them . . . the gun was not loaded," investigators quoted the 25-year-old youth.

Donovan told police the assault occurred while the couple were alone in the living room of the girl's home. There was a scuffle, he said, then Miss Leas ran from the room screaming hysterically and bleeding from nose and mouth.

He said he intervened and that Panagiotakos left the house, but returned in a few minutes with a revolver. Donovan said he ran a quarter mile to call police after the youth pointed the pistol at him and threatened him. Panagiotakos pulled the trigger, Donovan related, but the gun did not discharge.

Investigators said the youth was extremely jealous of the girl and insisted she remain home and follow the "Greek code." He had forced her to resign a bookkeeping position at her parents' sea food restaurant, police said, because he objected that she "came into contact with other men." The girl presently is unemployed.

Promises Action

Miss Leas, a Roman Catholic, was in the habit of going to church daily, but was forced to give up the practice because of her fiance's objections, police said.

Labor forces of Rochester last night were preparing their offensive to push ratification of the national Child Labor Amendment through the current session of the State Legislature.

Announcement by the Catholic Diocese of Rochester that it had launched its drive against ratification by New York State met the reply from the Committee for Industrial Organization, American Federation of Labor and American Labor Party that they would call meetings this week to open their 1938 counter drives.

"We've done our talking," said Abraham D. Chatham, CIO Amalgamated leader. "Monday we'll be in action."

The legislative committee of the CIO, headed by Hugh Thompson now is drafting plans for the renewed campaign to create public the Board of Education, said he did sentiment in favor of immediate ratification, Chatham said.

GOP Must Become 'Positive'

Discussion of the Rochester AFL campaign is expected to occupy a major place in Thursday night's regular meeting of the Central Trades and Labor Council.

Michael Reed, Labor Party leader, said illness among members had caused postponement of a special meeting called last week at which the ratification drive was to be speeded by appointment of a legislative committee. Another meeting will be called this week, he said.

Others in Rochester reported ready to fight for ratification are the Monroe County League of Woman Voters, Rabbi Philip S. Bernstein of Temple B'rith Kodesh, member of the State Child Labor Committee, and the Federation of Churches.

James E. Kittrell, chairman of not know whether the board would pupils—you can cross teacher off

Gunn is survived by his widow and five children, ranging in ages channels with regard to the ship, but it is believed generally here munication made to him in his that the American officers and terday in one of the most intense subsidies from the government. In air battles of the civil war while sailors will be released shortly. report said 3,000 were killed and a rabbit out with a stick. Martin

Park's Band Concerts Attract Large Crowds

Asserting "The people are in no mood right now for any 'I told you so's' " Colonel Knox suggested the States customs authorities had sealed the coach in which he was a day evening by insurgent bombs. The trucks were belived to have carried troop reinforcements. (One

Inside Today

Wednesday, April 6

Akron Briefs..........Page 8
Botzum's Column.....Page 11
Case Records.........Page 9
Clapper's Column.....Page 10
Crossword Puzzle.....Page 17
Donald Gray...........Page 9
Editorials ....Page 10
Frying Political Fat...Page 10
Foreign News.........Page 2
General Johnson......Page 10
Jimmie Fidler.........Page 6
Letters To The Editor.Page 10
Markets ....Page 14
Mrs. Ferguson.........Page 10
Mrs. Roosevelt........Page 9
Pegler's Column.......Page 9
Pyle's Column.........Page 10
News In Pictures......Page 9
O'Keefe Says..........Page 11
Radio News...........Page 7
Serial ....Page 14
Sermonette ....Page 11
Society and Clubs...Pages 4-5
Sports ....Pages 12-13-14
Theaters ....Page 6
Want Ads......Pages 14-15-16
Your Birthday........Page 17

Visting Here Today at City Club

John Smith of Omaha, who will speak to local business men today on national affairs

Twenty-six Local Boys Win College Degrees

Washington—A Spanish insur-where it was 32 degrees below zero night before last, came two Malone state troopers yesterday to Rochester's warmer climes to claim a man wanted in Franklin County on a contempt of court charge.

Bearing a warrant issued by Judge Carey of Children's Court, Troopers Thomas Hansen and H. J. Mayn of Troop B Malone, arrested Martin Bryan Cummings, 40, a lumberjack. The troopers rested here after their more than purveyors of the information. If it 300-mile ride in a curtained touring car, before starting the return where they lived. Eldon was poking

Out of the frozen north country, gent naval officer is in control of the American tanker Nantucket Chief, seized Jan. 18 by insurgent warships, T. Monroe Fisher, American vice-consul at Palma, informed the State Department yesterday.

Security Cost High

The ship is at Palma, Island of Majorca, together with 27 members of the crew who are American citizens, Fisher said in his cable.

The Nantucket Chief's manifest indicates the vessel has a cargo of gasoline and kerosene shipped from a Russian port destined for Barcelona, he added. The tanker was captured off Barcelona.

Secretary Hull's information is that the Nantucket Chief, although the property of an American corporation in New York, was chartered to the Spanish Loyalist government.

It is considered doubtful if much insurgent soldiers were lost there.

will be given a hearing next Thursday.

The "Greek code," he told the court, forbids an engaged woman to see or meet other men until after she is married.

Panagiotakos was seized at his home early yesterday after police

Twenty passengers were slightly shaken up when a southbound trolley split a switch at St. Paul and Andrews this afternoon.

Others Will Fight

The front trucks of the car, operated by Irvin Gibson, crossed the switch but the rear trucks swerved cut on an East Ave. automobile showroom when Supreme Court Justice John VanVoorhis an-down Andrews St. The trolley was hauled back on the St. Paul St. tracks by a traction company truck.

Harper Sibley, former president nounced he would appoint a ref-300 in the 1936 city tax assessment

Charged with criminal negligence in Rochester's fourth 1938 traffic fatality, Girard J. Dalle, 24, of 1580 Maiden Lane, Greece, pleaded not guilty in City Court yesterday and was granted adjournment until Feb. 21 by Judge Frederick J. Mix.

Police said Dalle's car struck and fatally injured Mrs. Mary Whalen, 63, of 1021 Campbell St., as she was crossing near 123 St. Paul St. after alighting from a bus at 2 p. m. Friday. She died of a fractured skull 40 minutes later in Highland Hospital. She was the third woman fatally hurt in traffic back by a withering counterfire.

Police Chief Jones Arrests Seventeen

Hendaye, France.—Government tion's policy, Superintendent James M. Spinning told school principals, is obvious: Many children can't afford even a few cents contribution—the question of a class collection would embarrass them deeply.

However, there is one exception to the otherwise ironclad rule. If children make something themselves, such as a desk blotter, teacher may accept it in the spirit offered.

But meanwhile, in the best interests of all—teachers, parents, fantry left 400 dead in the vicinity of Villabaja and Tortajada between Celadas and Teruel.

Planes carried the war again to middle Aragon base, said 100 government trucks moving up to the eastern front were destroyed Fri-

Insurgent columns led by tanks will be decidedly unwelcome. and insurgent airmen locked yes-

The new card, Miller said last of checking the men and their pay. ground forces fought bitterly on yesterday won the first round in the Teruel front. Civilian centers suffered new bombardments.

Government troops defending their newly-won foothold on the

Park's Band Concerts Attract Large Crowds

"The real reason I did it was she was failing to live up to the "Greek code" was blamed last night for a Massachusetts Institute of Technology instructor's alleged assault on his pretty fiancee.

Paul Panagiotakos, 25, brilliant institute graduate and candidate bail after pleading not guilty in toting, assault with a dangerous said brunet Ida Leas, 22, had been civilians far behind the front lines. provisional capital, Barcelona. lower Aragon front in Eastern Spain were reported to have repulsed three infantry attacks on

Police Chief Jones Arrests Seventeen

For gifts to teachers in the Rochester public school system this year again are under the Board of Education's traditional were clumsy with heavy mittens

This doesn't mean that pupils his heart he does not believe in them. If business will be reasonable in its demands, so will the farmer." cannot send Christmas greeting cards — if they are inexpensive cards. But it does mean that choc-with teacher—he'll have to find some other way than through the Christmas gift medium. assailed the government fortification only to be broken and turned

Eleven Men Try to Win Tournament

Capture Nine Firsts, Twenty Other Prizes In Rand City Games

Pale, sandy-haired Gordon Proctor, 42, on trial for his life, sat through his first day in a courtroom yesterday and "wished to heaven it could be my last."

With 11 jurors chosen at adjournment, the lawyers had moved speedily to decide whether the defendant, a truckman, will go to the chair for the slaying of Mrs. Alameda Griffiths, 35, and Ralph E. Hall, 30, her escort the night of Oct. 31 when both were shot.

"I'm tired," he said as guards clamped handcuffs on him for the ride back to the County Jail at the end of the day long session. "The sooner it's over with, the better."

Neatly dressed in a dark blue suit, dark tie and lighter blue shirt, Proctor had watched the proceedings calmly, almost without expression. He sat either with his hands folded in his lap, or leaning back, elbow on the chair arm and hand supporting his chin. He nodded briefly when the defense counsel, George D. Ogden, consulted him on the selection of jurors, but seldom spoke.

Hits at Monopoly

Whether temporary mental derangement will be the basis of the plea to save Proctor's life appeared to be uncertain late yesterday. Ogden said, however, he would not attempt to prove "insanity as such."

Prospective jurors were questioned as to prejudices against drinking and "the defendant's relations with a woman not in ac-standards." Police had attributed the double slaying to a love triangle.

Hall, an automoble salesman of 50 Spencer St. and Mrs. Griffiths were shot in the driveway of her home at 78 Jefferson Ter.

All but witnesses and veniremen were barred from the courtroom way at 11 a. m. today after selection of two jurors.

Liner on Mercy Errand

Return "to a certain and fixed dollar, redeemable in gold;" substitute for the undistributed profits cordance with accepted social liam C. Kohlmetz. A large group of cumulating excessive surpluses to spectators who arrived an hour before court opened had been reduced tax a "rational measure aimed only tered in the corridor outside.

Trial will probably get under avoid taxation;" let state and local governments handle relief of unemployment; reduce "waste and public squandering" to solve taxation problems; require union officials to account for finances and set up boards of inquiry in strikes. yesterday by order of Judge Wil-to prevent corporations from ac-by afternoon to a handful who loi-

Ladley Women Seek Honors

"If the Republican Party can point the way back to good times, the voters will restore our party to ods . . . must be stamped out by power," Colonel Knox said. "Unless it can become 'positive' again, its service is ended and the party will die.

"In the last campaign, the Republican Party came to be regarded, by millions of workers and farmers, as the special representative and spokeman of entrenched "artificial monopolies effected through improper, unsocial methto aim at the rabbit. His hands folks of America—the sort of people who gave it life 75 years ago

Freezes to Death

"The Republican Party must become again the party of the plain and the same sort of people who kept it in power most of that time."

Colonel Knox said "natural monopolies, such as telephones, street cars and electric power . . . must be regulated by law" while enforcement of existing anti-monopoly laws." He placed in another class those industries which, he declared "retiring" government in-

Twenty-six Local Boys Win College Degrees

Rochester's total of unemployed stood at 18,083 as 1937 neared its end, if figures released yesterday on the voluntary census taken Nov. 16 to 20 are correct.

Estimating the charting of jobless as 72 per cent correct, John D. Biggers, census administrator, made public the results of the nationwide count which shows the country's jobless number between 7,822,912 and 10,870,000.

Rochester's average of unemployment was lower than that of New York State as a whole and that of the other principal cities of the state, the figures reveal.

With a population of 328,132, Rochester, the tabulation revealed, had 12,465 males and 5,618 females totally jobless. Emergency work and part time occupations, engaged 11,817 others.

Buffalo, with a population of 573,076 had 37,613 out of work, and Syracuse's unemployed numbered 10,541 of the city's 209,326 population. Rochester's percentage of jobcent in comparison to the entire state's total of more than 6 per. cent.

Checking the approximately 12,000 total of state unemployment insurance applications filed here since the beginning of the year against Biggers' figures yesterday, Paul B. Smith, Rochester manager of the state unemployment and placement bureau, said the federal count was reasonably accurate.

In explanation the disparity between the two totals, Smith said persons filling out unemployment insurance form primarily are those paper reporter may be compelled to disclose the source of his inforwho either are or believe they are in covered employments.

For Monroe County, the figures were: Population, 423,881; totally unemployed, 19,919 (males, 13,838 mation, the persons giving it will refuse to supply the reporter with is known in advance that a newsfemales, 6,081); on emergency work, 5,670; partly employed, 7,-861. New York City numbered 514,-446.

EXAMPLE 236

BULLETINS

New Newspaper Home in Davenport

Front view of the building dedicated by the Davenport Times in October. See story on page two

The Reading (Pa.) Times has installed three Two-in-One Blue Streak Master Model 31 Linotypes, some twenty-five fonts of display matrices, and has adopted a modern head dress in Erbar Medium Condensed and Metromedium No. 2.

The Brooklyn Eagle has modernized its head dress and is now presenting most of its heads flush at the left in the Bodoni family.

The San Francisco Chronicle has adopted flush-left heads, most of them in Bodoni Bold or Poster Bodoni, and is departmentalizing news stories under such heads as "Foreign," "Science," "Education," "Crime," and so on.

The Kansas City (Mo.) Journal (formerly the Journal-Post) has installed many display sizes in the Memphis family and adopted a modern head dress that has attracted much favorable comment.

The Washington Star has installed twenty-five fonts of 7-point Ionic No. 5, many display fonts of Erbar Medium Condensed and Metromedium No. 2 with Italic, and is now presenting its heads flush at the left.

The Philadelphia Inquirer has added a Two-in-One Model 29 Linotype and fonts of 34- and 42-point Erbar Light Condensed, 24-point Metroblack No. 2 with Italic, and 14-point Metrolite No. 2 with Italic. The new faces are being used for flush-left heads on the Inquirer's sports pages.

The Washington Post has adopted flush-left heads, most of them in Bodoni Bold and Bodoni Bold Italic, and is setting its editorials in 9-point Excelsior on an 11-point body. Each line of each second deck presents a complete thought in bulletin form.

The Schenectady (N. Y.) Union-Star has installed thirteen fonts of 7½-point Ionic No. 5, several display sizes in the Bodoni family, and has adopted a flush-left head style.

The Winnipeg Tribune has adopted a flush-left head dress in Erbar Medium Condensed and Metromedium No. 2.

Thirty-five Kendall metal feeders are now in use in the plant of La Presse of Montreal, on all thirty-five of that paper's Linotypes.

New Structure for Allentown Papers

The accompanying picture shows the annex to the building of the Morning Call and the Chronicle and News of Allentown, Pa., which, as reported previously in The Linotype News, houses a new ninety-six page press and a well-equipped mailing room. Royal W. Weiler is president and manager of the Chronicle and News Publishing Company and of the Allentown Call Publishing Company, issuing the two papers. J. C. Shumberger is vice-president and comptroller; David A. Miller vice-president and managing editor; Ralph N. Mertz, secretary-treasurer; Percy B. Ruhe, editor, and William D. Reimert, executive editor. Harry W Sherman is mechanical superintendent

The Linotype News

VOLUME XVII — BROOKLYN, NOVEMBER 1938 — NUMBER THREE

1938 THE YEAR OF LINOTYPE'S MASTER MODELS

K. C. Journal Picks Memphis For New Dress

Modern Heads and Classified News Win Readers' Praise

KANSAS CITY, Mo.—One of the first acts of Orville S. McPherson after he became president of the Kansas City Journal-Post Company and publisher of the Journal-Post was to plan an effective new head dress for his paper

Mr McPherson had had much experience in newspaper re-styling in other parts of the country and so was well qualified to give the Journal-Post an unusually effective new dress

And when the new dress first appeared, October 4, it was greeted with enthusiasm by readers and advertisers, as well as by newspaper executives in many parts of the country

The issues of the Journal (the word "Post" had been dropped from the nameplate and masthead) for the next three days presented messages of commendation from more than 200 people in various walks of life, with many comments such as "I like it," "A hundred per cent improvement," "Best thing I've seen for some time," "I want that paper on my porch every day," "You can put me down as a regular subscriber," "I like its modern treatment of news," and "It's the talk of the town today"

Most of the heads in the new Journal are presented flush at the left in members of the Memphis family News heads are chiefly in Memphis Medium Condensed and Memphis Medium, and society and woman's page heads chiefly in Memphis Medium and Memphis Medium Italic On the sports pages many of the heads are in Memphis Bold Condensed, Memphis Bold and Memphis Bold Italic The Journal's editorial page is unusually attractive, with a three-column cartoon centered at the top and

(Continued on page two)

Washington Post Adopts New Dress

WASHINGTON, D C—The Washington Post, Eugene Meyer, publisher, which recently modernized its head dress by adopting simplified flush-left heads in the Bodoni family, is now setting its editorials in 9-point Excelsior on an 11-point body Each line of each second deck presents a complete thought in bulletin form.

In October the Post issued a twenty-page catalog that called attention to the many features that appear regularly in that paper

Atlanta Journal Adds Two-in-One

ATLANTA.—A Two-in-One Blue Streak Model 29 with a six-mold disk and a self-quadder has been added by the Atlanta Journal, making a total of twenty-three multiple-magazine Linotypes now in that plant.

The new Model 29 is used exclusively for the setting of heads

A short time ago the Journal added a Model 27 and a Model 28 both equipped with self-quadders and Mohr Lino-Saws and many extra fonts of two-letter display matrices

Inman Gray is president of the Journal, John A Brice, vice-president and general manager, James R Gray, vice-president and editor and George C Biggers, business manager Fred R Connell is superintendent

Union-Star Adopts New Type Dress

SCHENECTADY, N Y—Thirteen fonts of 7½-point Ionic No. 5—twelve fonts of Ionic in combination with Bold Face No 2 and one with Italic—have been installed for a new body dress for the Union-Star of this city and a new flush-left head style has been adopted.

Fonts of 18- and 24-point Bodoni Bold with Italic and 24-point Bodoni with Italic have been installed. Front-page heads are set in Bodoni Bold, Bodoni Bold Condensed and Bodoni Bold Italic. Society and woman's-page heads are set in Bodoni and Bodoni Italic

Fifteen Linotypes are operated by the Schenectady Union Publishing Company, issuing the Union-Star, including five Model 14s and a Two-in-One Model 26

Miss C W Callanan is president of the company and Paul L. Gross, treasurer and general manager Collaborating with them in making the change of type dress were Philip H Wertz, managing editor, and P H Bradley, city editor.

George W Wolfgang, foreman, and Gerald S Fuller, chief machinist, succeeded in making a layout of the Linotypes that obviates the necessity of changing liners, and has brought magazine changes down to the minimum.

For 5,000 Years From Now

Joe Mallen, Linotype operator who cast the famous slug, hands it to Grady Miller foreman of the Tuckahoe Record plant

Small-Town Linotype Man Casts Slug for Year 6939

Five thousand years from now barring too many earthquakes or other cosmic disturbances in the wrong place, a group of scientists will gaze on the handiwork of a small-town printer of today—on the work of Joe Mallen, Linotype operator with the Tuckahoe (N Y) Record

September 23 a "time capsule"—an 800-pound metal cylinder that contains much information about us and our times—was deposited fifty feet below the surface of the ground at the New York World's Fair, and in the cylinder, among other things, is a Linotype slug produced by Joe Mallen and that reads "This type was set on a Linotype machine"

In the "time capsule" are letters to the future from Dr Albert Einstein, Dr Robert A Millikan and Dr Thomas Mann Also included are newsreels and microfilm having to do with us and our times

The Book of Record

That people 5,000 years hence may know where to look for the "time capsule," a finely printed book "The Book of Record of the Time Capsule," has been published, and copies have been sent to leading libraries, museums and other repositories in various parts of the world The book contains a message to posterity, asking that it be preserved and translated into new languages as they arise, a description of the contents of the "time capsule," and detailed instructions for finding, raising and opening it in the year 6939.

To produce a book capable of surviving 5,000 years, the United States Bureau of Standards was consulted as to paper, ink and other matters The book, designed and set by Frederic W Goudy at the Village Press, Marlboro, N Y., was produced by G Leonard Gold of the Prestige Book Company, New York City The printing was done in Utica, N Y, by Howard Coggeshall, the frontispiece was produced by Charles Furth at the Photogravure and Color Company of New York City, and the binding was planned and produced by Randall W Bergmann of the Russell-Rutter Company, New York City The paper for the book was made by the Hurlbut Paper Company of South Lee, Mass., and the ink, black and red, by the International Printing Ink Corporation

The "time capsule, provided by the Westinghouse Electric & Manufacturing Company and deposited at the site of that company's exhibit at the fair, was made of a copper alloy known as cupaloy and has a pyrex glass crypt The cylinder is seven and one-half feet long and about eight inches in diameter

Can Opener and Woman's Hat

Among other things included in the "time capsule" are a can opener, a woman's hat of the latest style, a Bible, a toothbrush, a safety pin, a camera, a pipe, cigarettes, a fountain pen and a pencil Also included are bits of wool, silk, cotton, rayon, coal, asbestos, cement, metals, alloys, rubber and a variety of seeds

Scenes depicted in a representative newsreel were President Roosevelt speaking at Gettysburg on the seventy-fifth anniversary of the battle of Gettysburg, the return of Howard Hughes to New York from his record round-the-world flight, Jesse Owens's victory in the 100-meter dash in the 1936 Olympics at Berlin, a Harvard-Yale football game, a big-league baseball game, a review of the United States Fleet, and May Day in Moscow

Periscope at World's Fair

Visitors to the World's Fair will have the opportunity to see the "time capsule" through a periscope In the Westinghouse exhibit will be a replica of the cylinder, and duplicates of the items that make up the contents of the one fifty feet in the ground

Frank Mallen, publisher of the Tuckahoe (N Y) Record, whose plant was selected to provide the Linotype slug, says that a second slug was cast and will be placed on view at the World's Fair

"The assignment to set the type," says Mr Mallen, "came from Dr G. Edward Pendray, a nearby resident, who is assistant to the president of the Westinghouse Company Dr Pendray chose the Tuckahoe Record, because, he said, it was representative of the time in which we live that small establishments as well as the large ones possess the complex industrial machinery needed to carry on a successful commercial enterprise

"The operator who set the type, Joe Mallen, is a graduate of the Mergenthaler Linotype School The only comment Joe made when he cast the famous line was: 'Will there be any people left 5,000 years from now to see it?'"

La Presse of Montreal Using 35 Kendall Feeders

MONTREAL, Que —Thirty-five Kendall metal feeders are now in use in the plant of La Presse here, on all thirty-four of the paper's keyboard Linotypes and on its Linotype Lead and Rule Caster

La Presse ordered one Kendall feeder some time ago, and tested it thoroughly for three months on a Blue Streak Model 8 The composing-room men were so well pleased with it that six more were ordered, for application to six Model 9s And then they decided to equip the entire battery with Kendalls, and twenty-eight more were ordered, bringing the total to thirty-five.

In the meantime they were not idle at La Presse. Mr Lionais, general superintendent, who is a good draughtsman, got out his drawing board and designed a machine for quick and continuous casting of ingots for the Kendall feeders The machine consists of twelve double-sided water-cooled molds mounted on a frame to bring them to a height convenient to the big melting pot The molds are connected with gears, and fitted with cranks for easy dumping of the ingots There are twenty-four molds altogether, and twelve ingots are cast at one time Thus production is continuous and a week's supply of metal can be cast in half a day

Mr Lionais was assisted by "Pete" Poirier, chief machinist and Eugene Leverdure second machinist

Washington Star Adopts Modern Dress

Now Using Erbar, Metro for Heads, With Larger Ionic

WASHINGTON D C—The Star of this city came out October 31 with a modern head dress in Erbar Medium Condensed, Metromedium No 2 and Metromedium No 2 Italic, and with body matter in 7-point Ionic No 5 on an 8-point body

As the Star's presses were turning out the first copies in the new dress, a radio broadcast announcing the change was made from the composing room. Those taking part in the broadcast were Newbold Noyes, associate editor, B M McKelway, managing editor, Charles P Merkle, foreman of the composing room, Ralph McCabe, makeup editor, and "Bill" Coyle, radio announcer

For the new dress, the Star installed twenty-five fonts of 7-point Ionic No 5—twenty-four of them with Bold Face No 2 and one with Italic—and fonts of 18-, 24- and 34-point Erbar Medium Condensed, and 12-, 14-, 18- and 24-point Metromedium No 2 with Italic

Typographically Revitalized

On the radio broadcast Newbold Noyes stated, in part: "Today when you pick up your copy of the Star in your office, in your home, or at the newsstand, you will find a Star that is typographically revitalized. The headlines and news stories sparkle with readability The Star has lightened the optical task of absorbing the news."

Mr McKelway: "One big advantage of the new headlines is that they can be written faster, for they are simpler, you can get more words in them, and you don't have to spend so much time making each line exactly the same length"

Mr Merkle explained how the composing room got ready for and took care of the change "Everything we did was gotten out of the way yesterday. We had a battery of machinists headed by our chief machinist, William T Henderson, and under the supervision of Dave McCarty, news foreman."

Better Looking Paper

Mr McCabe: "Our new dress enables us to put out a much better looking paper There will be less eye strain"

A front-page story in the Star the day of the change stated, in part "In changing the dress of the Star it is felt that the finest typographic ability that specialists in newspaper type design have attained has been brought to the Star The result is to freshen the physical appearance of the paper"

The Evening Star and the Sunday Star, which operate forty-five Linotypes, are published by the Evening Star Newspaper Company, Inc Frank B Noyes is president of the company, Fleming Newbold, vice-president, R. M Kauffman, secretary, and Victor Kauffman, treasurer Capt Charles H Ruth is superintendent

Haddon Press, Inc. Adds 2 Linotypes

CAMDEN, N J—The Haddon Press, Inc., has added two Linotypes, and now operates sixteen Mergenthaler machines.

Ralph E Weeks is president of the company, C H. Wilhelm, vice-president; H C Rushmore, secretary and E H Beavers, treasurer J R Pratt is general superintendent of the plant C E. Nicholson is production manager J Troy Cobb is chief Linotype machinist

Washington, N. J., Star Marks 70th Birthday

WASHINGTON, N J—The Star of this community issued a sixty-four-page special edition in September to celebrate its seventieth anniversary

Since 1931 the Star has won five silver cups for general excellence and for its editorial page, and several ribbons for front and feature pages

The front page of the special carried several drawings contrasting the institutions of Washington in 1868 with those of 1938 More than 100 photographs were reproduced in the edition A large volume of advertising was carried

Four Linotypes are operated by the Star Operators are Howard Waters, William Griffith, Joseph Thatcher and Roger Smith Levi Cressman is composing-room foreman

This Issue, as Usual, Entirely Linotype Set

All lines of composition in this issue of THE LINOTYPE NEWS, as usual, were composed the Linotype way, even the biggest heads and the largest lines in display advertisements.

Most of the body matter is in 7½-point Excelsior with Memphis Bold on an 8½-point body, with some of the lines extra leaded, and most of the heads are in the Linotype Memphis family

See "Makeup of This Issue," on page four

3 Blue Streaks, New Dress For Times of Reading, Pa.

READING, Pa—The Times of this city has installed three Two-in-One Blue Streak Master Model 31 Linotypes, some twenty-five fonts of display matrices, and has adopted a modern head dress in Erbar Medium Condensed and Metromedium No 2

A front page story in the Times the day of the change stated, in part "Your Reading Times comes to you today dressed in still more modern clothes Our headlines are streamlined The new style of headline setting, and the Erbar and Metro types which compose the lines, make for more comprehensive headline writing, and for speedier and easier reading With the streamlined head type we also have modernized our masthead—that portion of page one above the dateline While Father Time and his part of the picture remain the same, the modern side of the world's affairs has been redesigned to include later developments in industry, commerce and agriculture among which is the airplane skyscrapers and the streamlined train

All three of the new machines are equipped with six mold disks, two of them with Mohr Lino-Saws, and one with an automatic ejector set A Reid magazine rack was included in the installation

Fifteen Linotypes are now operated

John H Perry is president of the Reading Times Publishing Company which publishes the Times Earl A. Kettel is secretary treasurer Eagle Freshwater is manager Abe Hurwitz is editor, and Charles W Detweiler is advertising director Harry Y Sterrett is mechanical superintendent, and George Schaaber is Linotype machinist

Mr Perry, who recently purchased control of the Western Newspaper Union, is head of the John H Perry Associates enterprises, which include the Jacksonville (Fla.) Journal, the Pensacola (Fla) News and the Journal, the Panama City (Fla) News-Herald, and radio station WCOA Pensacola

San Francisco Chronicle Modernizes Its Makeup

SAN FRANCISCO—"The Newspaper You've Been Waiting For" was the heading on the announcement by the Chronicle of this city that that paper had modernized its makeup and had departmentalized its news stories, classifying them under such heads as "Foreign," "Science," "Education, "Crime, "The Nation" and "Labor's Day"

Heads in the Chronicle are now set flush at the left, most of them in Bodoni Bold or Poster Bodoni

In the issue for the day before the change "30" dashes throughout the paper were made up of the words "Tomorrow" and "Streamline" and an announcement was made that the change was coming

W. D Chandler, managing editor, stated, "We are delighted with the reception. The reaction has been much more favorable than we had hoped"

"There is no doubt that streamlining will increase circulation," stated G E Gilroy, circulation manager

The changes in typography were made under the direction of Paul C Smith, general manager "We aim to classify news, to make it accessible and to make the relationship of one event to another readily discernible," Mr Smith stated

Inquirer Adds Model 29 And Fonts of Erbar, Metro

PHILADELPHIA—The Inquirer of this city has added a Two-in-One Model 29 Linotype and fonts of 34- and 42-point Erbar Light Condensed, 24-point Metroblack No 2 with Italic, and 14-point Metrolite No 2 with Italic. The new faces are being used for heads on the sports pages

M L. Annenberg is chairman of the board of the Philadelphia Inquirer Company and publisher of the paper Charles A Tyler is president and general manager of the company and Walter H Annenberg is vice-president John T Curtis is editor of the paper, and John J Fitzpatrick is managing editor

Leon Holtsizer is production manager, George W Hoesch, Jr., mechanical superintendent J F Agee, composing-room superintendent, and B J Farrell chief Linotype machinist

Sixty Linotypes are now operated by the Inquirer

M & L Company of Chicago Operates Fourteen Linos

CHICAGO—Fourteen Linotypes, including five mixers, two of them Blue Streak Models 30s and one a forty-two-pica machine, are operated by the M & L Typesetting and Electrotyping Company of this city

Lester A Neumann vice-president and general manager of the company, recently was re-elected president of the International Printers' Supply Salesmen's Guild For several years he has been active in organization work in this city and over the nation He recently completed a term as president of the Printers' Supply Salesmen's Guild of Chicago

He has proposed an active program to promote interest in the 1939 equipment show to be held during the New York World's Fair

The M & L Linotypes are arranged in a square formation, with magazine racks in the center Alleys between rows of magazines make them easily accessible to operators and machinists More than 350 fonts of matrices are available, and new fonts are added frequently

Approximately 15,500 square feet of floor space is required for the composing and makeup departments, both of which are under the direction of M J Capelle superintendent

One of the firm's Blue Streak Model 30s is shown in one of the accompanying pictures, in the foreground In the other picture Ed Wampole, in charge of the Linotype department, is shown standing behind the second machine from the front of the picture

M & L producers, with one of the company's Model 30s in the foreground

Another view of the plant, with Ed Wampole standing beside the second Lino

EXAMPLE 237

In Example 235 the heads in the last six columns were in 36-, 30-, 24- and 18-point Memphis Medium Condensed; 30-point Memphis Medium; 18-point Memphis Medium Italic, and 14-point Memphis Bold.

The use of Memphis Bold Condensed instead of Memphis Medium Condensed, and the use of Memphis Bold and Memphis Bold Italic instead of Memphis Medium and Memphis Medium Italic, was responsible for the stronger page suggested by Example 236.

In November, 1938, the *Linotype News* came out with a front page that presented another treatment of the high-double-column idea. See Example 237.

Observe that the high column was headed "Bulletins," and that it presented summations of ten stories, as well as two double-column pictures with overlines and legends.

Most of the heads on that page were in Memphis Bold Condensed. Single-column body lines were in 7½-point Excelsior on an 8½-point body, with subheads in 7½-point Memphis Bold. Double-column body lines were in 14-point Memphis Bold leaded 2 points.

Observe that in Examples 233 through 237 no dashes of any kind were employed, not even "30" dashes. Instead of "30" dashes, a pica of white space was employed in each instance. And notice how clearly following heads stand out, with no competition from dashes.

6

The Modern Tabloid

A FEW YEARS AGO the term "tabloid newspaper" meant many things to many people. To some it meant little more than "sensation sheet," "scandalmonger." To others it meant a newspaper with comparatively small pages that went in strong for pictures and "splashy" headlines. To some it meant all of those things. To some it still does.

But more and more people are coming to understand that there can be tabloids and tabloids. Of course, a newspaper can have a comparatively small page size and still be a conservative, dignified publication. Indeed, all our early newspapers were tabloids, and many of them were decidedly conservative.

In these busy times, when much of our newspaper reading is done on the way to and from work, in crowded railway trains, subways, trolley cars and buses, the newspaper with smaller size pages often is easier to handle than the large-page paper. Even many of our large-page papers publish some of their sections in tabloid size, for the convenience of readers. Witness the book sections, feature sections, magazine sections, of many of our otherwise "standard-size" newspapers.

It is the guess of this writer, and several others, as set forth in the last chapter of this book, that the page size of the newspaper of the future will approximate that of our present-day tabloid.

In January, 1939, the *Linotype News*, which, through the years, had suggested hundreds of different eight-column-page treatments, decided to demonstrate more frequently the many possibilities of tabloid-page makeup, without, however, neglecting its studies of eight-column possibilities.

Accordingly, the January, 1939, issue appeared in the form of a sixteen-page tabloid, but the center spread of that issue presented an eight-column "front-page" makeup. (Several other tabloid-size papers have since applied the standard-size-page idea to their center spreads.)

A front-page story in that issue explained: "This change of size finds us quite neutral in any discussion about 'standard' *versus* 'tabloid' papers. We sense a field for each and are well aware of our typographical responsibilities to both. So you will note a standard-size center spread, to present ideas about the format of the bigger page."

Example 238 presents a reduced showing of the front page of that issue. Heads were in various sizes of Memphis Bold, Memphis Bold Condensed and Memphis Medium Condensed. Cut legends were in 6- and 7-point Paragon Bold. Body lines were in 7-point Paragon on an 8-point body, and 10-point Paragon on a 12-point body.

The head on page two of that issue (see Example 239), a picture page, was in 30-point Memphis Bold, and cut legends were in 6- and 7-point Paragon Bold.

Example 240 suggests the editorial page of that issue, with four 15-pica columns and 12 points of white space between columns, instead of column rules. Most of the heads on that page were in 18-point Memphis Medium Italic, and body matter was in 9-point Paragon on an 11-point body.

Example 241 suggests a feature page in the March, 1939, issue, with four 15-pica columns to the page, separated by 12 points of white space. Most of the heads were in 14-point Memphis Bold and most of the body matter was in 9-point Paragon leaded 2 points.

The number for May, 1939, came out with the front page suggested by Example 242.

Heads were in various weights and sizes in the Bodoni family, legends were in 8- and 9-point Bookman, and body matter was in 7½-point Excelsior on a 9-point body.

Example 243 suggests the editorial page of that same issue, with most of the heads in 18-point Bodoni Bold Italic and with body matter in 9-point Excelsior on an 11-point body.

Example 244 suggests a feature page in that issue, with most of the heads in 12-point Poster Bodoni and with body matter in the same face and same sort of leading employed in Example 243.

The number for September, 1939, featured the front page suggested by Example 245.

Heads were in members of the Erbar, Metro and Spartan families, with single-column body matter in 7½-point Excelsior on a 9-point body. The double-column body lines were in 10-point Excelsior on a 12-point body, with subheads in 14-point Spartan Heavy.

The Linotype News

VOLUME XVII | BROOKLYN, JANUARY, 1939 | NUMBER FOUR

Morning News, Plymouth, Eng. Adds 16 Linos

22 Mergenthalers, New Press Operated In Modern Quarters

PLYMOUTH, England. — Sixteen new Linotypes have been installed in the new plant, in this city, of the Western Morning News, Western Evening Herald, Western Weekly News and United Services Review, associated newspapers. With the original six, all of which have been reconditioned, the plant now has a battery of twenty-two Linotypes.

Materials throughout the building are of the fire-resisting sort; the temperature is controllable, and the rooms are sound-proof.

Equipment includes a press capable of delivering 120,000 copies an hour, and new stereotyping machinery.

The plant has been named after Sir Robert Leicester Harmsworth, Bart., father of the present chairman of directors, Sir Harold Harmsworth.

This Issue, as Usual, Entirely Linotype Set

All lines of composition in this issue of The Linotype News, as usual, were composed the Linotype way, even the biggest heads and the largest lines in display advertisements.

Most of the body matter is 7-point Paragon with Paragon Bold on an 8-point body, with some of the lines extra leaded, and most of the heads are in the Linotype Memphis family.

See "Makeup of This Issue," on page six

Bishop Firm of Sydney Sets Handsome Booklet

SYDNEY, New South Wales, Australia.—A handsome booklet for the ceremony of installation and investiture of officers, at Masonic Hall, was produced recently by E. A. Bishop & Company, trade Linotypers at Perth. The booklet was set in Memphis Light and Metrolite and run in two colors and black.

In New Position

John J Shea

Shea Now With Hearst Papers

WORCESTER, Mass.—John J Shea, former production manager of the Telegram and the Evening Gazette of this city, is now general mechanical superintendent of the Hearst newspapers, with headquarters in New York City

Started With Telegram in 1916

Mr Shea, who was with the Telegram and the Gazette about twenty-three years, started in the mailing room of the Telegram in 1916, while he was still in high school. In 1918 he moved into the pressroom of the Telegram, and also held down a job in the delivery department of the Gazette.

He became foreman of the Gazette pressroom in 1925, and superintendent of the department, embracing both the Telegram and the Gazette, in 1929. In 1932 he became mechanical superintendent and production manager of both papers.

Active With A. N. P. A.

In the last ten years Mr. Shea has traveled extensively, making studies in leading newspaper plants of the newest developments in mechanical and production methods. Several times he has presided over, and presented papers at, meetings of the mechanical division of the American Newspaper Publishers' Association.

He has been president of the Wachusett Golf Club Associates the last two years, and is a member of the Worcester Y Athletic Club.

'Editor Tom Dreier Says 'It's a Shotgun Wedding'

Folks who have been receiving our *Shining Lines* got a card the other day announcing that hereafter our "little, intimate message" will become an editorial feature of The Linotype News.

When we began issuing *Shining Lines*, a couple of years back, we planned it for a limited list of leading executives in the printing and publishing fields. But the "limited list" kept on growing with requests from every branch of the industry and from without, too. And our publication for the industry as a whole has been, for many years, The Linotype News.

As the *Shining Lines* list grew and grew, it began to dawn on us that it might be a bit foolish to send out two publications when it was obvious that the two belonged together. Reader demand outside the executive list for whom *Shining Lines* was intended originally thus brought about what Editor Dreier promptly termed this "shotgun wedding."

So in this new version of The Linotype News you will find a special page devoted to *Shining Lines*, set forth in its own typography, as befits a feature possessing so many pre-marital friends. We hope you may find it equally interesting in this form.

Likewise do we hope that a new format for The Linotype News may seem significant in this laboratory newspaper. This change of size finds us quite neutral in any discussion about "standard" versus "tabloid" papers. We sense a field for each and are well aware of our typographical responsibilities to both. So you will note a standard-size center spread, to present ideas about the format of the bigger page.

All of which seems to be characteristic of the constant study and experimentation that must go on within an organization that would serve the graphic-arts industries. Your own reaction will be of interest. Please let us have it. J T Mackey President

Times-Picayune Company Completes Modern Annex; Installs Super-Display Lino

Southern Execs Meet Next Month

OKLAHOMA CITY, Okla.—The first meeting of the western division of the Southern Newspaper Mechanical Conference as now organized will be held in the Skirvin Hotel here February 20 and 21

Territory included in the conference is Texas, Oklahoma, Arkansas and Louisiana west of the Mississippi River, but the committee in charge hopes that many mechanical executives from the eastern-division territory of the Southern Newspaper Publishers' Association will attend.

It is also hoped that publishers and mechanical men will invite as guests representatives of engraving companies that do work for member newspapers.

Local arrangements for the conference are in charge of W. J. Phillips, mechanical superintendent of the Oklahoman and the Times of this city.

The executive committee in charge includes A. T Blease of the Corpus Christi (Texas) Caller and the Times, chairman; J. H. Gibson, Houston (Texas) Chronicle; Mr. Phillips; O. M. Harper of the Tulsa World; A. I Lundberg of the Fort Worth Star-Telegram, and Leven T Deputy of the Dallas News.

Charlotte News Marks 50th Year

CHARLOTTE, N. C.—The News of this city celebrated its fiftieth birthday November 15 with a 172-page golden anniversary edition.

Launched in the days when trains were looked on as Frankensteins, the Sherman Silver Purchase Bill was on every tongue, and Cleveland was on his way out of the White House, the News started right in to assert itself on controversial questions and has done so ever since.

Bought shortly after its birth, by W. Carey Dowd, from its founder, Wade H. Harris, the News has remained a Dowd family property. Today's publisher is W. Carey Dowd, Jr., and today's editor is James Edward Dowd.

In 1910 a Sunday edition was added, and in 1914 the Evening Chronicle, established in 1903, was absorbed.

The ten sections and a twenty-four-page tabloid gravure insert, of the golden anniversary edition, featured the past, present and future of Charlotte and the News. Advertising in the edition was heavy.

B. S. Griffith is managing editor, and E. H. Hall, Jr., is manager of the book-and-job-printing department. C. B. Capps is composing-room superintendent.

Two Australian Papers Publish Big Specials

Special issues of two Australian newspapers, the Daily Examiner at Grafton, New South Wales, and the Advertiser at Geelong, Victoria, marking the hundredth anniversaries of their respective communities, have been received by The Linotype News.

The Examiner's special consisted of fifty-six pages and included many features and pictures, among them a story about the installation of Linotypes in Grafton and a picture of five modern Linotypes now operated by the paper.

The centennial edition of the Advertiser, of fifty pages, carried many illustrated stories about the past growth and present development of Geelong and its surrounding territory

Praises Master 32

Eldon L. Martin, machinist in charge of the ten Linotypes operated by the Galesburg (Ill.) Register-Mail, who recently rounded out twenty years with that paper, says of a Blue Streak Master Model 32 installed last February: "It has been a marvelous addition. Our ads and jobs are being taken care of with a minimum of time and effort on the part of the operator and machinist"

Gage to Make 5 Talks In the Middle West

Harry L. Gage, Linotype vice-president, is scheduled for five talks in January, in Milwaukee, Indianapolis and Louisville.

January 18 he will speak on "Business—To the Rescue!" before the Milwaukee Typothetae and advertising executives; January 26 he will talk on "Typographic Sanity," at the Indianapolis Advertising Club, as a feature of "Advertising Week"; the evening of the same day he will address the Louisville Club of Printing House Craftsmen on "Tomorrow's Challenge to Craftsmen." The next day, in Louisville, he will talk on "Making Better Newspapers," before the Kentucky Press Association, and will address Louisville master printers on "The Master Printers' Responsibility for the Future."

New Blue Streak Being Used to Set Display Advertising

NEW ORLEANS.—Following completion of a five-story annex, which provides needed extra floor space, the Times-Picayune and the New Orleans States, published by the Times-Picayune Publishing Company, have added a Blue Streak Super-Display Model 27 Linotype, a new high-speed press, and other items of equipment.

Self-Quadder, Extra Magazines

The new Model 27 is equipped with a self-quadder, Mohr Lino-Saw, Margach metal feeder and twelve extra magazines. It is being used for display-advertising composition. Sixteen fonts of two-letter display matrices, and a wide range of food-store logotypes are included in the complement of matrices. A Reid magazine rack with a capacity for twenty extra Model 27 magazines is in use.

The new annex, of tapestry brick and steel construction, has a floor area of 38,400 square feet. The composing room occupies most of the fifth floor of the annex, as well as the major portion of the fifth floor of the main building.

The new press has a capacity of ninety-six pages. When printing forty-eight pages, it has a maximum speed of 100,000 copies an hour

Carefully Planned Program

These developments are part of a carefully planned expansion program laid out by executives of the Times-Picayune Publishing Company. The newspapers have consistently kept pace with modern trends both in equipment and typography. Recently the Times-Picayune and the States installed seventeen fonts of 7½-point Linotype Paragon for news body matter.

L. K. Nicholson is president of the Times-Picayune Publishing Company, and publisher of the papers. John F. Tims is business manager and treasurer.

Baker Is Superintendent

Claude Baker is mechanical superintendent. He is assisted by R. Hendrick, foreman of the Times-Picayune, and J. Powers, foreman of the States. The Linotypes are under the supervision of George E. Downes, head machinist.

The accompanying picture shows the new Super-Display Model 27, with Messrs. Baker and Downes standing at the left, Camile Lalonde at the keyboard, and John Kelley at the right. Messrs. Lalonde and Kelley are ad operators.

Messrs. Baker, Downes, Lalonde and Kelley at the Model 27

EXAMPLE 238

2 THE LINOTYPE NEWS, JANUARY, 1939

PICTURE PARADE OF THE LINOTYPE NEWS

Arne G. Rae, right, new executive secretary of the National Editorial Association, talks things over with Harry Schenk, who succeeds him as field manager for the Oregon Newspaper Publishers' Association and as assistant professor of journalism at the University of Oregon. Mr. Rae left Eugene, Ore., for Chicago, January 1, to take on his new duties

Presenting Herbert D. Hancock, managing editor of the Chelsea (Mass.) Evening Record, new president of the Massachusetts Press Association

Left to right: Clayton Rand, Dixie Press, Gulfport; Joe Dale, Lawrence County Press, Monticello, and Norman A. Mott, Yazoo City Herald—all elected to the Mississippi Press Association Hall of Fame for outstanding service to their communities, state and profession

Carl K. Towley (shown here with Violet M. Towley and their two children, Cathryn and Carl II) modestly states that the Clear Lake (Wis.) Star "isn't any great shucks as a paper, just a home-town sheet that wants to see the community happy and to record that happiness in its pages." Mr. and Mrs. Towley moved to Clear Lake in 1932 from Montevideo, Minn., where both had been teaching and he had been directing publication work in the high school

Fifty dollars for first prize in the best editorial contest conducted at the latest Texas state fair was won by R. B. Boyle (left), former publisher of the Heart O'Texas News, Brady. Mrs. A. V. Yeager, feature writer and columnist with that paper, who won the "best rural correspondent for Texas" contest conducted by Country Home, took third prize for a local column. Mr. Boyle's editorial was headed "What the State Fair Means to Texas and the Southwest." The contests aroused much interest not only in Texas but throughout the Southwest

The accompanying picture shows Tom Murry, head of the Linotype department at John Brown University, Siloam Springs, Ark., seated at one of the Linotypes in the institution's printing department. The university, founded in 1919, was started to carry out Mr. Brown's dream of what a modern education should be. There now is a junior college of the university, at Sulphur Springs, Ark., which also has a Linotype

The Connell Typesetting Company, recently established in Kansas City, Mo., by J. R. Connell, has installed two Linotypes, including a Blue Streak Model 31 with a self-quadder. Both machines are equipped particularly for telephone-directory work. The Martin Printing Company, for which the Connell Typesetting Company does composition, states that make-ready time has been greatly reduced. The accompanying picture shows, left to right: Frank Stevens, standing; Frank Murphy at the keyboard; J. R. Connell, standing, and John Rogers, operating the Blue Streak Master Model 31

The Independent Printing Company of Omaha recently replaced a Model 14 with a Blue Streak Master Model 32 with a self-quadder. Established in 1919 with two platens and a little type, by Bartolomew Caramello, the business has grown into a well-equipped and successful commercial-printing concern now headed by sons John and Paul. Shown here, left to right, are Frank Barnes, foreman; John Caramello, and Elmer Thoman, operator

R. V. Longwith, formerly an instructor at Shawnee High School, has been appointed instructor in the printing department of Okmulgee High School. His record: twenty years at teaching, printing and publishing in Oklahoma

Pictured here are some of the seventy employees and correspondents of the Lock Haven (Pa.) Express, snapped on their outing at Camp Rockypoint, Queens Run, last fall. Frank D. O'Reilly, Sr., publisher of the paper (third from the left in the third row from the top) served as master of ceremonies at the feast in the evening. First in the second row from the bottom is Miss Rebecca F. Gross, editor of the Express and secretary-treasurer of the company publishing it

Nearly nineteen years ago—May 19, 1920—members of the Mississippi Press Association enjoyed an outing at Pascagoula, where, among other things, they were taken on a sightseeing trip to the shipbuilding yards. George Wood, business manager of the Winona (Miss.) Times, who lent this picture to The Linotype News, wonders how many of our present readers (and so do we) faced the camera when this shot was taken

EXAMPLE 239

6 THE LINOTYPE NEWS, JANUARY, 1939

The Linotype News

Published regularly in the interests of many thousands of Linotype owners and those who work with the Linotype or its product.

Correspondence is invited. Specimens of Linotype composition, as well as brief accounts of experiences on or about the Linotype, are gladly received. News items are welcomed.

Address communications to the EDITOR OF THE LINOTYPE NEWS, 29 Ryerson Street, Brooklyn, N. Y.

PRINTED DIRECT FROM LINOTYPE SLUGS

JOHN E. ALLEN, *Editor*

Another New Makeup

A new year suggests new things—and here's THE LINOTYPE NEWS in another new makeup.

Through the years, we have presented many different forms of makeup in this typographic laboratory, and hundreds of newspapers have adopted some or all of those forms to the applause of readers and advertisers and with decided savings of time and money in editorial and composing rooms.

As MR. MACKEY states on the front page of this issue, "this change of size finds us quite neutral in any discussion about 'standard' *versus* 'tabloid' papers. We sense a field for each and are well aware of our typographic responsibilities to both. So you will note a standard-size center spread to present ideas about the format of the bigger page."

Shaw and Journalism

"Journalism," states GEORGE BERNARD SHAW, "is the highest form of literature; for all the highest literature is journalism. The writer who aims at producing the platitudes which are 'not for the age, but for all time' has his reward in being unreadable in all ages; whilst Plato and Aristophanes trying to knock some sense into the Athens of their day, Shakespeare peopling that same Athens with Elizabethan mechanics, Ibsen photographing the local doctors and vestrymen of a Norwegian parish, Carpaccio painting the life of St. Ursula exactly as if she were a woman living in the next street to him, are still alive and at home everywhere among the dust and ashes of thousands of academic punctilious, archæologically correct men of letters and art who spent their lives haughtily avoiding the journalist's vulgar obsession with the ephemeral.

"I also am a journalist, proud of it, deliberately cutting out of my works all that is not journalism, convinced that nothing that is not journalism will live long as literature, or be of any use whilst it does live. . . . The journalist writes about all people and about all time . . . let others cultivate what they call literature; journalism for me!"

Some Distribution!

From the WESTERN NEWSPAPER UNION offices in Chicago comes a story about setting type out of a barrel. The story was reported in the *Mulberry* (Ind.) *News* by DONALD CLARK, who with RAY CLARK, editor, and son ROBERT heard it in Chicago. It was told that:

"A tramp printer wandered into a small country town down south one day and was amazed to find a young man laboriously setting type out of a barrel. He poked around into the barrel, half full of type, until he found each letter wanted, and placed it in the proper position in his typesetting stick. After watching for some time, the tramp printer exclaimed:

" 'By gum, I've been in just about every country-newspaper office in this country, but this is the first time I ever saw anybody set type out of a barrel. Isn't it pretty slow going—take you a long time to get the paper out?'

" 'Yep,' grunted the young typesetter, 'takes a hell of a long time to set up all the type, but godalmity you ought to see us distribute it!' "

Makeup of This Issue

As usual, all lines in this issue of THE LINOTYPE NEWS were Linotype composed—all news and feature heads, as well as the largest display lines in advertisements. The larger lines were cast on the All-Purpose Linotype.

Most of the single-column body lines are in 7-point Paragon with Paragon Bold on an 8-point body, with some of the lines extra leaded.

Double-column body lines are in 10-point Paragon with Paragon Bold or with Italic and Small Caps on a 12-point body.

Brief items under state and sectional heads, and in the *Bookshelf* department, on page five, are in 6-point Paragon with Paragon Bold.

Body matter on page six is in 9-point Paragon with Italic and Small Caps on an 11-point body, and most of the heads on the same page are in 18-point Memphis Medium Italic.

The main head on the front page has a first deck in 36-point Memphis Bold, with a second deck in 14-point Memphis Bold.

The full-width head on page two is in 30-point Memphis Bold.

Some of the two-column heads are in 36-point Memphis Bold Condensed, and some are in 24-point Memphis Bold Italic.

Main single-column news heads are in 30-point Memphis Bold Condensed, with second decks in 14-point Memphis Bold.

Other single-column news heads are in 24- or 18-point Memphis Bold Condensed or 24- or 18-point Memphis Medium Condensed.

State and sectional heads are in 18-point Memphis Bold Italic.

Cut overlines are in 14- or 24-point Memphis Bold Italic, and cut legends are in 6- or 7-point Paragon Bold.

Running heads are in 12-point Memphis Bold.

The *Shining Lines* page carries its own descriptive matter, as also do all advertisements.

Somewhat Confused

It is said that someone once sent a newspaper editor a bottle of hard liquor and that shortly after its arrival he received for publication a wedding announcement and a notice of an auction sale, which later appeared in type as follows:

"William Smith and Miss Lucy Anderson are to be disposed of at public auction at my farm one mile east of a beautiful cluster of roses on her breast and two white calves, before a background of farm implements too numerous to mention in the presence of about seventy guests, including two milch cows, six mules and one bobsled. Rev. Jackson tied the nupital knot with 200 feet of hay wire and the bridal left on one good John Deere gang plow for an extended trip with terms to suit purchaser. They will be at home to their friends with one good baby buggy and a few kitchen utensils after date of sale to responsible parties and some fifty chickens."

Appearance Important

"Competition in typography and press renderings has made the newspaper of today incomparably superior in mechanical production to the papers of the pre-war period," states WILLIAM FEATHER of Cleveland. "It is significant that the most coveted awards in this field are those instituted by an advertising agency, N. W. AYER & SON, INC., a potent reminder that buyers of national space are thinking of the appearance of media and the production of their own advertising output quite as much as they think of circulation.

"The old-time newspaper management was content to produce a paper that looked as inviting as its immediate home rival. Today, papers must bear comparison with other papers produced hundreds or thousands of miles away."

NEWSPAPER MAKEUP

By JOHN E. ALLEN

No. 65—The Modern Newspaper

Another publication that has adopted to advantage the sort of modern front page originated by THE LINOTYPE NEWS is the *East Orange* (N. J.) *Record*.

As will be seen from the accompanying reduced showing of a front page from that paper, a high double column at the left presents a news picture under the head "In Today's News," followed by summations of leading stories under the head "Today's Headlines," followed by "Today's Editorial."

December 5, 1938, DONALD R. HASSELL, managing editor of the *Record*, wrote us as follows:

"For close to forty years the *Record* had had no live makeup. Last year it was purchased by two young Yale men, COLBURN HARDY and BALDWIN WARD, and it's beginning to look like a newspaper.

"My job, when I first came here, in May of this year, was to streamline the paper. First thing we did was flush all heads. And then we looked around for something that was really new.

"We found it in THE LINOTYPE NEWS, and October 14 saw the *Record* dressed up in modern style. Thus far we have received numerous favorable comments on the change.

"We have varied only once since we started using the new style. That was our issue immediately after election, when we used on page one a four-column picture layout of election scenes.

"Our left-hand double-column picture usually refers to an inside-the-paper story, generally a feature. That sends the reader inside to where the ads are, and the advertisers know it. They appreciate the new makeup, too."

In more recent issues the *Record* has occasionally presented in that high double column, in place of "Today's Headlines," brief items about coming events, under the head "Weekly Calendar," or items about fire alarms and arrests, under the head "From the Records."

East Orange Record

In Today's News

Today's Headlines

Today's Editorial

Welfare Federation Launches Campaign

Blood and Sinew

"We believe that no other single factor has done more toward building the Sears retail stores than the newspapers," says D. N. NELSON, merchandising vice-president of Sears, Roebuck & Company, who continues:

"Their generous consideration, their very concrete help were invaluable to us in creating a new instrument of distribution. We had something to sell and they, more than any other agency, provided us with a mass market place. Sears, Roebuck & Company is in their debt and knows it.

"I have always known that newspaper advertising was the backbone of our retail promotion, but not until now did I realize that it was the blood and sinew as well."

And MR. NELSON wasn't only saying it, either, for last year Sears, said to be the largest advertisers in the world, spent $11,261,763, or ninety-seven per cent of its advertising appropriation, in newspapers. Significantly, the Sears retail stores have weathered both the depression and recession with plenty to spare.

One Hundred Per Cent

"We studied the machine carefully before we installed our 'linoset,' about two years ago," states GEORGE WILLENS of Detroit in his house organ, *O. K.*, concerning his Forty-two-Pica Model 26.

"It has proved its worth 100 per cent," he continues. " 'Linoset' is a plain name for all the fancy things this device can do. It sets hand-set-quality type four to six times as fast; matches foundry type exactly; spaces down to 1/144 of an inch, which is even finer than a frog's hair; makes clean reproduction proofs; electrotypes perfectly; prints only once, then dies grandly in the melting pot!"

EXAMPLE 240

SHINING LINES

Edited by Thomas Dreier

Proposed Antidote for the "Isms"

Letters to the editors of *Colliers*, quoted in the February 18 issue, included this: "Our politicians and press are continually warning us against isms. I am a loyal American citizen, completely sold on the constitution and my country. I have a better than average job. I own my home, am married to the most intelligent and charming woman I ever met, am the father of three youngsters. My great desire is to perpetuate their happiness. But these isms scare me. The more I hear about them the more confused I become. What are these isms and what am I supposed to do about them? How many isms are there?"

All over the country thoughtful men and women are questioning the "isms" and wondering what's happened that strange philosophies and weird schemes should be getting so much attention in these United States.

Our diagnosticians classify these symptoms as a social afterphase of the World War. And our spiritual advisors tell us that these surges of emotion and mistrust will swing back and forth through the world until the calmer occupations of living reassert themselves.

Isn't the problem, then, how best to emphasize the homely affairs of daily life in our own communities? Here in New York, the nerve center of business palpitations, one wonders if leaders of business and finance might not well stop occasionally to appreciate the flow of life that goes on around them, regardless of the vagaries of the market.

Those obsessed with fear of the "isms" need a panorama of the every-day in America.

Coming down to work the other day, a traffic pause permitted a serene old mare to amble past my car window pulling the inevitable morning milk-wagon. But the streets were slippery and "Flossie Borden" had been safeguarded with equine galoshes to prevent her falling on the ice. In the summer she had worn rubber shoes, and her wagon, too, no longer rumbled and clacked over the pavements. It was equipped with pneumatic tires, and even the clatter of bottles had been reduced with insulated baskets. Perhaps you'll say that merely indicates the milk companies' business judgment in stopping morning assaults on city dwellers' sleep. But I like to feel, too, that the broader considerations of humane policy have given the lowly milk-wagon and its horse this modern share of creature comforts.

Then there's the story of Joe, aged seven, forced into the streets to sell papers when his father was killed and his mother bed-ridden. In a few weeks Joe had established himself at a corner, for the morning period before school. One day one of his new customers said: "Hello, son; what's your name?" Then, "Joe, is it? Well, mine's Jerry, and I hope business will be good with you today!"

The Joe and Jerry acquaintanceship grew apace, until the day when Jerry said, "Joe, have you folks a radio at home?" The gift of a simple set followed the query, and then Jerry said, "Now, Joe, you and the family listen carefully tomorrow evening at eight o'clock and you'll hear something interesting." Thus it developed that Joe's customer was Jerry Livingston, the song writer. The song he had written about Joe the newsboy became a hit. Jerry devoted its royalties to Joe's family and Joe's education. And if I were a "sob sister" I'd like to write the tale and point the moral.

I can't help feeling that such human occurrences are taking place constantly and it might be good for us all to hear more about them. Aren't the simplest emotions of every-day living the best antidote for the "isms"? Might it not be that more emphasis on the human side of life would help us find serenity to go ahead with our daily affairs? Forgetting the "isms," we might then buy the things we need from time to time—temperately but without fear. And if all America did that today, there would be no reception for the "isms."

J. T. MACKEY, President

There Are Great Editors In Every State

HARRIE B. COE, Maine's veteran publicity man who has done so much to popularize that state as a region for recreation, cites ARTHUR STAPLES, of the *Lewiston Journal* as one of his state's greatest assets.

ARTHUR STAPLES is to Maine what WILLIAM ALLEN WHITE is to Kansas. He's more than a mere person. He's an institution. His age is somewhere between seventy-five and eighty—but no one cares, least of all ARTHUR himself. Put him in a group for an all-night bull-session and not a man present will tell more stories or tell them better. He is "ARTHUR" to hundreds of men young enough to be his grandsons. It is the essential youthfulness of the man that appeals. Had he cared less for Maine and local affairs, a greater national reputation might be his. To sing Maine's praises (and to scold with a proper amount of indignation when discipline was required) has been his chief task.

ARTHUR STAPLES is one of the most lovable, most joyous, of men. He and the late HIRAM RICKER and HARRIE COE showed the country how it was possible to have lots of fun as leaders in state development work. Possibly every state has its own ARTHUR STAPLES. We'd like to have you tell us about the leading editorial personality in your state.

Seven "Musts" For Young Printers

There were about a hundred members of the Boston junior typographical union present at a meeting to hear a talk by C. A. MERRILL on "What a Superintendent Expects From an Apprentice." MR. MERRILL is superintendent of the printing department of the United Drug Company, and his hobby is helping boys develop into the right kind of men.

One rather astonishing statement made by him is that during the many years he has been in charge of the drug company's printing plant, not one of the many boys who have worked there ever "gave evidence of even a superficial understanding of the one tool he must use every day; namely, the English language. I have found an almost complete lack of knowledge of such books as he was supposed to study in high school—to say nothing concerning the broader field of general reading."

Here follows the list of qualities MR. MERRILL wants in his young helpers:

1. *I want loyalty*
2. *I want sustained interest*
3. *I want alertness*
4. *I want reliability*
5. *I want intelligence*
6. *I want effort*
7. *I want character*

The Rusty Folder That Never Worked

Years ago when he was a workman in a country printing plant, R. RANDOLPH KARCH was asked by the boss to stay and work Thursday night.

"The whole staff works Thursday nights," said the boss. "We've got to get the paper out." That meant most of them folded the paper by hand.

Seeing an old and rather rusty folder in one corner, MR. KARCH asked the manager why he didn't fix it up and fold the paper by macnine.

"Oh," he replied, "that folder never worked. It was busted when I came here, ten years ago."

Being practically friendless in a strange town, and having plenty of time, young KARCH asked the boss for permission to try his hand at fixing the folding machine. In a few weeks that folder was doing all the folding, just as its makers intended it to do.

"Now the moral of this story," writes MR. KARCH to us, "is that a poor punk operator who had never seen a folder before was able to fix it so it would do a creditable job. Any member of the force could have done a better job of it ten years before. They, too, were told that the folder 'never worked.' They believed it."

Young KARCH didn't. Perhaps that is why today he is head of the printing laboratory at the ROCHESTER ATHENÆUM.

The challenge of the machine is always before the alert executive.

Too Many Uncle Ezrys

Editors and advertising men would have much easier lives if there were not so many Uncle Ezrys at the heads of businesses. According to a story we picked up recently, old Uncle Ezry had been very much occupied all by himself over in a corner near the fireplace. He was working industriously with a stub of a pencil and a piece of paper. Suddenly he looked up happily.

"Doggone!" he exclaimed, "if I ain't learned to write."

Maw got up and looked over the scrawled lines across the paper.

"What do it say?" she asked.

"I don't know," replied Uncle Ezry, puzzled. "I ain't learned to read yit."

If copy could be released as written by men who know advertising and know how to write, without first being pawed over by Uncle Ezry executives whose skill lies in fields far from writing and editing, better advertisements might well result. We acknowledge in advance the applause of copy writers and contact executives.

More Than Eyes

Every newspaper editor, especially those who do their work in the smaller cities and towns, can appreciate the remark said to have been made by the movie director, William K. Howard, to a censor who had demanded that some important but innocuous scene be eliminated.

"Must you insist that we cut it?" asked Howard.

"Yes," answered the straight-laced critic. "After all, God gave me eyes."

"Yes, I know," said Howard, "but He also gave you eyelids."

We'd Like to Meet This Gas-Station Operator

There is a service station man who operates the Pureoil pumps at Mount Olive, a small town near Jackson, Miss., who actually knows the meaning of service. With men like him a world-conquering organization could be built. He was discovered for us by JOHN E. ALLEN, who ran across a press-bureau clipping from the *Jackson* (Miss.) *News* which told what happened to BOB BOWERS, one of our own southern representatives, who had stopped at Mount Olive to have his gas tank filled. Shortly after, he noticed that he was being frantically chased by the driver of a small car.

His first impulse was to step on the gas and make a getaway, believing it was a constable who wanted to nip him for speeding. However, he slowed down with a fervent hope in his heart that if it was a constable he would at least be reasonable.

The pursuer drew alongside, disembarked and said: "Friend, I sure had a race to overtake you. I had to find my son to take care of the station before I could start after you. Here's the cap off your gasoline tank and I'm sorry I overlooked it. I notice you have a Florida license on your car and I might never see you again, but, anyhow, I hate for anything to be wrong with my service."

Giants With Mysterious Forces

Speaking to the graduating class of CARNEGIE INSTITUTE OF TECHNOLOGY, the veteran Kansas editor WILLIAM ALLEN WHITE said: "The only hope for a better world is to make better people to live in it. Laws won't do it. Human nature changes only when the pressure of greeds is lifted, and men generally can afford to be neighborly and decent in their relations with one another without seeing their families suffer. We have made this a good world only in so far as we have made it possible for great masses of kindly, friendly individuals, good people, polite, courteous, thoughtfully generous people easily and comfortably to survive. That may be put down to the credit of these new giants which have come to live with man, giants motived with steam, electricity, and with the mysterious forces witched out of the ether about the earth."

A Crusader For More Libraries

By Harry L. Gage

M. M. HARRIS, editor of the *San Antonio* (Texas) *Express*, has exemplified for many years an ideal part to be played by leading journalists. MR. HARRIS is a virile crusader for more libraries in Texas, for the extension of library services to the rural sections of his state, and for state and federal support of libraries. His journalistic and publicity instincts have helped so well in this library movement that Texas has made substantial progress in providing books and reading for her citizens.

A prominent educator has said, "The prime object of education is to lead a boy or girl to the point at which he or she will not be afraid to be alone in a room with a book." And a great philosopher said, "Above all things else a child should be tumbled about in a library. All men are afraid of books who have not handled them from infancy." So we look to modern education to develop habits of reading in our young people—and to libraries to provide them with convenient services in books. For adult education, for the diverse masses of men and women in many parts of the world who are becoming newly conscious of themselves and the surrounding country, libraries are the vital center of development.

Says Lin Yutang in his *Importance of Living:* "The man who has not the habit of reading is imprisoned in his immediate world, in respect to time and space. His life falls into a set routine; he is limited to contact and conversation with a few friends and acquaintances, and he sees only what happens in his immediate neighborhood. From this prison there is no escape. But the moment he takes up a book, he immediately enters a different world, and if it is a good book, he is immediately put in touch with one of the best talkers in the world."

By Accident!

After working on an idea for some device for sixty years, and having made more than 300 models, a New England man sold his invention for a big fortune.

"Many times I was disheartened and was about to smash my models and give up," he said, "but when I thought that if I kept on trying I had a chance to win, while if I quit I had no chance at all, at last by accident I hit upon the secret."

EXAMPLE 241

The Linotype News

VOLUME XVII | BROOKLYN, MAY, 1939 | NUMBER SIX

Linotype Users Win All Honors In Ayer's Ninth Annual Contest

La Prensa Adds 3 Blue Streaks, Changes Dress

Big Buenos Aires Paper Now Using Modern Heads And Linotype Excelsior

BUENOS AIRES.—La Prensa of this city, one of the largest and most influential newspapers in the world, has added three Blue Streak Linotypes and 110 fonts of matrices, and is now appearing in a new type dress that is winning much praise from advertisers and readers.

Most of the heads in La Prensa are being given a modern flush-left treatment that saves time and money in the editorial department and in the composing room, and results in a much more attractive and legible paper.

Body matter is in various sizes of Linotype Excelsior.

Heads Scientifically Planned

The new head schedule has been scientifically planned. All heads on any one page have a definite and harmonious relationship to all other heads on the page, and nearly all of the heads throughout La Prensa are in capitals and lower-case, which are much easier to read than lines set entirely in capitals.

On the general-news pages, the heads are in members of the Erbar and Metro families, but on certain feature pages the heads are in members of the Memphis family.

Body Matter in Excelsior

Most of the news body matter is in 7-point Excelsior with Memphis Bold. Editorials are in 7½-point Excelsior. Classified advertising is in 5½-point Excelsior. Some of the provincial news is in 6-point Excelsior.

The Linotypes recently installed by La Prensa are two Two-in-One Blue Streak Model 31s and a Two-in-One Blue Streak Model 32. The paper now operates thirty-one Linotypes.

Sr. Ezequiel P. Paz is director-proprietor of La Prensa, and Dr. Alberto Gainza Paz is co-director.

Greenwich Journal Puts in Master Model 32

GREENWICH, N. Y.—A Master Model 32 has been installed by the Journal here.

Grant J. Tefft is editor and publisher of the paper. Raymond Robinson is foreman of the composing room, and Edward A. Barrie is machinist-operator.

ON THE INSIDE

A. N. P. A. Pictures	Page 2
Dream Plant	3
Commercial Printing	4
Legibility Group	4
Model 33 Linotype	5
Editorials	6
Newspaper Makeup	6
Shining Lines	7
Two World's Fairs	8
Books and Bookmakers	10
Easy-Grip	10
Recent Installations	10
Hints to Operators	11
Poster Bodoni Compressed	11
New Typo Developments	12
Flemco Rolls	14
Linotype Aids	15

A. N. P. A.

James G. Stahlman, publisher of the Nashville Banner and retiring president of the A. N. P. A., with John S. McCarrens, vice-president and general manager of the Cleveland Plain Dealer, the new president of the A. N. P. A. (See page two for many convention pictures)

Baltimore Firm Installs Five 31s

BALTIMORE.—Five Blue Streak Master Model 31s have been installed by the Monumental Printing Company of this city.

This well - known publication, book and commercial-printing plant occupies its own building, and all of its departments are modernly equipped.

J. H. Ferguson is president and general manager of the company, and his son John Ferguson, III, is vice-president. Miss M. McLaughlin is secretary-treasurer.

Theodore R. Brown is mechanical superintendent, and Joseph H. Yoash is machinist-operator.

Monitor Now Using Linotype Excelsior

BOSTON.—The Christian Science Monitor, which, with body matter in Linotype Ionic, won an honorable mention in the latest Ayer contest for typographic excellence, is now setting its news body matter in 7½-point Linotype Excelsior on an 8½-point body. Editorial body matter is set in 10-point Excelsior on an 11-point body, and markets are set in 6-point Excelsior on a 7-point body.

Before the new face was selected, the Monitor made test after test of available faces. Many different pages were made up and studied. And the visibility meter designed by Dr. Matthew Luckiesh and Frank Moss was brought into play.

The result was, as previously stated, the selection of Linotype Excelsior.

Composition Service Installs Master Model 31

Composition Service, Inc., New York City, has added a Master Model 31.

George K. Sackett is president and treasurer of this modern advertising-composition plant, and Roscoe Bishop is secretary. Composition Service, Inc., is well known for its quality work.

Toronto Star Adopts Linotype Opticon

TORONTO.—Eight fonts of 7½-point Linotype Opticon have been installed by the Star of this city.

The new face, which is being cast on a 9-point body, is being used for body matter in the Star Weekly.

A.N.P.A. Elects J.S. McCarrens And W.M. Dear

Chandler Is Treasurer; Parks Named Secretary; A. P. Re-elects McLean

John S. McCarrens, vice-president and general manager of the Cleveland Plain Dealer, is the new president of the American Newspaper Publishers' Association, so elected at the fifty-third annual convention of the association, in New York City, in April. Mr. McCarrens succeeds James G. Stahlman, publisher of the Nashville Banner.

Walter M. Dear, publisher and general manager of the Jersey City Jersey Journal and formerly treasurer of the A. N. P. A., is vice-president; William G. Chandler, general business manager of the Scripps-Howard papers, treasurer, and John S. Parks, publisher of the Fort Smith (Ark.) Southwest-American, secretary. Mr. Chandler and Mr. Parks were formerly directors.

A. P. Re-elects McLean

Robert R. McLean of the Philadelphia Bulletin was re-elected president of the Associated Press at that group's fortieth annual convention, held the week of the A. N. P. A. convention, in New York City.

E. Lansing Ray of the St. Louis Globe-Democrat was elected first vice-president of the Associated Press, and Stuart H. Perry of the Adrian (Mich.) Telegram, second vice-president. Kent Cooper was re-elected secretary; Lloyd Stratton, assistant secretary, and L. F. Curtis treasurer.

New members of the A. N. P. A. board, elected to two-year terms, are: Jerome D. Barnum, publisher of the Syracuse Post-Standard; Norman Chandler, publisher of the Los Angeles Times; David W. Howe, business manager of the Burlington (Vt.) Free Press; F. I. Ker, publisher of the Hamilton (Ont.) Spectator, and W. E. Macfarlane, vice-president of the Chicago Tribune. Howard Davis, business manager of the New York Herald Tribune, was elected director for a year.

Cranston Williams G. M.

Cranston Williams, for several years secretary-manager of the Southern Newspaper Publishers' Association, has been elected general manager of the A. N. P. A., to succeed Lincoln B. Palmer, on July 1. Mr. Palmer, who for the last thirty-four years served as general manager of the association, resigned recently following a long illness.

The six A. P. directors whose terms had expired were re-elected. They are: W. H. Cowles, Spokane Spokesman-Review; E. Lansing Ray; Col. Robert R. McCormick, Chicago Tribune; George B. Longan, Kansas City Star; L. K. Nicholson, New Orleans Times-Picayune, and Stuart H. Perry.

The Linotype News Entirely Linotype Set

All lines of composition in this issue of The Linotype News, as usual, were composed the Linotype way, even the biggest heads and the largest lines in display advertisements.

Most of the body matter is 7½-point Excelsior on a 9-point body, with some of the lines extra leaded, and most of the heads are in the Linotype Bodoni family.

See "Makeup of This Issue," on page six.

N. Y. Herald Tribune Captures Cup; N. Y. Times, Hartford Courant, Concord Monitor, N. Y. Daily News Attract First Honorable Mentions

All eleven of the winning newspapers in the latest Ayer contest for typographic excellehce are Linotype users, nine are composed chiefly in Linotype faces, and seven present their body matter in members of the Linotype Legibility Group.

In the nine typographic contests conducted by the Ayer organization, seventy-eight awards have been made. Seventy of these have been won by Linotype users, and fifty-seven of the winners have presented their body matter in members of the Linotype Legibility Group.

The cup winner in the latest contest is the New York Herald Tribune, with most of its heads in capitals and lower-case of Bodoni Bold and Bodoni Bold Italic, and with body matter in Linotype Ionic. The Herald Tribune operates seventy-five keyboard Linotypes, and an All-Purpose Linotype for large display.

Ten Honorable Mentions

In the group of papers with more than 50,000 daily circulation (121 entered), first honorable mention was won by the New York Times (thirty-three Linotypes); second, the Pittsburgh Press (forty-three Linotypes, Ionic); third, the Christian Science Monitor (thirty-one Linotypes, Ionic). The Monitor since has replaced its Ionic with Linotype Excelsior.

In the group with from 10,000 to 50,000 daily circulation (342 entered), first honorable mention was won by the Hartford Courant (twelve Linotypes, Ionic); second, the Chattanooga Daily Times (sixteen Linotypes, Ionic); third, the Bridgeport Telegram (sixteen Linotypes).

In the group with less than 10,000 daily circulation (834 entered), first honorable mention was won by the Concord (N. H.) Daily Monitor (seven Linotypes, Excelsior); second, the Hornell (N. Y.) Evening Tribune (five Linotypes, Ionic); third, the Meadville (Pa.) Tribune-Republican (seven Linotypes).

In the tabloid group (thirty-one entered), honorable mention was

(Continued on last page)

Seven Linos For Meio Dia

New Newspaper in Rio Using Bodoni and Ionic, And A-P-L for Big Heads

RIO DE JANEIRO.—Seven new Linotypes—five Model 8s, a Model 14 and an A-P-L—have been installed by a new newspaper here, Meio Dia.

The new journal, composed almost entirely the Linotype way, is presenting most of its heads in members of the Bodoni family. Body matter is in Linotype Ionic.

Dr. Joaquim Inojosa is director-owner of the paper; Dr. Lincoln Nery, managing director, and Dr. Mario de Henrique Trindade, director-secretary.

Buffalo Craftsmen To Entertain in May

BUFFALO.—Printing House Craftsmen of the Niagara District Conference will be the guests of the Buffalo club when the conference meets here Friday and Saturday, May 26 and 27, at the Statler.

Friday evening the Buffalo club will hold open house. Saturday morning will be taken up with a business session; afternoon, with clinic sessions, and evening, with a dinner-dance.

Richard H. Templeton, Jr., is general conference chairman, and Thomas L. Holling is honorary chairman.

A. N. P. A. Conference In Philadelphia June 5-7

PHILADELPHIA.—The thirteenth annual Mechanical Conference of the American Newspaper Publishers' Association will be held at the Benjamin Franklin Hotel here June 5 to 7.

Nine business associates felicitate W. V. Cowgill, mechanical superintendent of the Cleveland News, on his latest birthday. Seated, left to right, are L. R. Tracht, night foreman of the composing room; Mr. Cowgill, and Blanchard Wilson, stereotyping super. Standing, left to right, are W. J. Morrison, pressroom super; E. C. Bowles, day composing-room foreman; A. S. Ihlenfield, chief engineer; Frank Kreutz; C. L. Buttermore, composing-room super; O. J. Lange, engraving super, and C. L. Fanta, night engraving foreman

EXAMPLE 242

The Linotype News

Published regularly in the interests of the many thousands of Linotype owners and those who work with the Linotype or its product.

Correspondence is invited. Specimens of Linotype composition, as well as brief accounts of experiences on or about the Linotype, are gladly received. News items are welcomed.

Address communications to the EDITOR OF THE LINOTYPE NEWS, 29 Ryerson Street, Brooklyn, N. Y.

PRINTED DIRECT FROM LINOTYPE SLUGS

JOHN E. ALLEN, *Editor*

Watch Out for Them

Many times we have urged our readers to be careful about whom they employ to service their Linotypes, but we still occasionally hear from or of printers and publishers who have been victimized by unqualified machinists.

The latest story of this sort to come to us has to do with a man who has been going from plant to plant in New England selling sets of screw drivers that he states are made by the MERGENTHALER LINOTYPE COMPANY. He also states that he himself represents this company. Both of his statements are untrue.

So again we say:

There are several machinists traveling throughout the country, who, it is alleged, state either directly or indirectly that they are employed by the Linotype Company, and on the strength of this representation seek employment for the repairing or rebuilding of Linotypes.

Instances have been cited where these travelers have introduced themselves as "I am a Linotype man," thereby implying, or at least creating the impression, that they are in our employ.

In justice to hundreds of honest and capable Linotype machinists throughout the country whose services are available in emergencies, we feel that it is only fair again to warn Linotype users against employing persons unknown to them for the purpose of rebuilding or repairing their Linotypes.

Makeup of This Issue

All composition in this issue of THE LINOTYPE NEWS was produced the Linotype way—all news and feature heads, as well as the largest lines in advertisements. The larger lines were cast on the All-Purpose Linotype.

Most of the single-column body lines are in 7½-point Excelsior on a 9-point body, with some of the lines extra leaded. Double-column body lines on the center spread are in 12-point Excelsior on a 14-point body. The body matter of the panel on page seven is in 14-point Excelsior leaded two points. Some of the body matter on pages ten and eleven is in 7-point Excelsior No. 2 on an 8-point body, and brief items under state and sectional heads are in 6-point Excelsior on a 7-point body. Body matter on pages six and seven is in 9-point Excelsior on an 11-point body. Most of the heads on page six are in 18-point Bodoni Bold Italic, and most of the heads on page seven are in 12-point Poster Bodoni.

The main head on the front page has a first deck in 42-point Poster Bodoni and a second deck in 14-point Poster Bodoni.

The full-width head on page two is in 30-point Poster Bodoni Italic, and so is the three-column head on page three.

The main head on the center spread has a first deck in 36-point Poster Bodoni and second decks in 14-point Poster Bodoni. Cut overlines on the spread are in 24-point Poster Bodoni, and on other pages are in 14-point Poster Bodoni Italic. Cut legends are in 8- or 9-point Bookman.

Most of the two-column heads are in 18-point Poster Bodoni Italic.

Main single-column heads are in 30-point Bodoni Bold Condensed and 12-point Bodoni Bold.

Other single-column news heads are in 24- or 18-point Bodoni Bold Condensed or 18-point Bodoni Bold Italic.

Subheads are in 10-point Bodoni Bold, as also are the body lines of the front-page index.

State and sectional heads are in 18-point Poster Bodoni Italic.

Running heads are in 12-point Bodoni Bold.

Some of the department heads feature various sizes of the new Poster Bodoni Compressed.

Advertisements carry their own descriptions.

Five Generations

Into the sanctum of THE LINOTYPE NEWS, not long ago, came a young man who had just completed a course in journalism and who represents the fifth generation of a family of printers and newspaper people. The young man is A. VINCENT HARCOURT, JR., and he had with him a picture of the composing-room staff of the *Baltimore American* taken December 20, 1894. Among the men in the picture were his grandfather and his great-grandfather, along with the late BILLY STUBBS, a former "swift" at the keyboard and for many years, until his death, a MERGENTHALER representative. We wanted to run the picture, but knew that it was too faded to reproduce well.

Young HARCOURT'S great-great-grandfather, CAPT. WILLIAM HARCOURT, sailed under Commodore Perry on an expedition to Japan in 1852. In 1856 he worked in the composing and editorial rooms of the old *Baltimore Clipper and Argus*. Under Admiral Farragut he took part in the surrender of Mobile, and later was given command of the *Narcissus*, in recognition of his work at Mobile.

WILLIAM MANSFIELD HARCOURT, our young visitor's great-grandfather, was a proofreader with the *Baltimore American* about twenty years, and later worked on the *Baltimore Sun* as head proofreader many years.

ALBERT V. HARCOURT, the young man's grandfather, was one of the first compositors to learn the Linotype, and ran one of the first that was installed by the *Baltimore American*. In 1904, during the big fire in Baltimore that destroyed the business section and many of the newspaper plants, he worked on the *Baltimore Herald*. The Linotypes were running and the slugs were being carried out to be made up in another plant, even while firemen were placing dynamite throughout the building, preparatory to wrecking it, in the hope of stopping the fire.

A. VINCENT HARCOURT, our young visitor's father, also was a compositor, but for ten years has been typographic adviser with C. J. O'BRIEN, INC., New York City.

Neck and Ears

One morning sixty-eight years ago, thirteen-year-old J. HARRY DRECHSLER of Baltimore gave his neck and ears an extra-good scrubbing—or his mother did it for him—so he's been a printer ever since.

He's eighty-one now, and runs his own print shop, on Water Street in Baltimore. He's been deaf forty-five years, but says that being deaf is lots of fun, and that life begins at eighty. "They say the first 150 years are the hardest, so I only have sixty-nine to go until things ease up."

Sixty-eight years ago forty boys answered an ad in the *Baltimore Sun*. The ad had been placed by the DAUGHERTY, MAGUIRE & WRIGHT PRINTING COMPANY, for a printer's devil.

PAT MAGUIRE, one of the bosses, arranged the boys in a circle and gave each a good looking-over from the rear.

Presently he put his hand on the shoulder of J. HARRY DRECHSLER, the smallest of the lot, whose knees were shaking.

"You get the job," announced the boss. "You get it because you are the one boy here who has washed his neck and ears."

Makes Quite a Hit

"The new format of THE LINOTYPE NEWS," writes CHARLES FREDERICKSON, mechanical superintendent with WESTCHESTER COUNTY PUBLISHERS, INC., Yonkers, "makes quite a hit in all the plants."

NEWSPAPER MAKEUP

By JOHN E. ALLEN

No. 67—The Modern Newspaper

The *Brundidge* (Ala.) *Sentinel* is using on its front page the sort of high double column advocated by this department, and DEPEW MEREDITH, editor and publisher of the *Sentinel*, says: "I'm thoroughly sold on the new front page, and my readers and advertisers are pleased. No editor could ask for more than this."

MR. MEREDITH says that, before adopting the new plan, he had "tried everything" to capture the enthusiasm of readers. "Sensational front-page editorials got little response, and heavy use of pictures received little comment."

He decided to try one more experiment. If readers weren't favorably impressed with the double-column idea, it was to be abandoned after its second appearance.

"To my surprise," he says, "the new format received immediate commendation!

"Within two hours after the paper was in the mail, I had been stopped on the street at least ten times, and each person told me how good the issue was. There has been a steady stream of favorable comment since.

"The new plan gives me a chance to sum up the news of the world in a breezy, readable style. It allows me to use short, pithy comment on local happenings; short stories that would have had to be padded to make a regular length news story. And it greatly simplifies the front-page makeup.

"After adopting the new plan, I found that local stories were becoming more numerous, because we could use short items that, in the old-style sheet, had been used merely as fillers.

"We are now giving our readers a resume of state, national and international news, which we did not carry before. And this has simply replaced a batch of state department publicity that we used to set to make up for a lack of news in a town with a population less than 1,500.

"My makeup was patterned after a paper shown in your department in THE LINOTYPE NEWS, and I owe you a debt of gratitude.

"My readers are not familiar with the technicalities of makeup, but they know when they are pleased—and so do I."

Clever House Organ

Question: When is a house organ a galley proof? Answer: When it's as cleverly done, in text and typography, as *Ryder's Digest*, introduced last November by FREDERIC RYDER COMPANY, Chicago.

Bright copy appealingly dressed in several Linotype faces does an excellent job of acquainting RYDER clients with the excellence of the organization both in service facilities and equipment. And the format of *Ryder's Digest* is simple and inexpensive!

Praises Lino Service

"I want to compliment you for the finest service I have ever received from any company, barring none," writes ROBERT A. CONEVERY, business manager of the *Wellsboro* (Pa.) *Gazette*. "Yesterday afternoon at five-thirty the writer telephoned to your order department, in regard to heating units for our electric pot, and this morning at ten we had them in our office. After such consideration by your company for a backwoods publisher, I feel just as important as the big-city publisher. Thank you all."

EXAMPLE 243

THE LINOTYPE NEWS, MAY, 1939 7

EDITED BY THOMAS DREIER

SHINING LINES

The Whole Thing Is Ahead of Us

Month after month, with variations, we have been telling you that the supply of materials for the filling of all the needs of the world for generations yet unborn is limitless. Let a great need arise and, suddenly, there is a great supply. If we can't get one kind of thing, we get something just as good.

CHARLES F. KETTERING, the inventive genius of General Motors, knows that we need never worry over lack of a supply of what is needed. Natural resources are never exhausted. One particular thing may go, but before it goes something better has been discovered to take its place. There will always be plenty of work and plenty of materials for millions of men and women.

As an example of the KETTERING optimism based on scientific facts, let us tell you of the conversation with some of his engineering friends who wondered what could be done when the sources of gasoline were exhausted. We found this in a *New York World-Telegram* editorial:

"What is gasoline?" MR. KETTERING asked them. The reply was, "Petroleum."

"Well, what is petroleum?" "The product of decaying vegetable matter."

"How was the vegetable matter produced?" "By the growth of plants."

"What made the plants grow?" "The rays of the sun."

"And there," said the scientist, "you have it. We run our automobiles now by the stored-up radiant heat of the sun. All we need is to take out a few steps here and there to run them by ray-transmitted power direct. I haven't the slightest idea what we are going to do when the supply of oil runs out, but we are going to do something long before it runs out.

"If we scientists and industrialists could get out of our minds the idea that we know very much about anything, and realize that the whole thing is ahead of us, then, I think, we would have a shortage of labor in a brief time."

Perhaps Frustration Is Good Fortune

If it be true that there is good fortune in frustration, as the REV. RALPH SOCKMAN reminded us recently, executives in charge of big businesses are beloved of the gods. In golf the skilled player likes a course with sand traps, water holes, bunkers, valleys, side hills — all the things that enable him to show how well he can play the game. A level lawn acres in extent makes no appeal to him. But even the most skilled golfer likes more fairway than frustrating traps, *et cetera.*

During the last few years, the business executive has had comparatively little fairway on which to play. Those executives have succeeded who have maintained their sense of humor, their sense of proportion, and haven't lost their tempers.

In business, as in golf, to lose one's temper is to play the part of a damned fool. Let us keep thinking that the frustrations inflicted upon us are merely tests of our skill. We must find comfort in something.

They Gave the Answers

We who are puzzled by the answers given by the wise men of the ages to the perplexing questions about the meaning of life will not be less ignorant when we learn the answers given by the birds and beasts in ROBERT CLAIRMONT'S poem—but we may be ever so much more ready to laugh:

"When did the world begin, and how?"
I asked a lamb, a goat, a cow.

"What's it all about, and why?"
I asked a hog as he went by.

"Where will the whole thing end, and when?"
I asked a duck, a goose, a hen.

And I copied all the answers, too—
A quack, a honk, an oink, a moo.

A Man With a Hard Face

A salesman was describing a man to whom he had tried to make a sale. He described his hardness. "That fellow reminded me of Mr. Bodiham," said the salesman. "Mr. Bodiham is the rector in *Chrome Yellow*, by ALDOUS HUXLEY. He also had 'a grey metallic face with iron cheek-bones and a narrow iron brow; iron folds, hard and unchanging, ran perpendicularly down his cheeks; his nose was the iron beak of some thin, delicate bird of rapine. He had brown eyes, set in sockets rimmed with iron; round them the skin was dark, as though it had been charred. Dense wiry hair covered his skull; it had been black, it was turning grey. . . . His voice, when he spoke . . . was harsh; like the grating of iron hinges when a seldom-used door is opened.'"

Young Printing Executives

Every city in the country should have a Young Printing Executives' Club. This does not mean that the youngsters should not associate with the oldsters in other organizations. It simply means that the youngsters should get together for the discussion of their own problems and to help one another get the education they need to fit themselves for the responsibilities they must shoulder when they become more ancient. Let them get together and talk heatedly in discussions of problems of production, selling and management—especially the latter. The lone young executive often has a hard time of it. If he can associate regularly with others who have similar problems, he'll find his work easier and he'll do it better.

If They Expect—

Years ago an old salt who made his living by fishing told me, when I asked him why he was ashore mending his gear, "Young feller, them as can't fish while there's storms out there had better spend their time a-mendin' their nets if they expect to be all set when the blow's over 'nd the fish start runnin' agin."

He would have been a darn good business man in whatever line he followed.

J. T. MACKEY, *President*

Business Finds Its Voice

There's a new book on management's effort to sell the business idea to the public. It is by S. H. WALKER and PAUL SKLAR and is called "Business Finds Its Voice." Here is an objective account of the ways in which business organizations are interpreting their policies and activities to the public. HARPER & BROTHERS is the publisher. The book is written as a report—as a statement of current fact. It tells in more or less detail just what big and little organizations are doing in public-relations work, what they are spending, and just what reasons they have for making the effort. "Business Finds Its Voice" should be read and studied by every business executive.

When You Want Something From an Editor

When you want to get something from an editor, the easiest and best way to get it is to give something to the editor. MARK SULLIVAN achieved success as a young reporter and magazine writer because his way was not to ask an editor for anything, but to present him with something.

"My way," he writes in his autobiography, "was to study a paper until I knew what the editor wanted as well as he knew himself; then to suggest a topic that was within the editor's general field, but new; one that would not occur to the editor, but which would interest him when brought to his attention."

That formula may be useful to some of you young fellows who are trying to get ahead.

Men judge our quality by the quality of our associates. Eagles fly only with eagles. Sheep flock together. Pigs grunt together in the sty.

His associates were talking about him. One said, "He would make an uncommonly fine sour apple if he had happened to be born in that station in life."

A Comradely Library

The spirit of a library, like the spirit of any other institution from a home to a cathedral, is quite likely to be that of its chief executive. The late JOHN COTTON DANA, famous as the head of the Newark, N. J., library, wanted books to be a creative influence in his community. He thought of them as tools. He showed people how to make use of the ideas they contained.

LUCY STONE TERRILL, the brilliant short-story writer, believes that one of the most universally enjoyed diversions in any community is a cheerful library. She says even young people love a library and often prefer it to a public dance hall.

"A comradely library," she says, "with wise attendants, does more in a social way to combat human loneliness than any other institution. Without such an institution, the cultural life of a community is weak and stifled. Any city is benefited and benefits people when it provides an adequate, hospitable library building."

Free to Follow Folly As Well as Wisdom

By William Allen White

No architect, indeed no school of architecture, can draw the blueprint of human progress by which future men may work—even tomorrow. Yet man keeps on building. His unchecked greeds slow him down. But he never stops. He blunders toward the truth which is his light and leading. But to find the truth he must be free—free to follow folly as well as wisdom, until he knows which is which. Without truth, men can never find freedom. And in the binding rancor of chains, cramping economic chains or galling political chains, we can never be wise. We shall draw nearer to the brave new world only when economic liberty to be kind so unshackles the common man that he may walk upright in self-respect toward the vision of justice in his heart.

He Feels a Bit Apprehensive

After reading some of our editorials counselling some of the old folks to get out of the way and give the youngsters a chance, ALLAN K. DALBEY of the *Fallon* (Nev.) *Eagle*, is a bit apprehensive. He thinks we may be looking obliquely at him. But shucks, he's only a youngster. He's not yet fifty. A mere child, that's what he is. When he acquires our paunch, our bald head and our long white whiskers, then he can weep over his lost youth.

However, we'll be serious long enough to say that we are not at all interested in promoting the idea "that the man past forty is practically useless." We have sense enough to know that if men of forty and over were removed from their jobs, the industrial machinery of the world would come to an abrupt stop for a time. Then, when it started again, it would wobble terribly. Men over forty have experience. They have learned what judgment is. They also know the value of brakes.

MR. DALBEY needn't fret. Capable men of his age and much more advanced ages need not worry. The incompetent oldsters are the ones we are blowing peas against. Also those oldsters with plenty of money who are financially powerful but who are holding back the growth of their businesses by not giving control to younger men—men, let us say, in the forties and fifties.

May Polly Syllable's Tribe Increase

So many suggestions for the improvement of the printing business are duds. No one ever seems to get what may be called the true answer to the question: "How may the volume of printing be increased?"

A modest, shrinking, hermit-like printer by the name of ALBERT MURRAY, whose black-magic shop is in Cambridge, Mass., has the perfect solution. The trouble with the printing business is that there are too many short words used by writers.

"As printers," writes ALBERT, in his house organ, "we are in favor of writers who use long words. Polysyllables are the life of trade. Long titles, too, meet with our approval, our favorite being 'The Cambridge General Kosciusko Sesquicentennial Commission'—a hard name to write on a check, but an ideal one for using up type, ink and vast stretches of clean white paper."

Having said that, he sort of puts the skids under his own suggestion by adding that as a private citizen the more skeptical he becomes of drives, programs, campaigns or causes whose purpose cannot be stated in words of one syllable, or at least in words that make sense when one looks at them closely.

Gosh! Here we are right outside the door by which we entered.

So They Fly To Save Time, Do They?

Looking noble and serene, their faces washed and shining, both HARRY GAGE and WALTER PATTERSON return from trips and stride into their offices with brisk steps. They tell about flying hither and yon, doing so merely because of their love for their work and their devotion to duty. They wouldn't waste a single precious moment of the company's time! Oh, no! They've read the ALGER books. But they've also read other things. HARRY copied this tribute to the stewardess, pencilled in the guest book on one of the United Airline's planes:

The C. & O. has "Chessy,"
The Greyhound has its dogs,
The Pennsy has its lowers,
The Highway has its hogs.

Each route has its advantages,
Each has its drawbacks, too,
But I'll trade them to United
For one-third of its crew!

Says PATTERSON to TOM DREIER in rebuttal—

Mark Twain wrote much of his copy
While lolling around in his bed,
Now TOM confirms my suspicions
That we are 'way over his head.

EXAMPLE 244

Note that, while the first line of the banner was full five columns wide, the second line was held in to three columns, so that the story at the upper left could be featured high on the page.

September 28, 1939, the *Bay Ridge Record,* a New York City community tabloid, appeared with a front page like the upper half of an eight-column front page, but with all of its other pages tabloid.

J. Dee Sewell, associate editor of the *Record,* was quoted in *Editor & Publisher* of October 7, 1939, as saying of the new makeup: "We tried it out because it gives us the possibilities of news display of a standard-size paper, yet the inside pages have the readability of a tabloid."

In September, 1939, when a major war broke out in Europe and much of our alleged news from the warring countries was tinged with or steeped in propaganda, the *Los Angeles Evening News* and the *Los Angeles Daily News,* both tabloids, adopted a method of evaluating war news for readers.

At first those papers placed in parentheses at the ends of war stories key letters such as P, for propaganda; V, for verified; R, for rumor; SA for seems authentic, and OP, for official propaganda.

Soon, however, those papers abandoned the key letters in favor of more readily comprehended statements, usually presented in small bold-face lines just below the heads of stories—statements such as "Official propaganda," "Seems authentic," "Rumor," "Speculative," "Verified," "Unverified," and "Partially propaganda."

Some of those key statements were given comparatively large display by being presented within line-cuts of drawings of keys of the sort used for many locks.

The January-March, 1940, number of the *Linotype News* was a highly departmentalized number, with many stories on the same general subjects grouped under department heads.

All of the heads in that number were in modern sans-serif faces—attractive faces that afforded plenty of contrast but that got along together harmoniously.

Most of the department heads were in Metromedium No. 2, and subordinate heads were in various members of the Erbar, Metro and

The Linotype News

VOLUME XVIII — BROOKLYN, SEPTEMBER, 1939 — NUMBER TWO

New Linotype Developments Will Be Introduced At Exposition of Graphic Arts

The Indianapolis News Installs Ten More Blue Streak Linos

Having a look at one of the new Blue Streaks in the News lobby

INDIANAPOLIS.—The News of this city, which, earlier in the year, installed two Model 30 Linotypes, has added ten more Blue Streaks.

One of the new machines was temporarily installed near a large window in the lobby of the News building and operated there several days, to let the thousands of passersby know about the installation. A poster on the window presented these statements: "Mergenthaler Blue Streak Linotype Machine—one of ten new machines being installed in the composing room of the Indianapolis News. These machines set most of the reading matter for each daily issue."

In the accompanying picture, William Smith of the News composing room is shown operating the Linotype in the lobby, with, behind him, Charles Jones, old-timer with the News, who has been working on Linotypes since 1888. Looking on from the outside are some of the many Indianapolis citizens who paused to watch the new Blue Streak in operation.

Frederick C. Fairbanks is president of the News Publishing Company. William H. Williams is mechanical superintendent; Frank Butsch, composing-room foreman, and Maurice Geckler, head Linotype machinist.

Des Moines Register Adds Blue Streaks

DES MOINES.—Two new Blue Streak Linotypes, a Model 30 and a Model 8, and several fonts of matrices have been added by the job department of the Register and Tribune here. Both machines have self-quadders.

The Linotype News Entirely Lino Set

All lines of composition in this issue of The Linotype News, as usual, were composed the Linotype way, even the biggest heads and the largest lines in display advertisements.

See "Makeup of This Issue," on page six.

Argentina Company Adds 14 Linotypes

Publisher of Critica, B. A., Head of Group of Papers, Modernizing His Plants

BUENOS AIRES.—Fourteen Blue Streak Master Model Linotypes—thirteen Model 31s and a Model 32—have been purchased by Natalio Botana, owner and publisher of Critica here, and head of a newspaper group in Argentina

Mr. Botana's modernization program is in line with similar programs being followed by other papers here.

The famous La Prensa of this city recently added three Master Models, 128 fonts of matrices, and modernized its make-up. That paper is now appearing with flush-left heads in members of the Erbar, Metro and Memphis families.

La Razon has installed several new Linotypes, including a Blue Streak Model 33 and an All-Purpose Linotype, and has modernized its format. Practically all lines in that paper are now being produced from Linotype slugs.

77 Fonts of Ionic For Melbourne Age

MELBOURNE, Australia.—Seventy-seven fonts of Linotype Ionic No. 5 with Bold Face No. 2 have been ordered by the Age of this city for a new body dress.

Thirty-nine of the fonts are 7-point Ionic No. 5, for the news columns, and thirty-seven of the fonts are 5-point Ionic No. 5, for classified advertising and other uses. Included in the installation was a font of 8-point Ionic No. 5, for the news columns,

The Age operates thirty-two Linotypes.

Big Overseas Paper Installs 29 Linotypes

The Sunday Chronicle Is Using New Machines In Its Plant in London

MANCHESTER, England.—Twenty-nine more Linotypes have been added by the Sunday Chronicle and Sunday Referee, which is now being published both here and in London. The new machines are on duty in the paper's London plant.

Lord Kemsley, who owns the Sunday Chronicle and Sunday Referee, publishes papers in many parts of the country, particularly in the midlands and the north. The Kemsley group operates more than 300 Linotypes.

Industry to Observe Birthday of Printing

The year 1940 will be the five hundredth anniversary year of the invention of printing.

Aided by a grant from the Carnegie Corporation of New York, the American Institute of Graphic Arts has appointed a committee to coordinate a nation-wide celebration on the part of libraries, schools, newspaper, book and magazine publishers, and similar groups throughout the United States.

The chairman of the committee is Frederic G. Melcher of the R. R. Bowker Company; Elmer Adler, Pynson Printers, Inc.; John Archer, New York Public Library; Paul A. Bennett, Mergenthaler Linotype Company; George H. Carter, Lanston Monotype Machine Company; Melbert B. Cary, Jr., president of the Institute, Quincy P. Emery, Quincy P. Emery, Inc.; Otto W. Fuhrmann, New York University; Henry Watson Kent, Metropolitan Museum of Art; Dr. Harry M. Lydenberg, New York Public Library; F. Ronald Mansbridge, Cambridge University Press; William Reydel, Newell Emmett Company, and Monroe Wheeler, Museum of Modern Art.

The committee will act as a clearing house for the exchange and distribution of ideas, and will disseminate publicity.

Correspondence should be addressed to Will Ransom, secretary of the committee, at 285 Madison Avenue, New York City,

Premier Showings Will Be Made Of Two-in-One Model 33 Machine And Other Mechanical Equipment At Linotype Exhibit on Main Floor

When the doors of Grand Central Palace, New York City, swing open Monday afternoon, September 25, for the two-weeks' run of the Fifth Educational Graphic Arts Exposition, you'll lay eyes on the greatest display of modern printing equipment ever placed on exhibition.

And before the doors swing shut Saturday night, October 7, Fred W. Hoch, manager of the exposition, estimates, more than 100,000 people, yourself included, will have a better idea of the printing industry—where it is, and where it is going.

Premier Showings of Mergenthaler Features

The Linotype exhibit at the big exposition will introduce and demonstrate several new Mergenthaler developments.

Premier showings will be made of the new Two-in-One Model 33 Linotype, the new Linotype Thermo-Blo, the new Linotype Electric Pot with Micro-Therm Temperature Control, and the new Knife Block developed particularly for food-store and certain other kinds of advertising composition.

The new Two-in-One Model 33 carries new extra-wide 90-channel magazines, with 72-channel Super-Display magazines, all of them thirty-five per cent wider than standard. The 90-channel magazines carry sizes up to and including normal-width 24-point faces, and the 72-channel magazines carry full 36-point faces. This means that with this single-distributor machine an operator can produce both text and large display at Blue Streak speed. (See the announcement on page five of this issue.)

Thermo-Blo and New Knife Block

The new Linotype Thermo-Blo cools molds with a gentle stream of air, without hazard of moisture or forced draft, and thus makes for better Linotype slugs and faces.

On the new Knife Block a special lever makes it possible for the operator to shift knives quickly from open to trimming position while setting overhang and regular composition. A touch of the lever and the right-hand knife is opened so that overhanging characters may pass through untrimmed. Another touch and the right-hand knife is back at work again trimming in the usual manner, without loss of precision setting. A great time saver on food-store and certain other kinds of advertising composition.

New Pot With Micro-Therm Control

The new Electric Pot with Micro-Therm control of crucible, throat and mouthpiece temperatures carries sturdy and long-lasting calrod tubular immersion heaters, regulates the temperature of metal within a variation of less than two degrees, and thus makes for strong-bodied slugs with excellent printing surfaces, and economical performance.

But these are only some of the features that will be seen

(Continued on page sixteen)

Speakers at a meeting on Treasure Island for the San Francisco Book Club included J. R. Knowland, publisher of the Oakland Tribune; Miss Elna I. Keith, editorial representative for the Macmillan Publishing Company, and John B. Kaiser, Oakland City librarian. Mr. Kaiser acted as host

ON THE INSIDE

Some Lens Line-ups	Page 2
Recent Installations	3
Commercial Typography	4
Two-in-One Model 33	5
Editorials	6
Newspaper Makeup	6
Shining Lines	7
Book Department	10
Recent Visitors	10
Hints to Operators	11
Legibility Group	11
New Typo Developments	12
Linotype Aids	15
For Food-Store Ads	16

A view of the Press building at the Golden Gate International Exposition on Treasure Island in San Francisco Bay. The building, which was erected by the California commission and the exposition, for hospitality to visiting members of the press, is managed by the San Francisco Press Club

EXAMPLE 245

Spartan families. Most of the body matter was in 7½-point Excelsior on a 9-point body.

Example 246 presents a reduced showing of the front page of that issue.

And Example 247 presents a reduced showing of page four of that issue—one of the departmentalized pages.

An unusual front page was presented in the number for April-June, 1940, with a high first column filled with pictures and legends below a two-line head. See Example 248.

Heads were in members of the Franklin Gothic, Metro, Ryerson and Spartan families, and news body matter in 7½-point Excelsior on a 9-point body.

Members of the same type families were used for another lively looking front page, in the number for July-September, 1940, as suggested by Example 249.

The double-column body lines in columns two and three were in 10-point Excelsior on a 12-point body.

In the fall of 1940 the *Linotype News* adopted a three-way format. One section was in the form of a departmentalized news-magazine, and another section carried on the tabloid-newspaper idea, with a center spread that opened up into an eight-column page.

A skyline streamer was used across the top of the front page of the newspaper section for March-April, 1941, as suggested by Example 250.

Heads were in members of the Erbar, Franklin Gothic, Metro and Spartan families, with body matter in 7½-point Corona with Bold Face No. 2 on an 8½-point body.

An issue employing color—a bright blue—on every page in the newspaper section was the issue for May-July, 1941.

The front page of that section, as suggested by Example 251, featured two plates in color—the nameplate block just below the skyline streamer, and the arrow across the bottom of the page.

Again members of the Erbar, Franklin Gothic, Metro and Spartan families were employed for heads, and 7½-point Corona with Bold Face No. 2 for body matter, on an 8½-point body.

A front page with a high last column—a column given over to cuts and legends under a single-line head—featured the newspaper section for October-December, 1941. See Example 252.

The Linotype News

VOLUME XVIII | BROOKLYN, JANUARY-MARCH, 1940 | NUMBER FOUR

Boston Herald and Traveler Order 29 Linos; Chicago Tribune Adds 11; New York Times, 4

Lino-Set Books Score New High In Latest Fifty

At a preliminary showing (February 5) of the latest "Fifty Books of the Year" selected under the auspices of the American Institute of Graphic Arts it was disclosed that thirty-four of the fifty books were Linotype set.

Nine of the thirty-four were set in Janson; six in Granjon; five in Estienne; three in Caslon Old Face; two in Electra; two in Baskerville, and one each in Bodoni, Bodoni Book, Bookman, Garamond, Garamond No. 3, Memphis Light, and Scotch Roman.

Detailed stories about the 1940 "Fifty Books," with many illustrations, are presented in the supplement with this issue of The Linotype News.

Printer Patrons Vote for Electra

Last fall the Mills-Frizell-Evans Company, Baltimore trade composition house, asked Baltimore printers, through its house organ, "Face to Face," what new type face the company should add.

We quote from the January number of "Face to Face": "MFE is happy to announce the addition of Linotype Electra to its rapidly growing family of type faces. In choosing Electra rather than any of several other possibilities, we were guided largely by the preference of Baltimore printers, as expressed in the type 'poll' conducted by 'Face to Face' in November. Sentiment in favor of Electra was almost unanimous."

Launching a New Model 33 Linotype

In the Item composing room

Item Company, New Orleans Installs Four Blue Streaks

Four Blue Streaks—two Model 33s with self-quadders and Mohr saws, and two Model 31s—have been added by the Item Company Ltd., of New Orleans, which publishes the evening Item and the morning Tribune.

Coincident with the installation of the new machines, changes were made in the makeup of the Tribune, which now employs for some of its heads various sizes of Memphis Bold Condensed, Metroblack No. 2, and Poster Bodoni. The head dress of the Item makes use of various members of the Bodoni family. Heads in both papers are presented flush at the left.

Two of the new Blue Streaks—a Model 33 and a Model 31—have been equipped for heads, with many new fonts of duplex-display matrices. The other Model 33 has been added to the ad battery, along with several series of duplex-display matrices, extra magazines, and a Reid magazine rack.

The Item Company Ltd., which was among the first concerns to install Linotypes and, through the years, has been quick to avail itself of Mergenthaler improvements, is headed by James M. Thomson, publisher. Marshall Ballard is editor; Clarke Salmon, managing editor, and J. W. Fanz, business manager.

H. C. Alfred is superintendent; Walter Desforges, day foreman of the composing room, and Luther Alfred, head machinist.

The accompanying picture shows standing, left to right, Messrs. Fanz, H. C. Alfred and Desforges. Harry Cole is the ad operator at the new Model 33 Linotype.

500 Years

The year 1940 marks the five hundredth anniversary of the invention of printing from movable types, as well as several other anniversaries of importance in the graphic arts.

Printers and publishers, librarians and teachers, civic and church leaders—all who appreciate the significance of printing—are urged to unite in community observances to pay honor to the invention which, through five centuries, has contributed more than any other to the progress of civilization.

Besides the five hundredth anniversary of the beginning of printing as it is practiced today, these other anniversaries occur in 1940.

400 Years

The first printing in the New World was done 400 years ago in Mexico City.

300 Years

The earliest publication printed in colonial North America of which copies still remain was the Bay Psalm Book, printed by the Stephen Daye Press at Cambridge in 1640.

250 Years

The first paper mill in the United States was erected at Philadelphia 250 years ago.

100 Years

The first postage stamp was used in 1840, and practical photography was achieved at approximately the same time.

Montevideo Papers Order 10 Machines, 37 Fonts of Matrices

Twenty-nine Blue Streak Linotypes have been purchased by the Boston Herald and the Traveler—twenty-three Model 31s and six Model 29s.

This latest move in the modernization program being carried out by the Herald and the Traveler was preceded some six months ago by the adoption by both papers of new flush-left head dresses in members of the Linotype Erbar and Metro families. Most of the body matter in both is in 7-point Ionic No. 5 with Bold Face No. 2 on a 7¾-point body.

The Herald and the Traveler operate forty-five Mergenthaler machines, including two All-Purpose Linotypes.

Albert R. Hanley is superintendent of the composing room. William G. Thomas is day foreman; James E. Daley, night foreman, and James J. Hubbard, head machinist.

Chicago Tribune

Eleven Blue Streak Linotypes—nine Model 8s and two Model 31s—have been ordered by the Chicago Tribune, which, when the new machines have been installed, will operate a battery of seventy-seven Mergenthaler machines.

The Model 31s will be equipped with six-mold disks, self-quadders and Mohr saws.

Col. Robert R. McCormick is president of the Tribune Company and publisher of the paper. W. E. Macfarlane is business manager. Charles B. James is purchasing agent; J. W. Park is production manager; Roy Keeler is composing-room superintendent, and George Schmidt is head machinist.

New York Times

Four Mixer Model 29s, each with a six-mold disk and a Mohr saw, have been installed in the ad division of the New York Times composing room. Installed with the new machines were many extra magazines and display fonts for the setting of advertisements.

Arthur Hays Sulzberger is president of the New York Times Company and publisher of the paper. Col. Julius Ochs Adler is vice-president and general manager, and Godfrey N. Nelson is secretary. Harold Hall is assistant general manager. Cortland J. Strang is mechanical superintendent; Thomas J. Dillon, general foreman; Walter Johnson, machine foreman; Fred J. Schuyler, day foreman; Harry W. Dail, ad foreman; Fred Knowles and Walter Alderdice, head machinists.

(See, also, page five)

Penn Group to Mark Five Hundred Years

In co-operation with the nation-wide quincentennial celebration of the anniversary of printing, the Pennsylvania Newspaper Publishers' Association has chosen "Five Hundred Years of Progress in Printing" as the theme for its 1940 mechanical conference to be held at the Penn-Harris Hotel, Harrisburg, Monday and Tuesday, April 8 and 9.

Howard J. Lamade, business manager of Grit, Williamsport, chairman of the P. N. P. A. mechanical conference, has announced that plans are being completed to have outstanding speakers on composing-room, pressroom, stereotyping, picture and photo-engraving problems address the conference.

A feature of the meeting will be the observance of printing's five hundredth anniversary.

E. S. Upton of New Orleans Marks Two Anniversaries

December 4 was a day of dual celebration for Eldon Stephen Upton of New Orleans. It marked his eighty-ninth birthday anniversary and the fiftieth anniversary of his founding of the E. S. Upton Printing Company, of which he is vice-president.

His son E. C. Upton is secretary-treasurer of the company. Another son, the late George M. Upton, was president from 1907 until his death, in 1936, when he was succeeded by his son, John T. Upton, the present head.

The eldest Upton's father published the Bluffton (Ind.) Banner in pre-Civil War days; during the war the family lived in Vicksburg, Miss., and after the war, moved to New Orleans, where young Eldon, after working for this one and that, started the Upton Printing Shop and Religious Book Depository, later rechristened the E. S. Upton Printing Company, on Camp Street.

Later he moved the company to Poydras Street, and about twenty years ago moved it to its own four-story building on Magazine Street. The plant was remodeled about two years ago.

Mr. Upton takes pride in the fact that he pioneered the use of typesetting machines in commercial-printing plants.

E. S. Upton (center), E. C., left, and John T.

Franklin Typographers Issues Specimen Book

Franklin Typographers, Inc., the advertising-typography branch of Lino-Typography, Inc., New York City, has issued a sixty-four-page specimen book giving one-line showings of available faces, rules and borders.

The book is divided into two sections, the first being devoted to foundry type, and the second to faces on the machines, including two Linotypes. Reference is ready. And the book itself is an excellent piece of printing.

Emil Menlo owns the company.

The Linotype News Entirely Lino Set

All lines of composition in this issue of The Linotype News, as usual, were composed the Linotype way, even the biggest heads and the largest lines in display advertisements.

See "Makeup of This Issue," on page six.

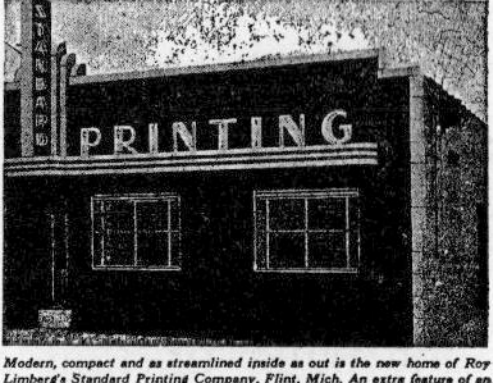

Modern, compact and as streamlined inside as out is the new home of Roy Limberg's Standard Printing Company, Flint, Mich. An extra feature of an extra service is the availability of parking space for customers

EXAMPLE 246

4 THE LINOTYPE NEWS, JANUARY-MARCH, 1940

Father Time and the Clicking Calendar

Jonesboro Gazette Ninety Years Old

JONESBORO, Ill.—But for a little fire started by some Union soldiers at one point in the Civil War, Perry C. Turner, publisher of the Gazette, would have a complete file of past issues of the paper, which passed the ninety-year mark in September. As it is, issues for six months are gone—issues that, among other things, contained much authentic data on the historic Lincoln-Douglas debate held here.

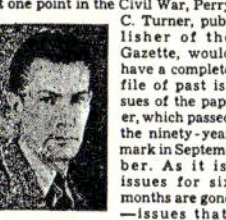

Perry C. Turner

Mr. Turner had been with the Anna (Ill.) Democrat for fourteen years prior to his purchase of the Gazette, last April.

Barry Bingham, publisher of the Louisville Courier-Journal and the Times, is shown here presenting William J. ("Bill") Lawler, former foreman, with a watch on behalf of the "bosses," and a chain on behalf of the "boys," in recognition of his fifty years of service with the papers. Bill, one of the first to qualify as a Linotype operator, went to Louisville fifty years ago from Columbus, Ohio, when he was nineteen

Washington, D. C.

The first lady of the land helped 700-odd Washington printers celebrate the hundred and twenty-fifth anniversary of the founding of Columbia Typographical Union, No. 101, at a banquet in the nation's capital January 7.

In her pre-dinner remarks, Mrs. Roosevelt said, "I feel you started a great many things that the government has done." She referred, she said, to the printers' own program of old-age and unemployment benefits and to their standards of wages and hours—ideas and ideals that began to take shape when a few men formed the Columbia Typographical Society January 7, 1815.

Other luminaries in the typo limelight were Miss Frances Perkins, secretary of labor; Frank Morrison, secretary emeritus of the American Federation of Labor; A. E. Giegengack, public printer; Mary Anderson, director of the women's bureau of the department of labor; Claude M. Baker, president of the I. T. U.; John B. Dickman, Sr., twice president of the local, and Woodruff Randolph, secretary of the I. T. U. . Most of the printers attending were from the Government Printing Office and the four Washington dailies. Charles Warren of the Washington Times-Herald composing room was toastmaster.

Clarence J. Desper is president of the local; John R. Evans, vice-president, and James I. Crockett, secretary-treasurer.

St. Paul

Bernard H. Ridder, publisher of the St. Paul Dispatch and the Pioneer-Press, was the honored guest at a dinner given by business men in November, marking the first anniversary of his arrival in St. Paul.

Ardmore, Okla.

Sam Blackburn, alias "The Wicked Flea," recently celebrated the twelfth anniversary of his column in the Ardmore (Okla.) Ardmoreite by writing another one and promising to continue as long as the readers show interest.

Gurdon, Ark.

December 7 the Gurdon (Ark.) Times celebrated its fifty-ninth anniversary. C. T. Key, publisher, bought the paper from B. H. Thomas eleven years ago. Thomas J. Key is editor; Mrs. C. T. Key is advertising manager; Mrs. Marcus L. Lowe is society editor and reporter; Mrs. Charles Hill is circulation manager, and Ellis McWhirter is Linotype operator.

Hornell, N. Y.

A. H. ("Lon") Howard, mechanical superintendent of the Hornell (N. Y.) Evening Tribune, and Mrs. Howard celebrated their fifty-seventh wedding anniversary November 28 by motoring to Elmira, N. Y., one of the places they visited on their honeymoon. Mr. Howard has been employed by the Tribune sixty-seven years.

Belleville, Ill.

The Belleville (Ill.) Advocate celebrated its centenary, last fall, with a 128-page special. The Advocate, the oldest paper in St. Clair County, was the first to publish a daily in Illinois, beginning in 1849.

Mrs. F. E. Evans is president of the publishing company; Mrs. W. W. Evans is vice-president, and Miss Anna L. Stolle is secretary-treasurer. C. J. Keller is managing editor and business manager. Miss Stolle has been an active executive of the paper since 1913. Mrs. F. E. Evans and Mrs. W. W. Evans became active following the deaths of their husbands, in 1936.

Dallas Center, Iowa

Elmer A. Emmert, publisher of the Dallas Center (Iowa) Times, celebrated the fiftieth anniversary of his printing-ink baptism last November 18.

Vandalia, Mo.

The Vandalia (Mo.) Leader, published by F. B. DeTienne, marked its sixty-fifth anniversary, last fall, by including a sixty-four-page magazine supplement with its regular edition.

If life begins at forty, then each of the three pictured here has had a double start in his race against the calendar. William Thomas (center), nearly eighty-five, composing-room foreman of the Boston Herald-Traveler, looks on smilingly as Weldon L. Crosman (left) and Thomas M. Nolan of that paper's composing room shake on their eightieth birthday and become members of the Herald-Traveler's Octogenarian Club. The new members are shown holding gifts that were presented by fellow workers along with clever verses about two young men who are still going strong

Akron, Ohio

The Akron Beacon Journal celebrated the hundredth anniversary of its founding, and its seventieth anniversary as a daily, December 6.

John S. Knight, who succeeded the late Charles L. Knight as managing editor in 1933, is president of the company and publisher of the paper. John H. Barry is business manager, and James P. Rosemond is managing editor.

J. M. Aylward is circulation manager; Roger Burrell, advertising manager; A. F. Falk, national ad manager; Robert Wheeler, classified ad manager; Earl Woodard, mechanical superintendent; James Curry, composing-room foreman, and James Horrigan, maintenance superintendent.

Nebraska City, Neb.

The Nebraska City (Neb.) Daily News-Press, born a year before the city, celebrated its eighty-fifth anniversary November 14 with a twenty-four-page special.

J. H. Sweet is president of the company and editor of the paper; John M. Scott is vice-president; Arthur R. Sweet is secretary and managing editor, and Marie Duncan is treasurer and advertising manager.

Stillwater, Okla.

John P. Hinkel, publisher of the Stillwater (Okla.) Gazette and the Press, and Mrs. Hinkel celebrated their golden wedding anniversary November 21. Mr. Hinkel started publishing the newspapers before Oklahoma became a state and is one of Oklahoma's oldest editors in point of continuous service. The Gazette is celebrating its fiftieth anniversary this year.

Indianapolis

Seventy years ago last December 7, the late John H. Holliday brought forth the first issue of the Indianapolis News, a four-page hand-set affair. The infant had good lungs, and has consistently increased their capacity. The past year's increase included the installation of twelve new Linotypes, among them two Model 30s.

Chillicothe, Ohio

"You may hear some say they 'learn the trade'; but I'll tell you, to me it's been just fifty years of apprenticeship," was the brief comment of Charles C. Metzger on rounding out fifty years in the printing industry January 5.

Mr. Metzger, for the last thirty-four years with the Scholl Printing Company, Chillicothe, Ohio, started in as a devil under George Tyler at the old Chillicothe Leader, where he acquired a certain finesse in shoveling snow, tending fires, cleaning the pressroom and delivering papers, and was the weekly heir to one dollar and one quarter.

He's an alumnus of Mergenthaler's school in Brooklyn, and will tell anyone, "I'm crazy about the business and it's really the only hobby I've ever had."

Springfield, Ohio

Friday, January 5, John F. O'Toole, Linotype operator with the Springfield (Ohio) News, began his fiftieth year as a member of Typographical Union No. 117. He is the oldest continuous member of the local.

Benton, Ill.

The Benton (Ill.) Standard celebrated its ninetieth anniversary last November. For more than fifty years the Standard was the only newspaper in Franklin County. It has had only six editors in its ninety years of publication.

Sioux City

Typographical Union No. 180, Sioux City, Iowa, rounded out sixty years December 28, but the anniversary was celebrated December 17. At the celebration A. F. Allen, who became a member of the I. T. U. in January, 1887, read a paper in which he talked about the tramp printer of other days and paid tribute to the Linotype and to the late George D. Perkins, editor and printer, in whose office the Sioux City union was organized.

Life, Type and the Pursuit Of Profits a la Diamant

By WALTER J. ELLIS

Stables, like the horses they housed, are fast disappearing from what professors are pleased to call the American scene.

No contemporary we know is more saddened by this passing than E. M. Diamant, one of New York

E. M. and Robert M. Diamant talking things over in their office

City's leading advertising typographers. For it was in a remodeled stable at the corner of Lexington Avenue and Thirty-second Street that E. M.'s typographic art flowered from 1924 to 1928.

And in spite of the insistent but good-natured razzing that came his way because of the stable's previous occupants, he likes to think of those years as "the good old days."

But if time and tide aren't in the habit of waiting, E. M. isn't given to lagging or floundering.

He rode business tides into his present spacious quarters at 191 Lexington Avenue. And recently he turned the clock ahead by installing his first typesetting machines, two Blue Streak Model 29s, which he has equipped with fifty fonts of Linotype matrices and Margach metal feeders.

We dropped by not long ago to see how things were going and

William H. Diamant at his desk

found E. M. at his board, buried in layouts. His son William H., a graduate of N. Y. U. and a partner in the business, was on the way out to make a sales call. The younger son, Robert M., also a partner, was checking some proofs.

Since Mr. Diamant's career as an advertising typographer goes back to 1907, when he helped A. Colish open the first advertising-typography shop in New York City, we thought he had probably come to a few conclusions while watching type metal flow over the typographic dam. He had.

"Slowly, but surely," he said, "the composing machines are pushing hand composition to the museum. In the old days it was easy to sell and convince the advertisers what hand composition could do for them. But the machine manufacturers have advanced with the times. They've improved the composing machines and the fonts of type, so that today the most complicated pieces of composition can be set on the machine in ridiculous time and be well comparable to hand composition.

"In the last few years typographers have invaded the field of booklet and magazine composition. And the growing influx of machines will open up new avenues for our shops."

Mr. Diamant, now fifty-six, came to New York from Holland, at fourteen. His first job was with the Pine

William Herold, night foreman; Irving Sunshine, day foreman, and Max Kolodny, Linotype operator with the Diamant Typographic Service

Hill (N. Y.) Optic (deceased), where "we wet down the paper Wednesday and printed 200 copies on the old hand press on Thursday."

In turn he worked as a hand comp with the John B. Watkins Company, Rogers & Company, the American Bank Note Company, and Mr. Colish, all in New York City.

He was working for Mr. Colish at the time, and there wasn't any reason for his reading want ads, but one evening in 1910 an ad placed by Conde Nast in the old Mail and Express stopped him cold. It seemed Vogue could use a man who was an expert on type, engraving, layout, processes, ad infinitum. The ad didn't state that a knowledge of plumbing and anthropology was necessary, but Mr. Diamant thought it might just as well have. "The job was impossible, no man could know or do all that. So, just for the heck of it, I took a chance." P.S.: He got the job.

In 1914 he went to the Carey Printing Company, and a year later joined the Cheltenham Advertising Agency as production manager under Ingalls Kimball. The following year Mr. Kimball sold out, and Mr. Diamant went in business for himself, as the fourth advertising typographer to set up shop in New York City.

His first shop was at 405 Lexington Avenue, a spot he held down until 1924, when the Chrysler building moved in.

Kansas City, Mo.

The Kansas City (Mo.) Journal wound up the old year by coming out December 31 with an eighty-sixth anniversary "Go, Kansas City" edition of twelve sections, 108 pages. Color was used in each section, and much advertising was carried. One section presented many pictures of Journal executives and production departments.

Orville S. McPherson is president of the Kansas City Journal-Post Company and publisher of the Journal. Russell H. Miles is vice-president and general manager; J. C. Johnsen, vice-president and editor; Ray Runnion, associate editor; J. W. West, managing editor, and Brewster P. Campbell, feature and Sunday editor. Gordon Elrod is the production manager; R. L. Adams is composing-room superintendent, and William Asbury is the assistant superintendent.

Bennington, Vt.

Frank E. Howe of the Bennington (Vt.) Banner has rounded out fifty years as a printer.

New Orleans

The New Orleans printing firm of Searcy & Pfaff, Ltd., celebrated its fiftieth anniversary November 1. Mrs. D. J. Searcy is president of the company; D. R. McGuire, Sr., is vice-president, and William Pfaff, Sr., one of the founders, is secretary-treasurer.

Mokena, Ill.

Mr. and Mrs. William Semmler, publishers of the Mokena (Ill.) News-Bulletin, celebrated their twenty-fifth wedding anniversary December 2 by holding open house in their newly completed home.

Excelsior Springs, Mo.

The Excelsior Springs (Mo.) Standard celebrated its fiftieth anniversary with a special edition last fall. W. N. McKinney, eighty-two, came out of retirement for the day to serve as honorary editor. Edward W. Sowers and E. L. Lawrence are the publishers.

EXAMPLE 247

The Four New Murals At New York Library

1—Moses and the Ten Commandments engraved on stone

2—A monk of the Middle Ages patiently copying a manuscript

3—Gutenberg, in his press, exhibiting a page of the Bible

4—Ottmar Mergenthaler at the first Linotype, with Whitelaw Reid

The Linotype News

VOLUME XVIII — BROOKLYN, APRIL-JUNE, 1940 — NUMBER FIVE

The Record, Philadelphia, Installs Sixteen Linotypes

National Editorial Association To Have Big Time in New York

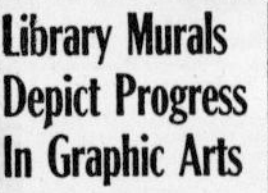

Library Murals Depict Progress In Graphic Arts

Pictures Suggest Story Of the Recorded Word From Moses to Lino

In April, four murals depicting "The Story of the Recorded Word"—from Moses to the Linotype—were unveiled in the third-floor lobby of the New York Public Library.

The murals, the work of Edward Laning of the New York City W. P. A. Art Project, show four stages in the development of written communication.

The first stage, when symbols were engraved on clay or stone, is represented by Moses bringing the Tablets of the Covenant down from Mt. Sinai.

The second stage, when reed pens or brushes were used to write on parchment, is depicted by a medieval monk copying a manuscript in his cell. In these two pictures the artist seeks to contrast the inspirational character of the Old Testament period with the patient conservatism of the medieval monasteries.

Johann Gutenberg is shown in the third panel, with the first Bible printed from movable type, in the fifteenth century, and the fourth deals with the invention of the Linotype, by Ottmar Mergenthaler, which the New York Tribune, in 1886, was the first newspaper to use. In this picture the late Whitelaw Reid, editor of the Tribune, who named the machine, is shown examining the first issue of the Tribune that was produced with the aid of the Linotype, with Mergenthaler at the keyboard.

Two lunettes by Mr. Laning also are in the third-floor lobby. One shows a mother teaching a child to read. The other shows a student reading.

The ceiling, when completed, will suggest the original inspiration of human culture in the gift of fire brought to earth by Prometheus.

See the illustrations at the left.

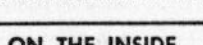

ON THE INSIDE

	Page
Picture Parade	2
Recent Installations	3
Spartan Duplicate	3
Buildings Activities	4
New Dresses	5
Editorials	6
Modern Newspaper	6
Book Department	7
Caravan	7
New Typo Developments	10
Some Anniversaries	10
Education	11
Hints to Operators	12
With the Ladies	12
Two-in-One Model 33	16

Program Will Feature Many Special Events And Fine Up-State Trip

Newspaper people in all parts of the country are planning to attend the fifty-fourth annual convention of the National Editorial Association, which will convene at the Roosevelt Hotel, New York City, Monday, June 17.

For many months, N. E. A. President Howard W. Palmer, members of his convention committee, the New York Press Association, New York City Merchants' Association, New York World's Fair officials, and other organizations have been busy with plans to make the twelve days, from time of arrival on the pre-convention tour in Washington, D. C., until time of departure from Lake Placid, filled with sightseeing, traveling, inspiring programs, entertainment, sports, and rest.

The pre-convention tour of Washington will afford a stay of a day and a half in the capital.

When the N. E. A. members arrive in New York City, they will embark on a program that calls for business sessions in the mornings, with many prominent people as speakers, with afternoons free for trips to the world's fair and other places of interest.

There will be several parties at the fair for the visitors, and at various places in New York City.

The annual banquet will be held Friday evening, June 21, and next morning the travelers will start on a leisurely trip along the Hudson River to Albany and on into the Adirondacks, with stays at the Sagamore Hotel at Lake George and three days at the Lake Placid Club.

Complete details about the convention and tour may be secured from N. E. A. headquarters, at 211 West Wacker Drive, Chicago.

Supplymen in Chicago Elect William R. Joyce

At a meeting May 17 of the Printers' Supplymen's Guild of Chicago, William R. Joyce of the Inland Printer was elected president.

A. E. Handschy of Martin Driscoll & Company is vice-president; Bernard Snyder of the American Typesetting Corporation, treasurer, and Charles Wallace of the Economy Printers' Products, secretary.

Members of the executive committee are: A. R Quaintance, J. D. Hennigan Company; W. C. Roddy, Metals Refining Company; Paul Roscher, Hyre Electric Company; W. C. Smith, Simonds-Worden-White Company, and D. H. Speidel, Kidder Press Company.

Emile Jean Now Heads. Canadian Daily Group

Emile Jean, general manager of Le Nouvelliste of Three Rivers, Que., is the new president of the Canadian Daily Newspapers Association.

William Wallace, advertising manager of the Toronto Star, is past president. W. J. Motz, manager of the Kitchener Record, is vice-president, and W. J. J. Butler of the Toronto Globe and Mail, continues as treasurer. R. B. Hara, advertising manager of the Toronto Telegram, has been re-elected chairman of the bureau of advertising. Arthur Partridge is secretary.

Fred B. Wachs (left), general manager of the Lexington (Ky.) Herald-Leader, receiving from Eldon S. Dummit the Optimist Club's trophy as Lexington's outstanding citizen

Hammond and Peay Buy in Montgomery

Stanley and Wilson Continue With Journal

The Montgomery Journal has been purchased by Col. James Hammond, former publisher of the Memphis Commercial Appeal, and Nicholas Peay of Little Rock.

Tom King, who was with Colonel Hammond at Memphis, has been made mechanical superintendent of the Journal. Robert F. Starr continues as foreman of the ad room, with Randle Smith as plant machinist.

C. M. Stanley, for thirteen years editor of the Journal, will continue in that capacity, and James Wilson remains as business manager and treasurer.

The Linotype News Entirely Linotype Set

All lines of composition in this issue of The Linotype News were composed the Linotype way, even the biggest heads and the largest lines in display advertisements. Many of the heads are in Linotype Ryerson Condensed, the brand-new display face.

See "Makeup of This Issue," on page six.

Many Other Plants, In Various Sections, Improve Equipments

Sixteen new Linotypes, fifteen of them with Micro-Therm electric metal pots, have been ordered by the Philadelphia Record, which, when the new machines have all been installed, will be operating twenty-two Linotypes.

J. David Stern, president of the Philadelphia Record Company and publisher of the paper, is also president of the Courier-Post Company of Camden, N. J. David Stern III is vice-president of the Philadelphia Record Company and publisher of the Courier-Post. Walter L. Tushingham is vice-president and secretary of the Record. Harry T. Saylor is editor of the Record; William F. Hawkes, managing editor, and David S. Loeb, business manager. Vincent B. Fuller is composing-room superintendent, and Charles W. Letsch is chief machinist.

A. E. Munyer, Brooklyn

Six Linotypes—five Blue Streak Master Model 31s and a Two-in-One Model 33—have been installed by the A. E. Munyer Electrotype Company, Inc., of 662-668 Pacific Street, Brooklyn, which will handle the composition and makeup for P. M., the New York tabloid that will make its initial appearance June 18. (See story on center spread of this issue.)

One of the Model 31s is a forty-two-pica machine. All six are equipped with Margach feeders.

A few months ago the Munyer concern installed four Linotypes, eighty fonts of matrices and seventy-five extra magazines.

A. E. Munyer is president and treasurer of the company; Frederick Hunter, vice-president, and Arthur A. Rasmussen, secretary. Joseph Hradecky is composing-room foreman, and Leo Kane is assistant foreman. John Loehner is machinist.

Staats-Herold Corp.

Six new Linotypes and many fonts of matrices, including eight fonts of Ionic No. 5 in the 7½- and 10-point sizes, have been installed by the Staats-Herold Corporation of New York City, which publishes the Staats-Zeitung und Herold.

Joseph E. Ridder is president of the corporation, and Victor F. Ridder is secretary. Charles J. Fuerst is business manager. Andrew J. Kurz is superintendent of the composing room, and Harry Scheidegger is head machinist.

(See, also, page three)

Seated at these four new Linotypes recently added by the Kansas City Star, front to rear, are: Henry J. Huckett, George Alwes, George W. Messick, and Charles H. Sharts. Standing is Chester S. Kelley, chief machinist. The superintendent of the plant is Daniel C. Carpenter

EXAMPLE 248

The Public Printer

Col. A. E. Giegengack

The Linotype News

VOLUME XVIII | BROOKLYN, JULY-SEPTEMBER, 1940 | NUMBER SIX

G. P. O., Washington, D. C. Adds 11 Mixer Linotypes

Southern Execs To Birmingham

The next mechanical conference of the eastern division of the Southern Newspaper Publishers' Association will be held September 16 and 17 at the Hotel Tutwiler, Birmingham, according to an announcement made by Walter C. Johnson, managing director of the S. N. P. A.

W. A. Carns, mechanical superintendent of the Birmingham Age-Herald, is in charge of the local committee on arrangements. Plans are now under way for a large and enthusiastic meeting.

The next mechanical conference of the western division of the S. N. P. A. will be held in Fort Worth, February 17 and 18, announces C. W. Tabb, Dallas, secretary.

A. I. Lundberg, superintendent of the Fort Worth Star-Telegram, will take a leading part in making arrangements for the sessions.

Plans for the conference will be made at a fall meeting of the executive committee to be set by J. H. Gibson of the Houston Chronicle, chairman.

The Linotype News Entirely Linotype Set

All lines of composition in this issue of The Linotype News were composed the Linotype way, even the biggest heads and the largest lines in display advertisements. Many of the heads are in Linotype Ryerson Condensed, the new sans-serif display face. Department heads are in Franklin Gothic Italic, with subheads in Spartan Heavy. The body lines are in various sizes of Excelsior.

See "Makeup of This Issue," on page six.

Short Now Heads Virginia Press

Carl B. Short, general manager of the Times-World Corporation of Roanoke, Va., is the new president of the Virginia Press Association. He succeeds Paul F. Watkins, publisher of the Ashland Herald-Progress. D. Tennant Bryan, general manager of the Richmond News Leader, is vice-president for Virginia dailies, and A. Robbins, publisher of the Hopewell News, is vice-president for Virginia weeklies. J. H. Thornton, publisher of the Salem Times-Register, continues as treasurer. James R. McKeldin, who in May was named secretary-manager to succeed Robert B. Smith, resigned, has been reappointed for another year.

Carl B. Short

Uncle Sam Orders 4 Model 31s For Navy and 1 for West Point

Here's a picture of the Model 32 Linotype that produces most of the modern heads (in members of the Erbar, Metro and Spartan families) for the Kankakee (Ill.) Republican-News. Standing, left to right: Albert P. Mayer, city editor; Leslie C. Small, managing editor, and H. B. DeSelm, national news editor. At the keyboard is Robert B. Moore, operator. David W. Wood is mechanical superintendent. Last year another Model 32 was installed, for the production of advertising composition.

New S. S. America Also Has Installed Blue Streak Lino

The United States government has ordered four more Linotypes for four of its naval vessels—for the California, the Oklahoma, the Curtiss and the Albemarle. All four of the machines are Blue Streak Model 31s.

Twenty-three other vessels in the United States Navy also are Linotype equipped. These are the Altair, Argonne, Arizona, Augusta, Canopus, Chicago, Dobbin, Houston, Idaho, Indianapolis, Lexington, Maryland, Melville, Nevada, New York, Northampton, Pennsylvania, Ranger, Richmond, Saratoga, Tennessee, West Virginia and Whitney.

A Model 31 also has been installed in the printing department of the United States Military Academy at West Point, which also operates a Model 26.

The S. S. America, the largest, fastest and most luxurious liner ever built in the United States, which sailed August 10 on her maiden voyage from New York City to West Indies ports, also has a Blue Streak Model 31 in her modern printshop. The new machine is equipped with a self-quadder and a thermo-blo mold cooler.

Eight other ocean liners also are Linotype equipped.

'Still Time to Buy'

"For more than a year *Editor & Publisher* has counseled, even urged, newspaper publishers to look to their heavy-machinery installations," ran an editorial, "Still Time to Buy," in *Editor & Publisher*, July 13. "We had no foreknowledge of the tremendous defense preparations which will shortly engage the facilities of the nation's industry, although it was obvious that the requirements of a European war might severely tax our production.

"The defense program is now moving through its preliminary stages. Orders for steel in behalf of the army and the navy will be in the works before autumn. Orders for guns and other ordnance material will come before winter. If past experience can be taken as a guide, these orders will be widely dispersed, with the probability that all of the concerns now making presses and other newspaper machinery will be running at capacity. Government work will have implied, if not absolute, priority over goods for private business.

"While it is also probable that orders for newspaper machinery placed in the near future will not obtain the speedy delivery that would have been possible a year ago, it is evident that business in hand soon will get much more prompt attention than that which comes when the heat goes on for defense manufacture. It may be expected also that prices will be better in the immediate future than they will be when military needs are making constantly heavier demands.

"The moment is opportune also for close examination of casting-metal stocks and equipment of which rubber is a major component. No one can predict the turn of events in the Asiatic areas from which most of the raw materials for these are drawn, but it is the part of prudence to assure protection now against events which may curtail these supplies or send their prices to the sky.

"No one appreciates more heartfully the dilemma in which newspaper publishers have found themselves in recent years, but it is *Editor & Publisher's* sincere counsel now that it is no longer prudent to delay replacement of old or obsolescent equipment."

Woodard Now Super Of Detroit Free Press

C. E. Woodard, former mechanical superintendent of the Akron Beacon-Journal, has been made mechanical superintendent of the Detroit Free Press.

Mr. Woodard joined the Beacon-Journal as a printer more than twenty-five years ago. In 1917 he was made assistant foreman; in 1927, foreman, and in 1939, mechanical superintendent.

He has been receiving congratulations from friends in many cities on his latest advancement and best wishes for success in the new job.

Bickelhaupt Heads The Times-Tribune

George B. Bickelhaupt, former business manager of the Minneapolis Times-Tribune, is now president of the company and publisher of the paper.

W. J. McNally is vice-president and general manager; C. K. Blandin, vice-president; Thomas J. Dillon, editor-in-chief; George H. Adams, executive editor, and Charles Arthur Peterson, business manager.

H. L. Foster, for many years mechanical superintendent with the Minneapolis Journal, is now production manager with the Times-Tribune, and George England, former night composing-room foreman with the Star-Journal, is now composing-room foreman with the Times-Tribune.

W. ("Billy") B. Hoke, for forty-one years a member of the Times-Tribune mechanical department, resigned as mechanical superintendent to devote himself to outside activities.

Many Other Plants, In Various Sections, Improve Equipments

The Government Printing Office at Washington, D. C., the largest printing plant in the world, has installed eleven new Mixer Model 25 Linotypes with self-quadders, micro-therm electric metal pots and thermo-blo mold coolers.

The G. P. O. now operates a battery of ninety-five Linotypes, including eighty-three mixer models.

The new machines have been installed in the $5,000,000 annex to the main G. P. O. building, a structure that Col. A. E. Giegengack, public printer, advocated building shortly after he became the head of the big plant and which he saw completed last winter.

The huge task of moving many Linotypes and much other machinery, as well as many galley racks, makeup banks, cabinets and other equipment from the old building to the new was started June 20.

"Great though that task was," writes Lawton W. Luther, an operator with the G. P. O., "it was accomplished speedily and without confusion.

Twenty Machines Moved Daily

"Twenty machines were moved daily, to avoid interruption of the usual large flow of composition through the office—some 25,000 folios a day, or an average of 8,000,000 ems of type daily.

"The typesetting machines, which were moved under the direction of Charles L. Nay, chief machinist, were shifted without being dismantled. A crew of electricians and plumbers disconnected all wires and pipes, after which each machine was raised onto a specially designed truck and hauled to an elevator. They were lowered from the seventh floor, or Linotype section, to the second floor, and then taken across into the new building and up to the sixth floor.

"The entire movement of the Linotype section was completed by Monday, June 24."

George Ortleb is deputy public printer; Col. E. M. Nevils, production manager; Raymond H. Lecraw, night production manager; E. E. Emerson, director of purchases; H. K. Stephens, superintendent of the composing division; Frank R. Horstman, foreman of the Linotype section, and James W. Broderick, foreman of the patent section.

(See, also, page three)

Arthur J. Mollman, editor and publisher of the Millstadt (Ill.) Enterprise, has served fifty years in the industry. He began his apprenticeship with the Mascoutah Herald in May, 1890. He formerly was co-publisher, with his brother Fred, of the East St. Louis Democrat, and of the Mascoutah Times. He purchased the Enterprise in 1906

EXAMPLE 249

Lino-Set Papers Again Win Most Ayer Honors

N. Y. Herald Tribune, Using Linotype Ionic, Again Captures Cup

Linotype users again won most of the honors in the latest Ayer contest for typographic excellence among English-language dailies of the United States

The New York Herald Tribune, which operates seventy-seven Linotypes and presents its body matter in Linotype Ionic and most of its heads in Bodoni Bold and Bodoni Bold Italic, won its second leg on the second Ayer trophy, having won the first leg in 1939 (In 1936 the Herald Tribune won permanent possession of the first Ayer cup by having won it three times)

Of the thirteen papers honored, eleven use Linotypes, and the body matter of eight of the papers is set in Linotype faces. Body matter of three is in Ionic, one in both Ionic and Opticon, one in Excelsior and one in Paragon, as well as one in Linotype Caledonia and one in Linotype Electra.

Many Modern Treatments

Twelve of the thirteen papers present most of their heads in capitals and lower-case, and eight of the thirteen employ the sort of flush-left heads pioneered by The Linotype News The eleven Linotype users operate a total of 188 Mergenthaler machines

In the latest contest, first, second and third honorable mentions in the group of standard-size papers with circulations of more than 50,000 were won by the Richmond Times-Dispatch, the New York Times, and the Milwaukee Journal

In the group with circulations of from 10,000 to 50,000, first, second and third honorable mentions were won by the Cape Cod Standard-Times of Hyannis, Mass; the Dayton (Ohio) Journal, and the Billings (Mont.) Gazette

In the group with circulations of less than 10,000, first, second and third honorable mentions were won by the Manchester (Conn) Evening Herald, the Alexandria (Va) Gazette, and the Troy (N Y) Record.

Caledonia and Electra

Winners of first, second and third honorable mentions in the tabloid group were PM of New York, the Newsday of Hempstead, N Y., and the Washington (D. C) News Body matter in PM is in Linotype Caledonia, and body matter in the Newsday is in Linotype Electra

Four of the place winners present most of their heads in members of the Erbar and Metro families, and five present most of their heads in Bodoni Bold and Bodoni Bold Italic

The judges for the latest contest were Raymond Clapper, Washington columnist, Melbert B Cary, Jr., president of the American Institute of Graphic Arts, and Herbert Brucker, assistant dean of the graduate school of journalism at Columbia University.

Tripp of Elmira, N. Y. Advances Bitner, Taft

Lynn N Bitner and Thomas V Taft have been named assistant publisher and business manager, respectively, of the Elmira (N Y.) Star-Gazette, by Frank E Tripp, publisher of that paper and general manager of all of the Gannett newspapers and radio stations

Mr Bitner joined the Gannett organization in 1928 with the Ogdensburg Journal For the last nine years he had been with the Rochester Gannett newspapers, and his most recent position there was as advertising manager of the Rochester Times-Union.

Mr Taft had been auditor for the Elmira Star-Gazette, and before that had been auditor for the Danville Commercial-News, another Gannett newspaper.

Western Star Issues A Progress Edition

The Western Star of Curling, Bay of Islands, Newfoundland, A. L Barrett, managing director, issued a progress edition of twenty pages March 26

The special featured several illustrated stories — one of them nearly a full page on the new sulphite mill at Corner Brook erected and operated by Bowater's Newfoundland Pulp and Paper Mills, Ltd And a large amount of advertising was carried.

The Linotype News

VOLUME XIX | BROOKLYN, MARCH-APRIL, 1941 | NUMBER THREE

Baltimore Sun Adds 5 Model 31s Lord Baltimore Press 5 Model 29s

To Duluth Herald

Albin E ("Al") Rosene, who had been with the Minneapolis Tribune papers since 1923, is now composing-room superintendent with the Duluth Herald and the News-Tribune In the seventeen years Mr Rosene was with the Tribune, he served in several capacities—the last seven and one-half as assistant composing-room foreman for the morning Tribune Mr Rosene was graduated from Roosevelt High School in Minneapolis and attended the University of Minnesota.

PM Setting Heads In Caledonia Bold

PM, the modern New York tabloid which, from its establishment, in June, 1940, has been appearing with body matter in 9-point Linotype Caledonia, is now presenting most of its heads in Linotype Caledonia Bold

The change was made March 27, and a story in PM of that date by T M Cleland, who designed the format of the paper, ran, in part, as follows

"With this issue PM takes an important step in the evolution of its typographic design Today appears for the first time a new roman heading type which has been in production for more than a year PM has had to wait while the skilled craftsmen who cut . . the steel master punches required for every letter and character in every size performed their miracle of patience These men, masters of a difficult art, are few in number and never to be hurried . .

"The new heading type is a bolder version of the design of PM's text type Originally suggested by PM, it has been developed through the co-operation of W A Dwiggins designer of the text face, and the Mergenthaler Linotype Company Far less rigidly mechanical than the types we have been using, it has a vivid 'speaking' quality ideally adapted to the rapid idiom of headlines in the news

"The simple use of only two types, this clear roman for stories that are news, and an italic face for commentary heads, is an important factor in PM's aim to establish typographic order and clarity in its columns It is PM's aim to make this the easiest of all newspapers to read—to bring order and more order out of the typographic chaos that confronts the reader in many newspapers—to spare him the abuse of emphasis and the bewildering variety of types which, like a confusion of tongues, makes more noise than sense"

Editor's Note The heads in the magazine section of this issue of The Linotype News are in various sizes of Caledonia Bold.

Linotype Corona Newest Member Of Famous Group

Has High Visibility, Yet Conserves Space, As May Be Seen Here

The body matter of this section of The Linotype News is set in the 7½-point size of Linotype Corona—the newest member of Linotype's famous Legibility Group for newspapers.

In most of the stories the 7½ point has been cast on an 8½-point body, but local items on the last page are in 7½ point on 8 point

Corona was designed to make available a newspaper body type that provides maximum visibility, or color, and which at the same time helps to conserve newsprint by saving space

"While the new Corona incorporates all of the basic legibility factors of other members of the group," says C H Griffith, Linotype vice-president in charge of typographic development, "it offers a higher unit count than many faces of comparable size, but still is not at all a condensed face

"The lower-case characters of Corona have been designed for maximum height, and all of its characters have been fitted to compensate for stereo shrinkage, with the result that to the hurrying reader this new body face seems really larger than it is

"This will recommend Corona to newspaper executives who want maximum legibility along with a saving of space—who want to run even more words than before to the column but want those words to be easier to read than the fewer were before"

The first newspapers to adopt 7½-point Corona with Bold Face No 2 were the Evening News of Paterson, N J, with fourteen fonts, and the Morning Call of the same city, with twelve fonts

Other newspapers that already have adopted the new face are the Asbury Park (N J) Evening Press, the Kent News of Chestertown, Md, and the Southside Virginia News of Petersburg, Va

U. T. A. Eastern Meet At Atlantic City, N. J.

The fourth annual Eastern Seaboard Conference of the United Typothetæ of America will be held at Haddon Hall, Atlantic City, N J, April 25 and 26

The theme this year will be "National Emergency and the Graphic Arts" One group will discuss the present situation, and another will discuss future possibilities.

Management, finance and taxes, equipment and supplies are other subjects to be discussed.

Harry L Gage, Linotype vice-president, will talk April 26 on "Cross Currents in the Industry"

A preliminary announcement about the conference states that "printers, lithographers, paper merchants, typesetters, binders, roller makers, machinery manufacturers, photo-engravers, electrotypers and people in all other branches of the industry will be invited to attend, as the subjects to be discussed will be of interest to everyone in the industry"

Those in charge of the program are expecting an unusually high attendance at the two-day sessions

Now at Louisville

R H Lane, the publisher of the Mount Sterling (Ky) Sentinel-Democrat is now serving as chief of the public-relations division for selective service, at state headquarters, in the city of Louisville

Mr. Lane has been connected with the Sentinel-Democrat since 1920, when he and G B Senff purchased that paper from Squire Turner In 1935 Mr Lane acquired Mr Senff's interest

Mr Lane was an officer in World War I, and formerly was post commander of the American Legion of Mount Sterling He is a past president of the local Kiwanis Club, and immediate past president of the local Rotary Club For ten years he was a member of the city council, and once filled out a term as mayor

Deacham of Toronto Now Licensed Pilot

Alex Deacham editor of the East Toronto Weekly of Toronto Canada, who has been interested in flying as a side line since May 1939, is now a fully accredited pilot for commercial planes He recently completed a course of instruction with the Toronto Flying Club and passed the required tests

Many Other Plants, In Various Sections, Improve Equipments

Five new Blue Streak Linotypes and some forty fonts of matrices have been ordered by the A S Abell Company of Baltimore which publishes the Baltimore Sun papers

All of the new machines are Master Model 31s with micro-therm heat control, but two of them are Two-in-One Master Model 31s and are equipped with self-quadders

Among the new fonts ordered are various members of the Erbar and Metro families for a new head dress for the Evening Sun, and members of various other type families for the Sun papers' ad department

Of the thirty-seven Linotypes now operated, two Mixer Model 29s and three Master Model 31s are kept busy in the ad department

Paul Patterson is president of the company William F Schmick is vice-president and general manager, Frank R Kent and J. Edwin Murphy are vice-presidents; Hamilton Owens is secretary, E Paul Flaherty, treasurer, and E P. Kavanaugh, assistant business manager

Louis F Fries is mechanical superintendent, William J Hebner, composing-room superintendent; D. M Hipsley, head Linotype machinist, and Charles Huebel, assistant machinist. Thirty-seven Linotypes are now operated.

Lord Baltimore Press

The Lord Baltimore Press, Baltimore, which in the last three years has installed five Blue Streak Mixer Model 29 Linotypes, has just ordered five more of the same model.

This concern, which is well known for its high-grade book, publication and commercial printing, has a large printing plant and bindery housed in a modern building that is one of the graphic arts show places in the East

Simon Dalsheimer is president of the company, and Hugo Dalsheimer is vice-president and treasurer. C. D Rose is superintendent; J G Thomas, composing-room foreman, and George Rein, Linotype machinist Fifteen Linotypes are operated.

(See, also, center spread)

Asheville Citizen-Times Co. Installs Master Model 32

The Asheville Citizen-Times Company of Asheville, N C, publishing the Asheville Citizen (morning) Times (evening), and Citizen-Times (Sunday), has installed a Two-in-One Blue Streak Master Model 32 with micro-therm heat control and a quick-opening knife block

The new machine is being used to produce a large amount of both text and display and is turning out lots of food-store composition

Charles A Webb is president of the company Don S Elias is vice-president D Hiden Ramsey, secretary and general manager, and W. Randall Harris, treasurer and assistant general manager Col Cleveland Baber is mechanical superintendent; J R. Hesse, day foreman, and Hugh D Creighton, machinist. Thirteen Linotypes are operated.

In the accompanying picture, Lawrence Sherrill, operator, is shown seated at the new machine. At the left is Machinist Creighton, and at the right is A T. Baber, son of Colonel Baber.

Messrs. Creighton, Sherrill and Baber

EXAMPLE 250

Uncle Sam Adds Nine Linotypes

The Linotype News

VOLUME XIX | SECOND SECTION | BROOKLYN, MAY-JULY, 1941 | SEE SECTION ONE | NUMBER FOUR

Louisville Courier-Journal, Newark News Each Installs Six Additional Blue Streaks

Army and Navy Printing Plants Get New Models

Two With Quadders; Four Naval Vessels Install Master 31s

Uncle Sam, the biggest user of Linotypes in the world, recently installed nine more Linotypes in various branches of the service.

A Forty-two-Pica Blue Streak Master Model 31 with a self-quadder has been put in at the Command and General Staff Press at Fort Leavenworth, Kan. The Army Printing Plant at Fort Benning, Ga., has installed a Two-in-One Master Model 32 with a self-quadder, and another Model 32 has been installed at the Naval Air Station at Jacksonville.

A Master Model 31 has been put in by the United States Naval Station at Guantanamo Bay, Cuba, and a Master Model 32 at the United States Navy Yard, Pearl Harbor, Hawaii.

Also, Master Model 31s have been installed on the U. S. S. Colorado, U. S. S. Griffin, U. S. S Mormacyork, and U. S. S. Wright, making thirty-one vessels in Uncle Sam's navy now Linotype equipped.

Montgomery Firm Now 75 Years Old

The Brown Printing Company of Montgomery, one of the South's outstanding printing concerns, is observing its seventy-fifth anniversary this year.

The firm was organized soon after the War Between the States, by Milo Barrett and Warren D. Brown, and was first known as Barrett and Brown. A few years later it became the Brown Printing Company when J. H. Crenshaw purchased Mr. Barrett's interest. Under the guiding hand of Mr. Chenshaw and his son, Henry C. Crenshaw, the business was built from a small upstairs shop to the outstanding organization it is today, occupying a concrete-and-brick building with some 20,000 feet of floor space.

Today active management of the company is in the hands of Mrs Henry C. Crenshaw, its president; Files Crenshaw, vice-president; Miss Kathleen Flinn, secretary and treasurer; Herbert R. Nations, manager and James C. Shepard, superintendent. Frank Avery is operator and machinist.

Milliken Now Heads Tri-State Printers

At the meeting of the Tri-State Printers' Association held in Omaha May 24, with 110 delegates present from Nebraska, Kansas and Oklahoma, Harvey E. Milliken of Omaha was elected president to succeed Charles H. Armstrong of Wichita, who became chairman of the board.

Bern Semtner of Oklahoma City; Herbert A. Carr of Hutchinson, Kan., and Kendrick Ott of Lincoln were elected vice-presidents. Harry R. Horner of Wichita is the new secretary-treasurer.

The next meeting of the group will be held in Wichita in May of next year.

New Superintendent

Clyde B. Daly, who has been with the Knoxville News-Sentinel since 1922, is now composing-room superintendent of that paper. Mr. Daly served his apprenticeship with the Knoxville Journal and Tribune and worked as a journeyman there from 1917 to 1922, when he joined the News-Sentinel.

Benjamin Rounds Out 50 Years in Industry

George E. Benjamin, superintendent of the Waterbury American and the Republican composing rooms, rounded out fifty years in the industry April 15. At that, he is only sixty-three years old, for he got an early start in the industry.

He began his apprenticeship with the Ridgefield Press in 1891, and went to work for the Waterbury Republican in 1903, before it was joined with the American: He has been composing-room superintendent of the papers nineteen years.

Miss Caroline Dikeman, who was a bookkeeper with the Republican when he joined the staff, soon became Mrs. Benjamin. She is now assistant treasurer of the American-Republican, Inc.

A couple of days after the fiftieth anniversary, employees of the two papers presented Mr. Benjamin, through William J. Pape, publisher, with a fine fishing outfit.

Old Ohio Papers Now Operating In Unique Home

Chillicothe Structure Looks Like Old Timer, But Is Ultra Modern

Publishers of the Chillicothe Gazette, News-Advertiser and Sunday Gazette and Advertiser held open house Sunday, April 6, to welcome visitors to their new home, a replica of Ohio's first capitol and reputed to be one of the most modern small-city plants in the nation.

Contrasting with its early American original, the three-story building contains such modern touches as air conditioning and dehumidification, glass-block areas in the production department, with end-grain wood-block flooring in the composing room and pressroom, fluorescent lighting, black-walnut woodwork, and many other features, such as a voice-intercommunication system and pneumatic-tube system for copy delivery from editorial department to composing room. The new plant is equipped with carefully planned, efficient steel filing facilities in every department.

Briar Hill sandstone, matching that of the first capitol, which stood a few hundred feet to the northeast, was used in the construction of the replica part of the building, which is surmounted by a cupola and a weather vane.

In the wall on each side of the main entrance is a stone from the first capitol, which was built in 1800, the same year the Chillicothe Gazette was founded by Nathaniel Willis of Boston Tea Party fame.

Inset in the walls on each side of the lobby are display cases filled with original specimens of early printing, collected by Dard Hunter, curator of the Dard Hunter Museum of Paper Making at the Massachusetts Institute of Technology. Mr. Hunter was commissioned to collect the exhibit by Merritt C. Speidel, president of the company.

Southern Leader

Adoption of a new title and election of officers featured the annual meeting of the Southern Master Printers' Federation in Birmingham. Henceforth the organization will be known as the Southern Graphic Arts Association. Tom L. Ketchings (above) of the Tom L. Ketchings Company of Natchez, Miss., is president; A. Toof Brown, S. C. Toof & Company, Memphis, vice-president, and V. C. Garriott, Southern School of Printing, Nashville, is secretary-treasurer. Next year's convention will be held in Jacksonville.

The News Gets Plaque From Sharon Herald

From the Sharon (Pa.) Herald The Linotype News has received a desk plaque headed "Lest We Forget" and quoting the first amendment to the Constitution of the United States: "Congress shall make no law respecting an establishment of religion, or prohibiting the free exercise thereof; or abridging the freedom of speech or of the press."

The plaque, made in the Herald plant, was presented by A. W. McDowell, president of the Herald Company, and C. B. Lartz, general manager, who have expressed the willingness to provide the plaques in three different sizes, for inside or outside use, at cost, to all organizations wishing to secure them.

Wolff Adds 5 Linos, Golden Eagle Press Puts in 3 Machines

The Louisville Courier-Journal and the Times, which in the last few years have added thirteen Blue Streak Linotypes (eight of them Master Models 31s), have ordered six more Model 31s, two of them with six-mold disks.

The Courier-Journal also operates a pair of mixers—a Model 29 and a Model 30—both with the two-in-one feature and equipped with self-quadders and six-mold disks. Two Super-Display Model 33s handle the bulk of the display composition.

Body matter in both the Courier-Journal and the Times is in 7½-point Excelsior.

Barry Bingham, now serving as an officer in the navy, is owner of the papers. Mark Ethridge is vice-president and general manager, and George M. Martin is production manager. C. Frank Mann is superintendent of the composing room; Parker Stodgill, foreman of the Times; Curtis Alcock, foreman of the Courier-Journal; William Embry, head machinist of the Times, and Tom Shircliffe, head machinist of the Courier-Journal.

Newark Evening News

Six Blue Streak Linotypes—five Mixer Model 29s and a Master Model 31—have been added by the Newark Evening News, which now operates forty Linotypes, including eight Model 29s and three Model 31s. The new machines were equipped with micro-therm heat controls and Mohr saws.

The News was among the first to use Spartan duplicate-character matrices for use in food-store composition—a procedure that since has become standard practice.

Edward W. Scudder is president and treasurer of the publishing company and publisher of the paper. William E Hocker is vice-president, and William L. Morgan is secretary. Benjamin J. Foley is general manager; Arthur J. Sinnott, editor-in-chief, and Lloyd M. Felmly, editor. Thomas Kenney is production manager; William E. Putscher, foreman of the composing room; William F. Becht, assistant foreman; James Clarkson, head machinist, and Earl V. Depew, assistant head machinist.

H. Wolff Company

Five Linotypes have been added by the H. Wolff Book Manufacturing Company, Inc., New York City, which now operates seven Linotypes.

This concern, established in 1893, is well known for its printing, publishing and binding of fine books. It occupies most of its own twelve-story building.

Bertram Wolff is president of the company. Nathan H. Shrifte is vice-president; Arthur Wolff, secretary; Louis J. Vorhaus, treasurer, and W. H. Wilkens, assistant treasurer. George Irving, superintendent, keeps the work flowing smoothly through the various stages of production. Joseph Whiteway is foreman of the composing room, and Joseph Hack is Linotype machinist.

Golden Eagle Press

Three Linotypes and several fonts of Baskerville, Caledonia, Estienne, Granjon and Janson have been installed by Samuel A. Jacobs, proprietor of the Golden Eagle Press, Mount Vernon, N. Y.

Note the many other installation stories on other pages of this issue of The Linotype News.

New England Execs Name Hutt

Members of the New England Daily Newspaper Composing Room Executives' Association, in session at Lodge Pole Ranch, Beverly, Mass., May 4, elected Edwin A. Hutt, composing-room foreman of the Beverly Evening Times, president to succeed Francis M. Britton, production manager of the Nashua (N. H.) Telegraph.

Raymond J. Cox of the Bangor Daily News was elected vice-president to succeed Daniel Stevens of the Middletown Press; William Madden of the Worcester Gazette was named secretary to succeed Joseph J. Mahoney of the Holyoke Transcript-Telegram, and Lewis R. Green of the Westerly (R. I.) Sun was elected treasurer to succeed J. Frank Coughlin of the Holyoke Transcript-Telegram. Mr. Stevens was named to the board of directors for three years, and Ralph Johnson of the Brockton Enterprise was named to fill an unexpired term as director.

Lewis R. Hovey, publisher of the Beverly Evening Times and Haverhill Sunday Record, welcomed the delegates to Beverly, and later paid tribute to the new president of the association. Laurence S. Hovey, business manager of the Times, and Carleton B. Hovey, managing editor of that paper, also spoke.

Treasurer Green, Secretary Madden, Vice-President Cox, President Hutt and Directors Johnson and Stevens

A BIG JOB IN A BIG WAY BY LINOTYPE

EXAMPLE 251

The Linotype News

VOLUME XX — BROOKLYN, OCTOBER-DECEMBER, 1941 — NUMBER TWO

Chicago News Adds 9 Linotypes For Setting of Field's Chicago Sun

New Morning Paper Using Excelsior, Ionic, Erbar, Memphis, Metro

Thursday morning, December 4, the Chicago Sun came up brightly over the City by the Lake, despite the fact that the skies in that part of the country were a bit soupy for several hours.

To many of the people who eagerly scanned the more than 900,000 copies of the first actual issue, the new paper was bright not only as to content but as to format.

The Sun, founded by Marshall Field and published by Silliman Evans, is being produced in the plant of the Chicago Daily News, which has installed and is installing much new equipment.

Nine New Linotypes Ordered

Eight Blue Streak Master Model 31s and an All-Purpose Linotype were installed for use on the first issue of the new paper

Most of the heads in the Sun are appearing in Erbar Medium Condensed and Metromedium No. 2, with heads on the women's pages in lighter members of the Memphis family. News body matter is in 7½-point Excelsior with Bold Face No 2, and classified is in 5½-point Ionic No 5 with Bold Face No 2.

Among the many display faces ordered for the A-P-L were series of Metroblack No 2 and Metromedium No 2 up to 144 point. The format was designed by Gilbert P Farrar of New York City, who has been warmly commended on the readability of the paper.

First Issue Seventy-two Pages

The first ready-for-the-public issue of the Sun (which had made up and printed but had not publicly distributed eight rehearsal issues) consisted of seventy-two pages. A twelve-page section devoid of advertising carried congratulatory messages from many people of prominence

Mr Evans announced the morning the new paper came out that half again as much advertising as appeared in the first issue was withheld for presentation later

Advertising in the first issue consisted of 82,862 lines of total display, covering 215 advertisers, and 8,531 lines of classified, for a total of 300 columns.

Good Job Well Done

Some idea of the production problems that were solved in the News plant in a matter of hours may be had when it is considered that the News of December 3 was a sixty-four-page paper with a run of more than 500,000, and that it was followed by a run of more than 900,000 copies of the seventy-two-page Sun.

Among those who deserve much credit for the good job well done, in addition to Founder Field, Publisher Evans, Ward Mayborn, assistant to Mr. Evans, and members of their staffs, are Herbert L. Fairfield, business manager of the News, and John W. Harm, mechanical superintendent.

THE CHICAGO SUN — TWO CENTS

REVOLT GROWS IN SERBIA

Labor to Ask Murphy Ouster

Anti-Strike Bill Passed By House

Federation Will Urge Green to Act

Air Raid Net Will Guard Chicago

Hitler Forced To Put Army On '3d Front'

Reds Reach Taganrog, Axis Holds Edge in Libya

See Ray of Hope In Pacific Crisis

S. N. P. A. Mechanical Executives To Stage Conference in Galveston

Western Division Men Will Conduct Sessions On February 16 and 17

Plans for the next annual Southern Newspaper Mechanical Conference (western division), to be held in Galveston, February 16 and 17, 1942, were discussed at a meeting of the conference's executive committee in Dallas, Sunday, November 23

Sessions of the conference will be held at the Galvez Hotel, and registration will begin at 3 p m Sunday, February 15. Delegates will also be registered, starting at 8 a m, each morning of the conference. Sessions will start at 9 30 and 2 p m each day

Topic leaders for the conference, which will be attended by representatives from newspaper mechanical departments in Texas, Oklahoma, Louisiana and Arkansas, are:

Composing Room—James A Cinnamon, mechanical superintendent of the Enid News and the Eagle. Machinist—E. R Turner, machinist of the Wichita Falls Times and the Record-News. Stereotype—E. A Turner, stereotype foreman of the Arkansas Democrat, Little Rock. Pressroom—E. C. George, pressroom foreman of the Houston Press. Photo-engraving—L C McMerrick, photo-engraving foreman of the Oklahoma City Oklahoman and the Times

Members of the executive committee of the conference are Bert Conner and A T Blease, Corpus Christi Caller-Times, J. M. Lighett, Beaumont Enterprise and the Journal. O M Harper, Newspaper Printing Corporation, Tulsa; R M Crawford, Shreveport Times, F J Williamson, San Antonio Express and the News. L W Culver, Fort Worth Star-Telegram. C C Washburn, Galveston News and the Tribune, and W F Thompson, Austin American-Statesman

C C Washburn of Galveston is in charge of local arrangements for the meeting

The conference last year was held in Forth Worth

Pandick Puts in Six Linos And Washington Post Five

The Pandick Press of New York City has installed six Forty-two-Pica Master Model 31s with thermo-blo mold coolers and now operates twenty-eight Linotypes

Miss A C Pandick is president of this concern, which turns out a large amount of book, job and law printing. A H G Hanning is vice-president, H Wayne Oakley, secretary and production manager, and Miss L R Wandell, treasurer. Julius Widemier is mechanical superintendent, Samuel Horowitz, foreman of the composing room, and Alexander P Basola and Ray J Remas, Linotype machinists

The Washington Post

The Washington Post, which recently remodeled its building, has installed five additional Master Model 31 Linotypes, each with a micro-therm heat control, Margach metal feeder and automatic ejector set. Thirty-six Linos are now operated, including two Mixer Model 30s and eight Master Model 31s

Eugene Meyer is publisher and editor, Alexander F Jones, managing editor, F R Harrison, treasurer, and C C Boysen, comptroller and business manager. T J Weir is production manager. E J Greenwald is assistant production manager. Thomas N Lynn, foreman of the composing room, and Paul Hysan, head machinist.

Three for Van Rees

Three Linotypes have been added by the Van Rees Book Composition Company of New York City, which now operates thirteen Linotypes

Richard Van Rees is president and secretary of the concern. A. Wilson Van Rees is production manager, Sterling Van Rees, mechanical superintendent, Vincent O'Connor, general foreman, Jerry Schonfeld, machine foreman, and Edward Kaag, machinist.

Plough of Memphis

Two Mixer Model 29s with self-quadders, six-mold disks, thermo-blo mold coolers have been installed by the Plough Printing and Box Company at Memphis. Included in the installation were eighteen extra magazines, two Reid magazine racks and many fonts of matrices.

George Krebs is general manager of the plant. R. L. Bryan is composing-room foreman, and Leo Scarborough is machinist-operator.

Burlington Free Press

Two Linotypes and several fonts of 7-point Excelsior No. 1 have been installed by the Burlington (Vt.) Free Press, David W. Howe, business manager.

Lewiston, Maine

Two Linotypes have been added by the Lewiston (Maine) Sun and the Journal

Russell Costello is the production manager, and Albert Shaw is the machinist.

Manchester, N. H.

Avenir National, French daily of Manchester, N H, has installed two Master Model 31s

Ernest Bournival is owner and publisher. Clarence Gamache is composing-room foreman and Linotype machinist

Poor Richard Club Honors W. M. Dear

The Poor Richard Club of Philadelphia will bestow its 1942 gold medal on Walter M Dear, publisher of the Jersey Journal of Jersey City, N J, and president of the American Newspaper Publishers' Association

The presentation will be made at the club's annual banquet, at the Bellevue-Stratford Hotel, Philadelphia, January 16, the day on which Benjamin Franklin's birthday will be celebrated in Philadelphia

Brooklyn Eagle Marks Centenary

The Brooklyn Eagle observed its hundredth anniversary by coming out Sunday, October 26, with a special issue of 138 pages that included an anniversary section of seventy-six pages and a reproduction of the first issue of the Eagle. The big paper was the largest in the history of the Eagle

A story headed "Brooklyn Furnishes World With Typesetting Machines" included this statement: "The great Mergenthaler plant at 29 Ryerson Street is the largest factory, in point of physical size, in Brooklyn and in the entire metropolitan area."

Linotypes Installed in 1894

Linotypes were first installed by the Eagle in August of 1894. Only news body matter and classified advertisements were set on them until 1898, when additional machines were purchased and equipped to set display up to 36 point. Thirty-nine Linotypes are now operated.

Among the Eagle people who played important parts in the production of the big special, in addition to Publisher Schroth, were William F Crowell, business manager; Andrew Bernhard, managing editor; John E. Dean, advertising manager; Charles A. Schoen, promotion manager; David George, editor of the anniversary section; Isadore Cohen, circulation manager; Stephen J. Lambert, production manager, and Thomas A Reddington, foreman of the composing room.

Installs Thermo-Blos On Eleven Linotypes

So well pleased was the Sharon Herald Company of Sharon, Pa., with a thermo-blo installed on one of its Linotypes several months ago it since has placed thermo-blos on all of its Linotypes—eleven of them

A. W. McDowell is president of the company, and A. C. Dickinson and J. S. Pharmer are vice-presidents. C. B Lartz is secretary and general manager, and W. L. Aiken is treasurer and editor. G. A. Harshman is business manager. M. T Alderman is foreman of the composing room, and A. T. Richards is machinist.

Kreiling Rounds Out 50 Years With Lino

Julius W. Kreiling, Chicago typesetting-machine engineer, was honored September 27, when a few of his friends gathered at his home to mark the fiftieth anniversary of his association with the Linotype.

Half a century ago he went to work in Baltimore with Ottmar Mergenthaler, inventor of the Linotype, and has kept up with Linotype mechanical developments since.

For several years he has been offering his services as a typesetting-machine consultant.

Some New Presidents

Mack F Denman, assistant editor of the News at Farmington, Mo., where his father, Harry Denman, is editor-in-chief, is the new president of the Southeast Missouri Press Association. Clint Denman of the Sikeston Herald and former president of the Missouri Press Association is an uncle

C H Dickinson, general manager of the Ryerson Press, Toronto, is the new president of the Toronto Graphic Arts Association. A. L. Lewis is honorary president, and A. Gordon Burns and Harold Dyment are vice-presidents. Alex. Gilchrist is treasurer, and R. E. Roddy is recording secretary. Miss Olive A. Ottaway continues as executive secretary

Herb G Grey, advertising manager of the Medford (Ore.) Mail-Tribune, is the new president of the Oregon Newspaper Publishers' Association. Jack B. Bladine of the McMinnville Telephone-Register is vice-president, and Palmer Hoyt of the Portland Oregonian is treasurer. Harry S. Schenk continues as secretary

William H Baldwin, composing-room superintendent of the Peoria Star, is the new president of the Peoria Club of Printing House Craftsmen. F. H. McCormick is vice-president; Sumner Stein, second vice-president; R O. Becker, secretary; Willard Fowler, associate secretary, and George Mebus, treasurer

EXAMPLE 252

Heads and body matter in that number were set in members of the same type families used for the numbers suggested by Examples 250 and 251.

A lively and forceful front page featured the newspaper section for March-May, 1942, with heads in members of the Bodoni family, and body matter again in 7½-point Corona with Bold Face No. 2 on an 8½-point body. See Example 253.

Observe the contrast between heads—harmonious contrast—with plenty of variety—all obtainable from a single good type family.

Newsprint shortages during World War II dictated the dropping, at least temporarily, of the newspaper section, but the typographic laboratory has continued to experiment with and to turn out many more tabloid and larger size pages.

In the summer of 1942, that laboratory co-operated with the *Daily Racing Form* of New York and other cities in the working out of a uniform head schedule to be followed for editions of the *Daily Racing Form* not only in New York City but in Chicago, Los Angeles and Houston as well.

That head schedule was planned for four 15-pica columns to the page, and held entirely to Metromedium No. 2 and Metromedium No. 2 Italic. All heads were in capitals and lower-case and set flush at the left, with white space taking the place of the jim dashes formerly used between and immediately below decks.

The schedule included three different banner treatments, one three-column head, five different two-column heads, and seven different single-column heads. Yet most of those sixteen different heads, which afforded the *Daily Racing Form* plenty of freedom for several different kinds of makeup, to meet the demands of any day's flow of news, could be produced from only five keyboard fonts in each plant —10-, 12-, 14-, 18- and 24-point Metromedium No. 2 with Italic.

The 30-, 36-, 48- and 60-point faces employed for the less frequently used heads were set up as needed from individual characters cast from matrices from an All-Purpose Linotype. (Those characters were cast on hard metal in New York City and an adequate supply sent to each of the four plants.)

Regular news body matter in all four papers was in 7½-point Ionic No. 5 on an 8½-point body, with leads and occasional other matter in 10-point Ionic No. 5 leaded 2 points.

The Linotype News

VOLUME XX | BROOKLYN, MARCH-MAY, 1942 | NUMBER FOUR

Linotype-Set Papers Again Win Leading Awards in Ayer Contest

Poughkeepsie Newspapers Add Eight New Linotypes

Company Also Installs Fourteen Thermo-Blos And Seventeen Fonts

Eight Linotypes, including three Master Model 31s and two Super-Display Mixer Model 35s, have been added by Poughkeepsie Newspapers, Inc., of Poughkeepsie, N. Y.

Included in the order were fourteen thermo-blo mold coolers for the fourteen Linotypes now operated by the company, and seventeen fonts of matrices. The Model 35s are equipped with six-mold disks.

Merritt C. Speidel is president of Poughkeepsie Newspapers, Inc., which publishes the New Yorker, the Eagle-News and the Hudson Valley Sunday Courier, all members of the Speidel chain of newspapers. Robert M. Speidel is vice-president of the Poughkeepsie company; Harry S. Bunker, secretary and general manager, and Edward A. Chappell, treasurer and publisher. Richard E. Coon is business manager, and Clifford J. Nuhn is editorial director. Frank Jacobs is mechanical superintendent; Clair S. Harrington, day machinist, and Ray Shepard, night machinist.

Farquharson M. E. Of Globe and Mail

Robert A. Farquharson, who has served many years with the Toronto Globe and the Mail and Empire but had been on a leave of absence, serving the Canadian Government, has been appointed managing editor of the Globe and Mail. Mr. Farquharson was on the staff of the Globe for nine years, and for nine years on the Mail and Empire, of which he was managing editor when it was purchased by the Globe Printing Company.

R. A. Farquharson

After the war started, Mr. Farquharson went to Ottawa as parliamentary correspondent for the Globe and Mail. Last year he was loaned to the government.

Many Publishers See Showing of War Work

A confidential demonstration of war material produced by the printing-equipment industry was presented April 21 to many newspaper publishers and manufacturers, at the Waldorf-Astoria, New York City.

Maj.-Gen. Levin H. Campbell, Jr., chief of the ordnance office, Washington, D. C., spoke "off the record" about the functions of the ordnance department, and paid tribute to the war work now being produced by the makers of printing machinery.

General Campbell speaking

New York ordnance district officers prepared a demonstration and arranged the program. Artillery and fire-control apparatus, in the hands of a special crew of army technicians, demonstrated extraordinary developments in defense against aircraft. Confidential moving pictures, made for army purposes, showed in field use some of the fifty-five kinds of war material now being made in plants formerly devoted to the graphic arts.

General Campbell stressed the unusual demands made by the ordnance department not alone for quantities of products but for extreme precision in their manufacture. He showed that the normal peacetime activities of these manufacturers had prepared them for this further demand upon their men and equipment.

The sponsoring manufacturers were American Type Founders, Dexter Folder Company, Duplex Printing Press Company, Goss Printing Press Company, Harris-Seybold Potter Company, R. Hoe and Company, Lanston Monotype Machine Company, Ludlow Typograph Company, Mergenthaler Linotype Company, Miehle Printing Press and Manufacturing Company, Mohr Lino-Saw Company, Walter Scott and Company, Wood Newspaper Machinery Company, and Vandercook and Sons. James Wright Brown of Editor & Publisher presided.

The guests received an interesting souvenir book with articles on the history and function of the ordnance department, printed by the Linotype Company.

At a dinner preceding the ordnance program, tendered by Joseph T. Mackey, Linotype president, to General Campbell and his fellow officers, the equipment manufacturers held a brief war-work convention with their new and most urgent customers, the representatives of Uncle Sam.

Some of those present at the Mackey dinner, left to right: Col. G. M. Welch, Frankford Arsenal; C. A. Hanson, Linotype vice-president in charge of works; General Campbell; Mr. Mackey; Col. J. K. Clement, deputy district chief, New York ordnance district; George W. Allison, Linotype assistant vice-president and assistant works manager, and Col. G. W. Trichel, Frankford Arsenal.—Pictures by U. S. Army Signal Corps.

Many Other Plants, In Various Sections, Improve Equipments

The News-Journal Company of Wilmington, Del., which in recent years has installed nine Linotypes, has added three more, two of them Master Model 31s with 30-pica six-mold disks and automatic ejectors.

Henry T. Claus is president of the company, and Henry Davis is treasurer. William F. Metten is business manager; W. Murray Metten, director of production; Harold C. Berg, assistant director, and William N. Reinhart, machinist.

Nashville, Tenn.

The Newspaper Printing Corporation of Nashville, which a few months ago installed two Mixer Model 29s, has put in two more Blue Streaks—a Two-in-One Mixer Model 29 and a Master Model 31.

The latest Model 29, to be used for heads, is equipped with a self-quadder, six-mold disk, Mohr saw, thermo-blo mold cooler and micro-therm heat control. Another Model 29 similarly equipped is also used for head production. All of the Linotypes in the ad room are equipped with self-quadders and Mohr saws.

The Newspaper Printing Corporation produces the Nashville Banner and the Nashville Tennessean.

New York City

Lenz & Riecker, Inc., of New York City, which in the last couple of years has added a Mixer Model 29 and a Mixer Model 30, both with 30-pica six-mold disks, self-quadders and automatic-ejector sets, has installed two more Mixer Linotypes with self-quadders.

William F. Riecker is president of the company, and Thomas A. Leonetti is vice-president. Raymond Scully is mechanical superintendent, John H. Lewys, composing-room foreman, and Harry Heik, machinist. Twelve Linotypes (five with self-quadders) are now operated.

Two Model 8s with Margach metal feeders and several fonts of matrices have been added by the F. & D. Printing Company, Inc., of New York City, which now operates eighteen Linotypes.

Arthur H. Stein is president of the company, and Morris Golos is secretary-treasurer. E. Weiman is Linotype machinist.

Auburn, Maine

Two Master Model 31s with Kendall metal feeders have been installed by the Merrill & Webber Company of Auburn, Maine. John H. Merrill is president of the organization.

Philadelphia

The Machine Composition Company of Philadelphia has added two Model 8 Linotypes.

Munyer Now Setting Several Magazines

The A. E. Munyer Electrotype Company, Inc., of Brooklyn is now producing the composition for several Munsey publications, chiefly in members of the Caledonia and Spartan families.

The publications are Argosy, Railroad, All-Star Love, All Story, Flynn's Detective, and Famous Fantastic Mysteries.

The company pulls stereo mats of made-up pages and sends them to the McCall Company at Dayton, Ohio, where the publications are printed.

Munyer also composes the Scholastic magazine, set in Caledonia.

Most Valuable

D. W. Grandon, co-publisher, with his son, P. F. Grandon, of the Grandon group of Illinois newspapers, has been voted the most valuable citizen of Sterling, Ill., by the Sterling Rotary Club. The elder Mr. Grandon is eighty-three years old, and has been in newspaper work sixty-nine years.

6 Indiana Papers Win Lino Awards

At the latest annual convention of the Hoosier State Press Association, in Indianapolis, February 20 and 21, handsomely printed certificates provided by the Linotype Company were awarded to six Indiana newspapers as first prizes in the association's latest better-newspaper contests.

The Lafayette Journal and Courier won a certificate for the best special edition among dailies, and the Tell City News a certificate for the best special among weeklies. The Gas City Journal was honored for the best feature story among weeklies with more than 1,500 circulation, and the Jonesboro Journal for the best feature story among weeklies with less than 1,500 circulation. The Corydon Democrat won a certificate for the best use of pictures among county-seat weeklies, and the Greenwood News won a certificate for the best use of pictures among non-county-seat weekly papers.

Canadians to Meet In Saskatoon, Sask.

The 1942 annual convention of the Canadian Weekly Newspapers Association will be held in Saskatoon, Sask., in August.

Walter Legge of the Granby (Que.) Leader-Mail is president of the association.

New York Times Has Second Leg On Second Cup

All eleven of the United States dailies honored in the latest Ayer contest for excellence in typography, makeup and presswork are Linotype users, and eight of them employ members of the famous Linotype Legibility Group for body matter. Three are set in Excelsior, three in Ionic, one in Paragon, and one in the new Corona. In addition, one of the winners uses Linotype Caledonia for body matter.

The New York Times came in first this year and now has two legs on the second F. Wayland Ayer cup. The New York Herald Tribune, which won permanent possession of the first cup by winning it twice, also has two legs on the second cup.

The Ten Honorable Mentions

First honorable mention this year among standard-size papers of more than 50,000 circulation was won by the New York Herald Tribune; second, Christian Science Monitor; third, Baltimore Evening Sun.

First honorable mention in the 10,000 to 50,000 circulation group went to the Lynchburg (Va.) News; second, Billings (Mont.) Gazette; third, Rutland (Vt.) Daily Herald.

First honorable mention in the group with circulations of less than 10,000 went to the Troy Record; second, Alexandria (Va.) Gazette; third, Public Opinion of Chambersburg, Pa.

PM of New York won honorable mention among tabloids.

The judges were Dr. M. F. Agha, art director of Conde-Nast publications; Ernest K. Lindley, chief of the Washington bureau of Newsweek, and Lewis W. Trayser, vice-president of the Curtis Publishing Company.

Missouri Paper In New Home

The Mansfield (Mo.) Mirror, Ralph O. Watters, publisher, is now operating in a new building. The structure is equipped with an automatic heating plant, fluorescent lighting, and an exposed east wall that provides an abundance of natural daylight and ventilation.

Ruth Carter is reporter and bookkeeper; John Hensley, shop foreman and operator; Bill Chester, compositor, and Don Cooley, apprentice.

Since Mr. Watters acquired the Mirror, five years ago, its circulation has been quadrupled, and the paper has increased from four to eight and ten pages. A thriving printing and office-supply business serves customers in more than thirty southeast Missouri counties.

The five pictured here were snapped at the latest annual meeting of the New Mexico Press Association. B. H. ("Doc") Kirby of the Portales Tribune, president of the association, is shown at the extreme right, and Earl Grau of the Tucumcari News, secretary, at the extreme left. In between them are Mrs. Grau, Mrs. Kirby and young Terry Kirby.

EXAMPLE 253

When the new head schedule was completed and approved, in the New York offices of the *Daily Racing Form*, proofs were pulled and sent to the offices in Chicago, Los Angeles and Houston.

Along with those proofs went proofs of seven different front-page makeups to suggest graphically and specifically some of the many possibilities of the new schedule.

Some of those proofs were posted in all four editorial offices and composing rooms, in advance of the change-overs, so that staff members might familiarize themselves with the new unit counts and other features of the head schedule and the new page makeups. Moreover, to make certain that the change-overs would go through without a hitch, the editor-in-chief of the papers visited the Chicago, Los Angeles and Houston plants and explained all details.

After the new head schedule had been put to work in all four plants of the *Daily Racing Form*, Kenneth Friede, publisher, informed this writer:

"Readers in all four cities are strong for the new dress. Plenty have let us know that they like our looks, but even more have told us that the papers are now much easier to read.

"Of course, that's what we hoped they'd do, and we're glad our efforts are appreciated. But there's another angle that's important, too —the speeding up of production and the cutting of production costs.

"Our new dress is a lot simpler than the old. It involves fewer type faces; a lot fewer magazine changes; less storage space; and it gets away from a lot of dead wood, or metal, that should have been tossed out long ago.

"We now have a head schedule as modern as next year's Derby winner and easy on the eyes—the same for each plant. And we have a production schedule as speedy as a fast track—the same for each plant."

One weekly newspaper publisher who changed from eight pages of eight columns each to sixteen pages of five columns did it, he explained, chiefly because he found it possible to present his thirty regular departments more effectively on the increased number of smaller pages than on half as many of the larger pages.

"We have a possible eighty top-column positions now," that publisher stated, "against only sixty-four before. The eighty columns are an aid also in placing advertising, particularly for the smaller ads, to which we devote a lot of attention, for getting results for small advertisers is calculated to transform them into larger users of space."

Another weekly publisher who changed to a tabloid did it, he said, because in addition to several reasons previously explained, many high-school students were used to the smaller page papers issued by their schools, and millions of service men and women had become used to the tabloid papers issued by and for members of various service organizations.

"From a strictly business angle," that publisher added, "an advertiser can buy visibility and dominance for his ad in a tabloid at much less cost than in a standard-sized paper. For example, a single-column 15-inch ad can dominate a tabloid page, whereas on a standard page it could not."

An attractive page size for a five-column paper with columns 12 picas wide is one with a width of 11½ inches and a depth of 15½ inches. This allows for four 6-point column rules, with side margins a little more than 3 picas wide, and a type-page depth of 86½ picas, with a 3-pica margin at the top and a 3½-pica margin at the bottom.

Of course head faces of the kind shown in Chapters 5, 16 and 17 of Part I of this book, and body faces of the kind shown in Chapters 6, 16 and 20 of Part I, can be just as effective for tabloid papers as for papers with larger page sizes.

7

Prize Winners

THE PRINTED PAGES of a newspaper should be attractive and easy to read. The reader should be able to get the message clearly and quickly.

Advertising-agency executives, who must get favorable results from advertising for their clients or lose the accounts, are well aware of this. They know that an advertisement that does not attract favorable attention and get itself read is not a good advertisement, even though the copy itself be excellent. They know that a well-planned and well-composed advertisement can be marred by poor presswork; by being placed on a poorly made up page; by many things in a newspaper plant.

Consequently, when agency space buyers compile a list of newspapers for an advertising campaign, they are inclined to favor the most attractive paper in a community, other things being equal or nearly so.

For many years many organizations have been encouraging newspaper executives to improve the appearance of their papers. National, regional and state associations of newspaper executives have conducted clinics and contests to encourage improvement. Trade journals have sponsored or encouraged improvement contests, and so have manufacturers of newspaper machinery and supplies.

The manufacturers, naturally, are just as interested in improvement as any others in the industry, for they realize that successful newspapers make much better customers than unsuccessful papers.

From its very beginning, the *Linotype News* has encouraged improvement contests and has provided many national, regional and state associations with loving cups and certificates of award for prize winners.

Back in 1931, when many of our newspapers were considerably less attractive than they are now; when many papers were presenting most of their headlines in capital letters, rather than in capitals and lower-case, which are easier to read; when many papers were employing small body faces with the thought, if they thought about it at all, that word count was more to be desired than legibility; when the advertising columns of many papers were considerably less effective than they are today, a big advertising agency in Philadelphia, N. W. Ayer & Son, Inc., introduced the first of its annual contests, open to all daily newspapers printed in English in the United States, for excellence in typography, makeup and presswork.

The Ayer trophy that first year (1931) was won by the *New York Herald Tribune*, which won it again in 1934 and in 1936. (Those three winnings gave the *Herald Tribune* permanent possession, and a second Ayer trophy was offered in 1937.)

Other newspapers that won "legs" on the first Ayer trophy were the *Hartford Courant*, in 1932, and the *New York Times*, in 1933 and in 1935.

In 1937 the *Los Angeles Times* won the first "leg" on the second Ayer trophy; in 1938 the *Newark Evening News* won first honors; in 1939 the *New York Herald Tribune;* in 1940, the *New York Times*; in 1941, the *New York Herald Tribune*; in 1942, the *New York Times*; in 1943, the *Christian Science Monitor*, of Boston; in 1944, the *Chicago Sun*, and in 1945, the *New York Herald Tribune*.

That third winning in the second series by the *New York Herald Tribune* gave that paper permanent possession of the second Ayer trophy, and a third trophy was offered by the Ayer people in 1946.

In the years from 1931 to and including 1938, issues of March 4 of each year were submitted for the contests, a date announced in advance.

In 1939, however, it was thought best by Ayer officials not to call for copies of a predetermined date, but to select by lot, after the date of issue, any week-day date in a two-weeks' period in March. (More recently, that period was shortened to one week.)

The idea of the two-week or one-week period, of course, was to encourage newspapers to pay close attention to production details for at least several days each year, rather than for a single day, as before.

Each year different men or women (usually three, but sometimes four and even five) have been invited by Ayer officials to judge the papers entered. While these people, of course, have personal likes and dislikes that undoubtedly play a part in their judgments, they are selected to bring to bear in each contest different points of view.

Among the judges, at various times, have been newspaper publishers, editors and writers, trade-journal editors, teachers of journalism, printers, typographers, and commercial designers.

In 1931 and again in 1932 the newspapers entered in the Ayer contests were judged in a single classification. In 1933 the contest was divided into three circulation groups; one group for newspapers with circulations of more than 50,000; one for newspapers with circulations between 10,000 and 50,000, and one group for newspapers with circulations less than 10,000.

In 1938 the judges began honoring ten newspapers each year, instead of nine. They named the trophy winner and nine others—first-, second- and third-honorable-mention winners in each of the three circulation groups.

The 1939 contest included a fourth division, for tabloid newspapers, and first honorable mention in that division was won by the *New York Daily News*. In 1940 the winner of first honorable mention in the tabloid division was the *Chicago Daily Times*; in 1941, 1942, 1943 and 1944, *PM* of New York City, and in 1945, the *Washington* (D. C.) *News*.

Most of the Ayer winners from the beginning have presented most of their heads in capitals and lower-case, rather than in capitals; most of them have presented most of their general-news heads in single or closely related type families, and most of them have employed body types that were specially designed for use by modern newspapers.

In referring to the Ayer contest in 1940, H. A. Batten, president of the Ayer organization, stated, in part:

"While the average reader might not be able to explain 'why' in so many words, there is no question that he reads more of the paper, and therefore sees more of the advertising, when the makeup is inviting and the typography is such that it is easy for him to follow the news from page to page.

"That the reader has become more discriminating with regard to the way in which printed material is presented can be verified readily through the experience of advertising. Survey after survey have shown that well-designed, good-looking, easily read advertisements do far better than those which are jumbled and hard to read. The reader's reaction is undoubtedly similar in the case of news.

"We are indeed gratified at the extent to which publishers have recognized the role of good typography in creating a product which is more attractive and interesting to the reader, and therefore more effective for the advertiser to use."

In referring to the Ayer contest in 1941, which was held some eight months before the attack on Pearl Harbor, Mr. Batten called attention to the big total circulation gain made by newspapers in the United States since the inauguration of the Ayer contests.

"This," he stated, "can be explained in part by the stirring news of our times. But I think a further explanation can be found in the steady improvement in newspaper makeup and general readability.

"Examining the more than 1000 entries in this year's exhibition, one is impressed with the progress being made now, when the flood of foreign and domestic news makes the job of putting together an attractive paper much harder than it would be under normal conditions. Actually, the advances this year by the papers on the whole, and especially by those of from 10,000 to 50,000 circulation, appear to have been greater than in any previous year.

"I believe one reason why the papers are able to continue improving, even under the pressure of unusual news demands, is that they paved the way in less active periods when there was time to study and adjust standards and facilities. They are a good example of the beneficial results any business can expect when it takes advantage of its opportunities to build constructively for the future."

In 1946 the winner of the Ayer trophy was the *Rochester* (Minn.) *Post-Bulletin*, which had been restyled some eight years before by Thomas F. Barnhart, professor of journalism at the University of Minnesota. Flush-left heads in capitals and lower-case of sans-serif and square-serif faces were used throughout the prize winner, and news body matter was set in 8-point No. 2 with Condensed Title No. 3 cast on a 9-point body.

Example 254 presents a reduced showing of the front page of the prize-winning *Post-Bulletin*.

The tabloid winner of first honorable mention in 1946 was the *York* (Pa.) *Gazette and Daily*, with flush-left heads chiefly in sans-serif capitals and lower-case, and news body matter in 8-point Regal cast on an 8-point body.

Example 255 presents a reduced showing of the front page of the prize-winning *Gazette and Daily*.

All fifteen of the newspapers honored in the 1946 contest presented

ROCHESTER POST-BULLETIN

VOL. 21, NO. 292 | ROCHESTER, MINNESOTA, WEDNESDAY, MARCH 13, 1946 | Full Leased Wire Service of the Associated Press | PRICE FIVE CENTS

GM Wage Agreement Reached

U. S. Troubled By Reported Iran Moves

Note Asks Soviet Reply to Report Of Reinforcements

By JOHN M. HIGHTOWER

WASHINGTON, (AP) — Reports of large Red army reinforcements moving into Iran put a new strain on Russian-American relations today and threatened a critical test of UNO's powers to preserve peace.

The reports have yet to be formally confirmed or officially denied, but this government has sent a note to Moscow asking what the Russians are up to and why.

Officials here are frankly puzzled as to the Russian objective in sending more troops into a country from which it was supposed by international agreement to have withdrawn all its forces by March 2.

Speculation on what the Russians may be up to covers three possibilities. Diplomats believe (1) they may be trying to force a pro-Soviet government on Iran, or (2) to bring sufficient threats of force against Turkey to win territorial concessions and rights in the Dardenelles, or (3) that they may have some designs on the Mosul oil fields of Iraq.

IN SHARP CONFLICT

If any of these or a combination is the answer, it seems certain that Russian aims will be in sharper conflict with British interests and with American pronouncements than at any time since war's end.

Top officials here firmly expect that unless the Russians change course and greatly modify their reported activities the whole issue again will be thrown into the United Nations security council, scheduled to open its next meeting in New York March 25.

The Iranian case was presented to the council at its recent London meeting by Iran itself with an appeal for some action to end alleged Soviet infringements on Iranian independence. The case finally was dismissed with a statement that Iran and Russia should try to settle their differences by direct negotiations. For that purpose Iran premier Ahmed Qavam es Sultaneh went to Moscow but failed to reach a settlement.

TEST OF UNO

While he was there the March 2 deadline passed and the Russians announced that while they would make a partial withdrawal they would keep some troops on hand until the troubled political conditions in the province of Azerbaijan were settled.

Speculation is that on any proposal for the council to take strong action, Russia would exercise its right of veto. Byrnes' declaration might be interpreted then as meaning that the United States and such other countries as hold the same view would act in spite of the veto.

Weather Forecasts

(U. S. Weather Bureau)

ROCHESTER AND VICINITY—Partly cloudy and mild tonight and Thursday, with occasional showers Thursday. Low temperature tonight 35; high Thursday upper 50's.

MINNESOTA—Partly cloudy and mild tonight and Thursday, except cooler in north portion Thursday. Occasional showers in extreme south portion Thursday.

Maximum yesterday, 52 at 4 p.m.
Minimum last night, 42 at 6 a.m.
At 6:30 a.m., 43. At 12:30 p.m. 55.

Sunset today 6:13
Sunrise tomorrow 6:25

A Year Ago
Maximum ....49 Minimum 32

	Min	Max	Pct
Chicago	48	67	.04
Denver	38	64	
Des Moines	49	60	.22
Duluth	33	41	
Indianapolis	47	68	
International Falls	30	47	
Kansas City	54	58	
Los Angeles	50	69	
Miami	67	72	
Minneapolis-St. Paul	36	48	.03
New Orleans	62	67	.16
New York	40	46	
Oklahoma City	53	60	.02
Seattle	—	56	
Phoenix	49	76	
Washington	43	60	
Winnipeg	39	33	

Selected in Yesterday's Charter Election

JOHN T. LEMMON • N. SMITH FRYER • AUSTIN A. KENNEDY • CLAUDE H. McQUILLAN • EDMUND A. ZUEHLKE

Incumbent Aldermen Win Re-election; Edmund Zuehlke Elected City Treasurer

The city council's membership remained unchanged today following yesterday's annual Rochester general election at which four of its members were re-elected.

Two World War II veterans ran for office, one winning and the other failing to gain office.

Edmund A. Zuehlke, a veteran, won a smashing victory in the contest for city treasurer, defeating G. H. McCarthy, 2,027 to 1,095.

EX-GI DEFEATED

Alderman-at-large J. T. Lemmon won re-election to the council presidency, defeating Willard H. Knapp, a veteran, 1,910 to 1,171.

Re-elected to the city council were Alderman S. Smith Fryer of the first ward, who defeated August F. Dornack, 724 to 557, Alderman Austin A. Kennedy of the second ward, who defeated Carlton Johnson, 521 to 364, and Alderman Claude H. McQuillan, who was re-elected third ward alderman without opposition. Alderman McQuillan, who was re-elected for a second term, polled 772 votes.

In the only board of education contest, U. W. Tervo polled an overwhelming vote to defeat Clare Healey, 640 to 249, for third ward school commissioner.

Mrs. M. M. Hargraves was elected school commissioner-at-large without opposition, polling 2,622 votes. Re-elected without opposition were Owen E. McCoy, second ward constable, 682 votes, Mark Fuller, third ward constable, 640, and Mrs. Ethel Osterreich Bray, third ward justice of the peace, 702.

31 PER CENT VOTE

The largest vote cast was in the treasurer contest, in which 3,122 voters participated. This represented only 31 per cent of the total registered vote of 10,153.

The council members re-elected yesterday will enter new terms April 1, with Aldermen Carl B. Kjerner of the first ward, John A. Yaeger of the second and Howard L. Narveson of the third holding over for another year.

Mr. Tervo will take office April 1 as third ward school commissioner, a post which Mrs. Hargraves left to run for commissioner-at-large to succeed Dr. George M. Higgins, who did not seek re-election. Holding over for another year will be Dr. William C. MacCarty, commissioner-at-large, Eugene Cutshall, first ward commissioner, and E. E. Harkness, second ward commissioner.

Continuing a long string of victories at the polls, Mr. Lemmon won re-election to the council presidency in a contest in which Mr. Knapp showed considerable strength.

The veteran council president, who has held office as mayor, second ward alderman or alderman-at-large almost continuously since 1922, won by a majority of 739 votes.

IDENTICAL PRECINCT VOTES

Mr. Knapp ran strongly in some sections, noticeably the third ward where he carried two precincts—both by two-vote leads and by identical votes of 66 to 64.

But Mr. Lemmon carried 14 of the 16 precincts, including all those in the first and second wards and four in the third. He continued unbroken his record of never having failed to carry his home ward—the second.

Mr. Zuehlke led throughout returns which were received in the office of City Clerk F. R. Finch, capturing majorities in 13 of the 16 precincts and losing to Mr. McCarthy only the fourth and fifth precincts of the first ward and the third precinct of the second ward. Mr. Zuehlke, an accountant and returned veteran who served in the army air forces in the Pacific, won by a majority of 932 and was elected treasurer in his first bid for public office.

The first ward contest for alderman was close until near the end. Mr. Dornack, who had the indorsement of the Rochester Central Labor union, was 32 votes ahead with the first four precincts reported, but an overwhelming 274-to-75 vote for Alderman Fryer in the fifth precinct was a decisive factor in sweeping the veteran council member back into office.

WINS SIXTH TERM

Alderman Fryer, who was re-elected for a sixth term, filed for the office after announcing that he would not be a candidate. He filed when urged publicly by a committee of citizens to seek re-election.

Mr. Dornack carried the first, second and third precincts and Alderman Fryer the fourth and fifth. The vote in the large first precinct was close—177 for Mr. Dornack and 174 for Alderman Fryer. The incumbent carried the ward by 167 votes.

The contest for alderman in the second ward was quiet, Alderman Kennedy carrying all but the first precinct, which Mr. Johnson won by 41 votes.

Alderman Kennedy, who has been in California on vacation and will return home later this month, encountered strong opposition in the second precinct, which he carried by five votes, but he rolled up large majorities in the third, fourth and fifth precincts. His majority was 157.

The school board contest in the third ward brought victory to Mr. Tervo by a majority of 391 votes. He won majorities in all the ward's six precincts and came out of the election with a smashing majority in his home precinct, the third, which gave him a vote of 190 to 37 for his opponent.

WAS SCHOOL TEACHER

Before coming to Rochester, Mr. Tervo served as a director of a junior college at Hancock, Mich., his

(continued on page 5)

President Withdraws Pauley Nomination

WASHINGTON, (AP)—President Truman today withdrew the nomination of Edwin W. Pauley, California oil man, to be undersecretary of the navy.

The president acted at Pauley's request. He said Pauley's defense of his "good name" has been "valiant and conclusive."

In a letter, Mr. Truman told Pauley that he "met the challenge" of his nomination "with facts" and added:

"You answered prejudice with a complete and forthright resume of your career and with an amazing patience under continued misrepresentation."

"COMMENDS PAULEY"

The first announcement of the withdrawal came from Chairman Walsh (Democrat - Massachusetts) of the Senate naval affairs committee after a 30-minute closed session of the group.

At the same time, Walsh handed reporters a statement declaring that the committee "commends" Pauley "for his patriotic action in requesting the president to withdraw his nomination."

The action wound up six weeks of controversy which boiled up at one point in the explosive resignation of Harold L. Ickes as secretary of interior. Ickes had criticized the nomination.

The White House made public an exchange of letters between the president and Pauly shortly after the note of withdrawal was sent to Leslie Biffle, secretary of the Senate.

After expressing his "full confidence" in Pauley, the president

(Continued on page 5)

Jap Torpedoes Rated Superior

Report Completed On Enemy Secrets

TOKYO, (AP)—Japanese torpedoes were better than American or British. They carried a larger explosive charge, had more range and greater speed, and left no air bubble train.

Captain Allan L. Dunning, who directed a U. S. navy technical mission to study closely guarded war secrets of the Japanese navy, announced those findings today upon completion of his project.

(Navy officials and correspondents had known of the Japanese torpedo's superiority since very early in the war but newsmen were not permitted even to hint at the fact).

An eye opener, Dunning said, was Japan's huge aircraft-carrying submarines. Japanese told him they had made reconnaissance flights over the Hawaiian islands in planes catapulted from submarines which could carry three planes each.

"The Japanese researchers had technical horizons as great as our own but they were unable to coordinate production with their findings," Dunning said. "In one laboratory, the Nipponese were making oil from rubber, exactly reversing a rubber from oil process developed in the United States."

Solons' Pension Bill Defeated; It's Election Year

WASHINGTON (AP) — Election-year jitters got the blame today for the latest defeat of "pensions-for-Congressmen."

At least that's the reason advanced by 79-year-old Representative Sabath (Democrat, Illinois), dean of the House, after his colleagues voted 217 to 116 yesterday against taking up a lawmakers' retirement bill. A similar measure failed four years ago.

The plan that was shelved, for the time being at least, would have allowed Senate and House members to become eligible for retirement benefits by paying five per cent of their $10,000 salaries, or $500 a year.

Filing for State Primary Begins

GOP Senate Fight Statements Due

ST. PAUL, (AP)—Minnesota's political pot reached an early boiling point today with the opening of filing for the July 8 primaries and scheduling of public announcements by principals in speculation over the U. S. senatorial contest.

Governor Thye set a press conference for 9 a.m. Thursday and former Governor Harold E. Stassen scheduled a radio broadcast over station KSTP for 6:30 p.m. Thursday.

The two are expected to disclose which, if either, has decided to contest for the Republican nomination for the U. S. Senate against Senator Henrik Shipstead. Both represent the faction of the party opposed to Shipstead for his stand on foreign policy as exemplified by his vote against United States participation in the United Nations organization.

JUDD ACCEPTS POST

Representative Walter Judd of Minneapolis, earlier regarded as a possible Republican senatorial candidate, indicated he had decided to seek re-election when he yesterday accepted appointment to a congressional committee being set up under the new employment act.

Nearly a dozen candidates for various posts, including four congressional aspirants, filed during the first few hours after filings opened.

Three of the first eight aspir-

(Continued on page 10)

Goering Defends Hitler's Grab of Power in 1933

By DANIEL DE LUCE

NUERNBERG, (AP)—Lecturing his Allied judges as if they were schoolboys, Hermann Goering testified today that Adolf Hitler seized power in 1933 "to make Germany free."

The leader among the 22 Nazis on trial for war crimes boastfully emphasized his own importance in snatching control for the Nazi party and asserted that an army plot against Hitler was barely averted a few hours before the first Hitler cabinet took its oath 13 years ago.

The former Reichsmarshal, dressed in a baggy, undecorated gray uniform with a red scarf about his neck, charged that the military plot was instigated by General Kurt von Schleicher—slain the following year in the Ernst Roehm blood purge—and General Curt von Hammerstein-Equord, former commander of the German army, with the help of the Potsdam garrison.

The prompt return of General Werner von Blomberg from a disarmament conference in Switzerland and his nomination as minister of war foiled the plotters, Goering said.

He started his testimony by telling of his career that started three decades ago in the Richthofen air squadron.

While his white-haired attorney slowly questioned him, Goering mentioned the medals he had won and a wound sustained in fighting for the Kaiser's Reich.

The court was packed for the dramatic moment of the three and a half months trial as the once flamboyant Reichsmarshal took his place before the microphone.

In a low, somber voice, Goering identified his father as a friend of the British empire builders, Cecil Rhodes and Joseph Chamberlain. He said the first world war left him "opposed in every way" to the Weimar republic.

McDonough Wins St. Paul Primary Race

Veteran Candidates Fail to Mark Up Victories in State

By Associated Press

Campaigning from a sickbed, Mayor John McDonough of St. Paul won nomination for re-election Tuesday by more than three to one over his nearest opponent as voters went to the polls in several Minnesota communities.

In unofficial returns, McDonough had 21,769 votes against 7,102 for Andrew Glenn, his closest rival from a field of nine candidates. All incumbent councilmen were renamed at the top of a record list of 28, topped by public safety commissioner Gus Barfuss with 25,625 votes.

The next five, in order of their ballot totals, were Fred Truax, William Parranto, John Findlan, Milton Rosen and Robert Peterson.

Chief interest at Owatonna centered in approval of an $800,000 bond issue for school improvements, including the building of a new grade school, and the uncontested election of Harold A. Kind, 37, veteran of World War II, as mayor.

VETERANS LOSE

A. H. Landdeck was named alderman-at-large, to serve with Vince Urban, Louis Kovar and Glenn Donnelly, a veteran, from the wards.

Andrew Meldahl was re-elected mayor of Northfield and three incumbent aldermen, all businessmen, were returned to office, despite the campaigns of four veterans of World War II for these posts.

Meldahl got 736 votes against 659 for Harvey P. Elling, who flew with the Flying Tigers in China. The successful aldermen were John Heyerholm, who bested Arthur Crawford 252-142, George Bickel, who won over Bernard Tralle 237-195, and H. B. Jacobson, who defeated Albert Hansen 278-174.

T. S. Silliman was elected municipal judge over T. R. McGuire, who had held the post for ten years, 772-361 in what was termed one of the main upsets of the voting. Another surprise came in the election of Dr. Nelson V. Russell, head of the Carleton college history department, to the school board over Marshall Diebold, who had held office for eight years, 175-154. Russell was a "sticker" candidate from the college section of the city.

SMALL TURN-OUT

Another veteran, Joseph Wang, lost out for the school board, 177-150, to incumbent Alfed J. Lashbrook.

Only ten per cent of the registered voters turned out at Alexandria to approve a charter change, extending the term of Mayor J. L. Fitzgerald from one to two years. The amendment got 172 of the 280 ballots cast, only five more than were needed for approval, while several other minor changes were defeated.

Alexandria aldermen chosen were

(Continued on page 5)

Samaritans' Efforts Fail To Save Girl

LOS ANGELES, (AP)—The many Christmas gifts that arrived from all over the nation for seven-year-old Margaret Eads were sent in vain.

Margaret died yesterday.

Last Christmas eve she was struck down in the street in front of Joe Passalacqua's cafe. A piece of automobile door handle pierced her brain. Passalacqua, knowing the circumstances of Margaret's widowed mother, Mrs. Hazel Eads, offered to pay medical expenses up to $10,000 to save the child's life.

A brain specialist accepted the case without fee. Joe and other persons contributed money for rent, grocery and hospital bills.

Mrs. Eads received an eviction notice almost at the hour of her child's death. Again, Passalacqua offered help and began raising a fund to buy a home for her and her two sons, Johnny, five, and Davis, 2.

Wallace Deplores A-Bomb Decision

Committee Gives Military Veto Power

WASHINGTON, (AP)—The issue of national safety gave the armed forces the decision today in an important preliminary test on post-war control of atomic energy.

The decision was hit immediately by secretary of commerce Wallace, who saw in it "the potentiality of delivering us into the hands of military Fascism in this nation."

Senator Vandenberg (Republican-Michigan), however held that military regulation is necessary until stabilized international control is developed effectively "to prohibit the use of atomic energy for military purposes by anybody at any time."

The test developed when the special Senate atomic committee voted six-to-one yesterday to incorporate into pending legislation a provision giving a presidentially-appointed military liaison committee a right to intervene before a civilian atomic control commission of five.

Wallace declared this was a vote "to place the control of atomic energy, in effect, in the hands of the military." He called it an "exceedingly unfortunate development."

The armed forces have taken the position all along that postwar atomic energy control should be their responsibility because of the importance of atomic weapons to the nations' defense. But numerous scientists and others have argued for complete civilian control to advance research and allay international suspicion.

Cherry Blossoms Will 'Bloom in Defeat'

TOKYO, (AP)—Japan's famed cherry blossoms will bloom April 2, "even in defeat," the newspaper Jiji Shimpo headlined today.

The paper explained Japanese like the blossoms because they die quickly, without lingering.

The cherry blossom was the symbol of the kamikaze and baka pilots who dived to their deaths during the war.

Soviet Papers Attack U.S. 'Businessmen' in Korea

By EDDY GILMORE

MOSCOW, (AP)—Articles attacking "American businessmen and politicians" in Korea and the continued presence of United States troops in Egypt were printed today in Soviet newspapers.

In an article in Pravda, Communist party newspaper, V. Smolensky described Dr. Syngman Rhee—who recently returned to Korea after 33 years of Japanese-imposed exile—as the leader of a group of Korean landowners and industrialists seeking to grab governmental power in Korea and control over mining enterprises there.

Describing Dr. Rhee and his followers as "old traders in the honor and freedom of their people," the article said the members of this group now were "coming out under the mask of strugglers for the independence of Korea."

Smolensky said Dr. Rhee had "directed his main effort toward establishing contact with anti-Soviet feeling in American circles and seeks" American support and help.

The article charged further that Dr. Rhee was working secretly behind the backs of the Korean people and was making deals with American businessmen and politicians who, it said, were rendering financial assistance to the Korean political leader and his followers.

"When will American troops leave Egypt?" was the title of an article by Kerim Thabet-Bey in the Cairo magazine Al Musavvar which was mentioned in the Soviet government newspaper Izvestia.

A Tass dispatch from Cairo, carried by Izvestia, quoted the article as saying that high British and American politicians were compelling Americans to remain in Egypt.

"The English look favorably upon the presence of American forces in Egypt as a justification of the impossibility" of evacuating English forces from that country, the Egyptian writer was quoted as saying.

All-Night Talks Bring Accord On Dispute

A Few Details Remain Unsettled, Says Spokesman

BULLETIN

DETROIT, (AP)—The General Motors strike was settled today on the basis of an 18½ cents an hour wage increase (18½ per cent.)

By Associated Press

A General Motors corporation official who asked that his name be withheld said today the company and the CIO United automobile workers had reached agreement on the wage issue, principal stumbling block in the 113-day old strike.

"A few other non-economic issues" remained to be resolved, the official said as a negotiation session that began yesterday afternoon continued through the night and into today.

Another management source who asked to remain anonymous said the negotiations contemplated a definite settlement of the entire dispute and "not just another deal." He did not elaborate.

Whether the reported agreement on wages was on the basis of an 18½ cents an hour increase or 19½ was not made known. The company has offered the lower figure, the union has demanded the higher.

IDLE SINCE NOVEMBER

Earlier a member of the union negotiating committee reported a settlement of the protracted strike of the nation's biggest union against the country's largest operating corporation appeared imminent.

The CIO spokesman, who asked that his name be withheld, came out of an unprecedented and dramatic conference that began behind locked doors at 9.20 p. m. (EST) yesterday in the GM administration building. Earlier yesterday afternoon GM officials had met with the UAW for three and half hours.

The meeting, interrupted for brief intermission for food and coffee, began with the two sides apparently deadlocked on numerous issues, including the UAW demand for a 19½ cents an hour wage increase. The corporation has offered 18½ cents.

The dispute has left 175,000 production workers idle since last November 21.

LEWIS GIVES DEMANDS

Meanwhile, actual negotiations between John L. Lewis' United mine workers and bituminous coal producers may not get started until next week. Yesterday Lewis submitted to the operators nine generalized demands for the new contract for the 400,000 soft coal miners. They included wage increases and shorter hours as well as a health and welfare fund for mine workers; adjustment of vacation, severance, and holiday pay, and "adjustment of the controversy" regarding unionization of supervisory, technical and clerical employes. Lewis has threatened a nationwide coal strike April 1, if necessary to enforce his demands.

The idle across the country because of labor disputes dropped to below 750,000, as more striking steelworkers reached agreements with employers.

Lehman to Leave UNNRA Post Because of Health

WASHINGTON, (AP)—Herbert H. Lehman is resigning, because of his health, from the post of UNRRA director general which he has held since the relief agency's birth.

Lehman's letter of resignation which he made public last night, noted that he resigned as governor of New York in 1942, three weeks before the end of his term, to take the helm of relief activities at the request of President Roosevelt.

BUTTER OUTPUT UP

CHICAGO (AP) — Butter production pushed up one per cent last week for the United States, the department of agriculture said today but still was 20 per cent under a year ago and offered little relief to harried butter-seeking housewives.

EXAMPLE 254

The Weather
Eastern Pennsylvania — Fair and warmer.

The Gazette and Daily

We print the news of the day without fear, bias or prejudice.

Vol. 117—No. 18985 — York, Pa., Wednesday Morning, March 13, 1946—Twenty-Eight Pages — Price 3c—15c a Week

—Photo by The Gazette and Daily

REROUTING STREAM—Work on changing the course of Willis run, north of Farquhar park, was completed this week. Picture shows last scoopfuls of ground being removed in the new channel.

The plot of ground bordering the run will be levelled into a recreation field. Watching operations are City Engineer Clyde F. W. Wallow, left, and two of his assistants, and at far right, Herbert F. Anderson, city director of parks and public properties.

Isolation Hospital Plan Step Nearer Realization

County Commissioners, prodded by Eyster, seem ready to meet with York hospital management. Action follows commissioners receipt of urgent letter from hospital asking action by April 1. Eyster avers he will act on own if Trout and McDowell won't agree to meet hospital authorities. Hospital outlines operational plan of proposed unit.

Definite and early action on an isolation hospital for York county entered the realm of possibility with the receipt by the county commissioners yesterday of an urgent letter from the York hospital management.

Concrete suggestions for an isolation unit on the hospital grounds were included with a request from Charles B. Wolf, president of the York hospital board, that a decision be forthcoming from the commissioners by April 1.

Commissioner Howard E. Eyster, president of the board, said at the session he would make an appointment to have the commissioners meet with the hospital board this week.

"If no conference is held," he added, "I will continue to make appointments to meet until a date suitable to all members of the board of county commissioners is fixed. * * * I'll go one step further. If the whole board doesn't go—if you won't go, I'll take it upon myself to go with our solicitor and bring the information back here to the board."

(Thus it is indicated that a showdown is imminent in the fight launched more than six years to have a contagious diseases hospital erected here. The movement has had the endorsement of civic, fraternal, veterans, medical and health and other organizations, as well as numerous individuals. Need of such a hospital was accentuated by a serious epidemic of infantile paralysis which broke out in York county in 1941.

No Pledge From Trout

County Commissioner Walter L. Trout, chairman of the Republican county committee, didn't pledge himself to go along, but remarked at the conclusion of the reading of the hospital communication: "I think that sounds pretty good."

And Commissioner James McDowell, lone Democrat, spoke up, "Well, I'll go along, if the whole board goes." Eyster reminded him, "You told me that once before."

(McDowell voted "No" to a resolution passed July 13, 1945, changing the proposed site from the county home to the hospital.).

The communication from the hospital was signed by President Wolf. The hospital group proposed in the letter and accompanying "Suggestions for Isolation Unit":

(1) An isolation unit on land furnished by the York hospital, with space for future expansion if needed.

(2) Operation by the hospital in keeping with suggestions made by the Hospital Association of Pennsylvania.

(3) A decision by the commissioners before April 1, because detailed plans and specifications for the Nurses home and hospital addition will be difficult to change after that date.

(4) A meeting of the county solicitor, Attorney Paul E. Stein, and the hospital's counsel, At-

(Continued on Page Twenty-seven)
See Isolation Hospital

Telephone Co. And Union To Confer Today

Federal labor conciliator will meet with company and union officials in attempt to settle strike which has affected calls to and from county exchanges.

Federal Labor Conciliator Adie S. Rush will meet this morning with company and union representatives in the first major attempt to settle the two-day old strike of employes of the York Telephone and Telegraph company.

The company asked for the joint meeting, it was stated by representatives of Local B-1451, International Brotherhood of Electrical Workers, who expressed the hope that this first overture on the part of the company meant a serious attempt to end the strike.

The strike was called Monday morning to back the union's demands for wage increases higher than the one-half-cent raise reportedly offered by the company and other benefits under a proposed new contract.

Union Always Ready To Meet

"We always were ready to meet at any time with Conciliator Rush and the company in an effort to bring about an end to the work stoppage," Budd Miller, president

(Continued on Page Twenty-seven)
See Telephone Strike

Selfish Pressure Group Termed Greatest Danger

The greatest danger to our nation now is the selfish pressure group, Rev. Clarence Rahn, of Temple, Pa., told the York Lions club at its luncheon meeting at Hotel Yorktowne yesterday.

For the nation's safety, he said, the Lions club should wave the guiding lanterns of imagination, honesty, bigness of spirit and good humor.

In a talk filled with humorous anecdotes and his interpretation of the Pennsylvania Dutch, he said that "We are living in an era of polished dishonesty," where there is a "crying need for simple honesty."

"We are living in a big country," he declared, "and we need big men, big enough to be unselfish. He asserted that if he had his way "I'd quarantine every sour-puss."

Senate Atomic Comm. Bill Can Lead To Military Fascism, Wallace Warns

Points to threat of military dictatorship after committee approves Vandenberg "compromise" measure to set up military liaison group to work with civilian commission.

Washington, March 12 (AP)—Secretary of Commerce Wallace said today that an atomic energy control bill drafted by a special Senate committee "has the potentiality of delivering us into the hands of military fascism."

Wallace commented with anger in his voice after the committee voted 6 to 1 to set up a military liaison committee to work with a control commission of five civilians. Chairman McMahon (D.-Conn.) cast the dissenting vote.

Wallace asserted that the committee had voted "to place control of atomic energy, in effect, in the hands of the military," and declared:

"This is an exceedingly unfortunate development. I hope that when the American people realize its significance they will rise up in their wrath and let the senators know what that action means.

"The peacetime uses of atomic energy can be of much more significance than its war. If the United Nations Organization develops in the way we have every reason to hope and believe it will, the great importance of atomic energy will be its peacetime use.

"We must be in the foretront of this peacetime use. We must not let other nations pass us in that respect. All of these ramifications of the peaceful use of this great energy can, if properly applied, bring about an era of unimagined abundance.

Will Arouse Suspicion

"If the military aspect of atomic energy is played up in the legisla-

(Continued on Page Twenty-seven)
See Wallace Warns

8 Arrested In Raids In City And West York

Five men taken into custody by state police and deputy sheriff in raid on alleged horse race betting room in B. & B. Cigar store in West York. Three city residents arrested by state officers for violations of liquor laws.

Law enforcement officers arrested eight persons in raids yesterday on an alleged horse race betting establishment in West York and on two places in the city where it is alleged liquor was sold illegally.

Acting on complaints, state police and a deputy sheriff visited the B. & B. cigar store, 1568 West Philadelphia street, arresting two men as the operators and three as frequenters of a room where, it is alleged, bets on horse races were taken.

State Liquor Control Board enforcement officers, unaccompanied by city police, meanwhile arrested a man and a woman at 141½ South Newberry street and another woman at 141 West Newton avenue for violations of the liquor laws.

Bets Were Received

Entering the B. & B. cigar store at 3 p. m., state police said the raiding party went to the second floor where they found five men in a room where bets on horse races were being received.

Officers said they arrested the proprietor, Robert Klinedinst, 112

(Continued on Page Twenty-Eight)
See 8 Arrested

Decision Due Today In Bus Co. Arbitration Case

Decision on the issues between the York Bus company and Local 858, Amalgamated Association of Street, Electric Railway and Motor Coach Employes of America, is expected today when a three-man arbitration board meets in Philadelphia.

The executive board of the union will be present at the meeting of the arbiters. The major issue is the union's demand for an increase in wages.

If two of the three arbiters—Herbert B. Cohen for the union, Henry Church Jr. for the company and Aaron Harovitz, neutral arbiter—fail to reach an agreement, further proceedings will be necessary.

The union executive board is composed of Roy E. Lightner, president of the local; Howard Shaffer, Charles Kindig and Harris Lichty.

Boy Dead, Sister And Mother Hurt In Tragic Blast

John Albert Bair, one year old, fatally burned as mother pours gasoline in mistake for kerosene into stove at their Hanover RD 1 home. Mrs. Bair and two-year-old daughter, Mildred Pauline, in hospital. Neighbors extinguish blaze which gutted three-room dwelling.

A one-year-old boy died and his two-year-old sister and mother suffered second degree burns as a result of a gasoline explosion in a kitchen stove, in their home, Hanover R. D. 1, east of the Beck Mill road, in Penn township, yesterday about 11:30 a. m.

John Albert Bair died at the Hanover General hospital two hours after the explosion. Chances for the recovery of his sister, Mildred Pauline, were described by hospital officials as "fair," and those of the mother, Mrs. Richard B. Bair, 28, as "good."

Mrs. Bair told County Detective John J. Karbon that she mistakenly used gasoline instead of kerosene in building a wood fire. Both had been kept in similar containers.

Clothing Ignited

John was sitting beside the stove, while Mildred was playing on the floor at the time of the explosion. The clothing of the children and mother as well as everything in the room was ignited.

Arthur Wilson, a next-door neighbor, rushed into the blazing building and carried the boy out. Mrs. Ruth Gladfelter, 26, Mrs. Bair's sister, carried Mildred out of the house. A bucket brigade consisting of Mrs. Gladfelter, Mr. Wilson, his father, Charles Wilson, and another neighbor, Irvin Lippy put out the fire. Karbon said the interior of the three-room home was "ruined."

Dr. Richard Dalrymple, resident physician at the hospital, said Mrs. Bair received first and second degree burns on both arms and both legs and first degree burns on her face and neck. She had not been told late yesterday afternoon that John had died.

Mildred received first and second degree burns on her face, neck, arms and body.

Injured When Thrown From Motor Scooter

Paul Wanbaugh, 23, of 1100 Mount Rose avenue, was seriously injured early yesterday afternoon when thrown from a motor scooter at the intersection of King and Duke streets.

York hospital attaches last night gave his condition as satisfactory. He is suffering from a possible skull fracture.

Thrown over the handle-bars of the scooter when it hit the curb at the north-west corner, Wambaugh, a grocery clerk, fell from a jack-knife position onto his head, an eyewitness said.

Edward Carpenter, who witnessed the sudden accident from his position at the Rex Hook and Ladder company, immediately summoned the city ambulance to take Wambaugh to the hospital. Carpenter said that there had been no blood but that foam appeared to be forming at the injured man's mouth.

Wanbaugh had been traveling west on King street, Carpenter said, stating that the chain which transmits power from the motor of the two-wheeled vehicle to the wheels had flown apart at the intersection. He said that the motor bike had swayed the wobbled precariously and that Wanbaugh apparently had tried to gain control or stop by placing his foot on the ground.

City police arrived on the scene shortly after the ambulance had taken Wanbaugh away. The motor scooter, which had not been badly damaged, had been placed at the rear of the Rex Hook and Ladder company until a friend of the injured man called for it later last night.

EXAMPLE 255

THE WEATHER
Increasing cloudiness and somewhat milder but turning colder at night; tomorrow fair with seasonable temperatures.

RUTLAND HERALD

ESTABLISHED IN 1794

LOCAL TEMPERATURES
Weather yesterday: Cloudy.

VOL. 94. NO. 93. RUTLAND, VERMONT, FRIDAY MORNING, APRIL 18, 1947. PRICE FIVE CENTS

Income Tax Bill's Power To Raise Money Sharply Cut By Senate Changes

Drastic Amendments Would Slash Estimated Revenue Nearly $1,000,000 Below House Version.

3 Revisions

Would Allow Deductions on U. S. Levies, Kill Withholding, Capital Gains and Losses Provisions.

(Vermont Press Bureau.)

Mobile Health Unit Bill Defeated, State Police Measure Gets Final OK

Emerson's Vote Needed to Break 14 to 14 Deadlock on Health Measure Which Was Up for Passage, But House Approves Senate Changes in Public Safety Dept. Bill, Sends It to Governor for Signature.

(Vermont Press Bureau.)

(Continued on Page Two.)

House Passes Bill to Curb Labor Unions

Measure Making Sweeping Changes in New Deal Laws Ok'd 308 to 107.

Bans Closed Shop

Milder Senate Measure Is Approved by Committee, Debate Scheduled.

BY DOUGLAS B. CORNELL.

Texas City Counts 650 Dead, 3000 Injured, Fears New Fires; Truman Offers Aid; Probe Looms

All Federal Agencies Ordered by President to Co-operate in Relief Activity.

Ask Inquiry

Senator O'Daniel Calls For Complete Investigation, Cites Number of Recent Wrecks, Fires, Blasts.

Explosion at a Glance

BY THE ASSOCIATED PRESS.

Order Lower Area of Port City Evacuated as Shifting Winds Pose New Fire Threats.

Oil Ablaze

Big Refinery Storage Farm Abandoned; Gas Masks Distributed as Flames Near Huge Gas Tanks.

Phone Union To Press For Settlement

Meanwhile Bell System Reports Some Workers Are Returning to Jobs.

Service Is Improving

State, RJC Vie for Big Estate Here

Seek Clementwood for New Woman's Reformatory, College Campus.

State Is High Bidder

Here's How To Get Information

Hopes Dim At Conference For Austrian Pact

Soviets Spurn Canadian Query On A-Issue

(Continued on Page Three.)

The Weather

Rutland Skies Today
FRIDAY, APRIL 18.

Attlee Shakes Up Cabinet But Move Strengthens Bevin's Hand

BY JACK SMITH.

Two Rutland Women Assail Proposed Rent Control Law

(Vermont Press Bureau.)

News at Glance

EXAMPLE 255A

most of their heads in capitals and lower-case, and twelve of the fifteen employed flush-left heads.

The 1947 winner of the Ayer trophy was the *Rutland* (Vt.) *Herald*, the basic typographic plan of which was worked out in 1938 by Carl Purington Rollins, printer to Yale University.

Most of the heads in the *Herald* were in members of the Garamond and Granjon families, and news body matter was in 7-point Excelsior No. 1 on an 8-point body. (See Example 255A.)

The tabloid winner of first honorable mention in 1947 again was the *York* (Pa.) *Gazette and Daily*, which won the same honor the year before. (See Example 255.)

Eight of the eleven papers honored by Ayer in 1947 presented most of their heads in capitals and lower-case, and six of the eleven employed flush-left heads.

At the conclusion of the 1947 contest, President Batten of the Ayer organization stated:

"This year's exhibition establishes beyond question the typographical excellence, improved appearance and readability of the nation's newspapers—large and small. Anyone examining the more than 1000 publications . . . in this exhibition cannot fail to be impressed with the high standards of typography and makeup that have been maintained in spite of continued shortages of paper and printing equipment.

"We at Ayer believe that constant improvement in general appearance and makeup, as well as presswork and typography, is absolutely necessary if newspapers are to preserve their effectiveness as an editorial and advertising medium."

To recapitulate, the winners of Ayer trophies from the beginning of the Ayer contest to this writing have been:

"Standard-Size" Newspapers

1931—*New York Herald Tribune*
1932—*Hartford Courant*
1933—*New York Times*
1934—*New York Herald Tribune*
1935—*New York Times*
1936—*New York Herald Tribune*
1937—*Los Angeles Times*
1938—*Newark Evening News*
1939—*New York Herald Tribune*
1940—*New York Times*
1941—*New York Herald Tribune*
1942—*New York Times*
1943—*Christian Science Monitor*
1944—*Chicago Sun*
1945—*New York Herald Tribune*
1946—*Rochester Post-Bulletin*
1947—*Rutland Herald*

Tabloid Newspapers

1939—*New York Daily News*	1943—*PM* of New York City
1940—*Chicago Daily Times*	1944—*PM* of New York City
1941—*PM* of New York City	1945—*Washington News*
1942—*PM* of New York City	1946—*York Gazette and Daily*

1947—*York Gazette and Daily*

In 1938, the *Linotype News*, which for many years had provided handsomely designed and printed certificates of award for winners in the annual better-newspaper contests conducted by the National Editorial Association, offered the first of a series of trophies in a new classification, open annually to all member-papers—dailies, weeklies, semi-weeklies, tri-weeklies or otherwise. The trophy was for general typographic excellence.

In 1938 the trophy was won by the *Cobb County Times* of Marietta, Ga., a weekly; in 1939, by the *Glendale* (Calif.) *News-Press*, a daily; in 1940, by the *Hastings* (Neb.) *Daily Tribune*; in 1941, by the *Ritzville* (Wash.) *Journal-Times*, a weekly; in 1942, by the *Lake Mills* (Iowa) *Graphic*, a weekly; in 1943, by the *Rochester* (Minn.) *Post-Bulletin*, a daily (which won the Ayer trophy in 1946), and in 1944, by the *Mission* (Texas) *Times*, a weekly.

From 1945 to date, the *Linotype News* has been offering two trophies annually to first-prize winners in the contests for general typographic excellence conducted by the National Editorial Association—one trophy for the best daily, and one for the best weekly.

In 1945 the *Morristown* (N. J.) *Daily Record*, and the *Scarsdale* (N. Y.) *Inquirer*, a weekly, won the N.E.A. first prizes for general typographic excellence.

In 1946 the N.E.A. first prizes for general typographic excellence were won by the *Bakersfield* (Calif.) *Californian*, a daily, and the *Mount Vernon* (Iowa) *Hawkeye-Record*, a weekly. Both papers employed flush-left heads.

Most of the heads in the *Californian* were set in sans-serif faces, but a few were in members of the Century family. News body matter was set in 7-point No. 2 with Bold Face No. 2 on a 7½-point body, with certain leads in 10-point No. 16 on a 12-point body, followed by 8-point No. 1 with Bold Face No. 2 on a 9-point body.

Heads in the *Hawkeye-Record* were set in sans-serif faces, and news body matter in 7-point Excelsior No. 2 with Bold Face No. 2 on an 8-point body.

Example 256 presents a reduced showing of the front page of the *Californian*, and Example 257 presents a showing of the front page of the *Hawkeye-Record*.

In 1947 the *Inglewood* (Calif.) *Daily News* won the N.E.A. first prize for general typographic excellence among dailies, and the *Scarsdale* (N.Y.) *Inquirer* repeated its success of 1945 in the weekly newspaper division.

Heads in the *Inglewood News* (see Example 257A) were presented flush at the left in various sans serifs, and news body matter was set in 8-point Regal on an 8-point body.

Most of the heads in the *Scarsdale Inquirer* (see Example 257B) were in members of the Bodoni family, and news body matter was in 8-point Ideal News on a 9-point body.

With three exceptions, only the more recent Ayer and N.E.A. prize winners are illustrated in this chapter, as several of the previous winners in both contests have been changed in appearance since they won the Ayer and N.E.A. prizes.

A front page from the *New York Herald Tribune*, which has won permanent possession of two Ayer trophies, is suggested by Example 258; a front page from the *New York Times*, which won two legs on the first Ayer trophy and two on the second, by Example 259, and a front page from *PM* of New York City, which won tabloid first honors four times, by Example 260.

In the issue of the *New York Herald Tribune* suggested by Example 258, general-news heads were in Bodoni Bold and Bodoni Bold Italic. News body matter was in 7½-point Ionic No. 5 cast on an 8-point body, with front-page body lines extra leaded 1 point.

In the issue of the *New York Times* suggested by Example 259, general-news heads were in Latin Condensed, members of the Century and Cheltenham families, and various sans serifs. News body matter was in 8-point Ideal News cast on an 8-point body, with front-page body lines extra leaded 1½ points.

In the issue of *PM* suggested by Example 260, general-news heads were in Caledonia Bold and members of the Bodoni family, with various sans serifs employed on the front page. Most of the news body matter was in 9-point Caledonia cast on a 9-point body.

The Bakersfield Californian

Kern Ranks First in Oil Output See Page 7

Vol. 57 | TWO SECTIONS | BAKERSFIELD, CALIFORNIA, WEDNESDAY, JULY 4, 1945 | 12 PAGES | No. 290

JAPS SINK 2 U. S. DESTROYERS

Tangier Problem for Big Three

Russia's Request for Voice in Restoration of International Status Delays Settlement

LONDON, July 4. (UP)—Russian insistence on a voice in discussions over restoration of Tangier to its prewar international status raised a new diplomatic problem for the Big Three today virtually on the eve of their Berlin conference.

A British foreign office commentator said the Russian request was "still under consideration" and "bound to cause delay in the settlement" involving the strategic ports on the straits of Gibraltar taken over in June, 1940, by Spain from the other co-guarantors, France, Britain and Italy.

NATIONAL GRAIN SCANDAL SEEN

LEADER IMPLICATES CAPITOL OFFICIALS

Attempt to Dynamite Mikado Reported

Americans Urged to Help Liberated

CRASH KILLS FIVE

INDEX TO ADVERTISERS

OLD GLORY WAVES IN MANY LANDS

U. S. FLAG IS HOISTED IN BERLIN FOR FOURTH

48-GUN SALUTE MARKS CEREMONIES; YANKS OBSERVE INDEPENDENCE DAY IN CAPITALS

Rains Impede Yanks Mopping Up Luzon

Tired Yanks Assume Berlin Duties After 30-Hour Trek

By DANIEL DE LUCE

BORNEO OIL CITY NEAR CAPTURE

AUSSIE TROOPS MENACE LAST JAP AIRFIELD

Navy Starts Air Preparatory Program

U. S. Fleet Invades Nip Waters

Ships, Subs Shell Karafuto Island, Tokyo Radio Says

Ship Carries Enemy Bomb for Month

Japs Nervous About Soong's Russia Visit

NIPPONESE DIPLOMATS FEAR PACT WHICH MIGHT AFFECT WAR

SOONG'S VISIT MAY MEAN MUTUAL AID PACT

CHIANG SENDS FOURTH MESSAGE

TRUMAN GIVEN PLEDGE OF MORE CO-OPERATION

Federal Employes to Get Half-Day Off

Connally Denies Bushfield's Blast on Charter Authority

By JOHN L. CUTTER

244 Lost in Blasts at Ships

Unidentified Missile, Suicide Bomber Hit Vessels at Okinawa

WASHINGTON, July 4. (UP)—The navy announced today that two United States destroyers were sunk by enemy action off Okinawa last month with combined casualties of 244.

Aided Bombardment

Commander Missing

Smith Lauds Marines in Farewell Message

17 Holiday Deaths Reported by Midday

London Laborites Jeer at Churchill

EXAMPLE 256

The Mount Vernon Hawkeye-Record

and The Lisbon Herald

MOUNT VERNON HAWKEYE, VOLUME LXXVI, NUMBER 28 — MOUNT VERNON, IOWA, THURSDAY, MAY 9, 1946 — MOUNT VERNON RECORD, VOLUME LII, NUMBER 37

Cornell Gets Allotment Of 6 More Buildings

Includes 19 Family Units, One Dormitory

BEGIN WORK ON FIRST ALLOTMENT

Collect For Milk Fund Sunday

DOGS—DOGS—DOGS

Mt. Vernon Enters District Track Meet

Returned GI's To Speak On Effect of Alcohol

Cancer Control Drive Closes This Week

Lester Notbohm Made Seaman First Class

91st Birthday Today

MRS. JANE WEST

B and N Cafe To Open Here On Wednesday

New Owners, Blackmer And Niles Take Over

Apologies, Apologies

Cedar Rapids Man Will Speak At Graduation

Dwight Krumbholtz To Deliver Address

Bread Situation Here Is Uncertain

Commencement Speaker

Mr. and Mrs. Nutt Return From California Trip

Mrs. Ink Will Attend Continental Congress

Ed Stinson Will Be Phone Service Chief

Complete Half Mile Of New Grading

Pour First Concrete At Ivanhoe Bridge

Will Meet Teachers Minus Three Regulars

Mrs. Johnson's Father Dies While Visiting Here

John L. Lewis Causes Reduced Mail Service

Mr. and Mrs. Willard Neal Buy Current House

Three Men Are Inducted

Fred Cooper Will Speak At Dinner For Rotary Anns

Good Reports Made At Linn Grove Church

Church Balance Is Largest In History

Honor Birthday Of Mrs. E. A. Johnson

Rotary Club Sees Movies Regarding Flood Control

Bohumil Mallie Will Have Closing Out Sale Friday

Ellabelle Davis Will Open May Music Festival

First Concert Occurs Here This Evening

Pops Harrison Will Speak At Activity Dinner

Annual Lisbon Affair Will Be Held Tuesday

Homemaker Classes To Present Fashion Show

Teachers and Wives Entertain Board Members

To Announce Decoration Day Committees Soon

Completes 50 Years As Pharmacist

Have Been Married For 70 Years

MR. AND MRS. HENRY OWENS

Ask $180 For Powdered Milk Fund In Lisbon

Churches Unite To Aid Starving Europeans

Mrs. Miles Dahn, English Bride, Arrives In Lisbon

Lisbon Senior Play Occurs Friday Eve

Services For Mrs. Tyson Were Held Thursday

Attend Eastern Star Meeting At Davenport

Bernard Gish Is Home With Navy Discharge

EXAMPLE 257

Only the Hometown Daily Newspaper Covers the Hometown Market

Inglewood Daily News

Serving the Centinela Valley since 1904

The Best-Informed People Read the Inglewood Daily News

Volume 44—No. 15 ★ 128 N. LA BREA ★ Inglewood, Calif., Friday, February 28, 1947 ★ PHONE OR. 7-2141 ★ Price Per Copy, 5c

LOCAL PILOT SETS NEW SPEED MARK IN P-82

Porter Hero When Pullman Car Runs Wild

Pennsy Coach Races 3½ Miles to Crash; 1 Killed, 11 Injured

ALTOONA, Pa., Feb. 28.—(U.P.)—A Pullman coach broke loose from the Pennsylvania railroad's Sunshine Special on Cresson mountain today and ran wild for 3½ miles as women passengers prayed and a heroic porter tugged helplessly at the emergency brake.

The porter, L. Keys, of Near Houston, Texas, was killed and 10 passengers and a flagman were injured when the car jumped the tracks and crashed into an embankment.

The car, the "Cascade Mirage," came uncoupled when the express, running from New York to Texas, stopped at Gallitzin tunnel to drop a "helper" locomotive after climbing the 11½-mile mountain grade.

In some, unaccountable manner, the last Pullman of the 13-car train came uncoupled. Without brakes it started drifting down the grade.

Flagman Edward J. Mulvihill, 46, of Pittsburgh, realized that the airbrakes had failed. He called to the passengers to lie flat on the floor. Several heeded and crawled from their berths. Mulvihill's warning was credited with saving them from serious injury or death.

Passes Gorge

The runaway car held the tracks for over five minutes. It sped past Bennington curve, where 10 days ago the Red Arrow Express leaped the tracks and plunged into a gorge, killing 24 persons.

At curve "109" the Pullman jumped the tracks and bounced over three other tracks to jam against the side of the mountain.

Harry Willis, of Jersey City, N.J., a passenger, said he heard Mulvihill's warning and jumped from his bed to crawl on the floor. He said the women were terrorized. Several prayed as the Pullman rocked down the steep grade.

"It was the longest five minutes of my life," Willis said.

He said the porter raced up and down the car trying to calm the passengers and pulling at the emergency brakes.

"He was a real hero," he said.

Chiang Kicks Out Commies

Delegation Told To Leave Nanking

NANKING, Feb. 28.—(U.P.)—The government of Gen. Chiang Kai-shek today ordered the communist delegation to leave Nanking before next Wednesday.

A curt, uncompromising letter from the nationalist garrison headquarters to the communist delegation and its liaison office served the notice to get out of Nanking.

A communist spokesman, commenting on the government order, said it completed the split between the two Chinese factions, "at least 99 per cent so. It will be 100 per cent if the communists set up their own government."

Communist sources expressed belief the withdrawal order meant that the government forces soon would begin a full scale attack with the primary objective of overrunning Yenan, the communist capital.

The letter to the communists said:

"Since your party closed the door to national peace by rejecting government proposals for peace talks, troops of your party have been engaged in open rebellion against the government, attacking troops of the national government throughout the country."

2000 Men Battling Hawaii Brush Fire

PEARL HARBOR, Feb. 28.—(U.P.)—Two thousand civilian and military firefighters battled in a gusty wind early today trying to prevent the spread of a huge brush fire on Halawa Ridge near here.

Five acres had been blackened by midnight last night. No one was reported injured and no buildings were damaged.

Weather Forecast

8 a.m. today 50
Yesterday's maximum 66
Yesterday's minimum 47

Scattered cloudiness this afternoon and tonight, followed by variable high cloudiness Saturday; slightly warmer afternoons today and Saturday.

COAST TO COAST

Movie Stunt Flier Smashes Record In Surprise West to East Flight

NEW YORK, Feb. 28.—(U.P.)—Paul Mantz, Hollywood stunt flier, today smashed the West-East cross-country record for propeller-driven single-engined planes when he flew from Burbank, Calif., to LaGuardia field, New York, in six hours, seven minutes, five seconds. Mantz roared his P-51 Mustang plane past the control tower at the New York field at 3:36:25 p.m. EST, according to a National Aeronautical Association timekeeper. He had left Burbank at 9:29:20 a.m. EST.

Mantz smashed the record set May 12, 1944, by Lt. Col. Jack Carter, of 6 hours, 39 minutes, 30 seconds. He did not, of course, even approach the jet plane record for the same flight made Jan. 26, 1946, by Col. William Council, who flew a jet-propelled P-80 the 2470 miles in four hours, 13 minutes, 30 seconds, for an average of about 585 miles an hour.

The record for multi-engine planes was set by the famous Dreamboat B-29 on Dec. 11, 1945, when it flew from west to east in five hours, 27 minutes.

Mantz was not reported along the entire route into LaGuardia.

His plane was the same ship with which he won the Bendix trophy race last year by covering the 2045 miles between Burbank and Cleveland at an average speed of 435.6 miles an hour.

He calls it "The Blaze of Noon." It is a low wing, single engine monoplane, powered by a new Packard-built Rolls Royce Merlin engine. Its 12-cylinder, liquid-cooled engine was said to have been capable of generating approximately 2,000 horsepower.

Mantz loaded it to capacity with 700 gallons of fuel, utilizing especially built tanks in the wing tips.

RECORD-MAKING FIGHTER—Here's the pride of Inglewood's North American Aviation company, the P-82 Twin Mustang "Betty Jo," which made the first non-stop flight from Honolulu to New York, landing at 11:08 a.m. (EST) today. It was the longest flight ever made by a fighter plane, and the initial Hawaii-New York trip by any kind of ship. The flight was made at altitudes varying from 19,000 to 22,000 feet, and with good tailwinds the "Betty-Jo" hung up an average speed of nearly 350 m.p.h.

Jail State Cop For Race Pool

Three Others Booked In Anita Derby Plot

SACRAMENTO, Feb. 28.—(U.P.)—Four men, including a California state policeman, were in jail here today for allegedly conducting a sweepstakes lottery scheme based on the $100,000 Santa Anita Derby March 8 in southern California.

Police said those under arrest included Walter Doyle, 46, of Hollywood; State Policeman Durwood McCord; Al Hahas, local concessionaire, and Lester Johnson, a bartender employed by Nahas. Formal charges had not been filed against them.

The suspects were rounded up and questioned by special agents of the state criminal and identification division.

George Brereton, chief of the CID, said the ring was promising sweepstake prizes of $278,000 based on results of the colorful closing day race at Santa Anita, but he said his department found no guarantee of their paying off.

He listed Doyle as the ringleader of the "racket." He said Doyle had a record of convictions for bunco and misdemeanors in Portland, Ore. Brereton said the sweepstakes ring apparently was in Hollywood and that additional arrests were expected.

Chief special agent Joseph McClellan said McCord confessed to getting rid of 200 books for a total of $12,500.

Local Woman Hurt In Auto Accident

Struck while crossing Manchester boulevard, a 36-year-old woman today was suffering from a bruised head, legs, and arms.

Aleta Nolte, 36, 508 West Magnolia street, was injured when a car driven by Anthony M. Emmanuel, 28, 954 Edgeware road, Los Angeles, collided with her last night at Manchester boulevard and Oak street last night.

Powerful Blasts Rock Harbor Area of Haifa

JERUSALEM, Feb. 28.—(U.P.)—A series of powerful explosions rocked the harbor area of Haifa today a few hours after a refugee ship carrying 1,350 uncertified immigrants was grounded off the nearby Palestine coast.

Two Jews were killed and one British Sixth Airborne trooper and one Transjordan Frontier Force man were wounded seriously when explosives wrecked the safe rooms of Barclay's Bank in the heart of the Haifa Port area.

Three blasts in the series were believed to be from bombs or land mines timed to explode with the expected arrival of the refugee ship, the Haim Arlosorov, formerly the Ulua, in Haifa Harbor.

The ship was intercepted by a British destroyer directed by a Royal air force plane. It was grounded off Bat Galim, a Jewish suburb south of Haifa.

The case of the refugees was taken to the Palestine Supreme court. It ordered British officials to show cause why they should not be allowed to land.

The court's show-cause order, the second it has issued in the long smouldering dispute over the legal status of Jewish refugees arriving without credentials, in effect prevented the British from moving the ship outside the port of Haifa.

One British seaman was wounded seriously when a naval party of 13 boarded the refugee ship, the Haim Arlosorov, this morning near Athlitm while the sailors were swarming aboard, an unknown number of refugees jumped overboard.

Evicted Landlady Sabotages Plumbing

LOS ANGELES, Feb. 28—(U.P.)—Dr. Manuel H. Haig charged today that when he finally evicted 38 boarders and the landlady from his recently purchased, $83,000 "Mt. Kalmia castle" overlooking the Sunset strip he found it not fit to live in.

Haig last month got possession of the home, built in the early 1930's by millionaire copper king George Campbell Carson.

He said toilets were plugged with knives and newspapers, costly rugs were ink-stained, wallpaper was torn, doors were yanked from their hinges, and a $400-stained glass window was missing.

He asked $7725 damages from Patricia Noblesse Hogan, whom he evicted after a nine-month court fight. He claimed the house was damaged by her 38 boarders.

Senate Votes Out Controls

OPA Gets Funds to Run Until June 30

WASHINGTON, Feb. 28—(U.P.)—The Senate Appropriations committee voted 8 to 5 today to allow OPA roughly $17,000,000 to operate to June 30 and then close up shop.

It voted 11 to 2 to force the entire office of temporary controls out of business as of June 30. This office includes OPA, the civilian production and the office of war mobilization and reconversion.

Sen. Styles Bridges, R., N. H., committee chairman, said the committee's action "in no way" means an immediate end of sugar, rice and rent controls.

He said Congress, between now and June 30, probably will transfer sugar controls to the agriculture department and rent controls to "some such agency" as the commerce department.

The committee's decision would give OPA only about $5,000,000 wtih which to operate until June 30, compared to $20,000,000 OPA claims it needs.

Bridges said that meant OPA must "start folding up immediately", and order into effect "a drastic reduction of their forces."

The committee over-rode a House decision to call back $9,000,000 of OPA funds.

Adm. King Minimizes A-bomb as Sole Weapon

ELGIN, Ill., Feb. 28.—(U.P.)—Fleet Adm. Ernest J. King, former naval commander in chief, said last night that it is "wholly unlikely" that the atomic bomb by itself can win a war.

Answering the question "why do we need a navy?" King told the Elgin academy winter forum that new weapons would modify that technique of warfare but would not affect the basic role of the navy "to carry the war overseas to the enemy."

★ ★ ★ ★ ★ ★

Ard Credited for Pressing Onward

NEW YORK, Feb. 28.—(U.P.)—Streaking in to an "emergency" landing at LaGuardia field, the army's twin-Mustang fighter plane Betty Jo today completed the first non-stop flight from Honolulu — 5,051 miles — in an official elapsed time of 14 hours, 33 minutes.

★ ★ ★

With only 60 gallons of gasoline in her tanks, the plane touched down here at 11:08 a.m. EST after passing the control tower at 11:06 a.m., EST, the latter figure being the one given officially by the National Aeronautical Association for the arrival here.

Lt. Col. Robert E. Thacker, chief pilot, believed he had completed the long flight in 14 hours, 32 minutes, but the NAA gave 14 hours, 33 minutes as official.

Longest Fighter Hop

It was the longest flight ever made by a fighter plane. On its takeoff last night from Hickam field, Honolulu, the strange twin-fuselaged plane carried the heaviest load ever lifted into the air by a fighter plane. And it was the first non-stop flight by any kind of a plane from Honolulu to New York.

Thacker dropped the "Flying Freak," as some of those seeing it for the first time today immediately named it, to a perfect landing as his wife, for whom the plane was named, and a crowd of more than 1,000 persons cheered and waved.

The El Centro, Calif., pilot, and his co-pilot, 1st Lt. John M. Ard, of Inglewood, were tired but happy as they slid from the cramped cockpits where they had sat for nearly 15 hours.

Flew It Their Way

"We flew it the way we wanted to fly it," Thacker said. "The engines ran sweet."

But for a time earlier today it had appeared that the fliers might have to give up before reaching their goal.

Thacker gave full credit to Ard for the decision to continue to La Guardia instead of landing at Erie or Wilkes-Barre, Pa., which they had considered. He quoted Ard as saying, when they discussed the dwindling gas supply as they roared over the Great Lakes area: "Colonel, we can do it."

Ard is a "very experienced" fighter pilot, Thacker explained, and the chief pilot made his decision then to continue to New York.

Weather As Briefed

The flight was made at altitudes ranging from 19,000 to 22,000 feet, Thacker said, and the "weather was exactly as briefed". He said they had good tailwinds, and occasionally reached a speed of 450 miles an hour. They averaged almost 350 mph.

One handicap in the latter stages of the flight was that one of the four auxiliary gas tanks affixed beneath the wings to carry a part of the seven-ton gasoline load with which the plane took off from Hickam field could not be jettisoned because of a mechanical failure.

Thacker said this slowed the plane perhaps as much as 40 miles an hour. The tank still hung beneath the wing as the plane came into the field.

Wives Greet Pilots

Wives of both fliers were at the field to greet them as they climbed from the plane's twin fuselages where they sat for nearly 15 hours of constant flying.

The strange plane left Hickam field at 8:34 p.m. EST yesterday, and spanned 2,483 miles of ocean to cross the coast of California at 2:25 a.m., EST, and then sped eastward 2,568 miles along the great circle route to New York. The total distance of the flight was 5,051 miles.

Leaving Hickam, the plane carried seven tons of gasoline in its regular tanks, and in four tanks attached beneath the wings. The flight was designed to test the possibiltiy of long range fighters with two pilots, accompanying new long range bombers on flights over great distances.

Test of Fatigue

It also was to test pilot fatigue, and various items of equipment designed for such long range flights.

The big ship taxied in and drew to a stop as a big crowd surged around it, straining at police lines. Photographers crushed in close for shots and Tracker emerged from one fuselage, slid smilingly down the wing and rushed to hug his wife.

The photographers pressed in close as they embraced and Thacker jostled with them, shouting, "Hey, look out. That's my wife."

The fliers' wives screamed with delight as the plane came in for a landing. Mrs Thacker cried, "Oh, isn't it wonderful," and waved wildly.

Ard, a tow-headed, blue-eyed youth, bare-headed and wearing a khaki flight jacket, appeared almost dazed as he slid from his cockpit. Someone on the ground yelled at him:

"Here's your wife."

Then Ard seemed to come awake, and slid down the wing and kissed his wife.

★ ★ ★

We Aren't To Blame

Doubtless many discerning readers are thinking the Inglewood Daily News has made a mistake in stories concerning Lieut. John Ard's adventures on the "Betty Jo," the Army's P-82 Twin Mustang that completed a record non-stop trip from Honolulu to New York today.

It's this way.

Pictures of the plane carried in this paper show the fighter with the name "Betty Joe" by Lieut. Col. Robert Thacker's cockpit. Caption for the picture, however, read "Betty Jo."

It wasn't a mistake by the Inglewood Daily News, nor by the photographer. Nope, it was a painter's error.

A check disclosed that a painter with a weakness in spelling thought that Colonel Thacker's wife, after whom the plane was named, spelled her name Betty Joe. She doesn't.

Why doesn't someone change the name on the plane? We don't know. Maybe it's bad luck.

Senate Group Votes Against TVA Hopeful

WASHINGTON, Feb. 28.—(U.P.)—The Senate public works committee today voted seven to five against the nomination of Gordon R. Clapp, who was nominated to succeed David E. Lilienthal. Clapp was TVA general manager under Lilienthal.

The Tennessee senator also has been opposing vigorously the nomination of Lilienthal to be chairman of the atomic energy commission.

Sen. Chapman Revercomb, R., W. Va., chairman of the public works committee, said he voted for confirmation. But he declined to disclose how the other members of the 12-man committee voted.

The committee's unfavorable report will go to the full Senate for final action.

Blast Chemicals Stored Without Refrigeration

LOS ANGELES, Feb. 28.—(U.P.)—Chemicals suspected of causing last week's fatal blast at the O'Connor Electroplating Co. lay for many months unrefrigerated on a Stanford university laboratory shelf, Dist. Atty. William E. Simpson said today.

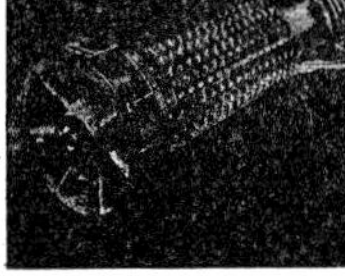

HERE'S NEW POWER—Unwrapped today after months of secret development, the Northrop-Hendy "Turbodyne" packs tremendous power in small, slender cylinder. Below, complete engine with bell-mouth intake at right where air enters and is compressed by hundreds of airfoil blades. Bulge is compression chamber, where air is mixed with fuel and is fired, whirling turbine blades at left end. At left, "Turbodyne" with top half of engine casing removed. (See complete story on page 3).

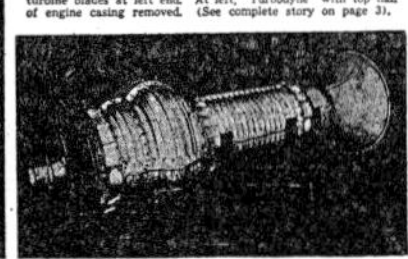

★ ★ ★ ★ ★ ★

SPEED KINGS—Lt. John Ard of Inglewood makes final check of North American Aviation's P-82 Twin Mustang with Lt. Col. Robert Thacker, in cockpit, before the Army Air Forces ace left Hawaii for a record-making non-stop flight to New York in 14 hours, 33 minutes. Thacker credited Ard, who acted as engineer, with decision to make La Guardia field when the chief pilot feared the "Betty Jo" would run out of fuel. The twin-engined ship landed with only 60 gallons of gasoline in its tanks.

Mother's Love Sent to Ard While Flying East

Inglewood friends of Lt. John Ard, engineer and co-pilot of the record-smashing "Betty Jo," heard two personal reports from the local ace by radio late last night and early this morning.

At 11:05 p.m. contact was established with the P-82 Twin Mustang as it neared the California coast.

"Hello, Johnny. I wish you the best of luck," said Mrs. Ada Ard, 420 East Arbor Vitae, the pilot's mother.

"Hello, Gloomy!" added Ard's brother, Louis.

Shortly after the "Betty-Jo's" 11:08 a.m. (EST) landing at La Guardia field, N.Y., today, Ard and Lt. Col. Robert Thacker, El Centro, broadcast impressions of their speed dash from Hawaii.

"I didn't think we would make it after we passed Chicago," said Thacker, "until Johnny (Ard) signaled from his cockpit that he was confident we could hit La Guardia. He's the engineer. I just went along for the ride," he added modestly.

Wives of both Army Air Forces pilots were at the New York field for a surprise welcome.

In an interview with the Daily News today, Mrs. Ard declared:

"I knew John would make it. He's got grit. Oh, yes, I'm extremely happy, but I'm not surprised. I knew my boy could do it."

Louis Ard, the pilot's brother, is a letter carrier at the Inglewood post office.

Casino Worker Faces Sentence for Slaying

LAS VEGAS, Nev., Feb. 28—(U.P.)—A jury today convicted Fred Teeter, Las Vegas casino worker, of second degree murder for fatally shooting a "pal" who objected to the division of loot from a jewelry store robbery.

Sentence was expected to be passed tomorrow.

Teeter shot Howard Linabury over division of $20,000 stolen from the Jerry Jerram jewelry store last November.

Newsman POW Drops Dead After Address

WASHINGTON, Feb. 28—(U.P.)—John B. Powell, American newspaperman who suffered Japanese torture in a prison camp during the war, dropped dead today at the close of an address to the University of Missouri Alumni Association.

Bevin Tells of French Treaty

Signing Slated For Next Tuesday

LONDON, Feb. 28.—(U.P.)—Foreign Secretary Ernest Bevin told the house of commons today that agreement has been reached with France on the terms of the Anglo-French alliance.

Bevin said that the terms of the treaty have been agreed upon and he hoped that the document would be signed Tuesday at Dunquerque.

Bevin told commons:

"There are a few adjustments now being made. The treaty will, I hope, be signed by the French foreign minister and myself on Tuesday, March 4, at Dunquerque."

Bevin's announcement was welcomed by Anthony Eden, acting conservative leader, who said that he was certain the house would share "the great satisfaction of his majesty's government at the successful outcome of these negotiations."

Bevin said a text of the treaty would be provided as soon as possible.

House Sends Portal Pay Bill to Senate

WASHINGTON, Feb. 28.—(U.P.)—The House today passed and sent to the Senate legislation to outlaw nearly $6,000,000,000 in labor claims for retroactive portal pay.

The only stubborn opposition came in an effort to increase from one year to two or three years the statutory time limit in which a worker could sue for back wages or other compensation.

Hoover Favors Pliable Foreign Relief Fund

WASHINGTON, Feb. 28—(U.P.)—Former President Herbert Hoover said today Congress would be justified in appropriating an additional $350,000,000 for foreign relief if the program is kept flexible to recapture any unneeded funds.

Today's Race Results

At Santa Anita Park

FIRST RACE—4½ furlongs. 2 year old maidens bred in Calif. purse $3000.

Roman In, 116 (Layton)	10.70	5.10	3.90
Top's Boy, 116 (James)		12.70	4.00
Fire Atom, 116 (Balaski)			2.50

Time: .53 2/5.

Also ran—Captain Perry, V Flag, Gay Countess, Pretty Gypsy, Vain Confetti, Isle of Skye, Wired Music, Watch Justice.

Scratched—Archaeologist, All Velvet, War Vistic, Maureen, Lucky Bob.

SECOND RACE—6 furlongs. Maiden 3 year olds and up. Allowances. Purse $3000.

Random Jest, 130 (E. Arcaro)	14.60	7.70	4.20
Family Circle, 107 (H. Trent)		5.50	4.00
Ocean Play, 113 (R. Campbell)			13.40

Time: 1.12 1/5.

Also ran—Black Fox, Connie Haines, Sandy James, Jogaway, Maria Del Ora, Beauty Queen, Perfecto, Fire Bee, Style Parade.

Scratched—Beats All, Handy Way, Mighty Falcon, Bionita.

EXAMPLE 257A

The Scarsdale Inquirer

VOLUME XXIX—NUMBER 10 SCARSDALE, NEW YORK, FRIDAY, MARCH 7, 1947 PRICE—TEN CENTS

Waste Paper Collection To Be Sunday, March 16

Weather Conditions Make Industry's Situation Critical; Need Generous Collection

Sunday, March 16, is the date set for Scarsdale's twenty-first waste paper collection.

Waste paper consuming mills for the sixth consecutive week had to dig further into their paper stock inventories in order to maintain production last week, according to J. Bradford Ricketts, waste paper salvage chairman. Weather conditions were blamed by dealers and collecting agencies for their inability to supply all the waste paper that was needed. Another heavy snow storm would cause many mills to shut down for lack of raw material which is now waste paper, he said.

Greenville and Green Knolls will also collect paper on March 16. The consuming mills are paying a price higher than they have paid for many years for waste paper—higher, indeed, than the price per ton of coal or oil, and every pound not saved and made available for collection is a direct financial loss to the local organizations.

The Girl Scouts will again distribute hand bills throughout the village this week announcing the coming collection. All residents in the areas to be collected are urged to continue their salvage efforts. A salvage box for paper only is located near Robison's garage on East Parkway for those who cannot conveniently store paper at home.

Benefiting from the drives are the following organizations: The Scarsdale Girl Scouts, Scarsdale Boy Scouts, American Red Cross, Scarsdale's Memorial Fund, and Post 52, American Legion.

Remember the date, says Mr. Ricketts—Sunday, March 16, one o'clock, rain or shine.

Deadline!

Several letters on the nonpartisan system of government and the forthcoming village election appear on the editorial page of this week's issue of The Inquirer. It is possible that they may bring forth more letters for next week's edition, the last before the election on March 18.

In accordance with long-standing practice, any letters which may introduce personalities or bring up new arguments will be submitted for rebuttal in the same edition. For that reason, any letters to the editor for insertion in next Friday's paper must be in the newspaper office by nine o'clock on Tuesday morning.

Union Conference Set for Tomorrow

In response to a request from Local 540, United Public Workers, village officials will meet in the Village Hall at ten o'clock tomorrow with representatives of the union to discuss its demands.

Employees in the water, highway and waste departments are asking a $250 emergency bonus and inclusion in permanent wages of the six dollar weekly cost of living increase granted last November. Other proposals are for shorter hours, longer vacations and more sick leave and holidays.

Village representatives at the conference will be Mayor H. Beach Carpenter, Acting Mayor Samuel E. Darby, Jr., Trustee Harry E. Humphreys, Jr. who is chairman of the Village Board's finance committee and Village Manager Reeves Newsom.

"Watching Brief" On Fare Increase

County Attorney Harry G. Herman was instructed, by a unanimous vote of the Board of Supervisors this week, to appear in any proceedings brought by the New York Central Railroad Company for increased fares and to fight raises found to be unjustified. It was pointed out by Robert Stewart of New Castle that the road has asked for an increase of $2.50 a month on regular commutation and about $2 on school commutations.

It was also suggested that this is the time to seek improvements in service and the county attorney was asked to consider this in any dealings with the company.

Paddle Tennis Tourney Is Marked by Upsets

Two upsets marked the semifinals of the national men's doubles tournament in paddle tennis last Sunday at the Fox Meadow Tennis Club. Both matches were played in the rain, since none of the contestants would have been able to play this week end.

Holbrook Hyde and Leland Wiley of the Hartford Golf Club defeated the champions for the past two years, Clifford Sutter and Basil Maguire of the Greenwich Field Club, 6-3, 6-2 to enter the finals. In the other semi-final, an all-Fox Meadow affair, John Grout and John Moses upset Clifford Couch and Charles M. O'Hearn, runners-up for the past two years, 6-0, 6-4.

Finals are scheduled for Sunday, March 16 at three p.m. on the Fox Meadow courts.

Arthur Manor Election

On Wednesday evening, March 12 at 8:15 the Arthur Manor Association will hold its annual meeting and election of officers at the Edgewood School. The nominating committee, under the chairmanship of J. R. Keith, is proposing James E. Daly of 168 Bell Road for president; Lloyd C. Carpenter, vice-president; Edward H. Jackson, treasurer; Paul M. Harwick, recording secretary; Mrs. Robert Jackson, corresponding secretary. The four nominees for two-year terms as directors are E. N. Wilmington, retiring president; C. T. Fuller, C. E. Darling, and Herman Zimmerman.

Committee Invites Parents to Tell All

The Town Club's education committee this year is asking questions about the foundation subjects of spelling, reading, grammar, study methods and discipline in Scarsdale schools. And, of course, they are looking over the school budget, too. But these other subjects have daily interest for many parents who are now invited to write, wire or phone their views on them to any sub-committee chairman or members.

If you have a triple-A-plus speller in your home or an audition winning reader or a Gettysburg grammarian or even a perfectly disciplined child, or would like one, and for which you are ready to give sole credit to our schools, tell the committee.

For reading and spelling, communicate with Nicholas W. Vancil, chairman or John H. Eisele. For grammar and study methods, see or call Paul S. Smith, chairman, Walter C. Howe or H. H. Thurlby. About discipline, approach William F. Reich, Jr., chairman, Malcolm Law or John R. Wood, Jr. The budget is being scrutinized by Albert C. Childs, chairman, Laurence B. Davis and Lewis V. Hohl.

A long succession of able and energetic committees of the Town Club have voiced the views of the community to the School Board to which, indeed, members of these education committees have often been promoted.

Edgemont Officers

William D. Gaillard, vice-president of the Edgemont Association, will continue in that office for the coming year, according to an announcement from the Association. John Van Norden has been appointed secretary of the group.

NEWS INDEX

Church News	Page 18
Editorials	Page 12
Obituaries	Page 19
Schools, Sports	Pages 10, 11
Society	Pages 13, 14
Theaters	Page 21
Woman's Club	Page 15

This is no unusual sight at the home of Mr. and Mrs. J. F. Gillis of Healy Avenue in Hartsdale. Their pet deer, well known to Scarsdale through the pictures of The Inquirer's photographer, John Gass, is now nine months old but still likes his bottle of powdered milk three times a day. He sleeps under Mrs. Gillis' bedroom window in a bed of honeysuckle and sumac, suitably trampled down for the greatest deer comfort. He feels free to enter the house through the French doors at any time, but usually makes straight for the kitchen where his milk is prepared. He pals about with the family's French poodle.

Humphreys Advocates 20% Tax Reduction

In the long run, a flat twenty per cent across-the-board decrease in Federal income taxes would provide more rather than less revenue, Harry E. Humphreys, Jr. of Brewster Road told a nation-wide radio audience recently while speaking on the National Association of Manufacturers' program "It's Your Business" over the ABC network. Mr. Humphreys, a member of the Village Board, is chairman of the association's government finance committee.

"There would be an immediate loss in revenue, but not for long," Mr. Humphreys stated. "With a twenty per cent tax reduction, we would increase our Federal revenue by reason of the increased volume of business. That's what happened after the first World War."

Declaring that NAM is opposed to "soaking" anybody, rich or poor, Mr. Humphreys advocated a plan of "quick action under which all will have some share in the tax relief, under which work and investment incentives will be quickened and under which the Federal revenues will be adequately protected."

Executive Committee

John A. Pearson, Scarsdale chairman for the forthcoming campaign for United Service to China, Inc., announced this week the names of those who will serve on his executive committee. They include the Reverend Adelbert R. Bryon, Mrs. Ruth Nash Chalmers, Mrs. Carl A. Evans, Mrs. George E. Hall, Mrs. Clark Harris and Lester R. Stewart.

Zoning Hearing Centers On Four-Story Limitation

Except for a few statements as to individual problems under the proposed new zoning ordinance, the public hearing held by the Village Board on Monday evening brought forth nothing except a brief discussion on the limitation of business and apartment buildings to four stories. Held at Dyckman Hall, in case large numbers of citizens wished to be heard, those attending could have been accommodated in the regular board room at the Village Hall.

Addison Wilson, speaking for the Parkway Spencer Corporation, largest owners of undeveloped property near the Scarsdale station, voiced his company's opposition to the proposal to change the ordinance which now allows six-story buildings back to the original limitation of four.

Walk-up apartments over stores would not attract Scarsdale residents, he said, or newcomers who were up to the Scarsdale "standard." Using the Scarsdale Chateaux as an example, he stated that many Scarsdale residents who wished to be relieved of the responsibilities of a private home, were prevented by old age or ill health from occupying apartments there because they had no elevators.

Step Backward

The change was a step backward, he continued, pointing out that the company's property south of Christie Place which would naturally be developed as stores and apartments, was protected from private homes on Chase Road by the roadways and by the Post Office. Popham Hall is a six-story building and with one already in the area, there is no sense in prohibiting six-story buildings, he concluded, pointing out that the actual height of a six-story building south of Christie Place would be no more than the Chateaux, since the latter are built on top of a hill.

Warren W. Cunningham of Autenrieth Road told the board that he might as well confess to being the member of the Town Club's zoning committee who had proposed the return to four-story buildings. I am not at all concerned about East Parkway, he said, but if the Residence A district east of Chase Road faces a six-story barricade, I don't see how you can keep business from spreading across Chase Road. That would be the end of zoning as we know it.

He pointed out that there was a 100-foot strip of Residence A land on the west side of Chase Road which was actually a buffer-strip for zoning since it was im-

(Continued on Page Two)

Teachers' Salaries Law Doesn't Affect Village

Arguments on teachers' salaries, raging throughout the State as the result of the report of special committee appointed by Governor Thomas E. Dewey which he urged the Legislature this week to vote into law, have no effect on the Scarsdale salary schedule. Its own schedule is already higher than the proposed schedule.

The education committee's report was hailed as revolutionary in two aspects. It recommends that all teachers, from kindergarten to high school, be paid on the same scale. It urges that, after six years of automatic pay rises, subsequent increases to teachers be made conditional on demonstrated superiority.

The Scarsdale school system has used a system of promotional increases after automatic increments for the past ten years and has had a single salary schedule since 1929.

Orchestra Concert

Annual concert of Scarsdale school orchestras will be held this Sunday afternoon, March 9 at three o'clock in the high school auditorium. The public is invited without charge. The orchestras will be directed by Morton Bley.

"Vox Pop" Program Draws Capacity Crowd to School

Abetted by good weather, Warren Hull's "Vox Pop" radio program and the Scarsdale Boy Scouts accomplished something which neither General Arnold nor the LWV's peace program managed to do—filled the Scarsdale High School auditorium practically to the roof. Moreover, in spite of a rather ticklish problem of selection, Scarsdale and its Scouts seemed pretty well satisfied with the program and its participants and brought in hearty applause with fine spirit at exactly the right moments as specified.

Troops whose boys may not make the program on the air were given a chance for participation during the half hour preceding and all troops were included in the repeating of the Scout Oath heard from coast to coast.

"Stars" included Robert Ormiston of Troop 1 and his father (who turned out to be a former school mate of Mr. Hull's); Jimmy Vickery of Troop 5, who told the United States that he intended to be a chemical engineer, that he liked the Dodgers, and that he found the Westerns in the movies "pretty mushy" these days; Rolf Monk of Troop 5, a lad from Brussels, Belgium, who belonged during the war to a "sort of underground Scout troop there" and who once gave a German the "wrong steer and then got out fast." Robert and Jonathan Leavitt, twin Cubs of Den 5, Pack 1 who were once neighbors of General Marshall on Fire Island; David Swanson of Troop 3, an Eagle Scout with four palms and a member of the Order of the Arrow and his father; and Mr. Hull's three sons, George and Paul of Troop 3 and Charles, a Cub Scout.

Milford Lester, a senior patrol leader of Troop 4, gave the commands and Dave Swanson was the bugler.

At the Court of Honor which preceded the program 134 merit badges were awarded; thirty-five second class, fourteen first class, eight star, seven life, one bronze palm and one second bronze palm awards were made.

Generous prizes were given all participants and a "shipment" of bubble gum for the Cubs created a near-riot from the boys in blue, who, said Justus H. Schwaner, Jr., master of ceremonies at the Court, "wanted their gum but now!" Mothers were plentifully supplied with Lipton's soup and Lipton's tea.

Ganzenmullers Reach Tennis Quarter-Finals

A former Scarsdale resident, the former Miss Louise Raymond of Colvin Road and her husband, Gus Ganzenmuller of Sea Cliff, Long Island both reached the quarter-final round in the national indoor tennis championships this week at the 7th Regiment Armory in New York.

Mrs. Ganzenmuller's triumph projected her into the unenviable role of being the opponent of Pauline Betz, American outdoor champion, in the quarter-finals. Miss Betz triumphed, 6-1, 6-3 on Tuesday afternoon. Mr. Ganzenmuller lost to Bob Falkenburg in the quarter-finals, 7-5, 5-6, 6-1.

Chamber of Commerce Will Hear Resident

The Scarsdale Chamber of Commerce will hold its monthly meeting next Tuesday evening, March 11 at the Scarsdale Lodge and will have as guest speaker, LeRoy McClary of Scarsdale who is affiliated with A. C. Nielsen, Market Research Analysts, Chicago, London and New York.

Mr. McClary will talk on market research and merchandising problems of interest to all Scarsdale merchants. The meeting will be preceded by dinner at The Lodge.

Two Meetings

Two village meetings are scheduled for next week. The Board of Education will meet on Monday evening at 8:15 in the High School and the Village Board on Tuesday evening at the same time in the Village Hall.

Archery Demonstration Tonight at High School

The Village Recreation Department will present an archery exhibition at the Scarsdale High School, this evening, March 7, at 8:30 p.m.

Charles Burdick of Yonkers has arranged this program. An array of some of the leading archers in the east will be presented at this time.

They include Natalia Clemson, Massachusetts state champion and national indoor and national intercollegiate champion, Adelaide Dickson, national competitor; William Sterner, Eastern champion; Dr. Joe Brussels, highest scorer of Westchester County; Chick Dodson, Yonkers; Harry Finney, junior Westchester County champion; Arthur Beman, Bronxville, and Fritz Touchenhagen, Port Chester. The program will consist of target and field shooting with the special attraction of blind shooting.

All high school students, as well as parents, are cordially invited to attend this show.

Draper Is Promoted

Brigadier General William M. Draper, Jr. of Scarsdale was named on Thursday of last week to the top economics post in the American Military Government as economics adviser to the theater commander. General Draper had been director of the economics division of the AMG.

Ralph McClelland Dies; Supervisor Here Since 1935

Col. Rodney Gott Put in Command Of Artillery Unit

Colonel Rodney C. Gott of 73 Greenacres Avenue, has been assigned by the First Army to command the 416th Field Artillery or "Westchester Group" of the 27th Artillery Corps, it was announced last Saturday by General Courtney H. Hodges. The 416th in common with all other groups, will be restricted to reserve officers. It will not be a National Guard unit.

The group headquarters will be in White Plains.

Colonel Gott was graduated from West Point in 1933 and served two years with the Engineers. He was then associated with the American Radiator Corporation and the Standard Sanitary Corporation. He reported for active duty again in May, 1941, as first lieutenant.

He served on the general staff at Army Ground Forces Headquarters, Washington, until he was assigned to the 12th Corps Artillery and sent to England in April 1944. The unit crossed the channel shortly after D-Day and spearheaded the Third Army drive across France. From September to December 1945, the Colonel commanded the artillery of the 79th Infantry.

He wears the Legion of Merit Medal, the Bronze Star Medal with Cluster, Purple Heart, the French Croix de Guerre with Palm, as well as his theater ribbons and battle stars.

Colonel Gott is manager of the commercial research department of the American Machine and Foundry Company in New York. He and Mrs. Gott have two sons, Peter H., eleven, and Rodney C., Jr., four.

Doctor Finds Him in Apartment with Gas Turned on; Services Held Yesterday

Residents of Scarsdale and of Westchester County thronged to the Church of St. James the Less yesterday morning to pay tribute to the memory of Ralph A. McClelland, supervisor of Scarsdale since 1935. The service was conducted by the Reverend James Harry Price, rector of the church, assisted by the Reverend Dr. George Hugh Smyth of the Hitchcock Memorial Church, and burial was in the family lot in the churchyard. Masonic services were conducted at the Bennett Funeral Home Wednesday night.

Honorary pallbearers at the service included Mayor H. Beach Carpenter, George W. Cornell, Thomas F. Croake, former Mayor Warren W. Cunningham, Village Manager Reeves Newsom, Waterbury Scott, State Senator Pliny W. Williamson and Addison R. Wilson.

Mr. McClelland was found dead in the kitchen of his home at 48 Garth Road on Monday morning with five jets of the gas range open. Efforts of Firemen Robert Auld and Arthur Nonemaker to revive him with a pulmotor were fruitless. Mr. McClelland was alone in the apartment at the time, his wife, who was recently a patient at the White Plains Hospital, being at her sister's home, recuperating.

Dr. Amos O. Squire, county medical examiner, ruled, after an examination, that Mr. McClelland had died "a suicide from illuminating gas poisoning while temporarily mentally disturbed." Mr. McClelland's body was found by Dr. Hugh McHugh, a psychiatrist, who was disturbed because Mr. McClelland had failed to keep an appointment, and came to Scarsdale to see him.

Flags at Half-Mast

At the public hearing on the zoning ordinance on Tuesday evening, Mayor H. Beach Carpenter expressed the shock and grief which Scarsdale, "the town which he has served so ably and so long," felt at Mr. McClelland's death. Flags were flown at half-mast in the village. The Village Board will adopt a formal resolution at its meeting next week.

In White Plains on Wednesday, sessions of the Supreme and County Court were adjourned out of respect to Mr. McClelland's memory. It is expected that a formal memorial service will be held later.

Born in Brooklyn in 1898, Mr. McClelland was graduated from Cornell University, where he received his law degree in 1921. During the first World War he served in the United States Naval Reserve. Beginning the practice of law in New York City, he later came to Westchester and joined the firm of Rounds, Dillingham, Mead and Neagle. In 1939 he became associated with the new firm of Dempsey, McClelland and Croake in White Plains.

In October, 1945, he severed his earlier business connections and entered a partnership with Waterbury Scott of 186 Lyons Road, under the firm name of McClelland and Scott, with offices at 175 Main Street, White Plains.

Record of Public Service

A Scarsdale resident for more than twenty years, Mr. McClelland served as Justice of the Peace here from 1930 to 1934 and as a member of the Town Board. Appointed to the Board of Supervisors to succeed State Senator Pliny W. Williamson, he was first elected to the board in the autumn of 1935 and had served as supervisor since then.

On the county board, he had been majority leader, chairman of the budget committee and chairman of the board for three years, beginning in 1938. Since that time he had held important committee posts on the board and also served as a member of the Board of Acquisition and Contract.

A staunch Republican, Mr. McClelland was Republican chairman

Hancock Honored At Luncheon Today

Former Mayor John M. Hancock of Mamaroneck Road, a partner in Lehman Brothers, investment bankers, is being honored today at a luncheon at the Hotel Commodore by the American Chemical Society. Mr. Hancock, who was associated with Bernard M. Baruch in formulating the American proposal for United Nations control of atomic energy, recently conducted a study of the chemical society's organization and functions.

He will speak on the role of science, scientists and scientific societies in achieving world peace. Other speakers will be Professor W. Albert Noyes, Jr., president of the society and head of the chemistry department at the University of Rochester and Dr. Charles Allen Thomas, president-elect and vice-president of the Monsanto Chemical Company at St. Louis and project director of the Clinton Laboratories at Oak Ridge, Tennessee, which are engaged in atomic research.

Awarded Legion of Honor

Craig Smyth — Robert Posey

The French Legion of Honor was awarded last week to Robert Posey, an architect, of Saxon Woods Road and to Craig Hugh Smyth, lecturer at the Frick Museum and the son of Dr. and Mrs. George H. Smyth of Walworth Avenue. The honor was accorded in recognition of their services with the Monuments, Fine Arts and Archives Division of the Third Army in France and Germany.

Presentation was made at the French Embassy's cultural center, 934 Fifth Avenue, on February 27, by General Maurice N. E. Mathenet, military attache to the embassy, in the name of Henri Bonnet, French ambassador, now in Europe.

Mr. Smyth lectured in Scarsdale recently, telling members of the Hitchcock Guild the story of the team work between the French authorities and the American Army in the recovery of works of art from Germany.

A graduate of Princeton University and of the Department of Fine Art and Archeology there, Mr. Smyth was, before the war a member of the staff of the National Gallery of Art in Washington, D. C. He served four years in the Naval Reserve as a lieutenant and in the Spring of 1945 became an officer in the department of Arts and Monuments in charge of the main collecting point in Munich.

Mr. Posey, who last year was made a Chevalier of the Order of Leopold, by Belgium, in reply to The Inquirer's question about his war service, said:

"During the early part of the

(Continued on Page Three)

EXAMPLE 257B

THE WEATHER
Today: Partly cloudy, with highest temperature near 75; fresh to moderate southwest winds.
Tomorrow: Partly cloudy and continued mild.
Detailed Report and Map—Page 45

NEW YORK Herald Tribune

LATE CITY EDITION

VOL. CVI No. 36,508 — WEDNESDAY, OCTOBER 30, 1946 — THREE CENTS In New York City

Baruch at Forum Bars Release of Atom Secrets Unless Veto Is Given Up

Asserts U. S. Will Sign No Pact Until Accord on Veto Is Arrived At

SpaakHailsTruman On Address to U. N.

BoydOrrUrges Action on Food; La Guardia Hits British Stand on D. P.s

THE PRESIDENT OF THE GENERAL ASSEMBLY—Paul-Henri Spaak, addressing the second session of the Forum yesterday

Citizens' Group Suing to Block Retroactive Subway Pay Rise

Challenges City's Right to Give 20c an Hour Back to July 1 and Manner of Raising $18,500,000; Council Asks Increase for 110,000 Workers

By David McConnell

Price Ceilings GoOffRadios. Fats and Oils

Kitchenware Also Freed Among Hundreds of Items in O. P. A. Order

Other Articles Still On the Waiting List

Small Hails Increase in Employment; Attacks 'Pessimistic Forecasts'

Atomic Board Asks Army to Carry On Now

Will Take Over Manhattan Project Gradually; Urges Scientists to Stay on Job

News on Inside Pages

Molotov Asks World Arms Cut, Calls for Ban on Atomic Bomb, Warns End of Veto Is End of U.N.

Stalin's Views Seen Echoing Byrnes Aims

Appraisal of Statements Shows Both Seek Unified Economy for Germany

By Bert Andrews

'Smart and Tough,' Says Austin, Liking Parts of Molotov Speech

Won't Answer Charges Now; Connally and Dulles Have No Comment; British Disappointed; India and Canada Are Impressed by Proposals

By Peter Kihss

Investigation of Britain's Press Ordered by Commons, 271-157

Royal Commission Created to Inquire Into Charges of Monopolistic Control, Which Government Holds Is Distorting Freedom of Press

TrucksRushing SuppliestoCity, EmbargoEased

Rail Shipments Will Be Freed; Warehouses and TerminalsNowHumming

$3,500 Left on L. I. Train Seat Ordered Split 5 Ways by Court

U.S.-to-Moscow Radiotelephone Open to Public for First Time

Russian Tells Assembly U. S. Atom Plan Would Upset Charter of U. N.

Delivers a Personal AttackUponBaruch

Says Other Side in a War May Use Bomb, Too, 'and Something Else'

By John G. Rogers

EXAMPLE 258

"All the News That's Fit to Print"

The New York Times.

LATE CITY EDITION
Partly cloudy and continued mild today and tomorrow.

Copyright, 1946, by The New York Times Company.

VOL. XCVI....No. 32,421. NEW YORK, WEDNESDAY, OCTOBER 30, 1946. THREE CENTS NEW YORK CITY

MOLOTOV URGES U. N. MOVE TO CUT WORLD ARMS; ASKS BAN ON ATOM BOMB, BUT SCORNS U. S. PLAN; BARUCH APPROVES SOVIET'S IDEA IF IT HAS TEETH

10 TO 35% PAY RISE ASKED BY COUNCIL FOR CITY WORKERS

Resolution Calls On Estimate Board to Increase All Wages Up to $5,550 a Year

TAXPAYER SUIT IS FILED

Trustee of Citizens Budget Group Would Enjoin Higher Rates to Transit Men

By ROBERT W. POTTER

Continued on Page 38, Column 1

'Fashions of Times' Shows Elegance of Pre-War Days

Style Leaders of the Nation, at Premiere of Lavish Display, Hail Imported Fabrics and End of Wartime Restrictions

By LUCY GREENBAUM

Continued on Page 35, Column 6

TRUMAN SUPPORTS LEWIS ON REOPENING FEDERAL COAL PACT

Clark Rules Against Krug in What Is Called 'Crassest Kind' of Deal to Elect Kilgore

MINERS NOW OPPOSE HIM

Secretary Expected to Return to Capital for 'Showdown' Meeting With Union Head

By LOUIS STARK

Continued on Page 23, Column 3

ADDRESSING THE UNITED NATIONS GENERAL ASSEMBLY

Foreign Minister Molotov speaking to the delegates yesterday

RUSSIAN IN WARNING

Foreign Minister Fights Veto Curb, Even on Atom—Assails Baruch

URGES TRUSTEE BODY

He Scores South Africa's Plan to Annex Area—For More WFTU Power

The text of the address by Mr. Molotov is on Page 12.

By THOMAS J. HAMILTON

Continued on Page 13, Column 5

DEWEY HERE TODAY TO END CAMPAIGN

Party Leaders Expect Speeches to Increase Republican Total in Legislature and Congress

By LEO EGAN

Continued on Page 20, Column 3

LEHMAN ASSAILS RIVALS ON TRADE

Asserts U. S. Can Prosper Only Under Foreign Policy of the Democratic Party

By WILLIAM R. CONKLIN

Continued on Page 20, Column 4

BARUCH RECEPTIVE TO SOVIET ON BOMB

Russian Proposal Acceptable, He Says, if Treaty Provides Compulsion of Obedience

By WILL LISSNER

Continued on Page 14, Column 5

Delegates Upset by Speech, Fear Allies Riven Further

By JAMES RESTON

Continued on Page 15, Column 3

CHURCHILL DOUBTS STALIN ON TROOPS

Says Even 60 War Divisions Would Outnumber U. S., British—London Impatient at Stalin

The text of Mr. Churchill's statement is on Page 4.

By EMANUEL R. FREEDMAN

Continued on Page 4, Column 4

World News Summarized

WEDNESDAY, OCTOBER 30, 1946

Allis Pickets Defy Sheriff's Force; 16 Workers Injured in Rioting

Continued on Page 33, Column 2

U. S. Accuses Rumania on Voting; Holds Coercion Violates Accord

TEXT OF U. S. NOTE

Continued on Page 7, Column 1

China Defends U. S. On Russian Charge

EXAMPLE 259

PM Daily
FIVE CENTS
(Copyright, 1946, by The Newspaper PM, Inc.)
Vol. VII – No. 114
Wednesday, October 30, 1946

☆ COMPLETE EDITION

Soviet Proposes World Arms Reduction

—Asks Ban on Atom for War

Molotov's disarmament proposals to the UN Assembly:

"1. In the interests of consolidating international peace and security and in conformity with the purposes and principles of the United Nations organization the General Assembly considers a general reduction of armaments necessary.

"2. The implementation of the decision on the reduction of armaments should include as a primary objective the banning of the manufacture and use of atomic energy for military purposes.

"3. The General Assembly recommends to the Security Council to provide for the practical achievement of the objectives set forth in the above-mentioned paragraphs 1 and 2.

"4. The General Assembly calls upon the governments of all states to render every possible assistance to the Security Council in this responsible undertaking, the accomplishment of which conforms to the establishment of stable peace and international security and also serves the interests of the peoples by lightening their heavy economic burden caused by excessive expenditures for armaments which do not correspond to peaceful postwar conditions."

Pages 3-4

By Max Lerner:

What Dewey Victory Would Mean

"A victory for Dewey and Ives will be a victory for the Republican policy of talking beautifully to labor, but not being there when trade unions must be defended. . . . He (Dewey) has promised, promised, promised. . . ."

Editorial on Page 2

From Rogge's Report:

Hate Campaign Against Minorities

"The weapon used incessantly and malevolently (by defendants in sedition case) . . . was incitement of hatred toward minority groups, especially Jews and Negroes"—Rogge names names.

Story on Page 9

Columns:

Jennings Perry:

Gordon Clapp will carry right on in TVA where Lilienthal leaves off in resigning to become head of the Atomic Commission. Perry takes stock of TVA.

Perry on Back Page

Billy Rose:

"This is the story of a fellow who had eighteen million dollars and thought he was a poor man. . . . He lived king-size. . . . And then came 1929 and Black Friday. . . .

Rose on Page 2

EXAMPLE 260

Of course, newspaper executives do not modernize the dresses of their papers merely to win prizes in contests. They do their sprucing up primarily to please readers and advertisers, and to attract more readers and more advertising. Yet it often happens that the modernizing done with only one objective in mind makes possible the achievement not only of that objective but of other goals equally desirable.

A few years ago, the typographic laboratory of the *Linotype News* helped a certain publisher to modernize his morning and evening papers.

Shortly after the new dresses appeared, that publisher was convinced that he had achieved the double objective of pleasing readers and advertisers, for many of each were quick to express appreciation. Moreover, he reported, "we have effected substantial savings in space formerly given to multiple banks, and are saving much time in the composing room."

Thus we see that, while that publisher did his modernizing primarily to please readers and advertisers, he not only accomplished that but, at the same time and by the same means, succeeded in bringing about two other desirable things—the saving of space and production time.

But this is not the end of the story.

A few months later, when the state press association of which that publisher was a member held its annual better-newspaper contest, those modernized papers ran away with every first prize in their division. One of the papers won a certificate for the best presswork, and the other paper won a treble-award certificate, for the best front page, best general makeup and best handling of display advertising.

A statistically minded person could carry this story along indefinitely.

He could score a point by referring to those handsome certificates on a wall in the business office of the papers that won them, with hundreds of visitors looking at them (and being favorably impressed) day after day. He could score another point by referring to the increased pride in craftsmanship felt by every staff member of those papers, and their determination to keep on producing prize winners.

He could logically assume that all of these things will help to attract more and more readers, more and more advertising, and to make those papers better and more profitable publications.

And he could conclude his statistical essay by stating, in all good faith, that many a publisher who started out merely to improve his type dress has, by that one action, helped to improve his paper all along the line. For one good thing has a way of leading to another and another and another.

8

The Newspaper of Tomorrow

WHAT ABOUT the newspaper of the future—of, say, 2000 A.D.? What will it be like?

Surely newspapers in the year 2000 A.D. will be different from those of today, just as many of those of today are different from what they were no longer than a few years ago. The papers that have not made decided changes for the better in recent years need not be considered in regard to the future, for they will not be here.

It seems to this writer that it may not be too unreasonable to think that:

The newspaper in the year 2000 A.D.—and perhaps considerably before that—will have a smaller page size—a size approximating our present-day tabloid.

It will have fewer and wider columns to the page, which, of course, will call for changes of the standard advertising widths that prevail at present.

It will have larger and generously leaded body lines, and fewer and simpler headlines.

Most of its news—and even much of its display advertising—will be classified—grouped in certain departments or sections—for the convenience of readers.

Its front page will afford the reader a quick preview of the most important stories and departments in the issue—not a mere prosaic index, but dramatized summations.

Its inside pages will be important pages—will be regarded as just as important as front pages.

It will employ better paper and better ink, and the pages will have a more attractive, uniform impression.

It will present more and better pictures.

And it will use more and better color.

Also, it may cost the reader more than his paper now does, but he probably will be glad to pay the higher price for the better value.

The New York World's Fair of 1939 had for its theme "The World of Tomorrow." And shortly before the opening of that fair, in April, 1939, Warren L. Bassett, then managing editor of *Editor & Publisher*, invited several newspaper people and others, including this writer, to participate in a symposium on "The Newspaper of Tomorrow."

The symposium was conducted by Bice Clemow in *Editor & Publisher* for April 22, 1939.

And what did those lookers-into-the-future prophesy?

Many, many things.

Some of the guesses volunteered were that by the year 2000 A.D. the radio, televised and untelevised, would be disseminating much of the spot news, and that facsimile would be flourishing in full color; but another was that the newspaper itself would be employing television to provide picture copy for its own engraving department.

Some of the lookers-ahead toyed with the idea that offset and gravure printing would be employed daily by many newspapers.

"Our prophets," stated Mr. Clemow, "are pretty much of a mind that there will still be plenty of room, plenty of fun and plenty of money for the printed paper sixty years hence. That is the kind of news diffuser they talk most excitedly."

He continued, in part, as follows:

"The newspaper in 2000 A.D. will be smaller than it is today. Whatever else, it will not be physically awkward.

"We couldn't stir up much argument about a format which classifies spot news and thus gives each item contrast and related meaning. Such a format pre-supposes integration of all phases of every story into a rounded whole.

"As news is classified in 2000 A.D., the advertising will be classified, and possibly indexed, too. Summary indices of the news will be fuller, brighter, more satisfying to the read-and-run reader.

"All our editorial experts want better paper for their perfect 2000 A.D. product.

"Pictures: Photographers will have learned how to take them, editors will have learned how to make sense with them, printers will have learned how to print them without that screen-door complexion. It's the consensus that pictures will fill half the editorial space in tomorrow's paper.

"Comics: By 2000 A.D., comics will be about as old as an elephant and about as much in the way.

"If we assembled our prophets, turned them loose without mechanical, editorial or business restriction, to create next week the paper they are talking about for 2000 A.D., we could defy any circulation wizard to set a maximum limit on the number of people who would buy such a paper at ten cents.

"Advertisers will pay, too. All our prophets who wanted to cut the paper size in half wanted to double our ad rates."

Some of the many other predictions individually made by the participating prophets were:

That "the character of newswriting will be vastly improved," and that there will be "actual use of experts in all lines of writing";

That "upon the reporters and editorial writers of 2000 A.D. will be an even greater burden than now to interpret, analyze and give the background of the spot news items published, as a matter of journalistic duty";

That effort will "be concentrated on further developing the technique of condensing news, making it more understandable, and presenting it more entertainingly";

That "what now passes for dull news, because it deals with economic and social complexities, will take on new life and vividness through expert handling";

That "better trained reporters will serve as 'transformers' in the process of apprising the lay public in the significant findings in the natural and social sciences";

That "editorial pages will be five inches or five columns, depending" —"the best editorials will be news-presented facts";

And that there "will be color on every page of the paper."

And there we have—or have we?—"The Newspaper of Tomorrow."

All of the men who participated in the symposium were well-informed, sincere newspaper executives or technicians. But January 1, 2000 A.D., is a long way ahead, and, of course, many things can happen between now and then.

Glossary of Technical Terms

agate: 5½-point type; unit of measurement used by most American daily newspapers in computing the depth of a page or an advertisement; weeklies usually compute depth in inches, as also do some of the small dailies; see type.

bank: a section of a multiple-section head; same as deck; a cabinet or bench designed to receive type or other units of composition; see drop.

banner: a large or comparatively large head extending across a page; a streamer; sometimes called a line; see sky-line streamer.

Ben Day pattern: a pattern of lines or dots used to tone down heavy types or rules or solid areas in cuts, or to provide a shaded background for types or pictures.

blanket sheet: a newspaper with unusually wide and deep pages.

Bodoni dash: a tapered dash thicker in the middle than at the ends; see French rule.

boilerplate: news or feature material received by publishers in the form of stereotype plates, or the casts from stereotype matrices received from outside sources; the term "boilerplate" was originated when the American Press Association established its Chicago office in the same building with a sheet-iron foundry, and a printer jokingly referred to the stereotypes as coming from a boilerplate factory.

border: a type-high typographic unit with an ornamental printing surface; several such units combined, with or without rules; the printed result secured from such units; a typographic frame; a border, shoulder or margin of white space; see rule.

box: news, feature or editorial matter enclosed by rules or borders and forming a square or oblong.

bumped heads: heads of the same structure, or nearly the same, placed side by side in a form; tombstone heads.

by-line: the signature line of the writer of a story—"By John Doe."

canopy head: a head with a first deck three or more columns wide, with subordinate decks dropping from the extreme left and right of the first deck; sometimes the same as a combination head.

chase: a metal frame into which a form is locked before being sent to the stereotyping department or pressroom.

column rule: a rule used to separate columns.

combination head: a head of two or more sections the first deck of which extends across two or more closely related stories.

composition: assembled types, slugs or other typographic units.

crossline: a single line of type (in a multiple-deck head) occupying the full width of the measure.

cut: a halftone, line-cut, plate or any other kind of engraving; an electrotype or stereotype.

cutoff rule: a rule used to separate advertisements or stories or other units of composition; a full-width rule in any given measure.

deck: see bank, and drop.

double rule: same as oxford rule, or Scotch rule, but not the same as parallel rule.

drop: a subordinate bank or deck, or sequence of such banks or decks.

drop-line head: a head of two or more type lines with second and following lines indented to the right to suggest a flight of stairs; a stagger, or step, head.

dummy: a chart, graph, or sketch, usually in miniature, outlining a makeup plan; see format, and layout.

ear: composition to the left or right or on each side of a nameplate, or title line.

em: the square of any type body size; in this country, straight composition usually is measured by ems, a 6-point line 1" wide containing 12 ems, a 12-point line containing 6 ems, and so on; a pica em, or pica, a standard unit of measurement among printers in this country, is 12 points, or approximately 1/6"; an em quadrat, or quad, is sometimes called a "mutton quad" to avoid confusion with the sound of en quad.

en: one-half of the width of an em in the same font; an en quad is sometimes called a "nut quad" to avoid confusion with the sound of em quad.

flag: statement of ownership, principles, and so forth, beneath the name of a newspaper, now usually placed on the editorial page; masthead.

flatbed press: a press that prints from flat forms.

flush head: a head the line or lines of which begin at the extreme left, or end at the extreme right, of any measure; usually meaning at the extreme left.

folio: a page number—"Page 2," or "2"; a size of paper.

font: an assortment of types of a single style and point size.

form: made-up composition.

format: the physical plan, or characteristics, of a publication or other item of printing; see dummy, and layout.

French rule: a tapered rule or dash thicker in the middle than at the ends; see Bodoni dash.

fudge: a mechanical device that fits into a printing press cylinder and that contains tapered slugs, or slugs or hand types supplemented with tapered leading material, for the printing of late news bulletins, in areas left blank on front pages, after the regular forms have gone to press; the printing secured from such a device.

galley: a three-sided metal or wooden tray used to contain composition before it is placed within a chase.

hanging-indention head: a head the first line of which is full width, with following lines uniformly indented to the right.

height to paper: type high; in this country, .918".

imposing stone: the stone-topped or steel-topped table or frame on which forms are locked in chases.

inverted-pyramid head: a head the first line of which is full width, with following lines centered and increasingly indented from line to line; a pyramid head.

jim dash: a comparatively narrow dash sometimes used between the decks of a multiple-deck head, or under a head, or between items in a column or department.

jump head: a head over part of a story continued from another page in the same issue.

layout: a sketched outline of a page, or part of a page, for the guidance of compositors or makeup men; a picture, or group of pictures, given special treatment for a story; see dummy, and format.

lead (pronounced led): a strip of metal less than type high, and that can be up to 4 points in thickness, used to separate type lines or other units of composition; strips 6 points or more in thickness are called slugs.

lead (pronounced leed): the first paragraph or first few paragraphs of a story.

leader: the most prominently presented story on a front page, or the leading editorial; a dot or hyphen, or sequence of dots or hyphens, used in some kinds of composition.

legend: the line or lines under an illustration; sometimes erroneously called a caption.

line-gauge: in this country, a printer's instrument of measurement usually marked off in picas, half-picas and agates, and sometimes, as well, in inches and fractions of inches; sometimes called a pica-stick, pica-rule, or rule.

logotype: a single type-high unit of composition incorporating two or more characters for use together; two or more characters somewhat cut away on one or both sides to bring about a closer fitting of the characters when used together; sometimes applied to a nameplate, or title line.

lower-case letters: the smaller letters (not capitals) in a font.

make-ready: the pressroom process of preparing a form and press for printing.

masthead: same as flag.

matrix, Linotype: a small brass mold bearing in intaglio on its casting edge one or two printing characters (or blank areas, in the case of spacing matrices); from such molds type characters on Linotype slugs are cast.

matrix slide: a brass mold several picas long, and that can be as long as 42 picas, from which a rule or border is cast on a slug-composing machine.

matrix, stereotype: a unit of specially prepared paper bearing the impression of a type form; from such units flat or curved stereotype plates are cast.

mitered rule: a rule one or both ends of which have been cut away at an angle.

mortise: an opening cut through an illustration for the insertion of type lines or ornaments, or through type lines for the insertion of other type lines or illustrations or ornaments.

must story: any story that the publisher or editor or someone else in authority has ordered inserted in a certain edition.

mutton quad: same as em quad.

nameplate: the line at or near the top of a front page, and sometimes at the top of other pages, presenting the name of a paper; title line; logotype; sometimes erroneously called the masthead, or flag.

nut quad: same as en quad.

over-banner: a banner above a nameplate; sky-line streamer.

overline or -lines: the line or lines immediately above and relating to an illustration.

oxford rule: a rule with one thick and one thin stroke running parallel with each other; sometimes called a Scotch rule, or double rule; not the same as parallel rule; a double oxford rule is a three-stroke rule with one central thick stroke and two outer thin strokes; see parallel rule.

parallel rule: a rule of two or more strokes of the *same weight* running parallel with each other; not the same as an oxford, or Scotch, or double rule, which incorporates both *thick* and *thin* parallel strokes.

patent-insides: sheets of printed pages of news and feature material, and sometimes advertising, purchased by some publishers from outside sources to form parts of their papers; such pages often are inside pages, and are used to back up outside pages of "home print"; same as ready-prints.

pica: in this country, 12-point type; approximately 1/6″; the standard now used by American type producers is .166″—the 12 points making a pica thus becoming, each, .01383″—for convenience usually called .014″; see type.

point: a unit of measurement for typographic material in this country, about 1/72″ or .01383″ or .014″.

pyramided advertisements: advertisements arranged upward and to the left or right on a page; usually meaning to the right, with the largest display in the lower-right corner.

pyramid head: when this term is used, inverted pyramid usually is meant.

quadrat: a quad; a less than type-high blank printing unit; see em, and en.

quotes: quotation marks.

ready-prints: same as patent-insides.

reverse plate: a printing plate photomechanically reversed from type or decoration or illustration so that black design on white paper becomes white design against black background; may also be printed in colored inks to change background.

R.O.P.: run of paper.

rule: a type-high printing unit consisting

of a line or lines; see border, and line-gauge.

running head: the name-and-date line usually at the top of all but front pages in a newspaper.

Scotch rule: same as oxford rule, or double rule, but not the same as parallel rule.

side head: a flush head.

sky-line streamer: same as over-banner.

slug: a line of composition produced on a slug-casting machine; a less than type-high blank printing unit 6 or more points thick; see lead (led).

spaceband: a steel device consisting of two co-operating wedges for the automatic spacing of lines on slug-composing machines.

spread head: a multiple-deck head with one or more decks three or more columns wide, but less than the full width of a page.

stagger head: a drop-line, or step, head.

step head: a drop-line, or stagger, head.

stick: a container in which a hand typesetter assembles types; on slug-composing machines, the container that receives the slugs after they have been ejected from the machines; on slug-casting machines, the container that carries matrices assembled by hand; about two inches of composition.

streamer: same as banner.

swash letter: any letter designed with a flourish or swinging loop for more decorative effect.

"30" dash: a dash used at the end of a story; many tales have been circulated as to why "30" came to mean the end of a story to journalists and printers, but the most generally credited is that the expression was adopted from the telegraphers' symbol "30," meaning the end of a message.

title line: same as nameplate; see logotype.

tombstone heads: same as bumped heads.

turtle: a curved container into which a type form was locked in the days of the type-revolving press; see turtle truck.

turtle truck: a movable table on which a form is moved about the composing room and to and from the stereotyping department; frequently abbreviated to "turtle."

type: before 1886, when a uniform point system was adopted by the United States Type Founders' Association, type sizes were designated by names. The most commonly used names and their nearest equivalents in point sizes were:

excelsior or minikin	3 point
brilliant	4 point
diamond	4½ point
pearl	5 point
agate or ruby	5½ point
nonpareil	6 point
emerald or minionette	6½ point
minion	7 point
brevier	8 point
bourgeois	9 point
long primer	10 point
small pica	11 point
pica	12 point
English	14 point
Columbian	16 point
great primer	18 point
paragon	20 point
double small pica	22 point
double pica	24 point
double English	28 point
double great primer	36 point
double paragon	40 point
meridian	44 point
canon	48 point

Types larger than 48 point were designated as 5-line pica (60 point), 6-line pica (72 point), and so on. Whereas, before 1886, excelsior and paragon represented *specific sizes of any type faces*, today Excelsior and Paragon are formal names of Linotype faces available in *various sizes*.

type high: in this country, a printing unit .918″ high; height to paper; in other countries, this measurement ranges from .918″ to .9893″.

upper-case letters: capital letters.

web perfecting rotary press: a press that prints from curved stereotype plates on rotating cylinders, on paper fed from a roll or rolls, and on both sides of the paper at one time.

well makeup: a page with advertisements to the left and right, with news and feature matter between.

widow: a line containing only one word, part of a word, or other brief sequence of type-high characters.

Index

Ackerman, Carl W., 364, 365
Acme News Pictures, 390
Acme Telephoto, 397
Adair County Democrat, Stilwell, Okla., 325
Advertising Federation of America, 314
Advertising Research Foundation, ix, 190, 191, 233
Airpress, 392
Albany Times-Union, 378
Alco Gravure, Inc., 265
Alexandria Gazette, 105, 106
Allen, Walter D., 195
American Association of Advertising Agencies, 190
American Institute of Graphic Arts, 156
American Newspaper Publishers' Association, 127, 190, 301, 390
American Press Association, 150
American Press Institute, 311
American Society of Newspaper Editors, 200, 304
American Telephone and Telegraph Company, 155
American Weekly, 272, 393
Anderson, Don, 150, 372
Andrews, Chauncey, 155
An Early Survey of the Newsprint Situation, 279-282
Art Gravure Corporation, 265
Associated Newspapers, Ltd., 379
Associated Press, 384, 395, 396, 398
Association of National Advertisers, 190
Atlantic Monthly, 364
Attractive, legible makeup, 5
Auburn (Wash.) *Globe-Republican*, 325
Auto talkie, 393-394
Ayer, N. W. & Son, Inc., 448

Bain, Alexander, 377
Baird, John Logie, 389
Bakersfield (Calif.) *Californian*, 455, 457
Balloon Hoax, 51
Baltimore Evening Sun, 374
Barnaby Rudge, 26
Barnhart, Thomas F., 450
Barnhill, Les, 393
Barthelme, George, 260
Bassett, Warren L., 466
Batten, H. A., 449-450, 454
Bay Ridge Record, New York City, 433
Beecher, The Rev. Henry Ward, 21
Bell, Alexander Graham, 29
Belleville (Ont.) *Daily Ontario*, 327
Ben Day, 161, 163
Bennett, James Gordon, 24, 155
Better Vision Institute, Inc., 94
Bingay, Malcolm W., 7
Bisbee, Ariz., *Brewery Gulch Gazette*, 111
Blair (Wis.) *Press*, 111
Blyth, F., 103, 105
Bodoni, Giambattista, 41
Body faces, 78
Bonaparte, Napoleon, 23
Book sections, 220
Boone, Nicholas, 14
Boston News-Letter, 11, 13-14, 101, 398
Boston Notion, 23
Boston, *Public Occurrences*, 11, 12, 101
Box effects, 131
Boxes and box effects, 131
Boz, 26
Bradford, William, 18
Brewery Gulch Gazette, Bisbee, Ariz., 111
Brink, R. L., 337
Brookline (Mass.) *Chronicle*, 195
Brooklyn Daily Eagle, 222-224, 258-260
Brown, Robert U., 171
Brown, Sevellon, 311-314
Brucker, Herbert, 364, 365, 368
Buchanan, President James, 21
Buenos Aires, *La Prensa*, 358, 359, 360, 361
Bullock, William, 29
Bureau of Advertising, 190, 301
Bureau of Censorship, 375
Burlingame (Kan.) *Enterprise-Chronicle*, 325
Burns, A. H., ix
Byrd, Rear Admiral Richard E., 397

Calder, Louis, 15
California Newspaper Publishers' Association, 337

California Publisher, 337
Cambridge University Press, ix
Campbell, Heyworth, 318
Campbell, John, 14, 398
Canham, Erwin D., 306-311
Carris, Lewis H., 93
Caslon, William, 41
Chandler, W. D., 374
Changing American Newspaper, The, 365, 368
Chicago Daily News, 284, 376
Chicago Daily Times, 449, 455
Chicago Sun, 448, 454
Chicago Tribune, 55-56, 265, 272
Christian Science Monitor, 150-153, 448, 454, 306
Classified advertising, 255
Clemow, Bice, 466-467
Cleveland News, 332, 333, 334, 337
Cleveland Press, 314
Cobb County Times, Marietta, Ga., 455
Color, 271-272
Columbia University, 311, 364, 365
Columbia University Press, 365
Column rules, 121, 126-130
Column widths, 10
Comics, 269
Compton's Pictured Encyclopedia, 10, 15, 29, 156
Continuing Study of Newspaper Reading, The, ix, 190-193, 301
Copyright Act (England), 382
Coster, Laurens Janszoon, 10
Cowles, Gardner Sr., 368
Cowles, John, 368, 370
Craske, Charles, 28
Crompton, James R. & Brothers, Ltd., 382
Cutoffs, 121, 124-126

Daily News Record, 390
Daily Racing Form, 443-445
Dashes, cutoffs and column rules, 121
Date lines and running heads, 115
Day, Ben, 161, 163
Day, Harry, ix
Daytona Beach Morning Journal, 372
Denman, F. T., 321, 330
De Smet (S. D.) *News*, 325
Des Moines Register, 368
Des Moines Tribune, 368
Detroit Free Press, 7, 375, 376
Detroit Sunday Free Press, 376
Dickens, Charles, 26
Dickey County Leader, Ellendale, N. D., 325
Dickman, O. Alfred, ix
Directory of Newspapers and Periodicals, 363, 373
Display advertising, 221
Dolan, P. A., 363
Dots and Dashes, 29
Dun & Bradstreet, Inc., 299

Ears, 101
Eastman Kodak Company, 396
Editor & Publisher, 7, 129, 171, 229-232, 305-306, 378, 388-392, 392-393, 395, 396-398, 433, 466
Editorial pages, 193
Ellendale, N. D., *Dickey County Leader*, 325
Elton Paper Mills, 382
English Newspaper, The, ix
Everett, Edward, 21
Eyes—No. 1 Production Tool, 94

Fairchild Publications, 390
Facsimile, 392
Feature heads, 137
Feature pages, 202
Federal Communications Commission, 390
Federal Telecommunications Laboratories, 395
Financial pages, 214
Financial Post, Toronto, 186-189, 196-200
Finch Telecommunications, Inc., 388-390
Finch, William G. H., 392
First Amendment, 392
1ste Mai, Stavanger, Norway, 357
Fitzpatrick, William H., 396-397
For More Effective Advertising, Don't Screen Type, 225-227
Franklin Institute of Philadelphia, 29
Fraser, Prime Minister Peter, 386
Friede, Kenneth, 445
Frischhertz, Raymond, 397
Front-page makeup, 172
Funk & Wagnalls, 10
Fust, Johann, 10

Gage, Harry L., ix, 83-86, 225-227, 232-234
Galignani's Messenger, 11
Gallup, Dr. George, 369, 375
General Electric Company, 378
Getting and Keeping Classified Advertising, 264
Gist, 365-367
Glendale (Calif.) *News-Press*, 455
Glossary of technical terms, 468
Goebbels, Paul Joseph, 312
Goudy, Frederic W., 105

Gowdy, Douglas M., 188-189, 196, 197, 200
Grantsburg, Wis., *Journal of Burnett County*, 327
Gravure, offset and color, 265
Gravure Service Corporation, 267
Great Falls (Mont.) *Tribune-Leader*, 207, 300
Greeley, Horace, 24
Green, B., 14, 398
Gregg Publishing Company, 156
Griffith, C. H., ix, 80-83, 86-87
Guillot, Jimmy, 397
Gutenberg, Johann, 10

Halifax, Viscount, 378
Harper & Brothers, vii, ix, 293
Harris, Benjamin, 11
Hartford Courant, 448, 454
Hastings (Neb.) *Daily Tribune*, 455
Hastings, Neb., *Tiger Cub*, 325
Head faces, 40
Hearst, William Randolph, 200, 272
Henry, M. R., 330
Hentschell, Charles J., 270
History of American Journalism, ix, 224
History of Printing in America, The, ix
History of the United States, for Families and Libraries, The, 23
Hitler, Adolf, 313
Hogan Faximile, 392
Hogan, John V. L., 392
Horan Engraving Company, ix, 157
Horgan, Stephen Henry, 154, 155-156
Houghton Mifflin Company, ix
How Many Sacred Cows Are You Feeding? 278, 289
Hudson, Frederic, ix, 11

Illuminated Quadruple Constellation, 121-123
Illustrations, 154
Imperial Type Metal Magazine, 8
Independent Journal of Columbia University, 364
Influences of World War II, 277
Inglewood (Calif.) *Daily News*, 456, 459
Inland Bulletin, 147-150
Inland Daily Press Association, 147-150
International Business Machines Corporation, 377
International News Service, 395
International Photo-engravers' Union, 156
International Telephone and Telegraph Corporation, 395
Iowa Publisher, 8
Ives, Frederic E., 156

Journal of Burnett County, Grantsburg, Wis., 327
Journalism in the United States from 1690 to 1872, ix, 11
Joyce, Maurice, 155
Jump heads, 142

Kal, Ehrlich & Merrick, 231
Kansas City Star, 8
Kimberly-Clark Corporation, 265
King Features Syndicate, 378
Knight, John S., 304-305, 375
Knight Newspapers, 368, 375, 376

La Farge (Wis.) *Enterprise*, 327
La Grange (Ill.) *Citizen*, 195
Lake Mills (Iowa) *Graphic*, 455
Lambert, Stephen J., 259
La Prensa, Buenos Aires, 358, 359, 360, 361
Larsson, A. Edwin, 195
Leading and spacing, 95
Lederer, Street & Zeus, 388
Lee, James Melvin, ix, 224
Legible makeup, 5
Life, 148, 303, 373
Life International, 373
Limitation Order L-240, 279
Lippmann, Walter, 368
Livermore (Calif.) *Herald*, 330
London Daily Express, 285, 288
London Daily Mail, 378-382
London Daily Mirror, 285, 288
London Daily Telegraph, 284-287
London, *News of the World*, 285, 288
London Packet, 101, 103, 104
London, *People*, 285, 288
London Times, 222, 382-383
London, *Typography*, 293
Look, 147, 148, 373
Loomis, William W., 195
Los Angeles Daily News, 433
Los Angeles Evening News, 433
Los Angeles Times, 260, 261, 337, 448, 454
Lossing, Benson J., 23
Louisiana Press Association, 304
Lownds, William G., 31
Luckiesh, Dr. Matthew, 225
Ludlow Typograph Company, 200

Magazine and book sections, 220
Makeup limitations, 37
Makeup of other pages, 190
Marconi, Guglielmo, 29

Marietta, Ga., *Cobb County Times*, 455
Marin Journal, San Rafael, Calif., 107, 108
Martin, Earle, 332-334, 337
Martin, John E., ix
Massillon (Ohio) *Guide*, 327
McArthur, General, 171
McDonald, Morton J. A., 264
McEachern, Ronald A., 188, 196, 197
McKelway, B. M., 371
McMurtrie, Douglas C., 200, 201
Mechanical Bulletin No. 266, 127
Medford (Wis.) *Star News*, 263
Men's Wear Manufacturing Association, 390
Metten, W. Murray, 279-282
Miami Herald, 393
Mich, D. D., 147-150
Michael Angelo, 23
Microwave facsimile, 392-393
Mikalson, Joh. B., 357-358
Milford (Conn.) *News*, 107, 108
Miller County Autogram, Tuscumbia, Mo., 327
Millersburg (Pa.) *Sentinel*, 325
Minneapolis Morning Tribune, 260, 262
Minneapolis Star, 368-371
Minneapolis Star-Journal, 374
Minneapolis Times, 155
Minneapolis Tribune, 374
Mission (Texas) *Times*, 455
Modern comment, 293
Modern Newspaper, The, vii
Modern pages, 411
Modern scene, 3
Modern suggestions, 399
Modern tabloid, 424
Montana State University, 207, 300
Moon Hoax, 23
Moore, Thomas, 26
Morison, Stanley, ix
Morning Courier and New-York Enquirer, 21
Morristown (N. J.) *Daily Record*, 455
Morse, Samuel F. B., 29
Moss, Frank K., 225
Mount Vernon (Iowa) *Hawkeye-Record*, 455, 456, 458
Multiplex broadcasting, 395

Nameplates and ears, 101
Napoleon Bonaparte, 23
National Broadcasting Company, 398
National Editorial Association, 195, 455
National Newspaper Promotion Association, 279
National Society for the Prevention of Blindness, 93
Nelson, William R., 8
Neo Gravure Corporation, 265
Newark Evening News, 448, 454
Newell, S. D., *Valley Irrigator*, 325
New Orleans Item, 270-271
New Orleans States, 396-397
News body faces, 78
News head faces, 40
News-Journal Newspapers, Wilmington, Del., 279
News of the World, London, 285, 288
Newspaper Advertising Executives' Association, 306
Newspaper Makeup, vii, 293
Newspaper-of-the-air, 390
Newspaper of tomorrow, 465
Newspaper wrappers, 272
New Standard Dictionary of the English Language, 10
New York City, *Bay Ridge Record*, 433
New York Daily Graphic, 154, 155
New York Daily News, 119-120, 449, 455
New York Daily Tribune, 26
New York Evening Journal, 337
New York Herald, ix, 24, 107, 155
New York Herald Tribune, ix, 24, 30, 31, 107, 109, 155-156, 180-182, 183, 184, 185, 314, 363, 365, 376, 377, 378, 382, 392, 393, 396, 448, 454, 456, 461
New York Morning Courier and Enquirer, 21
New York Morning Telegraph, 318, 319, 320
New York Post, 205, 206, 386-388
New York Semi-Weekly Tribune, 26
New York State Publishers' Association, 304
New York State Society of Newspaper Editors, 396
New York Sun, ix, 23, 50-55, 204, 206, 363
New York Times, 265, 374, 384-386, 448, 454, 456, 462
New York Tribune, 24-30, 155
New York University, 29
New York Weekly Tribune, 26
New York World, 111, 112
New York World's Fair, 376, 377, 378, 466
New York World-Telegram, 107, 109, 111, 112, 203, 206, 213-214, 393-394
Notizie Scritte, 11
Nuremberg Gazette, 11

Oakland, Calif., Roosevelt High School, *Roosevelt Crimson*, 327
Office of War Information, 308
Oklahoma Press Association, 296
Oklahoma Publisher, 296-297
Oswald, John Clyde, 156
Ottawa (Ont.) *Journal*, 105, 108

Page sizes and column widths, 10
Palm Beach Times, West Palm Beach, 372
Palo Alto (Iowa) *Reporter*, 325
Parade of progress—in other ways, 362
Parade of progress—typographic, 315
Park Falls (Wis.) *Leader*, 325
Patterson, Walter B., ix
Pearl Harbor, 278
Pelican Press Messenger, 304
Pennsylvania Journal, 18, 19
People, London, 285, 288
Perkins-Goodwin Company, 15
Pierce, R., 11
Placentia (Calif.) *Courier*, 337
Placing display advertisements, 239
Platt, Senator Thomas C., 155
PM, 449, 455, 456, 463
Pocahontas (Iowa) *Democrat*, 327
Poe, Edgar Allan, 51
Postal Laws and Regulations, 273
Postmaster General, 273
Post Office Department, 273
Powell, Gerry, ix
Preface, vii
Primm, Alex, 270
Printer's Ink Monthly, 265-267
Printing in the Americas, 156
Prize winners, 447
Proctor, Edna Dean, 224
Providence (R. I.) *Evening Bulletin*, 311
Providence (R. I.) *Journal*, 311
Publication Research Service, 190
Publick Occurrences, Boston, 11, 17, 101
Publishers' Auxiliary, 31-32, 284, 297-299
Pulse-time modulation, 395

Radio Corporation of America, 376, 398
Radio Inventions, Inc., 392
Radio newspaper, 389
Radio pages, 218
Radiophone, 393-394, 396-397
Radio Press, 376, 377
Radiotype, 378
Raytheon Manufacturing Company, 392, 394
Raytheon radio telephone, 393-394
Reid, Bill, 397
Reid, Whitelaw, 28
Research Company of America, 150
Rhinebeck (N. Y.) *Gazette*, 105, 106
Richmond (Calif.) *Independent*, 257-258, 384
Richmond News Leader, 364
Richmond Times-Dispatch, 373
Ritzville (Wash.) *Journal-Times*, 107, 109, 455
Robb, Arthur, 306
Roberts, George, 21
Rochester (Minn.) *Post-Bulletin*, 450, 451, 454, 455
Rollins, Carl Purington, 454
Roosevelt Crimson, Roosevelt High School, Oakland, Calif., 327
Rosenthal, Joe, 171
Rospaw, Frank, 337
Rothermere, Lord, 379-380
Run-of-paper color, 271-272
Running heads, 115
Rutland (Vt.) *Herald*, 453, 454

Saint Christopher, 10
San Diego (Calif.) *Daily Journal*, 107, 110-111
San Francisco Chronicle, 305, 373
San Rafael, Calif., *Marin Journal*, 107, 108
Saturday Evening Post, 148, 149
Scarsdale (N. Y.) *Inquirer*, 455, 456, 460
Schoeffer, Peter, 10
School papers, 275
Seattle Star, 334, 337
Seltzer, Louis B., 314
Sewell, J. Dee, 433
Shantytown, 155
Sherbow, Benjamin, 30, 31
Smith, Paul C., 305-306, 373-374
Society pages, 206
Soubiran, Julien J., ix, 157-158
Soundphoto System, 390
Southern Bell Telephone Company, 396, 397
So You Want to Change Your Head Dress! 77
Spacing, 95
Spartanburg (S. C.) *Herald*, 129
Spartanburg (S. C.) *Journal*, 129
Spartanburg (S. C.) *Sunday Herald-Journal*, 129
Speedwell Iron Works, 29
Sports pages, 210
Spring Valley (Wis.) *Sun*, 327
St. Louis Post-Dispatch, 269-270
Stanwood, August, 16
Stars and Stripes, 285
Station WGHF, 392

Stavanger, Norway, *1ste Mai*, 357
Stilwell, Okla., *Adair County Democrat*, 325
Strong, Jacob H., Jr., 105
Swanson, Neil H., 374
Syracuse University, 304

Tabloid, modern, 424
Technical terms, 468
Telephoto trans-ceivers, 397
Television, 378
Theatrical advertising, 252
Thomas, Isaiah, ix, 11
Thomas, Isaiah Jr., ix
Tierney, Paul A., 387-388
Tiger Cub, Hastings, Neb., 325
Time, 362-363, 373
Time, Inc., 373
Time-Life International, 373
Toronto Evening Telegram, 146
Toronto, *Financial Post*, 186-189, 196-200
Townes, William A., 129-130
Trammell, Niles, 398
Trans-Atlantic newspapers, 378-383
Truman, President Harry S., 171
Tuscumbia, Mo., *Miller County Autogram*, 327
Type-revolving presses, 48
Typography, London, 293

Ultrafax, 398
United Nations Conference, 384-388
United Press, 392, 395
University of Minnesota, 450
U.S.S. Mt. McKinley, 397
U.S.S. Mt. Olympus, 397

Vail, Alfred, 29
Vail, George, 29
Vail, Judge Stephen, 29
Valentino, Rudolph, 155
Valley Irrigator, Newell, S. D., 325
Veritas, 358
Virginia Gazette, 104, 105

Waldorf-Astoria, 390
Walker, Jerry, 388-392
Wall Street Journal, 272
Wallace, Ross, 23
Walters, Basil L., 368-371, 374-376
Warden, Alexander, 207-208, 300-304
War Production Board, 31, 279, 282
Warren (Ill.) *Sentinel-Leader*, 325
Washington Evening Star, 371
Washington News, 449, 455
Washington Post, 120, 202
Washington Times-Herald, 229-232
Watson, Campbell, 305
Webber, Clarence E., 130
Weekly Newspaper Bureau, 195
Wellesley (Mass.) *Townsman*, 195
Western Union Telegraph Company, 29
WGHF, Station, 392
What Makes Your Advertising Pull? 232-234
Whittier, John Greenleaf, 222
Williams, Gurney, 148, 149
Willing, J. Thomson, 267-268
Wilmington, Del., News-Journal Newspapers, 279
Wirephoto, 396, 397
Wisconsin State Journal, Madison, 147-150, 371-372
Woman's and society pages, 206
Women's Wear Daily, 390
Woodville (Wis.) *Times*, 327
World's Press News, 357
World War II, influences of, 277
Wortman, Elbert B. M., 388, 389-390
Wrappers, 272
Wright Company, Inc., 290

Yale University, 454
Yank, 285
York (Pa.) *Gazette and Daily*, 450, 452, 454, 455
Youngstown Vindicator, 155

Zwirner, Harry, 390